LIABILITY INSURANCE LAW IN CANADA

FOURTH EDITION

LIABILITY INSURANCE LAW IN CANADA

FOURTH EDITION

Gordon Hilliker, Q.C.

Member of the Bar of British Columbia

LexisNexis®
Butterworths

Liability Insurance Law in Canada, Fourth Edition
© LexisNexis Canada Inc. 2006
April 2006

Members of the LexisNexis Group worldwide

Canada	LexisNexis Canada Inc, 123 Commerce Valley Dr. E. Suite 700, MARKHAM, Ontario
Argentina	Abeledo Perrot, Jurisprudencia Argentina and Depalma, BUENOS AIRES
Australia	Butterworths, a Division of Reed International Books Australia Pry Ltd, CHATSWOOD, New South Wales
Austria	ARD Betriebsdienst and Verlag Orac, VIENNA
Chile	Publitecsa and Conosur Ltda, SANTIAGO DE CHILE
Czech Republic	Orac, sro, PRAGUE
France	Éditions du Juris-Classeur SA, PARIS
Hong Kong	Butterworths Asia (Hong Kong), HONG KONG
Hungary	Hvg Orac, BUDAPEST
India	Butterworths India, NEW DELHI
Ireland	Butterworths (Ireland) Ltd, DUBLIN
Italy	Giuffré, MILAN
Malaysia	Malayan Law Journal Sdn Bhd, KUALA LUMPUR
New Zealand	Butterworths of New Zealand, WELLINGTON
Poland	Wydawnictwa Prawnicze PWN, WARSAW
Singapore	Butterworths Asia, SINGAPORE
South Africa	Butterworth Publishers (Pty) Ltd, DURBAN
Switzerland	Stämpfli Verlag AG, BERNE
United Kingdom	Butterworths Tolley, a Division of Reed Elsevier (UK), LONDON, WC2A
USA	LexisNexis, DAYTON, Ohio

Library and Archives Canada Cataloguing in Publication

Hilliker, Gordon
   Liability insurance law in Canada / Gordon Hilliker. — 4th ed.

Includes bibliographical references and index.
ISBN 0-433-44959-4

   1. Insurance, Liability—Canada.   I. Title.

KE1198.H54 2006   346.71'0865   C2006-900980-5
KF1215.H45 2006

Printed and bound in Canada.

*In memory of my father, Robert John Hilliker,
and my mentor, David Alexander McDonald, Q.C.*

PREFACE TO THE FOURTH EDITION

Whether a claim involves professional negligence, product liability, securities fraud or a slip and fall at the local grocery store, there is often a liability insurer in the background providing both a defence and indemnity to the tortfeasor. Indeed, liability insurance is so pervasive that a basic understanding of the subject is essential for all civil litigation practitioners. Yet, surprisingly, when I began working on the first edition of this book there was no Canadian text that addressed this important part of our law. It has been a great privilege for me to attempt to fill that void and to carry this text into its fourth edition.

Consistent with the previous editions, I have not addressed the subject of automobile insurance. As a practical matter, the law relating to automobile insurance is simply too vast a subject, with the law varying significantly from province to province. Moreover, the subject of automobile liability insurance is in any event quite distinct from that of general liability insurance, which is what this book is mostly about. .

As before, where I consider it to be helpful I have made reference to American authorities. As anyone who practises in the insurance law field well knows, American authorities are routinely referred to by our courts in deciding issues relating to the interpretation of contracts of insurance, particularly where the Canadian authorities are either unclear or nonexistent. Fully cataloguing the American decisions and explaining the bases for the differences that exist among the various states, however, would take a book several times the size of this one. Of necessity, then, I have been selective in my treatment of American jurisprudence. My approach, on each topic, has been to refer to a few representative or leading cases that I believe will be of some assistance to Canadian practitioners.

Finally, I have not attempted to state the law in Quebec with respect to liability insurance contracts, which are governed by the *Civil Code*. Where decisions from the Quebec courts are illustrative of the common law position, however, I have included them in this text.

In the end, I have attempted to set out the law relating to liability insurance in a fashion that will be useful to lawyers and judges as well as to insurance personnel involved in the handling of claims.

As with previous editions, the Insurance Bureau of Canada has kindly granted permission to reproduce certain of the commercial liability policy forms it publishes for its members. Although not mandatory, these forms have gained widespread acceptance in Canada and are an invaluable tool for the study of this subject.

Gordon Hilliker, Q.C.
Belcarra, British Columbia
January 2006

ABOUT THE AUTHOR

Gordon Hilliker, Q.C., is recognized by his peers as one of the leading practitioners in British Columbia in both insurance and personal injury law. A graduate of the University of British Columbia, Mr. Hilliker obtained a Bachelor of Arts in Philosophy in 1974 and a Bachelor of Laws in 1976. He was called to the bar of British Columbia in 1977 and was appointed Queen's Counsel in 2001.

He has served as Chairman of the Insurance Law Section of the Canadian Bar Association, Chairman of the Insurance Law Section of the Canadian Bar Association, B.C. Branch, and Member of the Provincial Council, Canadian Bar Association, B.C. Branch. He also served for many years as the Head of Course, Civil Procedure for the Law Society of British Columbia's Bar Admission Program.

Mr. Hilliker practises with the firm of Watson Goepel Maledy in Vancouver.

TABLE OF CONTENTS

Part II — Commercial Liability Insurance

Chapter 6

Appendices

TABLE OF CASES

PART I

MATTERS OF GENERAL APPLICATION

Chapter 1

THE NATURE OF LIABILITY INSURANCE

1. LIABILITY INSURANCE DEFINED

At common law, contracts of insurance are rather vaguely defined as those under which the insurer, in consideration of a fee known as the "premium", undertakes to confer a benefit upon the insured on the happening of a specified event. There has to be either "uncertainty whether the event will ever happen or not, or if the event is one which must happen at some time there must be uncertainty as to time at which it will happen".[1] Further, the event "must be of a character more or less adverse to the interest of the person effecting the insurance".[2]

The insurance legislation in force in the various common law provinces provides a similar definition:

> "insurance" means the undertaking by one person to indemnify another person against loss or liability for loss in respect of certain risk or peril to which the object of the insurance might be exposed or to pay a sum of money or other thing of value on the happening of a certain event ...[3]

The class of liability insurance contracts comprises contracts in which the insurer undertakes to indemnify the insured with respect to the liability, either imposed by law upon the insured or assumed under contract, arising out of certain specified hazards or risks. Typically, liability insurance contracts provide further that the insurer will defend the insured against any claims which would fall within the coverage provided.

Liability insurance contracts are almost invariably evidenced by a written agreement known as the "policy". In most cases the policy is in a standard form prepared by the insurer. In some cases, however, particularly where the insured is a sophisticated business concern, the terms of the insurance contract are negotiated with the assistance of an insurance broker.

---

[1] *Prudential Ins. Co. v. Inland Revenue Commissioners*, [1904] 2 K.B. 658 at 663.

[2] *Ibid.*, at 664.

[3] *Insurance Act*, R.S.A. 2000, c. I-3, s. 1(*aa*). Comparable definitions are found in the following: *Insurance Act*, R.S.B.C. 1996, c. 226, s. 1(*b*); *Insurance Act*, C.C.S.M., c. I40, s. 1; *Insurance Act*, R.S.N.B. 1973, c. I-12, s. 1; *Insurance Contracts Act*, R.S.N.L. 1990, c. I-12, s. 2(*l*); *Insurance Act*, R.S.N.S. 1989, c. 231, s. 3(*k*); *Insurance Act*, R.S.O. 1990, c. I.8, s. 1; R.S.P.E.I. 1988, c. I-4, s. 1(*j*); *Saskatchewan Insurance Act*, R.S.S. 1978, c. S-26, s. 2(*gg*).

2. TYPES OF LIABILITY INSURANCE POLICIES

Liability insurance contracts are generally written according to the nature of the business, professional or personal risks undertaken by the insured. Within each of these three broad classifications a number of specialized policies are available. Thus, business liability policies include, in addition to the generalized Comprehensive General Liability and Commercial General Liability forms, a number of specialized policies such as:

- Manufacturers' and Contractors' Liability;
- Owners', Landlords', and Tenants' Liability;
- Products and Completed Operations Liability;
- Owners' or Contractors' Protective Liability;
- Contractual Liability;
- Personal Injury Liability;
- Garage Liability;
- Storekeepers' Liability;
- Employers' Liability;
- Druggists' Liability; and
- Farmer's Personal Liability.

Professional liability policies are underwritten according to the nature of the particular profession and provide coverage for lawyers, doctors, beauticians, dentists, nurses, optometrists, physiotherapists, chiropractors, veterinarians, architects, engineers, surveyors, real estate agents, insurance agents, accountants, directors and officers, and others. Personal liability policies are written both on a general basis, providing coverage for all types of liability with certain exceptions, and on a specialized basis, providing coverage for certain specified hazards such as automobile or aircraft liability.

3. INDEMNITY, LIABILITY AND CONTINGENCY CONTRACTS DISTINGUISHED

Insurance contracts are often classified according to whether or not they are contracts of indemnity.[4] Under a contract of indemnity the amount recoverable is measured by the extent of the insured's pecuniary loss. A policy of fire insurance, for example, falls within this classification, for the insured's entitlement is the value of the property destroyed by fire.[5] Contracts of non-indemnity are those in which payment is made upon the happening of a specified event, regardless of whether the insured has suffered a loss. Policies of life insurance

---

[4] *Glynn v. Scottish Union & National Ins. Co.*, [1963] 2 O.R. 705 (C.A.).

[5] Many fire insurance policies cover the replacement cost of the property destroyed, allowing new for old, without an allowance for depreciation. Such policies are nevertheless still generally considered to be policies of indemnity.

are the classic example of non-indemnity policies, for the beneficiary is entitled to collect even where the death of the person insured does not result in a pecuniary loss.

Liability insurance contracts are usually considered to be contracts of indemnity.[6] Unlike other contracts of indemnity, however, liability insurance contracts do not generally require that the insured actually suffers a pecuniary loss before being entitled to the benefits of the policy. Rather, it is sufficient, with some exceptions, that the insured merely be under a liability to another, and the policy is enforceable even though that liability has not been satisfied. In rare cases even proof of liability is not required. In *West Wake Price & Co. v. Ching*[7] an accountant's professional liability policy provided that the insurer must pay a claim unless a Queen's Counsel advised that the claim could be successfully contested. As Devlin J. noted,[8] this was not a policy of indemnity at all, rather it was a policy of contingency insurance.

A more precise classification, then, for the purposes of liability insurance contracts, is as follows:

(i) Contracts of indemnity — the insurer's obligations are triggered by the insured having sustained an actual loss (usually payment of a judgment);

(ii) contracts of liability — the insurer's obligations are triggered by the insured being liable to another even though no payment has been made;

(iii) contracts of contingency — the insurer's obligations are triggered by the making of a claim, subject to a determination as to whether the claim may be successfully defended.

The practical importance of the distinction between the various types of liability insurance contracts concerns the time at which the insured may enforce the insurer's obligations under the contract. Where the policy, on its true construction, is one of indemnity, then no action will lie against the insurer until the insured has paid the loss.[9] Where the policy is one where the indemnification is against liability, however, then, subject to the no-action clause,[10] a right of action accrues when liability attaches to the insured. With contingency contracts the insured's right of action accrues upon the happening of the contingency.

---

[6] *British Cash and Parcel Conveyors v. Lamson Store Service*, [1908] 1 K.B. 1006 at 1014 (C.A.); *Goddard and Smith v. Frew*, [1939] 4 All E.R. 358 (C.A.).

[7] [1957] 1 W.L.R. 45.

[8] *Ibid.*, at 51.

[9] *Greensboro (City) v. Reserve Insurance Co.*, 321 S.E.2d 232 (N.C. App. 1984).

[10] See Chapter 3, section 5: Action against Insurer.

4. STATUTORY REQUIREMENTS

Liability insurance contracts are regulated by provincial legislation. The common law provinces have worked closely together over the years in an attempt to enact more or less uniform legislation with respect to insurance contracts.[11] Under the scheme of this legislation, different classes of insurance are recognized and accorded separate treatment. While no separate provision is made for liability insurance contracts, they are subject to certain general requirements in the legislation.[12]

It must be noted that although the aim is that insurance legislation be uniform throughout the common law provinces, this has not been entirely achieved. There are certain provisions that have not been adopted in all of the provinces. Moreover, even where similar provisions are in force, there may be material differences in the wording of the legislation.

5. INJURED PERSON'S RIGHT OF ACTION

As a general rule, only the parties to a contract are entitled to enforce its provisions. With respect to liability insurance contracts, however, a statutory provision permits a third party to make a claim against the wrongdoer's insurer.[13] There are differences in the wording of this provision in the various provinces. In Manitoba, New Brunswick, Newfoundland, Nova Scotia and Ontario the section provides as follows:

> (1) Where a person incurs a liability for injury or damage to the person or property of another, and is insured against such liability, and fails to satisfy a judgment awarding damages against [the person] in respect of [the person's] liability, and an execution against [the person] in respect thereof is returned unsatisfied, the person entitled to the damages may recover by action against the insurer the amount of the judgment up to the face value of the policy, but subject to the same equities as the insurer would have if the judgment had been satisfied.
>
> (2) This section does not apply to motor vehicle liability policies.[14]

In Alberta the section states:

---

[11] See C. Brown & J. Menezes, *Insurance Law in Canada* (Scarborough: Carswell, 1997).

[12] See Chapter 2: The Contract of Insurance.

[13] The provision applies only with respect to liability insurance policies. A third party cannot make use of this provision to recover from the insured's property insurer. See *W.R. Scott Equipment Ltd. v. Guardian Insurance Co. of Canada*, [1998] A.J. No. 115, [1998] I.L.R. 1-3541 (Alta. C.A.).

[14] *Insurance Act*, C.C.S.M., c. I40, s. 127; *Insurance Act*, R.S.N.B. 1973, c. I-12, s. 104; *Insurance Act*, R.S.N.S. 1989, c. 231, s. 28. Virtually identical are: *Insurance Contracts Act*, R.S.N.L. 1990, c. I-12, s. 13; *Insurance Act*, R.S.O. 1990, c. I.8, s. 132.

In any case in which a person insured against liability for injury or damage to persons or property of others has failed to satisfy a judgment obtained by a claimant for the injury or damage and a writ of enforcement against the insured in respect thereof is returned unsatisfied, the enforcement creditor has a right of action against the insurer to recover an amount not exceeding the face amount of the policy or the amount of the judgment in the same manner and subject to the same equities as the insured would have if the judgment had been satisfied.[15]

The Saskatchewan statute is drafted in almost identical terms to that of Alberta:

(1) Where a person insured against liability for injury or damage to persons or property of others has failed to satisfy a judgment obtained by a claimant for the injury or damage and an execution against the insured in respect thereof is returned unsatisfied, the execution creditor has a right of action against the insurer to recover an amount not exceeding the face amount of the policy or the amount of the judgment in the same manner and subject to the same equities as the insured would have if the judgment had been satisfied.

(2) This section does not apply to contracts of automobile insurance.[16]

The British Columbia version of this provision differs materially. There is no requirement that the liability be for injury or damage to person or property:

24(1) If a judgment has been granted against a person in respect of a liability against which the person is insured and the judgment has not been satisfied, the judgment creditor may recover by action against the insurer the lesser of
(a)   the unpaid amount of the judgment, and
(b)   the amount that the insurer would have been liable under the policy to pay to the insured had the insured satisfied the judgment.

(2) The claim of a judgment creditor against an insurer under subsection (1) is subject to the same equities as would apply in favour of the insurer had the judgment been satisfied by the insured.
(3) This section does not apply in the case of a contract of automobile insurance.[17]

In order to establish liability against an insurer under these provisions, the third party must:

(i)   obtain a judgment against the insured in respect of injury or damage to person or property (with the exception of British Columbia, where any judgment will suffice);
(ii) attempt execution on the judgment but have it returned unsatisfied; and

---

[15]   R.S.A. 2000, c. I-3, s. 530.
[16]   R.S.S. 1978, c. S-26, s. 122.
[17]   R.S.B.C. 1996, c. 226, s. 24.

(iii) prove that the insured's liability falls within the coverage afforded by the policy.

In *Jones v. Kansa General Insurance Co.*[18] it was held that section 132 of the Ontario *Insurance Act* was not limited to judgments obtained in the province. A third party who obtained a judgment in the United States against the insured was able to rely on that section to obtain recovery in Ontario from an insurer residing in that province. In *Mueller v. Coronation Insurance Co.*,[19] the British Columbia Court of Appeal distinguished *Jones* in a case in which the plaintiff had obtained a default judgment in New Mexico against a B.C. company and there were issues both as to whether the company was properly served and whether the company may have had a defence under workers' compensation legislation. In the result, the plaintiff was required to pursue a separate action against the company in British Columbia to enforce her foreign judgment.

Since each section stipulates that the action is "subject to the same equities as the insured would have if the judgment had been satisfied", as a general rule the insurer may successfully resist payment in circumstances where it would have had a good defence against its own insured: for example, by showing that its insured was guilty of a material misrepresentation or a breach of condition.[20] The "equities", however, do not include all defences that might be available to the insurer in an action commenced by the insured rather than by the third party. In *Azevedo v. Markel Insurance Co. of Canada*[21] a majority of the Alberta Court of Appeal held that a judgment creditor could recover from the insurer even though after the loss the insured had waived all its rights under the policy and had released the insurer from its obligation of indemnity. The facts of the case are somewhat unusual. The insured, a transporter of mobile homes, was required by law to carry liability insurance. The plaintiffs were his customers. They claimed that he had damaged their mobile home in the course of transit. He denied the claim and advised his insurer that he would handle it personally and that he did not want them to make any payment on his behalf. The insurer responded by obtaining the insured's written confirmation that he was waiving all rights to indemnity and releasing the insurer from its obligations. When the plaintiffs later obtained a judgment against the insured, who could no longer be found, they sought to enforce the judgment against the insurer. At trial the action was dismissed on the basis that the insurer had been released from its obligations and the plaintiffs could have no better rights than those of the insured. The Alberta Court of Appeal, by a majority decision, allowed the appeal and permitted the plaintiffs to recover their judgment against the insurer. The Court

---

[18] [1992] O.J. No. 1597, 10 O.R. (3d) 56, supp. reasons 96 D.L.R. (4th) 286 (C.A.), leave to appeal to S.C.C. dismissed, [1993] 1 S.C.R. vii, 150 N.R. 397.

[19] [1995] B.C.J. No. 2973, 12 B.C.L.R. (3d) 90 (C.A.).

[20] *Frederick v. Aviation & General Ins. Co.*, [1966] 2 O.R. 356 (C.A.); *Sumitomo Canada Ltd. v. Canadian Indemnity Co.*, [1982] 5 W.W.R. 762 (B.C.C.A.).

[21] [1999] A.J. No. 1201, [2000] I.L.R. 1-3770 (C.A.).

of Appeal held that an "equity" was not something that two parties could deliberately create, and noted that any result that left open the possibility of collusion between the insurer and insured offended public policy.

In *J & P Holdings Ltd. v. Saskatchewan Mutual Insurance Co.*,[22] the Saskatchewan Queen's Bench held that the "equities" did not include a limitation defence available to the insurer under the policy. Some 13 months after being awarded judgment against the insured, and three months after a *nulla bona* return on a writ of execution, the plaintiff commenced a statutory action against the insurer. The policy contained a provision that any action for indemnity against the insurer had to be brought within one year of the date of judgment against the insured. Since the plaintiff's statutory right of action was subject to the "same equities as the insured would have if the judgment had been satisfied", the insurer applied to have the plaintiff's claim barred as not having been commenced within the one-year period. The application was dismissed on the basis that the policy condition referred only to a *contractual* action *by the insured*, whereas the action before the court was a *statutory action* commenced by a *judgment creditor*.

Except in British Columbia, the benefit of the statutory provision is available only where there has been loss or damage to person or property. It is unclear whether a purely economic loss meets this requirement. In *Starr Schein Enterprises Inc. v. Gestas Corp.*,[23] it was held that the section was not available to a corporation that had obtained judgment against its solicitor for negligence in failing to draft an enforceable agreement of purchase and sale. The majority of the British Columbia Court of Appeal held that the corporation's financial loss could not be characterized as "injury or damage to the person or property". A similar conclusion was reached by a majority of the Ontario Court of Appeal in *Perry v. General Security Insurance Co. of Canada.*[24] The contrary conclusion, however, was reached in the trial decisions of the Alberta Court of Queen's Bench in *Qualiglass Holdings Inc. v. Zurich Indemnity Company of Canada*,[25] in the Saskatchewan Court of Queen's Bench in *Kallos v. Saskatchewan Govt. Insurance*[26] and *63398 Alberta Ltd. v. Saskatchewan Government Insurance*[27] and the New Brunswick Court of Queen's Bench in *Caisse populaire de St-Isidore Ltée v. Assoc. d'assurance des juristes canadiens.*[28] Moreover, in

---

[22] [1990] S.J. No. 270, 44 C.C.L.I. 205 (Q.B.).

[23] [1986] B.C.J. No. 323, 18 C.C.L.I. 148 (S.C.), affd [1987] B.C.J. No. 803, 25 C.C.L.I. 240 (C.A.) (decided under the previous B.C. legislation. See also *Scurfield v. Assitaila-Le Assicurazioni D'Italia Sp.A.*, [1992] B.C.J. No. 759, 68 B.C.L.R. (2d) 174 (S.C.).

[24] (1983), 1 C.C.L.I. 227 (Ont. H.C.J.), affd (1984), 7 C.C.L.I. 231 (Ont. C.A.).

[25] [2004] A.J. No. 881, [2004] I.L.R. 1-4329 (Q.B.).

[26] (1984), 3 C.C.L.I. 65 (Sask. Q.B.).

[27] [1995] S.J. No. 7, [1995] I.L.R. 1-3177 (Q.B.), revd (on a different point), [1995] S.J. No. 760, [1996] I.L.R. 1-3309 (C.A.).

[28] [1992] N.B.J. No. 601, 15 C.C.L.I. (2d) 294, 129 N.B.R. (2d) 227, 325 A.P.R. 227 (Q.B.).

Reznick v. Zitzerman[29] the Manitoba Court of Appeal left the issue open and noted that in both the *Perry* and *Starr Schein* judgments, there was a dissent which raised cogent arguments.

Indeed, there is much to be said for the dissenting judgments in *Perry* and *Starr Schein*. The issue, simply put, is whether a purely pecuniary loss is caught by the words "injury ... to ... property". At common law "injury" has been held to extend beyond mere physical injury and include infringement of a right.[30] In the *Insurance Act* "property" is defined to include "profits, earnings and other pecuniary interests".[31] In this context, then, a client's financial loss resulting from the negligence of a solicitor can quite readily be said to constitute "injury ... to ... property". To hold otherwise goes against the very mischief which the statutory provision under consideration was intended to remedy.

In *Richards v. Continental Casualty Co.*[32] an issue arose as to whether the injury to person or property must be to the person or property of the claimant. The plaintiff, a firm of architects, was liable to the owner in respect of property damage to the project. After paying the owner's claim the plaintiff obtained judgment against a subcontractor and, upon execution on the judgment returning unsatisfied, brought proceedings against the subcontractor's insurer. The Alberta Court of Appeal held that the claim fell within the statutory provision, notwithstanding that the architects' loss was purely a pecuniary one, for the architects' judgment against the insured was properly characterized as an amount owing for damage to property and thus fell within the language of the statute.

The trial judge in *Richards v. Continental Casualty Co.*[33] drew attention to the differences in wording between the Ontario and British Columbia statutes on the one hand and the Alberta and Saskatchewan statutes on the other. These differences appear to support the decision in *Richards* but not that in *Kallos*.[34]

As an alternative basis for her judgment, the trial judge in *Richards* held that an injured person is a third party beneficiary to a policy of liability insurance and, as such, is entitled, by the device of a trust, to enforce the insurance contract directly. A similar argument was rejected by the British Columbia Supreme Court in *Freemont Development Co. v. Travellers Indemnity Co.*[35]

It is not entirely clear whether in the third party action against the insurer the claimant must lead evidence beyond the formal record in order to establish

---

[29] [1994] N.J. No. 611, 27 C.C.L.I. (2d) 58, 28 C.B.R. (3d) 234, 97 Man. R. (2d) 243, 79 W.A.C. 243 (C.A.), affg [1994] M.J. No. 267, 23 C.C.L.I. (2d) 86, 26 C.B.R. 125, 93 Man. R. (2d) 304 (Q.B.).

[30] See Chapter 7, section 4: Bodily Injury and Property Damage. In *Hildon Hotel (1963) Ltd. v. Dominion Insurance Corp.* (1968), 1 D.L.R. (3d) 214 (B.C.S.C.), it was held that the infringement of the right to enjoy unpolluted water was an "injury to property" in the context of the insuring agreement in a commercial liability policy.

[31] R.S.B.C. 1996, c. 226, s. 1.

[32] [1986] A.J. No. 643, 22 C.C.L.I. 91 (Q.B.), affd [1987] A.J. No. 454, 25 C.C.L.I. 237 (C.A.).

[33] *Ibid.* at 95.

[34] *Supra*, note 26.

[35] [1993] B.C.J. No., 1700, 23 C.C.L.I. (2d) 92 (S.C.).

the liability of the insured. In *Global General Insurance Co. v. Finlay*,[36] a case which dealt with statutory provisions regarding automobile insurance, the Supreme Court of Canada held that the claimant need only prove "the formal judgment, the reasons therefor and the record, including of course the pleadings, in the action in which the judgment was recovered".[37] In so holding, the Supreme Court of Canada found it necessary to distinguish the earlier decision of the Court in *Continental Casualty Co. v. Yorke*,[38] in which it was held that the claimant's judgment was not evidence of the circumstances upon which it was founded, thus requiring the claimant, in effect, to prove the case a second time. In *Global General Insurance Co. v. Finlay* the decision in *Continental Casualty Co. v. Yorke* was distinguished both on its facts and on the substantial differences in the legislation under consideration in the two cases. Subsequent decisions in lower courts have suggested that the decision in *Yorke* was overruled,[39] or at the very least, should be narrowly confined.[40]

In the Supreme Court of Canada's decision in *Joynt v. Canada Security Assurance Co.*, Judson J. explained the effect of a similar statutory provision, dealing with motor vehicle liability policies, as follows:

> The question in the statutory action is not whether the judgment in the liability action is correct but whether the plaintiff has a judgment against the insured for which indemnity is provided in the motor liability policy. A plaintiff in such an action proves his case by putting in the judgment against the insured, the insurance policy and proof of non-payment. All else is a matter of defence with the onus of proof on the insurance company.[41]

On its face, it would appear to make good sense that a claimant, having established a claim once against a wrongdoer, should not be required to prove the claim a second time against the wrongdoer's insurer.[42] That, however, is not the end of the matter. The underlying action does not deal with issues of coverage. The section provides that the claimant's rights against the insurer are "subject to

---

[36] [1961] S.C.R. 539.

[37] *Ibid.* at 551.

[38] [1930] S.C.R. 180.

[39] This appears to have been the view of O'Driscoll J. in *Romay Automotive Ltd. v. Dominion of Canada General Insurance Co.* (1974), 2 O.R. (2d) 506 at 513 (H.C.J.). See also Mitchell, "Rights of Unnamed Insurance and Third Parties", Law Society of Upper Canada, Special Lectures 1962 at 331.

[40] *Sedam v. Simcoe & Erie General Insurance Co.*, [1983] B.C.J. No. 1809, [1983] I.L.R. 1-1673 (S.C.).

[41] [1967] S.C.R. 110 at 113. See also *Rocovitis v. Dominion of Canada General Insurance Co.*, [2003] O.J. No. 297, 63 O.R. (3d) 402 (S.C.J.), affd [2004] O.J. No. 4326, 73 O.R. (3d) 735 (C.A.)

[42] Thus, in *Federated Insurance Co. of Canada v. Reliance Insurance Co.*, [2001] O.J. No. 4676 (S.C.J.), which addresses the duty to defend in a case involving overlapping coverage, the applicant sought and obtained an order that the respondent insurer was bound by any determination of fact or law in the underlying action.

the same equities as the insurer would have if the judgment had been satisfied". On this basis it has been held that it is open to the insurer to lead evidence to show that the claim does not fall within the coverage provided.[43] Further, even where the claim does fall within coverage, it may be open to the insurer to show that the underlying judgment was obtained by collusion between the claimant and the insured.[44]

Once the insurer participates as a party in the trial of the main action, however, it may be bound by the trial result. In *Bank of Montreal v. Pilot Insurance Co.*,[45] an action was commenced against the insured for negligently causing a fire at one of the plaintiff's branches. The insurer denied the claim on the basis that the fire was a deliberate act of the insured. Having been brought into the action by way of third party proceedings, the insurer availed itself of the procedural right to file a statement of defence in the main action. As a consequence, the insurer was bound by the result of the trial of the tort action even though, having obtained an order severing the third party proceedings, the insurer did not participate in the trial of that action. The decision turned on a provision in the Ontario Rules of Civil Procedure stipulating that a third party who delivers a statement of defence in the main action is bound by any order or determination made in that action. Whether the decision would have been the same had the insurer not delivered a statement of defence in the main action was not discussed. As a matter of principle, however, the same result would not have followed.

---

[43] *Hamilton v. Laurentian Pacific Insurance Co.*, [1988] B.C.J. No. 439, 30 C.C.L.I. 204 (S.C.), revd, [1989] B.C.J. No. 869, 37 C.C.L.I. 190 (C.A.); *Zegouras v. Pilot Insurance Co.*, [1987] I.L.R. 1-2211 (Ont. Dist. Ct.).

[44] See: *Litchfield Holdings & Management Corp. v. Kingsway General Insurance Co.*, [2002] B.C.J. No. 2807, 44 C.C.L.I. (3d) 238 (S.C.); *McKenna v. Reed*, [2001] O.J. No. 3513 I.L.R. 1-4005 (S.C.J.); and *Pepsi Co. Inc. v. Continental Casualty Co.*, 640 F. Supp. 656 (S.D.N.Y. 1986). Although these cases deal with alleged collusive *settlements,* the same principle should apply to a judgment obtained through collusion.

[45] [1993] O.J. No. 30, 16 C.C.L.I. (2d) 208 (Gen. Div.).

Chapter 2

THE CONTRACT OF INSURANCE

1. FORMATION OF THE CONTRACT

(a) Formal Requirements

The rules that govern the formation of liability insurance contracts are the same as those that govern the formation of contracts generally. There must be an offer and acceptance with agreement on all material terms.[1] With liability insurance contracts, the material terms would consist of the parties, the premium, the subject matter of the insurance, the nature and duration of the risk, and the limit of liability. It is unlikely that the parties will have reached an agreement on all the other terms of the insurance. Unless the circumstances dictate otherwise, the court will assume that the insured was seeking coverage on the basis of the insurer's usual or standard terms.[2]

There is no requirement at common law that a liability insurance contract be in any particular form. Oral contracts are permitted.[3] This has been carried over into the scheme of largely uniform insurance legislation in force in the common law provinces. The terms "contract" and "policy" are defined as follows:

> "contract" means a contract of insurance and includes a policy, certificate, interim receipt, renewal receipt or writing evidencing the contract, whether sealed or not, and a binding oral agreement; ...

> "policy" means the instrument evidencing a contract; ...[4]

---

[1] *Allis-Chalmers Co. v. Maryland Fidelity and Deposit Co.* (1916), 114 L.T. 433.

[2] *Rust v. Abbey Life Assur. Co. Ltd.*, [1979] 2 Lloyd's Rep. 334 (C.A.); *Acme Wood Flooring Co. Ltd. v. Marten* (1904), 9 Com. Cas. 157; *General Accident Ins. Corp. v. Cronk* (1901), 17 T.L.R. 233.

[3] *London Life Ins. Co. v. Wright* (1880), 5 S.C.R. 466; *Westminster Woodworking Co. and Graham v. Stuyvesant Ins. Co.* (1915), 9 W.W.R. 418; *Queen Ins. Co. v. Br. Traders Ins. Co.*, [1928] S.C.R. 9; *Taylor v. London Assur. Corp.*, [1935] S.C.R. 422.

[4] *Insurance Act*, R.S.B.C. 1996, c. 226, s. 1. Comparable definitions are found in the following: R.S.A. 2000, c. I-3, s. 1(*j*), (*uu*); C.C.S.M., c. I40, s. 1; R.S.N.B. 1973, c. I-12, s. 1; *Insurance Contracts Act*, R.S.N.L. 1990, c. I-12, s. 2(*f*), (*s*); R.S.N.S. 1989, c. 231, s. 3(*h*), (*q*); R.S.O. 1990, c. I.8, s. 1; R.S.P.E.I. 1988, c. I-4, s. 1(*d*.2), (*q*); *Saskatchewan Insurance Act*, R.S.S. 1978, c. S-26, s. 2(*m*), (*xx*).

(b) Interim Coverage

In practice, liability insurance coverage is usually bound well before the issuance of the policy. The insurer's agent may bind the risk either verbally or by the issuance of a binder or a receipt for the premium. A "binder" is a document that sets out the essential terms of the contract; it is generally subject to the terms and conditions of the policy to be issued.

As a general rule, the insurer's agent has authority to bind the insurer to the contract. Moreover, under a British Columbia statute, by issuing either a receipt for the premium or the policy itself, the agent binds the insurer to the contract whether or not there is actual authority to do so:

> If a policy or a receipt for the premium under a contract is delivered to the insured by the insurer or its agent, the insurer is bound by the contract, even though
> (a)   the delivery may have been made by the agent without authority, or
> (b)   the premium may not in fact have been paid.[5]

In the remaining common law jurisdictions a similar statutory provision applies with respect to delivery of the policy:

> When the policy has been delivered the contract is as binding on the insurer as if the premium had been paid, although it has not in fact been paid and although delivered by an officer or agent of the insurer who had not authority to deliver it.[6]

(c) Contents of the Policy

Notwithstanding that oral insurance contracts are permitted, the invariable practice of liability insurers is to issue a policy that sets out all the terms of the contract. By statute, once a policy has been issued there are certain provisions that it must contain:

> Every policy shall contain
> (a)   the name of the insurer;
> (b)   the name of the insured;
> (c)   the name of the person or persons to whom the insurance money is payable;
> (d)   the amount or the method of determining the amount of the premium for the insurance;
> (e)   the subject matter of the insurance;
> (f)   the indemnity for which the insurer may become liable;
> (g)   the event on the happening of which the liability is to accrue;

---

[5]   *Insurance Act*, R.S.B.C. 1996, c. 226, s. 14.

[6]   *Insurance Act,* R.S.A. 2000, c. I-3, s. 518(1). Comparable sections in other jurisdictions are as follows: C.C.S.M., c. I40, s. 125(1); R.S.O. 1990, c. I.8, s. 134(1); R.S.N.B. 1973, c. I-12, s. 102(1); R.S.N.S. 1989, c. 231, s. 20(1); *Insurance Contracts Act*, R.S.N.L. 1990, c. I-12, s. 15(1); R.S.P.E.I. 1988, c. I-4, s. 96(1); *Saskatchewan Insurance Act*, R.S.S. 1978, c. S-26, s. 112(1).

(h)   the date on which the insurance takes effect;

(i)   the date it terminates or the method by which that date is fixed or is to be fixed.[7]

Moreover, except in Nova Scotia, the insurer is precluded from setting up a term or condition of the contract that is not set out in full in the policy if doing so would be to the prejudice of the insured:

(1)   All the terms and conditions of a contract of insurance shall be set out in full in the policy or by writing securely attached to it when issued, and unless so set out no term of the contract or condition, stipulation, warranty or proviso modifying or impairing its effect is valid or admissible in evidence to the prejudice of the insured or any beneficiary.

(2)   Subsection (1) does not apply to an alteration or modification of the contract agreed on in writing by the insurer and the insured after the issue of the policy.[8]

It has been held in British Columbia that the provisions of this section may be satisfied by reference in the document received by the insured to another document containing the terms and conditions of the policy. In *Hwang v. Axa Pacific Insurance Co.*[9] the insured was bound by the terms set out in the policy booklet, which was referred to in the declarations pages he received upon successive renewals of the policy but which was apparently not delivered to him. A further basis for the decision was that in taking the benefit of the policy booklet the insured also took its burdens; he could not rely on the insuring provisions set out in the policy booklet without also being subject to the conditions and exclusions contained therein.

The interpretation given to this section by the British Columbia Court of Appeal in *Hwang v. Axa Pacific Insurance Co.*[10] may not necessarily apply with respect to the equivalent section in the other common law provinces. In Alberta, for example, unlike British Columbia, the legislature has included the following provision in the *Insurance Act*:

(5)   When a contract, whether it does or does not provide for its renewal, is renewed by a renewal receipt, it is a sufficient compliance with subsection (1)

---

[7]   *Insurance Act*, R.S.A. 2000, c. I-3, s. 513(3). Comparable sections in other jurisdictions are as follows: R.S.B.C. 1996, c. 226, s. 8; C.C.S.M., c. I40, s. 120(1); R.S.N.B. 1973, c. I-12, s. . 101(1); R.S.N.S. 1989, c. 231, s. 18; *Insurance Contracts Act*, R.S.N.L. 1990, c. I-12, s. 8(1); R.S.O. 1990, c. I.8, s. 127; R.S.P.E.I. 1988, c. I-4, s. 90(1); *Saskatchewan Insurance Act*, R.S.S. 1978, c. S-26, s. 107.

[8]   *Insurance Act*, R.S.A. 2000, c. I-3, s. 513(1), (2). Comparable sections in other jurisdictions are as follows: R.S.B.C. 1996, c. 226, s. 12; C.C.S.M., c. I40, s. 117; R.S.N.B. 1973, c. I-12, s. 98(1), (2); R.S.O. 1990, c. I.8, s. 124(1), (2); *Insurance Contracts Act*, R.S.N.L. 1990, c. I-12, s. 5(1), (2); R.S.P.E.I. 1988, c. I-4, s. 87; *Saskatchewan Insurance Act*, R.S.S. 1978, c. S-26, s. 103(1), (2).

[9]   [2001] B.C.J. No. 1217, [2002] I.L.R. 1-4056 (C.A.), revg [1998] B.C.J. No. 535, [1998] I.L.R. I-3565 (S.C.). See also *Youlden v. London Guarantee Co.* (1913), 12 D.L.R. 433 (Ont. C.A.).

[10]   [2001] B.C.J. No. 1217, [2002] I.L.R. 1-4056 (C.A.).

if the terms and conditions of the contract were set out as provided by that sub-section and the renewal receipt refers to the contract by its number or date.[11]

If the terms of subsection (1) can be met by incorporating a document by reference then subsection (5) would be rendered unnecessary.

(d) Amending the Contract

Liability insurance contracts generally contain a term to the effect that the policy may be amended only by the insurer's issuance of a written endorsement. It is further provided by legislation that:

(1) No term or condition of a contract shall be deemed to be waived by the insurer in whole or in part unless the waiver is stated in writing and signed by a person authorized for that purpose by the insurer.

(2) Neither the insurer nor the insured shall be deemed to have waived any term or condition of a contract by any act relating to the appraisal of the amount of loss or to the delivery and completion of proofs or to the investigation or adjustment of any claim under the contract.[12]

(e) Choice of Law

The proper law of an insurance contract is determined according to the same common law rules that apply to contracts generally. Unless the parties have stipulated in the insurance contract which law shall apply, the contract will be governed by the law of the jurisdiction that appears to have the closest and most substantial connection with the contract.[13]

Insurance contracts issued in Canada do not generally contain a term as to the choice of law. Rather, the various provinces, presumably in order to protect the interests of their residents in having their legal rights determined according to local law,[14] have enacted legislation on this subject. With the exception of Alberta, British Columbia and Nova Scotia, the insurance legislation in the common law provinces provides that:

Where the subject matter of a contract of insurance is property in the province, or an insurable interest of a person resident within the province, the contract, if

---

[11] *Insurance Act*, R.S.A. 2000, c. I-3, s. 513(5). Comparable sections are found in R.S.S. 1978, c. S-26, s. 103(3); C.C.S.M., c. I40, s. 117(2); R.S.O. 1990, c. I.8, s. 124(5); R.S.N.B. 1973, c. I-12, s. 98(3); R.S.N.L. 1990, c. I-12, s. 5(3).

[12] *Insurance Act*, R.S.A. 2000, c. I-3, s. 517. Comparable sections in other jurisdictions are as follows: R.S.B.C. 1996, c. 226, s. 11; C.C.S.M., c. I40, s. 123(1), (2); R.S.N.B. 1973, c. I-12, s. 109; R.S.N.S. 1989, c. 231, s. 35; *Insurance Contracts Act*, R.S.N.L. 1990, c. I-12, s. 12; R.S.O. 1990, c. I.8, s. 131; R.S.P.E.I. 1988, c. I-4, s. 94; *Saskatchewan Insurance Act*, R.S.S. 1978, c. S-26, s. 111.

[13] *Colmenares v. Imperial Life Assur. Co.*, [1965] 2 O.R. 465 (H.C.J.), affd [1966] 1 O.R. 553 (C.A.), affd [1967] S.C.R. 443.

[14] J.G. Castel and J. Walker, *Canadian Conflict of Laws*, 5th ed. looseleaf (Toronto: LexisNexis Butterworths, 2002) at pp. 31.38-39.

signed, countersigned, issued or delivered in the province or committed to the post office or to any person to be delivered to the insured, his assign or agent in the province, shall be deemed to evidence a contract made therein, and be construed according to the law thereof, and all moneys payable thereunder shall be paid at the head office or chief agency of the insurer in the province, in lawful money of Canada.[15]

This section is of general application. It is not directed at liability insurance contracts in particular. The subject matter of a liability insurance contract is not generally property in the province. Although the concept of insurable interest is seldom considered in the context of liability insurance contracts, however, it can be argued that a person's potential financial liability creates an insurable interest.[16] In this fashion, the section would apply to an insured resident in the province. In *Jones v. Kansa General Insurance Co.*[17] the Ontario Court of Appeal, without any discussion on the point, referred to this section in holding that a liability policy issued in Ontario was "made" in Ontario. It is not clear, however, whether the court relied upon the section as deeming that the liability insurance contract was made in Ontario or whether the court found, as a matter of common law, that an insurance contract negotiated in Ontario, issued in Ontario, and entered into between an Ontario insurer and a corporation with a business address in Ontario is a contract made in the province.

In *American Home Insurance Co. v. Drake International Inc.*[18] this section was considered in the context of an insurer seeking a declaration in Ontario that it had no duty to defend or indemnify the insured in proceedings brought against the insured in Australia. The policy was negotiated, delivered, received and financed in Ontario, apparently by the insured's parent company on its behalf. Thus, the Court held, the policy was "made" in Ontario. As is typical for a liability policy, however, the contract was silent as to the governing law of the contract. In these circumstances, the Court stated that the policy should be construed in accordance with the law of the jurisdiction having the closest and most real connection with the contract. Noting that the policy was stated to be of worldwide application, that the insured under consideration was an Australian corporation and that the insurer had a place of business in Australia, the Court apparently was of the opinion that Australian law should govern. The Court dismissed section 123 of the *Insurance Act*[19] on the basis that "The conditions

---

[15] *Insurance Act*, C.C.S.M., c. 140, s. 116. Comparable sections in other jurisdictions are as follows: R.S.N.B. 1973, c. I-12, s. 97; *Insurance Contracts Act*, R.S.N.L. 1990, c. I-12, s. 4; R.S.O. 1990, c. I.8, s. 123; R.S.P.E.I. 1988, c. I-4, s. 86; *Saskatchewan Insurance Act*, R.S.S. 1978, c. S-26, s. 102.

[16] This is implicit in the decision in *Re Laidlaw Inc.*, [2003] O.J. No. 1135, 46 C.C.L. 1 (3d) 263 (S.C.J.) and is consistent with the legislative purpose of the provision.

[17] [1992] O.J. No. 1597, 10 O.R. (3d) 56, supp. reasons 96 D.L.R. (4th) 286 (C.A.), leave to appeal to S.C.C. refd (1993), 98 D.L.R. (4th) *viii.*

[18] [2002] O.J. No. 333 (S.C.J.).

[19] R.S.O. 1990, c. I.8. Curiously, in quoting s. 123 the Court omitted the phrase "and the contract shall be construed according to the law thereof". This typographical error does not appear to

precedent for application of the constituent parts of s. 123 have, however, not been established within the context of these particular factual circumstances".[20] Presumably this is a reference to the requirement that the subject matter of the contract of insurance is property in Ontario or an insurable interest of a person resident in Ontario. Unfortunately, the Court did not explain the reasoning behind this conclusion. Perhaps the insured subsidiary was not resident in Ontario.[21] In any event, the Court went on to decline jurisdiction on the basis that Australia was the most convenient and appropriate forum in which to hear the dispute, which is a separate issue from that of determining the proper law of the contract.[22]

In Alberta and British Columbia the legislation is drafted in broader terms:

> A contract is deemed to have been made in British Columbia and must be construed accordingly if it
> (a)   insures a person domiciled or resident in British Columbia at the date of it, or
> (b)   has as its subject matter property or an interest in property located in British Columbia.[23]

Although this section clearly applies to policies of liability insurance, it differs from the legislation in force in the other provinces in that it does not stipulate that the contract shall be construed in accordance with the law of the province. Rather, as was noted in *Cansulex v. Reed Stenhouse Ltd.*,[24] the section simply deems that the contract was made in the province, which, albeit an important factor, is not determinative of the choice of law.

(f) Misrepresentation

The law regarding misrepresentation is the same with respect to liability insurance contracts as it is with respect to insurance contracts generally.[25] A material misrepresentation of fact by the insured, if relied upon by the insurer, will constitute grounds for avoiding the contract.[26] Materiality must be estab-

---

have affected the result in the decision, however, for the Court held that the condition precedent to the application of s. 123 had not been met.

[20]   *Supra*, note 18 at para. 28.

[21]   As noted in *Re Laidlaw Inc.*, [2003] O.J. No. 1135 at para. 8 (S.C.J.).

[22]   See, for example, *Zurich Insurance Co. v. Muscletech Research & Development Inc.*, [2004] O.J. No. 2739, 15 C.C.L. 1 (4th) 310 (S.C.J.).

[23]   *Insurance Act*, R.S.B.C. 1996, c. 226, s. 5. The comparable section in Alberta is R.S.A. 2000, c. I-3, s. 12(1).

[24]   [1986] B.C.J. No. 3125, 18 C.C.L.I. 24 at 41 (S.C.).

[25]   *Roumiani v. Fowler*, [1998] N.J. No. 347, 172 Nfld. & P.E.I.R. 337 (Nfld. S.C.T.D.).

[26]   The rule with respect to marine insurance is that a representation, however innocent it may be, vitiates the contract when it is materially and substantially incorrect: *Nova Scotia Marine Ins. Co. v. Stevenson* (1894), 23 S.C.R. 137. It is generally accepted that this rule applies to all classes of insurance. See *Graham v. Australian Ins. Co. Ltd.* (1931), 40 Lloyd's Rep. 64 at 66, Roche J.; *Golding v. Royal London Auxiliary Ins. Co.* (1914), 30 T.L.R. 350 at 351. See also

lished by the insurer. By statute, the insurer is prohibited from deeming that certain representations are material when, in fact, they are not:

> The proposal or application of the insured shall not, as against him, be deemed to be a part of or be considered with the contract of insurance except in so far as the Court determines that it contains a material misrepresentation by which the insurer was induced to enter into the contract.[27]

> No contract of insurance may contain or have endorsed on it, or be made subject to, any term, condition, stipulation, warranty or proviso providing that the contract is avoided by reason of any statement in the application for the contract or inducing the insurer to enter into the contract, unless the term, condition, stipulation, warranty or proviso is limited to cases in which the statement is material to the contract, and no contract may be avoided by reason of the inaccuracy of any such statement unless it is material to the contract.[28]

The test of materiality, as stated by the Privy Council in *Mutual Life Insurance Co. of New York v. Ontario Metal Products Co.* is:

> ... whether, if the matters concealed or misrepresented had been truly disclosed, they would, on a fair consideration of the evidence, have influenced a reasonable insurer to decline the risk or to have stipulated for a higher premium.[29]

Since materiality is measured by the standard of the reasonable insurer, the fact that either the insured or the insurer thought that the facts were or were not material is irrelevant. As noted by the Supreme Court of Canada in *Henwood v. Prudential Insurance Co.*,[30] a misrepresentation does not become material "simply because it has been elicited in answer to a question devised by the insurance company". In cases where materiality is an issue it is customary for expert evidence to be led on the point.[31]

Sayle v. Jevco Insurance Co. (1984), 58 B.C.L.R. 122 (B.C.S.C.) , affd, (1985), 16 C.C.L.I. 309 (B.C.C.A.) and *Fellowes, McNeil v. Kansa General International Insurance Co.*, [2000] O.J. No. 3309, 22 C.C.L.I (3d) 1 (C.A.).

[27] *Insurance Act*, R.S.A. 2000, c. I-3, s. 513(6). Comparable sections in other jurisdictions are as follows: C.C.S.M., c. I40, s. 117(3); R.S.N.B. 1973, c. I-12, s. 98(4); *Insurance Contracts Act*, R.S.N.L. 1990, c. I-12, s. 5(4); R.S.O. 1990, c. I.8, s. 124(4); R.S.P.E.I. 1988, c. I-4, s. 87(3); *Saskatchewan Insurance Act*, R.S.S. 1978, c. S-26, s. 103(4).

[28] *Insurance Act*, R.S.A. 2000, c. I-3, s. 513(7). Comparable sections in other jurisdictions are as follows: R.S.B.C. 1996, c. 226, s. 13; C.C.S.M., c. I40, s. 117(4); R.S.N.B. 1973, c. I-12, s. 98(5); *Insurance Contracts Act*, R.S.N.L. 1990, c. I-12, s. 5(5); R.S.O. 1990, c. I.8, s. 124(5); R.S.P.E.I. 1988, c. I-4, s. 87(4); *Saskatchewan Insurance Act*, R.S.S. 1978, c. S-26, s. 103(5).

[29] [1925] A.C. 344 at 351-52 (P.C.). See also *Fidelity & Casualty Co. of New York v. General Structures Inc.*, [1977] 2 S.C.R. 1098.

[30] [1967] S.C.R. 720 at 726.

[31] *Stevenson v. Simcoe & Erie General Ins.*, [1981] I.L.R. 1-1434 (Alta. Q.B.); *Fellowes, McNeil v. Kansa General International Insurance Co.*, *supra*, note 26.

Unlike property insurance policies, liability policies typically do not contain a condition requiring the insured to report material changes in the risk. In circumstances in which the risk has apparently changed after the policy has been issued this may well lead to a close examination of the description of the risk in the declarations portion of the policy[32] as well consideration being given to the statements made by the insured to the broker or the insurer at the time the policy was placed. An interesting example of this is provided by the decision in *Lafarge Canada Inc. v. Little Mountain Excavating Ltd.*[33] In seeking a quote for a liability policy the insured described its operations, in a broker's letter, as land clearing, site preparation, driveway installation, septic field installation, loading sand and gravel for Lafarge Concrete, decommissioning of logging roads, logging road repair and grounds maintenance. The insurer required the completion of a logging contractor form, on which the insured stated, in response to a question about welding activities, "No, doesn't weld". As a result, the insurer did not require a welding warranty and issued the policy describing the insured's operations as "repair contractor including grounds maintenance". Shortly afterwards the insured used a cutting torch in an operation for Lafarge Concrete, as a result of which a forest fire allegedly ensued. The insured sought coverage under the policy on the basis that the welding operation was incidental to the insured's stated business operations, that the answer to the welding question was true at the time it was given, that the welding operation was a singular event, taking place only after the policy was issued, and that the description of operations in the policy declarations superseded the description given by the insured in obtaining the quote. The court rejected these arguments, holding that the insured's representation amounted to a statement that it would not, in the future, undertake welding activities. There is no discussion in the reasons for judgment as to whether a statement about future intentions can properly be characterized as a representation.

Although the foregoing rules apply to insurance contracts generally, there may be an additional limitation on a liability insurer's right to avoid a contract by reason of the insured's misrepresentation. In *Coronation Insurance Co. v. Taku Air Transport Ltd.*,[34] the insurer sought to avoid a policy of aviation insurance, one of its grounds being the insured's misrepresentation of its accident record. The insured had disclosed only one of three prior accidents. Had the insurer checked either its own records, from a prior policy issued to the same insured, or the publicly available records of air carrier accidents, the true state of affairs apparently would have been revealed.[35] While the case was decided in the insurer's favour upon a different point, a majority of the Supreme Court of Canada stated that had the only issue been the misrepresentation as to

---

[32] See Chapter 6, Section 2: Structure of a Commercial Liability Policy.

[33] [2001] B.C.J. No. 732, [2001] I.L.R. 1-3977 (S.C.)

[34] [1991] S.C.J. No. 96, [1991] 3 S.C.R. 622, 61 B.C.L.R. (2d) 41.

[35] In Harris, "Fraudulent Misrepresentations and the Insurer's Duty to Investigate" (1992) 20 Can. Bus. L.J. 464, doubt is cast upon the extent to which the publicly available information would have provided the insurer with the requisite information.

the insured's accident record, then the insurer would have been unable to avoid the policy. The majority reasoned that in the case where a policy of liability insurance is required by statute for the protection of the public then different considerations apply than in the case where the policy is for the exclusive benefit of the insured. Justice Cory, after referring to the principle that the insured has no obligation to disclose to the insurer information which is generally available,[36] stated:

> The present situation can really be stated in this way. Insurance for passengers has been made a condition for licensing air carriers. A carrier, in order to obtain a licence, must seek out an insurer and obtain a policy. Without a policy they cannot fly. The Regulations provide the insurance companies with a captive clientele. Yet, on the strength of Lord Mansfield's doctrine the insurer is not bound to pay in case of death or injury of a passenger resulting from the negligence of the carrier if that carrier misrepresented the extent of its accident history on the application. This is so even if the insurer's own records would disclose the misrepresentation. It is a situation that discourages both investigation by the insurer and disclosure by the insured. In a highly regulated, and potentially dangerous, field the passenger is left unprotected. ...
>
> I would think that where the policy of insurance required by statute or regulation is primarily for the benefit of members of the flying public and not just the insured, the insurer must take some basic steps to investigate the flying record of the air carrier applying for insurance. At a minimum, it should review its own files on the applicant. Further the insurer should make a search of the public record of accidents of the air carrier....
>
> Surely the imposition of these modest requirements on the insurer is not placing too great a burden on an insurer entering the field of aviation insurance in which the passengers will be the beneficiaries. In this case the insurers had within their own grasp information which would have provided a more accurate assessment of the risk entailed by the policy. At a minimum, the insurers should have scrutinized their own records before issuing the policy. They did not meet the standards required of an insurer operating in this field. Having failed in exercising the required standard of diligence, the insurers cannot escape liability to the passengers on the policy because the insured also failed in its duty.[37]

The foregoing passages from the reasons for judgment of Cory J. consist of *obiter dicta*. Although the protection of the public is a laudable goal, the reasoning by which Cory J. reaches that goal is suspect. He takes the principle that an insured has no duty to disclose that which the insurer can reasonably be expected to know and elevates it to a duty on the insurer to carry out an investigation into the truth of the representations made by the insured in applying for the policy. Since a third party's right to the proceeds of a liability insurance policy is subject to the same equities which exist as between the insurer and the insured, it follows from the reasoning of Cory J. that an insured

---

[36] See section (g): Non-Disclosure.

[37] *Supra*, note 34 at paras. 31-35.

who knowingly misled the insurer would nevertheless be entitled to the benefit of the insurance policy in circumstances where a reasonably diligent insurer would have discovered the misrepresentation. With respect, this cannot be the law.

(g) Non-Disclosure

An insurance contract is a contract *uberrima fides*, of the utmost good faith.[38] The classic expression of this principle is that by Lord Mansfield in 1766 in *Carter v. Boehm*:

> Insurance is a contract upon speculation. The special facts, upon which the contingent chance is to be computed, lie most commonly in the knowledge of the insured only: the under-writer trusts to his representation, and proceeds upon confidence that he does not keep back any circumstances in his knowledge, to mislead the under-writer into a belief that the circumstance does not exist, and to induce him to estimate the risque as if it did not exist. The keeping back of such circumstance is a fraud, and therefore the policy is void. Although the suppression should happen through mistake, without any fraudulent intention; yet still the under-writer is deceived, and the policy is void; because the risque run is really different from the risque understood and intended to be run, at the time of the agreement. ... The governing principle is applicable to all contracts and dealings. Good faith forbids either party by concealing what he privately knows, to draw the other into a bargain, from his ignorance of that fact, and his believing the contrary. ...[39]

Although the rationale for the requirement of good faith is more clearly found in the context of marine insurance, where the insured is far more familiar with the subject matter of the risk than is the insurer, the principle of *uberrima fides* applies to all types of insurance and to the insurer as well as to the insured.[40] Each party to an insurance contract must disclose to the other all material facts concerning the risk. There is no duty, however, upon an insured to inform the insurer of matters of which the insurer either knows or ought to know:

> There are many matters, as to which the insured may be innocently silent — he need not mention what the under-writer knows — *Scientia untrinque par pares contrahentes facit.*
>
> An under-writer can not insist that the policy is void, because the insured did not tell him what he actually knew; what way soever he came to the knowledge.

---

[38] *Ford v. Dominion of Canada General Insurance Co.*, [1989] M.J. No. 674, 40 C.C.L.I. 313 (C.A.), revd [1991] S.C.J. No. 13, [1991] 1 S.C.R. 136.

[39] (1766), 97 E.R. 1162 at 1164.

[40] *London Assur. v. Mansel* (1879), 11 Ch. D. 363; *Joel v. Law Union and Crown Ins. Co.*, [1908] 2 K.B. 863 (C.A.); *Roumiani v. Fowler*, [1998] N.J. No. 347, 172 Nfld. & P.E.I.R. 337 (Nfld. S.C.T.D.).

> The insured need not mention what the under-writer ought to know; what he takes upon himself the knowledge of; or what he waves being informed of.[41]

The extent of the insurer's presumed knowledge was addressed by the Supreme Court of Canada in *Canadian Indemnity Co. v. Canadian Johns-Manville Co.*[42] Although the decision pertains to the Quebec *Civil Code*, the court gave extensive consideration to the position at common law.[43] The insured was in the business of mining, manufacturing and selling asbestos. When it applied for liability insurance coverage in 1970, the insured answered questions concerning its business operations and disclosed its claims history for the previous 24 years. No questions were asked, however, and the insured did not disclose details of the health risks associated with the inhalation of asbestos fibres. These risks were documented both within the industry and in medical literature, but were not known to the insurer, who had never before insured this type of risk and who assigned the investigation of the risk to a trainee. The Supreme Court of Canada held that the insurer could not use its own lack of due diligence as a basis for avoiding the policy. The Court held that if an insurer does not have the requisite degree of knowledge prior to considering a particular risk, then it must acquire that knowledge by means of inquiry or investigation. A reasonably competent insurer is expected to keep abreast of information concerning the industry it insures. In some cases this might go beyond that which is notorious to the general public, but the insurer is not expected to know facts which are known only to those within the industry and which are available only through a process of detailed research or in-depth investigation.

The principle of *uberrima fides* applies at the time the parties enter into the insurance contract. There is, in general, no obligation to disclose supervening facts which come to the knowledge of either party after the terms of the contract have been concluded.[44]

The remedy for a breach of the duty of good faith is, at the election of the aggrieved party, avoidance of the contract and return of the premium.[45]

(h) Public Policy

At law, a contract may be void as being contrary to public policy. Liability insurers sometimes invoke this doctrine not for the purpose of declaring their contracts void but to prevent a finding of coverage where there has been

---

[41] *Carter v. Boehm, supra*, note 39 at 1164-65.

[42] [1990] S.C.J. No. 82, 50 C.C.L.I. 95.

[43] In *Coronation Ins. Co. v. Taku Air Transport Ltd., supra*, note 34, the majority of the Supreme Court of Canada, in *obiter dicta*, accepted that the common law position was the same as the position was under the Quebec *Civil Code*.

[44] *Banque Financière de la Cité S.A. v. Westgate Ins. Co.*, [1990] 2 All E.R. 947 (H.L.); *Tumbers Video Ltd. v. INA Insurance Co. of Canada*, [1991] B.C.J. No. 3274, [1992] 2 W.W.R. 66 (C.A.).

[45] *Joel v. Law Union and Crown Ins. Co., supra*, note 40.

intentional or criminal conduct on the part of the insured or where the insured seeks indemnity with respect to fines, penalties or punitive damages.[46]

At one time the courts gave slack rein to this unruly horse. In *Home Insurance Co. and U.S. Fidelity & Guaranty Co. v. Lindal and Beattie*,[47] the insured, who was intoxicated, drove his car into a street railway standard and caused serious personal injury to his passenger. She recovered a judgment against him, following which both of them took proceedings against his insurer for indemnity. The majority of the Supreme Court of Canada held that although the insured did not intentionally cause harm to his passenger the rule of public policy prevented him from obtaining indemnity because his conduct constituted a criminal offence. The Court applied the principle stated by Kennedy J. in *Burrows v. Rhodes* as follows:

> It has, I think, long been settled law that if an act is manifestly unlawful, or the doer of it knows it to be unlawful, as constituting either a civil wrong or a criminal offence, he cannot maintain an action for contribution or for indemnity against the liability which results to him therefrom. An express promise of indemnity to him for the commission of such an act is void.[48]

The harshness of the decision in *Home Insurance and U.S. Fidelity & Guaranty Co. v. Lindal and Beattie* has been ameliorated by statute. The legislation in force in the common law provinces provides that:

> Unless the contract otherwise provides, a contravention of any criminal or other law in force in [the province] or elsewhere does not render unenforceable a claim for indemnity under a contract of insurance except when the contravention is committed by the insured, or by another person with the consent of the insured, with intent to bring about loss or damage.[49]

The effect of this section is that public policy may not be used as the basis for denying indemnity to the insured unless there was intent to bring about loss or damage. As the opening phrase in the section indicates, however, an insurer

---

[46] In many of the United States, coverage with respect to punitive damages is considered to be against public policy: see *Northwestern Nat. Casualty Co. v. McNulty*, 307 F.2d 432 (5th Cir. 1962); *Dorsey v. Honda Motor Co. Ltd.*, 655 F.2d 650 (5th Cir. 1981); *Public Service Mutual Ins. Co. v. Goldfarb*, 425 N.E.2d 810 (N.Y. 1981). For the contrary view see *Baker v. Armstrong*, 744 P.2d 170 (N.M. 1987). Many states that prohibit insurance coverage for punitive damages with respect to the wrongdoer nevertheless permit coverage for punitive damages imposed under the doctrine of vicarious liability; see *Beaver v. Country Mutual Insurance Co.*, 420 N.E.2d 1058 (Ill. 1981); *Magnum Foods v. Continental Casualty Co.*, 36 F.3d 1491 (10th Cir. 1994).

[47] [1934] S.C.R. 33.

[48] [1899] 1 Q.B. 816 at 828.

[49] *Insurance Act*, R.S.A. 2000, c. I-3, s. 529(2). Comparable sections in other jurisdictions are as follows: R.S.B.C. 1996, c. 226, s. 28; C.C.S.M., c. I40, s. 92; R.S.N.B. 1973, c. I-12, s. 2; R.S.N.S. 1989, c. 231, s. 13; *Insurance Contracts Act*, R.S.N.L. 1990, c. I-12, s. 18; R.S.O. 1990, c. I.8, s. 118; R.S.P.E.I. 1988, c. I-4, s. 107; *Saskatchewan Insurance Act*, R.S.S. 1978, c. S-26, s. 121. The history of this remedial legislation is briefly discussed in a note by G.W. Reed in (1953), 31 C.B.R. 319 at 325-26.

wishing to restrict coverage further may do so with the use of the appropriate policy language.

The application of the section requires the court to determine whether the insured intended to bring about loss or damage. It does not stipulate that the loss or damage intended must be the same as that which occurs. Thus, in *Co-operative Fire & Casualty v. Saindon*[50] it was held that the fact that a criminal act might have far more serious consequences than the insured intended does not prevent the application of the section. It is noted that the decision in *Saindon* has received substantial academic criticism[51] and, in subsequent cases, has more often than not been distinguished on its facts.[52]

Surprisingly, the section was not referred to in *Medhurst v. Children's Aid Society of London and Middlesex*.[53] The insured, a warden of a group home, was convicted of the sexual assault of a child in his care. In a civil action claiming damages for both physical and sexual assault it was held that the insurer was required to defend the insured because the insuring agreement in the policy extended coverage to claims for damages because of "assault and battery". For the purposes of the application, the learned judge conceded that the injuries were cause either intentionally or through the commission of a criminal act. The decision of the Supreme Court of Canada in *Non-Marine Underwriters, Lloyd's of London v. Scalera*[54] was distinguished on the basis that in the latter case the insuring agreement did not extend to assault and battery. Although that is so, the Supreme Court in *Scalera* also stated that one who engages in non-consensual intercourse will be presumed to have intended harm. Unfortunately, the pleadings filed on behalf of the plaintiff in *Medhurst* are not set out in sufficient detail in the reasons for judgment to permit a determination as to whether the result in the case would have been different had the learned judge given consideration to the statutory prohibition under discussion.

---

[50] (1975), 56 D.L.R. (3d) 556 (S.C.C.).

[51] See R.A. Hasson, "The Supreme Court of Canada and the Law of Insurance 1975" (1976) 14 Osgoode Hall L.J. 769; C. Brown & J. Menezes, *Insurance Law in Canada: A Treatise on the Principles of Indemnity Insurance as Applied in the Common Law Provinces of Canada* (Scarborough: Carswell, 1991) and Lee Stuesser, "Liability Insurance Covering Criminal Acts" (1989) 1 C.I.L.R. 131.

[52] *Devlin v. Co-op. Fire & Casualty Co.* (1978), 7 Alta. L.R. (2d) 155 (C.A.), leave to appeal to S.C.C. refd, 13 A.R. 18; *Long Lake School Div. No. 30 v. Schatz* [1984] S.J. No. 78, 6 C.C.L.I. 1 (Q.B.), affd [1986] S.J. No. 138, 18 C.C.L.I. 232 (C.A.), leave to appeal to S.C.C. refd, 22 C.C.L.I. xxxiii; *Taylor v. Co-op. Fire & Casualty Co.* [1984] A.J. No. 724, 10 C.C.L.I. 284 (Q.B.); *Newcastle (Town) v. Mattatall* [1987] N.B.J. No. 223, 25 C.C.L.I. 58 (Q.B.), affd [1988] N.B.J. No. 526, 33 C.C.L.I. 97 (C.A.); *Contra, Wawanesa Mutual Ins. Co. v. Thomas*, [1982] N.S.J. No. 402, [1982] I.L.R. 1-1559 (C.A.).

[53] [2001] O.J. No. 1382, 53 O.R. (3d) 631 (S.C.J.). See also *M. (E.) v. Reed*, [2000] O.J. No. 4791, [2001] I.L.R. 1-3947(S.C.J.).

[54] [2000] S.C.J. No. 26, [2000] 1 S.C.R. 551. See discussion in Chapter 5, Section 1 and Chapter 15, Section (d).

2. TERMS OF THE CONTRACT

(a) Express Terms

The express terms of a liability insurance contract will be set out in the policy, which, generally, consists of six sections:

   (i)   declarations;
   (ii) definitions;
   (iii) insuring agreement;
   (iv) exclusions;
   (v)   conditions;
   (vi) endorsements, if any.

(i) Declarations

The "declarations" consist of the representations by the insured to the insurer with respect to the nature of the risk to be insured along with a description of the type of coverage selected. In practice, these are often set out on the facing page of the policy and consist of the name of the insured(s), a description of the hazards, the nature of the coverage selected, any territorial limitation that may apply, and the limit of liability applicable to each occurrence as well as any aggregate or overall limit.

Depending upon the type of policy purchased, the representations by the insured in the declarations portion of the policy may not have contractual force. They are, however, relied upon by the insurer in considering whether or not to accept the policy and, if accepted, in establishing the premium. A misrepresentation in the declarations, if it is material, may be used by the insurer to avoid the contract.[55]

(ii) Definitions

Most liability insurance policies contain a "definitions" section in which special meanings are accorded to various terms used in the policy. In this fashion, the scope of the coverage provided under the policy may be defined with greater precision. The definitions themselves do not create coverage. Rather, all that the definitions do is give meaning to the words to be used in the policy — and nothing more.

(iii) Insuring Agreement

The insuring agreement is at the heart of the insurance contract. It establishes the areas for which coverage is granted. Logically, if coverage cannot be found under the insuring agreement there is no need to look elsewhere in the policy.

---

[55] See section 1(f): Misrepresentation.

The provisions of the insuring agreement vary according to the type of liability insurance policy involved. The forms of the insuring agreements used in the various types of policies are addressed in detail elsewhere in the text.

(iv) Exclusions

Liability insurance policies invariably contain a number of exclusions designed to limit the coverage provided under the insuring agreement. It is essential to note that the policy exclusions do not grant coverage; they merely take away from the coverage that has already been granted.[56]

(v) Conditions

Liability insurance policies contain a number of conditions governing various aspects of the contractual relationship. The policy will usually specify that coverage is contingent upon the insured having complied with all of the terms of the policy. Where there has been imperfect compliance, however, the court is empowered by legislation to grant relief against forfeiture.[57]

Although the policy conditions vary depending upon both the insurer and the type of policy involved, in most cases the conditions will be either the same as or similar to the form standardized by the Insurance Bureau of Canada ("I.B.C.") for use with commercial policies (which are addressed in detail in Chapter 3).

(vi) Endorsements, If Any

A policy of liability insurance, with the concurrence of the insured, may be modified with the issuance of a written endorsement by the insurer. In practice, endorsements are issued for a variety of reasons, including extending or restricting coverage, altering policy limits or adding additional insureds.

(b) Implied Terms

(i) Business Efficacy

As a general rule of contract law the courts may add a term where it is necessary to give business efficacy to a contract.[58] In the case of liability insurance contracts, however, terms are rarely implied. Moreover, although it may be open to the insured to assert the existence of an implied term to the insurance contract, it is arguable that the insurer does not have the same right.[59] It is provided by statute that:

---

[56] *Stillwater Condominium Assoc. v. Amer. Home Assur. Co.*, 508 F.Supp. 1075 (D. Mont. 1981); affd mem., 688 F.2d 848 (9th Cir. 1982); cert. denied, 103 S. Ct. 1429.

[57] See Chapter 3, section 11: Relief against Forfeiture.

[58] *The Moorcock* (1889), 14 P.D. 64 (C.A.); *Allan v. Bushnell T.V. Co.* (1969), 1 D.L.R. (3d) 534 (Ont. H.C.J.).

[59] *Re Canada 3000 Inc.*, [2003] O.J. No. 5143, 6 C.C.L.I. (4th) 169 (S.C.J.).

(1) A term or condition of a contract which is not set out in full in the policy or in a document in writing attached to it, when issued, is not valid or admissible in evidence to the prejudice of the insured or a beneficiary.

(2) This section does not apply to an alteration of the contract agreed on in writing between the insurer and the insured after the issue of the policy.[60]

(ii) *Implied Term of Good Faith and Fair Dealing*

In Anglo-Canadian jurisprudence, the doctrine of utmost good faith developed out of the duty to disclose all material facts: a duty which some say arises from an implied term of the contract and which others say is an independent rule of law.[61] In most of the American jurisdictions, an implied term of good faith and fair dealing is imported into every insurance contract.[62] In Canada, apart from the decision of the Supreme Court of Canada in *Whiten v. Pilot Insurance Co.*[63] there are two lines of authority. One line treats the duty of good faith, not as a contractual term, but as an obligation imposed by law as an incident of the insurance relationship.[64] The other line treats the duty of good faith as an implied term of the contract.[65] Under the first line of authority, breach of the duty of good faith is actionable in tort, but not in contract. While under the second line of authority a breach of good faith is actionable in contract, this does not necessarily preclude the existence of concurrent liability in tort.[66]

---

[60] *Insurance Act*, R.S.B.C. 1996, c. 226, s. 12. Comparable sections in other jurisdictions are as follows: R.S.A. 2000, c. I-3, s. 513(1), (2); C.C.S.M., c. I40, s. 117(1); R.S.N.B. 1973, c. I-12, s. 98(1), (2); *Insurance Contracts Act*, R.S.N.L. 1990, c. I-12, s. 5(1), (2); R.S.O. 1990, c. I.8, s. 124(1), (2); R.S.P.E.I. 1988, c. I-4, s. 87(1); *Saskatchewan Insurance Act*, R.S.S. 1978, c. S-26, s. 103(1), (2).

[61] *Banque Financière de la Cité S.A. v. Westgate Ins. Co.*, [1989] 2 All E.R. 952 (C.A.), affd [1990] 2 All E.R. 947 (H.L.); *Bank of N.S. v. Hellenic Mutual War Risks Assoc. (Bermuda) Ltd.*, [1988] 1 Lloyd's Rep. 514; E.R.H. Ivamy, *General Principles of Insurance Law*, 5th ed. (London: Butterworths, 1986) at 125. See also discussion in this chapter at section (g): Non-disclosure.

[62] *Bostwick v. Foremost Ins. Co.*, 539 F.Supp. 517 (D. Mont. 1982); *de Vries v. St. Paul Fire & Marine Ins. Co.*, 716 F.2d 938 (1st Cir. 1983); *Murphy v. Cincinnati Ins. Co.*, 772 F.2d 273 (6th Cir. 1985). This is a general requirement of contract law, apart altogether from the doctrine of *uberrima fides*. Article 2 of the *Uniform Commercial Code*, s. 205 Restatement of Contracts (1981) provides: "Every contract imposes upon each party a duty of good faith and fair dealing in its performance and enforcement".

[63] [2002] S.C.J. No. 19, [2002] I.L.R. 1-4048.

[64] *Burdan v Progressive Casualty Insurance Co.*, [1993] O.J. No. 2732, 20. C.C.L.I. (2d) 126 (Gen. Div.); *Lloyd's of London v. Norris*, [1998], N.B.J. No. 351, 8 C.C.L.I. (3d) 216 (C.A.); *Burke v. Buss*, [2002] O.J. No. 2938 (S.C.); *Spiers v. Zurich Insurance Company et al.*, [1999] O.J. No. 3683, 45 O.R. (3d) 726 (S.C.); *Green v. Constellation Assurance Co.*, [1993] O.J. No. 1445 (Gen. Div.). See also *Gibson v. Parkes District Hospital* (1991) 26 NSWLR 9 for support for the view that bad faith sounds in tort.

[65] *Thompson v. Zurich Insurance Co.* (1984), 45 O.R. (2d) 744, 5. C.C.L.I. 251 (Ont. H.C.J.); *Kantolic v. Peace Hills General Insurance Co.*, [2000] A.J. No. 67, 77 Alta. L.R. (3d) 221 (Q.B.).

[66] *Central Trust Co. v. Rafuse*, [1986] 2 S.C.R. 147; *Spiers v. Zurich Insurance Co.*, [1999] O.J. No. 3683, 45 O.R. (3d) 726 (S.C.J.).

In *Whiten v. Pilot Insurance Co.*[67] a majority of the Supreme Court of Canada accepted without discussion, the notion that the insurer's duty of good faith arises as an implied term of the insurance contract. The appeal was concerned primarily with the issue of punitive damages, which, pursuant to *Vorvis v. Insurance Corp. of British Columbia*,[68] are recoverable in contract only when there has been an independent, actionable wrong. The insured, in her pleadings, sought punitive damages on the basis that the insurer had breached an implied term of the contract, requiring the insurer to act fairly and in good faith. No claim was advanced in tort. The insurer conceded that the duty of good faith arose in contract and argued that, as a result, punitive damages should not be awarded, the insurer's contention being that punitive damages are recoverable only in tort. The latter proposition was rejected by the majority of the Supreme Court of Canada. The majority held that the obligation of good faith, although contractual, was nevertheless separate from the obligation to compensate the insured for the loss under the policy and, on that basis, a breach of good faith constitutes an independent, actionable wrong for the purpose of the test in *Vorvis*. Somewhat curiously, Lebel J., dissenting only as to the amount of the award for punitive damages, appears to have proceeded on the basis that a breach of the duty of good faith is actionable in tort.

In the result, the law in Canada is still somewhat unclear as to the proper legal basis for the insurer's obligation of good faith. Moreover, even if one accepts that the insurer's duty of good faith arises in contract, it is not at all clear that there is a reciprocal contractual obligation of good faith on the part of the insured. By legislation, the insurer cannot set up a breach of any contractual term not set out in writing in the policy.[69] It has been held, therefore, that an insurer cannot invoke an implied contractual term of good faith in order to compel the insured to submit to an interview for the purpose of determining whether ground exist to rescind the policy.[70]

With respect to liability insurance policies, issues as to the insurer's obligation of good faith typically arise in the context of the defence and settlement of third party claims.[71]

3. CONSTRUCTION OF THE POLICY

Although it is generally true that the principles of construction applicable to liability insurance contracts are the same as those applicable to contracts,[72] the

---

[67] [2002] S.C.J. No. 19, [2002] 1 S.C.R. 595, [2002] I.L.R. 1-4048. See also *I.C.B.C. v. Hosseini*, [2006] B.C.J. No. 6 (C.A.).

[68] [1989] S.C.J. No. 46, [1989] 1 S.C.R. 1085.

[69] See above at Section (b)(i): Business Efficacy.

[70] *Re Canada 3000 Inc.*, [2003] O.J. No. 5143, 6 C.C.L.I. (4th) 169 (S.C.J.)

[71] See Chapter 5, Section 3: The Scope of the Duty to Defend and Section 4: The Duty to Settle.

[72] *Pense v. Northern Life Assur. Co.* (1907), 15 O.L.R. 131 at 137 (C.A.), affd (1908), 42 S.C.R. 246; *Metropolitan Life Ins. Co. v. Frenette*, [1992] S.C.J. No. 24, [1992] 1 S.C.R. 647.

nature of the insurance contract is such that the principles of construction have undergone considerable refinement. The cardinal rule of construction is still that the intention of the parties must prevail.[73] Yet it is only in rare cases that the insured and the insurer combine to draft an insurance policy to meet the circumstances of the particular case. Rather, most insurance policies are standard forms drafted by the insurer and used in general application across the country.[74] In these circumstances, the parties to a policy of insurance may more properly be said to be the purchasing public on the one hand and the insurance industry on the other. Courts charged with the task of determining the intent of the parties must pay attention both to previous interpretations of the same wording[75] and to the effect of a particular construction upon other cases.[76]

The three primary rules of construction by which the courts are guided in the interpretation of liability insurance policies are:

(i) words in a policy are to be construed according to their plain, ordinary and popular sense;

(ii) the policy should be considered in its entirety and be construed liberally so as to give effect to the purpose for which it was written;

(iii) where, due to an ambiguity, the policy wording is susceptible to two reasonable but opposing interpretations, the construction to be adopted is the one most favourable to the insured.[77]

(a) Construction According to Ordinary Meaning

The general rule, subject to the qualifications discussed in this chapter, is that words in an insurance policy are to be construed according to their plain, ordinary and popular sense. As long ago as 1803, Lord Ellenborough stated that an insurance policy:

---

[73] *Pense v. Northern Life Assur. Co., ibid.* The intent of the parties is generally ascertained within the four corners of the policy. In *Vancouver General Hospital v. Scottish & York Ins. Co.*, [1988] B.C.J. No. 2619, 36 C.C.L.I. 1 (C.A.), however, it was held that previous policies between the same parties were admissible as an aid to the interpretation of a later policy. Moreover, in *Manufacturers Life Ins. Co. v. Can. General Ins. Co.*, [1988] B.C.J. No. 2007, [1989] I.L.R. 1-2394 (S.C.), the Court admitted into evidence correspondence between the insured and its brokers at the time when coverage was being placed.

[74] See Appendices A through K, which consist of a number of suggested policy forms published by the Insurance Bureau of Canada, an insurance industry association. Although individual insurers may vary their policy wordings somewhat there is a considerable degree of consistency among insurers both with respect to the type of coverage offered and the policy language used to achieve that end.

[75] *Glen v. Lewis* (1853), 8 Exch. 607 at 618; *Louden v. British Merchants Ins. Co.*, [1961] 1 Lloyd's Rep. 155 (C.A.); *Ronaghan v. Can. West Ins. Co.* (1957), 22 W.W.R. 337 (Alta. S.C.).

[76] *Re Etherington & Lancashire & Yorkshire Accident Ins. Co.*, [1909] 1 K.B. 591 at 597 (C.A.).

[77] *Wagner v. Commercial Union Assur. Co. of Can.* [1994] B.C.J. No. 1099, 95 B.C.L.R. (2d) 273, 27 C.P.C. (3d) 47 (S.C.); *D.P. Murphy Inc. v. Laurentian Casualty Co. of Canada*, [1992] P.E.I.J. No. 70, 14 C.C.L.I. (2d) 209, 99 Nfld. & P.E.I.R. 331 (P.E.I.T.D.).

is to be construed according to its sense and meaning, as collected in the first place from the terms used in it, which terms are themselves to be understood in their plain, ordinary, and popular sense, unless they have generally in respect to the subject matter, as by the known usage of trade, or the like, acquired a peculiar sense distinct from the popular sense of the same words; or unless the context evidently points out that they must in the particular instance, and in order to effectuate the immediate intention of the parties to that contract, be understood in some other special and peculiar sense.[78]

The rule is alternatively described as construing the words in a policy in accordance with "the natural and ordinary meaning of the words used".[79]

The "ordinary meaning" of a word would appear to be the meaning of that word in its popular sense as understood by ordinary lay people. In *Tomlinson v. Prudential Insurance Co.*,[80] however, the Ontario Court of Appeal, without purporting to introduce any modification to this principle, stated that words in an insurance policy should be interpreted in the sense in which they would be understood by "the ordinary policyholder". This view is similar to certain American authorities to the effect that words in an insurance policy shall be given that meaning which the average policyholder[81] or the average policyholder and insurer[82] would attach to them. Although this does not introduce a subjective element into policy interpretation (for it is the understanding of policyholders generally rather than the understanding of any particular policyholder which governs) it may lead to differing interpretations in those instances where the understanding of the average policyholder differs from that of the average lay person. Presumably, this would arise only with respect to certain specialized policies of insurance and with respect to words that have acquired a peculiar sense distinct from their popular meaning.

(b) Construction According to Purpose

The requirement that words are to be construed in accordance with their plain, ordinary and popular sense does not mean that one ignores the context in which the words are found. Rather, it is a cardinal rule that a contract of insurance should be considered in its entirety[83] and be construed liberally so as to give

---

[78]　*Robertson v. French* (1803), 102 E.R. 779 at 781, 782.

[79]　*Ocean Construction Supplies Ltd. v. Continental Ins. Co.*, [1978] 5 W.W.R. 681 at 686, [1978] I.L.R. 1-1035 (B.C.S.C.), affd [1981] 1 W.W.R. 60, 21 B.C.L.R. 194 (C.A.).

[80]　[1954] O.R. 508 (C.A.).

[81]　*Ames v. Baker*, 68 Wash.2d 713 (1966).

[82]　*Swindler v. St. Paul Fire & Marine Ins. Co.*, 223 Tenn. 304 (1969). See *Scott v. Wawanesa Mutual Ins. Co.*, [1989] S.C.J. No. 55, [1989] 1 S.C.R. 1445, 59 D.L.R. (4th) 660 at 666 in which La Forest J., in dissenting reasons, expressed his approval of this view.

[83]　*Sumitomo Can. Ltd. v. Can. Indemnity Co.*, [1982] 5 W.W.R. 762 (B.C.C.A.); *Hamlyn v. Crown Accidental Ins. Co.*, [1893] 1 Q.B. 750 at 754 (C.A.); *City Tailors Ltd. v. Evans* (1921), 126 L.T. 439 at 444 (C.A.); *Parsons v. Standard Fire Ins. Co.* (1880), 5 S.C.R. 233.

effect to the purpose for which it was written.[84] In *Consolidated Bathurst Export Ltd. v. Mutual Boiler & Machinery Insurance Co.*, Estey J., for the majority of the Supreme Court of Canada, stated the rule in this way:

> Even apart from the doctrine of *contra proferentem* as it may be applied in the construction of contracts, the normal rules of construction lead a Court to search for an interpretation which, from the whole of the contract, would appear to promote or advance the true intent of the parties at the time of entry into the contract. Consequently, literal meaning should not be applied where to do so would bring about an unrealistic result or a result which would not be contemplated in the commercial atmosphere in which the insurance was contracted. Where words may bear two constructions, the more reasonable one, that which produces a fair result, must certainly be taken as the interpretation which would promote the intention of the parties. Similarly, an interpretation which defeats the intentions of the parties and their objective in entering into the commercial transaction in the first place should be discarded in favour of an interpretation of the policy which promotes a sensible commercial result. It is trite to observe that an interpretation of an ambiguous contractual provision which would render the endeavour on the part of the insured to obtain insurance protection nugatory, should be avoided. Said another way, the Courts should be loath to support a construction which would either enable the insurer to pocket the premium without risk or the insured to achieve a recovery which could neither be sensibly sought nor anticipated at the time of the contract.[85]

The application of this principle usually works to the benefit of the insured — most commonly where a strict literal interpretation would render coverage illusory.[86] In *Weston Ornamental Iron Works Ltd. v. Continental Insurance Co.*,[87] a decision of the Ontario Court of Appeal, Lacourciere J. stated:

> The exclusion clause should not be interpreted in a way which is repugnant to or inconsistent with the main purpose of the insurance coverage but so as to give effect to it. Thus, even if the exemption clause were found to be clear and unambig-uous it should not be enforced by the courts when the result would be to defeat the main object of the contract or virtually nullify the coverage sought for protection from anticipated risks.[88]

---

[84] *Consolidated Bathurst Export Ltd. v. Mutual Boiler & Machinery Ins. Co.*, [1980] 1 S.C.R. 888, 112 D.L.R.*(3d) 49, 32 N.R. 488, [1980] I.L.R. 1-1176. See also *Campbell-MacIsaac v. Deveaux*, [2004] N.S.J. No. 250, 11 C.C.L. 1 (4th) 1 (C.A.); and *Ryan v. Sun Life Assurance Co. of Canada*, [2005] N.S.J. No. 24, 18 C.C.L. 1 (4th) 204 (C.A.).

[85] *Ibid.*, 112 D.L.R. (3d) 49 at 58.

[86] *Indemnity Ins. Co. v. Excel Cleaning Service*, [1954] 2 D.L.R. 721 at 728 (S.C.C.); *Total Cleaning & Security Services Ltd. v. Guardian Insurance Co. of Canada*, [1996] O.J. No. 4389 (C.A.); *Rayman v. Ontario Assn. of Architects*, June 25, 1997, Doc. No. RE 75554/97, Potts J., [1997] O.J. No. 2567 (*sub nom. Rayman v. Assn. of Architects (Ontario)*) 39 O.T.C. 382 (Gen. Div.); affd (1998), 108 O.A.C. 392, 39 O.R. (3d) 711, 38 C.L.R. (2d) 263 (Div. Ct.).

[87] [1981] I.L.R. 1-1430 (Ont. C.A.).

[88] *Ibid.* at 479.

In determining the purpose of the insurance coverage, consideration may be given to the nature of the hazard or risk for which insurance was sought and the description under which the policy was sold. In this fashion, even standard policy language may be given a different interpretation than would otherwise be the case. In *Grace Farms Ltd. v. Big A Tank Services*[89] the insured, who was in the manure disposal business, obtained a Comprehensive General Liability policy which listed only one hazard: "the operation of a manure spreader". The policy contained an exclusion in respect of damage "arising out of the discharge ... of ... waste materials or other irritants, contaminants or pollutants into or upon land" unless the discharge was sudden and accidental. It was held that the exclusion could not have been intended to apply to the most pervasive and obvious risk in the insured's business. The Court noted that one would anticipate that such a risk would be covered by a policy stated to provide "comprehensive" liability.

The decision in *Grace Farms Ltd. v. Big A Tank Services Ltd.* illustrates a difficulty created by the "one size fits all" approach used to market many modern day commercial liability policies. The standard provisions in the stock Comprehensive General Liability and Commercial General Liability policies are not necessarily applicable to every kind of business enterprise to which these policies are sold. It is not surprising, therefore, that on occasion the policy wording needs to be stretched somewhat to fit the circumstances in an individual case.[90]

The rule that policy provisions should be construed so as to give effect to the purpose for which the policy was written may also work in favour of the insurer. The most common example is where the loss has been occasioned by intentional or reckless conduct on the part of the insured. In *Acklands Ltd. v. Canadian Indemnity Co.*[91] the Manitoba Court of Appeal held that a comprehensive general liability policy did not provide coverage for wrongful dismissal, for to hold otherwise would distort the very nature and object of a liability policy. Similarly, in *Gray v. Barr*,[92] where the insured threatened another man with a loaded gun which discharged in an ensuing struggle, it was held that the death of the other man was not caused by the type of "accident" intended to be covered under a liability policy.

(c) Construction *Contra Proferentem*

Perhaps no principle of construction is more frequently cited in insurance cases than that of *verba chartarum fortius accipiuntur contra proferentem* — the words of a document are to be construed against the person proffering it. Yet, paradoxically, *contra proferentem* is often the least understood principle of

---

[89] (1984), 6 C.C.L.I. 136 (B.C.S.C.).

[90] *Kingsway General Insurance Co. v. Lougheed Enterprises Ltd.*, [2004] B.C.J. No. 1606, 13 C.C.L. 1 (4th) 173 (C.A.).

[91] [1985] M.J. No. 506, 8 C.C.L.I. 163 (C.A.).

[92] [1971] 2 All E.R. 949 (C.A.).

construction. It does not mean that the policy will generally be interpreted in favour of the insured. Neither does it mean that all ambiguities are to be resolved in the insured's favour. Rather, *contra proferentem*, properly applied, is a rule for resolving a conflict between two reasonable but opposing interpretations of the policy wording.[93] In such cases the interpretation to be adopted is that which favours the insured.

The courts will not resort to a strained construction for the purpose of creating an ambiguity where none exists. As Laidlaw J.A. noted in *Kruger v. Mutual Benefit Health & Accident Assn.*:

> The contract of insurance should be given a reasonable interpretation. The Court should endeavour to see that the insured obtains all the benefits fairly and reasonably in contemplation of the parties at the time the policy was issued. In a case of doubt or uncertainty, the Court should not readily be persuaded to negative or minimize the obligation of the insurer. But the application of the principle mentioned requires that there should be an obscurity, uncertainty or ambiguity in the policy. The doubt or difficulty in construction must not be fanciful, it must be real.[94]

The existence of different dictionary meanings of a word does not mean that its use in a policy is ambiguous. As Bull J.A. noted in *Pentagon Construction (1969) Co. v. U.S. Fidelity & Guaranty Co.*:

> It is true that the word "design" has many dictionary meanings, as have a large percentage of words in everyday use. But the existence of different dictionary meanings of a word does not mean that it is ambiguous. Whether or not a word is ambiguous involves the consideration of its use in its place and context. It is only when two or more different meanings are equally, reasonably and sensibly applicable that it can be said to be ambiguous.[95]

Thus, *contra proferentem* cannot be applied where the meaning of the words is plain.[96] Nor, if there is ambiguity, may *contra proferentem* be applied to resolve the ambiguity in favour of the insured where to do so would be inconsistent with the purpose for which the policy was written.[97]

The rationale behind the application of *contra proferentem* in the insurance context is that the insurer is responsible for the policy language. Typically, insurance policies are contracts of adhesion. They are drafted by insurers and presented to prospective insureds on a "take it or leave it" basis. In some cases,

---

[93] *Wawanesa Mutual Insurance Co. v. Hewson,* [2004] S.J. No. 534, 13 C.C.L. 1 (4th) 189 (C.A.).

[94] [1944] O.R. 157 at 161 (S.C.); see also *Kekarainen v. Oreland Movers Ltd.*, [1981] 3 W.W.R. 534 (Man. Q.B.).

[95] [1977] 4 W.W.R. 351 at 353 (B.C.C.A.).

[96] *Harbour Machine Ltd. v. Guardian Ins. Co. of Can.*, [1985] B.C.J. No. 2876, 10 C.C.L.I. 72 at 80 (C.A.).

[97] *Fitzpatrick v. Red River Valley Mutual Insurance Co.*, [2004] S.J. No. 453, 14 C.C.L. 1 (4th) 296 (Q.B.); *Consolidated Bathurst Export Ltd. v. Mutual Boiler & Machinery Ins. Co.*, *supra*, note 84.

however, either the entire policy (as in the case of government automobile insurance issued by a Crown Corporation), or certain of its terms (as in the case of statutory conditions), may be set by statute. In such cases the rationale for construing ambiguities against the insurer may be absent, for neither party may have had any involvement in choosing the language of the policy. Thus, in *Lloyd's London Non-Marine Underwriters v. Chu*[98] the Supreme Court of Canada stated that *contra proferentem* did not apply in the case of an exclusion in an automobile policy, the wording of which was mandated by statute.

The decision in *Chu,* however, does not represent the final word on the subject. In *Wigle v. Allstate Insurance Co. of Canada*[99] the Ontario Court of Appeal considered the application of the *contra proferentem* rule for resolving an ambiguity in an underinsured motorist endorsement in a standard form automobile insurance policy. The ultimate responsibility for the wording of the endorsement lay with the Superintendent of Insurance. The Court, noting that the insurance industry had the opportunity to make submissions to the Superintendent of Insurance and that an insurer could choose whether or not to offer the endorsement, held that the ambiguity should be construed against the insurer. No reference was made to the decision of the Supreme Court of Canada in *Lloyd's London Non-Marine Underwriters v. Chu.*[100]

In *Donovan v. McCain Foods Ltd.*[101] the Court of Appeal for Newfoundland and Labrador chose not to follow the Ontario Court of Appeal decision in *Wigle v. Allstate Insurance Co. of Canada.* The Court in *Donovan* held that the *contra proferentem* rule had no application with respect to a provision which the insurer, by statute, was required to include in a motor vehicle liability policy. The decision in *Wigle* was distinguished on the basis that there was no evidence that the insurer had played any role in the drafting of the statutory provision under consideration. Yet, in fact, it does not appear that such evidence was ever presented in *Wigle*; rather, the Ontario Court of Appeal appears to have proceeded on the basis of a general understanding that the insurance industry is involved in the drafting of the forms approved by the Superintendent of Insurance.

The decisions in *Chu, Wigle* and *Donovan* involved private insurers. In *Martin v. Manitoba Public Insurance Corp.*[102] and *Squire v. Insurance Corp. of British Columbia*[103] consideration was given as to whether *contra proferentem* applied to automobile insurance policies issued by provincial Crown corporations. In both cases the policy wording was contained entirely in statutes and

---

[98] [1977] 2 S.C.R. 400.

[99] (1984), 49 O.R. (2d) 101 (Ont. C.A.), leave to appeal to S.C.C. dismissed, S.C.C. Bulletin, 1985, p. 374.

[100] [1977] 2 S.C.R. 400.

[101] [2004] N.J. No. 70, 234 Nfld. & P.E.I.R. 122 (C.A.).

[102] [1988] M.J. No. 529 (Q.B.). See also *DePape v. M.P.I.C.* (1980), 7 Man. R. (2d) 119 (Q.B.); *Huff v. Mireault*, unreported Manitoba Q.B., April 28, 1980; *Hoeffer v. M.P.I.C.*, unreported, County Court of Winnipeg, October 21, 1981; *Thiessen v. Manitoba Public Insurance Corp.*, 1989 CarswellMan 93.

[103] [1990] B.C.J. No. 633, 44 B.C.L.R. (2d) 65 (C.A.).

regulations enacted by the province. In *Martin*, the Manitoba Court of Queen's Bench concluded that *contra proferentem* applied because the Manitoba Public Insurance Corporation was either wholly or partly responsible for the drafting of the regulation under consideration. In *Squire*, on the other hand, the British Columbia Court of Appeal, in *obiter dicta*, stated that the *contra proferentem* rule has no application to the statutory terms of a contract of insurance, for neither party can choose the language of the contract between them. No evidence was led, in *Squire*, as to the involvement of the Insurance Corporation of British Columbia in the drafting of the regulation. One might well expect that involvement to have been considerable.

In the result, the law is unclear as to when, if ever, the *contra proferentem* rule applies to a statutory provision in an insurance policy. Apart altogether from *contra proferentem*, however, there is much to be said for a uniform approach to the interpretation of the provisions of insurance policies, whether statutory or otherwise, especially when the policies use similar language to express the insuring intent.

(d) The Doctrine of Reasonable Expectations

In some American jurisdictions the courts apply a rule of construction that has become known as the doctrine of reasonable expectations.[104] This doctrine began as a rule for resolving ambiguities in wording — in such cases the policy was to be construed in a fashion consistent with the reasonable expectations of the ordinary person as to the coverage purchased.[105] Some courts and commentators, however, have argued for a broader application of the doctrine, suggesting that it should apply even in the absence of an ambiguity.[106] The latter approach is fraught with difficulties. It introduces a substantial element of uncertainty in ascertaining the terms of the contract. Moreover, it requires the court to ignore the plain wording of the contract, even where the insured has read the policy and is aware that it does not apply to the loss.

In Canada, some courts have expressed approval of the doctrine of reasonable expectations, either as a means of resolving ambiguities or, in its broader formulation, as a rule for honouring the insured's expectations in purchasing the

---

[104] See Robert H. Jerry, "Insurance, Contract, And The Doctrine Of Reasonable Expectations" (1998) 5 Conn. Ins. L.J. 21; Roger C. Henderson, "The Doctrine of Reasonable Expectations in Insurance Law After Two Decades" (1990) 51 Ohio St. L.J. 823; Eugene R. Anderson & James J. Fournier, "Why Courts Enforce Insurance Policyholders' Objectively Reasonable Expectations of Insurance Coverage" (1998) 5 Conn. Ins. L.J. 335; Stephen J. Ware, "A Critique of the Reasonable Expectations Doctrine" (1989) 56 U. Chi. L. Rev. 1461.

[105] See *Atwater Creamery Co. v. Western Nat. Mutual Ins.*, 366 N.W.2d 271 (Minn. 1985).

[106] Keeton, "Reasonable Expectations in the Second Decade" (1976) 12 Forum 275; Keeton, "Insurance Law Rights at Variance with Policy Provisions" (1970) 83 Harvard L. Rev. 961; Shinevar, "A Reasonable Approach to the Doctrine of Reasonable Expectations as Applied to Insurance Contracts" (1980) 13 U. Mich. J.L. Ref. 603.

policy.[107] Other courts, however, have declined to rule on the extent, if any, to which the doctrine of reasonable expectations forms a part of our law.[108]

In recent years various members of the Supreme Court of Canada have discussed the doctrine of reasonable expectations, but to date no particular formulation of the doctrine has been adopted.[109] The Ontario Court of Appeal, in *Chilton v. Co-operators General Insurance Co.*[110] suggested in *obiter dicta* that the doctrine be restricted to those circumstances in which the insured has a reasonable coverage expectation that the insurer contributed to by way of either marketing practices or language that makes the policy difficult to read or understand.

It is submitted that, properly applied, the doctrine should be no more than an alternate expression of the principle propounded by the Supreme Court of Canada in *Consolidated Bathurst Export v. Mutual Boiler Insurance*,[111] namely, that the policy should be construed liberally so as to give effect to the purpose for which it was written.[112] On this basis, the doctrine would be helpful in the interpretation of vague or uncertain policy wording. The doctrine could not be used to override clear and unambiguous terms unless the failure to do so would defeat the main object of the insurance contract.

(e) Construction of Exclusion Clauses

It is sometimes said to be a rule of construction that coverage provisions should be construed broadly and exclusion clauses narrowly.[113] Although this is often

---

[107] *Pettit v. Economical Mutual Ins. Co.* (1982), 143 D.L.R. (3d) 752 (Ont. H.C.J.); *White v. Dom. of Can. General Ins. Co.* (1985), 11 C.C.L.I. 121 (Ont. H.C.J.); *Wigle v. Allstate Ins. Co. of Can.* (1985), 10 C.C.L.I. 1 (Ont. C.A.), leave to appeal to S.C.C. refd (1985), 14 D.L.R. (4th) 404*n*; *Tinmouth v. Groupe Desjardins Assur. Generales* [1986] O.J. No. 899, 19 C.C.L.I. 268 (H.C.J.), affd [1988] O.J. No. 1169, [1988] I.L.R. 1-2359 (C.A.), leave to appeal to S.C.C. refd (1988), 32 O.A.C. 80*n*; *Selig v. 31390 Sask. Ltd.* [1986] S.J. No. 549, 22 C.C.L.I. 175 (C.A.) (see dissenting judgment); *Gatzke v. Ins. Corp. of B.C.*, [1989] B.C.J. No. 866, [1989] I.L.R. 1-2480 (B.C.S.C.); *Scott v. Wawanesa Mutual Ins. Co.*, *supra*, note 82.

[108] *Elite Builders Ltd. v. Maritime Life Assur. Co.*, [1984] B.C.J. 2896, 52 B.C.L.R. 251 (S.C.), affd [1985] B.C.J. No. 2617, 68 B.C.L.R. 273 (C.A.), leave to appeal to S.C.C. refd (1986), 70 B.C.L.R. xl.

[109] *Brisette Estate v. Westbury Life Ins. Co.*, [1992] S.C.J. No. 86, [1992] 3 S.C.R. 87; *Simcoe & Erie General Ins. Co. v. Reid Crowther & Partners Ltd.*, [1993] S.C.J. No. 10, [1993] I.L.R. 1-2914.

[110] (1997), 41 C.C.L.I. 35, 32 O.R. (3d) 161, [1997] I.L.R. 1-3423, 143 D.L.R. (4th) 647 (C.A.), revg (July 5, 1993), Doc. 15927/86 (Ont. Gen. Div.).

[111] *Supra*, note 84. This is the view expressed by La Forest J. in *Scott v. Wawanesa Mutual Ins. Co.*, *supra*, note 82.

[112] This appears to be the view of Iacobucci J. in *Non-Marine Underwriters, Lloyd's of London v. Scalera*, [2000] S.C.J. No. 26, [2000] 1 S.C.R. 551, 185 D.L.R. (4th) 1, [2000] I.L.R. 1-3810, 253 N.R. 1, affg, [1988] B.C.J. No. 834, 48 B.C.L.R. (3d) 143, 158 D.L.R. (4th) 385, [1998] I.L.R. 1-3568, [1998] 9 W.W.R. 209 (C.A.), revg, [1997] B.C.J. No. 2481, 47 B.C.L.R. (3d) 187, [1998] I.L.R. 1-3519 (S.C.).

[113] *Madill v. Chu* (1977), 71 D.L.R. (3d) 295 (S.C.C.); *Simcoe & Erie General Ins. Co. v. Reid Crowther*, *supra*, note 109.

the result of applying the rules of construction set out above, one must be careful not to be misled. Unless it is repugnant or inconsistent with the main purpose of the insurance coverage, a plainly worded and unambiguous exclusion clause will be effective.

(f) Use of American Authority

Where little or no Canadian authority can be found on a point of insurance law our courts have, for several decades, turned to American authorities for assistance. As MacDonald J. noted in *Cunningham v. St. Paul Fire Co.*:

> In coming to a conclusion as to the result which follows from my finding that the defendant did not fulfill its bond of indemnity as to repairs, I have followed American decisions, and am led to take such a course in this insurance action by the remarks of Lord Justice Brett in *Cory v. Burr* (1882) L.R. 9 Q.B., at p. 469:
>
> > "If I thought that there were American authorities clear on this point I do not say I would follow them but I would try to do so, for I agree with Chancellor Kent, that, with regard to American Insurance law, it is most advisable that the law should, if possible, be in conformity with what it is in all countries. I must therefore add that, although American decisions are not binding on us in this country, I have always found those on insurance law to be based on sound reasoning and to be such as ought to be carefully considered by us and with an earnest desire to endeavour to agree with them."[114]

In *Commerce Capital Trust Co. v. Continental Insurance Co.* Callaghan J. commented that:

> In my view this reasoning is particularly compelling when as in this case, there are well-reasoned United States authorities which construe insurance policies which are virtually identical to the one in dispute.[115]

The reasoning in these cases is sound. The various forms of liability insurance policies sold in Canada are the same as or similar to their counterparts in the United States. In the commercial context at least, the policies are designed to cover very much the same set of risks.[116] Although in both countries insurance

---

[114] (1914), 5 W.W.R. 1098 at 1102 (B.C.S.C.). See also *Berry v. Confederation Life Assoc.*, [1926] 3 W.W.R. 670 (Alta. C.A.); revd on another point [1927] 3 D.L.R. 945 (S.C.C.); *Fingard v. Merchants Casualty Ins. Co.*, [1928] 2 W.W.R. 609 (Man. K.B.); *Co-operative Fire and Casualty v. Saindon*, [1975] I.L.R. 1-669 at 1157 *per* Laskin J.; *Clarkson Co. v. Can. Indemnity Co.* (1979), 25 O.R. (2d) 281 (S.C.); *Morguard Bank of Can. v. Guarantee Co. of North America* [1987] B.C.J. No. 323, 12 B.C.L.R. (2d) 137 (C.A.).

[115] (1982), 36 O.R. (2d) 38 at 42 (H.C.J.).

[116] In *Re Partners Investments Ltd. and Etobicoke* (1981), 33 O.R. (2d) 195 at 197 (H.C.J.) Cory J., then of the Ontario High Court, took the novel approach that since the insurer carried on business in the United States as well as Canada, it must have intended that our courts interpret its policy on the same basis as it had been interpreted by American courts:

contracts are regulated by statute, most matters pertaining to insurance contracts are governed by principles of common law and equity. When giving consideration to American authorities, however, care must be taken to ensure that the rules of construction applied by the American court are not materially different from our own,[117] for that may have a profound effect on the result in the case.

4. BURDEN OF PROOF

The rules relating to the burden of proof in insurance cases are as laid down by Bailhache J. in *Munro, Brice & Co. v. War Risks Assn.*:

1. The plaintiff must prove such facts as bring him *prima facie* within the terms of the promise.
2. When the promise is qualified by exceptions, the question whether the plaintiff need prove facts which negative their application does not depend upon whether the exceptions are to be found in a separate clause or not. The question depends upon an entirely different consideration, namely, whether the exception is as wide as the promise, and thus qualifies the whole of the promise, or whether it merely excludes from the operation of the promise particular classes of cases which but for the exception would fall within it, leaving some part of the general scope of the promise unqualified. If so, it is sufficient for the plaintiff to bring himself prima facie within the terms of the promise, leaving it to the defendant to prove that, although prima facie within its terms, the plaintiff's case is in fact within the excluded exceptional class. ...
3. When a promise is qualified by an exception which covers the whole scope of the promise, a plaintiff cannot make out a prima facie case unless he brings himself within the promise as qualified. There is *ex hypothesi* no unqualified part of the promise for the sole of his foot to stand upon. ...
4. Whether a promise is a promise with exceptions or whether it is a qualified promise is in every case a question of construction of the instrument as a whole. ...
5. In construing a contract with exceptions it must be borne in mind that a promise with exceptions can generally be turned by an alteration of phraseol-

---

The insurer carries on business in the United States of America as well as Canada. The same all-risk policy with precisely the same exclusion clauses has been interpreted by American Courts. It might then be assumed that the insurer, and perhaps also the insured, would expect the policy to be interpreted in a similar manner in Canada as in the United States. It would be in the best interests of both the insurer and its clients in the business community if the interpretation of the policy was the same on both sides of the border. With this in mind, it might be helpful if I indicate what I take to be the position set forth by the American cases and then determine whether the reasoning in those cases is contrary to Canadian authorities that are binding upon me.

[117] Many of the American jurisdictions differ from each other, as well as from the provinces in Canada, in their approach to the construction of insurance contracts. See the remarks of Scrutton L.J. and Duke L.J. in *Re Hooley Hill Rubber and Chemical Co. and Royal Ins. Co.*, [1920] 1 K.B. 257 at 272, 274 (C.A.).

ogy into a qualified promise. The form in which the contract is expressed is therefore material.[118]

Although initially formulated for policies of marine insurance, it is well established that these rules apply generally to all classes of insurance.[119]

Applying these rules to liability policies, the burden, as a general rule, will be on the insured to show that the claim falls within the insuring agreement,[120] on the insurer to show that a claim falls within an exclusion,[121] and on the insured to show that it falls within an exception to an exclusion.[122]

---

[118] [1918] 2 K.B. 78 at 88, 89, revd on the facts [1920] 3 K.B. 94 (C.A.).

[119] *Bjorkman and Toronto Flying Club Ltd. v. Br. Aviation Ins.*, [1953] O.R. 231 (H.C.J.), affd [1954] 3 D.L.R. 224 (Ont. C.A.), affd [1956] S.C.R. 363.

[120] *ING Insurance Co. of Canada v. Sportsco International L.P.*, [2004] O.J. No. 2254, 12 C.C.L.I. (4th) 86 (S.C.J.).

[121] *Dewar v. Zurich Ins. Co.*, [1966] I.L.R. 1-165 (B.C.S.C.); *Hardrock Construction Co. v. Sun Alliance Ins. Co.* (1980), 28 N.B.R. (2d) 665 (Q.B.); *Lawrence v. Kansa General International Insurance Co.*, [2000] Q.J. 615 (S.C.).

[122] *Model Jewellery Mfg. Co. v. Western Assur. Co.*, [1962] O.R. 293 (H.C.J.), affd [1962] O.R. 1099 (C.A.), affd [1963] S.C.R. vi.

Chapter 3

CONDITIONS OF THE POLICY

Liability insurance policies invariably contain a variety of conditions designed to govern various aspects of the contractual relationship between the parties. Generally, the policy will stipulate that coverage is contingent upon the insured having complied with all of the terms of the contract,[1] although this is subject to the courts' statutory power to relieve against forfeiture.[2]

The discussion that follows is based upon the conditions that have been standardized by the Insurance Bureau of Canada for use with commercial liability policies.[3] The conditions which appear in other forms of liability policies are usually drafted in substantially similar terms.

1. PREMIUM

The premiums due under a liability insurance policy, rather than being for a fixed sum, are often calculated according to the amount of business carried out by the insured. The policy, therefore, provides that the insured is obliged to maintain the records necessary for premium computation:

1. Premium and Adjustment of Premiums:
   (a) Unless otherwise stated, the premium stated in the declarations is an estimated deposit premium only. Adjustment of premium shall be made at least annually and for this purpose the premium bases and rates shown in the declarations or in any endorsement attached hereto, shall be used in ascertaining the earned premium with respect to the specific hazards mentioned herein.
   (b) In the case of any hazards existing and covered under coverage rider(s) attached but not specified in the declarations, or in any endorsement the earned premium with respect thereto shall be computed in accordance with the Insurer's rules, rates, rating plans and minimum premiums applicable to such hazards.
   (c) Subject to the retention by the Insurer of the minimum premium provided for in the declarations, if the earned premium for this policy thus computed exceeds the estimated deposit premium paid, the Named Insured

---

[1] Whether a condition in a policy is a true condition precedent, however, is in each case a matter of construction. See *Re Bradley and Essex & Suffolk Accident Indemnity Soc.*, [1912] 1 K.B. 415 (C.A.).

[2] See section 13: Relief against Forfeiture.

[3] I.B.C. Form 2000, June 1978; revised, January 1983 and I.B.C. Form 2001, revised March, 2005. See Appendices A and K.

shall pay such excess to the Insurer; on the other hand, if the estimated deposit premium exceeds the earned premium, the Insurer shall return to the Named Insured such excess.

(d) The Named Insured shall maintain for each hazard hereby insured against, a record of the information necessary for premium computation on the basis stated, and shall submit such record to the Insurer at the end of the policy period and at such other times during the policy period as the Insurer may direct.[4]

9. Premium Audit

a. We will compute all premiums for this policy in accordance with our rules and rates.

b. Premium shown in this policy as advance premium is a deposit premium only. At the close of each audit period we will compute the earned premium for that period. Audit premiums are due and payable on notice to the first Named Insured. If the sum of the advance and audit premiums paid for the policy period is greater than the earned premium, we will return the excess to the first Named Insured subject to the retention of the minimum retained premium shown in the Declarations of this policy.

c. The first Named Insured must keep records of the information we need for premium computation, and send us copies at such times as we may request.[5]

In *Re Bradley and Essex & Suffolk Accident Indemnity Society*[6] it was held that non-compliance with a similar clause did not entitle the insurer to deny coverage, for the sole object of the condition was to provide for the adjustment of premiums. Although the policy stipulated that the insured's observance of all of the conditions in the policy was a condition precedent to the liability of the insurer, the Court held, on a construction of the policy as a whole, that the condition with respect to the keeping of books for the purposes of premium adjustment could not be so read.

2. INSPECTION AND AUDIT

Insurers will often inspect the insured's premises or operations before issuing a policy. The purpose of the inspection is to determine whether or not to accept the risk and, if it is to be accepted, upon what terms. Insurers may also require access to the insured's books and records in order to confirm the premium basis for the policy. Accordingly, the policy provides that the insurer has the right to conduct both an inspection and audit:

2. Inspection — Audit
The Named Insured shall permit the Insurer to inspect the insured premises, operations and elevators and to examine and audit the Named Insured's books

---

[4] Appendix A.
[5] Appendix K.
[6] *Supra*, note 1.

and records at any time during the policy period (and any extension thereof and within one year after the termination of this policy), as far as they relate to the premium basis or the subject matter of this insurance. The Insurer assumes no responsibility and waives no rights by reason of such inspection, examination, audit or the omission thereof.[7]

5. Examination Of Your Books and Records
We may examine and audit your books and records as they relate to this policy at any time during the policy period and up to three years afterward.[8]

6. Inspections and Surveys
   1. We have the right to:
      a. Make inspections and surveys at any time;
      b. Give you reports on the conditions we find; and
      c. Recommend changes.
   2. We are not obligated to make any inspections, surveys, reports or recommendations and any such actions we do undertake relate only to insurability and the premiums to be charged. We do not make safety inspections. We do not undertake to perform the duty of any person or organization to provide for the health or safety of workers or the public. And we do not warrant that conditions:
      a. Are safe or healthful; or
      b. Comply with laws, regulations, codes or standards.
   3. Paragraphs 1. and 2. of this condition apply not only to us, but also to any rating, advisory, rate service or similar organization which makes insurance inspections, surveys, reports or recommendations.
   4. Paragraph 2. of this condition does not apply to any inspections, surveys, reports or recommendations we may make relative to certification, under provincial or municipal statutes, ordinances, bylaws or regulations, of boilers, pressure vessels or elevators.[9]

During the course of an inspection, the insurer may notice that certain operations are being carried out in an unsafe or unlawful manner and may direct that these practices be changed. This could, conceivably, expose the insurer to an action in negligence where the insured relies upon the insurer's inspection as a representation that the premises and operations are safe and are in compliance with any applicable laws or regulations.[10] In this regard it is noted that the Commercial General Liability policy provisions set out above specifically state that any inspection is only in relation to insurability and that the insurer does not warrant that conditions are safe or healthful or in compliance with legal requirements. It is somewhat surprising that the term "warranty" is used in this context. A warranty is a term of a contract. The exclusion of a warranty does not act to exclude a claim for negligent misstatement. With respect to the latter, the insurer's defence would have to be that, given the limited purpose for which the

---

[7] Appendix A.

[8] Appendix K.

[9] Appendix K.

[10] See *Newton v. Liberty Mutual Ins. Co.*, 252 S.E.2d 199 (Ga. 1979).

statement was made, the insured could not reasonably rely upon the statement for any other purpose.

3. NOTICE OF ACCIDENT, OCCURRENCE, CLAIM OR SUIT

One of the most important conditions in a liability insurance policy relates to the insured's duty to give notice to the insurer of an accident, occurrence, claim or suit. The standard Comprehensive General Liability policy provides as follows:

> 3.   Insured's Duties in the event of Accident, Occurrence, Claim or Suit:
>
> (a) In the event of an accident or occurrence, written notice containing particulars sufficient to identify the Insured and also reasonably obtainable information with respect to the time, place and circumstances thereof, and the names and addresses of the injured and of available witnesses, shall be given promptly by or for the Insured to the Insurer or any of its authorized agents.
>
> (b) If claim is made or suit is brought against the Insured, the Insured shall immediately forward to the Insurer every writ, letter, document or advice received by him or his representative. ...[11]

The "plain language" version of this condition appears in the Commercial General Liability policy as follows:

> 4.   Duties In The Event Of Occurrence, Offense, Claim or Action
>
> a.   You must see to it that we are notified as soon as practicable of an "occurrence" or an offense which may result in a claim. To the extent possible, notice should include:
>
> (1) How, when and where the "occurrence" or offense took place;
>
> (2) The names and addresses of any injured persons and witnesses; and
>
> (3) The nature and location of any injury or damage arising out of the "occurrence" or offense.
>
> b.   If a claim is made or "action" is brought against any insured, you must:
>
> (1) Immediately record the specifics of the claim or "action" and the date received; and
>
> (2) Notify us as soon as practicable.
>
> You must see to it that we receive written notice of the claim or "action" as soon as practicable.

The purpose behind paragraph (a) of the condition is to permit the insurer to conduct an investigation while the facts are still fresh and, where appropriate, to mitigate damages. The standard to which the insured is held is that of the reasonable person. If the accident or occurrence is one in respect of which the insured, if liable, would be covered under the policy, then the insured must give notice if a person of ordinary prudence would foresee that a claim could arise.[12]

---

[11] Appendix A.

[12] *Marcoux v. Halifax Fire Ins. Co.*, [1948] 4 D.L.R. 143 (S.C.C.); *Moore v. Can. Lawyers Ins. Assn.*, [1993] N.S.J. No. 290, 18 C.C.L.I. (2d) 1 (C.A.). But *cf. Eastend School Division No. 8 v. Commonwealth Insurance Co.*, [1989] S.J. No. 623, 43 C.C.L.I. 57, 81 Sask. R. 150, [1990]

The fact that the insured may be of the view that any such claim would be unfounded is immaterial,[13] for the obligation to give notice must be read in conjunction with the insurer's obligation to defend the insured with respect to groundless claims.[14]

The test applied by the courts in determining whether there has been a breach of the notice requirement thus combines both a subjective and an objective element. The subjective element is that the insured must be actually aware of the circumstances which gave rise to the claim. The objective element is whether a reasonably prudent person, with knowledge of those circumstances, would consider that they would likely give rise to a claim.15

The leading case with respect to the duty to give notice of an accident to a liability insurer is the decision of the Supreme Court of Canada in *Marcoux v. Halifax Fire Insurance Co.*[16] The insured's truck driver struck a pedestrian. The driver, noticing that the pedestrian "looked as if something were the matter", offered to drive him to the hospital. The pedestrian replied that nothing was the matter and that he preferred to go home. The driver related the details of this incident to the insured, expressing the opinion that the pedestrian was not hurt. No notice of the accident was given to the insurer until two months later when the pedestrian advanced a claim. The insurer, in these circumstances, declined to defend or indemnify the insured with respect to the claim on the basis that prompt notice had not been given.

The insurer's position was upheld at trial in the Quebec Court of Appeal[17] and in the Supreme Court of Canada. In the latter Court, Taschereau J., with whom Rinfret C.J.C., Kerwin and Locke JJ. agreed, noted that:

> The policy of insurance is a contract between the parties. The respondent undertook to indemnify the appellant; but on a condition, that is, that it be given prompt notice of the accident. One readily understands the reason justifying this clause of the contract. It is for the purpose of permitting the insurance company to make an investigation immediately, to check the facts, to seek the names of witnesses who later on may not be discoverable, and thus not to be at the mercy of the claimant. This is a protection justly claimed in the contract, and of which the insured cannot deprive his insurer with impunity. In the present case, the appellant said that the accident was not serious, that he had been informed by his employee that the victim was all right.
>
> The appellant or his employee knew however that the truck had "hit someone," that he had "fallen down," that he "looked as if something were the mat-

---

I.L.R. 1-2571 (Q.B.), supp. reasons (1990), 81 Sask. R. 150 at 152 (Q.B.), affd, [1990] S.J. No. 674, 86 Sask. R. 317, 46 C.C.L.I. 197 (C.A.), where the Court states that the failure to discover the magnitude of the loss by reason of neglect or incompetence does not amount to a breach of condition.

[13] *Glenburn Dairy Ltd. v. Can. General Ins. Co.*, [1953] 2 D.L.R. 445 (B.C.C.A.); *Moore v. Can. Lawyers Ins. Assn., ibid.*; *Can. Shade Tree Service Ltd. v. Northern Assur. Co.*, [1987] A.Q. No. 2255, [1987] I.L.R. 1-2171 (C.A.).

[14] See Chapter 5: The Duty to Defend.

[15] *Moore v. Can. Lawyers Ins. Assn., supra*, note 12.

[16] *Supra*, note 12.

[17] [1947] Que. K.B. 637 (C.A.).

ter", which warranted calling an ambulance as well as a doctor. In the circumstances, as Mr. Justice Demers said, a man of ordinary prudence would have foreseen that a claim could arise therefrom.

It is not the assured who is to determine the gravity of the injuries, and decide whether or not the insurance company should make an investigation. His obligation is to give notice, the company will take measures it deems necessary. The appellant perhaps acted in good faith, but the events demonstrated he was wrong, that he was ill-informed, as the evidence has revealed that as a result of this accident Roger had three ribs fractured and suffered other bodily injuries. It is the appellant who must suffer the consequences and not the respondent.

The notice was a condition precedent to any recourse the appellant could exercise against the respondent, and as he did not give it, his claim must be dismissed.[18]

Justice Rand, in a concurring judgment, stated:

For the purposes of the appeal I will assume, as Mr. Samson contended, that the language of the condition must be interpreted not absolutely but in the background of the ordinary and reasonable understanding of such a requirement on the part of persons who enter into such contractual relations; and that if the truck driver, acting with the intelligence and prudence of the ordinary, reasonable man, in the light of all the circumstances, was satisfied that no bodily injury had been suffered by the person struck, the situation was not one where the notice should at that time have been given. But the appellant must be charged with the appreciation of the circumstances that such a person would have had. It may be that the driver here was dull or unimaginative; but the employer cannot avail himself of that fact for his own advantage. The latter, too must in learning the bare and sketchy details of an accident be sufficiently alert to imagine likely facts which the report of his employee may not adequately convey.[19]

The condition requires that notice be given to the insurer or its authorized agent. In *Sumitomo Canada Ltd. v. Canadian Indemnity Co.*[20] the insured notified its broker of the claim but the broker notified the wrong insurers. Applying the test of Rand J. from *Marcoux v. Halifax Fire Insurance Co.*[21] noted above, the court held that the condition as to notice must be interpreted against the background of the ordinary and reasonable understanding of such a requirement on the part of persons who enter into such contractual relations. On this basis, since the insured acted reasonably and, moreover, had not prejudiced the insurer, the condition was satisfied and the insurer was liable on the policy.

As noted in *Hogan v. Kolisnyk*,[22] the reported cases are of little assistance in establishing a general rule for what constitutes prompt notice. In one case[23] a

---

[18] *Supra*, note 12 at 146.

[19] *Ibid.* at 149.

[20] (1981), 125 D.L.R. (3d) 356 (B.C.S.C.), affd 138 D.L.R. (3d) 173 (B.C.C.A.).

[21] *Supra*, note 12 at 149.

[22] [1983] 3 W.W.R. 481 (Alta. Q.B.).

[23] *Duchene v. General Accident Assur. Co.* (1926), 31 O.W.N. 59 (H.C.J.).

delay of five weeks was held to be a breach of a condition while in another case[24] a delay of four months was held to be sufficiently prompt. "Prompt" is therefore a relative term, dependent upon the circumstances of each case.[25] Indeed, in *Pribyl v. Wilson-Murray*[26] it was held that a delay of over six years was "as soon as practicable" in circumstances where an unnamed insured was unaware that he was covered under his mother's policy until he had consulted a lawyer.

The purpose of paragraph (b) of the condition, requiring the insured to immediately forward suit papers, is to allow the insurer to investigate the claim and to facilitate settlement. Unless and until the suit papers have been forwarded, the insurer has no obligation to defend the claim. Moreover, failure to forward suit papers in accordance with the condition will relieve the insurer from the obligation to indemnify the insurer. This is subject, of course, to the court's power to relieve against forfeiture.[27]

4. ASSISTANCE AND CO-OPERATION

Liability insurance contracts generally stipulate that the insured must co-operate with the insurer with respect to the defence of all claims made against the insured which are covered under the policy. In the forms recommended by the Insurance Bureau of Canada for use with commercial liability policies the "co-operation clause" is in the following terms:

> 3. Insured's Duties in the event of Accident, Occurrence, Claim or Suit: ...
>
> (c) The Insured shall co-operate with the Insurer and, upon the Insurer's request, assist in making settlements, in the conduct of suits and in enforcing any right of contribution or indemnity against any person or organization who may be liable to the Insured because of injury or damage with respect to which insurance is afforded under this policy; and the insured shall attend hearings and trials and assist in securing and giving evidence and obtaining the attendance of witnesses. The Insured shall not, except at his own cost, voluntarily make any payment, assume any obligation or incur any expenses other than for the first aid to others at the time of accident.[28]

> 4. Duties In The Event Of Occurrence, Offense, Claim or Action...
>
> c. You and any other involved insured must:
>
>   (1) Immediately send us copies of any demands, notices, summonses or legal papers received in connec-tion with the claim or "action";
>
>   (2) Authorize us to obtain records and other information;

---

[24] *Filiatrault v. Zurich Ins. Co.* (1981), 126 D.L.R. (3d) 555 (B.C.S.C.).

[25] *Duchene v. General Accident Assur. Co.*, *supra*, note 23. See also *Hogan v. Kolisnyk*, *supra*, note 22 at 499; *Filiatrault v. Zurich Ins. Co.*, *ibid.* at 558.

[26] [1993] B.C.J. No. 2968, 21 C.C.L.I. (2d) 205 (C.A.).

[27] See section 13: Relief against Forfeiture.

[28] Appendix A.

    (3)   Cooperate with us in the investigation or settlement of the claim or defense against the "action"; and

    (4)   Assist us, upon our request, in the enforcement of any right against any person or organization which may be liable to the insured because of injury or damage to which this insurance may also apply.

    d.   No insured will, except at that insured's own cost, voluntarily make a payment, assume any obligation, or incur any expense, other than for first aid, without our consent.[29]

The duties imposed upon the insured by clause 3 (c) above are not limited to the matters enumerated after the first "and"; rather, as indicated in the opening phrase of the clause, the insured is placed under a general duty to co-operate.[30]

    Under paragraph 4 above the provisions apply with respect to offences as well as occurrences because, under the 2005 Commercial General Liability form, Coverage B, dealing with personal injury and advertising injury, applies to offenses rather than occurrences.

The purpose behind the co-operation clause is readily apparent. Since the insurer is liable to indemnify the insured in respect of the claim it is vital that the insurer have the insured's assistance and co-operation both in conducting a proper defence of the claim and in concluding a settlement on advantageous terms. Without the insured's assistance in securing and giving truthful evidence and obtaining the attendance of witnesses the insurer may be unable to mount an effective defence.[31] Without the insured's assistance in concluding a settlement the insurer may be forced into taking the claim to trial and risk incurring a greater liability.

An example of a breach of the duty to co-operate is provided by the decision of the Ontario Court of Appeal in *Canadian Newspapers Co. v. Kansa General Insurance Co.*[32] The insured, a newspaper publisher, had an arrangement with its insurer whereby the publisher would conduct the defence of libel actions brought against it but would keep the insurer informed of any substantial developments in the course of an action. An action was brought against the insured which, in accordance with this arrangement, was defended by the insured. Accounts for legal fees were sent to the insurer from time to time for payment. Contrary to the arrangement, however, the insurer was not kept advised of significant developments in the litigation which materially affected the insurer's position with respect to risk and expense. All of this information

---

[29]   Appendix K.

[30]   *Canadian Newspapers Co. v. Kansa General Insurance Co.*, [1996] O.J. No. 3054, 30 O.R. (3d) 257 (C.A.); Application for leave to appeal to S.C.C. dismissed, [1996] S.C.C.A. No. 553.

[31]   *Satter v. Pafco Ins. Co.*, [1993] S.J. No. 253, [1993] I.L.R. 1-2984 (Q.B.); In *Richards v. Continental Casualty Co.* [1993] A.J. No. 198, 14 C.C.L.I. (2d) 202 (Q.B.) it was held that the insured breached the co-operation clause by perjuring himself on examination for discovery and in making a deliberately false diary entry.

[32]   [1996] O.J. No. 3054, 30 O.R. (3d) 257 (C.A.), application for leave to appeal to S.C.C. dismissed, [1996] S.C.C.A. No. 553.

would have been made available to the insurer upon request. The onus, however, was upon the insurer to keep the insured informed; its failure to do so resulted in a forfeiture of coverage.

The requirement that the insured assist in enforcing any right of contribution or indemnity against any such person or organization who may be liable to the insured must be read in conjunction with the subrogation provision of the policy. This permits the insurer, by way of subrogation, to recover sums that it has paid on the insured's behalf.

The requirement that the insured "shall not, except at his own expense, voluntarily make any payment, assume any obligation, or incur any expense other than for the first aid to others at the time of accident" prevents the insured from making a payment in respect of the claim and then seeking indemnity from the insurer. This is designed both to protect the insurer's right to investigate, defend, and settle claims and to prevent collusion between the insured and the claimant. The stipulation does not apply, however, when the insurer has wrongfully denied coverage under the policy. In such cases the insured may recover the amount of the settlement, provided it is reasonable and the settlement was made in good faith.[33]

Under the terms of the policy, compliance with the co-operation clause is stated to be a condition precedent to the insurer's liability to the insured. Thus, where the insured is in breach of the co-operation clause, the insurer is entitled to withdraw from the defence and deny indemnity to the insured. As a matter of practice, in such cases the insurer may also cancel the policy.

It is not every breach, however, that gives the insurer this right. In order for the insurer to withdraw from the defence and deny indemnity, the breach must be substantial and material. An inconsequential or trifling breach does not serve to exonerate the insurer from its contractual responsibilities under the policy.[34]

In addition, even when there has been a substantial and material breach of the co-operation clause, the insured may, in appropriate circumstances, obtain relief against forfeiture.[35]

Where there is more than one insured a question may arise as to whose co-operation is required. In the United States it has been held that co-operation is required of anyone who reaps the benefit of the policy and is named as a defendant in the law suit.[36] This requirement is plainly set out in the wording of the Commercial General Liability form noted above, where, on its face, the condition applies to "you and any other involved insured". It is not as clearly set out in the Comprehensive General Liability policy, which requires co-operation by the "Insured", which is not a term defined in the policy (which defines only "Named Insured" and "insured"). Given that the insuring agreement in the

---

[33] See Chapter 5, section 7: Consequences of the Refusal to Defend.

[34] *Travelers Indemnity Co. v. Sumner Co.* (1960), 27 D.L.R. (2d) 562 (N.B.C.A.); *Hanson v. Yorkshire Ins. Co.* (1964), 49 W.W.R. 603 (Alta. S.C.).

[35] *Colliers McClocklin Real Estate Corp. v. Lloyd's Underwriters*, [2003] S.J. No. 581, I.L.R. 1-4246 (Q.B.) See also section 13: Relief against Forfeiture.

[36] *St. Paul Fire & Marine Insurance Co. v. Albany Emergency Center, Inc.*, 361 S.E.2d 687 (1987).

Comprehensive Liability Policy provides coverage only for the "Insured", however, it is likely that the courts will hold that the term "Insured" refers to both the named and unnamed insureds under the policy.

Co-operation is not required by an insured who has no relationship to the action. Thus, where a policy covered a number of medical doctors, the insurer, in investigating the claim, could not require the assistance of a doctor named in the policy but not in the law suit.[37]

Nor, with respect to the language under consideration, is co-operation required for the insurer's purpose of examining the insured in order to determine whether there is a basis to rescind the policy.[38]

5. ACTION AGAINST INSURER

Liability policies generally provide that the insurer may not sue the insured unless there has been full compliance with the policy terms and the amount of the insurer's obligation to pay has been finally determined, either by a judgment or written agreement. In the Comprehensive General Liability policy the "no-action" clause is worded as follows:

> 4. No action shall lie against the Insurer unless, as a condition precedent thereto, there shall have been full compliance with all of the terms of this policy, nor until the amount of the insured's obligation to pay shall have been finally determined either by judgment against the Insured after actual trial or by written agreement of the Insured, the claimant and the Insurer. Every action or proceeding against the Insurer shall be commenced within one year next after the date of such judgment or written agreement and not afterwards. Nothing contained in this policy shall give any person or organization any right to join the Insurer as a co-defendant in any action against the Insured to determine the Insured's liability.
>
> Bankruptcy or insolvency of the Insured or of the Insured's estate shall not relieve the Insurer of any of its obligations hereunder.[39]

In the newer Commercial General Liability policy, the bankruptcy provision has been made into a separate condition. The "no action" condition is worded as follows:

> 7. Legal Action Against Us
> No person or organization has a right under this policy:
>   a. To join us as a party or otherwise bring us into an "action" asking for "compensatory damages" from an insured; or
>   b. To sue us on this policy unless all of its terms have been fully complied with.

---

[37] *Ibid.*

[38] *Re Canada 3000 Inc.*, [2003] O.J. No. 5143 (S.C.J.)

[39] Appendix A.

A person or organization may sue us to recover on an agreed settlement or on a final judgment against an insured; but we will not be liable for "compensatory damages" that are not payable under the terms of this policy or that are in excess of the applicable limit of insurance. An agreed settlement means a settlement and release of liability signed by us, the insured and the claimant or the claimant's legal representative.[40]

The provision that no action lies against the insurer until there has been full compliance with all the terms of the policy is subject to the Court's power to relieve against forfeiture where there has been imperfect compliance on the part of the insured.[41] The further stipulation in the condition, that the insured may not commence action against the insurer until the amount of its obligation to pay has been finally determined, has, in the province of Ontario, been negated by statute.[42] Prior to the enactment of the statute, however, it was held by the Ontario Court of Appeal[43] that such clauses apply only with respect to the indemnity provisions of the contract. Although the British Columbia Court of Appeal did not agree with this interpretation,[44] neither did it hold that the no-action clause was automatically a bar to third party proceedings against the insurer. Rather, it was but one of several factors to take into account.

By denying coverage and invoking the no-action clause an insurer is not taken to have repudiated the policy. Any action must be brought against the insurer within the contractual limitation period, if one exists.[45] Typically, the limitation date is one year from the date at which the insured's liability has been established either by judgment or by written agreement of the insured, the claimant and the insurer.

In *Canadian Northern Shield v. Demers*[46] the insurer sought a declaration that it was not required to defend the insureds in proceedings brought against them for damages for negligence. After being denied a defence, the insureds, representing themselves, waited 18 months before issuing third party proceedings against the insurer. The policy apparently did not contain a contractual limitation period. It did, however, provide that the insureds:

---

[40] Appendix K.

[41] See section 13: Relief against Forfeiture.

[42] *Courts of Justice Act*, R.S.O. 1990, c. C.43.

[43] *Great West Steel Industries v. Simcoe & Erie General Ins. Co.* (1979), 106 D.L.R. (3d) 347, 27 O.R. (2d) 379, [1980] I.L.R. 1-1167 (C.A.). See also *SCS Western Corp. v. Dominion of Canada General Ins. Co.*, [1998] A.J. No. 180, [1998] 7 W.W.R. 570, 59 Alta. L.R. (3d) 73, [1998] I.L.R. 1-3561 (Q.B.).

[44] *Svetlichny v. Overend* (1982), 131 D.L.R. (3d) 664, 24 C.P.C. 309, [1982] I.L.R. 1-1518, 33 B.C.L.R. 214 (C.A.). See also *Conrad v. Snair*, [1994] N.S.J. No. 231, 25 C.P.C. (3d) 1, 115 D.L.R. (4th) 414, 132 N.S.R. (2d) 126, 376 A.P.R. 126 (C.A.) and *Yacht Harbour Pointe Development Corp. v. Architectura Waisman Dewar Grout Carter Inc.*, [1999] B.C.J. No. 675, 69 B.C.L.R. (3d) 334 (S.C.).

[45] *Guarantee Co. of North America v. Gordon Capital Corp.*, [1999] S.C.J. No. 60, [1999] 3 S.C.R. 423, 178 D.L.R. (4th) 1, [2000] I.L.R. 1-3741, revg (1998), 38 O.R. (3d) 563, 157 D.L.R. (4th) 643, [1998] I.L.R. 1-3555 (C.A.), revg (1997), 32 O.R. (3d) 428, 33 B.L.R. (2d) 310 (Gen. Div.).

[46] [2004] B.C.J. No. 650, 10 C.C.L.I. (4th) 230 (S.C.).

... shall not bring suit against us until you have fully complied with all the terms of this policy, nor until the amount of your obligation to pay has been finally determined, either by judgment against you or by an agreement which has our consent.

Notwithstanding this provision, the court held that the limitation period started to run from the time at which the insurer had unequivocally denied coverage. In the absence of a contractual limitation period the court held that the matter was governed by the following provision in the *Insurance Act*:

Every action on a contract must be commenced within one year after the furnishing of reasonably sufficient proof of a loss or claim under the contract and not after.[47]

In the result, the court found that the limitation period had expired and the insured's third party action was time-barred.

With respect, the decision in *Canadian Northern Shield v. Demers* is plainly wrong. Even assuming that the one year limitation period in the *Insurance Act* applies, the cause of action does not accrue until the liability of the insured has been established by a judgment or by an agreement with the consent of the insurer. Moreover, as noted in *Qualiglass Holdings Inc. v. Zurich Indemnity Company of Canada*,[48] the insuring agreement stipulates that it will indemnify the insured against sums which the insured is legally obligated to pay. Although a claim for defence costs may arise earlier, a cause of action for indemnity does not arise until the insured's legal obligation to pay damages has been determined.

6. SUBROGATION

As is the case with property insurance policies, liability insurance policies provide that, having made a payment under the policy, the insurer is subrogated to the insured's rights of recovery against others:

5. Subrogation
In the event of any payment under this policy, the Insurer shall be subrogated to all the Insured's rights of recovery therefor against any person or organization and the Insured shall execute and deliver instruments and papers and do whatever else is necessary to secure such rights. The Insured shall do nothing after loss to prejudice such rights.[49]

14. Transfer Of Rights Of Recovery Against Others To Us

---

[47] R.S.B.C. 1996, c. 226, s. 22(1).

[48] [2004] A.J. No. 881, [2004] I.L.R. 1-4329 (Q.B.).

[49] Appendix A.

If the insured has rights to recover all or part of any payment we have made under this policy, those rights are transferred to us. The insured must do nothing after loss to impair them. At our request, the insured will bring "action" or transfer those rights to us and help us enforce them.[50]

With respect to liability insurance policies, the issue of subrogation does not often arise. The condition is useful, however, where the insured has a right to claim indemnity from someone in addition to the insurer making payment.

7. OTHER INSURANCE

(a) Types of Policies

In general terms, liability policies are written on a primary, excess or umbrella basis. A primary policy is one that, subject to any applicable deductible, attaches upon the happening of a loss. Excess policies are written on the basis that the insured has underlying insurance and generally do not apply until the underlying insurance is exhausted.[51] Umbrella policies have features of both forms. They provide excess coverage for claims that fall within the underlying insurance but also, in certain circumstances, "drop down" and provide primary coverage.[52] Whether primary, excess or umbrella, most liability insurance policies contain a clause designed to determine the manner in which the policies apply when there is other insurance applicable to the loss.

(b) Types of Clauses

There is a considerable variation in the language used in the drafting of "other insurance" clauses. The types of clauses which are in general use can be broadly categorized as primary, excess, and escape clauses. As a caution, it must be noted that not all "other insurance" clauses fit within this classification and, moreover, even clauses which do fall within the same category may, as a result of differences in wording, be materially different in certain respects.

(i) Primary Clauses

A primary clause provides that the insurance afforded under the policy applies first to any loss. Typically, such clauses also provide that if the other insurance applies on the same basis then the insurers shall contribute rateably to the loss. The "other insurance" clause found in the Insurance Bureau of Canada's Comprehensive General Liability policy is a primary clause:

---

[50] Appendix K.

[51] *Plaza Fibreglass Manufacturing Ltd. v. Cardinal Insurance Co.*, [1994] O.J. No. 1023, 18 O.R. (3d) 663 (C.A.).

[52] *Trenton Cold Storage Ltd. v. St. Paul Fire and Marine Insurance Co.*, [2001] O.J. No. 1835, I.L.R. 1-3990 (C.A.).

6.   Other Insurance

The insurance afforded by this policy is primary insurance, except when stated to apply in excess of or contingent upon the absence of other insurance. When this insurance is primary and the Insured has other insurance which is stated to be applicable to the loss, on an excess or contingent basis, the amount of the Insurer's liability under this policy shall not be reduced by the existence of such other insurance. When both this insurance and other insurance apply to the loss on the same basis, whether primary, excess or contingent, the Insurer shall not be liable under this policy for a greater proportion of the loss than that stated in the applicable contribution provision below:

(a)   Contribution by Equal Shares:

If all of such other valid and collectable insurance provides for contribution by equal shares, this Insurer shall not be liable for a greater proportion of such loss than would be payable if each insurer contributes an equal share until the share of each insurer equals the lowest applicable limit of liability under any one policy or the full amount of the loss is paid, and with respect to any amount of loss not so paid the remaining insurers then continue to contribute equal shares of the remaining amount of the loss until each such insurer has paid its limit in full or the full amount of the loss is paid.

(b)   Contribution by Limits:

If any of such other insurance does not provide for contribution by equal shares, this Insurer shall not be liable for a greater proportion of such loss than the applicable limit of liability under this policy for such loss bears to the total applicable limit of liability of all valid and collectible insurance against such loss.[53]

In the Commercial General Liability form the "other insurance" clause is a, with certain exceptions, also a primary clause:

8.   Other Insurance

If other valid and collectible insurance is available to the insured for a loss we cover under Coverages A, B or D of this policy, our obligations are limited as follows:

a.   Primary Insurance

This insurance is primary except when b. below applies. If this insurance is primary, our obligations are not affected unless any of the other insurance is also primary. Then, we will share with all that other insurance by the method described in c. below.

b.   Excess Insurance

This insurance is excess over:

(1) Any of the other insurance, whether primary, excess, contingent or on any other basis:

   (a)   That is Fire, Extended Coverage, Builder's Risk, Installation Risk or similar coverage for "your work";

   (b)   That is Fire insurance for premises rented to you or temporarily occupied by you with permission of the owner;

---

[53] Appendix A.

(c) If the loss arises out of the maintenance or use of watercraft to the extent not subject to Exclusion e. of Section I – Coverage A – Bodily Injury and Property Damage Liability.

(2) Any other primary insurance available to you covering liability for "compensatory damages" arising out of the premises or operations or products-completed operations for which you have been added as an additional insured by attachment of an endorsement.

When this insurance is excess, we will have no duty under Coverages A, B or D to defend the insured against any "action" if any other insurer has a duty to defend the insured against that "action". If no other in-surer defends, we will undertake to do so, but we will be entitled to the insured's rights against all those other insurers.

When this insurance is excess over other insurance, we will pay only our share of the amount of the loss, if any, that exceeds the sum of:

(1) The total amount that all such other insurance would pay for the loss in the absence of this insurance; and

(2) The total of all deductible and self-insured amounts under all that other insurance.

We will share the remaining loss, if any, with any other insurance that is not described in this Excess Insurance provision and was not bought specifically to apply in excess of the Limits of Insurance shown in the Declarations of this policy.

c. Method Of Sharing

If all of the other insurance permits contribution by equal shares, we will follow this method also. Under this approach each insurer contributes equal amounts until it has paid its applicable limit of insurance or none of the loss remains, whichever comes first.

If any of the other insurance does not permit contribution by equal shares, we will contribute by limits. Under this method, each insurer's share is based on the ratio of its applicable limit of insurance to the total applicable limits of in-surance of all insurers.[54]

(ii) Excess Clauses

An excess clause provides that the insurer's liability is limited to the amount by which the loss exceeds the coverage provided by all other insurers. A typical example of what might be termed a "pure excess" clause is as follows:

If, at the time of an accident or occurrence covered by this Section II, there is any other insurance which would attach if this insurance had not been effected, the Insurer under this Section II shall be liable only for the excess, if any, of any loss, over the applicable limit of the other insurance covering such loss.

Under this language the entire policy limit will be available, but as excess rather than primary coverage. Some excess clauses, however, purport to limit coverage even further.

---

[54] Appendix K.

(iii) Escape Clauses

An escape clause purports to avoid all liability for a loss that is covered under any other policy. The following is an example of such a clause:

> If any other Assured included in this insurance is covered by valid and collectable insurance against a claim also covered by this Policy, he shall not be entitled to protection under this Policy.

Sometimes the "other insurance" clause incorporates features of both excess and escape clauses. Such was the case in *Manitoba Public Insurance Corp. v. Scottish & York Insurance Co.*[55] A teacher was insured under two primary policies; the M.P.I.C. policy was stated to be excess to any other insurance, whereas the Scottish policy had a provision that it was null and void whenever other insurance was available, except that it would provide excess insurance, so as to give the insured a combined amount of protection equal to the limits of the Scottish policy. The loss was within the limits of the M.P.I.C. policy. The Court held that in these circumstances the escape provisions of the Scottish policy operated to exclude it from liability.

This decision was distinguished in *Wawanesa Mutual Insurance Co. v. Commercial Union Assurance Co.*[56] The Wawanesa policy had an excess clause; the Commercial Union policy contained a clause which was similar in meaning except for the last sentence, which read: "In no event shall this policy be construed as contributing insurance". It was contended on behalf of Commercial Union that the last sentence constituted an escape clause and that Wawanesa was solely liable. The Court disagreed. The clause in question did not purport to avoid all liability and therefore could not be considered an escape clause. It was held that the excess clauses in both policies cancelled each other out and both policies contributed on a primary basis.

In the United States, some courts have treated escape clauses with disfavour, finding it "unacceptable for an insurance company to provide no coverage under a policy for which it received premiums".[57] In Canada, however, the courts have continued to give effect to an appropriately worded escape clause.

(c) Resolving Coverage When Policies Overlap

Liability policies are said to overlap when they are in force at the relevant time and insure the same insured against the same peril.[58] Where two or more

---

[55] [1991] M.J. No. 212, I.L.R. 1-2733 (Q.B.).

[56] [1994] M.J. No. 565, [1994] 10 W.W.R. 701, 27 C.C.L.I. (2d) 15, 96 Man. R. (2d) 284, [1995] I.L.R. 1-3174 (Q.B.).

[57] *Contrans Inc. v. Ryder Truck Rentals, Inc.*, 836 F.2d 163 at 166. For the American position see, generally, G.J. Couch, *Couch Cyclopedia of Insurance Law*, 2nd ed. (Revised) (Rochester: Lawyers Co-operative Publishing Co., 1984) at para. 62.71 *et seq.*

[58] *Simcoe & Erie General Ins. Co. v. Kansa General Ins. Co.*, [1994] B.C.J. No. 1442, [1994] I.L.R. 1-3110, 93 B.C.L.R. (2d) 1, [1994] 9 W.W.R. 712 (C.A.), leave to appeal to S.C.C. refd, [1994] S.C.C.A. No. 438, 27 C.C.L.I. (2d) 195, 188 N.R. 400; *Aetna Ins. Co. v. Can. Surety Co.*,

policies apply in this fashion to a loss, the traditional approach has been that the liability of the respective insurers is determined by their intent, as manifested by the terms of the policies which they have issued. An alternative approach, developed in the United States and sometimes referred to as the "Minnesota approach", is to determine, in all of the circumstances, which policy is closer to the risk: the carrier whose coverage was placed for the primary purpose of insuring the risk will be liable first for payment and the carrier whose coverage of the risk was the most incidental to the basic purpose of its insuring intent will be liable last.[59]

In *Family Insurance Corp. v. Lombard Canada Ltd.*[60] the Supreme Court of Canada expressly rejected the Minnesota approach in favour of the traditional approach. The Court accepted as correct the following statement of the law from *Couch Cyclopedia of Insurance Law*:

> There is authority that the liability of insurers under overlapping coverage poli-cies is to be governed by the intent of the insurers as manifested by the terms of the policies which they have issued. Thus, it has been said that where two or more lia-bility policies overlap and cover the same risk and the same accident, the respective liabilities of the insurers must rest upon a construction of the language employed by the respective insurers and not upon the so called "pri-mary tort-feasor doctrine" or upon any other arbitrary rule or circumstance.[61]

The insured in *Family Insurance Corp. v. Lombard Canada Ltd.* owned a stable. She had liability coverage under a homeowner's policy as well as under a "Comprehensive Business Liability" policy issued to all members of the Horse Council of British Columbia, of which she was a member. A person injured at the insured's stable commenced an action against her. After the action was settled the insurers litigated the issue of whether one or both of the policies responded to the claim. On their face both policies were primary and the "other insurance" clauses in both policies were in the nature of excess clauses. Thus, going strictly by the policy wordings, the loss should be prorated. This was the approach taken by the trial judge.[62] The British Columbia Court of Appeal, however, eschewed the traditional approach, preferring to go beyond an interpretation of the policy language and give broader consideration to the circumstances under which the respective polices were placed. On this basis the Court ruled that the homeowner's policy should be regarded as primary and the business policy as providing excess coverage. Because the latter policy was offered through a group and it could be expected that many members of the

---

[1994] A.J. No. 399, 114 D.L.R. (4th) 577, [1994] 8 W.W.R. 63 at 114, [1994] I.L.R. 1-3119, 114 D.L.R. (4th) 577, 19 Alta. L.R. (3d) 317, supp. reasons, [1995] 1 W.W.R. 108, 23 Alta. L.R. (3d) 182 (C.A.); *Eagle Star Ins. Co. v. Provincial Ins. Plc.*, [1993] 3 All E.R. 1 (P.C.).

[59] See, for example, *Nordby v. Atlantic Mutual Ins. Co.*, 329 N.W.2d 820 (Minn. 1983).

[60] [2002] S.C.J. No. 49, [2002] 2 S.C.R. 695.

[61] C.J. Couch, *Couch Cyclopedia of Insurance Law*, 2nd ed. (Revised) (Rochester: Lawyers Co-operative Publishing Co., 1984) at para. 62:44.

[62] [1999] B.C.J. No. 515, 10 C.C.L.I. (3d) 58 (S.C.), affd [2002] S.C.J. No. 49, [2002] 2 S.C.R. 695.

group would have their own homeowner's policies, the Court concluded that the group's insurer must have intended that its policy be excess to any such individual policies.[63] The Court also opined, although no evidence was led on the point, that the premium charged by the group's insurer was likely based upon a claims experience which took into account the existence of other policies.

The Supreme Court of Canada restored the trial judgment. The Minnesota approach was rejected in favour of the traditional approach, which is to determine intent on the basis of the terms of the respective policies. Moreover, said the Supreme Court of Canada, when the contest is between insurers, intent must be ascertained from the four corners of the contract, without reference to any surrounding circumstances:

> Thus, while it remains true that the intentions of the insurers prevail, the inquiry is of necessity limited to the insurers' intentions vis-à-vis the insured. In the case of an insurance contract, the entire agreement between the insurer and the insured is contained within the policy itself and evidence of the parties' intentions must be sought in the words they chose. Were the dispute between the insurer and the insured, reference to surrounding circumstances may be appropriate if provisions of the policy are ambiguous. Once the interest of the insured is no longer at stake, that is, where the contest is only between the insurers, there is simply no basis for looking outside the policy. In the absence of privity of contract between the parties, the unilateral and subjective intentions of the insurers, unaware of one another at the time the contracts were made, are simply irrelevant.[64]

This statement by the Supreme Court of Canada is *obiter dicta.* In the case before the Court no issue of ambiguity arose. There is earlier authority, albeit from the lower courts, which was not considered by the Supreme of Court of Canada and which takes a contrary position.

In *Manufacturers Life Ins. Co. v. Can. General Ins. Co*,[65] which involved a contest between two insurers as to which policy was primary, the British Columbia Supreme Court admitted into evidence correspondence between the insured and its brokers that took place while the insured was in the process of placing coverage. In *Sun Alliance Ins. Co. v. Commercial Union Assur. Co. of Can*,[66] the court accepted both oral evidence and a memorandum of an insurance manager as to the purpose for which the policy was obtained. In *Healy v. Prefontaine*,[67] a case which involved a contest between a strata corporation's liability insurer and an individual strata owner's policy, the Court took into

---

[63]   [2002] B.C.J. No. 1076, 18 C.C.L.I. (3d) 165 (C.A.).

[64]   [2002] S.C.J. No. 49, [2002] 2 S.C.R. 695 at para. 19.

[65]   [1988] B.C.J. No. 2007, [1989] I.L.R. 1-2394 (S.C.).

[66]   [1991] O.J. No. 425, [1991] I.L.R. 1-2746 (Gen. Div.).

[67]   [1989] A.J. No. 579, 98 A.R. 54, [1989] I.L.R. 1-2502, 43 C.C.L.I. 117 (Q.B.).

account both the by-laws of the strata corporation and the provisions of the Alberta *Condominium Property Act* in determining which policy was primary.[68]

Admittedly, an inquiry into the surrounding circumstances will be rare, particularly where "stock" or standardized policies are concerned.[69] Indeed, in *Simcoe & Erie v. Kansa*,[70] the British Columbia Court of Appeal went so far as to note that rather than simply relying upon a standard type of "other insurance" clause, an insurer who wishes to avoid contribution should include an endorsement specifically referring to the other policy in place. Nevertheless, with respect, there are cases in which the Supreme Court of Canada's prohibition against extrinsic evidence in a contest between insurers may lead to the obvious injustice of one insurer having greater rights against another insurer than does the insured. This is illustrated by the following example. The insured purchases two liability policies, policy A to cover operations generally and policy B to provide coverage for a specific project. Both policies are in stock form and both policies are stated to be primary. Extrinsic evidence, however, makes it plain that the intent of all parties was that policy B was intended to provide primary coverage for the specific project and that, as far as the project was concerned, policy A was intended to be excess to policy B. Applying the reasoning in *Family Insurance Corp. v. Lombard Canada Ltd.*,[71] insurer B can pay out a claim in respect of the project and then obtain contribution from insurer A. In this suit the extrinsic evidence would not be admissible. The case would be determined solely by the policy wordings, on the basis of which insurer B would succeed. Yet, if the insured were to sue insurer A in these circumstances, the extrinsic evidence would be admissible and the suit would fail. Surely, this is a result that should not be countenanced. Insurer B's rights against insurer A should be no greater than the rights of the insured.

The traditional approach does not limit itself to a comparison of the "other insurance" provisions in the respective policies; rather, the policies must be construed in their entirety. In *Trenton Cold Storage Ltd. v. St. Paul Fire and Marine Insurance Co.*[72] the insured had purchased a "Warehouseman or Bailee Liability" policy from I.A.R.W. and an "Umbrella Excess Liability Policy" from St. Paul. The I.A.R.W. policy provided primary coverage but, with respect to other insurance, incorporated three provisions: a clause stating that the I.A.R.W. policy was excess to any other policy which would apply in the absence of the I.A.R.W. policy, a clause granting permission for the insured to purchase excess insurance and a clause which provided as follows:

---

[68] R.S.A. 1980, c. C-22.

[69] *McGeough v. Stay 'N Save Motor Inns Inc.*, [1994] B.C.J. No. 1374, 116 D.L.R. (4th) 137, [1994] 8 W.W.R. 295, 92 B.C.L.R. (2d) 288, 25 C.C.L.I. (2d) 165 (C.A.).

[70] *Simcoe & Erie General Insurance Co. v. Kansa General Insurance Co.*, [1994] B.C.J. No. 1442, [1994] 9 W.W.R. 712, 93 B.C.L.R. (2d) 1, [1994] I.L.R. 1-3110 (C.A.), leave to appeal to S.C.C. refd, [1994] S.C.C.A. No. 438, 27 C.C.L.I. (2d) 195, 188 N.R. 400.

[71] [2002] S.C.J. No. 49, [2002] 2 S.C.R. 695.

[72] [2001] O.J. No. 1835, [2001] I.L.R. I-3990 (C.A.).

> This insurance does not cover any loss, which at the time of the happening of such loss, is insured by or would but for the existence of this Policy, be insured by any other existing Policy or Policies except in respect of any excess beyond the amount which would have been payable under such other Policy or Policies had this insurance not been effected.

The St. Paul policy provided coverage in excess of the insured's retained limit, which was defined as including the limits of any underlying insurance. Certain underlying policies were set out in a schedule to the St. Paul policy, but the I.A.R.W. policy was not one of these. The St. Paul policy contained an "other insurance" clause stating that it was excess to any other valid and collectible insurance.

After paying a claim, I.A.R.W. sought contribution from St. Paul. Taking all of the provisions of the policies into account, however, including the respective premiums payable, the Ontario Court Appeal determined that the I.A.R.W. policy was primary and that the St. Paul policy did not apply until the I.A.R.W. limits were exhausted.

The traditional approach of determining intent from the language of the policy works well where the overlapping policies have complementary "other insurance" clauses. For example, where there are two policies, both of which contain primary clauses with identical wording, then the loss will be prorated between the two insurers on the basis specified in that clause.[73] Similarly, where one policy contains a primary clause and the other an excess clause, the policy containing the primary clause will apply first to the loss.[74]

The traditional approach does not lend itself well, however, to cases where the "other insurance" clauses in the overlapping policies are in conflict. For example, where both policies contain escape clauses, a literal reading would lead to the absurd conclusion that neither policy applied to the loss. Similarly, where both policies contain excess clauses the language of those clauses will generally create the paradox that each of the policies provides only excess coverage to the amount covered under the other policy.

The conflict between policies that both contain either escape or excess clauses is generally resolved on the basis that the clauses cancel each other out and the insurers share the loss rateably.[75] Unlike a primary clause, however,

---

[73] *American Lumbermens Mutual Casualty Co. v. Lumber Mutual Casualty Ins. Co.*, 295 N.Y.S. 321 (1937); *Neice v. Nation Wide Mutual Ins. Co.*, 419 N.Y.S.2d 799 (1978).

[74] *Seagate Hotel Ltd. v. Simcoe & Erie General Ins. Co.*, (1981), 27 B.C.L.R. 89, [1982] 1 L.R. 1-1470 (C.A.), affg (1980), 22 B.C.L.R. 374 (S.C.). This is also the majority view in the United States: see *Jones v. Medox Inc.*, 430 A.2d 488 (D.C. 1981). The minority American position, expressed in *Lamb-Weston Inc. v. Oregon Automobile Ins.*, 341 P.2d 110 (1959), modified and rehearing denied, 346 P.2d 643 (1959), is that *pro rata* and excess clauses are irreconcilable and therefore both policies must contribute *pro rata* to the loss. The minority American position was rejected in *Caldor Inc. v. Kansa General Ins. Co.*, [1988] O.J. No. 334, 31 C.C.L.I. 69 (H.C.J.).

[75] *Wawanesa Mutual Insurance Co. v. Commercial Union Assurance Co.*, [1994] M.J. No. 565, [1994] 10 W.W.R. 701, 96 Man. R. (2d) 284, [1995] I.L.R. 1-3174, 27 C.C.L.I. (2d) 15 (Q.B.); *Wawanesa Mutual Ins. Co. v. Co-op. Fire & Casualty*, [1980] S.J. No. 614, [1981] I.L.R. 1-1349

neither an excess clause nor an escape clause contains a formula setting out the basis upon which the overlapping policies are to contribute to the loss. In the absence of such a formula the three methods of prorating which have been considered by the courts are the maximum liability, equal shares and the independent liability approaches:

(i)   Maximum liability approach — each insurer's contribution to the loss is in the same proportion as the limits of that insurer's policy bears to the aggregate limits of all of the available insurance;

(ii) Equal shares — the insurers contribute equally to the loss up to the limits of their respective policies;

(iii) Independent liability approach — each insurer contributes to the loss according to the ratio that such insurer's independent liability to pay the loss bears to the independent liability of the other insurer(s) to pay the loss.

The differences between these three approaches may be illustrated by a simple example. Suppose there are two policies, one issued by insurer A for $100,000 and the other issued by insurer B for $300,000. A loss is incurred in the amount of $200,000. Under the maximum liability approach, insurer A would pay one-quarter of the loss or $50,000. Under the equal shares approach, the insurers would each pay $100,000. Under the independent liability approach, insurer B would be independently liable for the entire claim, or $200,000, whereas insurer A would be independently liable for only $100,000, being the policy limits. Accordingly, the ratio of insurer A's contribution to insurer B's contribution would be 1:2; thus, insurer A would pay one-third of the loss and insurer B would pay the remaining two-thirds.

The American decisions employ both the maximum liability and equal shares approaches.[76] In England and Canada, however, the independent liability approach has been favoured. In *Commercial Union Assurance Co. v. Hayden*[77] the insured was covered by two policies, one with a limit of £10,000, the other with a limit of £100,000. Both policies contained an "other insurance" clause which provided that if there was any other insurance covering the risk then the insurers would not be liable for more than "a rateable proportion". Neither policy, however, defined what "rateable proportion" should mean. A claim against the insured was settled for £4,425.45. The insurer with the lower limit argued that it was required to contribute only one-eleventh of the claim, which is

---

(Q.B.); *Pacific Power & Light Co. v. Transport Indemnity Co.*, 460 F.2d 959 (9th Cir. 1972) (excess clauses); *Travelers Indemnity Co. v. Chappell*, 246 So. 498 (Miss. 1971) (escape clause).

[76] *St. Paul Mercury Ins. Co. v. Underwriters of Lloyd's of London*, 365 F.2d 659 (10th Cir. 1966) (maximum liability); *Liberty Mutual Ins. Co. v. Pacific Indemnity Co.*, 557 F.Supp. 986 (W.D.Pa. 1983) (equal shares). The equal shares method is now gaining favour as being a more equitable basis for sharing the loss than the basis of policy limits: See *Reliance Ins. Co. v. St. Paul's Surplus Lines Ins. Co.*, 753 F.2d 1288 (4th Cir. 1985). A minority of American courts have prorated the loss on the basis of the amount of the premium paid by each insurer. See *Ins. Co. of Texas v. Employers' Liability Ins. Corp.*, 163 F.Supp. 143 (S.D. Cal. 1958).

[77] [1977] 1 All E.R. 441 (C.A.).

the ratio which the limits of its policy bore to the total available insurance. This argument was accepted by the trial judge. In the Court of Appeal, however, the independent liability approach was preferred. Cairns L.J. reasoned as follows:

> The issue being one of construction and the language being, as it seems to me, equally capable of either suggested meaning, I ask myself which meaning is that more likely to be intended by reasonable businessmen. The documents to be construed are policies, the parties to each of which are an assured and an insurer. It is not to be supposed that when either policy is issued the insurer knows that there is, or is going to be, another policy covering the same risk. Each limit of liability and each premium may be taken to be fixed without knowledge of the limit under any other policy that may have been, or be going to be issued. It is difficult to suppose that when a limit of £10,000 was fixed by Lloyd's it could be intended that if there happened to be another policy with a limit of £100,000, Lloyd's underwriters should be liable for only one-eleventh of any claim, however small. The independent liability basis is much more realistic in its results. In the case of these two policies, any loss up to £10,000 would be shared equally, and it is only with larger losses that the proportion of Commercial Union's share to Lloyd's share steadily increases until with a loss of £110,000 or more, ten-elevenths of the liability falls on Commercial Union. The obvious purpose of having a limit of liability under an insurance policy is to protect the insurer from the effect of exceptionally large claims: it seems to me artificial to use the limits under two policies to adjust liability in respect of claims which are within the limits of either policy.[78]

Lawton L.J. noted that using the policy limits as the basis for apportionment was unfair to the insurer who gave a much higher limit for a small increase in premium:

> What is the "burthen" under an indemnity liability policy? It is the claim which is made, not the claim which could be made. This kind of policy may be unlimited as to the amount of the indemnity, as it always is under motor car policies and often is under employers' liability policies, or limited as it almost always is under professional negligence policies. Even when a policy limits the amount of the indemnity, it is a matter of judicial experience that most claims are well below the limit. To ascertain the proportions of contribution by reference to the limits of indemnity would, in my judgment, be an odd way of sharing the "burthen" in equity between insurers; and in cases where there was a limit under one policy but none under another, it would be a difficult judicial task, probably an impossible one, to assess, as counsel for Lloyd's suggested should be done and Donaldson J. agreed (I quote from the judgment):
>
> > "... the maximum cover which will ever be likely to be provided by the unlimited policy and to compare this figure with the sum specified in the other policies."

Further, using the limits as the basis for apportionment of contributions would be unfair to the insurer who gave a much higher limit for a small increase in

---

[78] *Ibid.* at 447.

premium. This case provides an example. The Commercial Union gave the assured a limit of £100,000; Lloyd's a limit of £10,000. The difference in premium was £1.

It is a matter of my experience both as a judge and a practitioner that the assessment of premiums under liability policies is based on underwriting experience backed up by statistical information and actuarial projections.

The risk underwritten is at its greatest with small claims and at its least with large claims. It follows that the upper limits for claims can be increased with only a small increase in premiums. When there are two insurers with differing upper limits for claims, the inference I would draw is that they were both accepting the same level of risk up to the lower of the limits. If this be so, in my judgment, "a ratable satisfaction", to use Lord Mansfield CJ's phrase, would be an equal division of liability up to the lower limit; the "burthen" of meeting that part of the claim above the lower limit would fall on the insurer who had accepted the higher limit.[79]

The decision in *Commercial Union v. Hayden* was applied by the British Columbia Supreme Court in *Dominion of Canada General Insurance v. Wawanesa Mutual Insurance Co.*[80] Liability insurance coverage extended to the insured under two policies, both of which contained an excess clause. One policy had a limit of $100,000, the other of $300,000. The insured was liable, with reference to a boating accident, for damages in the approximate amount of $130,000. The two insurers could not agree on the basis upon which the liability to pay damages should be apportioned. Dominion favoured the maximum liability approach. Wawanesa argued that the loss should be apportioned equally. The Court rejected both approaches in favour of the independent liability method, stating that the effect of this would be that the two insurers would share equally to the lower limit of $100,000. This curious way of stating the effect of the independent liability method comes from the judgment of Lawton L.J. in *Commercial Union v. Hayden.*[81] Although this language might suggest that the entire burden of the judgment in excess of the lower limit should fall upon the insurer with the higher limit, it is plain from a consideration of the other judgments in *Commercial Union v. Hayden* that on the application of the independent liability method in *Dominion of Canada General Insurance Co. v. Wawanesa Mutual Insurance Co.* the ratio of Dominion's contribution to Wawanesa's contribution would be 1:1.3.

---

[79] *Ibid.* at 53.

[80] [1985] B.C.J. No. 1394, 16 C.C.L.I. 69 (S.C.). Followed by the British Columbia Court of Appeal in *Simcoe & Erie General Insurance Co. v. Kansa General Insurance Co., supra*, note 70.

[81] *Supra*, note 77 at 453.

8. CHANGES TO THE POLICY

Liability insurers generally insert a provision in the policy to protect them against any verbal waivers or changes to the policy:

> 7. Changes
> Notice to any agent or knowledge possessed by any agent or by any other person shall not effect a waiver or a change in any part of this policy or estop the insurer from asserting any right under the terms of this policy; nor shall the terms of this policy be waived or changed, except by endorsement issued to form a part of this policy.[82]

> 3. Changes
> This policy contains all the agreements between you and us concerning the insurance afforded. The first Named Insured shown in the Declarations is authorized to make changes in the terms of this policy with our consent. This policy's terms can be amended or waived only by endorsement issued by us and made a part of this policy.[83]

To some extent this condition duplicates what has been provided by statute:

(1) No term or condition of a contract shall be deemed to be waived by the insurer in whole or in part unless the waiver is stated in writing and signed by a person authorized for that purpose by the insurer.

(2) Neither the insurer nor the insured shall be deemed to have waived any term or condition of a contract by any act relating to the appraisal of the amount of loss or to the delivery and completion of proofs or to the investigation or adjustment of any claim under the contract.[84]

The limit that the condition purports to place on the doctrine of estoppel is most likely ineffective since the doctrine of estoppel is not based simply on notice or knowledge. Rather, an estoppel arises in circumstances where the insurer has, by its words or conduct, made a representation of fact that the insured has acted upon to his or her detriment.[85]

---

[82] Appendix A.

[83] Appendix K.

[84] *Insurance Act*, R.S.A. 1980, c. I-5, s. 207. Comparable sections in other jurisdictions are as follows: R.S.B.C. 1996, c. 226, s. 11; R.S.M. 1987, c. I40, s. 123; R.S.N.B. 1973, c. I-12, s. 109; R.S.N.S. 1989, c. 231, s. 35; *Insurance Contracts Act*, R.S.N.L. 1990, c. I-12, s. 12; R.S.O. 1990, c. I.8, s. 131; R.S.P.E.I. 1988, c. I-4, s. 94; *Saskatchewan Insurance Act*, R.S.S. 1978, c. S-26, s. 111.

[85] See Chapter 5, section 6(b): Estoppel by Representation.

9. CANCELLATION AND TERMINATION

Liability insurance policies customarily contain provisions regarding the cancellation or termination of the policy. The wording typically found in commercial policies is as follows:

10. Cancellation — Termination
(a) This policy may be terminated,
    (i)   by the Insurer giving to the Named Insured 15 days' notice of termination by registered mail or 5 days' written notice of termination personally delivered;
    (ii) by the Named Insured at any time on request.
(b) Where the policy is terminated by the Insurer,
    (i)   and where the premium is developed on other than an estimated basis, the Insurer will refund the excess of the paid premium for the time the policy has been in force, calculated pro rata, or
    (ii) where the premium is developed by an estimated basis, the Insurer will refund the excess of the premium above the premium earned, when determined.
(c) Where the policy is terminated by the Named Insured,
    (i)   and where the premium is developed on other than an estimated basis, the Insurer will refund the excess of the paid premium above the short rate premium, for the time the policy has been in force calculated in accordance with the short rate premium table in use by the Insurer, subject to the retention of the minimum premium, if any, provided by the policy, or
    (ii) where the premium is developed by an estimated basis, the Insurer will refund the excess of the paid premium above the premium earned, when determined, subject to the retention of the minimum premium, if any, provided by the policy.
(d) Refund of premium may be made by money, postal or express company money order or by cheque payable at par.
(e) The 15 days mentioned above in this condition commences to run on the day following the receipt of the registered letter at the post office to which it is addressed.
(f) Premium adjustment may be made at the time cancellation is effected and if not then shall be made as soon as practicable after cancellation becomes effective but payment or tender of unearned premium is not a condition of cancellation.[86]

It has been held that a policy cancellation by registered mail is effective even when it is not actually received by the insured.[87] In British Columbia in such circumstances the *Insurance Act*[88] provides for relief against forfeiture.

---

[86] Appendix A.

[87] *Lumbermen's Mutual Casualty Co. v. Stone*, [1955] S.C.R. 627.

[88] R.S.B.C. 1996, c. 226, s. 10. See *Rokanas v. Co-op. Fire & Casualty Co.* (1977), 1 B.C.L.R. 85 (S.C.).

10. ASSIGNMENT

Liability insurance policies typically provide that the insured cannot assign the policy without the insurer's consent. There may be an exception for a transfer of interest by operation of law, such as in the case of death or bankruptcy. The rationale for this condition is that the risk characteristics of the particular insured determine whether the insurer will provide coverage, and, if so, at what premium.[89]

A typical clause prohibiting assignment without the insurer's consent is as follows:

> 8. Assignment
> Assignment of interest under this policy shall not bind the insurer until its consent is endorsed hereon; if, however, the Named Insured shall die or be adjudged bankrupt or insolvent within the policy period, this policy, unless cancelled, shall, if written notice be given to the Insurer within sixty days, after the date of such death or adjudication, cover the Named Insured's legal representative as the Named Insured except in the Province of Quebec, where no notice is required.[90]

A clause somewhat similar in intent was considered in *Gosse v. Juany Inc.*,[91] where a town was disestablished by Order in Council and all of its assets and liabilities transferred to the City of St. John's. It was held by the trial judge that in the absence of consent this transfer was not binding on the town's liability insurer. The Newfoundland Court of Appeal expressed some unease with this conclusion but found in favour of the insurer on another ground.

The prohibition against assignment of the policy without the insurer's consent is not generally considered to apply in the case of the assignment of an existing claim. As stated in the *Couch Cyclopedia of Insurance Law*:

> The great weight of authority supports the rule that general stipulations in policies prohibiting assignments thereof except with the consent of the insurer apply to assignments before loss ... and do not prevent an assignment after loss, for the obvious reason that the clause by its own terms ordinarily prohibits merely the assignment of the policy, as distinguished from a claim arising thereunder, and the assignment before the loss involves the transfer of a contractual relationship, while the assignment after loss is the transfer of a right to a money claim.[92]

---

[89] *Northern Ins. Co. of N.Y. v. Allied Mutual Ins. Co.*, 955 F.2d 1353 (9th Cir.), cert. denied, 112 S. Ct. 3033 (1992).

[90] Appendix A.

[91] [1995] N.J. No. 294, 134 Nfld. & P.E.I.R. 15 (Nfld. C.A.).

[92] G.J. Couch, 2nd ed. (Revised) (Rochester: Lawyers Co-operative Publishing Co., 1984) at para. 63.40.

11. SEPARATION OF INSUREDS AND CROSS LIABILITY

Liability policies typically provide that, except with respect to monetary limits, coverage applies separately with respect to each insured. Thus, the Commercial General Liability policy provides as follows:

> 12. Separation Of Insureds, Cross Liability
> Except with respect to the Limits of Insurance, and any rights or duties specifically assigned in this policy to the first Named Insured, this insurance applies:
>> a. As if each Named Insured were the only Named Insured; and
>> b. Separately to each insured against whom claim is made or "action" is brought.[93]

The significance of these provisions is discussed in Chapter 6.[94]

12. REPRESENTATIONS

Liability insurance policies typically provide that the policy is issued in reliance upon the accuracy of the statements made by the insured in the policy Declarations:

> 11. Representations
> By accepting this policy, you agree:
>> a. The statements in the Declarations are accurate and complete;
>> b. Those statements are based upon representations you made to us; and
>> c. We have issued this policy in reliance upon your representations.[95]

The stipulation that the policy was issued in reliance upon the insured's representations, however, does not necessarily mean that the policy is void in the event that one or more of the representations is determined to be inaccurate. In order to avoid coverage on this basis the insurer must be able to prove that the misrepresentation is material.[96]

13. RELIEF AGAINST FORFEITURE

Liability insurance policies generally provide that no action shall lie against the insurer under the policy unless there has been full compliance by the insured with all of the terms of the policy. By statute, however, the courts are given the power to relieve against the consequences of imperfect compliance. In the common law provinces, except British Columbia, the legislation provides:

---

[93] Appendix K.

[94] See Chapter 6, section 3(i): Severability of Insureds or "Cross-Liability".

[95] Appendix K.

[96] See Chapter 2, section 1(f): Misrepresentation.

When there has been imperfect compliance with a statutory condition as to the proof of loss to be given by the insured or other matter or thing required to be done or omitted by the insured with respect to the loss and the consequent forfeiture or avoidance of the insurance in whole or in part and the Court considers it inequitable that the insurance should be forfeited or avoided on that ground, the Court may relieve against the forfeiture or avoidance on any terms it considers just.[97]

In British Columbia, the legislation is drafted in somewhat broader terms:

If there has been imperfect compliance with a statutory condition as to the proof of loss to be given by the insured or other matter or thing required to be done or omitted by the insured with respect to the loss, and a consequent forfeiture or avoidance of the insurance in whole or in part, or if there has been a termination of the policy by a notice that was not received by the insured owing to the insured's absence from the address to which the notice was addressed, and the court deems it inequitable that the insurance should be forfeited or avoided on that ground or terminated, the court may, on terms it deems just, relieve against the forfeiture or avoidance or, if the application for relief is made within 90 days of the date of the mailing of the notice of termination, against the termination.[98]

The statutory provision regarding relief against forfeiture, which is drafted in language that is more suited to property policies, has been held to apply to policies of liability insurance.[99] Although the legislation refers to statutory conditions, of which there are none in a non-automobile liability insurance policy, the phrase "or other matter or thing" has been held to encompass the non-statutory conditions in a liability insurance contract.[100]

The section creates a distinction between imperfect compliance and non-compliance. It is only in the former case that relief from forfeiture may be granted. In *Falk Bros. Industries Ltd. v. Elance Steel Fabricating Co.* the Supreme Court of Canada described the distinction between imperfect compliance and non-compliance as follows:

The distinction between imperfect compliance and non-compliance is akin to the distinction between breach of a term of the contract and breach of a condition precedent. If the breach is of a condition, that is, it amounts to non-compliance, no relief under s. 109 is available.[101]

---

[97] *Insurance Act*, Alta., s. 205. Comparable sections in other jurisdictions are as follows: Man., s. 130; N.B., s. 110; Nfld., s. 10; N.S., s. 33; Ont., s. 129; Sask., s. 109.

[98] *Insurance Act*, B.C., s. 10.

[99] *Minto Const. Ltd. v. Gerling Global General Ins. Co.* (1978), 86 D.L.R. (3d) 147 (Ont. C.A.); *Falk Bros. Industries Ltd. v. Elance Steel Fabricating Co.*, [1989] S.C.J. No. 97, 2 S.C.R. 778.

[100] *Ibid.*

[101] *Ibid.*, at para. 17.

Applying this logic, cases in which there has been failure to give notice of a claim under an occurrence based policy are generally treated as imperfect compliance,[102] whereas cases in which there has been a failure to give notice during the policy period under a claims-made policy are treated as non-compliance,[103] against which relief from forfeiture is not available. The reason for this distinction is that, unlike an occurrence policy, coverage under a claims-made policy is triggered by the claim being made during the policy period. Thus, a failure to give notice during the policy period in the case of a claims-made policy amounts to non-compliance with a condition precedent for coverage. Under either type of policy, the section does not apply to the insured's failure to take proceedings against the insurer within the limitation period, for that is neither a matter or thing "with respect to the loss" or imperfect compliance, nor has there been a forfeiture.[104]

It has been held by the Saskatchewan Court of Queen's Bench that the duty to co-operate is not a condition precedent to coverage so as to preclude the availability of relief against forfeiture when a breach has occurred.[105] The Ontario Court of Appeal arguably reached the contrary conclusion in *Canadian Newspapers Co. v. Kansa General Insurance Co.*[106] The insured, a newspaper publisher, had an arrangement with its insurer whereby the publisher would conduct the defence of libel actions brought against it but would keep the insurer informed of any substantial developments in the course of an action. An action was brought against the insured which, in accordance with this arrangement, was defended by the insured. Contrary to the arrangement, however, the insured failed to keep the insurer informed as to certain matters which materially affected the insurer's position. The insured failed to report on the progress of the litigation, to convey offers to settle and to inform the insurer of the theory of the defence and did not even advise the insurer that the action had proceeded to trial until after the trial had begun. It was held that this constituted a breach of the policy condition requiring the insured to co-operate[107] and, further, that it went beyond imperfect compliance and was a substantial breach of the policy, so as to preclude any consideration of relief against forfeiture. In the alternative, the

---

[102] *Canadian Equipment Sales & Service Co. v. Continental Insurance Co.* (1975), 59 D.L.R. (3d) 333 (Ont. C.A.); *Minto Construction Ltd. v. Gerling Global General Insurance Co.* (1978), 86 D.L.R. (3d) 147 (Ont. C.A.); *Moxness v. Saskatchewan Government Insurance Office*, [1977] 3 W.W.R. 393 (Sask. D.C.); *Janet Estate and Kallos v. Saskatchewan Government Insurance* (1984), 30 Sask. R. 185 (Q.B.); *North Lethbridge Garage Ltd. v. Continental Casualty Co.*, [1930] 1 W.W.R. 491 (Alta. S.C., App. Div.).

[103] *Stuart v. Hutchins* [1998] O.J. No. 3672, 164 D.L.R. (4th) 67, 40 O.R. (3d) 321, [1999] I.L.R. 1-3619, 27 C.P.C. (4th) 1 (C.A.).

[104] *Nat. Juice Co. v. Dominion Ins. Co.* (1978), 81 D.L.R. (3d) 606 (Ont. C.A.); *Wilson v. Zurich Ins. Co.*, [1981] I.L.R. 1-1447 (Sask. Q.B.).

[105] *Colliers McClocklin Real Estate Corp. v. Lloyd's Underwriters*, [2003] S.J. No. 581, [2003] I.L.R. 1-4246 (Q.B.).

[106] [1996] O.J. No. 3054, 30 O.R. (3d) 257 (C.A.), application for leave to appeal to S.C.C. dismissed, [1996] S.C.C.A. No. 553.

[107] See section 4: Assistance and Co-operation.

Ontario Court of Appeal noted that there was ample evidence that the insurer had been prejudiced by the non-reporting and that relief against forfeiture would not have been available in any event.

One Court has suggested that the primary basis for the decision in *Canadian Newspapers Co. v. Kansa General Insurance Co.*[108] is inconsistent with the reasoning found in the Supreme Court of Canada's decision in *Falk Bros. Industries Ltd. v. Elance Steel Fabricating Co.*[109] In *Colliers McClocklin Real Estate Corp. v. Lloyd's Underwriters*[110] the Saskatchewan Court of Queen's Bench suggested that the Ontario Court of Appeal considered a substantial breach of a condition to be tantamount to a condition precedent, and, therefore, one with respect to which relief against forfeiture would not be available. The Ontario Court of Appeal, however, did not express its decision in those terms. The decision may be explained on the basis that a breach of the duty to cooperate is a breach of a true condition precedent, so as to amount to non-compliance and therefore not subject to relief against forfeiture. The decision may alternatively be explained on the basis that "imperfect compliance", as that phrase is used in the statute, denotes a trifling or immaterial breach. On such reasoning, relief from forfeiture would never be available in the case of a substantial breach even though it did not involve a condition precedent.

Neither alternative, with respect, is compelling. In reaching the conclusion that relief against forfeiture is not available in a case where there has been a substantial breach the Ontario Court of Appeal relied upon the decision in *Travellers Indemnity Co. v. Sumner Co.*[111] Yet, the latter decision does not stand for that proposition. The case involved a motor vehicle liability policy. The insured was in an automobile accident. He told his insurer that shortly before starting his journey he had consumed alcohol. In his initial statement he did not tell the insurer that during the journey he had also taken one drink from a bottle. This information was revealed later, after a passenger had commenced legal action. The evidence plainly showed that the insured was not intoxicated. The trial judge, Anglin J., held that in these circumstances the insured had not violated a term or condition of the policy or made a wilfully false statement. Alternatively, if there had been a breach, it at most was imperfect compliance, in respect of which relief against forfeiture would lie. The New Brunswick Court of Appeal upheld the trial decision, noting:

> The statutory conditions are essential terms of every contract of automobile insurance and a violation of them will, unless relief is granted by the Court, destroy any right of the insured to indemnity under the policy. The duty of the insured to co-operate with the insurer, being a condition precedent to his right to recover, requires him to assist willingly and to the best of his judgment and

---

[108] *Supra*, note 106.

[109] [1989] S.C.J. No. 97, 2 S.C.R. 778 at para. 17.

[110] [2003] S.J. No. 581, I.L.R. 1-4246 (Q.B.), revd [2004] S.J. No. 308.

[111] (1960), 27 D.L.R. (2d) 562, [1961] I.L.R. 1-037, 45 M.P.R. 332 (N.B.C.A.), affd [1961] S.C.R. viii.

ability. If in this connection a breach occurs in some material respect the insurer is entitled even to refuse to defend an action. Lack of co- operation, however, must be substantial. No inconsequential or trifling breach of such
obligation should serve to exonerate the insurer from his contractual liabilities
under the policy.[112]

If this passage is read as indicating that relief against forfeiture does not lie for a
substantial breach, then the statement is either *obiter dicta,* for on the facts of the
case no breach was found, or amounts to a conflation of the concept of substantial breach with that of prejudice to the insurer. The passage may also be read,
however, as indicating that as a matter of contract, a trifling or immaterial
breach of condition does not give rise to the insurer's right to deny coverage. On
this latter reading, relief against forfeiture is available in respect of a substantial
breach, provided that the insured is able to show that such relief is just and
equitable in the circumstances.

As a matter of principle, relief against forfeiture should not be limited to
cases involving a trifling or immaterial breach by the insured. By its terms, the
statute applies in cases of "imperfect compliance", a phrase which, considered
both on its plain meaning and in accordance with the aim of the statute, would
include a material breach. As the Supreme Court of Canada noted in *Falk Bros.
Industries Ltd. v. Elance Steel Fabricating Co.*:

> The purpose of allowing relief from forfeiture in insurance cases is to prevent
> hardship to beneficiaries where there has been a failure to comply with a condi-
> tion for receipt of insurance proceeds and where leniency in respect of strict
> compliance with the condition will not result in prejudice to the insurer.[113]

In a case involving a substantial breach it may well be difficult for the insured to
demonstrate that it is just and equitable for relief to be granted. The fact that a
substantial breach has occurred, however, should not preclude a court from
considering the exercise of its equitable jurisdiction.

It should be noted that this is not simply an exercise in semantics. The Ontario Court of Appeal, in *Canadian Newspapers Co. v. Kansa General Insurance
Co.*,[114] did not approach the case from the perspective that a substantial breach
was, by definition, one which prejudiced the position of the insurer so as to
make relief against forfeiture unavailable. Nor would such a perspective be open
in any event, for it is not until the statute is invoked that any issue of prejudice
can arise.

In determining whether or not to grant relief against forfeiture under the
legislation, the courts are guided by equitable considerations. The test to be
applied is whether, in all of the circumstances of the case, it is just and equitable
that relief be granted. From the cases, the two factors most often considered by

---

[112] *Ibid.* at 565.

[113] *Supra*, note 109 at para. 17.

[114] *Supra*, note 106.

the courts in granting relief are the insured's conduct[115] and lack of prejudice to the insurer:

> Section 103 is an ameliorating clause. It is not to be used to allow contracts entered into in good faith to be broken with a careless disregard for the rights of the insurer so as to cause actual or potential injury to the insurer's position. On the other hand it should not be so encrusted with authorities as to become a circumscribed rule of law rather than a principle of equity to be exercised with judicial discretion. ...
>
> I have reviewed dozens of cases and it has become clear that recourse to s. 103, and its counterpart in other jurisdictions with relation to other kinds of insurance, has always depended on the particular facts of the case, and on whether there was clearly some actual proven prejudice to the insurer, or potential prejudice which could not be quantified after the event. In addition, regard was had to the conduct of the insured, whether he had, for example, deliberately misled or lied to the insurer. There is no suggestion in this case that the plaintiff has been guilty of bad faith, or deliberate misrepresentation or concealment.[116]

The onus of establishing grounds for relief against forfeiture rests with the insured.[117] In *W. Schoeler Trucking Ltd. v. Markel Insurance Co. of Canada*[118] it was held that because lack of prejudice to the insurer was a "critical factor" in the granting of such relief, the onus on the insured extended to showing that the insurer was not prejudiced by the insured's breach of condition. As a statement of law this is surely correct, for the insured has the burden of coming within the terms of the section. As a practical matter, however, evidence of prejudice, if any, will likely lie with the insurer, and it behooves the insurer to bring the evidence forward.

The nature of the prejudice to the insurer that will prevent the application of the section will, of course, depend upon the particular circumstances of the case. In *Canadian Equipment Sales & Service v. Continental Insurance Co.*[119] it was stated that either an "actual proven prejudice" or a "potential prejudice which could not be quantified" would suffice. An example of such a potential prejudice is provided by the decision in *W. Schoeler Trucking Ltd. v. Markel Insurance Co. of Canada.*[120] The insured sought indemnity from its insurer with respect to

---

[115] *Saskatchewan River Bungalows Ltd. v. Maritime Life Assurance Co.*, [1994] S.C.J. No. 59, 2 S.C.R. 490, 115 D.L.R. (4th) 478, 20 Alta. L.R. (3d) 296, 168 N.R. 381, revg. [1992] A.J. No. 512, 92 D.L.R. (4th) 372, [1992] I.L.R. 1-2895 (C.A.).

[116] *Can. Equipment Sales & Service Co. v. Continental Ins. Co.* (1975), 59 D.L.R. (3d) 333 at 342, 343 (Ont. C.A.).

[117] *Hogan v. Kolisnyk*, [1983] 3 W.W.R. 481 (Alta. Q.B.); *Gulf Plastics Ltd. v. Cornhill Ins. Co.* (1990), 46 C.C.L.I. 144, 47 B.C.L.R. (2d) 379 (S.C.), affd (1991), 3 C.C.L.I. (2d) 203, 61 B.C.L.R. (2d) 64 (C.A.) *Kelowna (City) v. Royal Ins. Co. of Can.*, [1992] B.C.J. No. 147, 9 C.C.L.I. (2d) 236 (S.C.).

[118] [1980] I.L.R. 1-1210 (Alta. Dist. Ct.).

[119] *Supra*, note 116 at 343.

[120] *Supra*, note 118.

a claim for damages arising from an accident involving the insured's truck. The insured had considered the accident to be trivial and not worth reporting. This was a clear breach of the policy condition requiring prompt notice. It was held that there was sufficient potential prejudice to preclude the granting of relief against forfeiture, for the insurer was denied the opportunity to interview the driver, who had since left the insured's employ, and decide whether or not to contest the claim. The Court noted that the insurer could not be called upon to retry the case and show a basis upon which it would have succeeded had prompt notice of the accident been given.

If the case is one in which the insurer has denied coverage for reasons other than late notice then it will be difficult for the insurer to claim prejudice, for had notice been given in a timely fashion it is unlikely that the insurer's position would have been any different.[121]

With respect to liability insurance contracts, the power to relieve against forfeiture is often invoked where there has been a failure to give timely notice of an incident giving rise to the claim. In such circumstances, the courts frequently grant the relief sought,[122] provided there is no bad faith[123] on the part of the insured or prejudice to the insurer.

---

[121] *International Comfort Products Corp. (Canada) v. Royal Insurance Co. of Canada*, [2000] O.J. No. 893 (S.C.J.).

[122] See, for example, *Cook v. Gold Circle Ins. Co.*, [1987] O.J. No. 665, 26 C.C.L.I. 173 (H.C.J.); *Vallabh v. Kay*, [1986] O.J. No. 1922, 19 C.C.L.I. 163 (Dist. Ct.); *Qualiglass Holdings Inc. v. Zurich Indemnity Co. of Canada*, [2004] A.J. No. 881, [2004] I.L.R. I-4329 (Q.B.). Note the distinction, referred to above, between occurrence based policies and claims-made policies. In the latter case relief against forfeiture may not be available with respect to the failure to give notice of a claim within the policy period.

[123] In *Terry v. L.S.U.C.*, [1992] O.J. No. 1678 (Gen. Div.) it was held, following *Perry v. General Security Ins. Co. of Can.* (1984), 47 O.R. (2d) 472 (C.A.), that despite the absence of any prejudice, a deliberate decision not to notify the insurer of the claim nevertheless voided coverage. Relief was granted, however, where the decision not to report was not characterized as a deliberate refusal to abide by the terms of the policy: *Feature Foods v. Landau*, [1995] O.J. No. 4899, 23 O.R. (3d) 147, 20 C.L.R. (2d) 94, 27 C.C.L.I. (2d) 179, [1995] I.L.R. 1-3221 (Gen. Div.). Similarly, relief was granted where the insured's decision not to report a claim was made in good faith and not with the intent to take advantage of the insurer: *Gulf Plastics Ltd. v. Cornhill Ins. Co.*, [1990] B.C.J. No. 1541, 46 C.C.L.I. 144 (S.C.), affd, [1991] B.C.J. No. 3310, 3 C.C.L.I. (2d) 203 (C.A.).

Chapter 4

LIMITS OF LIABILITY

Liability insurance contracts in North America typically place monetary limitations on the insurer's obligation to indemnify the insured. There is often a lower limit, known as a deductible, which must be borne by the insured. Invariably there is an upper limit, beyond which the insurer's obligation to indemnify the insured will cease.

1. DEDUCTIBLE PROVISIONS

There is no uniform practice among liability insurers with respect to the provision of a deductible clause in their insurance agreements. In some policies, the Comprehensive General Liability (or "CGL") policy for example, there is no deductible whatsoever. In other policies — for example, professional liability policies — it is not uncommon for there to be a substantial deductible that, may or may not include defence costs.

Where a policy does contain a deductible clause it is generally stipulated that the deductible applies on a per claim rather than on a per occurrence basis. Hence, if one incident gives rise to several claims the insured will have to pay the deductible in respect of each claim.[1] This was the situation in *R.A. Kerschbaumer Painting Contractors Ltd. v. Canadian Indemnity Co.*[2] In the course of painting a bridge, the insured allowed paint to spray onto 25 cars parked below. The policy provided that:

> 1. The Insured shall pay the first $250.00 of each and every claim arising out of damage to the property of others unless otherwise stipulated in this policy and the Insurer shall be liable only for the difference between such deductible amount and the limit of the Insurer's liability for each accident as stated in the Policy.

The insured maintained that this clause is ambiguous in that it begins with a reference to "claim" and concludes with a reference to "accident". On behalf of the insured it was submitted that on its proper interpretation the policy required the insured to pay only the first $250 in respect of all claims arising out of each occurrence. The Court rejected this submission, holding that the insured was

---

[1] *Lamberton v. Travelers Indemnity Co.*, 325 A.2d 104, affd 346 A.2d 167 (Del. 1975).

[2] [1977] I.L.R. 1-905 at 772 (B.C.S.C.). See also, *Park & Derochie Decorating Co. v. Employers' Liability Assur. Corp.* (1963), 40 D.L.R. (2d) 653 (Alta. S.C.).

obliged to pay the first $250 of each claim made by the owners of the vehicles damaged by the plaintiff's spray painting operation.

A remarkably similar case, on its facts, was before the courts of Virginia in *Atlas Underwriters Ltd. v. Meredith-Burde Inc.*[3] A manufacturers' and contractors' liability policy provided coverage to a painting contractor subject to a "$250.00 deductible for each and every claim". It was held that the deductible applied to each claim of 40 vehicle owners whose cars were sprayed with paint while the insured was engaged in painting two water towers at the premises of the vehicle owners' employer. The fact that the owners had each assigned their claims to the employer, who recovered a judgment against the contractor for the entire damage to all of the vehicles, did not convert the 40 claims into a single claim for the purposes of the policy deductible. The Court noted that:

> "Claim" contemplates the assertion of a legal right by a third person for damages caused by conduct of the named insured. It means a demand by one to whom a right has accrued for payment of a loss suffered due to acts of the insured that are covered by the policy ... The term "claim," unlike policy provisions dealing with limits of liability, does not refer to the aggregate of all claims arising from a single incident or transaction, as the plaintiff's argument implicitly suggests. "Claim" does not mean "cause." One cause frequently spawns many claims.[4]

In *Canadian Gas Assn. v. Guardian Insurance Co. of Canada*[5] the insurer declined to defend a class action on the basis that the $25,000 deductible applied separately to each of the 10,000 claims comprised in the class action and each of those claims was less than the deductible. The insured responded that some of the individual claims could conceivably exceed $25,000 and that, in any event, the Ontario legislation permitted an aggregate assessment of damages to be made in the action, in which case there would be no assessment of individual claims. In these circumstances the Court held that for the purposes of the duty to defend the deductible applied once to the entire action. The Court did not rule on the issue of indemnity.

Where a claim which is entirely within the deductible is brought against the insured, an issue may arise as to whether the insurer is required to defend the claim on the insured's behalf. Although generally speaking the duty to defend is co-extensive with the duty to indemnify, the policy language may, nevertheless, require the insurer to incur the costs of investigation and defence for a claim which falls within the deductible.[6]

The items included in the deductible for which the insured bears the responsibility to pay will be a matter of construction in each case. In *Swan Wooster*

---

[3]   343 S.E.2d 65 (Virg. 1986).

[4]   *Ibid.* at 67.

[5]   [1999] O.J. No. 5260, [1999] I.L.R. 1-3633 (S.C.).

[6]   *Swan Wooster Engineering Co. v. Continental Casualty Co.*, [1971] I.L.R. 1-406 (B.C.S.C.).

Engineering Co. v. Simcoe & Erie General Insurance Co.,[7] on the wording of the particular policy under consideration, it was held that the deductible provision did not apply to the taxed costs that the insured had to pay as a result of a judgment obtained against it. In *Pafco Insurance Co. v. Zagora Holdings Ltd.*,[8] the Court held that the insurer could not recover under the deductible provisions of the policy for expenses which were incurred after notice of the claim was received but before an action was commenced. In *Kansa General Insurance Co. v. Elbow Skiing Ltd.*,[9] the insurer successfully defended the insured and then sought to recover its deductible on the basis of a clause stating that the deductible amount applied "to all damages ... including legal expenses and adjusters' fees".[10] The court held that the legal expenses and adjusting fees incurred by the insurer could not be characterized as "damages". Accordingly, the insurer's claim was dismissed.

2. UPPER LIMITS

(a) Policy Language

The upper limit of the insurer's liability to indemnify the insured is generally specified in the declarations. Typically, separate limits will apply depending upon the number of persons injured, the number of accidents or occurrences, and the aggregate of claims during the policy period. In the CGL policy the limits are specified in the declarations as follows:

SCHEDULE

The insurance afforded is only with respect to such of the following Coverages as are indicated by specific premium charge or charges. The limit of the Insurer's liability against each such Coverage shall be as stated herein, subject to all the terms of this policy having reference thereto.

	Coverages	Limits of Liability	Advance Premiums
Separate Limits	A. Bodily Injury Liability	$ each person $ each occurrence $ aggregate	
	B. Property Damage Liability	$ each accident $ aggregate	
Inclusive Limit	A. Bodily Injury Liability and B. Property Damage Liability	$ { bodily injury each occurrence property damage each accident $ { aggregate	
Minimum Premium $		Total Advance Premium	$

[11]

---

[7] (1981), 30 B.C.L.R. 1 (C.A.).

[8] [1991] B.C.J. No. 666, 54 B.C.L.R. (2d) 367 (S.C.).

[9] [1991] O.J. No. 1174, 6 C.C.L.I. (2d) 299, [1991] I.L.R. 1-2753 at 1478 (Gen. Div.).

[10] *Ibid.*

[11] Reproduced in Appendix B.

The policy sets out the basis upon which the various limits are to apply: Regardless of the number of (1) insureds under this policy (2) persons or organizations who sustain bodily injury or property damage or (3) claims made or suits brought on account of bodily injury or property damage, the Insurer's liability is limited as follows:

1. Limits of Liability: Coverage A — The limit of bodily injury liability stated in the schedule as applicable to "each person" is the limit of the Insurer's liability for all compensatory damages, including compensatory damages for care and loss of services, arising out of bodily injury sustained by one person in any one occurrence; the limit of such liability stated in the schedule as applicable to "each occurrence" is, subject to the above provision respecting each person, the total limit of the Insurer's liability for all compensatory damages, including compensatory damages for care and loss of services, arising out of bodily injury sustained by two or more persons in any one occurrence.

2. Limits of Liability: Coverage B — The limit of property damage liability stated in the schedule as applicable to "each accident" is a total limit of the Insurer's liability for all compensatory damages arising out of property damage, as a result of any one accident, or series of accidents arising out of one event.

3. Subject to the above provision respecting "each person" and "each occurrence" under Coverage A, and "each accident" under Coverage B, the limits of bodily injury liability and property damage liability stated in the schedule as "aggregate" are respectively the total limits of the Insurer's liability for all compensatory damages arising out of the products hazard and completed operations hazard in any one period of twelve months terminating on an anniversary of the inception date of the policy.

4. Limits of Liability: Coverages A and B — The inclusive limit of liability stated in the schedule as applicable to "bodily injury each occurrence property damage each accident" is the total limit of the Insurer's liability under Coverages A or B or Coverages A and B combined for all compensatory damages, including compensatory damages for care and loss of services, arising out of bodily injury in any one occurrence or property damage as a result of any one accident or series of accidents arising out of one event.

5. Subject to the above provision respecting "bodily injury each occurrence property damage each accident" under Coverages A and B combined, the limit of bodily injury and property damage liability combined stated in the schedule as "aggregate" is the total limit of the Insurer's liability for all compensatory damages arising out of the products hazard and completed operations hazard in any one period of twelve months terminating on an anniversary of the inception date of the policy.

6. All compensatory damages arising out of one lot of goods or products prepared or acquired by the Named Insured or by another trading under his name, shall be considered as arising out of one occurrence as regard bodily injury liability and one accident as regards property damage liability.

7. For the purpose of determining the limit of the Insurer's liability, all bodily injury arising out of continuous or repeated exposure to substantially the same general conditions shall be considered as arising out of one occurrence.

(b) Limit per Person

The limit of liability set out in the declarations for "each person" is intended to apply to all claims which may arise from the injury or death of any one person as a result of a single occurrence.[12] Some courts, however, have held that the policy language is ambiguous and that the single person limit does not apply where others have sustained a loss as a result of the injury — for example, where a spouse has a claim for loss of consortium[13] or a parent has incurred expenses as the result of an injury to a child in an automobile accident.[14]

(c) Limit per Accident or Occurrence

If two or more persons sustain bodily injury as a result of an occurrence then, in addition to the limit per person, the insurer's total liability under a CGL policy is limited to the amount specified in the declarations as the limit for "each occurrence". The policy further stipulates that "all bodily injury arising out of continuous or repeated exposure to substantially the same general conditions shall be considered as arising out of one occurrence".

The limit of the insurer's liability with respect to property damage claims is expressed on a similar basis. The limit stated for "each accident" is the total limit of the insurer's liability for all claims concerning property damage resulting either from one accident or a series of accidents arising out of one event.

Determining the number of accidents or occurrences for the purpose of applying the policy limits is often a difficult task. At one time, under markedly different policy language, the approach was to equate the number of claims with the number of accidents. In *South Staffordshire Tramways Co. v. Sickness & Accident Assurance Assn.*[15] the insured, a tramcar company, had coverage against "claims for personal injury ... in respect of accidents caused by vehicles ... to the assured sum of £250 in respect of any one accident". One of the plaintiff's tramcars was overturned, 40 persons were injured, and the plaintiff became liable to pay claims in the amount of £833. The court held that on the true construction of the policy each injury constituted an accident; therefore, the policy limits of £250 were available to each of the 40 injury claims.

Under modern policy language, however, the approach taken in *South Staffordshire* is no longer applicable. Instead of focusing on the number of injuries or claims, the courts instead focus on the cause of the injuries — all injuries

---

[12] See also G.J. Couch, *Couch Cyclopedia of Insurance Law*, 2nd ed. (1966), vol. 15A, para. 56:22, and *Richie v. American Cam. Mutual Ins. Co.*, 409 N.W.2d 146 (Wis. 1987).

[13] *Atellon v. Hartford Ins. Co.*, 212 Cal. Rptr. 852 (Ct. App. 1985).

[14] *Spaete v. Automobile Club Inter-Ins. Exchange*, 736 S.W.2d 480 (Mo. 1987).

[15] [1891] 1 Q.B. 402 at 403 (C.A.).

which flow from one cause (or event) are considered to result from one occurrence and are therefore subject to one policy limit.[16] Thus, where a single fire caused damage to several parties it was held that one limit applied.[17] Similarly, one limit applied where the negligent sale of firearms by the insured sporting-goods store allegedly resulted in a shooting spree in which several persons were injured.[18] Where, however, separate injuries result from separate acts, even though the acts may be of the same nature, each act constitutes a separate occurrence. Thus, where the insured fired three shotgun blasts, each causing injury, it was held that each act of firing the shotgun was a separate occurrence.[19] Similarly, where an insured restaurant served customers with tainted food over a three day period, each instance in which a customer was served constituted a separate occurrence.[20]

The issue of whether to apply the policy limits per accident or per occurrence frequently arises in the context of bodily injury and property damage claims involving continuous or repeated exposure to hazardous substances.[21] The resolution of this issue will, of course, depend upon an analysis of the facts and the policy wording in each case. With respect to the policy language noted at the outset of this section, it seems clear that the intent of the insurer is to treat claims arising from the continuous or repeated exposure to hazardous substances as arising from one accident or occurrence.

(d) Aggregate Limit

An aggregate limit is the limit of the insured's liability in respect of all claims of a certain nature resulting from occurrences during the policy period. In the CGL policy aggregate limits are provided with respect to:

(1) the insurer's liability for all compensatory damages for bodily injury arising out of the products hazard and completed operations hazard in any one period of twelve months terminating on an anniversary of the inception date of the policy;

(2) the insurer's liability for all compensatory damages for property damage arising out of the products hazard and completed operations hazard in any one period of twelve months terminating on an anniversary of the inception date of the policy;

---

[16] See M. Sullivan, "What Constitutes Single Accident or Occurrence within Liability Policy Limiting Insurer's Liability to a Specified Amount per Accident or Occurrence" (1988), 64 A.L.R. 4th 668, annotation.

[17] *Travelers Indemnity Co. v. New England Box Co.*, 157 A.2d 765 (New Hampshire, 1960).

[18] *Travelers Indemnity Co. v. Olive's Sporting Goods Inc.*, 764 S.W.2d 596 (Ark., 1989).

[19] *American Indemnity Co. v. McQuaig*, 435 So.2d 414 (Fla. App. 1983).

[20] *Mason v. Home Ins. Co. of Illinois*, 532 N.E.2d 526 (Ill., 1988).

[21] See Chapter 7, section 7(a): Occurrence Policies.

(3) the insurer's liability for compensatory damages arising out of bodily injury in any one occurrence, or property damage as a result of any one accident or a series of accidents arising out of one event;

(4) the insurer's liability for all compensatory damages arising out of the products hazard and completed operations hazard in any one period of twelve months terminating on an anniversary of the inception date of the policy.

Three of these four aggregate limits are confined to the products hazard and completed operations hazard. The scope of these hazards is discussed in Chapter 6.

The issue of applying the aggregate limit in respect of the products hazard arose in *Mason v. Home Insurance Co. of Illinois*, referred to earlier.[22] Where a number of persons became ill with botulism after having been served tainted food at the insured's restaurant, it was held that the claims were not subject to the aggregate limit specified in respect of the product hazard for the bodily injury did not occur away from the insured's premises. The Court reasoned that injury from the botulin toxin occurs at the time that it is consumed rather than at the time that the symptoms of botulism poisoning become apparent.

In *Richardson Construction Co. v. London & Lancashire Guarantee & Accident Co. of Canada*[23] a contractor's liability policy limited the insurer's liability to "$1,000.00 for any one accident or series of accidents arising out of one cause". In the course of pile driving the insured caused damage to three neighbouring homes. It was held that vibrations from the pile driver constituted one cause of damage; accordingly the aggregate liability of the insurer was limited to $1,000.

---

[22] *Supra*, note 20.

[23] (1939), 6 I.L.R. 97 (Ont. H.C.J.).

Chapter 5

THE DUTY TO DEFEND

In addition to providing for indemnity with respect to claims, liability insurance policies almost invariably contain provisions requiring the insurer to defend certain types of law suits brought against the insured,[1] notice of which has been provided to the insurer.[2] As a general rule, the duty to defend is co-extensive with the duty to indemnify. There are, however, exceptions to this rule.[3] Particular consideration must be given to those instances where the pleadings contain multiple allegations, are ambiguous, contain allegations contrary to fact, or where the limits of coverage have been exhausted. In such cases an issue may also arise as to who has the right to appoint and instruct counsel.

1. WHEN THE DUTY TO DEFEND ARISES

(a) The Pleadings Rule

Liability insurance policies are usually written in a manner that ties the insurer's duty to defend to the obligation to indemnify the insured against various types of claims. A typical defence clause reads as follows:

---

[1] The insurer's obligation with respect to directors' and officers' liability policies is to reimburse the insured for defence costs. The conduct of the defence remains with the insured. See the discussion in Chapter 13. Where the policy is silent as to a duty to defend, it has been held that the policy is one of indemnity only. See G.J. Couch & R.A. Anderson, *Couch Cyclopedia of Insurance Law*, 2nd ed. (Rochester: Lawyers Co-operative Publishing Co., 1984) para. 51:35 at n. 14, and *W. (T.) v. W. (K.R.J.)* [1996] O.J. No. 2102, 29 O.R. (3d) 277, 39 C.C.L.I. (2d) 272, 5 O.T.C. 306, [1996] I.L.R. 1-3351 (Gen. Div.). In *Asleson v. Continental Insurance Co.*, [1995] B.C.J. No. 1334, I.L.R. 1-3130 (S.C.), however, in the absence of express words the Court was prepared to imply a duty to defend.

[2] The duty to defend will arise only where notice of a claim is given: *ING Insurance Co. of Canada v. Federated Insurance Co. of Canada*, [2005] O.J. No. 1718, 75 O.R. (3d) 457 (C.A.).

[3] For example, in *British Columbia v. Surrey School District No. 36*, [2005] B.C.J. No. 364, 21 C.C.L.I. (4th) 157 (C.A.), having regard to the particular circumstances of the case, it was held that the insurer was required to indemnify the insured with respect to the insured's liability to the third party but was not required to pay the insured's costs of defence. On the other hand, in *Thorne v. Royal & Sun Alliance Insurance Co. of Canada*, [2003] N.B.J. No. 322, 261 N.B.R. (2d) 119 (C.A.) which deals with the self-defence exception to the intentional injury exclusion (see Chapter 8 at section 7: Intentional Injury), it was held that the insurer was required to defend the insured even though the only basis for a finding of liability would be one for which indemnity was not available under the policy.

As respects such Insurance as is afforded by the other terms of this Policy, the Insurer agrees to defend in the name of and on behalf of the Insured, claims, suits, or other proceedings which may at any time be instituted against the Insured for any occurrence covered by this Policy, although such claims, suits, proceedings or allegations and demands may be groundless, false or fraudulent.

The traditional view is that whether or not an insurer is required to defend a particular claim is determined strictly from the allegations made in the pleadings filed against the insured. When the pleadings allege facts which, if true, would require the insurer to indemnify the insured in respect of the claim, the insurer must provide a defence. This is generally so notwithstanding that the facts may differ from those as pleaded. In the leading American decision in *Lee v. Aetna Casualty & Surety Co.*[4] Learned Hand J. stated that a defence clause such as that set out above

... means that the insurer will defend the suit, if the injured party states a claim, which ... is for an injury "covered" by the policy; it is the claim which determines the insurer's duty to defend; and it is irrelevant that the insurer may get information from the insured, or from anyone else which indicates, or even demonstrates, that the injury is not in fact "covered".[5]

The rule that the pleadings govern the insurer's obligation to defend (which I shall refer to as the "pleadings rule") was accepted by the Supreme Court of Canada in *Nichols v. American Home Assurance Co.*[6] In the leading decision of *Bacon v. McBride*[7] the rule is stated in this fashion:

The pleadings govern the duty to defend — not the insurer's view of the validity or nature of the claim or of the possible outcome of the litigation. If the claim alleges a state of facts which, if proven, would fall within the coverage of the policy the insurer is obliged to defend the suit regardless of the truth or falsity of such allegations. If the allegations do not come within the policy coverage the insurer has no such obligation: see *Couch on Insurance,* 2nd revised ed. (1982), vol. 14, p. 706, para. 51:149. In this respect the duty to defend may well be broader than the insurer's obligation to indemnify the insured for liability imposed by law. The insurer's obligation to defend arises when notice of the claim is received and continues as long as it is outstanding even though the insurer may consider the allegation to be groundless.[8]

The statement that the duty to defend is broader than the obligation to indemnify is capable of being misunderstood. The duty to defend is tied to the obligation to indemnify in that the only claims that the insurer must defend are

---

[4] 178 F.2d 750 (2nd Cir. 1949).

[5] *Ibid.* at 751.

[6] [1988] O.J. No. 90, 30 C.C.L.I. 79 (H.C.J.), affd, [1989] O.J. No. 238, 36 C.C.L.I. 204 (C.A.), revd [1990] S.C.J. No. 33, 68 D.L.R. (4th) 321.

[7] (1984), 5 C.C.L.I. 146 (B.C.S.C.).

[8] *Ibid.* at 151.

those which, if proven, would require the insurer to indemnify the insured.[9] If the claim ultimately proven against the insured falls outside of coverage, then there will be no requirement on the insurer to indemnify the insured against either the judgment or any corresponding award of costs.[10]

The insurer is not obliged to defend claims which fall wholly outside of the coverage provided by the policy. Thus, in *Nichols v. American Home Assurance Co.*,[11] the Supreme Court of Canada held that a lawyer's professional liability insurer was not required to defend the insured in respect of a groundless allegation of fraud.[12]

It has been held that the rule that the pleadings govern the duty to defend applies even where the plea is one which is bad in law.[13] Whether, in such a case, the insurer could properly instruct counsel to apply to strike the offending plea raises an interesting issue.[14]

The pleadings filed against the insured are usually in the form of a statement of claim, but may include a counter-claim or set-off.[15] There is some confusion as to whether the duty to defend can be founded on the pleadings filed *on behalf* of the insured.[16] As a general rule it is only the pleading filed *against* the insured which should be taken into account.[17] An insured cannot, in a statement of defence, create coverage where none is found in a statement of

---

[9] *Thames Steel Const. Ltd. v. Northern Assur. Co.* [1988] O.J. No. 2055, 34 C.C.L.I. 320 (C.A.).

[10] *Hersh v. Wawanesa Mutual Ins. Co.*, [1994] B.C.J. No. 10, 89 B.C.L.R. (2d) 225, [1994] I.L.R. 1-3071, 22 C.C.L.I. (2d) 242 (S.C.).

[11] (1990), 68 D.L.R. (4th) 321 (S.C.C.).

[12] Note that in some professional liability policies, as long as a covered claim is alleged, the fraud exclusion does not come into play unless fraud is established by a judgment. See *Wisebrod v. American Home Assurance Co.*, [1997] O.J. No. 3862, 35 O.R. (3d) 733, 104 O.A.C. 229, [1998] I.L.R. 1-3499 (C.A.).

[13] *Smrekar v. Co-op. General Ins. Co.*, [1986] O.J. No. 2654, 18 C.C.L.I. 201 (Dist. Ct.).

[14] See section 9: Duty of Counsel.

[15] *Myers v. Simcoe and Erie General Ins. Co.* [1994] O.J. No. 1354, 115 D.L.R. (4th) 607, 19 O.R. (3d) 257 (C.A.), leave to appeal to S.C.C. refd (1994), 21 O.R. (3d) xvin.

[16] See *Wlasichuk v. Citadel General Insurance Co.*, [1999] A.J. No. 665, [2000] I.L.R. 1-3759 (Q.B.); *Reform Party of Canada v. Western Union Insurance Co.* [1999] B.C.J. No. 2794, 3 C.P.R. (4th) 289, (S.C.), revd, [2001] B.C.J. No. 697, 26 C.C.L.I. (3d) 1; *Kerr v. Law Profession Indemnity Co.* [1994] O.J. No. 2, 22 C.C.L.I. (2d) 28 (Gen. Div.), revd (on a different point), [1995] O.J. No. 2823, 128 D.L.R. (4th) 269, [1995] I.L.R. 1-3250, 25 O.R. (3d) 804 (C.A.); *Societa Italiana Assicurazioni Trasporti v. Canadian Marine Underwriters Ltd.* (1994), 26 C.C.L.I. (2d) 274 (Gen. Div.); *Daher v. Economical Mutual Ins. Co.*, [1993] O.J. No. 2361, 19 C.C.L.I. (2d) 106, [1994] I.L.R. 1-3007 (Gen. Div.), affd [1996] O.J. No. 4394, 31 O.R. (3d) 472, 96 O.A.C. 255, [1997] I.L.R. 1-3414 (C.A.); and *Shragie v. Tanemura*, [1987] B.C.J. No. 2582, 32 C.C.L.I. 126, 22 B.C.L.R. (2d) 64, [1988] I.L.R. 1-2278 (S.C.).

[17] *Westridge Construction Ltd. v. Zurich Insurance Co.*, [2004] S.J. No. 43, 15 C.C.L.I. (4th) 262 (Q.B.), revd, [2005] S.J. No. 396, 25 C.C.L.I. (4th) 182 (C.A.); *A.R.G. Construction Corp. v. Allstate Insurance Co. of Canada*, [2004] O.J. No. 4517 (S.C.J.); *Dionne Farms Ltd. v. Fermes Gervais Ltée*, [2002] N.B.J. No. 402, 43 C.C.L.I. (3d) 1 (C.A.); *Hamel Construction Inc. v. Lombard Canada Ltd.*, [2005] N.S.J. No. 151, 21 C.C.L.I. (4th) 44 (C.A.).

claim.[18] Occasionally, however, as in *Reform Party of Canada v. Western Union Insurance Co.*,[19] reference to the statement of defence may be helpful in understanding the nature of the allegations made in the statement of claim.

When determining whether the insurer is under a duty to defend, one must look beyond legal labels and examine the substance of the factual allegations in the pleadings.[20] Particular care must be taken when it appears that an attempt is being made in the pleadings to manipulate coverage so as to convert an uncovered claim, such as an intentional tort, into a covered claim, for example, negligence. In a case in which the statement of claim contained pleas of both battery and negligence arising out of allegedly non-consensual sexual relations, Iacobucci J. of the Supreme Court of Canada, in a concurring judgment, enunciated a three-step process for determining whether the duty to defend arises:

> ... First, a court should determine which of the plaintiff's legal allegations are properly pleaded. In doing so, courts are not bound by the legal labels chosen by the plaintiff. A plaintiff cannot change an intentional tort into a negligent one simply by choice of words, or vice versa. Therefore, when ascertaining the scope of the duty to defend, a court must look beyond the choice of labels, and examine the substance of the allegations contained in the pleadings. This does not involve deciding whether the claims have any merit; all a court must do is decide, based on the pleadings, the true nature of the claims.
>
> At the second stage, having determined what claims are properly pleaded, the court should determine if any claims are entirely derivative in nature. The duty to defend will not be triggered simply because a claim can be cast in terms of both negligence and intentional tort. If the alleged negligence is based on the same harm as the intentional tort, it will not allow the insured to avoid the exclusion clause for intentionally caused injuries.
>
> Finally, at the third stage the court must decide whether any of the properly pleaded, non-derivative claims could potentially trigger the insurer's duty to defend. ...[21]

---

[18] An exception to this rule is found in the case of the self-defence exception to the intentional injury exclusion. A plea of self-defence is typically found in a statement of defence rather than a statement of claim. In order to give meaning to the exception, then, the statement of defence must be taken into account in determining the duty to defend. See *Thorne v. Royal & Sun Alliance Insurance Co. of Canada*, [2003] N.B.J. No. 322, 230 D.L.R. (4th) 587 (C.A.).

[19] *Ibid.* See also *Unrau v. Canadian Northern Shield Insurance Co.*, [2004] B.C.J. No. 2409 at para. 34: "In some cases it might be helpful in defining the nature of the claims to analyze the defences".

[20] *Non-Marine Underwriters, Lloyd's of London v. Scalera*, [2000] S.C.J. No. 26, [2000] 1 S.C.R. 551, 185 D.L.R. (4th) 1, [2000] I.L.R. 1-3810; *Buchanan v. GAN Canada Insurance Co.*, [1999] O.J. No. 436, 10 C.C.L.I. (3d) 205 (Gen. Div.), affd, [2000] O.J. No. 2616, 50 O.R. (3d) 89, [2000] I.L.R. 1-3876 (C.A.); *Long v. Dominion of Canada General Insurance Co.*, [1998] O.J. No. 4346, [1999] I.L.R. 1-3611, 9 C.C.L.I. (3d) 81 (Gen. Div.).

[21] *Scalera, ibid.*, at paras. 50-52.

The concept of "derivative" claims, in this context, is new to Canadian jurisprudence. In *Godonoaga v. Khatambakhsh*,[22] the Ontario Court of Appeal described the concept as "problematic" and stated that it was probably confined to the facts in *Scalera*. The *Godonoaga* case involved a claim by an injured child against another child for battery and against that child's parents for negligence in raising their child. The claim against the parents was covered but not the claim against the child. Despite the concern raised by the Ontario Court of Appeal, however, the negligence claim in *Godonoaga* could not be derivative of the intentional tort, for the negligence was not based on the same act as the intentional tort, nor did it involve the same actor. The only common element of the separate torts was that they caused the same harm. That is not sufficient to render the negligence derivative according to the test formulated by the Iacobucci J.

The concept of derivative claims is problematic when extended beyond claims involving sexual battery. The assumption that apparently underlies the concept is that the claim in negligence would not succeed if the claim based on the intentional tort failed. Although that was true in *Scalera*, it is not always the case. Consider, for example, a claim made against a realtor for fraudulent or, alternatively, negligent misrepresentation. Assume that the realtor has a liability policy which covers negligent misrepresentation but excludes fraud. Applying the reasoning of Iacobucci J. in *Scalera*, it would seem that the insurer is not obliged to defend the claim, for the negligence claim is derivative — it arises out of the same act as the intentional tort and causes the same harm. Yet the pleadings clearly present a claim potentially within coverage, for at trial the fraud claim may fail and the negligence claim succeed.

One might argue that this example does not set out a truly derivative claim. Although in the case of negligent and fraudulent misrepresentation at one level the action is the same — making a statement — it might be argued that at another level the two torts involve entirely different actions based upon the tortfeasor's state of mind.[23] In the case of a fraudulent misrepresentation the tortfeasor either has knowledge of the falsity of the statement or is reckless as to its truth, whereas in the case of a negligent misrepresentation the tortfeasor believes the statement to be true. Yet, if such fine distinctions are to be made

---

[22] *Godonoaga (Litigation Guardian of) v. Khatambakhsh*, [2000] O.J. No. 2172, 188 D.L.R. (4th) 706, 49 O.R. (3d) 22, [2000] I.L.R. 1-3864 (C.A.).

[23] This distinction was recognized in *Morrison v. Co-operators General Insurance Co*, [2004] N.B.J. No. 290, 12 C.C.L.I. (4th) 171 (C.A.) in which it was held that the insurer was required to defend a claim which included elements of both negligence and an intentional tort. The Court noted at para. 29:

> Having said all this, I am not convinced that, in a case such as this, a plaintiff could not claim that Mr. Morrison intentionally caused the collision in an attempt to stop the Dedam vehicle from leaving his property or, in the alternative, that he caused the injuries by driving his vehicle in a negligent manner. It is arguable, in my view, that the two torts involve different acts or conduct based upon Mr. Morrison's state of mind, one being an intentional tort and the other a non-intentional tort. The Statement of Claim would obviously contain a claim potentially within coverage. At trial, the claim based upon the intentional tort could fail and the negligence claim succeed.

whenever deciding whether a claim is derivative, the concept would lose its meaning almost entirely.

It is submitted that Iacobucci J.'s concept of a derivative claim is not helpful. The better approach is that provided by the British Columbia Court of Appeal in *Unrau v. Canadian Northern Shield Insurance Co.*[24] The question posed by the Court was whether, if the facts necessary to support the claim for an intentional tort are taken out of the pleadings, there remains any basis for a claim in negligence. If the question is answered in the affirmative then the insurer is under a duty to defend. This is consistent with the reasoning in *Scalera*. As recognized both in the majority decision by McLachlin C.J.[25] and in the concurring reasons by Iacobucci J.,[26] the negligence claim was not legally viable. The defendant had engaged in sexual relations with the plaintiff and said that she consented. Either there was consensual sexual intercourse, in which case the claim would be dismissed, or there was non-consensual intercourse, in which case the claim in battery would succeed. Thus, in *Scalera* there was no possibility of a claim within coverage succeeding.

The same analytical framework can be used to explain the subsequent decisions that have either followed or distinguished *Scalera*. In *Lee v. Townsend*,[27] for example, it was held that a tenant's liability policy did not respond to a claim by the plaintiff against the defendant for malicious prosecution, in which it was alleged that the defendant had given a statement to the police falsely accusing the plaintiff of an assault in respect of which he was subsequently acquitted. The statement of claim also included an allegation that the defendant had been negligent in failing to disclose to the police her history of emotional and psychiatric problems. The apparent theory of the negligence claim was that if the defendant had disclosed her history to the police then charges would not have been laid. Yet the negligence claim was plainly untenable. Malice, which is an essential component of a claim for malicious prosecution, requires that the tortfeasor act with the intent to cause harm. Although reckless indifference may amount to such intent, negligence does not. Thus, once the allegation of malice is taken out of the statement of claim, no basis would remain for a claim in negligence.

(b) Where the Pleadings Are Ambiguous

Pleadings are not, unfortunately, always framed with sufficient precision to determine whether the claim falls within coverage. In such cases, the insurer is obliged to defend where, on any reasonable reading of the pleadings, a claim within coverage could be inferred. In the United States one court described the rule in this fashion:

---

[24]   [2004] B.C.J. No. 2409, 15 C.C.L.I. (4th), 89 (C.A.).

[25]   *Scalera, supra,* note 20, at para. 39.

[26]   *Ibid.* at para. 109.

[27]   [2002] O.J. No. 4304, 43 C.C.L.I. (3d) 261 (S.C.J.).

... the insurer's duty to defend suits brought against its insured is determined by the allegations of the injured plaintiff's petition, with the insurer being obligated to furnish a defense unless the petition unambiguously excludes coverage.[28]

In *Opron Maritimes Construction Ltd. v. Canadian Indemnity Co.*,[29] the New Brunswick Court of Appeal expressed the same rule, but in somewhat different language:

Any doubt as to whether the pleadings bring the incident within the coverage of the policy ought to be received in favour of the insured.[30]

In *Nichols v. American Home Assurance Co.*,[31] the Supreme Court of Canada stated:

I conclude that considerations related to insurance law and practice, as well as the authorities, overwhelmingly support the view that the duty to defend should, unless the contract of insurance indicates otherwise, be confined to the defence of claims which may be argued to fall under the policy. That said, the widest latitude should be given to the allegations in the pleadings in determining whether they raise a claim within the policy.

In the same judgment the Supreme Court also said:

... it is not necessary to prove that the obligation to indemnify will in fact arise in order to trigger the duty to defend. The mere possibility that a claim within the policy may succeed suffices.[32]

Some courts have stated that the foregoing passage indicates that if there is any possibility of the claim falling within coverage then the insurer must defend.[33] Other courts, however, have noted that the passage in question refers

---

[28] *Sherman v. Embassador Ins. Co.*, 670 F.2d 251 (D.C. Cir. 1981).

[29] [1986] N.B.J. No. 111, 19 C.C.L.I. 168, [1986] I.L.R. 1-2108 (C.A.), leave to appeal to S.C.C. refd [1987] 1 S.C.R. xi.

[30] *Ibid.* at 173.

[31] *Supra*, note 11, at 327.

[32] *Ibid.* at 329.

[33] *Uniroyal Chemical Ltd. v. Kansa General Ins. Co.*, [1996] O.J. No. 644, [1996] I.L.R. 1-3285 (C.A.); *R. v. Kansa General Ins. Co.*, [1994] O.J. No. 177, 111 D.L.R. (4th) 757, 17 O.R. (3d) 38, [1994] I.L.R. 1-3031, 21 C.C.L.I. (2d) 262 (C.A.), leave to appeal to S.C.C. refd, [1994] S.C.C.A. No. 123, 25 C.C.L.I. (2d) 23*n*; *St. Paul Fire & Marine Ins. Co. v. Durabla Can. Ltd.*, [1994] O.J. No. 1727, 118 D.L.R. (4th) 273, 19 O.R. (3d) 631, [1994] I.L.R. 1-3101 (Gen. Div.), vard [1996] O.J. No. 2505 137 D.L.R. (4th) 126 (C.A.); *Slough Estates Can. Ltd. v. Federal Pioneer Ltd.* (1994), 20 O.R. (3d) 429, [1995] I.L.R. 1-3129 (Gen. Div.); *Moncton Wesleyan Church (Trustees) v. Ecclesiastical Ins. Office plc.*, [1992] N.B.J. No. 497, 13 C.C.L.I. (2d) 231 (Q.B.).

to the proof of the underlying claim rather than to its character.[34] Whatever the case, a court should not engage in a fanciful reading of the statement of claim merely for the purpose of requiring the insurer to defend.[35] It is only where there is true ambiguity or doubt that the duty to defend must be resolved in favour of the insured.

The duty to defend with respect to ambiguous allegations does not, however, extend indefinitely. Should it become clear, either through the provision of particulars or the amendment of pleadings, that the claim is not one for which coverage is provided, then the obligation to defend will cease.

(c) Burden of Proof

The rules which govern the burden of proof with respect to the duty to defend are the same as those which apply generally to contracts of insurance.[36] In applying these rules in this context, however, one must bear in mind that the threshold the insured must meet is that of possibility, not probability. Thus, as noted by the Ontario Court of Appeal in *Trafalgar Insurance Co. of Canada v. Imperial Oil Ltd.*:

> The onus is on the insured to establish that, on a possibility basis, the allegations made by the plaintiff, if proved, bring the claim within the four corners of the relevant policy. Once that threshold is met, the onus shifts to the insurer to show that the claim made falls outside the coverage provided by the policy because of an applicable exclusion clause. If there is an exception to an exclusion, the insured bears the burden of establishing that the exception applies.[37]

(d) The Underlying Facts Exception

The pleadings rule is based on the wording of the insurance policy itself, which typically obliges the insurer to defend claims alleging matters which, if true, would fall within coverage. The rule is convenient in that the issue of whether the insurer is required to defend can be determined simply by reference to the

---

[34] *Ellett Industries Ltd. v. Laurentian P & C Ins. Co.*, [1994] B.C.J. No. 1540, 95 B.C.L.R. (2d) 169, 26 C.C.L.I. (2d) 258 (S.C.), revd, [1996] B.C.J. No. 500, 17 B.C.L.R. (3d) 201, 34 C.C.L.I. (2d) 294, 120 W.A.C. 72 (C.A.); *Privest Properties Ltd. v. Foundation Co. of Can.*, [1991] B.C.J. No. 2313, 6 C.C.L.I. (2d) 23 (S.C.).

[35] *Monenco Ltd. v. Commonwealth Insurance Co.*, [2001] S.C.J. No. 50, [2001] I.L.R. 1-3993; *Groupe DMR inc. c. Kansa General International Insurance Co.*, [2004] Q.J. No. 8523 (S.C.); *Kingsway General Insurance Co. v. Lougheed Enterprises Ltd.*, [2004] B.C.J. No. 1606, 13 C.C.L.I. (4th) 173 (C.A.); *Jesuit Fathers of Upper Canada v. Guardian Insurance Co. of Canada*, [2003] O.J. No. 4534, 6 C.C.L.I. (4th) 276, (S.C.J.), appeal dismissed [2004] O.J. No. 4641 (C.A.), leave to appeal to S.C.C. granted [2005] S.C.C.A. No. 5; *Galerie Claude Lafitte inc. c. R.H.C. Hotels inc.*, 2005 CarswellQue 11696 (S.C.); *Djepic v. Kuburovic*, [2006] O.J. No. 97 (C.A.).

[36] See Chapter 2, section 4: Burden of Proof. See also *Alie v. Bertrand & Frère Construction Co.*, [2003] I.L.R. I-4146 (Ont. C.A.).

[37] [2001] O.J. No. 4936, 57 O.R. (3d) 425 at para. 18. See also *A.R.G. Construction Corp. v. Allstate Insurance Co. of Canada*, [2004] O.J. No. 4517, 17 C.C.L.I. (4th) 262 (S.C.J.).

wording of the complaint, thereby avoiding the difficulties inherent in investigating and assessing the facts underlying the claim. Yet for precisely this reason, there are instances where a strict application of the pleadings rule may lead to an unjust result.[38] In *Cansulex Ltd. v. Reed Stenhouse Ltd.*,[39] the Chief Justice of the Supreme Court of British Columbia noted in an *obitur dictum* that, in an appropriate case, it should be open to the parties to go behind the pleadings:

> If a claim is pleaded which is covered, then the insured is unquestionably entitled to succeed on that narrow ground. Most cases are not so simple, but I have the view that neither the insured nor the insurer are always in the hands of the third party pleader, and it is open to an insured to show he is covered for the claim even if it is not correctly pleaded, and it is equally open to an insurer to show that a claim, however pleaded, is not one for which indemnity is furnished or, if covered, is excluded by another provision of the policy.[40]

This was the view of Devlin J. in *West Wake Price & Co. v. Ching*[41] as stated in the headnote, which appears to accurately express his Lordship's views:

> PER CURIAM: underwriters were not bound by the way in which a claimant chose to formulate his claim, but could properly invite the court to ascertain the true nature of the claim and to make such an inquiry as might be necessary for that purpose. ...

These sentiments were echoed in *Kates v. Hall*:

> While it remains the ordinary rule that the duty of an insurer to defend will depend on the claims made by the plaintiff against the insured, there are recognized dangers in applying this test uncritically. Both insured and insurer are entitled to protection from deprivation of benefits or imposition of obligations as the mere result of calculated pleading. It is not difficult to contemplate a situation in which an insured might be deprived of the defence for which he has paid because of inept or malicious pleading on the part of the plaintiff.[42]

The scope of this rule, which may be referred to as the "underlying facts exception" in that it operates as an exception to the pleadings rule, remains a matter of controversy. Some courts have stated that it is not appropriate to look behind the pleadings;[43] other courts have stated that, depending on the circum-

---

[38] *International Radiography and Inspection Services (1976) Ltd. v. General Accident Assurance Co. of Canada*, [1997] A.J. No. 1053, 4 W.W.R. 115, 47 Alta. L.R. 137 (C.A.).

[39] [1986] B.C.J. No. 3125, 70 B.C.L.R. 273 (S.C.).

[40] *Ibid.*, at 294.

[41] [1957] 1 W.L.R. 45, [1956] 3 All E.R. 821 at 822 (Q.B.).

[42] (1990), 46 C.C.L.I. 186 at 194 (B.C.S.C.).

[43] *Karpel v. Rumack* [1994] O.J. No. 1617, 19 O.R. (3d) 555 (Gen. Div.); *Jon Picken Ltd. v. Guardian Ins. Co. of Can.*, [1993] O.J. No. 1952, [1993] I.L.R. 1-2973 (C.A.); *Leger v. Canadian Lawyers Ins. Assoc.*, [1993] N.B.J. No. 23, 17 C.C.L.I. (2d) 61 (Q.B.), affd, [1993] N.B.J.

stances, it may be preferable for the underlying facts to determine the duty to defend rather than the pleadings.[44] In *Monenco Ltd. v. Commonwealth Insurance Co.*[45] the Supreme Court of Canada declined to rule upon the scope of the exception, although, in order to determine the duty to defend the underlying action in the case, the Court did permit consideration of extrinsic evidence that had been explicitly referred to in the pleadings. In *Dionne Farms Ltd. v. Fermes Gervais Ltée* [46] the New Brunswick Court of Appeal applied this principle so as to take into account federal regulations which all parties agreed were essential to a resolution of the duty to defend and which were implicitly referred to in the statement of claim.

It is submitted that the better view is that reference to the underlying facts is permissible in certain limited circumstances. As should be apparent from the discussion which follows, and as the New Brunswick Court of Queen's Bench has noted: "There are surely instances where the application of the 'underlying facts exception' is the only solution in order to reach an equitable result."[47] When the facts are not in dispute and bring the claim within coverage, it is indeed difficult to accept that the insurer nevertheless has the right to deny a defence simply because of careless pleading on the plaintiff's part.[48] Where there is a dispute as to the underlying facts, however, then the pleadings rule must apply.[49] Judging from the reported cases, this latter point is far too often overlooked by counsel and even by some judges. An application to determine the duty to defend must not become a trial within a trial.[50]

In jurisdictions where the courts are prepared to look at the underlying facts there are four separate situations to be considered:

(i) where the underlying facts bring the claim within the insuring agreement;

(ii) where the underlying facts take the claim outside of the insuring agreement;

No. 600, 140 N.B.R. (2d) 395 (C.A.); *Halifax Insurance Co. of Canada v. Innopex Ltd.*, [2004] O.J. No. 4178, 15 C.C.L.I. (4th) 159 (C.A.).

[44] *Bathurst (City) v. Royal Ins. Co. of Can.*, [1994] N.B.J. No. 474, 154 N.B.R. (2d) 86 (C.A.); *Privest Properties Ltd. v. Foundation Co. of Can.*, [1992] B.C.J. No. 6 C.C.L.I. (2d) 15, 4 C.P.C. (3d) 313 (S.C.); *Kates v. Hall, supra*, note 42; *Cansulex v. Reed Stenhouse Ltd., supra*, note 39; *Heck v. Prudential Ins. Co.*, [1991] M.J. No. 540, 5 C.C.L.I. (2d) 138 (Q.B.); *Thorne v. Royal & Sun Alliance Insurance Co. of Canada*, [2003] N.B.J. No. 322, 261 N.B.R. (2d) 119 (C.A.).

[45] [2001] S.C.J. No. 50, [2001] 2 S.C.R. 699.

[46] [2002] N.B.J. No. 402, 43 C.C.L.I. (3d) 1 (C.A.).

[47] *Bathurst (City) v. Royal Ins. Co. of Canada, ibid.*, at 91.

[48] *Advanced Laser and Fusion Technology, Inc. v. Guardian Insurance Co. of Canada*, [2001] O.J. No. 3268, 31 C.C.L.I. (3d) 307 (S.C.J.).

[49] *Sam Ermen Plumbing & Heating Ltd. v. Canadian General Insurance Co.*, [1999] N.B.J. No. 58, 535 A.P.R. 94, 209 N.B.R. (2d) 94, (Q.B.); *Privest Properties Ltd. v. Foundation Co. of Canada, supra*, note 44; *Cooper v. Farmer's Mutual Insurance Co.*, [2002] O.J. No. 1949, 59 O.R. (3d) 417 (C.A.).

[50] *Monenco Ltd. v. Commonwealth Insurance Co.*, [2001] S.C.J. No. 50, [2001] 2 S.C.R. 699; *Halifax Insurance Co. of Canada v. Innopex Ltd.*, [2004] O.J. No. 4178, 15 C.C.L.I. (4th) 159 (C.A.).

(iii) where the underlying facts bring the claim within a policy exclusion;

(iv) where the underlying facts bring the claim within an exception to an exclusion.[51]

(i) *Where the Underlying Facts Bring the Claim within the Insuring Agreement*

A rigid adherence to the pleadings rule leads to the conclusion that the insurer can rightfully deny a defence to an insured on the basis of an unskillfully drawn pleading, even though, on the underlying facts, the claim is one for which indemnity would be provided. In such cases, many courts in the United States have held that the underlying facts must prevail and the insurer is required to defend.[52]

An example of this exception to the pleadings rule is provided by the decision in *American Motorist Insurance Co. v. South Western Greyhound Lines Inc.*[53] In that case the defendant bus company's liability policy expressly excluded coverage in respect of injuries sustained by passengers alighting from buses. A passenger brought an action against the bus company alleging that he had been injured while alighting from a bus. The actual facts were otherwise. The Court held that the bus company's insurers were required to defend since the actual facts were within coverage even though the claim, as pleaded, was not.

In circumstances such as these, the underlying facts exception might, arguably, be seen as following from the duty of good faith which the insurer owes to the insured.[54] An insurer, acting fairly, ought to defend the insured where the facts known to the insurer bring the claim clearly within coverage. As one American court noted, "the insurer cannot rely on the pleadings alone where the allegations are in conflict with facts known or reasonably ascertainable by the insurer."[55] Where the facts are in dispute, however, until that dispute is resolved the pleadings will continue to govern the duty to defend.[56]

---

[51] Extrinsic evidence of an admission by the insurer that there was a duty to defend was permitted in *Uniroyal Chemical Ltd. v. Kansa General Insurance Co.*, [1996] O.J. No. 644, 89 O.A.C. 311 (C.A.). See also *Uniform Developments & Leasing Ltd. v. Issac*, [1998] O.J. No. 1768, 7 C.C.L.I. (3d) 290 (Gen. Div.). The latter cases are not examples of the underlying facts exception, for they relate not to the facts of the underlying claim but, rather, to statements made by the insurer to the insured regarding the former's obligations under the policy.

[52] J. Appleman, *Insurance Law and Practice*, revised ed. (St. Paul: West Publishing Co., 1981), at para. 4683.

[53] 283 F.2d 648 (10th Cir. 1960).

[54] See Chapter 2, section 2(b)(ii): Implied Term of Good Faith and Fair Dealing.

[55] *Baugh Construction Co. v. Mission Ins. Co.*, 836 F.2d 1164 at 1168 (9th Cir. 1988).

[56] *Supra*, note 49.

(ii) *Where the Underlying Facts Take the Claim outside the Insuring Agreement*

Some authorities suggest that the underlying facts exception may operate in favour of the insurer, permitting the insurer to decline a defence, notwithstanding the pleadings, where the known facts indicate that the claim does not fall within the insuring agreement in the policy.[57] Yet whether this situation, which must be distinguished from the situation where the facts bring the claim within one of the policy exclusions, is a proper application of the underlying facts exception is a matter of considerable doubt. The defence clause usually stipulates that the insurer will defend even where the allegations are "groundless, false or fraudulent". The intention is that the insured be given coverage with respect to the costs which are incurred in the defence of an unmeritorious claim. Indeed, the very cases that the insurer is most likely to defend through trial, rather than settle, are those cases where the plaintiff is not likely to succeed.

Thus, in *Shragie v. Tanemura*[58] the insurer was required to defend, notwithstanding that the insured himself acknowledged that the actual facts brought the claim outside of the insuring agreement. The allegation against the insured was that, in his capacity as a chartered accountant, he negligently advised the plaintiff to make an improvident investment. If this were true then the claim would fall within his professional liability policy. Yet in his defence the insured denied that he provided professional services to the plaintiff — on examination for discovery he was extensively cross-examined on this point and consistently maintained that he was simply a co-investor with the plaintiff. There was no evidence to the contrary. In these circumstances, the third party insurer declined to defend the action. Nevertheless, on the insured's motion the Court required the insurer to assume conduct of the defence. The Court noted that the insurance contract required the insurer to defend the action irrespective of whether the insured would ultimately be found liable to the plaintiff or not, and further noted that the facts underlying the claim were to be determined by the trial judge, who would not be bound by the insured's evidence on discovery.

The decision of the Ontario Court of Appeal in *Halifax Insurance Co. of Canada v. Innopex Ltd.*[59] can be explained on the same basis. The insured, a distributor, sold watches to a purchaser in the United States. Gucci America, Inc. brought a trademark infringement action against the insured, alleging that the watches were a 'knock-off' of a Gucci product and that the insured had falsely marketed the watches under the Gucci name. If proven, certain of the allegations in the complaint would have triggered coverage under the advertising liability

---

[57] *Cansulex Ltd. v. Reed Stenhouse Ltd.*, *supra*, note 39.

[58] [1987] B.C.J. No. 2582, 32 C.C.L.I. 126 (S.C.). See also *Renco v. The Fitness Institute Ltd.*, [1995] O.J. No. 2295, 25 O.R. (3d) 88, [1996] I.L.R. 1-3271 (Gen. Div.) and *Palmieri v. Misir*, [2003] O.J. No. 3518 (S.C.J.). In the latter decision the insured, a lawyer, advised the insurer that he acted as an investment and business advisor, not as a lawyer. Nevertheless, the Statement of Claim, which alleged negligence as a lawyer, was controlling, and the insurer was obliged to defend the claim.

[59] [2004] O.J. No. 4178, 72 O.R. (3d) 522 (C.A.).

provisions of the insured's policy. The insurer, however, was of the view that the 'true facts' revealed that the insured simply purchased and sold the watches and did not engage in any advertising activity so as to come within the coverage afforded by the policy. On this basis the insurer brought declaratory proceedings seeking an order that it was not under a duty to defend with respect to the Gucci complaint. Affidavit evidence was presented by the insurer to establish the underlying facts which, according to the insurer, brought the complaint outside of coverage. The motion judge admitted the extrinsic evidence and found in favour of the insurer. On appeal, however, the finding was reversed. The Court of Appeal considered that an inquiry into whether the insured had in fact engaged in the conduct complained of in the underlying action should not be undertaken in an application to determine the duty to defend. As a general principle this is correct. Gucci America, Inc. was not a party to the declaratory proceeding. Thus, the judge trying the underlying action would not be bound to accept the findings of fact made in the course of the declaratory proceeding.

To many insurers this will be considered an entirely unsatisfactory state of affairs, placing them wholly at the mercy of the third pleader and forcing them to defend a misconceived or unmeritorious claim. In some cases, however, there may be a way out for the insurer. Provided that the underlying facts are not in dispute, it may be possible for the insurer, in the course of its conduct of the defence of the insured, to bring a summary application on behalf of the insured which will be binding on the third party and which will dispose of the allegations in the complaint which have triggered the defence obligation. The insurer could then either withdraw from the defence of the claim or bring declaratory proceedings seeking an order to that effect. In proceeding in this fashion, of course, the insurer would have to be mindful of the duty of good faith it owes to the insured in the defence of the claim.[60] The insurer would also have to take care to use separate counsel for the defence and coverage proceedings.

(iii) Where the Underlying Facts Bring the Claim within a Policy Exclusion

Where, on the pleadings, a claim is presented which falls within one of the policy exclusions, then it is clear that the insurer is not obliged to defend.[61] Where the pleadings are either silent or unclear, however, some courts have permitted the insurer to decline a defence where the underlying facts indicate that one of the policy exclusions will apply to the claim.[62] Whether this is a proper application of the underlying facts exception is an interesting and

---

[60] See discussion at Chapter 2, section 2(b)(ii): Implied Term of Good Faith and Fair Dealing.

[61] *Opron Maritimes Const. Ltd. v. Can. Indemnity Co.*, [1986] N.B.J. No. 111, 19 C.C.L.I. 168 (C.A.).

[62] See, for example, *Heck v. Prudential Ins. Co.*, *supra*, note 44; *Cincinnati Ins. Co. v. Mallon*, 409 N.E.2d 1100 (Ind. 1980); *Kepner v. Western Fire Ins. Co.*, 509 P.2d 222 (Ariz. 1973); *Monenco Ltd. v. Commonwealth Insurance Co.*, [1997] B.C.J. No. 1971, 42 B.C.L.R. (3d) 280, 47 C.C.L.I. (2d) 12, supp. reasons 19 C.P.C. (4th) 66 (S.C.), affd [1999] B.C.J. No. 568, 64 B.C.L.R. (3d) 307, 29 C.P.C. (4th), 8 C.C.L.I. (3d) 11 (C.A.), leave to appeal to S.C.C. granted March 16, 2000.

unresolved question, the answer to which may very well depend upon the nature of the exclusion and the manner in which it is tied to the allegations against the insured.[63]

It is common, for example, for policies issued to hotel owners to contain a "forcible ejection" exclusion, excluding coverage where a patron is injured while being forcibly removed from the premises.[64] Where a patron brings an action in respect of such injuries, the pleadings may or may not disclose sufficient facts to bring the forcible ejection exclusion into play. Yet if those facts are not in dispute then it seems reasonable to permit the insurer to decline the defence, for the insurer will have no economic interest in the outcome of the action.[65] As the Supreme Court of Canada noted in *Nichols v. American Home Assurance Co.*:

> The insurer's interest in defending a claim is related to the possibility that it may ultimately be called upon to indemnify the insured under the policy. It is in the insurer's interest that if liability is found, it be on a basis other than one falling under the policy. Requiring the insurer to defend claims which cannot fall within the policy puts the insurer in the position of having to defend claims which it is in its interest should succeed.[66]

This type of case, where the claim falls within the insuring agreement but the facts bring it within a policy exclusion, is logically distinct from the case where the claim falls within the insuring agreement, but, on the facts, is groundless, false or fraudulent. In the latter case, the wording of the defence clause requires the insurer to defend the claim. In the former case, however, if the evidence that establishes the plaintiff's claim also establishes the application of a policy exclusion, then the claim is not one which, if proven, would fall within coverage.

In most cases, of course, the facts relating to the application of the policy exclusion will be in dispute. This raises the issue of whether the insurer will be responsible for the costs of defence pending the resolution of the dispute. If the

---

[63] As McLachlin J. observed in *Nichols v. American Home Assur. Co.*, [1990] S.C.J. No. 33, 68 D.L.R. (4th) 321 at 326 the exclusion clause may be worded in such a way as to be concerned only with the duty to indemnify:

> As I read the policy, the exclusion clause is primarily concerned with the duty to indemnify. For this reason, it refers to actual acts or omissions, which are the precondition of the duty to indemnify. The scope of the duty to indemnify, in turn, triggers the application of the defence clause, through use of the phrase in the defence clause limiting the duty to claims for "damages which are or may be payable under the terms of this Policy". The duty to defend, unlike the duty to indemnify, is triggered not by actual acts or omissions, but by allegations, applying "even if any of the allegations of the suit are groundless, false or fraudulent". Thus the scope of the duty to defend is not conditioned directly by the exclusion clause, but only indirectly through that clause's definition of the scope of coverage.

[64] See, for example, *Hamilton v. Laurentian Pacific Ins. Co.*, [1988] B.C.J. No. 439, 30 C.C.L.I. 204 (S.C.), revd, [1989] B.C.J. No. 869, 37 C.C.L.I. 190 (C.A.).

[65] Appleman, *supra*, note 52, para. 4683 at 53.

[66] *Supra*, note 63, at 328.

pleadings rule is strictly applied, then the insurer will be required to defend the action at its own expense. In principle this is the correct approach, for if the underlying facts are in dispute then the pleadings should govern the duty to defend.[67] Nevertheless, recognizing that a strict application of the pleadings rule may require the insurer to defend some claims which may ultimately prove to be excluded from coverage, some courts have held that the issue of defence costs cannot be determined until the claim is finally resolved. In such cases two options are available:

(i) the insured should pay the costs of the defence, subject to reimbursement by the insurer, should it be determined that the claim falls within coverage;

(ii) the insurer should pay the costs of defence, subject to being reimbursed by the insured should it be determined that the claim does not fall within coverage.[68]

In *Stout v. Grain Dealers Mutual Insurance Co.*[69] the Court opted for the first approach, requiring the insured to defend until the issue of coverage was decided in his favour. The insured had entered a plea of guilty to manslaughter for shooting a prowler at his home. The prowler's estate brought a wrongful death action, alleging negligence against the insured in respect of which the insurer declined to defend. In declaratory proceedings, the Court held that the insurer was not required to pay the costs of defence until it could be established that coverage was available under the policy:

> This does not mean that by a mere assertion of a conflict of interest the insurer may excuse itself from its contractual obligation to defend. It means only that, when there is an unresolved dispute as to the existence of this obligation, the insurer is not required to participate in a tort proceeding where the insurer's interest would be to prove a state of facts which would establish or magnify the damaged party's claim against the insured. Simply, the law will recognize the practicalities of the situation. But, if it should be later determined that there is coverage, the insurer would be liable for the cost of the defense independently arranged for by the insured, as well as any judgment against him.[70]

In Canada, this issue was touched upon in *Schwartz v. Kuszko Estate.*[71] Unfortunately, the basis of the decision is somewhat difficult to determine. After an

---

[67] Note that this is a different issue than that of the allocation of defence costs between covered and uncovered claims, discussed in section 8(c): Covered and Uncovered Claims.

[68] G.W. Mayo, Jr., "Defense Cost Reimbursement to Insurers When Lack of Coverage is Established After Reservation of Rights" (Winter 1993) *FICC Quarterly* 175-89; M.J. Brady and S.H. Handelman, "Insurer's Right to Reimbursement: Neglected But Valuable Remedy" (Oct. 1992) *Defense Counsel Journal* 547-53.

[69] 307 F.2d 521 (5th Cir. 1962).

[70] *Ibid.*, at 523.

[71] [1988] O.J. No. 611, 32 C.C.L.I. 42 (Dist. Ct.).

altercation the plaintiff was shot and seriously wounded by the defendant. The plaintiff commenced an action alleging, alternatively, the intentional use or the negligent handling of a firearm. The defendant's insurer declined to defend the claim, citing an exclusion in the policy with respect to "bodily injury ... caused intentionally by you or at your direction". The defendant then commenced third party proceedings against the insurer and brought an application to require the insurer to defend the main action or, alternatively, to pay the defendant's costs of defence on a solicitor and client basis. The Court declined to grant either form of relief. Although the Court apparently accepted the argument that the duty to defend must be determined strictly from the pleadings, from which it follows that the insurer should have been required to defend the claim, the Court held that it would create a conflict of interest for the insurer to conduct the insured's defence. As discussed below, it is submitted that this reasoning is erroneous.[72] The Court further held that it would not be appropriate to make an order that the insurer pay the costs of defence on a solicitor and client basis, for it would be up to the trial judge to determine the remedy for the insurer's "anticipated breach of contract."[73] In the result, the insured was required to bear the burden of defending the action, but with the right to seek damages from the insurer at the conclusion of the litigation. It is not clear from the judgment, however, whether any damages would be awarded should it be found that the claim fell within the policy exclusion.

The issue was also before the Court on the facts (although not discussed in the reasons for judgment) in *Heck v. Prudential Insurance Co.*[74] Again, the basis of the decision is not entirely clear. Following a shooting incident the insured was convicted of assault with a weapon. The victim brought a civil action, initially alleging both negligence and the intentional infliction of bodily harm. He later amended the statement of claim, ostensibly so as to plead only negligence, but as the Court noted, despite the use of the word "negligence", the substance of the claim clearly was that the defendant intentionally shot the plaintiff. Relying upon an exclusion with respect to claims arising from intentionally inflicted bodily harm, the insurer declined a defence to its insured. The insured then brought an application for an order requiring the insurer to defend the action. No affidavit evidence was given by the insured, who chose instead to simply rely upon the pleadings rule. The Court noted that, although not conclusive, the certificate of conviction was *prima facie* proof of the facts upon which it was based. Accordingly, on the basis of the material before the Court, it was held that the claim by the plaintiff was in respect of the defendant's intentional tort. The insured was required to defend the action at his own expense.

---

[72]　See section 8: Right to Select and Instruct Counsel.

[73]　*Supra*, note 44, at 47.

[74]　[1991] M.J. No. 540, 5 C.C.L.I. (2d) 138 (Q.B.).

One might be tempted to explain the decision in *Heck v. Prudential*[75] on the basis of the pleadings rule, namely, that despite its form, the substance of the claim was in respect of an intentional tort. Yet in a subsequent decision,[76] the same Court ruled that Prudential could participate in the action as a third party because there was a possibility that the insurer might be adversely affected by a finding at trial that the injuries were inflicted through the insured's negligence.[77] This leaves the decision in *Heck v. Prudential* as being an application of the underlying facts exception. It cannot be said, however, that the underlying facts were not in dispute, for at trial it was open to both the plaintiff and the defendant to lead evidence that the injuries were inflicted through negligence. Unfortunately, the Court did not address the issue of responsibility for defence costs should it be determined at trial that the exclusion was not applicable.

(iv) *Where the Underlying Facts Bring the Claim within an Exception to an Exclusion*

On their face the pleadings may allege liability on a basis which is excluded from coverage, yet the underlying facts may reveal that an exception to the exclusion applies. Applying the pleadings rule, the insured would not be entitled to a defence. Should the claim proceed to trial, however, and the insured held liable on a basis that falls within the exception, then indemnity would be provided.

As in the first situation discussed above, an insured in these circumstances ought to be entitled to obtain a defence by showing that the undisputed facts indicate that the exception applies. Should the facts be in dispute, however, then the pleadings rule must govern until the dispute is resolved.

A unique situation exists in the case of the self-defence exception to the intentional injury exclusion. In *Thorne v. Royal & Sun Alliance Insurance Co. of Canada*[78] the insured was alleged to have assaulted an opposing player in a hockey game. The insured's homeowner's policy provided coverage for bodily injury but excluded liability in cases in which the bodily injury was expected or intended from the standpoint of the insured. The exclusion contained the proviso that it did not apply to bodily injury "...resulting from the use of reasonable force to protect persons or property." On its face the claim fell within the exclusion. The insured, however, claimed to have acted in self-defence, so as to fall within the exception to the exclusion. The Court noted that an unusual feature of the exception is that, for all practical purposes, it could not be used to bring a claim within the indemnity provisions of the policy. The use of reason-

---

[75] *Ibid.*

[76] *Block v. Heck*, [1991] M.J. No. 539, 5 C.C.L.I. (2d) 134 (Q.B.).

[77] The Court is mistaken in this view, for the decision between the plaintiff and the defendant would not be binding upon the insurer, given that the Court had already ruled that the insurer had no duty to defend. Moreover, and in any event, a finding of negligence in the main action would not preclude the insurer from raising the intentional injury exclusion in subsequent litigation to determine coverage. See section 7: Consequences of the Refusal to Defend.

[78] [2003] N.B.J. No. 322, 261 N.B.R. (2d) 119 (C.A.).

able force in self-defence is an answer to a claim for battery. Thus, the only basis for a finding of liability would be one for which indemnity was not available under the policy. Nevertheless, the Court required the insurer to provide a defence to the insured.

In reaching its decision in *Thorne v. Royal & Sun Alliance Insurance Co. of Canada* the Court took into account the uncontradicted affidavit evidence from the insured establishing that he acted in self-defence. Yet, plainly, this was a matter which was in dispute in the underlying action. The insured, however, had not filed a statement of defence. The affidavit thus merely set out the basis upon which the insured intended to defend the claim. In these circumstances the decision is not an example of the application of the underlying facts exception to the pleadings rule. Rather, the case illustrates the unique nature of the self-defence exception to the intentional injury exclusion, which requires the insurer to defend an action alleging an intentional tort when the insured claims to have acted in self-defence.

(e) Claims within the Deductible

Many liability insurance policies contain a deductible provision. Where a claim is brought which is entirely within the deductible amount, the insurer has no financial interest in defending the lawsuit. Nevertheless, the policy language may require that the insurer provide a defence. In *Swan Wooster Engineering Co. v. Continental Casualty Co.*[79] the insured was covered under a professional liability policy with a $100,000 deductible. The defence clause (under Insuring Agreement II of the policy) provided that the insurer would defend "as respects such insurance as is afforded by this Policy ...". A policy condition provided that:

> The Company agrees to pay the amount incurred under Insuring Agreement II of this Policy, entitled Defence, Settlement, and Supplementary Payments in addition to the limit of liability stated in the Declarations and it is agreed that the deductible amount shall not apply to Insuring Agreement II.

The Court held that this condition had the effect of requiring the insurer to incur the costs of investigation and defence relating to a claim which was clearly within the deductible.

(f) Where Policy Limits Have Been Exhausted

Whether the insurer's duty to defend continues after the policy limits are exhausted depends upon the wording of the policy in question. Many modern policies specifically provide that the insurer "shall not be obligated to pay any claim or judgment or to defend any suit after the applicable limit of the company's liability has been exhausted by payment of judgments or settlements". Other policies, however, are silent on the issue. With respect to the latter policies, in American jurisprudence two conflicting lines of authority have

---

[79] [1971] I.L.R. 1-406 (B.C.S.C.).

developed. One line holds that the insurer must continue to defend even after it has paid the policy limits; the other line holds that upon payment of the policy limits, the insurer is relieved of the obligation to defend.[80] The Canadian authorities, although not entirely consistent, favour the latter view.

The opinion that the duty to defend does not extend beyond the exhaustion of indemnity limits is exemplified by the decision in *Keene Corp. v. Insurance Co. of North America*,[81] a decision arising out of industry-wide asbestos litigation. The policy provided in its introductory sentence that the contract was "subject to the limits of liability, exclusions, conditions and other terms of this policy". The duty-to-defend provision was prefaced by the phrase, "with respect to such insurance as is provided by this policy ...". It was held that this language was unambiguous and was susceptible only to one reasonable interpretation: namely, that the duty to defend was limited to both the nature and the amount of insurance provided.

The opposing viewpoint is represented by *Commercial Union Insurance Co. v. Pittsburgh Corning Corp.*,[82] which holds that the policy phrase "with respect to such insurance as is provided by this policy" is ambiguous and should be construed against the insurer. The duty to defend in that case was held to apply to all claims that were in litigation at the time that the indemnity limits were exhausted. It was further held, however, that no duty to defend arises with respect to any claims subsequently asserted against the insured.

There are two reported Canadian cases from the province of Quebec dealing with this issue. In *Yorkshire Insurance Co. v. Turgeon*[83] an automobile liability insurer, without the insured's consent, settled a dubious claim within the policy limits, after which it tendered the balance of the limit and refused to defend a second, meritorious claim. The majority of the Quebec Court of Appeal held that the insured was not bound by the settlement of the dubious claim, and the Court went on to state, in what must be regarded as an *obitur dictum*, that in any event the policy language required the insurer to defend claims after the policy limits had been exhausted.

A similar issue arose in *Les Mines d'Amiante Bell Ltée v. Federal Insurance Co.*,[84] a decision of the Quebec Superior Court. In that case, after some $8,000,000 were expended in the defence of asbestos litigation claims, the policy indemnity limits of $4,000,000 were finally exhausted. The insurer then refused to defend any further claims, taking the position that the policy had come to an end. The Court agreed, holding that the obligation to pay defence costs arises only where there is or may be an obligation to provide indemnity.

---

[80] Zulkey and Pollard, "The Duty to Defend after Exhaustion of Policy Limits" *For the Defence*, June 1985, 21-28.

[81] 597 F.Supp. 946 (D.D.C. 1984).

[82] 553 F.Supp. 425 (E.D.Pa. 1981).

[83] [1962] B.R. 625 (Que. C.A.).

[84] [1986] I.L.R. 1-1995 (Que. S.C.).

The issue came before the Alberta Court of Appeal in *Co-operators General Insurance Co. v. Johnson*,[85] however, with a different result. The insurer sought a declaration that it could pay the policy limits into court and thereby avoid having to defend the action. The Court refused the application on the basis that the defence provisions of the policy, including the provisions to pay costs, were not stated to be subject to the policy limits. Unfortunately, the somewhat meagre reasons for judgment do not set out the provisions of the policy under consideration. Nevertheless, the decision may alternatively be explained on the basis that an insurer cannot, in good faith, escape the defence obligation simply by tendering limits.[86]

In *Boreal Insurance Inc. v. Lafarge Canada Inc.*,[87] after exhausting its limits a primary insurer sought a declaration that an excess insurer assume responsibility for the defence of the action. The primary policy did not contain any language specifically addressing the issue of whether the defence obligation ended once the limits of indemnity were reached. The preamble to the primary policy, however, provided that the policy was "subject to the limits of liability ... and other terms of the policy..." and the defence obligation was stated to be "...with respect to such insurance as is afforded by this policy ...". The excess carrier asserted that this language, which is general in nature, was ambiguous and did not clearly relieve the primary insurer from its defence obligation, notwithstanding the exhaustion of the limits of liability. The court did not agree. Noting that the purpose underlying the duty to defend was to require the participation of the insurer in the defence of cases for which there may be indemnity under the policy, the court considered that it would illogical to require the insurer to defend a claim for which indemnity could never be provided. The court further stated that, read in this context, the prefatory language to the policy and the defence obligation was not ambiguous and should be interpreted so as to relieve the insurer of the defence obligation upon the exhaustion of the limits of liability.

Whether, once the limits have been exhausted, the duty to defend extends to execution proceedings against the insured was considered in *Regency Plymouth Chrysler Inc. v. I.C.B.C.*[88] A number of claims arose out of a single accident. Two of the claims were quantified by judgments. Although the balance of the claims remained unquantified, it was clear that the total would exceed the limits of the primary policy. I.C.B.C., the primary insurer, pursuant to a statutory right, paid the policy limits into court. The insured incurred legal expenses to obtain orders that the judgment creditors obtain payment from the moneys in court. This was allowed on the basis that the insured had purchased excess coverage from different carriers and that the excess carriers had filed undertakings to pay

---

[85] [1992] A.J. No. 162, 7 C.C.L.I. (2d) 183 (C.A.).

[86] See *Boreal Insurance Inc. v. Lafarge Canada Inc.*, [2004] O.J. No. 1571 at para. 44, 10 C.C.L.I. (4th) 212 (S.C.J.).

[87] [2004] O.J. No. 1571, 10 C.C.L.I. (4th) 212 (S.C.J.).

[88] *Regency Plymouth Chrysler Inc. v. Insurance Corp. of British Columbia* [1999] B.C.J. No. 639, 69 B.C.L.R. (3d) 342, [1999] I.L.R. 1-3694 (S.C.).

up to the limits of their policies. I.C.B.C. refused to pay for these legal expenses, arguing that its duty to defend did not extend to execution proceedings. The Court agreed, noting that the insured was in the same position as one who has insufficient insurance to cover the claims against him, determined or undetermined. The case is silent with respect to any obligations of the excess carriers to pay the expenses in question.

(g) Multiple Causes of Action, One or More of Which Is Outside Coverage

It is not uncommon for a complaint to allege multiple or alternative causes of action, one or more of which is outside coverage. In these circumstances it is clear that the insurer is required to defend the claims that are within coverage, but there is conflicting authority as to how the defence of the uncovered claim is to be handled. Some of the courts in the United States hold that the insurer owes the insured the unqualified duty to defend the entire suit, including claims that are not covered under the policy,[89] while other courts hold that the insurer may leave the defence of the uncovered claims to the insured.[90]

This issue was addressed by the British Columbia Supreme Court in *Bacon v. McBride*,[91] which has become recognized as one of the leading decisions in Canada on the matter of the duty to defend. The statement of claim alleged various grounds of liability against the insured, some of which were within the coverage provided under an automobile liability policy and some of which were outside that cover. The insurer took the position that it was not required to defend. The Court held that the insurer was thereby in breach of contract, for it was required to defend those allegations that fell within the coverage afforded under the automobile policy. With respect to the allegations that fell outside of the cover, however, the Court stated that the insurer would have been within its rights to decline the defence of those issues and require the insured to obtain separate counsel in that regard:

> In refusing to conduct the defence of the litigant, I.C.B.C. committed a breach of the insurance agreement contained in Reg. 6.18. The presence of allegations in the pleadings relating to claims outside the coverage might reasonably have induced I.C.B.C. to decline to defend the insured on those issues (because of a possible conflict of interest) and advise it to retain its own lawyer for that aspect of the defence or, alternatively, to defend all claims under a non-waiver agreement with the insured. Such allegations did not, however, justify I.C.B.C.'s breach of contract in refusing to defend the insured regarding those allegations which advanced claims for which insurance coverage was provided. Accordingly, I.C.B.C.'s unjustified refusal to defend obligates it to pay the

---

[89] See, for example, *Garden Sanctuary Inc. v. Ins. Co. of North America*, 292 So.2d 75 (Fla. 1974).

[90] *Town of Tieton v. General Ins. Co.*, 380 P.2d 127 (Wash. 1963).

[91] (1984), 5 C.C.L.I. 146 (B.C.S.C.).

insured the reasonable expenses to which it was put by reason of having to employ its solicitor to defend the claim.[92]

The same approach has been taken by other courts.[93] Unfortunately, there is no discussion in these decisions on the practical consequences of having two counsel defend the claim on behalf of the insured. In two British Columbia decisions the court considered it to be "unworkable" for there to be two lawyers, one instructed by the insured and the other instructed by the insurer, defending an action.[94] In an Ontario decision, however, the master declined an application by the plaintiff in a sexual abuse case to restrict the defendant to one solicitor of record.[95] A key issue, for the purpose of coverage, concerned the dates upon which the abuse occurred. Since the insurer and the insured had competing interests with respect to this issue, the court permitted the school board defendant to be represented at trial by two lawyers, one appointed by the defendant and the other by the defendant's insurer. The master noted that the trial judge would be able to control any abuse of process at trial.

In cases in which the insured and insurer are in agreement it may arguably be appropriate for their separate interests to be separately represented. In a case in which the insured objects to there being two counsel of record, however, it is unlikely that the court would permit the insurer, as a non-party, to be separately represented in the guise of counsel ostensibly appointed by the insurer to represent the insured. Moreover, counsel appointed by the insurer to defend the insured in these circumstances would be in the position of potentially acting against the interests of the very client he or she has been appointed to represent. For these reasons, absent agreement, it would not be appropriate for one action to be jointly defended by separate counsel appointed by the insurer and the insured. Rather, one counsel should be appointed to defend the entire proceeding. Issues as to apportionment of defence costs[96] and who has the right to select and instruct counsel, as well as the duties of counsel with respect to potential conflicts of interest[97] are discussed later in this chapter.

(h) The Duty to Defend Where There Are Multiple Insurers

In some cases, there may be more than one insurance policy responding to all or part of a claim. Four situations may arise:

---

[92] *Ibid.*, at 152.

[93] *American Home Assur. Co. v. Stinchcombe*, [1992] A.J. No. 1052, 13 C.C.L.I. (2d) 79 (Q.B.); *Waterloo (Regional Municipality) v. Guarantee Co. of North America*, [1990] O.J. No. 1443, 1 C.C.L.I. (2d) 290 (H.C.J.).

[94] *Continental Ins. Co. v. Dia Met Minerals Ltd.*, [1994] B.C.J. No. 1724, 5 B.C.L.R. (3d) 222, [1995] I.L.R. 1-3150 (S.C.); *Wear v. Robertson*, [1996] B.C.J. No. 1627, 27 B.C.L.R. (3d) 192 (S.C.); *cf. Sam Ermen Plumbing & Heating Ltd. v. Canadian General Insurance Co.* [1999] N.B.J. No. 58, 209 N.B.R. (2d) 94 (Q.B.).

[95] *J.L. v. Sabourin*, [2002] O.J. No. 445, [2002] I.L.R. 1-4043 (S.C.J.).

[96] See section 2: Apportionment and Reimbursement of Defence Costs.

[97] See section 8: Right to Select and Instruct Counsel, and section 9: Duty of Counsel.

(i) There may be overlapping policies, that is, policies that respond to the same item of loss;

(ii) There may be excess coverage, that is, coverage that applies after the limits of the primary policy or policies have been exhausted;

(iii) Coverage may be several, that is, one policy responds to one part of the claim and another policy responds to a separate part of the claim;

(iv) There may be alternative coverage, that is, one or the other policy responds to the loss, but not both;

The obligation to defend the claim and the right to control the defence will depend upon into which of these four situations the case falls.

(i) Overlapping Coverage

It follows from the pleadings rule that every insurer whose policy contains a duty to defend provision must defend the insured whenever a claim is presented that, if proven, would fall within the coverage afforded by the policy. On this basis the courts may require overlapping insurers to defend jointly and to agree upon the selection of counsel.[98] If the insurers are unable to agree, then the insured will have the right to select counsel and seek reimbursement for the reasonable costs incurred in defending the action.[99] Should one insurer defend and the other refuse to defend, then the insurer defending is entitled to seek contribution,[100] the determination of which may have to await the outcome of the underlying action.[101] In the absence of a compelling reason to apportion

---

[98] *Prudential Assur. Co. v. Manitoba Public Ins. Corp.* (1976), 67 D.L.R. (3d) 521 (Man. C.A.); *Berezin v. Firestone Ins. Co.*, [1992] O.J. No. 1033, [1992] I.L.R. 1-2841 (Gen. Div.); *Economical Mutual Insurance Co. v. 856742 Ontario Inc*, [2001] O.J. No. 3235, [2001] I.L.R. 1-3991 (S.C.J.). But see *Royal Ins. Co. of Can. v. Manitoba Public Ins. Corp.*, [1989] M.J. No. 490, 40 C.C.L.I. 223 (Q.B.), the facts of which are not entirely clear, in which a "pragmatic approach" was followed, with the result that one insurer was required to defend, with a right to later claim indemnity for defence costs from the other insurer.

[99] *Prudential Assur. Co. v. Manitoba Public Ins. Co.*, *ibid.*; *Economical Mutual Insurance Co. v. 856742 Ontario Inc.*, *ibid.*

[100] *Ecclesiastical Ins. Office plc. v. Sun Alliance Ins. Co.*, [1993] N.B.J. No. 149, 17 C.C.L.I. (2d) 66 (Q.B.). But *cf. Royal Ins. Co. of Can. v. Coronation Ins. Co*, [1993] N.B.J. No. 102, 17 C.C.L.I. (2d) 131 (Q.B.); affd, [1993] N.B.J. No. 570, 141 N.B.R. (2d) 9 (C.A.), where it was held that an insurer defending an action in the absence of a duty to defend (there being no coverage under the policy) was a volunteer and was not entitled to recover its defence costs to date from a different insurer which was required to defend. In *Aetna Ins. Co. v. Canadian Surety Co.*, [1991] A.J. No. 267, 4 W.W.R. 750, 79 Alta. L.R. (2d) 252, 2 C.C.L.I. (2d) 215 (Q.B.), vard in part, [1994] A.J. No. 399, 114 D.L.R. (4th) 577, 19 Alta. L.R. (3d) 317, [1994] I.L.R. 1-3119, 24 C.C.L.I. (2d) 257 (C.A.), however, an excess insurer required by law to defend in the face of the primary insurer's refusal was able to obtain indemnity from the primary insurer under the law of restitution.

[101] *Canadian Indemnity Co. v. Royal Ins. Co.*, [1993] A.J. No. 56, 4 W.W.R. 57, 7 Alta. L.R. (3d) 337, [1993] I.L.R. 1-2958, 14 C.C.L.I. (2d) 240 (Q.B.), affd, [1994] A.J. No. 411, 7 W.W.R. 607, 19 Alta. L.R. (3d) 406, 157 A.R. 267, 24 C.C.L.I. (2d) 102 (C.A.).

defence costs on some other basis, the courts will order the insurers to share equally.[102]

(ii) Excess Coverage

The circumstances under which excess coverage arises vary. The insured may purchase both primary and excess coverage, in which case the policy language will usually require the primary carrier to provide the sole defence of claims within the limits of its policy. A situation which often arises in the context of automobile liability policies is that the driver and the owner of the vehicle are separately insured. In that case, legislation generally provides that one policy is to be treated as first loss insurance and the other as excess insurance.[103] Legislation may also provide that the costs of defence be borne according to each insurer's liability to pay the judgment against the insured.[104]

Typically, when the limits of the primary policy have been exhausted the terms of the excess coverage will require the excess insurer to defend.[105] Where the limits of the primary policy have not been exhausted but claims have been presented which have the potential to exceed the primary limit, the issue of whether the excess insurer has the right to control the defence of the action may arise. In *Economical Mutual Insurance Co. v. Insurance Corp. of B.C.*[106] the Court held that as between a primary insurer and an excess insurer who both wish to defend, the one with the greater risk of loss should have the right to control the conduct of the defence. The excess insurer, who in this case had the greater risk, was directed by the Court, however, to maintain full consultation with the first loss insurers and their legal representatives.

But what if the excess insurer, although at risk, does not wish to participate in the defence? Provided that both policies contain a defence provision,[107] the primary insurer, by the principle of equitable subrogation, may be able to compel the excess insurer to contribute to defence costs. This issue arose in *Broadhurst & Ball v. American Home Assurance Co.*[108] The insured, a law firm, was exposed to a claim for $20 million. Its insurance coverage consisted of a primary policy with American Home for $500,000 and an excess policy with Guardian for $9,500,000. It was common ground that if the claim succeeded

---

[102] *Skyline Gold Corp. v. American Home Assurance Co.*, [1997] B.C.J. No. 2609, 50 B.C.L.R. (3d) 81, [1998] I.L.R. 1-3518 (S.C.); *Ayr Farmers Mutual Insurance Co. v. CGU Group Canada Ltd.*, [2003] O.J. No. 1523, 64 O.R. (3d) 340 (S.C.J).

[103] See, for example, *Insurance Act*, R.S.A. 1980, c. I-5, s. 335.

[104] *Ibid.*, s. 319.

[105] *Boreal Insurance Inc. v. Lafarge Canada Inc.*, [2004] O.J. No. 1571, 10 C.C.L.I. (4th) 212 (S.C.J.).

[106] [1986] A.J. No. 248, 18 C.C.L.I. 134 (Q.B.).

[107] In the absence of a defence provision an excess insurer is under no duty to defend: *ING Insurance Co. of Canada v. Federated Insurance Co. of Canada*, [2005] O.J. No. 1718, 22 C.C.L.I. (4th) 1 (C.A.).

[108] [1990] O.J. No. 2317, 4 C.C.L.I. (2d) 89 (C.A.), leave to appeal to S.C.C. refd (1991), 79 D.L.R. (4th) vin.

then the damages awarded would likely exceed the combined coverage. Both policies provided that the insurer had the obligation to defend claims which, if proven, would fall within coverage. After an initial denial American Home agreed to defend the claim. Guardian, however, demurred. The Ontario Court of Appeal held that in these circumstances, notwithstanding the lack of any contractual relationship between the two insurers, the primary insurer was entitled under the doctrine of equitable subrogation to compel the excess insurer to pay its fair share of the defence costs. The decision was followed in *Federated Insurance Co. of Canada v. Reliance Insurance Co.*,[109] with the proviso that the ultimate allocation of defence costs would be a matter to be determined after judgment.

(iii) Where Coverage Is Several

On the basis of the decision in *Bacon v. McBride*,[110] where one policy responds to another part of the claim, each insurer is responsible for defending that part of the claim covered under its policy. Where the court does not permit representation by separate counsel, it would be in order for the insurers to retain counsel jointly.[111]

(iv) Where Coverage Is in the Alternative

In some cases, a claim will be such that it falls within one or the other, but not both, of two policies. In *Station Square Developments Inc. v. Amako Construction Ltd.*[112] the insured, a firm of professional engineers, was covered under both a professional liability policy and a comprehensive general liability wrap-up policy. The latter policy contained an exclusion with respect to professional services. An action was brought against the insured arising out of the collapse of a building, the essential allegations being ones of error or omission in the provision of engineering services. Accordingly, the professional liability insurer undertook the defence of the action. Part way through the proceedings, however, counsel for the professional liability insurers sought an order requiring the comprehensive general liability insurer to contribute to the costs of the defence. The Court accepted that there was some possibility that part of the claim might fall within the comprehensive liability coverage and outside of the professional liability coverage. The Court nevertheless refused to grant the relief sought:

> The substance of the claims as put forward to this stage are clearly within the insuring agreements in the Simcoe & Erie and Kansa policies and equally clear within the exclusionary provisions of the Continental policy. So the duty of the professional liability insurers to defend is clear, that of Continental is at best problematical. ...

---

[109] [2001] O.J. No. 4676, [2002] 1 L.R. 1-4054 (S.C.J.).

[110] *Supra*, note 91.

[111] *Prudential Assur. Co. v. Man. Public Ins. Corp.* (1976), 67 D.L.R. (3d) 521 (Man. C.A.).

[112] [1989] B.C.J. No. 1533, 40 C.C.L.I. 292 (S.C.).

... What appears from the cases is that, on an issue of this kind, the court will approach it in a manner which takes into account the realities of the situation, and attempt to balance as best it can the interests of the various parties. The interests of the insured are, as I said earlier, not involved in this issue. The professional liability insurers appear to be much more clearly at risk than is Continental. That is because the claim, in large part if not entirely, falls within the professional liability coverage, and not within the comprehensive liability coverage.

In these circumstances, I consider it appropriate that the professional liability insurers continue to defend. I see no rational basis upon which I could order Continental to contribute to the costs of defence as they are incurred. I think, therefore, that the proper disposition of the matter at this stage is to refuse the declarations sought by the defendants against Continental, but without prejudice to their right at the end of the case to claim indemnity against defence costs in light of the actual outcome of the action, or for the professional insurers who are the real parties in interest against Continental to directly seek contribution.[113]

The decision in *Station Square Developments Inc.* may be seen as an application of the underlying facts exception. As noted earlier,[114] where the insurer takes the position that the claim falls within a policy exclusion some authorities permit the insurer to decline the defence of the claim, subject to the requirement that the insured be reimbursed should it later be determined that the claim is within coverage.

2. APPORTIONMENT AND REIMBURSEMENT OF DEFENCE COSTS

The issue of apportionment of defence costs may arise either (a) when one counsel defends an action that presents both covered and uncovered claims against the insured or (b) when there is more than one policy imposing a defence obligation in respect of the underlying claims.

In the first situation the rule is that the insurer must pay all of the defence costs except those which are solely and undeniably referable to the uncovered claims.[115] The burden of proving which costs are payable by the insured rests with the insurer. If it is not possible to fairly allocate the defense costs between

---

[113] *Ibid.*, at 297, 299.

[114] See section 1(d)(iii): Where the Underlying Facts Bring the Claim within a Policy Exclusion.

[115] *St. Andrews Service Co. v. McCubbin*, [1987] B.C.J. No. 2636, 22 B.C.L.R. (2d) 38, [1988] I.L.R. 1-2305, 31 C.C.L.I. 166 (S.C.), additional reasons at [1988] B.C.J. No. 3117, 29 B.C.L.R. (2d) 305, 31 C.C.L.I. 161 (S.C.); *Surrey (District) v. General Accident Assur. Co. of Can.*, [1994] B.C.J. No. 27, 7 W.W.R. 226, 92 B.C.L.R. (2d) 115, 24 C.C.L.I. (2d) 34, supp. reasons (1994), 24 C.C.L.I. (2d) 50 (S.C.), affd, [1996] B.C.J. No. 849, [1996] 7 W.W.R. 48, 19 B.C.L.R. (3d) 186, 35 C.C.L.I. (2d) 154, [1996] I.L.R. 1-3325 (C.A.); *Continental Insurance Co. v. Dia Met Minerals Ltd.*, [1996] B.C.J. No. 1293, 7 W.W.R. 408, 20 B.C.L.R. (3d) 331 (C.A.); *Gosse v. Huemiller*, [1988] O.J. No. 1595, [1988] I.L.R. 1-2372, 34 C.C.L.I. 265 (H.C.J.).

the covered and the uncovered claims then they must be borne by the insurer.[116] The mere fact that the insured has received an incidental benefit from the defence is not a sufficient basis upon which to order apportionment.[117]

In the second situation the insurers are required to share the defence costs in accordance with the provisions of their respective policies. If the insurers are unable to agree upon the appropriate formula then the court, on an application either by the insured or by one of the insurers, will impose a distribution that is considered equitable in all of the circumstances of the case.[118]

Typically, an insurer will not seek a determination as to apportionment of defence costs against the insured until the underlying action has been resolved,[119] although it is open to the parties either to agree in advance upon a formula or to seek directions from the court.[120] The rationale for a retrospective rather than a prospective determination of the apportionment of defence costs is that it is generally possible to make a fair allocation between covered and uncovered claims only in hindsight.[121] Thus, as a general rule of practice, an insurer faced with defending an action asserting both covered and uncovered claims will agree to defend the entire action subject to a reservation of rights permitting the insurer to seek an allocation of the defence costs at the conclusion of the case.[122] The exception to this general rule will be a case in which, in all of

---

[116] *McRae v. Kitching*, [1997] O.J. No. 4436, 49 C.C.L.I. (2d) 93 (Gen. Div.); *St. Paul Fire & Marine Insurance Co. v. Durabla*, [1994] O.J. No. 1727, 118 D.L.R. (4th) 273, [1994] I.L.R. 1-3101, 19 O.R. (3d) 631 (Gen. Div.), vard [1996] O.J. No. 2505, 137 D.L.R. (4th) 126, 29 O.R. (3d) 737, 92 O.A.C. 157, 36 C.C.L.I. (2d) 25 (C.A.); *Kerr v. Law Profession Indemnity Co.*, [1994] O.J. No. 2, 22 C.C.L.I. (2d) 28 (Gen. Div.), revd, [1995] O.J. No. 2823, 128 D.L.R. (4th) 269, 83 O.A.C. 394, 25 O.R. (3d) 804, [1995] I.L.R. 1-3250 (C.A.); *Daher v. Economical Mutual Ins. Co.*, [1993] O.J. No. 2361, 19 C.C.L.I. (2d) 106, [1994] I.L.R. 1-3007 (Gen. Div.), affd, [1996] O.J. No. 4394, 31 O.R. (3d) 472, 96 O.A.C. 255, [1997] I.L.R. 1-3414 (C.A.); *Hanis v. University of Western Ontario*, [2003] O.J. No. 4167, 5 C.C.L.I. (4th) 277 (S.C.J.); *Ayr Farmers Mutual Insurance Co. v. CGU Group Canada Ltd.*, [2003] O.J. No. 1523, 47 C.C.L.I. (3d) 66 (S.C.J.); *Conservation Council of New Brunswick Inc. v. Encon Group Inc.*, [2005] N.B.J. No. 109, 19 C.C.L.I. (4th) 312 (Q.B.).

[117] *Coronation Insurance Co. v. Clearly Canadian Beverage Corp.*, [1999] B.C.J. No. 43, 168 D.L.R. (4th) 366, [1999] 6 W.W.R. 189, [1999] I.L.R. 1-3651, No. 109, 19 C.C.L.I. (4th) 312 (Q.B.) (C.A.); *New Zealand Forest Products v. New Zealand Insurance Co.*, [1997] 3 N.Z.L.R. 1 (P.C.).

[118] *Alie v. Bertrand & Frère Construction Co.*, [2003] I.L.R. I-4146; *Ayr Farmers Mutual Insurance Co. v. CGU Group Canada Ltd.*, [2003] O.J. No. 1523, 47 C.C.L.I. (3d) 66 (S.C.J.).

[119] *F.W. Hearn/Actes - A Joint Venture Ltd. v. Commonwealth Insurance Co.* [2000] B.C.J. No. 964, 75 B.C.L.R. (3d) 272, [2000] I.L.R. 1-3870, (S.C.); *Continental Insurance Co. v. Dia Met Minerals, Ltd.*, *supra*, note 115.

[120] *Sommerfield v. Lombard Insurance Group*, [2005] O.J. No. 1131, 74 O.R. (3d) 571 (S.C.J.); *Alofs v. Temple Insurance Co.*, [2005] O.J. No. 4372 (S.C.J.).

[121] This is implicitly recognized in *Kelly Panteluk Construction Ltd. v. AXA Pacific Insurance Co.*, [2005] S.J. No. 370, 26 C.C.L.I. (4th) 271 (Q.B.) at para. 28.

[122] The alternative, discussed earlier (See: G. Multiple Causes of Action, One or More of Which Is Outside Coverage) is for the insurer to defend only those claims which it asserts are covered under the policy. This is often impractical for any of a number of reasons, including uncertainty as to which claims are not covered, the existence of overlapping claims, and the difficulties inherent in having two lawyers being separately instructed in the defence of the action.

the circumstances, an equitable allocation of the burden of paying defence costs can be arrived at in advance.[123]

In the situation in which more than one insurer is required to defend the action it is not unusual to see an application brought early on by one insurer against the other seeking an order for an equitable allocation of defence costs, subject to a reapportionment upon the conclusion of the action.[124] On such an application the court may be required to give consideration to the provisions of the respective policies concerning "other insurance".[125]

The issue of reimbursement of defence costs may arise in a variety of circumstances. There is a considerable body of American law with respect to this issue.[126] Great care must be taken in the application in Canada of the American authorities in this regard. Not only may the policy provisions differ substantially,[127] but the issue is often clouded by the related issue of reimbursing settlement moneys. As a matter of principle there is in Canada at least a limited basis upon which an insurer would be entitled to reimbursement of defence costs. Where, for example, the insured has been guilty of a breach of condition with respect to the handling of the claim (for example, making a false report to the insurer regarding the circumstances of the loss) then the insurer may have a claim against the insured for damages from breach of contract, which damages might very well include the defence costs incurred in the underlying action. But if the insurer has, out of caution, defended a claim pending a determination of the duty to defend, then, in the absence of a reimbursement provision either in the insurance policy or in a non-waiver agreement, the insurer should not be entitled to subsequently obtain reimbursement from the insured for the costs of the defence. Such a claim for reimbursement would have to be presented in equity under the law of restitution. Yet, in the absence of mistake, coercion or request, the insurer is in the position of a volunteer and, therefore, should not be able to succeed under equitable principles.

Some Canadian courts have contemplated reimbursement of defence costs in circumstances where the insurer has been required to defend an action notwithstanding an alleged breach of condition by the insured.[128] As noted below,[129] however, the better view is that upon alleging a breach of condition, an

---

[123] *Sommerfield v. Lombard Insurance Group, supra,* note 120.

[124] *Ayr Farmers Mutual Insurance Co. v. CGU Group Canada Ltd., supra,* note 116. *Federated Insurance Co. of Canada v. Reliance Insurance Co.,* [2001] O.J. No. 4676, [2002] 1 L.R. 1-4054 (S.C.J.).

[125] See Chapter 3, section 7: Other Insurance.

[126] *Knapp v. Commonwealth Land Title Ins. Co.,* 932 F. Supp. 1169 (D. Minn. 1996); *Buss v. Superior Court,* 16 Cal. 4th 35, 65 Cal. Rptr. 2d 366, 939 P.2d 766 (Cal. 1997).

[127] Some policies expressly provide for reimbursement: see Annotation, *Validity and Construction of Liability Policy Provision Requiring Insured to Reimburse Insurer for Payments Made under Policy* (1970) 29 A.L.R. (3d) 291.

[128] *SCS Western Corp. v. Dominion of Canada General Insurance Co.,* [1998] A.J. No. 180 [1998] 7 W.W.R. 570, 59 Alta. L.R. (3d) 73, [1998] I.L.R. 1-3561 (Q.B.).

[129] See section 5(b): Where There Has Been a Misrepresentation or a Breach of a Policy Condition.

insurer is not obliged to defend, and thus the issue of reimbursement does not arise.

3. THE SCOPE OF THE DUTY TO DEFEND

The contractual obligation to investigate and defend the action carries with it the obligation to exercise reasonable care and skill in so doing.[130] In *Fredrikson v. Insurance Corp. of B.C.*[131] the Court adopted the following passage from Appleman's *Insurance Law and Practice*:

> It is not an extraordinary degree of care but the care that is required under these particular circumstances. It must use skill diligently and adequately to investigate a case, it must use skill in negotiation, it must select skilled trial counsel — not the lowest priced member of the bar — and that individual, so selected by it, may bind the insurer by his derelictions. It is not a comfortable spot for a liability insurer to occupy, but it seeks the business upon the basis of its skill. Even an attorney, abstractor, accountant, or physician may be liable if he fails to use the degree of skill in the handling of a professional matter which one is entitled to expect of one possessing like training and abilities, so must the insurer accept legal duties commensurate with its responsibilities. A declaration which alleged that the insurer negligently failed to use proper care in the preparation of a case, and that as a result a judgment was recovered against the insured in excess of the policy limits, was held to state a cause of action both in tort and for breach of contract.[132]

In *Shea v. Manitoba Public Insurance Corp.*[133] the British Columbia Supreme Court emphasized that the insurer's duty to defend carried with it an obligation to disclose with reasonable promptitude to the insured all material information touching upon the insured's position both in the litigation and in the settlement negotiations, as well as a duty to ensure that defence preparations and settlement negotiations take place in a timely way. The insurer must advise the insured of the nature and extent of any conflicting interests and must instruct counsel to treat the interests of the insured equally with its own.[134] The insurer's duty to defend includes the obligation to defend on the issue of damages, and to attempt to minimize by all lawful means the amount of any judgment awarded against the insured.[135]

---

[130] *Joe v. Ins. Corp. of B.C.* (1984), 55 B.C.L.R. 118 at 121 (C.A.).

[131] [1990] B.C.J. No. 717, 44 B.C.L.R. (2d) 303 (S.C.).

[132] J. Appleman, *Insurance Law and Practice*, revised ed. (St. Paul: West Publishing Co., 1981) para. 4687 at 181-3.

[133] [1991] B.C.J. No. 711, 55 B.C.L.R. (2d) 15 (S.C.). See also *I.C.B.C. v. Hosseini*, [2006] B.C.J. No. 6 (C.A.).

[134] *Ibid.*, at 69-70.

[135] *Ibid.*

An insurer defending an action on behalf of the insured must therefore carry out a reasonable investigation into the complaint and retain competent counsel on the insured's behalf.[136] Where the claim exceeds the policy limits, a breach of this duty may result in the insurer being held responsible for the excess.[137]

4. THE DUTY TO SETTLE

Unlike the defence clause, which stipulates that the insurer "shall defend" claims on behalf of its insured, the typical clause in a liability insurance policy provides that the insurer may settle any claim "as may be deemed expedient by the insurer". Standing alone, such language gives the insurer the right, but not the duty, to effect a settlement on behalf of its insured. In both the United States and Canada, however, insurers have been held liable in circumstances where they have refused a settlement offer within the policy limits, and an excess judgment has gone against the insured.[138] Liability may similarly be imposed in circumstances involving both covered and uncovered claims, when the insurer has refused to settle the covered claim, with the result that the insured is held liable for the claim that falls outside of coverage.

The American cases do not proceed from a common principle. The insurer's liability for failing to settle a claim has been expressed in terms of tort and also breach of contract.[139] In either case, the courts generally hold that there must be bad faith or lack of due care before liability may be imposed,[140] although some courts have suggested that strict liability should be the rule.[141] Since the duty is one which is owed to the insured, an injured person has no cause of action against an insurer for failing to settle within the policy limits.[142]

In Canada, the issue of the insurer's duty to settle was first touched upon in *Pelky v. Hudson Bay Insurance Co.*,[143] a case in which counsel appointed by the

---

[136] *Travelers Ins. Co. v. Lesher*, 187 Cal. App. 3d 169 (1986).

[137] *McNally v. Nationwide Ins. Co.*, 815 F.2d 254 (3rd Cir. 1987).

[138] G.J. Couch & R.A. Anderson, *Couch Cyclopedia of Insurance Law,* 2nd ed. (Rochester: Lawyers Co-operative Publishing Co., 1984) at para. 51:1; *Shea v. Manitoba Public Ins. Corp., supra,* note 133; *Drummond v. Fortune,* [1994] O.J. No. 2805 (Gen. Div.), affd [1998] O.J. No. 622 (C.A.).

[139] *Venturi v. Zurich General Accident & Liability Ins. Co.*, 57 P.2d 1002 (1936) (breach of contract); *Dumas v. Hartford Accident & Indemnity Co.*, 56 A.2d 57 (1947) (negligence); *Gideon v. State Farm Mutual Automobile Ins. Co.*, 188 A.2d 320 (1963) (bad faith). See generally, R. Andal, "The Insurer's Duty to Settle within Policy Limits: Learning from the American Experience" (1989) 1 C.I.L.R. 233.

[140] Couch, *supra*, note 138, para. 51:1, 51:7.

[141] *Crisci v. Security Ins. Co.*, 426 P.2d 173 (1967).

[142] *Karamanolis v. Prudential Ins. Co.* (1983), 42 O.R. (2d) 752 (H.C.J.). *Cf. Drummond v. Fortune, supra*, note 138, in which it was held that the insurer was liable to the plaintiffs for pre-judgment interest in addition to the policy limits. The insurer knew that the claim would exceed the limits and ignored a demand by plaintiff's counsel to place the limits in an interest-bearing account. Apparently the insurer preferred to maintain the funds for its own use as long as possible.

[143] (1981), 35 O.R. (2d) 97 (H.C.J.).

insurer to defend the action on behalf of the insured negligently failed to relay to either party the plaintiff's offer to settle the claim for the policy limits. The action proceeded to trial, with the result that an excess judgment was awarded against the insured. The insured then sought an order that the insurer pay the excess and referred the Court to American authority dealing with the obligation of the insurer to settle claims within the policy limits. It was conceded by counsel for the insurer, however, that the insurer was vicariously liable for the negligence of the lawyer appointed to assume conduct of the defence. Since the insurer acknowledged that it would have accepted the settlement offer had it been received, the Court chose not to reach any conclusion on the obligation of the insurer to settle claims within the policy limits. Instead, the Court simply held the insurer vicariously liable for the negligence of its lawyer.

The issue next arose for consideration in *Dillon v. Guardian Insurance Co.*[144] Although the Court in *Dillon* held that the insurer was under a duty to settle claims within the policy limits, the Court, unfortunately, did not consider it necessary to reach a conclusion as to the basis for that duty. The facts of the case are somewhat sketchy in the reasons for judgment. The insurer apparently could have settled a claim for $45,000, which was within the policy limits of $50,000. Counsel appointed by the insurer to defend the claim had expressed the opinion that liability would be found against the insured and that damages would be assessed at $43,000. The insurer's instructions were, apparently, to go no higher than $40,000. When the case went to trial, the injured party obtained a judgment for $78,000. In the insured's action against the insurer for payment of the excess portion of the judgment, the Court made note of the various standards applied in the United States. The Court stated that the strict liability approach was persuasive but found that, on the facts, the insurer acted both negligently and in bad faith. Accordingly, the Court chose not to reach a conclusion as to which standard should be applied in Canada.

The strict liability approach, which received favourable consideration in *Dillon*, was rejected by the British Columbia Supreme Court in *Fredrikson v. Insurance Corp. of B.C.*[145] The trial judge found, on the facts, that the insurer had acted in a fair and open manner and had followed the course that its insured wished it to take. In the circumstances, although the Court recognized that in some cases there could be a basis for holding the insurer liable for failing to settle a claim within policy limits, the Court did not consider it appropriate to reach a conclusion as to the basis upon which that duty arises.

In *Shea v. Manitoba Public Insurance Corp.* the British Columbia Supreme Court summarized the law touching upon the insurer's duty to settle as follows:

1. The relationship between the insurer and insured is a commercial one, in which the parties have their own rights and obligations;

---

[144] (1983), 2 C.C.L.I. 227 (Ont. H.C.J.).

[145] *Supra*, note 131. See also *Adams v. Confederation Life Ins. Co.*, [1994] A.J. No. 308, [1994] 6 W.W.R. 662, 18 Alta. L.R. (3d) 324, [1994] I.L.R. 1-3096, 25 C.C.L.I. (2d) 180 (Q.B.).

2. Within the commercial relationship, special duties may arise over and above the universal duty of honesty, which do not reach the fiduciary standard of selflessness and loyalty;

3. The exclusive discretionary power to settle liability claims given by statute to the insurer in this case, places the insured at the mercy of the insurer;

4. The insured's position of vulnerability imposes on the insurer the duties:
   a) of good faith and fair dealing;
   b) to give at least as much consideration to the insured's interests as it does to its own interests; and
   c) to disclose with reasonable promptitude to the insured all material information touching upon the insured's position in the litigation, and in the settlement negotiations.

5. The fact that the insured is at the mercy of the insurer for the purposes of settlement negotiations gives rise to a justified expectation in the insured that the insurer will not act contrary to the interests of the insured, or will, at least, fully advise the insured of its intention to do so;

6. While the commercial nature of the relationship permits an insurer to assert or defend interests which are opposed to, or are inconsistent with, the interests of its insured, the duty to deal fairly and in good faith requires the insurer to advise the insured that conflicting interests exist, and of the nature and extent of the conflict;

7. The insurer's statutory obligation to defend its insured imposes on the insurer, where conflicting interests arise, a duty to instruction counsel to treat the interests of the insured equally with its own; and where one counsel cannot adequately represent both conflicting interests, an obligation to instruct separate counsel to act solely for the insureds, at the insurer's own costs;

8. The insurer's duty to defend includes the obligation to defend on the issue of damages, and to attempt to minimize by all lawful means the amount of any judgment awarded against the insured. In this case that would include arguing that court order interest and no fault benefits are payable in addition to the policy limits, where such an argument is available in law; and

9. Defence preparations and settlement negotiations must take place in a timely way, and, where last minute negotiations are required, advance planning must be made to ensure that the insured's interests are given equal protection with those of the insurer.[146]

The facts in *Shea* are somewhat complicated by the byzantine provisions of British Columbia's motor vehicle insurance legislation.[147] The Manitoba Public Insurance Corporation ("M.P.I.C.") had issued to its insured a motor vehicle policy with a $300,000 third party limit. It was not clear whether accident benefits and pre-judgment interest were payable in addition to that limit. The plaintiff, an injured infant, took tort proceedings against the insured and separate no-fault proceedings against the insurer. M.P.I.C. appointed one counsel to defend both actions. It became apparent early on that the insured was liable and that damages would greatly exceed the third party limit. The insurer then

---

[146] [1991] B.C.J. No. 711, 55 B.C.L.R. (2d) 15 at 69-70, [1991] I.L.R. 1-2721 (S.C.). See also *I.C.B.C. v. Hosseini, supra*, note 133.

[147] See the comments of Seaton J.A. in *Shea v. Shea* (1985), 66 B.C.L.R. 92 at 96 (C.A.).

instructed counsel to maintain the position that the no-fault benefits were deductible from the third party limit. The insured was not notified of this position, even though it plainly affected the insured's interests, for it exposed him to a larger excess judgment. The plaintiff offered to accept the third party limit of $300,000 in full settlement of the tort action, provided that he was free to pursue the action for no-fault benefits. The offer was refused and the tort action went to trial. Judgment went against the insured for an amount in excess of $900,000. In subsequent litigation the insurer was required to pay the entire amount of the judgment. It was held that in the settlement negotiations the insurer had an obligation to give at least as much consideration to the insured's interests as to its own and that it had failed to do so.

The standard applied in *Shea* was that the interests of the insurer and the insured are entitled to equal protection. This "balancing of interests" approach is also found in some of the American jurisprudence.[148] Yet other courts in the United States have adopted a different standard. The test applied by the latter courts in determining whether an insurer ought to have accepted a settlement offer is whether a prudent person would have accepted the offer if he or she were solely liable for the claim.[149] In a given case these two tests may yield different results, for a consideration of the insured's interests may lead to the conclusion that the case should be settled, although if one were solely liable for the claim it may be preferable to take the case to trial.

The insurer's duty to settle is based upon the facts that are or should be known to the insurer on the basis of a reasonable investigation.[150] Thus, one of the consequences of failing to adequately investigate and defend a claim is that an insurer may unwittingly find itself in breach of the duty to settle and be liable for an excess judgment.

In addition to the situation presented by a claim in excess of the policy limits, the duty to settle may arise in circumstances in which the claim is within the policy limits but asserts both covered and non-covered causes of action. An example would be where punitive damages are claimed.[151] In these circumstances the insurer is obliged to give due regard to the interests of the insured and to work cooperatively and in good faith with the insured to settle the entire claim.

Moreover, an insurer cannot, in good faith, pressure the insured into a settlement which does not reasonably take the insured's interests into account. In *West American Insurance Co. v. Freeman*[152] the insurer, under a reservation of rights, defended a third party action on behalf of its insured contractor. The action included both covered and non-covered claims. The insurer obtained numerous experts exonerating the insured. One of these reports cast blame upon

---

[148] *Petts v. Allstate Ins. Co.*, 154 Cal. App.3d 688 (1984).

[149] *United States Fire Ins. Co. v. Royal Ins. Co.*, 759 F.2d 306 (3rd Cir. 1985).

[150] *Riske v. Truck Ins. Exch.*, 490 F.2d 1079 (8th Cir. 1974).

[151] *Magnum Foods, Inc. v. Continental Casualty Co.*, 36 F.3d 1491 (10th Cir. 1994).

[152] 37 Cal. App. 4th 1469 (1995).

the structural engineer. The insurer, concerned by the costs of defending the action chose not to join the engineer in the action and instead proposed to settle with the plaintiff for $40,000, being the cost of structural repairs. The proposed settlement preserved the insurer's right to seek recoupment of the settlement proceeds from the insured. The insurer advised the insured that if it did not agree with this settlement then it would cease paying defence costs and would pay no more than $40,000 in the event of a judgment being granted in favour of the plaintiff. The insured succumbed to this financial pressure and entered into the settlement. The insurer then sued the insured for recoupment of the settlement moneys and defence costs. The insured counterclaimed for damages for bad faith. The counterclaim succeeded; the insured was awarded compensatory damages of $1,316,000 and punitive damages of $12 million.

5. PROCEEDINGS TO DETERMINE THE DUTY TO DEFEND

Where proceedings have been brought against the insured and an issue arises as to whether or not the insurer is required to defend, the issue is often resolved either by way of third party proceedings or by declaratory proceedings. It is usually in the interest of both parties to have an early determination of this issue.[153] The insured is often not easily able to bear the financial burden of defending a claim. In such cases, the insurer will be reluctant to leave the defence in the hands of the insured, for if it is later found that there *is* coverage under the policy then the insurer will not be heard to say that the claim should have been defended differently.[154] Although it has been held that the limitation period for commencing a proceeding to enforce the duty to defend is one year from the date of an unequivocal denial,[155] the decision is of dubious authority.[156]

Proceedings by the insured to enforce the defence provisions of the insurance contract have been permitted notwithstanding the "no-action" clause in the insurance contract. Such clauses typically provide that no action may be brought against the insurer until the insured's liability has been determined by a judgment. It has been held by the Ontario Court of Appeal[157] that such clauses apply only with respect to the indemnity provisions of the contract. Although the British Columbia Court of Appeal did not agree with this interpretation,[158]

---

[153] *Hironaka v. Co-Operators General Insurance Co.*, [2005] A.J. No. 1313 (Q.B.).

[154] *Davis v. Associated Indemnity Corp.*, 56 F. Supp. 541, affd 150 F.2d 1005 (3rd Cir. 1945).

[155] *Canadian Northern Shield v. Demers*, [2004] B.C.J. No. 650, 10 C.C.L.I. (4th) 230 (S.C.).

[156] See Chapter 3, section 5: Action Against Insurer.

[157] *Great West Steel Industries v. Simcoe & Erie General Ins. Co.* (1979), 106 D.L.R. (3d) 347 (Ont. C.A.); *Tinker v. Zurich Ins. Co.*, [1990] O.J. No. 1119 [1990] I.L.R. 1-2622 (C.A.). See also *SCS Western Corp. v. Dominion of Canada General Insurance Co.*, [1998] A.J. No. 180, 7 W.W.R. 570, 59 Alta. L.R. (3d) 73, [1998] I.L.R. 1-3561 (Q.B.); *cf. Svetlichny v. Overend, Davidson & Co.* (1982), 33 B.C.L.R. 214 (C.A.); and *Rivtow Straits Ltd. v. Commonwealth Ins. Co.*, [1992] B.C.J. No. 3052, 7 C.C.L.I. (2d) 184 (S.C.).

[158] *Svetlichny v. Overend, Davidson & Co., ibid.* See also *Conrad v. Snair*, [1994] N.S.J. No. 251, 115 D.L.R. (4th) 414, 376 A.P.R. 126, 132 N.S.R. (2d) 126, 25 C.P.C. (3d) 1 (C.A.).

neither did it hold that the no-action clause was automatically a bar to third party proceedings against the insurer. Rather, it was but one of several factors to take into account. In Ontario, legislation has been enacted providing that such clauses are void.[159]

There are two mechanisms available for determining the duty to defend. One method, which is open only to the insured, is to issue third party proceedings against the insurer in the underlying action. The other method, which is available to both the insurer and the insured, is to take declaratory proceedings seeking a summary determination of the duty to defend.

In the United States, rather than being dealt with in the underlying action, issues regarding the duty to defend are usually the subject of separate declaratory proceedings. This is now becoming the norm in Canada.[160] In *Axa Pacific Insurance Co. v. Elwood*[161] the Supreme Court of British Columbia concluded that the proper forum for determining the issue of the duty to defend is in separate declaratory proceedings rather than by way of third party proceedings[162]. The advantage of a declaratory proceeding, commenced by a petition, is that it provides for a summary resolution of the issue, without the need for discovery of documents and examination for discovery. As the Ontario Court of Appeal noted in *Halifax Insurance Co. of Canada v. Innopex Ltd.*:

> Motions or applications to determine whether an insurance company has a duty to defend a policyholder who is a defendant in an underlying lawsuit are intended to be decided expeditiously. Invariably, such proceedings are decided by reading the claim or claims asserted in the statement of claim in the underlying action with the coverage provided by the insurance policy. If one or more of the claims in the underlying action fall within the coverage, the insurer has a duty to defend the action on behalf of the insured. As the Supreme Court of Canada has observed, a duty to defend application should not be permitted to become "a trial within a trial". does not in the underlying action.[163]

The ordinary rules of practice regarding third party procedure, however, are not necessarily appropriate for the proper determination of this sort of dispute. An insured, for example, subject to the applicability of the no-action clause, has the right to commence third party proceedings against the insurer, but where the insured fails to do so it is questionable whether the insurer can add itself either

---

[159] *Courts of Justice Act*, R.S.O. 1990, c. C.43.

[160] See, for example, *Danric Construction Ltd. v. Canadian Surety Co.*, [2002] B.C.J. No. 2699, 50 C.C.L.I. (3d) 201 (S.C.); *Federated Insurance Co. of Canada v. Reliance Insurance Co.*, [2001] O.J. No. 4676, [2002] 1 L.R. 1-4054 (S.C.J.); *East Kootenay Realty Ltd. v. Gestas Inc.* (1986), 21 C.C.L.I. 230 (B.C.S.C.).

[161] [2000] B.C.J. No. 1738, 20 C.C.L.I. (3d) 168.

[162] In *Unrau v. Canadian Northern Shield Insurance Co.*, [2004] B.C.J. No. 2409, 15 C.C.L.I. (4th) 189 (C.A.), the British Columbia Court of Appeal questioned whether third party proceedings would have been a more appropriate method for determining an issue as to the duty to defend. The parties in *Unrau*, however, had proceeded by way of petition and there was no issue before the Court as to the appropriateness of that form of proceeding.

[163] [2004] O.J. No. 4178 at para. 1, 15 C.C.L.I. (4th) 159 (C.A.).

as a defendant[164] or third party[165] on its own volition. Moreover, once having been added as a third party it may not be appropriate for the insurer to have the right, usually given to third parties, to defend the main action, for in so doing the insurer might act in a fashion contrary to its insured's interests.[166] Further, third party proceedings typically provide the parties with rights of discovery, which are not usually necessary for the purpose of determining the duty to defend and may hinder or delay a timely and efficient resolution of the issue.

Although in some cases the insured will ask the court to rule on whether there is a duty to indemnify as well as to defend, it is generally considered to be inappropriate to rule on indemnity at this stage. Rather, indemnity can usually not be determined until after the findings at trial.[167]

If successful in proceedings to establish the duty to defend, the insured may be entitled to solicitor and client costs.[168] In *E.M. v. Reed* the Ontario Court of Appeal stated:

> Entitlement to solicitor-and-client costs in the third party proceeding flows directly from the unique nature of the insurance contract which entails a duty to defend at no expense to the insured. The obligation to save harmless the insured from the costs of defending the action is sufficiently broad to encompass the third party proceedings. It is the contractual basis for the claim to solicitor-and-client costs that justifies the award and therefore constitutes an exception to the usual rule that solicitor-and-client costs will not be awarded except in unusual circumstances.
>
> ·   I note that English jurisprudence also appears to support the award of solicitor-and-client costs in such situations. See R. Merkin, *Colinvaux's Law of Insurance*, 7th ed. (London: Sweet & Maxwell, 1997) at 405:

---

[164] *Waterloo Ins. Co. v. Zurbrigg* (1983), 43 O.R. (2d) 219 (C.A.), leave to appeal to S.C.C. refd (1984), 2 O.A.C. 320. *Cf. Bryant v. Korres Moving & Transfer Ltd.*, [1989] B.C.J. No. 1694 (Co. Ct.).

[165] *Evans v. Steinberg Inc.* (1988), 35 C.C.L.I. 119 (Ont. Dist. Ct.); *cf. Block v. Heck*, [1991] M.J. No. 539, 5 C.C.L.I. (2d) 134 (Q.B.).

[166] *Gatt v. Rumack*, [1994] O.J. No. 3054, 21 O.R. (3d) 655 (Gen. Div.); *Waterloo Ins. Co. v. Zurbrigg, supra*, note 164; *Porretta v. Stock* (1989), 67 O.R. (2d) 736 (C.A.). See also *Tilbury Cement Ltd. v. Seaspan International Ltd.*, [1991] B.C.J. No. 3473, 8 B.C.A.C. 74 (C.A.). There is an exception in this regard with respect to automobile liability policies where, by statute, the insurer may add itself as a third party in order to contest the insured's liability in the underlying action, which right, it must be noted, does not extend to any determination of the issues as between the insurer and the insured: see *Parlee v. Pembridge Insurance Co.*, [2005] N.B.J. No. 74, 22 C.C.L.I. (4th) 223 (C.A.); *McMurachy v. Red River Valley Mutual Ins. Co.*, [1994] M.J. No. 220, 115 D.L.R. (4th) 220, [1994] 6 W.W.R. 99, 92 Man. R. (2d) 225, [1994] I.L.R. 1-3093 (C.A.), leave to appeal to S.C.C. refd [1994] S.C.C.A. No. 267, 178 N.R. 396*n*; and *Evans v. Steinberg Inc.*, [1988] O.J. No. 1366, 35 C.C.L.I. 119 (Dist. Ct.).

[167] *Kamco Installation Ltd. v. Chilliwack (District)*, [1991] B.C.J. No. 2438, [1992] I.L.R. 1-2790 (S.C.); *British Aviation Insurance Group (Canada) Ltd. v. West Central Air Ltd.*, [1997] S.J. No. 357, 156 Sask. R. 77 (Q.B.).

[168] *E.M. v. Reed*, [2003] O.J. No. 1791 (C.A.); *Godonoaga (Litigation Guardian of) v. Khatambakhsh*, [2000] O.J. No. 3807, 191 D.L.R. (4th) 221 (C.A.); *Carwardine (Litigation Guardian of) v. Northumberland Clarington Board of Education*, [2001] O.J. No. 63 (C.A.); *Dionne Farms Ltd. v. Fermes Gervais Ltée*, [2002] N.B.J. No. 402 (C.A.).

> The assured is entitled to any costs reasonably incurred by him in re-
> sisting a claim, by way of damages, where the insurers wrongfully
> repudiate liability on the policy, and the insurers will face liability for
> any costs incurred by the assured in forcing the insurers to admit li-
> ability under the policy. [emphasis added]

> The American case law similarly favours the view that where an insurer
> breaches its duty to defend and the insured is required to bring a declaratory
> action to establish the duty, the insured should be reimbursed for those costs
> that are attributable to establishing the duty.[169]

In the United States it is common for the insurer, rather than the insured, to
be the one seeking a determination on the duty to defend.[170] In such proceedings
the insurer will typically seek a declaration that it is not required to defend·on
one or more of the following grounds:

(i) The allegations do not present a claim within coverage;
(ii) The insured is guilty of either a misrepresentation or a breach of a
policy condition;
(iii) Although the allegations present a claim within coverage, the
underlying facts establish that an exclusion applies.

(a) Where the Allegations Do Not Present a Claim within Coverage

Where the basis for the insurer's refusal to defend is that the allegations do not
present a claim within coverage, the issue as to whether or not that refusal is
justified can usually be readily determined in a summary fashion. The court will
be called upon to decide only one issue: whether the pleadings disclose a claim
that, if proven, would fall within the coverage afforded under the policy.[171] This
situation arose in *Opron Maritimes Construction Ltd. v. Canadian Indemnity
Co.*[172] The insured declined to defend various claims brought against the
insured, who, as a result, commenced proceedings seeking a declaration that the
insurer was obliged to defend. In the declaratory proceedings, the Court held
that the pleadings in the main action disclosed a claim which was clearly outside
coverage. Accordingly, the insured's application was denied.

In a somewhat unusual case,[173] notwithstanding that the claim, as pleaded,
fell within a policy exclusion, the insured asserted that the scope of coverage
had been misrepresented by the insurer's agent and, accordingly, sought a
declaration that the insurer provide a defence. Faced with conflicting evidence,

---

[169] [2003] O.J. No. 1791 at para. 22 (C.A.).

[170] In *Comeau v. Roy*, [1999] N.B.J. No. 365, 178 D.L.R. (4th) 115, 555 A.P.R. 242, [2000] I.L.R.
1-3743 (C.A.) the New Brunswick Court of Appeal favoured the view that an insurer seeking to
deny coverage for breach of condition should promptly take proceedings to seek a declaratory
order. Failure to do so in a timely fashion may be result in the court refusing to grant costs.

[171] See section 1(a): The Pleadings Rule.

[172] (1986), 19 C.C.L.I. 168 (N.B.C.A.).

[173] *Farrant v. Low*, [1998] O.J. No. 449 (Gen. Div.).

the Court was unable to make any finding with respect to the alleged misrepresentation, and concluded that until such determination had been made the insurer was required to provide a defence. The decision is based upon a misunderstanding of the pleadings rule. The rule that an insurer must defend a claim potentially within coverage arises from the contractual obligation imposed on the insurer by the defence clause, which in the *Farrant* case required the insurer to "... defend you against any suit which makes claims against you for which you are insured under Coverage E ...". Since the claim in question was not covered under Coverage E the insured was not entitled to a defence. The insured cannot create a contractual obligation simply by alleging a misrepresentation.

(b) Where There Has Been a Misrepresentation or a Breach of a Policy Condition

Although the claim may fall within coverage, the insurer may nevertheless decline to defend the proceeding on the basis that there has been a misrepresentation or a breach of a policy condition — for example, the condition requiring the timely reporting of the incident which gave rise to the claim. In such cases it may or may not be convenient, depending upon the extent to which the facts concerning the alleged breach are in dispute, to determine in a summary proceeding the merits of the insurer's refusal to defend.

In *East Kootenay Realty Ltd. v. Gestas Inc.*,[174] for example, the insurer refused to defend on the basis of an alleged non-disclosure by the insured in its application for liability insurance. In a summary proceeding brought by the insured for a declaration that the insurer was obliged to defend, the Court granted the relief sought on the basis that sufficient facts were available, by way of affidavit evidence, to determine the issue of non-disclosure in the insured's favour. Had the insurer been able to establish the non-disclosure, then the insurer would have been released from the duty to defend. Had a triable issue been raised, then a separate trial would have been directed to deal with the issue of non-disclosure.

Where the issue of the insurer's obligation to defend cannot be determined summarily, there is conflicting authority as to whether the insurer must defend the action in the interim. As discussed below, some courts have held that in these circumstances the insurer must defend, other courts have held that the insurer cannot be compelled to defend unless and until the issue has been resolved in the insured's favour and other courts support a flexible approach, namely, that the issue should be determined upon a consideration of the circumstances of each case, including the relative strength of the positions asserted by the insurer and the insured and the necessity and urgency of furnishing the insured with a separate defence.

---

[174] [1986] B.C.J. No. 1569, 21 C.C.L.I. 230 (S.C.).

In *Agassiz Enterprises (1980) Ltd. v. General Accident Assurance Co. of Canada Ltd.*,[175] the insured ski resort operator, contrary to the terms of its liability insurance policy, failed to report an incident to the insurer until an action was commenced almost three years later. The insurer, citing the policy breach, declined to defend. The insured then brought an action for a declaration that the policy required the insurer to defend. The facts concerning the alleged breach of condition were hotly disputed and could not be resolved by way of affidavit evidence in a summary hearing. In these circumstances, the Manitoba Court of Appeal held that the insurer could not be obliged to defend until the issue had been determined following a trial. Until such time the burden of defending the claim fell upon the insured.

The opposite conclusion was reached by the Nova Scotia Court of Appeal in *Dominion of Canada General Insurance Co. v. MacCulloch.*[176] The insurer declined to defend under a garage policy on the basis that the insured had breached a policy condition requiring the prompt reporting of accidents. In the Court's view, however, under the policy wording in question the insurer could rely upon a breach of condition only for the purpose of denying indemnity. With respect, the Court of Appeal's reasoning in this regard is erroneous. If the Court's reasoning were correct it would follow that the insurer would have to defend even though, due to a breach of condition, there could be no possibility of indemnity. Yet that is not what the policy provided. The conditions were stated to be applicable to Coverage III of the policy, which contained the indemnity provisions. The defence provisions were in a separate part of the policy, but were prefaced by the phrase, "As respects insurance against legal liability for compensatory damages afforded by this policy, under Coverage III (Liability), the Insurer shall ... defend ...". Provided the insured was in breach of a policy condition it would follow, in the absence of relief against forfeiture, that indemnity was no longer available. Since the defence provision was expressly limited to the insurance afforded under Coverage III, neither would there be a duty to defend.

The same result, but with different reasoning, was reached by the Alberta Court of Queen's Bench in *Canadian Linen Supply Co. v. Canadian Indemnity Co.*[177] The insurer declined to defend a claim for damages arising out of a motor

---

[175] [1988] M.J. No. 118, 49 D.L.R. (4th) 415 (C.A.), revg [1987] M.J. No. 462, 43 D.L.R. (4th) 757 (Q.B.). See also *Continental Ins. Co. v. M.T.C. Electronic Technologies Co.*, [1995] I.L.R. 1-3238 (B.C.S.C.); *Veillieux (Litigation Guardian of) v. Chambers*, [1995] O.J. No. 2755, 25 O.R. (3d) 538, [1996] I.L.R. 1-3262 (Gen. Div.); *Societa Italiana Assicurazioni Trasporti v. Canadian Marine Underwriters Ltd.*, [1994] O.J. No. 3130, 26 C.C.L.I. (2d) 274 (Gen. Div.); *Laughlin v. Sharon High Voltage Inc.*, [1993] O.J. No. 73, [1993] I.L.R. 1-2934 (Gen. Div.); *Litton Systems Canada Ltd. v. Olympia Engineering Ltd.*, [1990] O.J. No. 2428, 1 O.R. (3d) 780 (Gen. Div.); *Carter v. Kerr*, [1990] B.C.J. No. 715, 69 D.L.R. (4th) 542 (C.A.).

[176] [1991] N.S.J. No. 78, 2 C.C.L.I. (2d) 267 (C.A.).

[177] [1987] A.J. No. 951, 27 C.C.L.I. 248 (Q.B.). See also the trial decision in *Hamilton v. Laurentian Pacific Ins. Co.*, [1988] B.C.J. No. 439, 30 C.C.L.I. 204 (S.C.) in which the trial judge was apparently of the view that an insurer must defend notwithstanding an allegation that the insured was in breach of a condition. On the appeal, reported at [1989] B.C.J. No. 869, 37

vehicle accident, citing an alleged breach of a policy condition. On the insured's application for an order directing the insurer to defend, the Court was not able to determine whether a breach of condition had taken place. In these circumstances, the Court held that the insurer was required to defend although it may have had an enforceable claim against the insured by reason of a breach of the policy. Mr. Justice McLean stated as follows:

> If the insurer is entitled to refuse to defend then the only remedy for such a breach of the policy is by way of damages after the primary lawsuit is over. Such an approach would render the insurer's duty to defend meaningless and capable of being dealt with arbitrarily to the prejudice and detriment of the insured.[178]

A similar sentiment was expressed in *Slough Estates Canada Ltd. v. Federal Pioneer Ltd.*[179] The insurer refused to defend an action brought against its insured on the basis that the allegations, if proven, would fall outside of the insuring agreement and that, in any event, the policy was void for material non-disclosure. The Court held that the allegations did raise a claim potentially within coverage and ordered the insurer to defend, notwithstanding its assertion of material non-disclosure, for:

> If this argument were correct and the Federal application should be dismissed simply on the basis of the pleading of material nondisclosure, then any insurer could so plead and avoid the separate and distinct obligation to the insured to defend. That is not the law. The material non-disclosure can be part of the summary judgment motion as it is in this case or can be determined at trial as it may be if the motion for summary judgment is unsuccessful. The mere pleading of material non-disclosure should not defeat the plaintiff's right to have the insurer defend the action.[180]

Yet in *Continental Insurance Co. v. M.T.C. Electronic Technologies Co.*[181] the British Columbia Supreme Court declined to follow *Slough*, noting:

> ... where an insurer has placed at issue, in proceedings commenced for that purpose, the essential validity of the policy, the issue as to the obligation to defend or indemnify must be resolved within the action by judgment before the

---

C.C.L.I. 190, the British Columbia Court of Appeal declined to deal with that aspect of the case, noting that the duty to defend had not been determined in the court below.

[178] *Ibid.* at 249.

[179] [1994] O.J. No. 2147, 20 O.R. (3d) 429, [1995] I.L.R. 1-3129 (Gen. Div.). Followed in *SCS Western Corp. v. Dominion of Canada General Ins. Co.*, [1998] A.J. No. 180, [1998] 7 W.W.R. 570, 59 Alta. L.R. (3d) 73, [1998] I.L.R. 1-3561. *Cf. Royal & Sun Alliance Ins. Co. of Canada v. Fiberglas Canada*, [1999] O.J. 1275 (C.A.), [1999] I.L.R. 1-3698, 2 C.C.L.I. (3d) 282 (Gen. Div.).

[180] *Slough Estates v. Federal Pioneer, ibid.* at 443.

[181] *Supra*, note 175.

insurer can be compelled to either defend or indemnify with reference to separate proceedings.[182]

In *Veillieux (Litigation Guardian of) v. Chambers*, which was decided without reference to *Slough Estates*, an Ontario court noted:

> The Ontario cases make it clear that once the insurer alleges breach of contract then the insurer owes no duty to defend pending a determination of the alleged breach of condition by the insured. All that is required in this regard to suspend the duty to defend is a simple assertion on the part of the insurer of an alleged breach.[183]

These conflicting authorities were reviewed by the Ontario Court of Justice in the 1999 decision in *Royal & Sun Alliance Insurance Co. of Canada v. Fiberglas Canada Inc.*[184] The Court noted that the preponderance of authority supports the view that where there is an alleged breach of a policy condition the insurer should not be compelled to defend the underlying action. The Court considered this to be the correct approach and purported to distinguish the decision in *Slough* on the dubious ground that it involved an allegation of material non-disclosure rather than a breach of condition. Since both matters provide grounds upon which the insurer can forfeit coverage there is no valid basis for drawing a distinction between the two insofar as the duty to defend is concerned.

In *Longo v. Maciorowski*,[185] which involved a motor vehicle liability policy, the Ontario Court of Appeal expressed a preference for a flexible approach to this issue:

> It is apparent that the preponderance of authority is consistent with the order made by Kiteley J. in the present case. As the division of judicial opinion makes clear, however, different fact situations raise different policy considerations that must be examined in order to determine whether, in any particular case, the insurer should be compelled to furnish, or excused from furnishing, a separate and independent defence for its insured. For that reason, I have reservations about the wisdom of establishing any hard and fast rule on the subject.
>
> Suppose, for example, that the rule would be that the insurer is never obliged to defend in any case upon the mere allegation of breach of condition. Assume, as well, an insured person who is without income and without assets. It cannot be of much comfort to that insured to be told that, while his insurer cannot be compelled to defend him and that he must provide and finance his own defence, he can — if the alleged breach of condition is not proven or if estoppel is established or relief from forfeiture is granted — sue his insurer

---

[182] *Ibid.*, at 3631.

[183] [1995] O.J. No. 2755, 25 O.R. (3d) 538 at 547 (Gen. Div.).

[184] *Supra*, note 179.

[185] [2000] O.J. No. 3632, 23 C.C.L.I. (3d) 1 (C.A.), application for leave to appeal dismissed [2000] S.C.C.A. No. 620. See also *Drane v. Optimum Frontier Insurance Co.*, [2004] N.B.J. No. 251, 11 C.C.L.I. (4th) 163 (C.A.); *Bejinariu v. Primmum Insurance Co.*, [2004] O.J. No. 516 (S.C.J.).

later to recoup the costs of his defence and perhaps damages for breach of his insurer's obligation to him.

Suppose, conversely, that the rule would be that the insurer is always obliged to defend, notwithstanding its allegation of breach of condition, so long as the plaintiff's claim falls within the policy coverage. Assume, again, an impecunious insured. It cannot be of much comfort to the insurer to be told that, while it is obliged to provide its insured with a defence, it can — if the alleged breach of condition is proven and if estoppel is rejected and relief from forfeiture is denied — sue its insured later to recover the costs of that defence.

With respect, I do not place much confidence in the solution suggested in Featherstone, endorsed in Laughlin and followed in Colitti, that the tort action should be put on hold while the breach of condition issue is decided "on an expedited basis". That solution may be practical where the issue admits of summary disposition: where the breach of condition is clear and the case for estoppel or relief from forfeiture unmeritorious or, conversely, where the breach of condition is technical or insubstantial and the case for estoppel or relief from forfeiture overwhelming. But in the many cases that are not clear — where the alleged breach of condition, the basis of the alleged estoppel or the grounds for relief from forfeiture are in serious dispute and require the testimony of witnesses and the resolution of conflicting evidence — there seems to me to be no justification for compelling the trial of the plaintiff's tort action to await the final disposition of the breach of condition issue.

Thus, rather than establishing an immutable legal principle, I would suggest that the question should be determined upon consideration of the circumstances of each case, including the relative strength of the positions asserted by the insurer and the insured and the necessity and urgency to furnish the insured with a separate defence.[186]

The court in *Longo* found against the insured on the basis that the insurer had made allegations of clear and uncontested breaches of condition on the part of the insured, no material had been put forward to support a claim for estoppel or relief from forfeiture, the insurer had invoked the statutory mechanism to be added as a third party in the action and, as statutory third party, the insurer had contested both the liability of the insured and the amount of the claim made against him in language that was congruent with the interests of the insured and adopted by him almost verbatim in the preparation of his own statement of defence.

As a matter of public policy there is much to commend the flexible approach. The refusal of the insurer to provide a defence has the potential to cause considerable harm to the insured. Where the refusal to defend is without merit this could result in a substantial injustice. Nevertheless, the flexible approach must be supported on a proper juridical foundation. An order requiring the insurer to defend an insured alleged to be in breach of the policy of insurance amounts to the issuance of a mandatory interlocutory injunction, a remedy

---

[186] *Ibid.*, at paras. 32 *et seq.*

which is granted only in exceptional circumstances.[187] As a general rule, an injunction is not an appropriate remedy if an award of damages can afford adequate relief. Thus, in the absence of irreparable harm, the correct approach in these circumstances is to refuse an order requiring the insurer to defend an insured alleged to be in breach. Should the insurer's assertion of a breach of condition by the insured later prove to be erroneous, however, the consequences for the insurer could be very serious.[188] An insurer is therefore well-advised to be very sure of its ground before denying coverage for an alleged breach of condition.

(c) Where the Underlying Facts Establish That the Claim Is Excluded

Some authorities suggest even when the pleadings present a claim that is within coverage the insurer is not required to defend the claim if the underlying facts bring the claim within one of the policy exclusions.[189] In cases of this sort, the determination of the duty to defend is often not amenable to resolution in a summary fashion. The facts giving rise to the exclusion are often inextricably bound up with the facts of the claim itself. The court is thus being asked in declaratory proceedings to resolve the same issues that will be determined between the insured and the claimant upon a trial. In these circumstances, some courts have required the insurer to defend, although others have permitted the insurer to decline to defend, subject to later reimbursing the insured should it be determined that the claim falls within coverage.[190] The latter view is contrary to sound principle, for if the underlying facts are in dispute then the duty to defend must be determined on the pleadings.

It should be noted that the circumstances under consideration are logically distinct from the situation presented when the insurer denies coverage on the basis of an alleged breach of condition. In the latter case the issue is not whether the claim is covered; rather, the issue is whether coverage has been forfeited. In the case under consideration, however, no issue of forfeiture arises. Instead, it is given that the claim as pleaded falls within coverage and that under the defence clause the insurer is obliged to defend. The issue is whether the insurer can avoid its contractual obligation to defend on the basis that further facts, which have not been pleaded, bring the claim within a policy exclusion.

---

[187] *Traynor v. Unum Life Insurance Co. of America*, [2003] O.J. No. 2252 (C.A.); *Hedstrom v. Manufacturers Life Insurance Co.*, [2002] B.C.J. No. 2463, 2 C.C.L.I. (4th) 175 (S.C.).

[188] See section 7: Consequences of the Refusal to Defend.

[189] *Cansulex Ltd. v. Reed Stenhouse Ltd.*, [1986] B.C.J. No. 3125, 70 B.C.L.R. 273 (S.C.).

[190] See section 1(d)(iii): Where the Underlying Facts Bring the Claim within a Policy Exclusion.

6. ELECTION, WAIVER AND ESTOPPEL

By undertaking the defence of an action on behalf of its insured, an insurer may, in certain circumstances, lose the right to subsequently deny coverage.[191] The insurer, in some cases, is said to have "waived" the right to deny the claim. In other cases the insurer may be estopped from asserting a right under the policy. Statements made by the insurer may amount to an admission of its obligations under the policy.[192] Insurers often seek to avoid these consequences through the use of a reservation of rights letter or a non-waiver agreement.

(a) Election and Waiver

When the insurer becomes aware of a breach of condition on the part of the insured, then the insurer has the option of repudiating its liability. Under the contractual doctrine of election of remedies, if, in the face of the breach, the insurer nevertheless decides to carry on with the defence of the action against the insured, then the insurer has thereby elected to undertake liability in respect of the claim. Where such an election is made, it is sometimes said that the insurer has "waived" the right to rely upon the policy breach.

The doctrine of election is significantly different from the doctrine of estoppel by representation, although courts have not always been careful to observe the distinction.[193] An election is an intentional act by an insurer. An insurer making an election must know of the policy breach and must make an unequivocal decision to waive its right to rely upon that breach. Prejudice to the insured need not be established for a waiver to be effective, whereas it is a necessary ingredient of estoppel.[194]

The application of the doctrine of election to insurance contracts has been modified by the largely uniform insurance legislation in force in the common law provinces:

(1) A term or condition of a contract is not deemed to be waived by the insurer in whole or in part unless the waiver is stated in writing and signed by a person authorized for that purpose by the insurer.

(2) Neither the insurer nor the insured are deemed to have waived any term or condition of a contract by any act relating to the appraisal of the

---

[191] *Rowe v. Mills*, [1986] N.B.J. No. 798, 21 C.C.L.I. 112 (Q.B.).

[192] *Uniroyal Chemical Ltd. v. Kansa General Insurance Co.*, [1996] O.J. No. 644, 89 O.A.C. 311 (C.A.); *Uniform Developments & Leasing Ltd. v. Issac*, [1998] O.J. No. 1768, 7 C.C.L.I. (3d) 290 (Gen. Div.).

[193] C. Brown & J. Menezes, *Insurance Law in Canada: A Treatise on the Principles of Indemnity Insurance as Applied in the Common Law Provinces of Canada* (Scarborough: Carswell, 1991) at para. 14:1:2.

[194] *Western Can. Accident & Guarantee Ins. Co. v. Parrott*, [1921] 2 W.W.R. 569 (S.C.C.); *cf. Rosenblood Estate v. Law Soc. of Upper Can.*, [1989] O.J. No. 240, 37 C.C.L.I. 142 (H.C.J.), affd, [1992] O.J. No. 3030, 16 C.C.L.I. (2d) 226 (C.A.).

amount of loss or to the delivery and completion of proofs or to the investigation or adjustment of any claim under the contract.[195]

This legislation may first appear to be quite far-reaching. It has been held, however, that the section does not apply to the doctrine of estoppel.[196] The only circumstance in which the section would operate to the benefit of the insurer, therefore, would be one in which the insured was unable to establish that it had relied to its detriment upon the insurer's conduct.

(b) Estoppel by Representation

The doctrine of estoppel by representation was succinctly stated by Lord Birkenhead in *Maclaine v. Gatty* as follows:

> Where A has by his words or conduct justified B in believing that a certain state of facts exists, and B has acted upon such belief to his prejudice, A is not permitted to affirm against B that a different state of facts existed at the same time.[197]

In general terms, there are three elements to an estoppel by representation:

(i) there must be a representation of existing fact made by the defendant

(ii) with the intention that the plaintiff should act upon the faith of the representation, and

(iii) the plaintiff must act upon the representation to his or her detriment.[198]

The representation may be given orally, in writing or by conduct. Even silence or inaction may be held to constitute a representation.[199]

In the context of liability insurance contracts, the doctrine of estoppel most often arises in circumstances where the insurer, by its words or deeds in conducting the defence of an action on the insured's behalf, leads the insured to believe that the claim is covered under the policy. In such cases, detriment to the insured is usually established by the fact that the insurer, by taking control of the

---

[195] *Insurance Act*, R.S.B.C. 1996, c. 226, s. 11. Comparable sections in other jurisdictions are as follows: R.S.O. 1990, c. I.8, s. 131; R.S.A. 1980, c. I-5, s. 207; *Saskatchewan Insurance Act*, R.S.S. 1978, c. S-26, s. 111; R.S.M. 1987, c. I40, s. 123(1), (2); R.S.N.B. 1973, c. I-12, s. 109; R.S.P.E.I. 1988, c. I-4, s. 94; R.S.N.S. 1989, c. 231, s. 35; *Insurance Contracts Act*, R.S.N.L. 1990, c. I-12, s. 12.

[196] *McKenzie v. Jevco Ins. Management Inc.*, [1986] B.C.J. No. 1212, 28 C.C.L.I. 358 (S.C.), affd, [1988] B.C.J. No. 568, 32 C.C.L.I. 78 (C.A.).

[197] [1921] 1 A.C. 376 at 386, [1920] All E.R. Rep. 70 (H.L.).

[198] G.S. Bower & A.K. Turner, *The Law Relating to Estoppel by Representation*, 3rd ed. (London: Butterworths, 1977) at para. 3.

[199] *Tattersall v. People's Life Ins. Co.* (1904), 9 O.L.R. 611 (Dist. Ct.), affd (1905), 11 O.L.R. 326 (C.A.); affd (1906), 37 S.C.R. 690; *Globe Indemnity Co. v. Blomfield*, 562 P.2d 1372 (Ariz. 1977).

defence, thereby usurps the insured's right both to conduct the defence and to negotiate terms of settlement as he or she sees fit.[200]

An example of the application of the doctrine of estoppel in the context of a liability insurance policy is provided by the decision in *Rosenblood Estate v. Law Society of Upper Canada*.[201] A lawyer's professional liability insurer denied coverage on the grounds that the lawyer's conduct was dishonest and that he failed to give notice of a potential claim within a reasonable time. Although the insurer was correct on both counts, it was held that the insurer was estopped from raising these defences because, with knowledge of the facts giving rise to the exclusion of coverage, the insurer continued to defend the action, conduct examinations for discovery, and conduct settlement negotiations, all without giving notice to the insured of any issue concerning coverage. Although the insured could not point to any actual prejudice, the Court presumed prejudice on the basis that had the insured been advised of the off-coverage position earlier, the defence could well have been conducted differently. The Court offered the following sage advice for insurers:

> When a claim is presented to an insurer the facts giving rise to the claim should be investigated. If there is no coverage then the insured should be told at once and the insurer should have nothing further to do with the claim if it wishes to maintain its off-coverage position. If coverage is questionable the insurer should advise the insured at once and in the absence of a non-waiver agreement or of an adequate reservation of rights letter defends the claim at its risk.[202]

(c) Reservation of Rights and Non-Waiver Agreements

Where doubts exist as to either the duty to defend or the obligation to indemnify, insurers often resort to either a reservation of rights letter or a non-waiver agreement. A reservation of rights letter is a unilateral communication by the insurer to the insured stating that by carrying out an investigation and by defending the action, the insurer does not waive its right to deny coverage at a later time. A non-waiver agreement is, as the name suggests, a contract between the insurer and the insured generally stipulating that the insurer may investigate, defend and settle the claim without prejudice to any of its rights under the policy.

In most cases, a reservation of rights letter and a non-waiver agreement have the same effect. Since the insurer undertakes the defence of the action on the clear basis that it reserves the right to later deny coverage, the insured is

---

[200] *Western Can. Accident & Guarantee Ins. Co. v. Parrott, supra,* note 194; *Rosenblood Estate v. Law Soc. of Upper Canada, supra,* note 194; *Canada Trustco Mortgage Co. v. Kansa General Ins. Co.,* [1994] M.J. No. 276, [1994] 6 W.W.R. 225, 93 Man. R. (2d) 306, [1994] I.L.R. 1-3099, 25 C.C.L.I. (2d) 97 (Q.B.); *Snair v. Halifax Ins. Nationale-Nederlanden North America Corp.,* [1995] N.S.J. No. 424, 418 A.P.R. 132, 145 N.S.R. (2d) 132, [1996] I.L.R. 1-3286 (S.C.).

[201] *Supra,* note 194. See also *Antiaris v. Lawrence Park X-ray & Ultrasound,* [1994] O.J. No. 3196 (Gen. Div.).

[202] *Rosenblood Estate v. Law Soc. of Upper Can., supra,* note 194 at 157.

precluded from using the fact of investigation and defence by the insurer as the basis for a successful plea of estoppel. Where the reservation of rights letter and non-waiver agreement may differ, however, is that the latter can give the insurer rights which are not found in the policy. A non-waiver agreement, for example, may provide the insurer with the right to unilaterally settle the claim and obtain reimbursement from the insured for the amount of the settlement,[203] a right which is not available to the insurer under a mere reservation of rights.[204] As a matter of law insureds are not obliged to enter into a non-waiver agreement and in most cases they are better advised to simply require the insurer to fulfill its obligations under the policy.

A non-waiver agreement, of course, is subject to the law regarding contracts in general. Particular care must be taken by insurers not to misrepresent the purpose or effect of these documents or to otherwise take advantage of the insured, who, having usually just been named in a law suit, is in a peculiarly vulnerable position. Claims adjusters often require the insured to sign a non-waiver agreement on the basis that it is a formality and is a condition precedent to the insurer undertaking an investigation of the claim. This practice is plainly not acceptable. An insurer seeking to gain additional rights to those granted by the policy would be well-advised to make a full disclosure to the insured of its intentions in that regard. Failure to do so may result in the non-waiver agreement being declared unenforceable.

In order for a reservation of rights letter to be effective it must be given in reasonable time and must contain adequate notice of the coverage issue. What constitutes reasonable time and adequate notice will, of course, vary according to the circumstances of the particular case. Often, an initial investigation will be required before the insurer is able to make an assessment of the coverage issues in the case. Once the insurer has sufficient information to make a decision on coverage, it must then make its position known to the insured; failing this an estoppel may arise.[205]

Both a reservation of rights letter and a non-waiver agreement may be rendered ineffective by the insurer's subsequent conduct. For example, in *Federal Insurance Co. v. Matthews*[206] it was held that an insurer cannot both defend an action under a non-waiver agreement and, at the same time, commence separate proceedings for a declaration that it is not liable under the policy. The insured in that case was, while driving under the influence of alcohol, involved in an accident in the state of Washington. Proceedings were brought against him in Washington, which the insured defended under a non-waiver agreement. While

---

[203] See, for example, *Canadian Mercantile Insurance Company v. Clark*, [1946] 1 W.W.R. 673, 13 I.L.R. 73 (Man. K.B.), affd [1946] 3 D.L.R. 702, [1946] 2 W.W.R. 656, 54 Man. R. 308, 13 I.L.R. 99 (C.A.).

[204] *Allstate Insurance Co. v. Foster* (1971), 24 D.L.R. (3d) 9, [1972] 1 O.R. 653, I.L.R. 1-470 (Co. Ct.).

[205] *Rowe v. Mills, supra*, note 191; *Wawanesa Mutual Insurance Co. v. Buchanan* (1976), 74 D.L.R. (3d) 330, 14 O.R. (2d) 644 (Co. Ct.).

[206] (1956), 18 W.W.R. 193 (B.C.S.C.).

still defending that action on behalf of the insured, the insurer brought proceedings in British Columbia for a declaration that coverage was avoided by reason of the insured's intoxication. The Court held that by bringing the declaratory proceedings the insurer had repudiated the non-waiver agreement. The continued defence of the Washington action after that time then amounted to an election to affirm the contract, with the result that the insurer was bound to provide coverage.

7. CONSEQUENCES OF THE REFUSAL TO DEFEND

Serious consequences flow from an insurer's refusal to defend its insured in circumstances where the policy stipulates that a defence is required. In addition to being in breach of contract, the insurer will have lost certain of its rights under the policy and may be exposed to a bad faith claim.

(a) Loss of Policy Rights

By taking the position that the policy does not respond to the claim, the insurer forgoes both its right to defend the action[207] and its exclusive right to settle the action on behalf of its insured.[208] If the denial is wrongful then the insurer may also lose the right to insist upon the insured's compliance with the terms and conditions of the policy, including conditions establishing a limitation period for suits against the insurer.[209] With the exception of automobile liability policies,[210] a liability insurer has no statutory right to add itself as a third party for the purpose of contesting the plaintiff's claim against the insured.[211] Under the applicable rules of civil procedure, however, the insurer may be able to add itself to the action as an interested party.[212]

---

[207] *Passarell v. Taku Air Transport Ltd.* (1988), 30 C.C.L.I. 272 (B.C.C.A.); *Heads v. Brownlee,* [1943] 4 D.L.R. 513 (B.C.C.A.); *Ward Estate v. Olds Aviation Ltd.,* [1996] A.J. No. 791 (Q.B.), 40 C.C.L.I. (2d) 119 (C.A.).

[208] *Shore Boat Builders Ltd. v. Can. Indemnity Co.* (1975), 51 D.L.R. (3d) 628 (B.C.S.C.); *Cansulex Ltd. v. Reed Stenhouse,* [1986] B.C.J. No. 3125, 70 B.C.L.R. 273 (S.C.); *McMurachy v. Red River Valley Mutual Ins. Co.,* [1994] M.J. No. 220, 115 D.L.R. (4th) 220, [1994] 6 W.W.R. 99, 92 Man. R. (2d) 225, [1994] I.L.R. 1-3093 (C.A.), leave to appeal to S.C.C. dismissed [1994] S.C.C.A. No. 267, 178 N.R. 396*n*.

[209] *Co-opérative Avicole de St. Isidore Ltd. v. Co-Operators General Insurance Co.* [1997] O.J. 2550, 44 C.C.L.I. (2d) 1, (Gen. Div.).

[210] *Insurance Act,* R.S.O. 1990, c. I.8, s. 258(14); R.S.A. 1980, c. I-5, s. 320(14); *Saskatchewan Insurance Act,* R.S.S. 1978, c. S-26, s. 210(14); R.S.M. 1987, c. I40, s. 258(14); R.S.N.B. 1973, c. I-12, s. 250(14); R.S.P.E.I. 1988, c. I-4, s. 240(13); R.S.N.S. 1989, c. 231, s. 133(14); *Automobile Insurance Act,* R.S.N.L. 1990, c. A-22, s. 28(14); *Insurance (Motor Vehicle) Act,* R.S.B.C. 1996, c. 231, s. 21(7).

[211] *Evans v. Steinberg Inc.,* [1988] O.J. No. 1366, 35 C.C.L.I. 119 (Ont. Dist. Ct.).

[212] *Young v. Young,* [1993] S.J. No. 54, 13 C.C.L.I. (2d) 324 (Q.B.); *Bryant v. Korres Moving & Transfer Ltd.,* [1989] B.C.J. No. 1694 (Co. Ct.); *York Region Condominium Corp. No. 772 v. Richmond Hill (Town),* 2003 CarswellOnt 4899 (S.C.J.).

As a general rule, an insurer in breach of the duty to defend will not be permitted, in subsequent proceedings for coverage, to dispute the insured's liability to the plaintiff as established in the underlying action.[213] The doctrine of issue estoppel does not, however, apply where the insurer seeks to lead evidence to show the application of a policy exclusion, for the issue of coverage is not one which is properly before the court in the underlying action. Thus, in *Hamilton v. Laurentian Pacific Insurance Co.*[214] an insurer that denied a defence to its insured was permitted in coverage proceedings to lead evidence that an assault for which the insured was held liable arose out of a forcible ejection (thereby bringing a forcible ejection exclusion into play), notwithstanding that in the tort action the Court found that the assault occurred outside the premises and that no ejection, forcible or otherwise, was involved.

Where the insured enters into a reasonable settlement of the claim the insurer will not be able to resist indemnity on the basis of a policy condition stipulating that judgment against the insured is a condition precedent to taking action against the insurer.[215] Rather, the insurer, by its wrongful denial of coverage, is taken to have excused the insured from having to run the risk of going to trial and facing the possibility of a judgment for a greater sum.[216]

(b) Breach of Contract

The duty to defend is a contractual duty, the breach of which gives rise to a claim by the insured for any recoverable damages resulting therefrom. Those damages will include defence costs at least and, where indemnity is required, the amount for which the insured is liable on a settlement or judgment. Punitive damages may also be awarded where appropriate.

Liability insurance policies frequently do not place any limit on defence costs. The insurer's obligation is to defend the action in good faith and in the best interests of the insured. Accordingly, where the insurer is in breach of the duty to defend, the insured will be entitled to all of the expenses, as damages, that were incurred in the defence of the action, the only limitation being that the expenses be reasonable.[217] Where the underlying action included both covered and uncovered claims there is authority that, having wrongfully refused to

---

[213] *Chemetics International Ltd. v. Commercial Union Assur. Co. of Can.* (1981), 31 B.C.L.R. 273 (S.C.), affd (1984), 6 C.C.L.I. 196 (B.C.C.A.); *Global General Ins. Co. v. Finlay,* [1961] I.L.R. 1-036 (S.C.C.); *Milne v. Wall,* [1966] 2 O.R. 862 (S.C.), *Boutique 21 ans Inc. c. Chaussures Bruno Scola (1985) Inc.,* [1996] A.Q. No. 2741. Neither can the insured dispute the basis upon which liability was found: *Balzer's Canada Inc. v. Sovereign General Insurance Co.* [1998] S.J. No. 865, 174 Sask. R. 158, (Q.B.).

[214] [1989] B.C.J. No. 869, 37 C.C.L.I. 190 (C.A.).

[215] *Supra,* note 207.

[216] *Stevenson v. Reliance Petroleum Ltd.,* [1953] 4 D.L.R. 755 at 765 (Ont. H.C.J.), revd in part [1954] 4 D.L.R. 730 (Ont. C.A.), affd (1956), 5 D.L.R. (2d) 673 (S.C.C.); *Cansulex Ltd. v. Reed Stenhouse, supra,* note 208.

[217] See G.J. Couch & R.A. Anderson, *Couch Cyclopedia of Insurance Law,* 2nd ed. (Rochester: Lawyers Co-operative Publishing Co., 1984) at para. 51:60, 51:61; R. Long, *The Law of Liability Insurance* (New York: Matthew Bender & Co., 1966) at para. 5:30.

defend the covered claims, the insurer must pay all of the costs of the defence, including those costs incurred with respect to the uncovered claims.[218] Yet other authorities have held in such circumstances that the insurer is responsible only for those costs associated with the covered claims.[219] As a matter of principle, the latter are correct. The insurer's liability is for damages stemming from its breach of contract. The insured is entitled to be put back in the position it would have been in had no breach occurred. In the absence of circumstances justifying punitive damages, the insured is not entitled to be placed in a better position than if the contract had been fulfilled.

Where the insured has settled the action and the claim is one for which indemnity is provided under the policy, the insurer will be liable for the amount of the settlement, provided that the settlement is for a reasonable amount and was made in good faith.[220]

In cases where a judgment has gone against the insured and is one for which indemnity is provided in the policy, then the insurer will be liable for the amount of the judgment to at least the monetary limit specified in the policy. The insurer will be additionally liable for the excess where it ought to have settled the action within the policy limits.[221]

As a general rule, punitive damages are not awarded in respect of the insurer's breach of the duty to defend. Where there is malice on the part of the insurer, however, an award of punitive damages may be made.[222]

(c) Bad Faith

In the liability insurance context the term "bad faith" is used to refer to conduct of an insurer that gives rise to the insured's right to claim damages in addition to the benefits by the policy. Such damages are usually either consequential or

---

[218] *Hanis v. University of Western Ontario*, [2003] O.J. No. 4167 (S.C.J.); *Modern Livestock Ltd. v. Kansa General Insurance Co.*, [1993] A.J. No. 575, 11 Alta. L.R. (3d) 355, 143 A.R. 46, 18 C.C.L.I. (2d) 266 (Q.B.), affd (1994), 77 W.A.C. 167, 24 Alta. L.R. (3d) 21, 157 A.R. 167, 24 C.C.L.I. (2d) 254 (C.A.). On this point the latter decision can be said to be *obiter dicta*, for the court found as a fact that Kansa had failed to discharge the onus of allocating a portion of the defence costs to the uncovered claims.

[219] *Surrey (District) v. General Accident Assurance Co. of Canada*, [1994] B.C.J. No. 27, [1994] 7 W.W.R. 226, 92 B.C.L.R. (2d) 115, 24 C.C.L.I. (2d) 34 (S.C.), supp. reasons (1994), 24 C.C.L.I. (2d) 50, affd, [1996] B.C.J. No. 849, 7 W.W.R. 48, 19 B.C.L.R. (3d) 186, 35 C.C.L.I. (2d) 154, [1996] I.L.R. 1-3325 (C.A.); *St. Andrews Service Co. v. McCubbin*, [1987] B.C.J. No. 2636, 22 B.C.L.R. (2d) 38, 31 C.C.L.I. 166, [1988] I.L.R. 1-2305, supp. reasons, [1988] B.C.J. No. 3117, 29 B.C.L.R. (2d) 205, 31 C.C.L.I. 161 (S.C.).

[220] *Stevenson v. Reliance Petroleum Ltd.*, *supra*, note 216; *Cansulex Ltd. v. Reed Stenhouse*, [1986] B.C.J. No. 3125, 70 B.C.L.R. (2d) 273 (S.C.); *Jon Picken Ltd. v. Guardian Ins. Co. of Can.*, [1993] O.J. No. 1952, I.L.R. 1-2973 (C.A.); Couch, *supra*, note 217, at para. 51:57. A reasonable settlement may include an assignment of the insured's bad faith claim against the insurer: *McMurachy v. Red River Valley Mutual Ins. Co.*, *supra*, note 208.

[221] See section 4: The Duty to Settle.

[222] *Thompson v. Zurich Ins. Co.* (1983), 45 O.R. (2d) 744 (H.C.J.); *Rosenblood Estate v. Law Society of Upper Can.*, [1989] O.J. No. 240, 37 C.C.L.I. 142 (H.C.J.), affd, [1992] O.J. No. 3030, 16 C.C.L.I. (2d) 226 (C.A.).

punitive in nature. The law in Canada with respect to bad faith on the part of the insurer is still in its infancy.[223] There is a considerable body of American jurisprudence with respect to bad faith claims, but one must be careful when analyzing this jurisprudence from a Canadian perspective. In several of the American jurisdictions issues concerning bad faith claims involve both statutory and common law considerations which may not apply in Canada. Although, in Canada, it is clear that an implied term of good faith and fair dealing is imported into every insurance contract,[224] it is not clear whether the same duty arises in tort,[225] nor is it clear whether the duty extends to adjusters.[226] In the United States the insurer and the insured are sometimes considered to be in a fiduciary relationship, a view which has been rejected by some Canadian courts.[227] There has also been considerable legislative intervention in the United States, with a number of jurisdictions enacting statutes regulating unfair claims handling practices.

8. RIGHT TO SELECT AND INSTRUCT COUNSEL

The right of the insurer to select and control defence counsel raises complex and controversial issues[228] which require careful analysis. The discussion which

---

[223] See, generally, G. Hilliker, *Insurance Bad Faith* (Markham: LexisNexis Butterworths, 2004).

[224] *Whiten v. Pilot Insurance Co.*, [2002] S.C.J. No. 19, [2002] I.L.R. 1-4048.

[225] One line of authority, pre-*Whiten,* treats the duty of good faith, not as a contractual term, but as an obligation imposed by law as an incident of the insurance relationship: *Burdan v Progressive Casualty Insurance Co.*, [1993] O.J. No. 2732, 20. C.C.L.I. (2d) 126 (Ont. Gen. Div.); *Lloyd's of London v. Norris*, [1998] N.B.J. No. 351 (C.A.); *Burke v. Buss*, [2002] O.J. No. 2938 (S.C.); *Spiers v. Zurich Insurance Co.*, [1999] O.J. No. 3683, 45 O.R. (3d) 726 (S.C.); *Green v. Constellation Assurance Co.*, [1993] O.J. No. 1445; *Gibson v. Parkes District Hospital* (1991), 26 NSWLR 9. Another line of authority treats the duty of good faith as an implied term of the contract: *Thompson v. Zurich Insurance Co.* (1984), 5 C.C.L.I. 251 (Ont. H.C.); *Kantolic v. Peace Hills General Insurance Co.*, [2000] A.J. No. 67 (Q.B.). One does not preclude the other: *Central Trust Co. v. Rafuse*, [1986] S.C.J. No. 52, [1986] 2 S.C.R. 147; *Spiers v. Zurich Insurance Co.*, [1999] O.J. No. 3683, 45 O.R. (3d) 726 (S.C.J.).

[226] *Bullock v. Trafalgar Insurance Co. of Canada*, [1996] O.J. No. 2566 (Ont. Gen. Div.); *Spiers v. Zurich Insurance Co.*, [1999] O.J. No. 3683 (S.C.); *Bush v. Continental Insurance Co.*, [2001] O.J. No. 3315 (S.C.J.); *Burke v. Buss*, [2002] O.J. No. 2938 (S.C.J.); *Abbasi v. Portage La Prairie Mutual Insurance Co.*, [2003] A.J. No. 1118, 5 C.C.L.I. (4th) 34 (Q.B.); *Noble v. Riddell*, [2003] O.J. No. 3053 (S.C.J.); *Dick v. ING/Halifax Insurance Co.*, [2002] O.J. No. 3258 (S.C.); *Kogan v. Chubb Insurance Co. of Canada*, [2001] O.J. No. 1697, I.L.R. 1-3987 (S.C.); *Walsh v. Nicholls*, [2004] N.B.J. No. 281, 14 C.C.L.I. (4th) 6 (C.A.).

[227] *Fredrikson v. Ins. Corp. of B.C.*, [1990] B.C.J. No. 717, 44 B.C.L.R. (2d) 303 (S.C.); *Plaza Fiberglass Manufacturing Ltd. v. Cardinal Ins. Co.*, [1994] O.J. No. 1023, 115 D.L.R. (4th) 37, 18 O.R. (3d) 663, [1994] 1-3067, 56 C.P.R. (3d) 46 (C.A.); *Canadian Newspapers Co. v. Kansa General Ins. Co.*, [1991] O.J. No. 1078, 5 C.C.L.I. (2d) 66 (Gen. Div.).

[228] See B. Billingsley, "Caught in the Middle: When Insurance Defence Counsel Encounter Coverage Problems" (2000) 79 C.B.R. 221; M.B. Snowden, "When Coverage Is in Dispute: The Conduct of Insurers and Counsel in Canada" (1992) 4 C.I.L.R. 1; D.S. Ferguson, "Conflict Between Insured and Insurer: An Analysis of Recent Canadian Cases" (1990-91) 12 Adv. Q. 129.

follows must be read in conjunction with the next section, "Duty of Counsel", for these issues are inextricably bound with the ethical obligations placed upon lawyers both by their governing bodies and by the courts. In addition, throughout this discussion, it must always be kept in mind that modern liability insurance policies create two distinct aspects of coverage, namely, the duty to defend and the requirement to indemnify.[229]

With the exception of certain professional liability policies and directors' and officers' liability policies, liability insurance policies generally provide that the insurer has the exclusive right to select and instruct counsel to defend on behalf of the insured. There are two reasons for this provision. First of all, it is in the interest of the insurer, as the potential indemnitor, that competent counsel be retained to defend the claim. Second, it is in the interest of the insurer, as the one responsible for paying defence costs, that the expenses be kept within reason.

In cases where the insurer acknowledges that the claim is covered under the policy, the insurer's right to select and control counsel rarely presents any difficulty to the insured. In cases where coverage is reserved, however, that right is sometimes challenged on the basis that counsel appointed by the insurer will be representing conflicting interests. The law in this regard is still somewhat unsettled. In the United States, in these circumstances, the authorities range from giving the insured the unfettered right to select counsel,[230] to requiring that this right be exercised in good faith so that reasonably competent counsel is selected,[231] to leaving the insurer with the residual right to approve the insured's selection of counsel (such approval not to be unreasonably withheld),[232] to allowing the insurer to retain the right to select counsel so long as certain criteria are met.[233] Unfortunately, when analyzing this issue, many courts, perhaps influenced by the positions taken by the litigants and counsel before them, have either proceeded upon a mistaken view as to the role of defence counsel or have overlooked the distinction between selecting counsel and controlling the defence. Defence counsel's ethical obligations are the same regardless of whether counsel is selected by the insurer or the insured. In either case, counsel must defend the case on the basis that is most favourable to the insured.[234] Even though the insurer may have the right to select counsel, it is not necessarily appropriate for that counsel to be instructed solely by the insurer. In some instances, where the conduct of the defence may affect the issue of indemnity, then the insured should be given the right to direct counsel.[235]

Perhaps the most celebrated and controversial decision with respect to the right of the insured to select defence counsel is the decision of the California

---

[229] *Renaud and Jacob v. Zurich of Canada*, [1996] A.Q. No. 2670 at para. 38 (C.A.).

[230] *Maryland Casualty Co. v. Peppers*, 355 N.E.2d 24 (Ill. Sup. 1976).

[231] *CHI of Alaska Inc. v. Employers Reinsurance Co.*, 844 P.2d 1113 (Al. 1993).

[232] *Fireman's Fund Ins. Co. v. Waste Management*, 777 F.2d 366 (7th Cir. 1985).

[233] *Johnson v. Continental Casualty Co.*, 788 P.2d 598 (Wash. App. 1990); *National Union Fire Ins. Co. v. Circle Inc.*, 915 F.2d 986 (5th Cir. 1990).

[234] See section 9: Duty of Counsel.

[235] See section 8(c): Covered and Uncovered Claims.

Court of Appeal in *San Diego Navy Federal Credit Union v. Cumis Insurance Society Inc.*[236] An action for wrongful dismissal seeking both compensatory and punitive damages was brought against the insured credit union. Since their policy did not provide coverage for punitive damages, the insured defended under a reservation of rights letter. The defence was assigned to counsel selected by the insurer. The insured objected on the basis that counsel so appointed would be required to serve conflicting interests. The Court agreed:

> We conclude the Canons of Ethics impose upon lawyers hired by the insurer an obligation to explain to the insured and the insurer the full implications of joint representation in situations where the insurer has reserved its rights to deny coverage. If the insured does not give an informed consent to continued representation, counsel must cease to represent both. Moreover, in the absence of such consent, where there are divergent interests of the insured and the insurer brought about by the insurer's reservation of rights based on possible non coverage under the insurance policy, the insurer must pay the reasonable cost for hiring independent counsel by the insured. The insurer may not compel the insured to surrender control of the litigation (*Tomerlin v. Canadian Indemnity Co., supra,* 61 Cal. 2d 638, 648, 39 Cal. Rptr. 731, 394 P.2d 571; and see *Nike Inc. v. Atlantic Mut. Ins. Co.* (1983) 578 F. Suppl. 948, 949). Disregarding the common interests of both insured and insurer in finding total nonliability in the third party action, the remaining interests of the two diverge to such an extent as to create an actual, ethical conflict of interest warranting payment for the insured's independent counsel.[237]

While the effect of the decision in *Cumis* has been restricted by subsequent legislation in California,[238] *Cumis* was followed by the Ontario High Court in *Laurencine v. Jardine.*[239] The facts in *Laurencine* are not entirely clear from the judgment. The plaintiff was injured while riding the defendant's motorcycle. There was an issue as to whether the motorcycle was taken with consent and, if

---

[236] 208 Cal. Rptr. 494 (1984).

[237] *Ibid.,* at 506.

[238] Section 2860 of the California Civil Code provides that:

  (a) If the provisions of a policy of insurance impose a duty to defend upon an insurer and a conflict of interest arises which creates a duty on the part of the insurer to provide independent counsel to the insured, the insurer shall provide independent counsel to represent the insured unless, at the time the insured is informed that a possible conflict may arise or does exist, the insured expressly waives, in writing, the right to independent counsel. An insurance contract may contain a provision which sets forth the method of selecting that counsel consistent with this section.

  (b) For purposes of this section, a conflict of interest does not exist as to allegations of facts in the litigation for which the insurer denies coverage; however, when an insurer reserves its rights on a given issue and the outcome of that coverage issue can be controlled by counsel first retained by the insurer for the defense of the claim, a conflict of interest may exist. No conflict of interest shall be deemed to exist as to allegations of punitive damages or be deemed to exist solely because an insured is sued for an amount in excess of the insurance policy limits.

  See also *Foremost Insurance Co. v. Wilks,* 253 Cal. Rptr. 596 (Cal. C.A. 1989).

[239] [1988] O.J. No. 302, [1988] I.L.R. 1-2292 (H.C.J.).

so, whether instructions for use were given to the plaintiff and whether a helmet was offered and refused. The defendant's motor vehicle insurer declined to defend on the basis that the action did not arise from the ownership, use or operation of a motorcycle. On the defendant's application, however, the insurer was ordered to defend, with the question of indemnity left to be determined by the trial judge. The insurer then appointed counsel to defend, but the insured objected on the basis that he would be obliged to advise counsel of the circumstances surrounding the accident and in so doing might provide information that would be used by the insurer in denying indemnity. The Court agreed with the insured and granted an order permitting the insured to appoint counsel of his own choice at the insurer's expense. The Court further directed that counsel not be required to report to the insurer with respect to any matters bearing on the issue of coverage, and permitted the solicitors for the insurer to participate in the defence of the action, subject to the control of counsel appointed by the insured.

The decision in *Laurencine v. Jardine* was followed in *Gosse v. Huemiller.*[240] After a motor vehicle accident, the plaintiff and the defendant became involved in a physical altercation. The plaintiff commenced an action against the defendant claiming damages for assault as well as damages with respect to the negligent operation or deliberate operation of a motor vehicle so as to cause harm. Only the claim in negligence fell within the coverage provided by the defendant's insurer. Given these circumstances, the insurer chose not to defend the action but applied instead to be added as a third party pursuant to a statutory provision in that regard. On the insured's application, however, the Court held that the insurer was responsible for defence costs that were incurred in that aspect of the claim relating to the negligent operation of the motor vehicle and that, in that regard, the insured was entitled to be separately represented by counsel of his own choice.

To be properly understood, the decisions in *Laurencine* and *Gosse* must be placed in context. With respect to liability insurance policies in general, the insurer has no unilateral right to add itself as a party to the action against its insured in order to contest issues of either liability between the plaintiff and defendant or coverage between the defendant and the insurer.[241] Any findings on liability in the underlying action will not ordinarily bind the insurer in subsequent litigation to determine coverage.[242] In *Gosse v. Huemiller,* however, the motor vehicle liability insurer had availed itself of its statutory right to add itself as a third party. The purpose of this statutory provision is to permit the insurer, where it has denied coverage, to contest the liability of the insured to the plaintiff. It is not intended as a method for the determination of the coverage dispute between the insurer and the insured.[243] It appears from the reasons in *Gosse* that the insurer, as third party, had filed a statement of defence alleging

---

[240] [1988] O.J. No. 1595, 34 C.C.L.I. 265 (H.C.J.).

[241] *Evans v. Steinberg Inc.*, [1988] O.J. No. 1366, 35 C.C.L.I. 119 (Dist. Ct.).

[242] *Hamilton v. Laurentian Pacific Ins. Co.*, [1989] B.C.J. No. 869, 58 D.L.R. (4th) 760, [1989] 5 W.W.R. 467, 37 B.C.L.R. (2d) 30, 37 C.C.L.I. 190 (C.A.).

[243] *Bliefernich v. Freeman*, [1989] B.C.J. No. 1133, 60 D.L.R. (4th) 385, 38 B.C.L.R. (2d) 128, [1989] I.L.R. 1-2504 (C.A.).

that the plaintiff's injuries resulted from an assault by the insured, which, if proven, would result in a lack of coverage for the insured under the motor vehicle liability policy. In these circumstances, the insurer having taken a position in the action adverse to the interests of the insured, the Court was of the view that it would be clearly inappropriate for the insured to be represented by the lawyer representing the insurer or by some other lawyer appointed and instructed by the insurer. Accordingly, the court directed that the insured be at liberty to appoint counsel who would not seek to represent conflicting interests.

The decision in *Laurencine v. Jardine* also arose out of rather special circumstances. There was a clear appearance of impropriety in that counsel appointed by the insurer opposed the insured's application (even though the insured was, as a matter of law, his client) and apparently could not satisfy the Court's wish that confidential information regarding the issue of coverage not be disclosed to the insurer.

In subsequent cases the decision in *Laurencine* has been followed,[244] explained[245] and distinguished.[246] Although the law in this regard is still somewhat unsettled, it is clear that the mere fact that there is a reservation of coverage by the insurer does not give the insured the right to control the defence.[247] Rather, the right to control the defence is determined by whether or not there exists a conflict of interests which overrides the insurer's right to select and control counsel to defend the claim.[248] As a general rule, where the insured's status

---

[244] *Desmond v. Guardian Insurance Co. of Canada*, [1995] N.B.J. No. 378, 427 A.P.R. 93, 167 N.B.R. (2d) 93, 15 M.V.R. (3d) 314 (Q.B.); *Incerto v. Landry*, [2000] O.J. No. 861, 47 O.R. (3d) 622, [2000] I.L.R. 1-3827, 2 M.V.R. (4th) 264 (S.C.J.).

[245] *Brockton (Municipality) v. Frank Cowan Co.*, [2002] O.J. No. 20, 34 C.C.L.I. (3d) 1 (C.A.); *Zurich du Canada, Cie d'Indemnité v. Renaud & Jacob*, [1996] A.Q. No. 2670, DRS 97-08820, [1996] R.J.Q. 2160 (Que. C.A.). For an English summary of this decision see case comment A. Legrand, "The Duty to Defend: The Quebec Court of Appeal Takes a Stand" (1996) 6 C.I.L.R. 307.

[246] *Ontario v. Kansa General Ins. Co.*, [1991] O.J. No. 757, 3 O.R. (3d) 543 (Gen. Div.).

[247] *Zurich du Canada, Cie d'Indemnité v. Renaud & Jacob*, [1996] A.Q. No. 2670, DRS 97-08820, [1996] R.J.Q. 2160 (C.A.); *Brockton (Municipality) v. Frank Cowan Co.*, [2002] O.J. No. 20, 57 O.R. (3d) 447 (C.A.); *Roman Catholic Episcopal Corp. of St. George's v. Insurance Corp. of Newfoundland*, [2003] N.J. No. 324, 6 C.C.L.I. (4th) 83 (C.A.); *Morrison v. Co-operators General Insurance Co.*, [2004] N.B.J. No. 290, 12 C.C.L.I. (4th) 171 (C.A.).

[248] See *Brockton (Municipality) v. Frank Cowan Co.*, [2002] O.J. No. 20 at para. 43 (C.A.):

The issue is the degree of divergence of interest that must exist before the insurer can be required to surrender control of the defence and pay for counsel retained by the insured. The balance is between the insured's right to a full and fair defence of the civil action against it and the insurer's right to control that defence because of its potential ultimate obligation to indemnify. In my view, that balance is appropriately struck by requiring that there be, in the circumstances of the particular case, a reasonable apprehension of conflict of interest on the part of counsel appointed by the insurer before the insured is entitled to independent counsel at the insurer's expense. The question is whether counsel's mandate from the insurer can reasonably be said to conflict with his mandate to defend the insured in the civil action. Until that point is reached, the insured's right to a defence and the insurer's right to control that defence can satisfactorily co-exist.".

An example of such a conflict of interest is provided by *Svishchov v. Corol*, [2003] O.J. No. 4745 68 O.R. (3d) 19 (S.C.J.).

regarding coverage will not be adversely affected by the actions of defence counsel in the underlying action, and where counsel appointed by the insurer properly restricts the retainer to defending the issues in the underlying action (and avoiding any coverage issues between insurer and insured), the insured will rarely have the right to either select or instruct counsel. Although each case will depend upon its own peculiar facts, it is possible to categorize the areas in which a perceived conflict may arise.

(a) Breach of Condition

Where coverage has been reserved because of an alleged breach of condition on the part of the insured, it is unlikely that the facts surrounding that breach will be at issue in the underlying liability action. Where counsel's retainer is restricted to defending the liability action, as it ought to be, there should be no real possibility of counsel being placed in a position of representing conflicting interests. In *Desmond v. Guardian Insurance Co. of Canada*[249] the Court reached the contrary conclusion, but the decision can be explained on the basis that the insurer apparently proposed that the lawyer representing the insurer in the third party proceedings should also represent the insured. This created an appearance of impropriety, thus giving the insured the right to appoint and instruct counsel.

(b) Claims in Excess of Policy Limits

Where a claim is brought that is in excess of the policy limits, the insurer and the insured will have the same interest in securing an outright dismissal of the action. The insurer will have an interest in keeping the claim below the policy limits, if that is possible. The insured, of course, will also have an interest in minimizing the claim. Accordingly, in most cases there will be no basis for the insurer's losing the right to instruct counsel. Where it is clear, however, that, if successful, the claim will exceed the policy limits, then the interests of the insured and insurer will diverge, for the insurer will no longer have any financial interest in the assessment of damages. In these circumstances, a case can be made for the insured having the right to instruct counsel.[250]

(c) Covered and Uncovered Claims

Where the plaintiff presents multiple claims, one or more of which is not covered under the defendant's insurance policy, some courts require that the insurer defend only those claims that are covered,[251] leaving it to the insured to

---

[249] *Supra*, note 244.

[250] An analogous situation is where the claim exceeds the primary layer and the excess insurer asserts the right to control the defence. See *Economical Mutual Ins. Co. v. Ins. Corp. of B.C.*, [1986] A.J. No. 248, 18 C.C.L.I. 134 (Q.B.).

[251] *Gosse v. Huemiller*, [1988] O.J. No. 1595, 34 C.C.L.I. 265, [1988] I.L.R. 1-2372 (H.C.J.); *Bacon v. McBride*, [1984] B.C.J. No. 2813, 5 C.C.L.I. 146 (B.C.S.C.); *P.C.S. Investments Ltd. v.*

secure counsel to defend the remaining claim or claims. Although it may be impractical[252] to permit two counsel to represent the insured, this should prevent any conflict from arising. Where only one counsel is appointed, however, and the claims are separate and discrete, sole counsel defending the action on behalf of the insured will not be in the position of representing conflicting interests. If there is any overlap with respect to the claims, however, then the insurer and the insured may be adverse in interest, for the insurer's interest may be better served by defending the covered claim at the expense of the uncovered claim. In these circumstances counsel instructed by the insurer would be unable to represent both interests unless provided by the insurer with a mandate and instructions entirely compatible with the interests of the insured.[253]

(d) Alternative Claims — One Covered, One Not Covered

A claim may be presented under alternative heads, one covered and one not. If so, the interests of the insurer and the insured are clearly in conflict with regard to the issue of coverage. This should not affect the insurer's right to select counsel, however, although it may require that counsel take instructions from the insured rather than from the insurer. The determining factor in the latter regard will be whether in the specific case the issue of coverage may be affected by the conduct of the defence in the underlying action.

This issue arose both in *P.C.S. Investments Ltd. v. Dominion of Canada General Insurance Co.*[254] and *Karpel v. Rumack.*[255] In the former case an action for defamation and wilful interference with contractual relations was brought against the insured. The insurer declined to defend both claims. The Court agreed that there was no duty to defend the claim with respect to interference with contractual relations but held that the insurer was required to defend the defamation action. The Court further held that in order for there to be no appearance of conflict, the insured had the right to select and control counsel in defence of the defamation action:

> There is an appearance of conflict. The applicants would prefer an adverse finding based on negligent defamation. The respondent insurer would prefer an adverse finding against the applicants based on fraudulent defamation as there would then be no obligation to indemnify.

Dominion of Can. General Ins. Co., [1994] A.J. No. 204, 18 Alta. L.R. (3d) 270, 153 A.R. 187 (Q.B.), vard [1996] A.J. No. 33, 110 W.A.C. 274, 37 Alta. L.R. (3d) 38 (*sub nom. Dominion of Can. General Ins. v. P.C.S. Investments Ltd.*), [1996] A.J. No. 33, [1996] I.L.R. 1-3308, 34 C.C.L.I. 113 (2d) (C.A.).

[252] *Continental Insurance Co. v. Dia Met Minerals Ltd.*, [1994] B.C.J. No. 1724, 5 B.C.L.R. (3d) 222, [1995] I.L.R. 1-3150 (S.C.).

[253] *Morrison v. Co-operators General Insurance Co.*, [2004] N.B.J. No. 240, 12 C.C.L.I. (4th) 171 (C.A.); *Lee v. Townsend*, [2002] O.J. No. 4304, 43 C.C.L.I. (3d) 261 (S.C.J.); *Zurich du Canada, Cie d'Indemnité v. Renaud & Jacob*, *supra*, note 247; *Conservation Council of New Brunswick Inc. v. Encon Group Inc.*, [2005] N.B.J. No. 109, 19 C.C.L.I. (4th) 312 (Q.B.).

[254] *Supra*, note 251.

[255] [1994] O.J. No. 1617, 19 O.R. (3d) 555 (Gen. Div.).

> If the respondent insurer has the right to conduct the defence, its counsel would be in an untenable conflict situation. As between the fraudulent defamation claim and the negligent defamation claim counsel would be inclined to pursue the defence of the latter at the expense of the former. The issue of indemnity may well be determined by the actions of the defence counsel in the third party action. This aspect of the defence is difficult to prevent. While there are valid concerns by the insurers they are, I believe, superseded by the need to protect the rights of the insured.[256]

It is clear from the foregoing passage that the Court proceeded on the basis that counsel appointed by the insurer could prejudice the insured's right to indemnity by taking steps which would result in a judgment against the insured for "fraudulent" rather than "negligent" defamation. This is so. Yet, with respect, one must be careful not to confuse the separate issues of selecting counsel and instructing counsel, and one must not ignore the matter of counsel's ethical obligations. Whether appointed by the insurer or the insured, counsel has the same ethical obligations towards the insured, for in both cases the insured is a client.[257] Counsel appointed by the insurer must give undivided loyalty to the insured. It would be entirely improper for counsel to prepare and present the insured's case so that it fell outside rather than inside coverage. The only true basis for rejecting the insurer's choice of counsel will be where there is either actual mischief or the appearance of impropriety,[258] an obvious example of which would be where counsel is also representing the insurer with respect to the coverage issue. It may be arguable in some circumstances that the mere fact that counsel routinely acts for the insurer is a sufficient basis for finding an appearance of impropriety.[259]

The right to instruct counsel, however, is a separate matter. It is not appropriate for the insurer to provide instructions to counsel as to the conduct of the defence when doing so may enable the insurer to manipulate the coverage result. In the event that the insurer does not provide counsel with a mandate and instructions entirely compatible with the interests of the insured, then, in order to ensure that a proper defence is provided, the right to instruct counsel should be relinquished in favour of the insured.[260]

---

[256] *P.C.S. Investments*, *supra*, note 251, at 199-200.

[257] See section 9: Duty of Counsel.

[258] *MacDonald Estate v. Martin*, [1990] S.C.J. No. 41, 77 D.L.R. (4th) 249.

[259] Given the economic pressures placed upon defence counsel by insurers there is a risk that counsel will, wittingly or not, favour the insurer. In *United States Fidelity & Guar. Co. v. Louis A. Roser Co.*, 585 F.2d 932 (8th Cir. 1978) the Court noted at 938 that: "Even the most optimistic view of human nature requires us to realize that an attorney employed by an insurance company will slant his efforts, perhaps unconsciously, in the interest of his real client — the one who is paying his fee and from whom he hopes to receive future business — the insurance company". See also section 9(d): Insurer-Imposed Guidelines.

[260] *Brockton (Municipality) v. Frank Cowan Co.*, [2002] O.J. No. 20, 34 C.C.L.I. (3d) 1 (C.A); *Morrison v. Co-operators General Insurance Co.*, [2004] N.B.J. No. 290, 12 C.C.L.I. (4th) 171 (C.A.); *Lee v. Townsend*, [2002] O.J. No. 4304, 43 C.C.L.I. (3d) 261 (S.C.J.); *Zurich du Canada, Cie d'Indemnité v. Renaud & Jacob*, *supra*, note 253.

In *Karpel v. Rumack*[261] the insured was a lawyer and mortgage broker. An action was brought against him for negligence and breach of fiduciary duty. His professional liability insurer declined to defend on the basis that the impugned conduct did not fall within the insuring agreement's definition of "professional services" and, moreover, fell within an exclusion with respect to fraudulent, dishonest or malicious acts. The insured took third party proceedings against the insurer and in the course of those proceedings sought an order that the insurer provide his defence. The Court agreed that the insurer was required to defend but held that the choice of counsel rested with the insured. The Court went on to direct that counsel should consult with the insurer before "committing to any large or unusual disbursement or initiating any unusual proceeding".[262] With respect, the learned judge has overlooked both the matter of counsel's ethical obligations to the insured and the fact that, being an action for negligence, the issue of whether or not the insured's actions were fraudulent would not be before the Court. Indeed, in a subsequent decision[263] in the same action it was held that the third party insurer was not entitled, in the main action, to raise the issue of fraud. Rather, that issue would be dealt with after the trial of the underlying action was concluded, the result of which would not prevent the insurer, in the indemnity proceeding, from seeking to show that the claim fell within the exclusion.

(e) Punitive Damages

It is almost commonplace in these times for punitive damages to be included in the relief sought by the plaintiff. Rarely, if ever, are punitive damages covered under an insurance policy.[264] Yet, in most cases this should not prevent the insurer from retaining the right to select and instruct defence counsel. Usually it will be in the insurer's interest to vigorously resist any suggestion that the insured's misconduct merits an award of punitive damages, for such conduct may very well increase the insurer's exposure to pay compensatory damages.

9. DUTY OF COUNSEL

Liability insurance policies generally give the insurer the right and obligation to select and instruct counsel to defend on behalf of the insured. In most cases, the interests of the insured and the insurer will be the same; that is, both will want to have the action dismissed, and, if it is not dismissed, the insurer will pay the judgment. Occasionally, however, the insurer and the insured will have diverging interests. Perhaps only part of the claim is covered. Perhaps the claim exceeds the policy limits. Perhaps there has been a breach of policy conditions.

---

[261] *Supra*, note 255.

[262] *Ibid.*, at 572.

[263] *Gatt v. Rumack*, [1994] O.J. No. 3054, 21 O.R. (3d) 655 (Gen. Div.).

[264] See Chapter 7, section 3: Damages.

In such circumstances, serious questions have been raised, particularly in recent years, concerning the duty of counsel appointed to defend on behalf of the insured. On the one hand, lawyers are required by ethical considerations to give undivided loyalty to the insureds whom they represent, even where this may be contrary to the interests of the insurer.[265] On the other hand, as noted in *San Diego Navy Federal Credit Union v. Cumis Insurance Society*:

> Insurance companies hire relatively few lawyers and concentrate their business. A lawyer who does not look out for the carrier's best interest may soon find himself out of work.[266]

(a) Acting for Two Clients

The relationship of insurer, insured and defence counsel is unique. Although to the world at large it will appear that counsel is representing only the insured in the action, the fact is that in the course of that representation counsel will give advice to and take instructions from the insurer. Thus most American courts considering the question have held that defense counsel appointed by the insurer to defend the insured has two clients, the insurer and the insured. There is a minority view, however, with a substantial number of proponents, which holds that the only client is the insured.[267]

In Canada the issue was dealt with in *Chersinoff v. Allstate Insurance Co.*[268] in which the Court held that counsel appointed to defend a wrongful death action on behalf of the insured must be regarded as having been jointly retained, the scope of the retainer being the defence of the insured in respect of the claim for damages:

> I now turn to the second question which I posed earlier. The starting point now must be that the solicitors were acting as solicitors for both insurer and insured in respect to the claims for damages brought against the latter. Although the insured did not select the solicitors himself but was represented by them and became their client because of the contractual right of the insurer to conduct the defence and select the solicitors, the insured agreed as a condition of being indemnified that the insurer should have the right to select solicitors so I think the insured may properly be taken to be a party to the employment of the so-licitors selected. While the employment of the same solicitors for both parties came about because of the condition, the position of the solicitors in my view is that they must be regarded as having been jointly retained to represent both parties on the issues of whether or not the insured was liable to pay damages in respect to the motor accident and the amount of the damages.[269]

---

[265] *Zurich of Canada v. Renaud & Jacob*, [1996] A.Q. No. 2670 R.J.Q. 2160 (C.A.); *Brockton (Municipality) v. Frank Cowan Co.*, [2002] O.J. No. 20, 57 O.R. (3d) 447 (C.A.); *Parlee v. Pembridge Insurance Co.*, [2005] N.B.J. No. 174, 22 C.C.L.I. (4th) 223 (C.A.).

[266] 208 Cal. Rptr. 494 at 498 (Cal.Ct. App. 1984).

[267] *Atlanta International Ins. Co. v. Bell*, 448 N.W.2d 804 (Mich. C.A. 1989).

[268] (1968), 69 D.L.R. (2d) 653 (B.C.S.C.), revd in part (1969), 3 D.L.R. (3d) 560 (B.C.C.A.).

[269] *Ibid.*, at 660-61.

Notwithstanding the decision of the British Columbia Court of Appeal in *Chersinoff*, the Supreme Court of British Columbia, in *Hopkins v. Wellington*,[270] reached the conclusion that insurance defence counsel has only one client, the insured. It does not appear from the reasons in *Hopkins*, however, that the court considered the decision in *Chersinoff*, which, pursuant to the principle of *stare decisis*, it was bound to follow.[271]

In Canadian jurisdictions other than British Columbia, the courts have been strangely silent on this issue. The one thing that can be safely said is that the insured is, at least, a client of defence counsel appointed by the insurer.[272] Except in British Columbia, whether the insurer is also a client is still an open question.

The rules of professional conduct in the various law societies in Canada, as well as the Canadian Bar Association's *Code of Professional Conduct*, addresses the duties owed by counsel when acting for two clients. Unfortunately, these rules are of a generic nature and were not devised to specifically address the unique role of insurance defence counsel.

As a general rule, a lawyer cannot act or continue to act for two parties in a matter where there is a conflict of interest between them. The Canadian Bar Association's 1987 *Code of Professional Conduct* provides as follows:

> The lawyer must not advise or represent both sides of a dispute and, save after adequate disclosure to and with the consent of the client or prospective client concerned, shall not act or continue to act in a matter when there is or there is likely to be a conflicting interest.
>
> *Commentary*
>
> Guiding Principles
>
> 1. A conflicting interest is one that would be likely to affect adversely the lawyer's judgment or advice on behalf of, or loyalty to a client or prospective client. ...
>
> 5. Before the lawyer accepts employment for more than one client in the same matter, the lawyer must advise the clients that the lawyer has been asked to act for both or all of them, that no information received in connection with the matter from one can be treated as confidential so far as any of the others is concerned, and that if a dispute develops that cannot be resolved the lawyer cannot continue to act for both or all of them and may have to withdraw completely. If one of the clients is a person with whom the lawyer has a continuing relationship and for whom the lawyer acts regularly, this fact should be revealed to the other or others with a recommendation that they obtain independent representation. If, following such disclosure, all parties are content that the lawyer act for them, the lawyer should obtain their consent, preferably in writing, or record their

---

[270] [1999] B.C.J. No. 1164, 68 B.C.L.R. (3d) 152 (S.C.).

[271] The *Hopkins* decision has been criticized by B. Billingsley in "Caught in the Middle: When Insurance Defence Counsel Encounter Coverage Problems" (2000) 79 C.B.R. 221.

[272] *R. Sherwin Enterprises v. Municipal Contracting Services,* [1994] O.J. No. 2233, 20 O.R. (3d) 692, 33 C.P.C. (3d) 244 (Gen. Div.).

consent in a separate letter to each. The lawyer should, however, guard against acting for more than one client where, despite the fact that all parties concerned consent, it is reasonably obvious that an issue contentious between them may arise or their interests, rights or obligations will diverge as the matter progresses.[273]

The principle that a lawyer representing two clients inform them at the outset of the nature and consequences of the retainer, while salutary, is seldom followed by insurance defence counsel.[274] This is unfortunate, for adherence to this principle would avoid many of the problems that may arise.

(b) Avoiding Conflicts

In most cases the interests of the insurer and the insured coincide. Whenever an issue arises as to coverage, however, or whenever the claim exceeds the policy limits, then the potential exists for a conflict of interest between the two parties to the insurance contract.

Counsel appointed by an insurer to defend the claim on behalf of the insured must be careful to avoid representing the insurer in those areas where its interests are at odds with those of the insured. As a practical matter, this is accomplished at the outset by a clear delineation of the scope of the retainer. Counsel appointed to defend the claim against the insured should restrict the retainer to the defence of issues of liability and damages in the underlying action. Issues as to coverage or as to the obligations of one party to the other under the insurance contract must be considered to be outside the scope of counsel's retainer.

In the past, there was a practice among some insurance defence counsel to continue to advise the insurer on matters of coverage while at the same time acting for the insured on the issue of liability. This practice, which even in the past was described as one that would often raise "substantial difficulties",[275] is no longer acceptable. In such cases there is an obvious appearance of impropriety. The insured cannot be expected to rely upon defence counsel to defend the claim in the best interests of the insured when, at the same time, counsel may be assisting the insurer to avoid coverage.[276]

A conflict of interest between insurer and insured may also arise where the plaintiff has alleged two grounds of liability, one which is covered under the policy and the other which is not. Perhaps the most common example of this sort of conflict is where the claim involves allegations of both negligence and

---

[273] Canadian Bar Association, *Code of Professional Conduct*, revised ed. (Ottawa: Canadian Bar Association) at 17-18.

[274] This observation is based upon the writer's own experience as to the practice generally followed by insurance defence counsel and is supported by discussions with other insurance law practitioners.

[275] *Chersinoff v. Allstate Ins. Co.* (1968), 69 D.L.R. (2d) 653 at 663, revd in part (1969), 3 D.L.R. (3d) 560, 67 W.W.R. 750 (B.C.C.A.).

[276] This paragraph was adopted by the New Brunswick Court of Appeal in *Parlee v. Pembridge Insurance Co.*, [2005] N.B.J. No. 174, 22 C.C.L.I. (4th) 223 (C.A.).

intentional wrongdoing. As noted earlier,[277] in these circumstances some courts permit the insured to select and control counsel to defend the action, while others have held that the right to select counsel still remains with the insurer. In either case, the duty on counsel is the same: namely, to defend the case on the basis that is most favourable to the insured:

> The defendants [*i.e.*, the insurers] undertake the defence in the name of the insured. Their duty and the duty of the solicitors is to defend him as an independent solicitor would.[278]

(c) Confidentiality

As with any lawyer-client relationship, the relationship between the insured and counsel appointed to defend the claim on behalf of the insured is a confidential one. The insurer is also a party to that relationship and is entitled to receive information that bears upon the issues in the underlying action. The insurer is not, however, entitled to receive information that is outside the scope of the retainer and that may prejudice the insured's position with respect to coverage.

It is both an ethical rule and a rule of evidence that information and communications passing between counsel and one client on the subject matter of the joint retainer must be disclosed in favour of the other client. In *Chersinoff v. Allstate Insurance Co.*,[279] the Court adopted as correct this statement of the rule from *Phipson on Evidence*:

> *Joint Retainer.* When two parties employ the *same solicitor*, the rule is that communications passing between either of them and the solicitor, in his *joint capacity*, must be disclosed in favour of the other — *e.g.*, a proposition made by one, to be communicated to the other; or instructions given to the solicitor in the presence of the other; though it is otherwise as to communications made to the solicitor in his *exclusive* capacity.[280]

On the basis of this rule, the Court in *Chersinoff*[281] held that communications between counsel and the insurer which dealt exclusively with matters of coverage need not be disclosed to the insured, but communications which were relevant both to the conduct of the defence and to the coverage issue had to be provided to the insured.

A breach of confidence by counsel appointed by the insurer to defend a claim on behalf of the insured may have serious repercussions for the insurer. In

---

[277] See section 8(d): Alternative Claims — One Covered, One Not Covered.

[278] *Federal Insurance Co. v. Matthews* (1956), 18 W.W.R. 193 at 212 (B.C.S.C.).

[279] *Supra*, note 275 at 661.

[280] S.L. Phipson & M.V. Argyle, *Phipson on Evidence*, 10th ed. (London: Sweet & Maxwell, 1963), at 253, para. 589.

[281] Followed in *Browne v. Cigna Insurance Co. of Canada*, [2000] B.C.J. No. 1606, 20 C.C.L.I. (3d) 257 (Master).

Citadel General Assurance Co. v. Wolofsky[282] the insured signed a non-waiver agreement and then proceeded to discuss the case with the lawyers appointed by the insurer. At counsel's request, the insured signed a statement indicating when he had received notice of the loss. This statement was passed on to the insurer and was used for the purpose of denying coverage on the basis of late reporting. When the insured then took proceedings against the insurer for coverage it was held that the statement was confidential as it was given to the lawyers in their capacity as counsel for the insured and was not to have been passed onto the insurer. In the result, the insurer was not permitted to decline coverage.

As a corollary of the rule against the disclosure of confidential information from one client to the other, the courts will generally not permit defence counsel to represent the insurer in subsequent litigation with the insured arising out of the same matter. Thus, in *Szebelledy v. Constitution Insurance Co. of Canada*[283] it was held that it was not proper for counsel defending the insurer against the insured's claim for accident benefits to also defend the claim brought against the insured arising out of the same motor vehicle accident.

Nor is it proper for the insurer, in subsequent litigation, to use against its own insured privileged information obtained from the insured in a related matter. In *Walker v. Wilson*,[284] I.C.B.C. provided insurance coverage to both drivers involved in a motor vehicle accident. The drivers commenced separate actions against each other for damages for personal injuries. I.C.B.C. appointed counsel to defend Mrs. Walker in the action commenced against her by Mr. Wilson. Then, in the action commenced by Mrs. Walker against Mr. Wilson, I.C.B.C. provided Mr. Wilson's lawyer with a copy of the file they had maintained in defending Mrs. Walker, including details of privileged communications between Mrs. Walker and her I.C.B.C.-appointed lawyer. I.C.B.C. attempted to support this practice on the basis that doing otherwise would fetter their ability to provide Mr. Wilson with a complete defence. The Court did not agree, noting that the privilege belonged to Mrs. Walker and that it could not be waived by I.C.B.C. Accordingly, I.C.B.C. was required to appoint new counsel for Mr. Wilson and to refrain from providing new counsel with any privileged information contained in the defence file maintained on behalf Mrs. Walker.

---

[282] [1984] 2 R.D.J. 440 (Que. C.A.).

[283] (1985), 11 C.C.L.I. 140 (Ont. Dist. Ct.). In theory, counsel selected by the insurer should be able to abide by this precept. Some courts, however have suggested that counsel who regularly act for an insurer will not be able to loyally represent the insured in a case in which the insurer's interests are not aligned:

> Even the most optimistic view of human nature requires us to realize that an attorney employed by an insurance company will slant his efforts, perhaps unconsciously, in the interests of his real client — the one who is paying his fee and from whom he hopes to receive future business — the insurance company.

United States Fidelity & Guar. Co. v. Louis A. Roser Co., 585 F.2d 932, 938 n.5 (8th Cir. 1978).

[284] [2000] B.C.J. No. 220 (S.C.).

(d) Insurer-Imposed Guidelines

A considerable controversy has arisen in the United States,[285] and more recently in Canada, concerning the imposition by insurers of strict guidelines for defence counsel in the handling of cases on behalf of insureds. Some insurers have implemented a variety of cost-saving measures that arguably intrude upon the ability of defence counsel to properly represent the insured. Examples of such measures include the refusal to pay for legal research unless pre-approved, the refusal to pay lawyers to draft documents deemed by the insurer to be routine, restrictions on investigations and on the selection and use of experts, and the refusal to pay for trial preparation until so instructed by the insurer. Some insurers have gone beyond this and have placed restrictions on the submissions which counsel are permitted to make to the court, for example, a blanket rule forbidding counsel from putting forward a suggested figure for the quantum of damages greater than the insurer's last offer.

In years past, in Canada at least, defence counsel's independent judgment was almost invariably respected. If that is no longer to be the case then the danger is that the insured may receive a less than adequate defence. As a Texas Supreme Court justice noted in *State Farm Mutual Automobile Insurance Co. v. Traver*:

> I am concerned that defense lawyers may be reluctant to resist cost-cutting measures that detrimentally affect the quality of the insured's defense. There is a real risk that these efforts at cost containment compromise a lawyer's autonomy and independent judgment on the best means for defending an insured.[286]

An example of insurer guidelines impeding the proper defense of an action is provided by the decision in *Frederick v. Unum Life Insurance Co. of America*.[287] Unum's guidelines subjected defense counsel to pre-approval and control by an in-house lawyer and paralegal. As a result defense counsel was unable to meet discovery deadlines. When defense counsel applied to extend the deadlines, the Court refused to grant relief, despite the fact that the motion was unopposed. The Court noted:

> The problem as I see it is that UNUM's bottom line is in conflict, not only with the local rules of practice, but also with the Federal Rules of Civil Procedure. The guide hamstrings the lawyer charged with defending the claim.

A lawyer whose independent judgment concerning the proper defence of an action conflicts with insurer imposed guidelines is in an impossible position. If

---

[285] See, generally: R. Mallen, "The Changing Profession: Recognizing the Defense Lawyer" (Insurance Coverage and Practice, Defense Research Institute, Chicago, 1999); W.T. Barker, "The Tripartite Relationship: Who Is the Client and to Whom Does the Attorney Owe Ethical Duties" (Insurance Coverage and Practice Symposium, Defense Research Institute, 1997).

[286] 980 S.W.2d 625 (Tex. 1998).

[287] 180 F.R.D. 384 (D.Mont. 1998).

the interests of the insured will be adversely affected then the lawyer must so inform the insured, even though by so doing there is the risk that this will poison the lawyer's relationship with the insurer and result in the lawyer losing the insurer as a client.[288] Understandably, although regrettably, there are lawyers who are not prepared to take such a risk. For this reason, a strong case can be made for the insured having the right to select counsel whenever the claim is one which exposes the insured to personal liability, whether due to issues of coverage or of limits.

---

[288] See James, Ugrin & Zadick, "The Montana Decision, Experience of the Litigants" (June 2000) 42 For the Defense, No. 6, p. 10, in which the authors relate the experience of two long-standing insurance defence firms that questioned whether an insurer's litigation guidelines complied with the rules of ethics imposed by their state bar. The insurer refused to submit the matter to the State Bar Ethics Committee and ended its relationship with the firms in question. The Montana Supreme Court subsequently ruled that the guidelines violated the Montana Rules of Professional Conduct. What is particularly chilling about this experience is that the lawyers who acted ethically by raising concerns about the insurer's guidelines were punished by the loss of a longtime client. This does not bode well for the independence of the insurance defence bar.

PART II

COMMERCIAL LIABILITY INSURANCE

Chapter 6

Introduction to Commercial Policies

1. TYPES OF COMMERCIAL POLICIES

Business risks form the largest portion of liability risks underwritten in Canada and the United States. Due to the diversity of business interests, a number of separate forms are available, including:

(i)   Aircraft Liability;
(ii)   Boiler and Machinery Liability;
(iii)   Commercial General Liability;
(iv)   Comprehensive General Liability;
(v)   Contractors' General Liability;
(vi)   Druggists' Liability;
(vii)   Elevator Public Liability;
(viii) Employers' Liability;
(ix)   Farmers' Personal Liability;
(x)   Garage Liability;
(xi)   Manufacturers' and Contractors' Liability;
(xii)   Owners' or Contractors' Protective Liability;
(xiii) Owners', Landlords' and Tenants' Liability;
(xiv)   Storekeepers' Liability.

For many years the form of policy most commonly issued has been the Comprehensive General Liability (or "CGL") policy. This form of policy was first standardized in the United States in 1940 by the National Bureau of Casualty Underwriters and the Mutual Casualty Insurance Ratings Bureau. The policy underwent major revisions in the United States in 1943, 1955, 1966 and 1973.[1] The 1973 revision was the final one in the United States, for in 1986 a new program, the Commercial General Liability policy, was introduced by the Insurance Services Office, Inc. ("ISO") as a replacement for the CGL form. In 1996, ISO issued a new, substantially revised edition of its standard Commercial General Liability Coverage Form. Various additional endorsements have been issued since.

---

[1]   G.H. Tinker, "Comprehensive General Liability Insurance — Perspective and Overview" (1975) 25 Federation of Insurance Counsel Quarterly 217.

In Canada, the standardization of liability policies has been carried out under the auspices of the Insurance Bureau of Canada.[2] In 1971, the Insurance Bureau issued uniform general liability policy forms for Comprehensive General Liability, Manufacturers' and Contractors', and Owners', Landlords' and Tenants' liability policies. Over the years the Insurance Bureau of Canada has made a number of changes to these forms and has also recommended several additional forms, including Garage Liability, Storekeepers' Liability, Employers' Liability, Farmers' Personal Liability, and various professional liability policies.

In 1986, the Insurance Bureau of Canada recommended a Canadian version of the Commercial General Liability policy program that had been introduced in the United States. This form, IBC 2100, underwent a number of revisions in 2005.

Although uniform liability policy wordings have received substantial acceptance in the insurance industry, differences between the same type of policy issued by different underwriters often exist. In addition, particularly with large business concerns, the policy terms may have been negotiated, resulting in a so-called "manuscript" policy which may provide markedly different coverage from the standard form. When considering any question of interpretation, therefore, one must pay careful attention to the particular wording of the policy at hand as well as to the context in which the wording is used. A case on the interpretation of words in one insurance contract is not necessarily an authority for the interpretation of similar words in another insurance contract if the context has changed.[3]

In this part the focus will be on the CGL form. Many of the same concepts, and often the same wording, found in other forms of liability policies are also in the CGL form. Any substantive differences between the CGL form and the other forms generally available will be noted.

2. STRUCTURE OF A COMMERCIAL LIABILITY POLICY

Despite various differences in wording, the structure of commercial liability policies is generally the same. Most insurers utilize a policy "shell", which is the same for their various liability policies, containing the declarations, definitions and conditions.[4] To this shell are added coverage riders for the particular forms of coverage purchased by the insured.

There are six sections to a standard commercial liability policy:

(i) declarations;

---

[2] The Insurance Bureau of Canada was formed in 1964 and includes in its membership a majority of the property and casualty underwriters in Canada.

[3] *Dominion Bridge Co. v. Toronto General Ins. Co.* (1962), 37 W.W.R. 673 at 682 (B.C.C.A.) *per* Davey J.A., affd [1963] S.C.R. 362.

[4] See Appendix A for an example of a policy "shell".

(ii) definitions;
(iii) insuring agreement;
(iv) exclusions;
(v) conditions;
(vi) endorsements, if any.

When analyzing coverage in a particular case one will likely have to give consideration to each of these six parts of the liability policy.[5]

The starting place is with the declarations. These are the representations by the insured with respect to the nature of the risk to be insured and the type of coverage selected. In a commercial liability policy they will include the name of the insured(s), a description of the premises and operations or hazards, the nature of the coverage selected, any territorial limitation that may apply, and the limit of liability applicable to each occurrence as well as any aggregate or overall limit. The form in which the declarations are printed may vary with the insurer. Often, the declarations are printed on the first page of the policy shell. Additional declarations may, however, be found in the coverage rider itself, or in a separate endorsement.

One must then look at the insuring agreement, which establishes the parameters within which coverage is available. If coverage is not found within the insuring agreement then, logically, it cannot be found elsewhere.[6]

The next step is to consider the exclusions, which operate to narrow the coverage provided under the insuring agreement. The exclusions are to be read separately. Often more than one exclusion applies. It takes only one exclusion to apply, however, in order to avoid coverage.

Several of the terms used in the insuring agreement and in the exclusions are given specific definitions in the definition section of the policy. Obviously, the terms must be used in accordance with their assigned definitions.

The conditions of the policy must then be examined in order to determine whether coverage may be avoided by reason of the insured's breach of condition. The condition to which one must often refer in analyzing a coverage question is the condition requiring notification to the insurer of an accident or occurrence.[7]

The final step is to review the endorsements, if any, in order to determine whether any of the terms of the policy have been modified.

---

[5]   *Jesuit Fathers of Upper Canada v. Guardian Insurance Co. of Canada*, [2003] O.J. No. 4534, 6 C.C.L.I. (4th) 276 (S.C.J.), appeal dismissed [2004] O.J. No. 4641 (C.A.), leave to appeal to S.C.C. granted [2005] S.C.C.A. No. 5.

[6]   *Weedo v. Stone-E-Brick Inc.*, 405 A.2d 788 (N.J. 1979). Note, however, that one may need to examine the wording of the exclusions in order to place the language of the insuring agreement in context. See Chapter 7, section 2: Liability Imposed by Law.

[7]   See Chapter 3, section 3: Notice of Accident, Occurrence, Claim or Suit.

3. PERSONS INSURED

(a) Policy Language

Commercial liability policies contain a section setting out the persons insured under the various provisions of the policy. The standard CGL policy wording provides that:

> Each of the following is an Insured under this insurance to the extent set forth below:
>
> (1) if the Named Insured is designated in the declarations as an individual, the person so designated but only with respect to the conduct of a business of which he is the sole proprietor;
> (2) if the Named Insured is designated in the declarations as a partnership or joint venture, the partnership or joint venture so designated and any partner or member thereof but only with respect to his liability as such;
> (3) if the Named Insured is designated in the declarations as other than an individual, partnership or joint venture, the organization so designated and any executive officer, director, or stockholder thereof while acting within the scope of his duties as such;
> (4) any person (other than an employee of the Named Insured) or organization while acting as real estate manager for the Named Insured. This insurance does not apply to bodily injury or property damage arising out of the conduct of any partnership or joint venture of which the insured is a partner or member and which is not designated in this policy as a Named Insured.

"Named Insured" and "insured" are defined in the definition section of the policy:

> "insured" means any person or organization qualifying as an Insured in the "Persons Insured" provision of the applicable coverage rider. The insurance afforded applies separately to each Insured against whom claim is made or suit is brought, except with respect to the limits of the Insurer's liability.

> "Named Insured" means the person or organization named in the Declarations of this policy.

In the Commercial General Liability policy the definition of "insured" has been expanded to include spouses of proprietors and partners as well as, in certain circumstances, employees of corporations. In addition, coverage is extended for the first 90 days to newly acquired but otherwise uninsured organizations:

> SECTION II — WHO IS AN INSURED
> 1. If you are designated in the Declarations as:
>   a.   An individual, you and your spouse are insureds but only with respect to the conduct of a business of which you are the sole owner.

  b. A partnership or joint venture, you are an insured. Your members, your partners, and their spouses are also insureds, but only with respect to the conduct of your business.

  c. An organization other than a partnership or joint venture, you are an insured. Your executive officers and directors are insureds, but only with respect to their duties as your officers or directors. Your stockholders are also insured, but only with respect to their liability as stockholders.

2. Each of the following is also an insured:

  a. Your employees, other than your executive officers, but only for acts within the scope of their employment by you. However, none of these employees is an insured for:

    1) "Bodily injury" or "personal injury" to you or to a co-employee while in the course of his or her employment; or

    2) "Bodily injury" or "personal injury" to any person who at the time of injury is entitled to benefits under any workers' compensation or disability benefits law or a similar law; or

    3) "Bodily injury" or "personal injury" arising out of his or her providing or failing to provide professional health care services; or

    4) "Property damage" to property owned or occupied by or rented or loaned to that employee, any of your other employees, or any of your partners or members (if you are a partnership or joint venture).

  b. Any person (other than your employees), or any organization while acting as your real estate manager.

  c. Any person or organization having proper temporary custody of your property if you die, but only:

    1) With respect to liability arising out of the maintenance or use of that property; and

    2) Until your legal representative has been appointed.

  d. Your legal representative if you die, but only with respect to duties as such. That representative will have all your rights and duties under this policy.

3. Any organization you newly acquire or form, other than a partnership or joint venture, and over which you maintain ownership or majority interest, will be deemed to be a Named Insured if there is not other similar insurance available to that organization. However:

  a. Coverage under this provision is afforded only until the 90th day after you acquire or form the organization or the end of the policy period, whichever is earlier;

b.   Coverages A and D do not apply to "bodily injury" or "property damage" that occurred before you acquired or formed the organization;
and

c.   Coverage B does not apply to "personal injury" arising out of an offence committed before you acquired or formed the organization.
No person or organization is an insured with respect to the conduct of any
current or past partnership or joint venture that is not shown as a Named
Insured in the Declarations.[8]

(b) Proprietorships

Where the named insured is a proprietorship, coverage under the CGL policy is
provided to the person appearing in the declarations as the proprietor. Coverage
is limited, however, to liability arising out of the operation of the designated
proprietorship. Thus, in *Consolidated American Insurance Co. v. Landry*[9] it was
held that a policy in which the named insured was designated as the proprietor
of an apartment rental business did not extend to the insured's liability arising
out of his operation of a lumber yard, which was a separate business.

Under the Commercial General Liability policy, coverage is extended to the
spouse of the proprietor, and, with certain limitations, to the employees of the
proprietorship.[10]

(c) Partnerships and Joint Ventures

If the named insured is a partnership or joint venture then, under the CGL
policy, coverage is provided to the persons declared as partners or joint ventur-
ers but is limited to the liability arising out of the designated partnership or joint
venture. Under the Commercial General Liability policy coverage extends to the
spouses of the partners or members of the joint venture and also, with certain
limitations, to the employees of the partnership or joint venture.

Both the CGL and the Commercial General Liability policies provide that
they do not apply to any bodily injury or property damage arising out of the
conduct of any partnership or joint venture of which the insured is a partner or
member and which is not designated in the policy as a named insured. The
meaning of this provision was considered by the British Columbia Court of
Appeal in *Kingsway General Insurance Co. v. Lougheed Enterprises Ltd.*[11]
Three corporations formed a partnership in connection with a real estate
development. The project consisted of residential apartment buildings which
were sold to strata owners. Shortly after completion of the development one of
the corporate partners was dissolved. Several years later a fire occurred in one of
the buildings. An action was commenced by the strata owners against the

---

[8]   For the whole policy, see Appendix I of this book.
[9]   525 So.2d 567 (La. 1988).
[10]   See section 3(e): Employees.
[11]   [2004] B.C.J. No. 1606, 13 C.C.L.I. (4th) 173 (C.A.).

partnership and the two remaining corporate partners alleging negligence in the development, design, construction, inspection and approval of the building. The two corporate defendants tendered the defence of the action to their liability insurer under a policy which was in place at the time of the fire. The policy made no mention of the partnership. Nevertheless, the corporate insureds argued that the "No person" clause[12] applied solely in respect of an individual partner's vicarious liability for the actions of the partnership and did not extend to a partner's direct liability to the plaintiffs. The Court rejected this argument, noting that the clause under consideration excluded the insured's liability with respect to the conduct of the partnership, which would encompass both direct and vicarious liability. Although the Court expressed concern that the clause in question was contained in a policy definition rather than an exclusion, the Court noted that the rules of construction require that effect be given to all words used in a contract, if at all possible, and that the plain meaning of the words used should be given effect unless the result would be commercially unreasonable or absurd.

(d) Corporations and Other Organizations

Under the CGL policy, where the named insured is an organization other than an individual, partnership or joint venture, coverage is extended to that body and to its executive officers, directors and stockholders engaged in their duties as such. The types of organizations fitting this description include corporations, societies and co-operative associations.

It is, of course, easy to determine if one is a director or stockholder. Determining whether one is an *executive officer*, however, may be somewhat more difficult. Some assistance may be obtained from the articles of the company and the incorporation legislation, in either of which the term "officer" (although probably not "executive officer") will likely be defined. This may place too great a restriction on the term, however, for in the United States the courts have generally extended the designation of "executive officer" to those engaged in the management or supervision of a group or department, regardless of whether within the company the person actually holds the designation "officer".[13]

In the Commercial General Liability policy, coverage is additionally extended to employees of the organization, subject to the limitations discussed below.

(e) Employees

Under the standard CGL policy wording, employees are not included as insured persons. This often leads to practical difficulties. Since the named insured is

---

[12] "No person or organization is an insured with respect to the conduct of any current or past partnership or joint venture that is not shown as a Named Insured in the Declarations".

[13] *Argonaut Ins. Co. v. Colonial Ins. Co.*, 70 Cal. App.3d 608, 138 Cal. Rptr. 855 (1977). See Annotation, "Who Is 'Executive Officer' of Insured within Coverage of Liability Insurance Policy" (1971) 39 A.L.R. (3d) 1434.

vicariously liable for the acts or omissions of employees, the insurer will likely want to secure the employees' co-operation in the defence of an action. Additionally, if the employee is named in the law suit, it will be in the insurer's interest for the employee to be adequately represented. In these circumstances, provided the employee does not carry separate insurance, a CGL insurer may very well undertake to defend and indemnify both the employee and the employer, notwithstanding that the employee is not covered under the policy.

In the Commercial General Liability policy, coverage is extended to employees, but only with respect to acts within the scope of their employment and, in any event, not with respect to:

(1) bodily injury or personal injury to an employee;

(2) bodily injury or personal injury to any person entitled to benefits under any Workers' Compensation legislation or similar law;

(3) bodily injury or personal injury arising out of providing or failing to provide professional health care services;

(4) property damage to property owned or occupied by or rented or loaned to an employee or a partner or member of an insured partnership or joint venture.

(f) Insured's Real Estate Manager

Under both the CGL and Commercial General Liability policies, coverage is extended to the named insured's real estate manager, other than an employee, while acting as a real estate manager for the named insured.

Whether a person is a "real estate manager" for the purposes of this provision is a question of fact to be determined in light of the circumstances. In *McDermott v. Smith*,[14] where the person occupying the premises did so for his own benefit and was not under any instructions with respect to the maintenance or care of the property, it was held that he was not a "real estate manager" and was therefore not insured under the owner's policy.

The real estate manager need not have been appointed by the insured. In *Fireman's Fund Insurance Co. v. Vordemeier*[15] it was held that coverage extended to a court-appointed receiver who was responsible for the management of the insured's building during foreclosure proceedings.

Coverage is extended to the insured's real estate manager only while he or she is acting in that capacity. Thus, the policy does not afford coverage where the manager uses the insured's property for personal business.[16]

---

[14] 364 So.2d 141 (La. 1978).

[15] 415 So.2d 1347 (Fla. 1982).

[16] *Nourighe v. Preferred Risk Mutual Ins. Co.*, 650 P.2d 1075 (Ore. 1982).

(g) Newly Acquired Organizations

Under the Commercial General Liability policy, coverage is automatically extended for 90 days (or the expiration of the policy, whichever is earlier) to any newly acquired or newly formed organization other than a partnership or joint venture. Coverage is excluded, however, with respect to bodily injury or property damage that occurred before the acquisition or formation, and neither does it apply where similar insurance is available to the organization.

(h) Additional Insureds by Endorsement

Frequently, additional insureds are added by an endorsement to the policy. In such cases it is customary for the endorsement to limit the nature of the risks for which the additional insured is covered. Common limitations are to restrict the additional insured's coverage to vicarious liability arising from the negligence of the named insured[17] or to liability arising out of the operations of the named insured.[18] In the absence of any limitation,[19] or if the limitation is not clearly worded,[20] it may be argued that the additional insured is also covered for its own independent negligence.

This presents fertile ground for coverage disputes. The additional insured may well have its own liability policy. An issue may often arise as to whether one or both of the policies apply to a particular claim.

(i) Severability of Insureds or "Cross-Liability"

Commercial liability policies generally provide that the insurance afforded under the policy applies separately to each person insured. This provision is sometimes referred to as a "cross-liability" clause. In the Insurance Bureau of Canada's standard form for use with commercial liability policies the cross-liability clause appears in the definition of the term "insured":

> ... the insurance afforded applies separately to each Insured against whom claim is made or suit is brought except with respect to the limits of the Insurer's liability.

In the Commercial General Liability policy there is a separate clause with respect to cross-liability:

> 13. Separation of Insureds, Cross Liability
>
> Except with respect to the Limits of Insurance, and any rights or duties specifically assigned to the first Named Insured, this insurance applies:

---

[17] *Harbor Insurance Co. v. Lewis*, 562 F.Supp. 800 (E.D.Pa. 1983).

[18] *Cowichan Valley School District No. 79 v. Lloyd's Underwriters, Lloyd's London*, [2003] B.C.J. No. 1964, 2 C.C.L.I. (4th) 170 (S.C.).

[19] *Mercer v. Paradise (Town)*, [1991] N.J. No. 126, [1991] I.L.R. 1-2740 (Nfld. T.D.).

[20] *Philadelphia Electric Co. v. Nationwide Mutual Insurance Co.*, 721 F.Supp. 740 (E.D.Pa. 1989).

(a) As if each Named Insured were the only Named insured; and

(b) Separately to each insured against whom claim is made or "action" is brought.

The cross-liability clause affects the policy in two significant respects. First, since the policy is to be read as applying to each insured separately, a breach by one insured will not affect another insured's coverage.[21] Further, since the exclusions are to be read as applying separately to each person insured under the policy, on the facts of any particular case an exclusion may apply to one insured but not to another.[22] Hence, it was held that an assault committed by a partner in the regular course of the business of the partnership did not affect coverage for the co-partner who had nothing to do with the assault but was nevertheless liable in respect of it.[23] Similarly, an assault by a taxi driver did not affect his employer's coverage, for the nature of vicarious liability is that the liability rather than the act is attributed to the employer.[24]

4. PREMISES AND OPERATIONS COVERED

The CGL and Commercial General Liability policies do not contain any restriction as to either premises or operations. Coverage is extended in respect of all of the insured's premises and operations, subject, however, to the requirement that all hazards known to exist at the effective date of the policy be disclosed in the policy declarations. As noted earlier,[25] under the Commercial General Liability policy, coverage is automatically extended for 90 days in respect of newly acquired organizations.

In other forms of commercial liability insurance policies, however, coverage may be restricted both with respect to the premises occupied by the insured and the operations which the insured carries on. A useful description of the various forms of coverage available is set out in the decision in *Tucker Construction Co. v. Michigan Mutual Insurance Co.* as follows:

> A manufacturer or a contractor or other person performing services for others faces two types of potential liability. One is contractual liability for failure to perform the contractual obligation and to deliver a product or service as agreed. The other is the usual potential tort liability attendant to all activity that results when one fails to use due care and thereby causes others personal injury or property damage. As a practical matter the potential for tort liability is different

---

[21] *Broquedis v. Employers Mutual Liability Ins.*, 360 N.Y.S.2d 735 (1974).

[22] *ING Insurance Co. of Canada v. Sportsco International L.P.*, [2004] O.J. No. 2254, 12 C.C.L.I. (4th) 86 (S.C.J.). This may be the result even in the absence of a cross-liability clause. See *Stolberg v. Pearl Assur. Co.*, [1971] I.L.R. 1-415 (S.C.C.). But *cf.*, *Romay Automotive Ltd. v. Dominion of Can. General Ins. Co.* (1974), 2 O.R. (2d) 506 (H.C.J.).

[23] *Morgan v. Greater New York Tax Payers Mutual Ins. Assn.*, 112 N.E.2d 273 (N.Y. 1953).

[24] *Bluebird Cabs Ltd. v. Guardian Insurance Co. of Canada*, [1999] B.C.J. No. 694, 173 D.L.R. (4th) 318, 66 B.C.L.R. (3d) 86, [1999] I.L.R. 1-3688 (C.A.).

[25] See section 3(g): Newly Acquired Organizations.

and greater during the manufacturing or service performing activity than it is thereafter and different liability insurance coverage applies while the work is in progress than applies after the work is completed; but in either event, liability coverage does not cover the contractual liability involved.

Liability insurance protection for a manufacturer arising out of the process of producing or manufacturing goods is generally termed "premises liability" while liability protection coverage for the manufacturer once the goods are finished and moved away from the manufacturing premises is called "products liability." Similarly, a person who performs a service on the premises of others, such as a building contractor, can obtain coverage while his work is in progress in the form of an "operations liability" insurance policy and, after work is completed, by a "completed operations" policy. Since a "premises liability" policy provides a manufacturer with the same type of coverage that an "operations liability" policy provides the service performer, some policies lump such coverage together as "premises/operations" coverage. Likewise, "products liability" for manufacturers equates with "completed operations" coverage for the service performer. However the "premises/operations" coverage and the "products liability/completed operations" coverage are mutually exclusive, each coverage protecting against a separate liability situation and each carrying a separate premium. Where tort liability results from poor workmanship or other activity on the contractor's part, whether the contractor's liability policy provides coverage or not depends on which of the two coverages is carried and when the injury or damage occurs. A premises/operations policy does not provide coverage as to an incident or accident giving rise to injury or damages which occurs after the work is completed.[26]

(a) Premises and Operations Coverage

In the early part of the century, when products liability was still in its infancy, commercial liability coverage was generally purchased with respect to the risk of bodily injury or property damage occurring on or in connection with the insured's "premises and operations".[27] This form of coverage applied only where the insured's liability arose out of accidents which occurred on the insured's premises or in connection with the insured's operations, wherever they were located. Coverage was not provided with respect to the risk that an accident might have occurred off the insured's premises and after the insured's operations were complete.

This limited form of "premises and operations" coverage is still available today under certain types of policies. In the Owners', Landlords' and Tenants' Liability policy, for example, coverage is limited to claims arising out of:

> ... the ownership, maintenance or use of the insured premises and all operations necessary or incidental thereto.

The term "insured premises" is defined as follows:

---

[26] 423 So.2d 525 (Fla. 5th DCA 1982) at 526-27 (footnotes omitted).

[27] See, generally, Landis & Rahdert, "The Completed Operations Hazard" (Summer 1984) The Forum 570.

"insured premises" means (1) the premises designated in the schedule, and (2) premises as to which the Named Insured acquires ownership or control provided the Named Insured notifies the Insurer within 30 days following the effective date of such acquisition, but the insurance with respect to the newly acquired premises does not apply to any loss against which the Named Insured has other valid and collectable insurance; and includes the ways immediately adjoining such premises.[28]

It has been held that this form of policy contemplates coverage against liability arising from the condition or use of the premises as distinct from the nature of the enterprise or activity conducted therein.[29] Thus, such a policy did not respond to a claim against an insured hotel by a fashion model who alleged that the stage upon which she was performing had become slippery because of the use of certain props in the production of the show.[30]

The definition of "insured premises" extends to the premises designated in the schedule and those to which the named insured acquires ownership or control and in respect of which notice is given to the insurer within 30 days. In addition, coverage is extended in respect of "the ways immediately adjoining such premises". This has been interpreted as referring to the ways which touch or abut the premises. Coverage, therefore, was not afforded in respect of an incident that occurred two and one-half blocks away from the insured premises.[31]

(b) Completed Operations

For several decades, insurers have recognized that "completed operations" pose a separate category risk from that of "premises and operations".[32] The classic example of the need for completed operations coverage is that of the contractor who is liable in respect of a structural defect which does not result in the building collapsing until many years after completion.

Unfortunately, the manner in which the "completed operations" concept is often addressed in modern liability policies is somewhat convoluted. Ordinarily, if "completed operations" is shown on the face page as an included form of coverage, one would expect to see separate policy provisions setting out the scope of the coverage provided. Yet that is often not the case. Instead, "completed operations" will often appear simply as a defined term in the policy and the parameters of the coverage will appear not in the insuring agreement but, rather, in the exclusions and other provisions of the policy. In some forms, the

---

[28] I.B.C. Form 2004, June 1978; reproduced in its entirety in Appendix D of this book. See also the form of "Shiprepairers' Liability Insurance Policy" under consideration in *Nanaimo Shipyard (1985) Ltd. v. Underwriters, Lloyd's London*, [1992] B.C.J. No. 597, 66 B.C.L.R. (2d) 162, 7 C.C.L.I. (2d) 1, 12 B.C.A.C. 179 (C.A.); leave to appeal to S.C.C. refd (1992), 17 B.C.A.C. 320*n*, 29 W.A.C. 320*n*, 70 B.C.L.R. (2d) xxxii*n*, 12 C.C.L.I. (2d) 102*n*.

[29] G.J. Couch, *Couch Cyclopedia of Insurance Law*, 2nd ed. (Rochester: Lawyers Co-operative Publishing Co., 1984) at para. 44:379.

[30] *Harvey v. Mr. Lynn's Inc.*, 416 So. 2d 960 (La. 1982).

[31] U.S. Fire Ins. Co. v. Schnackenberg, 429 N.E.2d 1203 (Ill. 1981).

[32] *Supra*, note 27.

Owners', Landlords' and Tenants' Liability policy being an example, liability in respect of completed operations is excluded in its entirety. The CGL and Commercial General Liability forms, on the other hand, do not contain a blanket exclusion in respect of completed operations, although the scope of certain exclusions may be expressed in terms of the completed operations hazard. Such policies may also contain an extended period of coverage in respect of completed operations. For example, the policy may be subject to a one year term in respect of all hazards except that of completed operations, in respect of which a three year period may apply.

In modern policies the term "completed operations hazard" is usually defined as follows:

"completed operations hazard" includes bodily injury or property damage arising out of operations, but only if the bodily injury or property damage occurs after such operations have been completed or abandoned and occurs away from premises owned by or rented to the Named Insured. Operations include materials, parts or equipment furnished in connection therewith. Operations shall be deemed completed at the earliest of the following times:

(i)   when all operations to be performed by or on behalf of the Named Insured under the contract have been completed;

(ii) when all operations to be performed by or on behalf of the Named Insured at the site of the operations have been completed;

(iii) when the portion of the work out of which the bodily injury or property damage arises has been put to its intended use by any persons or organization other than another contractor or sub-contractor engaged in performing operations for a principal as a part of the same project.

Operations which may require further service or maintenance work, or correction, repair or replacement because of any defect or deficiency, but which are otherwise complete shall be deemed complete.

The completed operations hazard shall not include:

(i)   operations in connection with the pick up and delivery of property;

(ii) the existence of tools, uninstalled equipment or abandoned or unused materials.[33]

In determining when operations can be considered complete the courts have applied a test of factual rather than legal completion. Thus, in *Baynes Manning (Alta.) Ltd. v. Employers' Liability Assurance Corp.*,[34] coverage was not available where the insured contractor (whose policy did not cover completed operations) had left the job site and received a certificate of completion but remained contractually liable to remedy any potential deficiencies. The decision in *Baynes* was followed by the Supreme Court of Canada in *Western Pile & Foundation (Ont.) Ltd. v. Canadian General Insurance Co.*[35] In the latter case,

---

[33] See Appendix A of this book.

[34] [1960] I.L.R. 1-371 (B.C.C.A.).

[35] [1972] S.C.R. 175, 20 D.L.R. (3d) 325, [1971] I.L.R. 1-429.

coverage was denied to an insured contractor, even though the certificate of completion had not been issued, where the contractor had left the job and had been paid the amount owing, less a holdback. Ritchie J., for the Court, noted:

> To conclude, as did the Court of Appeal for Ontario [the court below], that "construction operations" are incomplete simply because the insured has the intention to remedy any defects which become apparent even though all men and equipment have been removed from the job site, is to confuse the question of the legal relationship between the insured and a third person who might or might not have required work to be done in the future with the question of the actual performance of the work itself. Here it was clear that the actual work or "construction operation" in which the appellant was involved was the sinking of piles in an interlocking pattern to specified depths. This "operation" was "completed" by January 29th, 1964, and it was out of this operation, negligently performed, that the respondent's claim arose.[36]

In *Conacher Construction Ltd. v. Canadian Surety Co.*,[37] it was held that an exclusion with respect to completed operations did not apply where the insured had removed its workers and equipment from the site but had agreed to remedy a list of deficiencies at a later date when it was going to undertake a further extension of its contract. The distinction between the decisions in *Conacher* and those in *Baynes* and *Western Pile* seems to be that in the former case there was an actual intent to return to the site to remedy known deficiencies, whereas in the latter two cases there was only a legal requirement to remedy such deficiencies as might arise.

(c) Products Hazard

The first products liability policies are said to have been issued in England, in the latter part of Queen Victoria's reign, for the purpose of insuring bakers against liability for accidents which sometimes occurred when roach powder found its way into their pie dough.[38] Today, coverage with respect to the so-called "products hazard" is available under a variety of forms, including the CGL and Commercial General Liability policies, but may be excluded under other forms, such as the Owners', Landlords' and Tenants', and Manufacturers' and Contractors' policies. The definition of "products hazard" found in commercial policies is as follows:

> "products hazard" includes bodily injury and property damage arising out of the Named Insured's products but only if such bodily injury or property damage occurs away from premises owned by or rented to the Named Insured and after physical possession of such products has been relinquished to others.

---

[36] *Ibid.*, I.L.R. at 173.

[37] (1965), 47 D.L.R. (2d) 237, [1965] I.L.R. 1-132 (Alta. C.A.).

[38] Anderson, "Current Problems on Products Liability Law and Products Liability Insurance" (1964) 31 Ins. Counsel Journal 436 at 441.

"Named Insured's products" means goods or products manufactured, sold, handled or distributed by the Named Insured or by others trading under his name, including any container thereof (other than a vehicle), but shall not include a vending machine or any property other than such container, rented to or located for use of others but not sold.[39]

Coverage with respect to the products hazard does not, by definition, arise where the injury or property damage occurs on the insured's premises. Rather, products hazard coverage applies only with respect to the risk that the insured's products will cause bodily injury or property damage away from the insured's premises and after physical possession of the products has been relinquished to others.

Since the products hazard may operate either as an insuring clause or as an exclusion, depending upon the type of policy purchased, it is not surprising that there is disagreement on the scope of the hazard. While some courts suggest that a claim cannot arise out of the products hazard unless the product is defective,[40] others have held that the products hazard embraces the risk of negligently recommending the wrong product for use or failing to warn with respect to a dangerous product, even though the product itself contains no defect.[41]

---

[39] I.B.C. Form 2000, May 1978. See Appendix A of this book.

[40] See, for example, *Lessak v. Metro. Casualty Ins. Co.*, 151 N.E.2d 730 (Ohio 1958).

[41] See, for example, *Abbot v. Meacock*, 746 P.2d 1 (Ariz. 1987). See, generally, Harvey, "Products Liability Insurance Coverage" (1980) 31 South Carolina Law Review 718, and Henderson, "Insurance Protection for Products Liability and Completed Operations: What Every Lawyer Should Know" (1971) 50 Nebraska Law Review 415.

Chapter 7

THE INSURING AGREEMENT

1. STRUCTURE OF THE INSURING AGREEMENT

In order for coverage to exist under a liability policy, it must be found within the insuring agreement. The primary risk covered under business liability policies is usually tortious liability. However, as discussed below, certain forms of statutory and contractual liability may also be covered.

The wording of the insuring agreement may differ from policy to policy and from insurer to insurer. Nevertheless, there are certain common elements. The insuring agreement defines coverage in terms of:

    (i)   The theory of liability (usually "liability imposed by law" or "legally obligated to pay");

   (ii) The type of obligation (usually "to pay damages");

 (iii) The type of damage (usually "bodily injury" or "property damage");

 (iv) The type of event giving rise to the claim (usually "accident" or "occurrence");

  (v) The place where the damage occurs (the "policy territory");

 (vi) The period of coverage (either the date of the accident or occurrence, or the date when the claim was made).

An example of the most common insuring agreement found in a commercial liability policy is the form of CGL rider published by the Insurance Bureau of Canada:

Coverage A — Bodily Injury Liability

To pay on behalf of the Insured all sums which the Insured shall become legally obligated to pay as compensatory damages because of bodily injury.

Coverage B — Property Damage Liability

To pay on behalf of the Insured all sums which the Insured shall become legally obligated to pay as compensatory damages because of property damage caused by accident.[1]

---

[1] I.B.C. Form 2001, June 1978. The discussion throughout this chapter will be based in large part on this form, which is found at Appendix B. The Commercial General Liability form, I.B.C. 2100 is found at Appendix I. Both forms are in general use and, while similar in terms of coverage, there are differences which may be of significance in an individual case.

In conjunction with the definitions of "bodily injury" and "property damage", the coverage provided under this form of insuring agreement may be conveniently analyzed as follows. For coverage to obtain there must be:

(i) liability imposed by law
(ii) to pay damages
(iii) because of bodily injury or
(iv) because of property damage occasioned by an accident or occurrence
(v) in the policy territory
(vi) during the policy period.

2. LIABILITY IMPOSED BY LAW

The insuring clause in commercial liability policies is expressed in terms either of the "liability imposed by law" on the insured to pay damages, or in terms of damages which the insured is "legally obligated to pay". It has been held that the meaning of both phrases is the same,[2] although arguably the latter is consistent with any form of legal obligation whereas the former only with liability which is *imposed upon* as distinct from being *assumed by* the insured.

Historically, the expression "liability imposed by law" was considered to refer to tortious liability, and statutory liability akin to tort, as distinct from liability arising in contract.[3] Over the years, however, policy wordings have been modified so as to provide coverage with respect to certain types of contractual liability. These modifications have been accomplished in two ways: either (i) by including a specific reference to contractual liability in the insuring clause, or (ii) by inserting in the policy an exclusion with respect to liability arising in contract, with certain specified exceptions. From a drafting standpoint, the latter approach leaves much to be desired, for in order to extend coverage to the exceptions to the exclusion one is required to read the expression "liability imposed by law" as including contractual liability although, standing alone, the phrase refers solely to liability arising in tort. This has been the source of considerable confusion to courts, commentators and practitioners.

As a result, having regard to the context in which it is used, the phrase "liability imposed by law" may be held in one policy to include contractual liability and in another policy to extend only to claims arising in tort. Where the phrase "liability imposed by law" is accompanied by wording such as "or assumed under contract (as defined herein)" then it is plain that the former wording is restricted to tortious liability.[4] Where, on the other hand, the phrase

---

[2] *Ben's Ltd. v. Royal Ins. Co.*, [1985] N.S.J. No. 47, [1985] I.L.R. 1-1969 (T.D.); *Kentville (Town) v. Gestas, Inc.*, [1989] N.S.J. No. 234, 96 N.S.R. (2d) 339, [1989] I.L.R. 1-2519 (S.C.), affd, [1990] N.S.J. No. 64, 253 A.P.R. 338, 96 N.S.R. (2d) 338 (C.A.).

[3] *Foundation of Can. Engineering Corp. v. Can. Indemnity* (1977), 13 N.R. 282 at 289 (S.C.C.).

[4] *Capital Regional Dist. v. General Accident Assur. Co. of Can.*, [1985] B.C.J. No. 345, 15 C.C.L.I. 193 (S.C.), affd, [1987] B.C.J. No. 1301, 39 D.L.R. (4th) 619, [1987] I.L.R. 1-2210, 27

"liability imposed by law" stands alone, and an exclusion exists with respect to some (but not all) types of contractual liability, then the phrase has been held to include liability arising pursuant to a contract that has not been excluded.[5]

The meaning of the phrase "liability imposed by law" in the context of personal injury[6] (as distinct from bodily injury) liability insurance has been considered in a number of recent cases. In each of the decisions in *Neiman v. CGU Insurance Co.,*[7] *Capital Regional District v. General Accident Assurance Co. of Canada,*[8] *Ben's Ltd. v. Royal Insurance Co.,*[9] and *Acklands Ltd. v. Canadian Indemnity Co.,*[10] it was held that both "liability imposed by law" or "legally obligated to pay" referred to tortious liability and therefore did not extend coverage to claims for compensation in lieu of notice as a result of wrongful dismissal. In *Cultus Lake Park Board v. Gestas Inc.,*[11] however, it was held with respect to a Municipal Liability Insurance Policy which made no mention of "contract" in either the insuring agreement or the exclusions, that the phrase "legally obligated to pay" encompassed a claim arising in contract for the breach of a restrictive covenant in a lease.

The issue of whether the liability imposed on the insured must be a liability to a third party arose in *Northwood Mills Ltd. v. Continental Insurance Co.*[12] In that case a manuscript policy provided coverage as follows:

Coverage D — Forest Fire Fighting Expenses

> To pay on behalf of the insured all sums which the insured shall become obligated to pay by reason of the liability imposed upon the insured by a law or statute for the cost of fighting forest fires.[13]

The insured was required by statute to directly incur the expenses of fighting various forest fires. The insurer argued that the coverage afforded under the policy extended only to liability to third parties, which may be imposed by a law or statute, and not to the direct cost of fighting forest fires, even though that cost may be imposed by statute. It was held, however, having regard to the context of the policy, that the expenses were recoverable from the insurer.

C.C.L.I. 81 (C.A.); *Acklands Ltd. v. Can. Indemnity Co.*, [1984] 4 W.W.R. 764, 4 C.C.E.L. 324 (Man. Q.B.), affd 16 D.L.R. (4th) 637, [1985] 4 W.W.R. 71 (Man. C.A.).

[5] *Moffat Tank Co. v. Can. Indemnity Co.*, [1974] 1 W.W.R. 688 (Alta. C.A.).

[6] See Chapter 10.

[7] [2002] O.J. No. 2215 (S.C.J.).

[8] *Supra*, note 4.

[9] *Supra*, note 2. See also *Kentville (Town) v. Gestas, Inc., supra*, note 2.

[10] *Supra*, note 4.

[11] [1995] B.C.J. No. 2595, 15 B.C.L.R. (3d) 89, [1996] I.L.R. 1-3293, (C.A.). Applied in *Surrey (District) v. General Accident Assur. Co. of Can.*, [1996] B.C.J. No. 849, 7 W.W.R. 48, 19 B.C.L.R. (3d) 186, [1996] I.L.R. 1-3325 (C.A.), in which the Court held that an award for unjust enrichment was "liability imposed by law" in the context of a CGL policy.

[12] [1973] 5 W.W.R. 144, [1973] I.L.R. 1-543 (B.C.S.C.).

[13] *Ibid.*, at 647.

The phrase "liability imposed by law" has also been held to apply to the insured's liability for the costs of execution.[14]

3. DAMAGES

Most liability policies, including the initial version of the CGL policy, provide coverage in respect of "damages". In 1977, the Insurance Bureau of Canada amended its CGL policy so as to restrict coverage to "compensatory damages". The intent of this amendment was to exclude from coverage punitive damages, which, by definition, are not compensatory in nature.[15]

The word "damages" is usually left undefined in a liability policy. To a lawyer, "damages" has a technical meaning — it refers to compensation payable on a wrong that is either a tort or a breach of contract. Under this definition, "damages" does not encompass sums payable under a statute where the claim is made independently of a wrong that is either a tort or a breach of contract.[16]

The meaning accorded to the term "damages", however, depends upon the context in which the term is used.[17] When interpreting policies of liability insurance the courts, for the most part, have not been constrained by the technical meaning of "damages". Rather, the term has generally been interpreted in accordance with its plain, ordinary, and popular sense and has been applied accordingly to sums payable by way of compensation, whether at law, or under statute.

The issue of whether "damages" includes sums payable as "compensation" under workers' compensation legislation was addressed by the Alberta Court of Appeal in *Chamberlain v. North American Accident Assurance Co.*[18] The plaintiff was required by the *Workmen's Compensation Act* of Alberta to provide "compensation" to the widow of an employee killed on the job. The employer's liability insurer denied coverage under an employer's liability policy on the basis that "compensation" under a strict liability workers' compensation scheme was not liability imposed by law to pay damages and, therefore, did not fall within the policy. The Alberta Court of Appeal categorically rejected this contention and held that the policy responded to the claim:

> Then it is said that compensation under the Act is not covered by the policy at all, inasmuch as its indemnity to the plaintiff is against loss from liability for *damages* and that the word is not broad enough to cover what the Act calls compensation. If we are forced to give to the word "damages" as used in this

---

[14] *Davies v. Safeco Ins. Co. of America*, [1982] B.C.J. No. 1653, 137 D.L.R. (3d) 66 (S.C.).

[15] For cases concerning whether insurance for punitive damages is against public policy see Chapter 2, section 1(h): Public Policy.

[16] H. McGregor, *McGregor on Damages*, 15th ed. (London: Sweet & Maxwell, 1988), at para. 1-6.

[17] *Ukrainian (Fort William) Credit Union Ltd. v. Nesbitt, Burns Ltd.*, [1997] O.J. No. 4282, 152 D.L.R. (4th) 640, 36 O.R. (3d) 311 (C.A.), leave to appeal to S.C.C. granted [1997] S.C.C.A. No. 672, 289 N.R. 201.

[18] (1916), 28 D.L.R. 298 (Alta. C.A.).

policy the strict technical meaning first given to it generations ago and which undoubtedly still attached to it in comparatively modern times, this contention, unmoral and iniquitous though it may be, under the circumstances must prevail. The almost universal definition of the word given by text writers is that it is a recompense for a wrong done. ... This definition, though, had its origin before the days of Workmen's Compensation Acts and at a time when a man's only liability to another in any form of action for the recovery of money except one arising *ex contract* was for a wrong done to him by that other. Its meaning should, I think, be extended to keep pace with the development of our law which now gives to a workman something which it calls compensation for injuries sustained by him in his masters' employ, but which might just as well have been called damages. The two words are, in many cases, used interchangeably by legislators and by Judges and by authors.[19]

A contrary result, however, appears to have been reached in *Neiman v. CGU Insurance Co.*[20] The insured sought an order requiring the insurer under a personal injury liability policy[21] to provide a defence to the insured in proceedings before a human rights tribunal which was authorized to impose an award of compensation for workplace discrimination. The insured had coverage for an award of compensatory damages resulting from discrimination. Although the court was of the view that any difference between "compensation" and "damages" was ephemeral at best, the court nevertheless felt constrained by the decisions in *Piazza v. Airport Taxicab*,[22] *Akey v. Encon Insurance Managers Inc.*[23] and *Brockton (Municipality) v. Frank Cowan Co.*[24] to construe the term "damages" "in accordance with its legal, technical meaning in law". With respect, the reliance on the referenced decisions to reach this conclusion is misplaced. In the *Piazza* case an employee was terminated from her employment by reason of sex discrimination. At issue was the correct measure of compensation: was it limited to lost wages during a period of reasonable notice or was the employee entitled to be restored, by compensation, to the position she would have been in had the discriminatory act not taken place? The Ontario Court of Appeal held in favour of the latter. Although the learned judge in *Neiman* views the decision in *Piazza* as establishing a difference between "damages" and "compensation", this must be placed in context. *Piazza* established that compensation for *discrimination* under the human rights legislation under consideration differed from compensation (described as damages) for *wrongful dismissal* under contract law. Thus, the contract action and the discrimination proceeding addressed different wrongs. In both cases, however, the compensation matched the wrong being alleged. The insurance policy in *Neiman* provided coverage for

---

[19] *Ibid.*, at 300-301.

[20] [2002] O.J. No. 2215 (S.C.J.).

[21] See Chapter 10.

[22] [1989] O.J. No. 994, 69 O.R. (2d) 281 (C.A.).

[23] [2001] O.J. No. 2184, 28 C.C.L.I. (3d) 63 (S.C.J.).

[24] [2000] O.J. No. 4455, [2001] I.L.R. 1-3905 (S.C.J.), vard on appeal, [2002] O.J. No. 20, [2002] I.L.R. 1-4097 (C.A.).

discrimination but not for wrongful dismissal. It was surely the reasonable expectation of both the insurer and the insured that compensation to restore the complainant to the position she would have been in had the discrimination not occurred constitutes "compensatory damages".

The decisions in *Akey* and *Brockton* deal with a different issue than was before the court in *Neiman*. In *Akey* the insured sought coverage for legal fees in connection with a coroner's inquest. Since the applicable legislation specifically precluded a finding of liability, the court found that there was no claim made against the insured to which the insurer must respond. The decision in *Brockton* similarly deals with the recovery of defence costs associated with a public inquiry which could not result in the imposition of civil liability. Again, the insurer was not required to respond. Neither decision, with respect, stands for the proposition that the term "damages" in a policy of insurance, must be accorded its narrow, technical meaning in law.

"Damages" does not include a claim that is akin to debt. In *Moore (Township) v. Guarantee Co. of North America,*[25] a claim was brought against the insured by a taxpayer for moneys "illegally" had and received in respect of the overpayment of municipal taxes. The Ontario Court of Appeal held that this was not a claim for "damages"; rather, it was a claim in respect of taxes unlawfully collected and held.

The "debt" argument, however, did not succeed in *Peterborough (City) v. General Accident Assurance Co.*[26] The city was insured under an Errors and Omissions Liability policy in respect of "compensatory damages which the Insured shall become obligated to pay by reason of the liability imposed upon the Insured by a court of civil law because of a wrongful act". An action was commenced against the city by lien claimants who alleged that the city, in breach of statute, had made payments to a contractor at a time when it had written notice of the liens. The insurer, denying both a defence and indemnity, maintained that liability arising from the failure to comply with the statutory hold-back requirements was not liability to pay "damages", but rather was in the nature of the payment of a debt. This argument was rejected. The Court noted that it was open to the trial judge to make a finding that the city was negligent in failing to withhold sufficient moneys to satisfy the lien claims and that the city's liability in this regard would sound in damages.

In *Bridgewood Building Corp. (Riverfield) v. Lombard General Insurance Co. of Canada,*[27] it was held that "legally obligated to pay as damages" encompassed warranty obligations imposed upon contractors pursuant to the Ontario *New Home Warranties Plan Act.*[28] The Court viewed with favour the approach taken by a number of American courts that have held that statutorily imposed environmental clean-up costs are covered under CGL policies.

[25] [1995] O.J. No. 3702, 26 O.R. (3d) 733, [1996] I.L.R. 1-3275 (C.A.).

[26] [1994] O.J. No. 1041, I.L.R. 1-3083 (Gen. Div.), affd [1998] O.J. No. 1506, I.L.R. 1-3553, 38 C.L.R. (2d) 84 (C.A.).

[27] [2005] O.J. No. 2083 (S.C.J.).

[28] R.S.O. 1990, c. O.31.

In British Columbia, two cases have addressed the issue of whether "damages" includes clean-up and remedial costs payable under environmental protection legislation. In *Hildon Hotel (1963) Ltd. v. Dominion Insurance Corp.*[29] fuel from a storage tank on the insured's premises had leaked, causing wharves and the surface of the ocean to become polluted by oil. The spill was cleaned up by the National Harbours Board pursuant to legislation which provided that this was "at the risk and expense of the person in contravention of the Act". The British Columbia Supreme Court held that these expenses constituted "damages" according to the ordinary and popular sense of that term and, accordingly, the claim was covered under the policy.

The decision in *Hildon Hotel* was followed in *Greenwood Forest Products Ltd. v. U.S. Fire Insurance Co.*[30] In that case a dangerous chemical (pentachlorophenate) leaked from the insured's lumber dip tank, contaminating the surrounding soil and groundwater as well as polluting a nearby river and lake. Both the federal and provincial governments took steps to clean up the spill and prevent further contamination. In addition, the insured was ordered by the Environmental Protection Service of Canada to take certain clean-up and remedial steps. All expenses incurred in this regard, including the moneys expended to prevent future potential or threatened injury, were held to be "damages because of injury to property" and were covered under the insured's liability policy.

In both *Hildon Hotel* and *Greenwood* the issue of whether or not clean-up costs and expenses are "damages" did not receive extensive consideration. The Courts' attention focused mainly on other issues in each case. In the United States, in similar cases, the courts have been sharply divided on the issue of whether costs of response payable under the *Comprehensive Environmental Response, Compensation and Liability Act*[31] are "damages" for the purposes of a CGL policy.[32] Care must be taken when attempting to apply the American experience in the Canadian context. Those courts in the United States which hold that response costs are not damages may do so on the basis that the costs sought are not based simply on compensation for an injury done but consist, instead, of remedial costs which may far exceed what would be recoverable as damages at common law and can be assessed even when there is no injury in fact but only the threat of an injury.[33] Whether the same situation exists in a Canadian case will depend upon the particular facts of the case and the nature of the legislation under consideration. Those courts in the United States which hold that response costs are "damages" may do so on the basis that the policy shall be

---

[29] (1968), 1 D.L.R. (3d) 214 (B.C.S.C.).

[30] [1982] 3 W.W.R. 739 (B.C.S.C.).

[31] 42 U.S.C. s/s 9601 *et seq.* (1980), chapter 103.

[32] For a summary of the American position see M.G. Lichty & M.B. Snowden, *Annotated Commercial General Liability Policy* (Aurora: Canada Law Book, 1997) at para. 8:20.6 *et seq.*

[33] See, for example, *Maryland Casualty Co. v. Armco*, 822 F.2d 1348 (4th Cir. 1987), cert. den., 108 S.Ct. 703.

) as to adhere to the reasonable expectations of the insured.[34] The
hich the doctrine of reasonable expectations applies in Canada is
....

The issue of whether or not sums payable in equity constitute "damages"
for the purpose of a liability policy was addressed by the Manitoba Court of
Queen's Bench in *Wolinsky v. General Security Insurance Co.*[36] In that case, the
solicitor for the mortgagor undertook, as part of the mortgage transaction, to
apply the proceeds firstly in payment of outstanding taxes. He failed to do so
and paid out the funds to his client instead. When the error was discovered (and
the client by this time had disappeared) the solicitor paid the taxes himself and
sought indemnification from his insurer. Coverage was denied by the insurer on
the basis that the lawyer's obligation arose in equity for breach of an undertaking and was not one for which an award of damages would lie. The Court
rejected this argument, holding that a breach of an undertaking gave rise to a
claim for damages. The trial judge, however, went on to state that:

> Whatever the earlier narrow technical meaning which limited "damages" to
> pecuniary satisfaction on account of a wrong done to the plaintiffs, liability for
> damages now extends indifferently to money payable by way of recompense
> for a wrong done, or for any other form of liability which may be imposed by
> law upon the defendant.[37]

This *obiter dictum* states the principle far too broadly. "Damages" does not
extend indifferently to all forms of monetary liability. No one would suggest, for
example, that criminal or quasi-criminal fines or penalties fall within the ambit
of "damages". Nor can the cost of complying with an injunction be categorized
as damages.[38] Damages awarded in lieu of an injunction, however, would
generally be covered.

In *Macmillan Bloedel Ltd. v. Youell*[39] an issue arose as to whether the insured could claim against a liability insurer for expenses incurred to minimize
the extent of a liability which had already arisen. Although the decision
concerned a charter-party hull agreement, the Court stated that the same
principles would apply as with respect to non-marine liability coverage. The
insured had chartered a freighter to carry a cargo of coal from New Orleans to
Taiwan. Part way through the voyage the insured learned that the coal was

---

[34] See, for example, *Newcastle County v. Hartford Accident & Indemnity Co.*, 673 F. Supp. 1359 (1987).
[35] See Chapter 2, section 3(d): The Doctrine of Reasonable Expectations.
[36] [1983] 2 W.W.R. 761 (Man. Q.B.).
[37] *Ibid.*, at 767.
[38] *Hwang v. AXA Pacific Insurance Co.*, [1988] B.C.J. No. 535, 53 B.C.L.R. (3d) 119, 5 C.C.L.I. (3d) 227 (S.C.), revd on other grounds [2001] B.C.J. No. 1217, 32 C.C.L.I. (3d) 201 (C.A.); *Vancouver General Hospital v. Scottish & York Insurance Co.*, [1988] B.C.J. No. 2619, 55 D.L.R. (4th) 360, 36 C.C.L.I. 1 (C.A.), leave to appeal to S.C.C. refd [1989] 1 S.C.R. *xvi.*
[39] (1993), 23 C.C.L.I. (2d) 18 (B.C.C.A.), leave to appeal to S.C.C. refd (1994), 23 C.C.L.I. (2d) 18*n.*

overheating and was in danger of spontaneously combusting. The ship put into Long Beach in order to offload the coal and prevent what could have been a catastrophic loss for which the insurer would have been responsible. The insured then claimed from its liability insurers the expenses incurred in minimizing the loss. The British Columbia Court of Appeal denied the claim. Justice Southin framed the issue as follows:

> Is a person insured under a policy covering his liability at law to third persons entitled to recover from his insurer as a matter of law expenses which he incurs to minimize the amount of that liability when his breach of contract or tortious act has occurred and damage to a third person is occurring?[40]

The policy wording in question provided for the insurer "to cover the assured's legal liability for loss of or damage to the chartered vessel". On this wording it was held that the insured's expenses in minimizing the loss were not recoverable. Whether the same result would apply in the case of the standard CGL wording is not clear.[41]

4. BODILY INJURY AND PROPERTY DAMAGE

Most commercial liability policies limit coverage to those instances where damages are payable because of "bodily injury" or "property damage".[42] A separate form of coverage, however, is available in respect of "personal injury", which is usually defined to include defamation of character, false arrest and imprisonment, and discrimination.[43]

(a) Bodily Injury

The standard form of the CGL policy defines "bodily injury" as:

> Bodily injury, sickness or disease sustained by any person which occurs during the policy period, including death at any time resulting therefrom.

In the United States there is conflicting authority as to whether, for the purposes of this definition, "bodily" modifies solely "injury" or whether it also

---

[40] *Ibid.*, at 38.

[41] There is American jurisprudence in favour of coverage in these circumstances: see *Broadwell Realty Services Inc. v. Fidelity & Casualty Co. of New York*, 528 A.2d 76 (N.J.S.C. 1987); and *Leebov v. United States Fidelity & Guaranty Co.*, 165 A.2d 82 (Pa. S.C. 1960).

[42] The damages claimed must be caused by bodily injury or property damage. In *G.B. Catering Services Ltd. v. Beckley*, [1994] O.J. No. 699, 18 O.R. (3d) 135, [1994] I.L.R. 1-3079 (Gen. Div.) it was held that a claim for pure economic loss by a caterer against the insured food manufacturer was not covered. The cause of the loss was the bad publicity attendant upon a food poisoning incident involving the caterer's customers as a result of eating contaminated meat supplied by the insured.

[43] See Chapter 10: Personal Injury and Advertising Injury Liability Coverage.

modifies "sickness" and "disease".[44] In Canada it has been held that the definition extends "bodily injury" beyond mere physical trauma, such that any sickness or disease, physical or mental, is included. The Manitoba Queen's Bench, in *Victoria General Hospital v. General Accident Assurance Co. of Canada*,[45] held that the insuring agreement in a comprehensive general liability policy with respect to "bodily injury, sickness or disease" provided coverage for a claim for severe emotional trauma consequent upon incidents of sexual abuse. The British Columbia Court of Appeal, in *Wellington Guarantee v. Evangelical Lutheran Church in Canada*,[46] held that nervous shock, depression and psychological trauma resulting from sexual abuse amounted to "bodily injury, sickness or disease" for the purposes of an *exclusion* in a directors' and officers' liability policy. Both Courts noted that "sickness" includes the impairment of mental health. Although both decisions stand for the proposition that "bodily" modifies solely "injury" they could arguably be alternately explained on the basis that severe psychological trauma is often accompanied by physical symptoms so as to result in "bodily injury".[47]

In the United States there is conflicting authority as to whether mere emotional distress (that is unaccompanied by any physical manifestations), not triggered by any physical contact, is covered under an extended definition of "bodily injury".[48] The only Canadian decision to date to deal with this issue is *Elmford Construction Co. v. Canadian Indemnity Co.*,[49] in which it was held, for the purpose of the duty to defend, that a claim for emotional distress resulting from a fear that a retaining wall might collapse could conceivably fit within coverage in respect of "... bodily or mental injury or illness ...".

An injury to a fetus subsequently born alive would likely be considered an injury to a "person" for the purposes of the insuring agreement under consideration.[50]

A claim for damages arising from injury to reputation does not fall within an insuring agreement providing coverage for "bodily injury".[51]

---

[44] See, for example *Lavanant v. General Accident Insurance Co.*, 584 NYS.2d 744 (1992) and *Lanigan v. Snowden*, 938 SW.2d 330 (Mo.App. WD 1997) ("bodily" modifies "injury"); *Knapp v. Eagle Property Mgt. Corp.*, 54 F.3d 1272 (7th Cir. 1995); and *E-Z Loader Boat Trailers, Inc. v. Travelers Indemnity Co.*, 726 P.2d 439 (Wash. 1986) ("bodily" modifies "injury, sickness or disease").

[45] [1995] M.J. No. 276 [1995] 8 W.W.R. 106, 103 Man. R. (2d) 168 (Q.B.).

[46] [1995] I.L.R. 1-3236, 29 C.C.L.I. (2d) 93 (B.C.S.C.), revd, [1996] B.C.J. No. 872 [1996] 9 W.W.R. 373, 35 C.C.L.I. (2d) 164, [1996] I.L.R. 1-3334 (C.A.), leave to appeal to S.C.C. refd (1996), 207 N.R. 79*n*, 138 W.A.C. 160*n*, 39 C.C.L.I. (2d) 12*n*.

[47] *Voorhees v. Preferred Mutual Insurance Co.*, 607 A.2d 1255 (N.J. 1992).

[48] M.F. Aylward, "What Me Worry? Insurance Coverage For Mental Distress" (*Insurance Coverage and Practice Symposium*, Defense Research Institute, December, 1997).

[49] [1995] O.J. No. 1022, [1995] I.L.R. 1-3191 (Gen. Div.).

[50] *Breau (Litigation Guardian of) v. General Accident Assurance Co. of Canada* [2000] N.B.J. No. 454, 194 D.L.R. (4th) 105 (C.A.).

[51] *Maillet v. Halifax Insurance ING Canada*, [2003] N.B.J. No. 5 (Q.B.).

(b) Property Damage

A number of older business liability policies did not define the term "property damage", and simply provided coverage with respect to "damages because of injury to or destruction of property, including loss of use thereof ...". This form of insuring agreement, with its unqualified use of the word "injury", provides coverage with respect to infringement of a right as well as physical injury to property. In *Hildon Hotel (1963) Ltd. v. Dominion Insurance Corp.* it was noted that the distinction between "injury" and "damage" is fundamental. The Court adopted the following definition of "injury" from Jowitt's *Dictionary of English Law*:

> *Injuria; Injury*, the infringement of some right. Hence "injury" is opposed to "damage," because a right may be infringed without causing pecuniary loss *(injuria sine damno)*: thus, the pollution of a clear stream is to a riparian proprietor below both injury and damage . . .[52]

Thus, it was held that the infringement of the right to enjoy unpolluted wharves and water was an "injury to property" as that phrase is used in a CGL policy. The decision in *Hildon Hotel* was followed in *Greenwood Forest Products Ltd. v. U.S. Fire Insurance Co.*,[53] where it was held that chemical pollution of the groundwater, a river and a lake constituted an infringement of the Crown's right to a clean water system and was therefore "injury to property".

In the 1971 and subsequent versions of the standard CGL policy, the term "property damage" has been defined so as to limit the coverage available where no physical injury has occurred:

> "property damage" means (1) physical injury to or destruction of tangible property which occurs during the policy period, including the loss of use thereof at any time resulting therefrom, or (2) loss of use of tangible property which has not been physically injured or destroyed provided such loss of use is caused by an accident occurring during the policy period.[54]

The decision in *Canadian Equipment Sales & Service Co. v. Continental Insurance Co.*[55] does not deal with the 1971 policy wording but does provide an illustration of what constitutes physical injury. The insured was responsible for negligently permitting a piece of pipe known as a "coupon" to fall into a water line. The presence of the coupon was a potential danger in that it might have jammed in the water line and caused damage. Efforts were made to locate the coupon, but to no avail. A judgment was granted against the insured for the amount of the search costs, including x-rays of the pipeline. The insurer resisted coverage on the basis that there was no injury to the pipeline. The trial judge

---

[52] Quoted in *Hildon Hotel* (1968), 1 D.L.R. (3d) 214 at 217 (B.C.S.C.).

[53] [1982] 3 W.W.R. 739 (B.C.S.C.).

[54] See Appendix A of this book.

[55] (1975), 59 D.L.R. (3d) 333, 9 O.R. (2d) 7, [1975] I.L.R. 1-680 (C.A.).

agreed but the Court of Appeal for Ontario did not, holding instead that there was "injury" to both tangible and intangible property. The injury to tangible property was to the pipeline, which, from the moment the coupon dropped into it was an imperfect or impaired pipeline. The injury to intangible property was to the owner's "property right" to a free flow of water through its pipeline. This right, the Court held, was clearly impeded or interfered with by the dropped coupon.

A similar conclusion, in a non-insurance context, was reached by the Supreme Court of Canada in *Ontario (Attorney General) v. Fatehi*.[56] The Court held that debris and gasoline spread upon a highway following a motor vehicle accident constituted property damage such that the clean-up monies expended could not be categorized as pure economic loss and thus be non-recoverable. Applying the same logic in the context of liability insurance policies it has been held that property damage had occurred when pieces of the roof fell onto the floor of the SkyDome,[57] when a caisson sunk, impairing the use of a navigable waterway,[58] and when several rolls of paper, weighing 6,000 pounds each, were deposited in a lake.[59]

In cases involving faulty workmanship or the supply of a defective product the courts will frequently find against coverage either on the basis that such cases do not present a claim for "property damage" or on the basis of the product and performance exclusions typically found in liability policies.[60] This may lead to some confusion as to the proper basis upon which such claims fall outside of coverage. As noted by the Saskatchewan Court of Appeal in *Westridge Construction Ltd. v. Zurich Insurance Co*:

> The definition of property damage in the policy in this case is not qualified to mean physical injury to property other than the insured's own work product and cannot be read as though it were so qualified (subject, of course, to the exclusion clause which will be referred to later.)[61]

Nevertheless, it has generally been held that the supply of a defective product by the insured does not, standing alone, constitute property damage under the first branch of the 1971 definition.[62] Nor, with respect to the first branch, is faulty

---

[56] [1984] 2 S.C.R. 536, 15 D.L.R. (4th) 132, 56 N.R. 62, 6 O.A.C. 270.

[57] *ING Insurance Co. of Canada v. Sportsco International L.P.*, [2004] O.J. No. 2254, 12 C.C.L.I. (4th) 86 (S.C.J.).

[58] *Hamel Construction Inc. v. Lombard Canada Ltd.*, [2005] N.S.J. No. 151, 21 C.C.L.I. (4th) 44 (C.A.).

[59] *Westside Transport v. Continental Insurance*, [2005] B.C.J. No. 1971, [2005] I.L.R. I-4357 (S.C.).

[60] See Chapter 8, section 4: Product and Performance.

[61] [2005] S.J. No. 396, 25 C.C.L.I. (4th) 182 at para. 38 (C.A.).

[62] *Ray Electric Ltd. v. Zurich Ins. Co.*, [1993] O.J. No. 1620, [1993] I.L.R. 1-2989 (Gen. Div.); *Privest Properties Ltd. v. Foundation Co. of Can.*, [1991] B.C.J. No. 2213, 57 B.C.L.R. (2d) 88, 6 C.C.L.I. (2d) 23 (S.C.). *Cf. Hironaka v. Co-Operators General Insurance Co.*, [2005] A.J. No. 1313 (Q.B.).

workmanship by itself generally considered to be property damage.[63] Where, however, the defective product or faulty workmanship causes injury to other property, then the definition of "property damage" will be satisfied. This was the issue before the court in *Carwald Concrete & Gravel Co. v. General Security Insurance Co. of Canada.*[64] The insured supplied defective cement which resulted in a concrete pad having insufficient compressive strength. The components of the pad (rebars, reinforcing steel, ducting, wiring, plumbing and anchor bolts) became useless for the purposes for which they were installed. It was held that this constituted physical injury to tangible property.

Some courts have held that the "property damage" requirement is not satisfied in cases in which one part of the insured's product or work has caused damage to another part of the same product or work. In *Swagger Construction Ltd. v. ING Insurance Co. of Canada*[65] the insured, a general contractor, was responsible for the construction of a building. It was alleged that one component of the building leaked, resulting in water damage to other parts of the building. After noting that the Supreme Court of Canada rejected the complex structure theory in *Winnipeg Condominium Corp. No. 36 v. Bird Construction Co.*,[66] the learned judge in *Swagger* stated that it is not appropriate to divide the insured's work into component parts so as to find coverage when a defect in one part causes damage to another part of the same structure.

The decision in *Winnipeg Condominium* does not address coverage issues under a liability insurance policy; rather, the case concerns a claim against a general contractor, in tort, by a subsequent purchaser of a building. The Supreme Court of Canada characterized the purchaser's claim for the cost of remedying the construction defects as a claim for pure economic loss rather than a claim for damage to property. The Manitoba Court of Appeal, in *Bird Construction Co. v. Allstate Insurance Co. of Canada,*[67] which is the insurance companion to the tort action, appeared to apply the tort law concept of pure economic loss to its interpretation of the insurance policy in arriving at the conclusion that there was no "property damage" within the meaning of the contractor's liability insurance policy. The Manitoba Court of Appeal, however, also relied upon the performance exclusion for the conclusion that the loss was not covered. In the result, it is not clear whether the conclusion was arrived at (i) by interpreting "property damage" so as not to include the insured's own defective work or (ii) by the application of the performance exclusion. Nevertheless, the Court in *Swagger,* on the basis of the former interpretation, concluded that the claim against the

---

[63] *Bird Construction Co. v. Allstate Insurance Co. of Canada,* [1996] M.J. No. 363 [1996] 7 W.W.R. 609, 110 Man. R. (2d) 305 (C.A.); *Carleton Iron Works Ltd. v. Ellis Don Construction Ltd.,* [1996] O.J. No. 2427 [1996] I.L.R. 1-3373 (Gen. Div.).

[64] (1986), 17 C.C.L.I. 241 at 261 (Alta. C.A.), leave to appeal to S.C.C. dismissed (1986), 17 C.C.L.I. 241*n.* See also *Gulf Plastics Ltd. v. Cornhill Ins. Co.,* [1990] B.C.J. No. 1541, 46 C.C.L.I. 144 (S.C.), affd, [1991] B.C.J. No. 3310, 3 C.C.L.I. (2d) 203 (C.A.).

[65] [2005] B.C.J. No. 1964, [2005] I.L.R. 1-4445 (S.C.).

[66] [1995] S.C.J. No. 2, [1995] 1 S.C.R. 85.

[67] [1996] M.J. No. 363 [1996] 7 W.W.R. 609, 110 Man. R. (2d) 305 (C.A.).

general contractor for damage to part of the building caused by a defect elsewhere in the building was not "property damage".

With respect, the decision in *Swagger* in this regard should be regarded as being erroneous. Liability insurance policies do not define "property damage" in terms of whether or not the loss is characterized, under tort law, as being in respect of economic loss. Rather, the policies typically define "property damage" as including "physical injury to property", which must surely apply to a building, the structural components of which have been damaged by water penetration. Further, the conclusion that damage to the insured's own work can never constitute property damage renders meaningless the "work" exclusion invariably found in such policies. The typical wording of this exclusion is that the policy does apply not in respect of "property damage" to "your work".[68] If damage to "your work" can never be "property damage" then the exclusion is meaningless. Further still, if *Swagger* is correct it makes nugatory the exception often found in the work exclusion to the effect that the exclusion does not apply in cases in which the property damage to the insured's work is the result of defective work performed on the insured's behalf by a subcontractor.[69] In other words, even though the exception says that the contractor is covered for "property damage" to "your work" arising out of defective work performed "on your behalf" by a subcontractor, if *Swagger* is correct, the exception is illusory, for "your work" can never be the subject of "property damage". With respect, this simply cannot be correct.

The correct approach, it is submitted, is that taken by the Ontario Court of Appeal in *Alie v. Bertrand & Frère Construction Co.*[70] The court noted that drawing a distinction between property damage and economic loss is not a useful tool for analyzing coverage under liability insurance policies. Rather, the focus must be on the policy language itself. The defendant Bertrand had supplied defective concrete, which was used in the construction of foundations for new homes. The defect was traced to the presence of fly ash in cement which had been sold to Bertrand by another defendant, Lafarge. The foundations consisted of concrete with other components, such as tie rods, reinforcing steel and anchor bolts. In addition, parging was placed on the outside of the founda-tion. The defective concrete resulted in cracking of the foundation and delamina-tion of the parging and permitted excessive moisture to enter the homes, which led to the growth of mildew and toxic moulds. The foundations were determined to constitute a major structural defect and required replacement. The defendants' insurers, relying upon the decision of the Supreme Court of Canada in *Winnipeg Condominium Corp. No. 36 v. Bird Construction Co.*[71], argued that the case was one of pure economic loss, that the structural defect created a risk of future harm

---

[68] See Chapter 8, section 4: Product and Performance.

[69] See Chapter 9, section 4: Broad Form Property Damage Endorsement.

[70] [2003] I.L.R. I-4146 (Ont. C.A.), leave to appeal to S.C.C. dismissed [2003] S.C.C.A. No. 48. See also *Westridge Construction Ltd. v. Zurich Insurance Co.*, [2005] S.J. No. 396, 25 C.C.L.I. (4th) 182 (C.A.).

[71] [1995] S.C.J. No. 2, [1995] 1 S.C.R. 85.

but did not, by itself, constitute property damage. The Court did not agree with this position. There was property damage to the foundations and to the buildings. The insured's product was the defective concrete, not the foundation. Coverage in respect of the concrete was excluded, but the balance of the claim was covered.

The second branch of the definition of "property damage" extends coverage in respect of the loss of use of tangible property which has not been physically injured or destroyed. An example of this situation is provided by the decision in *International Radiography and Inspection Services (1976) Ltd. v. General Accident Assurance Co. of Canada.*[72] Using radiography, the insured carried out a non-destructive inspection of certain steel fittings at Suncor's oil extraction plant. During a subsequent, unrelated shutdown Suncor carried out its own inspection and came up with different readings, indicating that the fittings would require heat treatment. This led to an extension of the shutdown while the fittings were treated and a claim was made against the insured for the resulting business losses. The Court noted that there was no physical injury to any tangible property. There was, however, a loss of use of tangible property which had not been physically injured; hence the second branch of the definition of "property damage" was satisfied.

Unlike previous policy versions, the 1971 definition of "property damage" is restricted to claims involving tangible property. Thus, interference with intangible property, such as a patent,[73] is not covered. Nor does conversion of the proceeds of a negotiable instrument constitute damage to tangible property.[74]

In construction cases the interplay between the insuring agreement in respect of property damage caused by an accident and the exclusions with respect to product and performance requires careful analysis. Many courts approach these cases from the perspective that a liability insurance policy is not a performance bond,[75] which, of course, is correct. Yet, it does not follow that a performance bond and a liability insurance policy are mutually exclusive instruments. A performance bond is not an insurance policy; rather, it is an agreement pursuant to which a surety (typically an insurance company) guarantees satisfactory completion of a project by the principal (typically, in this context, a general contractor). In such arrangements the principal will generally be required to indemnify the surety against any losses by reason of issuing the bond. Certain of the events to which the performance bond applies will, plainly, not fall within the coverage afforded under a liability policy. For example,

---

[72] [1997] A.J. No. 1170, 4 W.W.R. 115, 47 Alta. L.R. (3d) 137, 40 C.C.L.I. (2d) 282 (C.A.).

[73] *Canadian Universities Reciprocal Insurance Exchange v. GAN Canada Insurance Co.*, [1999] O.J. No. 1276 [1999] I.L.R. 1-3700 (Gen. Div.).

[74] *Ritchie (Litigation Guardian of) v. Barill*, [2002] O.J. No. 1778, [2002] I.L.R. I-4115 (S.C.J.).

[75] For a discussion of the exclusion designed to achieve this end see Chapter 8, section 4(a): Damage to Product. Decisions referring to the notion that a liability insurance policy is not a performance bond include: *Hamel Construction Inc. v. Lombard Canada Ltd.*, [2004] N.S.J. No. 65, 8 C.C.L.I. (4th) 120 (S.C.); *Celestica Inc. v. ACE INA Insurance*, [2003] O.J. No. 2820, 50 C.C.L.I. (3d) 190 (C.A.); and *Pier Mac Petroleum Installation Ltd. v. Axa Pacific Insurance Co.* [1997] B.C.J. No. 1611, 41 B.C.L.R. (3d) 326 (S.C.).

should the contractor become insolvent then the performance bond will require the surety to complete the contract, which is not something which would fall within the liability policy. On the other hand, there are other events to which both a performance bond and a liability policy would respond. For example, if a subcontractor should install a leaky roof, as a result of which the interior of the building becomes damaged, then the general contractor will be in breach of the construction contract, thus bringing the performance bond into play, but may also be entitled to indemnity under the liability policy, which, in many cases, will extend coverage to a general contractor's work in circumstances in which the loss arises from work performed by a subcontractor.[76]

One must therefore take care not to allow the perspective that an insurance policy is not a performance bond to lead to an overly narrow interpretation of the insuring agreement when, on a proper interpretation, the claim falls within the insuring agreement but is captured by one or more of the policy exclusions.[77]

An example of such an overly narrow interpretation of the insuring agreement is provided by the decision in *Tsubaki of Canada Ltd. v. Standard Tube Canada*.[78] The defendant improperly performed heat treating procedures on the plaintiff's steel chain links, which the plaintiff then marketed to its customers. After receiving complaints from its customers of premature chain wear, the plaintiff commenced an action against the defendant for damages for the cost of replacing the defective steel, lost profits and loss of future business. The defendant sought indemnity from its insurer in respect of this claim. The Court held in favour of the insurer, however, on the basis that there was no accident, there was no property damage and the claim fell within a number of exclusions. With respect, the Court is in error in its finding that the claim did not fall within the insuring agreement. As will be seen from the discussion below[79] there was clearly an "accident", in the sense that the improper application of heat to the steel chain links was an unlooked for mishap or occurrence. There was also, plainly, property damage, for the plaintiff's steel was damaged during the heating process, resulting in premature failure. The proper basis for the decision, it is submitted, is that the claim fell within the care, custody or control exclusion.[80]

---

[76] See Chapter 8, section 4(b): Work Performed and Chapter 9, section 4: Broad Form Property Damage Endorsement.

[77] *Westridge Construction Ltd. v. Zurich Insurance Co.*, [2005] S.J. No. 396, 44 C.L.R. (3d) 204 (C.A.).

[78] [1993] O.J. 1855 (Gen. Div.).

[79] See section 5(b): Meaning of "Accident".

[80] For a discussion of the treatment of the exclusions in this case see Chapter 8, section 3(c): Damage to Property in the Care, Custody or Control of the Insured.

5. ACCIDENT AND OCCURRENCE

(a) Accident versus Occurrence

Commercial liability policies generally express coverage for property damage in terms of it having been either "caused by accident" or "caused by an occurrence". While some courts have held that the terms "accident" and "occurrence" are interchangeable,[81] the view generally held is that the change from "accident" in older policies to "occurrence" in the more recent policies manifests an intention to broaden coverage.[82]

In the United States, the "occurrence" wording has been in general use since it was first introduced in 1966. At that time "occurrence" was defined thus:

> "occurrence" means an accident including injurious exposure to conditions, which results, during the policy period, in bodily injury or property damage neither expected nor intended from the standpoint of the insured.

In 1973, in conjunction with a number of changes to the CGL policy language, the definition of occurrence was revised as follows:

> "occurrence" means an accident including continuous or repeated exposure to conditions which results in bodily injury or property damage neither expected nor intended from the standpoint of the insured.

This revision was designed for at least two purposes: (i) to negate the element of suddenness which has sometimes been associated with "accident", thereby extending coverage to property damage which takes place over a long period of time, and (ii) to ensure that all injury or damage resulting from continuous or repeated exposure to substantially the same general conditions would be considered as arising from one occurrence for the purposes of both the deductible provisions and the policy's limits of liability.[83]

In Canada, the standard form of the CGL policy provides coverage with respect to damage caused by "accident", which term is not defined in the policy. The Property Damage Endorsement, however, which is generally included with the CGL policy, provides an extended definition of the term:

> "Accident" includes continuous or repeated exposure to conditions which results in property damage neither expected nor intended from the standpoint of the Insured.[84]

---

[81] See, for example, *Hartford Accident & Indemnity Co. v. Wesolowski*, 350 N.Y.S.2d 895 (1973).

[82] See, for example, *Lombard v. Sewerage & Water Bd.*, 284 So.2d 905 (La. 1973).

[83] J. Tarpui, "The New Comprehensive Policy: Some of the Changes" (April, 1966), Insurance Counsel Journal 223 at 224; Reichenberger, "The General Liability Insurance Policy: Analysis of 1973 Revisions" *Insurance Law: General Liability Insurance*, 1973 Revisions, (Chicago, Ill.: The Defence Research Institute, Inc., 1974) No. 1, 5 at 10; *Carter Lake (City) v. Aetna Casualty & Surety Co.*, 604 F.2d 1052 (U.S.C.A. 8th Cir. 1979).

[84] I.B.C. Form 2009, February 1979.

The effect of this definition is to bring the accident-based wording of the Canadian policy in line with the occurrence-based wording of the American policy.

In the Commercial General Liability policy the "occurrence" wording has been retained, but the definition of the term again has been changed:

> "occurrence" means an accident, including continuous or repeated exposure to substantially the same harmful conditions.

(b) Meaning of "Accident"

The term "accident" has likely generated more litigation than any other word used in an insurance policy. "Accident" and its derivatives are found in various types of insurance contracts, including liability, life, and accident and sickness policies. Although these various policies are drafted with somewhat different purposes in mind, the courts generally interpret "accident" in the same fashion, regardless of the type of policy in which it is found.[85]

Any attempt to provide a comprehensive definition of "accident" has proved a monumentally difficult task. As the noted American Judge Oliver Wendell Holmes once stated, "a word is not a crystal, transparent and unchanged, it is the skin of a living thought and may vary greatly in colour and content according to the circumstances and the time in which it is used".[86] The remarks of Holmes J. are particularly apposite with respect to "accident", which has been described as:

> ... a chameleonic term, taking on different hues and shades of meaning in different circumstances, context and classes of cases ... It is indeed a term "susceptible of being given such scope that one would hardly venture to define its boundaries".[87]

As a non-technical word, "accident" is interpreted in accordance with its popular and ordinary sense,[88] a sense which, obviously, will change according to the context and the circumstances. In *Trim Joint District School Board v. Kelly*, Earl Loreburn cautioned against any attempt to define "accident" by way of a formula:

> In short, the common meaning of this word is ruled neither by logic nor by etymology, but by custom, and no formula will precisely express its usage for all cases.[89]

---

[85] *Mutual of Omaha Ins. Co. v. Stats* (1978), 87 D.L.R. (3d) 169 at 181-82 (S.C.C.) *per* Spence J. *Cf.*, the remarks of Rae J. in *Ocean Const. Supplies Ltd. v. Continental Ins. Co.*, [1978] I.L.R. 1-035 at 1292 (B.C.S.C.).

[86] *Towne v. Eisner*, 245 U.S. 418 (1917).

[87] *White v. Smith*, 440 S.W.2d 497 at 511 (Mo. 1969).

[88] *Mutual of Omaha Ins. Co. v. Stats, supra*, note 85.

[89] [1914] A.C. 667 at 681 (H.L.).

The courts have, nevertheless, invariably attempted to construct a formula for "accident", the test most often cited being that expressed by Lord MacNaghten in *Fenton v. J. Thorley & Co.*:

> I come, therefore, to the conclusion that the expression "accident" is used in the popular and ordinary sense of the word as denoting an unlooked-for mishap or an untoward event which is not expected or designed.[90]

On this test, "accident" connotes both lack of intent and lack of expectation. Both of these concepts are retained in the definition of "occurrence" found in most modern commercial liability policies, in which coverage is extended to "continuous or repeated exposure to conditions which results in property damage neither expected nor intended from the standpoint of the insured".[91]

"Accident" is also sometimes explained by the "fortuity principle".[92] As a general rule, the function of an insurance policy is to transfer fortuitous contingent risks.[93] Although there may be coverage for the unintended consequences of an intentional act, liability insurance policies are not generally designed to provide coverage in respect of harm that is deliberately brought about by the insured.[94]

(c) Causation

The language of causation is found in both the insuring agreement and in certain exclusions. Careful attention must be paid to this language, for it will determine the test to be used in establishing causation. For example, the phrase "arising out of" does not mean the same as "directly caused by".[95] The latter phrase imports a more stringent causation requirement.

The insuring agreement in a commercial liability policy typically requires that the loss be "caused by" an accident or an occurrence. This language invokes the concept of proximate cause, which is common to all branches of insurance law.[96] Under the doctrine of proximate cause, the courts are required to ascertain

---

[90]   [1903] A.C. 443 at 448 (H.L.).

[91]   *Coalition pour la protection de l'environnement du parc linéaire "Petit train du Nord" c. Laurentides (Municipalité régionale de comté des)*, [2004] J.Q. No. 13133 (Que. S.C.).

[92]   *Liberty Mutual Insurance Co. v. Hollinger Inc.*, [2004] O.J. No. 481, 10 C.C.L.I. (4th) 200 (C.A.).

[93]   See *Non-Marine Underwriters, Lloyd's of London v. Scalera*, [2000] S.C.J. No. 26, [2001] 1 S.C.R. 551 at paras. 68-9, citing C. Brown and J. Menezes, *Insurance Law in Canada*, 2nd ed. (Scarborough Ont.: Carswell, 1991) at pp. 125-26.

[94]   See, in this chapter, section 5(e): Accident and Deliberate Acts. See also, Chapter 8, section 7: Intentional Injury and Chapter 2, section 1(h): Public Policy.

[95]   *Amos v. Insurance Corp. of British Columbia*, [1995] S.C.J. No. 74, [1995] 3 S.C.R. 405; *Greenhalgh v. ING Halifax Insurance Co.*, [2004] O.J. No. 3485, 13 C.C.L.I. (4th) 292 (C.A.).

[96]   E.R.H. Ivamy, *General Principles of Insurance Law*, 5th ed. (London: Butterworths, 1986) at 381.

the dominant or effective cause of the loss, which is said to be determined by common sense.[97]

The proximate cause of the loss is not ascertained in isolation. One must look at the facts surrounding the loss in light of the purpose for which the policy was written and determine whether the loss can fairly be attributed to the peril insured against. In the context of liability insurance policies, this requires one to pay particular attention to the actions of the insured that gave rise to the loss, and determine whether they constitute the sort of activity for which coverage was intended. Hence, in *Gray v. Barr*,[98] where the insured, armed with a shotgun, entered the home of a neighbour, and in the ensuing struggle the gun accidentally discharged and killed the neighbour, Lord Denning was of the view that the proximate cause of the loss was not the accidental discharge of the gun, but the insured's deliberate act in entering the premises with a loaded weapon and that, therefore, the death was not caused by accident.

There is often more than one cause of a loss. In a case in which there are concurrent causes, one an included peril and the other an excluded peril, then coverage will depend upon the wording of the exclusion clause. There is no general presumption that, where there are concurrent causes, all coverage is ousted if one of the concurrent causes is an excluded peril. An insurer wishing to oust coverage in cases where covered perils operate concurrently with excluded perils should insert express language to that effect in the insurance policy.[99]

(d) "Accident" and Negligence

The fact that damage is caused by the insured's negligence and is therefore reasonably foreseeable does not preclude a finding that the damage is caused by accident. Since the main purpose of a commercial liability policy is to provide protection to the insured in respect of certain types of damage caused by the insured's negligence, to use reasonable foreseeability as a test for determining whether or not there has been an accident would frustrate the object of the insurance. Justice Macfarlane of the British Columbia Supreme Court noted in *Straits Towing Ltd. v. Washington Iron Works*:

> ... if there was no liability under an accident policy for damage flowing from a reasonably foreseeable event then there would be no indemnity for liability arising from the negligence of the insured. The object of the insurance would thereby be frustrated because, in essence, the result of negligence of the insured is the risk insured against.[100]

---

[97]   *Nadorfsky Steel Erecting Ltd. v. Hartford Fire Ins. Co.*, [1980] I.L.R. 1-222 (Ont. H.C.J.).

[98]   [1971] 2 All E.R. 949 (C.A.).

[99]   *Derksen v. 539938 Ontario Ltd.*, [2002] S.C.J. No. 27, [2002] I.L.R. 1-4029.

[100]   (1970), 74 W.W.R. 228 at 231 (B.C.S.C.), affd [1973] 5 W.W.R. 212 *(sub nom. Straits Towing Ltd. v. Walkem Machinery & Equipment Ltd.)* (B.C.C.A.), affd (1975), 53 D.L.R. (3d) 1 (S.C.C.) *(sub nom. Can. Indemnity Co. v. Walkem Machinery & Equipment Ltd.)*. See also *Modern Livestock Ltd. v. Kansa General Ins. Co.*, [1994] A.J. No. 654, 24 Alta. L.R. (3d) 21, 24 C.C.L.I. (2d) 254 (C.A.); *J & P Holdings Ltd. v. Sask. Mutual Ins. Co.*, [1990] S.J. No. 270, 44 C.C.L.I.

Not all acts of negligence, however, may be characterized as "accidental" for the purposes of a liability insurance policy. There are certain business risks which, although negligence on the part of the insured is involved, are not considered to give rise to bodily injury or property damage "caused by accident" as that phrase is used in a commercial liability policy.[101] Additionally, where the insured courts the risk, the resulting damage is not caused by accident even though the insured may be held liable in negligence.[102]

(e) "Accident" and Deliberate Acts

Where the insured acts with deliberation, the resulting loss may nevertheless still be accidental. As Cardozo J. noted in *Messersmith v. American Fidelity Co.*:

> Injuries are accidental or the opposite, for the purpose of indemnity, according to the quality of the results rather than the quality of the causes. ... A driver turns for a moment to the wrong side of the road, in the belief that the path is clear and deviation safe. The act of deviation is willful, but not the collision supervening. The occupant of a dwelling leaves a flower pot upon the window sill, and the pot, dislodged by wind, falls upon a passing wayfarer. The position of the flower pot is intended, but not the ensuing impact.[103]

When the loss is the natural and probable consequence of the insured's deliberate act, however, a number of courts have held that the loss is not caused by accident. An example of the application of this principle is provided by the decision of the English Court of Appeal in *Gray v. Barr*.[104] The insured, Barr, was covered under a homeowner's policy in respect of his legal liability to pay damages because of "bodily injury to any person ... caused by accident". In the mistaken belief that his wife had resumed her affair with Gray and was at Gray's home, Barr went to the house armed with a loaded shotgun. He went inside the house and asked whether his wife was there. From the top of the stairs Gray replied that she was not. Barr, wishing to see for himself, proceeded up the stairs, firing a shot into the ceiling to frighten Gray. The two then struggled, during which the gun went off, and Gray lay dead. In a wrongful death action commenced by Gray's widow, Barr was held liable for damages. He then sought indemnity from his insurer.

The Court of Appeal held in favour of the insurer on two grounds: the first being that the death was not caused by accident; the second, that the action was barred by a rule of public policy. There are three concurring judgments in the case, the basis for each judgment, however, being somewhat different.

Lord Denning M.R. acknowledged that the immediate cause of the death was the accidental discharge of the shotgun, but stated that the dominant or

---

205 (Q.B.); *Prince George White Truck Sales Ltd. v. Can. Indemnity Co.*, [1974] I.L.R. 1-583 (B.C.S.C.); *Tiko Electric v. Can. Surety*, [1973] I.L.R. 1-573 (Ont. Co. Ct.).

[101] See section 5(g): "Accident" and Business Risks.

[102] See section 5(f): "Accident" and Courting the Risk.

[103] 133 N.E. 432 at 443 (N.Y. 1921).

[104] *Supra*, note 98.

proximate cause of loss, which is the cause that must be considered for the purposes of coverage, was the insured's deliberate act in going up the stairs with a loaded weapon:

> Ever since that case in 1918 it has been settled in insurance law that the "cause" is that which is the effective or dominant cause of the occurrence, or, as it is sometimes put, what is in substance the cause, even though it is more remote in point of time, such cause to be determined by common sense: see also *Canada Rice Mills Ltd v Union Marine & General Insurance Co Ltd* [[1940] 4 All E.R. 169 at 178, [1941] A.C. 55 at 71] per Lord Wright. Thus, when a ship was torpedoed and sea water entered, but afterwards a gale sprang up and she was lost, it was held that the loss was due to the torpedoing and not to perils of the sea: see *Leyland Shipping Co v Norwich Union Fire Insurance Society* [[1918] A.C. 350, [1918-19] All E.R. Rep. 443]. And when a ship was scuttled by the crew so that sea water entered and she sank, it was held that the loss was due to the scuttling, and not to perils of the sea: see *P Samuel & Co Ltd v Dumas* [[1923] 1 K.B. 592 at 619, [1924] A.C. 431 at 459, [1924] All E.R. Rep. 66 at 82] per Scrutton LJ and per Viscount Finlay. Applying this principle, I am of opinion that the dominant and effective cause of the death was Mr Barr's deliberate act in going up the stairs with a loaded gun determined to see into the bedroom. The whole tragic sequence flows inexorably from that act. It was because of that loaded approach that Mr Gray grappled with Mr Barr. It was because of the grappling that Mr Barr fell and the gun went off. There was no new intervening cause at all.[105]

Salmon L.J. took a different view. Unlike Lord Denning, Salmon L.J. held that the proximate cause of the injury was the accidental discharge of the shotgun. On this basis, Salmon L.J. accepted that Gray's injuries were "caused by accident". The learned judge went on to state, however, that this was not the type of "accident" referred to in the policy:

> *Was this accident an accident of a kind intended to be covered by the policy of insurance?* This is a difficult question. I incline to the view that, although the accident in question was of the genus "accident" referred to in the policy, it was not a species of that genus which the policy was intended to cover. No doubt, the language of the policy is wide enough to cover any kind of accident. I think, however, that it should be read as subject to an implied exception. The exception being that the policy does not apply to injuries caused by an accident occurring in the course of threatening unlawful violence with a loaded gun. It is, of course, well settled that no term can be implied into a contract unless necessary to give it ordinary business efficacy. I doubt whether from the point of view of ordinary business the parties can be taken to have intended to cover such a risk as this unless at any rate they had stated such an intention in express words. Put in another way, if the officious bystander had asked the parties when the policy was written, "Do you intend to cover such an accident as this?" they would have both unhesitatingly have answered "No."[106]

---

[105] *Ibid.*, at 955.

[106] *Ibid.*, at 963-64.

Phillimore L.J. took yet another approach. On the basis that the incident should be regarded as a whole rather than being dissected into its constituent parts, he was of the view that the injury could not be characterized as having been caused by accident:

> Was the fact that the shot so fired actually killed Mr Gray an accident in the true sense? Could Mr Barr have said it was an accident if it had merely wounded Mr Gray or if it had killed somebody else who happened to be nearby? No doubt the word "accident" involves something fortuitous or unexpected, but the mere fact that a wilful and culpable act — which is both reckless and unlawful — and has a result which the actor did not intend surely does not, if that result was one which he ought reasonably to have anticipated, entitle him to say that it was an accident. After all, an unlawful and reckless act may result in death albeit the actor did not intend to cause that death — if he had it would, of course, have been murder. If he did not is it automatically an accident? If anyone who saw him doing it could foresee that it was dangerous and reckless and might result in harm to another and in the event it did so and thus caused a death which the law terms manslaughter, does the ordinary citizen term it an accident? I think not.[107]

The decision in *Gray v. Barr*, which has been described by one commentator as "a combination of bad law and bad policy",[108] was received favourably by the majority of the Supreme Court of Canada in *Co-operative Fire & Casualty Co. v. Saindon*,[109] a decision which pertains to the intentional injury exclusion[110] rather than to the insuring phrase "caused by accident". Adopting the test laid down in *Gray v. Barr*, the majority of the Supreme Court of Canada held that a person carrying out an illegal act must be taken to intend any resulting harm which ought reasonably to have been anticipated. Chief Justice Laskin dissented on the basis that there was a middle ground between "accident" and "intent" and that although injury caused recklessly could not be said to be "caused by accident" neither could such injury be said to have been intentionally caused.[111]

The majority decision in *Saindon* has been criticized by various commentators who prefer Laskin C.J.'s dissent.[112] For the purposes of the present discussion, however, it must be remembered that *Saindon* concerns an intentional injury exclusion. With respect to the meaning of "caused by accident", both the majority and minority opinions in *Saindon* appear to proceed on the basis that an injury that is the natural and probable consequence of a deliberate act cannot be said to have been caused by accident.

---

[107] *Ibid.*, at 969.

[108] R.A. Hasson, "Supreme Court of Canada and the Law of Insurance 1975" (1976) 14 Osgoode Hall L.J. 769 at 777.

[109] (1975), 56 D.L.R. (3d) 556 (S.C.C.).

[110] See Chapter 8, section 7: Intentional Injury.

[111] *Supra*, note 109 at 560.

[112] R.A. Hasson, "Supreme Court of Canada and the Law of Insurance 1975", *supra*, note 108; L. Stuesser, "Liability Insurance Covering Criminal Acts" (1989) 1 C.I.L.R. 131.

(f) "Accident" and Courting the Risk

Where the insured is engaged in conduct that carries with it a significant and known risk of causing loss or damage, then the insured may, in some circumstances, be said to be acting recklessly or "courting the risk". Whether in such a case the loss or damage is "caused by accident" and therefore covered under a liability policy is often a vexing question. The answer cannot depend simply on the degree of likelihood of the harm, for someone who dies in a game of Russian Roulette does not die by accident, even though there is only one chance in six of a bullet being in the chamber.[113] Nor is the question answered by the notion of assumption of risk, for there are risks which are assumed in the course of daily living, which, when they do arise, are said to be accidental. In the end, then, questions as to courting the risk are perhaps best resolved by considering all of the circumstances, including the purpose for which the policy was placed, and determining whether the actions of the insured giving rise to the loss fall within the sort of activity that the policy intended to cover.

The classic illustration in Canada of courting the risk is provided by the decision of the Ontario High Court in *Candler v. London & Lancashire Guarantee & Accident Co. of Canada*,[114] Mr. Candler was insured for a sum in the event of his death from bodily injuries caused solely by accident. In a state of intoxication, and for the purpose of showing off his nerve to a friend, Candler walked out onto the balcony of his 13th-floor hotel suite and attempted to balance himself on the railing. He slipped onto the coping, where he tried valiantly to hang on. Eventually, however, unable to hold on any longer and his friend unable to pull him to safety, Candler plunged to his death. The Court held that for the purposes of the insurance policy Candler's death could not be characterized as "accidental", for he realized the obvious dangers of his actions and assumed the risk that he might slip and fall to his death.

The decision in *Candler* accords with common sense. Obviously, Candler did not intend to fall, neither can one even say that it was substantially certain that a fall would occur. Yet, even though the death was not intended, it was not accidental. The proximate cause of the loss was Candler's deliberate decision to place himself in danger for the purpose of courting the very risk that tragically materialized.

In *Mutual of Omaha Insurance Co. v. Stats*[115] the majority of the Supreme Court of Canada considered the assumption of risk test enunciated in *Candler* but distinguished the case on its facts. The insured, who was grossly intoxicated, insisted on driving her own motor vehicle. She was involved in a collision, killing both herself and her passenger. It was held by the majority that her death resulted from "accidental bodily injuries". Justice Spence, who delivered the reasons for the majority, stated as follows:

---

[113] *Thompson v. Prudential Ins. Co.*, 66 S.E.2d 119 (Ga. 1951).

[114] (1963), 40 D.L.R. (2d) 408 (Ont. H.C.J.).

[115] (1978), 87 D.L.R. (3d) 169 (S.C.C.).

Negligence is a finding made whereby the conduct of a person is judged by the concept of a reasonable man under certain circumstances. A person may be found to have been negligent or even grossly negligent but at the time that person performed the acts in question he might never have thought himself to be negligent. If, on the other hand, the person realized the danger of his actions and deliberately assumed the risk of it, then in Grant, J.'s view his actions could not be characterized as accidental. I agree with the Court of Appeal that such analysis does not apply to the circumstances in this case and I agree, therefore, with the view of the Court of Appeal that this occurrence was an "accident" within the words of this policy.[116]

In the context of a commercial liability policy, the assumption of risk test was applied by the Ontario Court of Appeal in *Crisp v. Great American Indemnity Co.*[117] The insured contractor, in the course of installing a terrazzo floor, permitted dust to spread throughout the owner's home. The insured knew that the dust would spread unless precautions were taken, yet not only did the insured not take the appropriate precautions but his employees, against the owner's wishes, deliberately left open a door and a window, which facilitated the dust's dispersal. The Ontario Court of Appeal held that the resulting damage, for which the insured was liable, was not "caused by accident":

> In our view, on the particular facts of this case, there was no accident within the meaning of that word as it appears in Coverage B of the policy. That which happened, in our opinion, was the natural, foreseeable and probable consequence of the defendants' acts. The defendants should have foreseen that such natural and probable consequences would ensue because the defendant and the defendant's workmen, on the evidence, had actual knowledge of what would happen if the precautions, which they failed to take, were not taken. There was, in this sense, a deliberate courting of the risk with knowledge of the risk, there was an element of reckless conduct in the sense that they could not have cared whether or not the dust damage would ensue when they proceeded with the work in the way they did with the knowledge which they had.[118]

The decision in *Crisp* was followed in *R.D. McCollum Ltd. v. Economical Mutual Insurance Co.*,[119] a case in which the insured contractor sand-blasted the brick and stone exterior of an office building and was held responsible for damage done to a number of windows. The Court held that the plain and ordinary meaning of "accident" included negligence but precluded wilful and deliberate acts or acts of gross negligence. In the result, the Court held that damage resulting from negligent conduct was covered under the policy but that damage resulting from reckless conduct was not. On this test, the insured's claim was allowed in part.

---

[116] *Ibid.*, at 183.

[117] [1961] I.L.R. 1-1046 (Ont. C.A.).

[118] *Ibid.*, at 230.

[119] [1962] O.R. 850 (H.C.J.).

Mere advertence to a risk, however, does not preclude a finding that a loss was caused by accident. In *Marshall Wells of Canada Ltd. v. Winnipeg Supply & Fuel Co.*[120] the Manitoba Court of Appeal addressed the issue of coverage in circumstances where the insured did not act deliberately or recklessly but, nevertheless, took a "calculated risk". The insured contractor left unsupported a hot water tank which later collapsed and caused damage. The contractor knew the situation was dangerous but failed to take any remedial steps, apparently because he felt that to do so he should receive additional money under his contract. The trial judge held that these circumstances did not come within the term "accident" and that the policy therefore did not cover. The test applied by the trial judge to determine whether there was an accident was whether the damage was "the result of an unanticipated mishap".[121]

The majority of the Manitoba Court of Appeal agreed with the trial decision. The majority judgment contains a detailed analysis of the meaning of the phrase "caused by accident" and concludes that to be considered accidental an event must have been unanticipated by an ordinary, reasonable and prudent person. Since the insured had adverted to the very risk in question, the collapse could not be said to be unanticipated, and therefore coverage was denied. Justice Freedman, in dissent, held that the insured's actions were not deliberate or reckless but were merely negligent and, as such, the resulting damage was "caused by accident".

Ten years later, the views of Freedman J. would prevail in the Supreme Court of Canada. The case was that of *Canadian Indemnity Co. v. Walkem*,[122] being the insurance companion to the decision of the Supreme Court of Canada in *Rivtow Marine Ltd. v. Washington Iron Works*.[123] Walkem, as a distributor of barge cranes, was held liable for failing to warn a customer of certain defects in the cranes which had come to Walkem's attention. As the trial judge noted:[124]

> Walkem knew of the dangerous condition of the crane, but nevertheless pawned off on an unsuspecting customer an inadequately and negligently re-paired piece of equipment. Walkem sought indemnity from its liability insurer. Coverage was denied on the ground that Walkem had taken a calculated risk and that the damage was therefore not "caused by accident". Reliance was placed by the insurer on the decision of the Manitoba Court of Appeal in *Marshall Wells of Can. Ltd. v. Winnipeg Supply & Fuel Co.*[125]

The Supreme Court of Canada overruled the decision in *Marshall Wells* and held in favour of the insured. The basis of the Supreme Court's decision,

---

[120] [1965] I.L.R. 1-131 (Man. C.A.).

[121] *Ibid.*, at 655.

[122] (1976), 53 D.L.R. (3d) 1 (S.C.C.).

[123] (1973), 40 D.L.R. (3d) 530 (S.C.C.).

[124] (1970), 74 W.W.R. 228 at 229 (B.C.S.C.).

[125] *Supra*, note 120.

however, is left in doubt. Justice Pigeon, for the majority, referred to the reasons of Guy J.A. in *Marshall Wells* and stated:

> With respect, this is a wholly erroneous view of the meaning of the word "accident" in a comprehensive business liability insurance policy. On that basis, the insured would be denied recovery if the occurrence is the result of a calculated risk or of a dangerous operation. Such a construction of the word "accident" is contrary to the very principle of insurance which is to protect against mishaps, risks and dangers. While it is true that the word "accident" is sometimes used to described unanticipated or unavoidable occurrences, no dictionary needs to be cited to show that in everyday use, the word is applied as Halsbury says in the passage above quoted, to *any unlooked for mishap or occurrence*. That this is the proper test rather than the words italicized by Guy, J.A., is apparent from a reading of the two cases on which that passage is based. ...
>
> However, I wish to add that, in construing the word "accident" in this policy, one should bear in mind that negligence is by far the most frequent source of exceptional liability which a businessman has to contend with. Therefore, a policy which would not cover liability due to negligence could not properly be called "comprehensive". But foreseeability is an essential element of such liability. If calculated risks and dangerous operations are excluded, what is left but some exceptional causes of liability?[126]

In the passage above, Pigeon J. applied the traditional definition of "accident" as "any unlooked for mishap or occurrence". He went on, however, to formulate a different test, one which he derived from the statutory provision[127] modifying the common law rule by which public policy barred indemnity with respect to the consequences of an unlawful act:

> In my view, the test laid down by the statute, namely, whether or not something was done by or for the insured "with intent to bring about loss or damage" is the very same test which must be applied to decide whether the occurrence is an accident or whether it is a crime barring recovery.[128]

On this basis, unless the insured intended to bring about loss or damage, the damage must be said to have been "caused by accident".

Ritchie J., while in agreement with Pigeon J., had this to say:

> I have had the advantage of reading the reasons for judgment prepared for delivery by my brother Pigeon and I agree with him that this appeal should be dismissed and that the damages sustained by the respondent were due to an "accident" in the sense of "an unlooked for mishap or occurrence" which occurred during the policy period and which was attributable to the respondent's negligence.
>
> I do not, however, agree that the word "accident" as used in a comprehensive business liability insurance policy includes a "calculated risk" which phrase ap-

---

[126] *Supra*, note 122 at 6, 7.

[127] See Chapter 2, section 1(h): Public Policy.

[128] *Supra*, note 122 at 7.

pears to me to imply the very antithesis of an "unlooked for mishap or occurrence". I know of no principle of insurance law which would compel such a construction in such a policy, but as I regard my brother Pigeon's expression of the contrary view as being an *obiter dictum* which is not necessary to his decision in this appeal, it does not prevent me from agreeing with his reasons for judgment in all other respects. I would accordingly dismiss this appeal with costs.[129]

Thus, two tests of "caused by accident" emerge from the reasons for judgment in *Canadian Indemnity Co. v. Walkem*. The test of "any unlooked for mishap or occurrence" is applied by both Ritchie J. and Pigeon J. On this test, damage caused recklessly, albeit unintentionally, could still fall outside of the insuring phrase "caused by accident". Yet, Pigeon J. proposes a second test, namely, that unless the insured intended to bring about loss or damage, the damage must be said to have been "caused by accident". On this basis, unless one extended the notion of intent so as to include recklessness, damage caused recklessly would not fall outside of coverage. Unfortunately, there is no further elaboration of the second test, nor is any note taken of its inconsistency with the traditional test of "any unlooked for mishap or occurrence". Moreover, in *Co-operative Fire & Casualty Co. v. Saindon*,[130] Pigeon J. concurred with the dissenting reasons of Laskin C.J.C., in which the Chief Justice noted that "accident" and "intent" are not exhaustive complements:

> What is evident to me, and is, I think, supported by case law apart from the cases referred to here, is that "accident" and "intent" are not exhaustive complements. It follows that where intent to cause injury is relied upon by an insurer as an exclusion from otherwise comprehensive coverage, it cannot succeed merely by showing that a deliberate act was involved which was not an accident, without also showing that there was an intent to cause the injury and not merely that there was a likelihood that injury might result from the act.[131]

In the passage quoted, Laskin C.J.C. is clearly of the view that there is a middle ground between "accident" and "intent": that damage caused recklessly is not caused intentionally, but neither is it caused by accident.[132] That this is correct is illustrated by the decision in *Candler v. London & Lancashire Guarantee & Accident Co. of Canada*[133] noted earlier.

(g) "Accident" and Business Risks

It is often said that commercial liability policies are not intended to cover "business risks". The term "business risk" is not one that is either defined or

---

currently used in liability policies,[134] nor is it a concept that can be defined with any degree of precision. What is generally meant by the term is the kind of risk that is inherent to doing business and which it is management's function to control or avoid.

The concept of business risk has been used, both explicitly and implicitly, as a guide to the interpretation of the insuring phrase "caused by accident". The first such attempt in the Supreme Court of Canada was in *Canadian Indemnity Co. v. Andrews & George Co.*[135] The decision is comprised of four separate judgments which concur in result but not in reasoning. In the circumstances, the comments as to the meaning of "accident" are merely *obiter*.

Andrews & George Company Limited, a manufacturer, delivered defective glue to a customer. The defect arose due to a testing machine being out of order and yielding a misleading result. The customer used the glue for making plywood, which then had to be sold at a lower price because the glue lacked adhesive strength. Judgment was awarded against the insured and indemnity was sought from the insurer.

Justice Kerwin, with whom Estey J. concurred, held that the defective condition of the glue was "unsuspected and undesired and, therefore, there was an accident which caused the damage to 'property of others'".[136] An exclusion to the policy, however, precluded coverage for liability assumed by contract, so the claim was not covered.

Justice Rand agreed that the exclusion applied but he was of the view that the damage was not caused by accident:

> What is meant is something out of the ordinary or the likely, something fortuitous, unusual and unexpected, not, in the ordinary course, guarded against.
>
> ... what the parties had in mind were possibilities difficult if not impossible to foresee: what they clearly did not aim at were direct and expectable damages from the daily risks which it was part of their business of production and sale to face and eliminate. These are the ordinary consequences of a breach of warranty of fitness, a liability as old as warranty itself.[137]

Justice Kellock held that on the wording of the particular policy, coverage was provided only for accidents that occurred after the goods had left the insured's possession. Since the accident in this case happened before the glue had left the insured's possession, Kellock J. held in favour of the insurer.

Justice Cartwright, agreeing with Kerwin J. and Rand J., held that the exclusion applied, and did not express an opinion on the meaning of "accident".

---

[134] At one time the predecessor to the performance exclusion was known as the "business risk" exclusion. In modern policies, however, the wording of that exclusion has been considerably altered. From an underwriting standpoint the notion of business risk pervades the entire policy. As imprecise as the concept may be, it is nevertheless used by underwriters as a description of the sort of risk that they do not intend to insure.

[135] [1953] 1 S.C.R. 19.

[136] *Ibid.*, at 22.

[137] *Ibid.*, at 27.

In the result, it was only Rand J. who attempted to formulate an analysis of "caused by accident" so as to exclude business risks on the basis of foreseeability. This analysis has been criticized as being unduly restrictive[138] in that certain risks are foreseeable, yet are nevertheless clearly intended to be covered under a commercial liability policy. This criticism is well-taken, for commercial policies are obviously designed to provide coverage with respect to negligence, and liability in negligence is based on the loss or damage being reasonably foreseeable to the insured. However, Rand J.'s views cannot be so easily disposed of. In the context of a commercial liability policy there is a sense of "caused by accident" which would eliminate coverage for risks that, although neither probable nor substantially certain to occur, are nevertheless expectable and are considered to be the sort of business risks which the parties did not intend the policy to cover. An example of such a risk is provided by the decision of the Ontario Supreme Court in *Erie Concrete Products Ltd. v. Canadian General Insurance Co.*[139] The insured, a pipe manufacturer, supplied pipe which cracked while in use. No damage occurred other than to the pipe itself. The cracking was the result of a shortcoming in the insured's manufacturing process coupled with a lack of inspection. Clearly there was negligence or a lack of care in the insured's business practices. Nevertheless, it was held that the cracking was not caused by an "accident" according to the common usage of the term. Implicit in the Court's reasoning was the notion that the insured's technical shortcomings were a business risk not intended to be covered by the policy.

Similar logic was employed in the decision in *A.R.G. Construction Corp. v. Allstate Insurance Co. of Canada.*[140] The decision illustrates a weakness in the business risks analysis of "accident" in that it holds that the same act is both "an accident" and not "an accident", depending upon the particular property which is damaged. The insured was the general contractor responsible for the construction of a commercial and retail building complex. An action was commenced against the insured asserting liability in both contract and tort as a result of certain alleged construction deficiencies. It was claimed that these deficiencies permitted the ingress of water into the building, causing extensive damage to various components of the building as well as causing damage to vehicles in the parking garage. The court held that the damage to the building did not result from an "accident"; rather, the court reasoned, the damage resulted from faulty workmanship. The court held in the alternative that if there was an accident then the claim was excluded by a number of exclusions, including the faulty workmanship exclusion. On the other hand, the court held that the damage to the vehicles did result from an "accident" and was covered under the policy. With

---

[138] D. Barlow, Case Comment (1953) 31 Can. Bar Rev. 429.

[139] [1969] I.L.R. 1-270 (Ont. H.C.J.). See also *Avalon (Consolidated School Board) v. McNamara Industries Ltd.*, [1975] I.L.R. 1-649 (Nfld. S.C.); *Supercrete Precast Ltd. v. Kansa General Ins. Co.*, [1990] B.C.J. No. 1132, 45 C.C.L.I. 248 (S.C.); *Kitchener Silo Inc. v. Cigna Ins. Co. of Can.*, [1991] O.J. No. 280, [1991] I.L.R. 1-2764 (Ont. Gen. Div.); *Greenan v. R.J. Maber Construction Co.*, [1992] N.B.J. No. 552, [1993] I.L.R. 1-2899 (C.A.).

[140] [2004] O.J. No. 4517, 17 C.C.L.I. (4th) 262 (S.C.J.).

respect, this reasoning exhibits a logical inconsistency. The same "unlooked for mishap or occurrence" (*i.e.*, "accident") that led to water penetrating the garage and damaging vehicles also led to water penetrating other portions of the building and causing other damage. The true issue in the case, it is submitted, is not whether there was an accident, but, rather, whether the claim was excluded by the other provisions of the policy.[141]

The same logic applies with respect to the decision in *Swagger Construction Ltd. v. ING Insurance Co. of Canada.*[142] A general contractor was responsible for the construction of a building. Defects in one portion of the work caused damage to other portions of the building. In addition to holding that this did not constitute property damage, the court also suggested that there was no occurrence. Yet, with respect, applying the classic formulation by Lord MacNaughten, the event was clearly "an un-looked for mishap or an untoward event which is not expected or designed".[143] Again, the real issue, it is submitted, ought to be whether or not the claim falls within the policy exclusions.

A similar difficulty arises with respect to the decision by the Ontario Court of Appeal in *Celestica Inc. v. ACE INA Insurance.*[144] The insured supplied a module which was incorporated into Xerox photocopiers. A transformer, purchased by the insured from its supplier and incorporated into the module, was defective in that it lacked double insulation and could result in an electrical shock. After the defect was discovered the insured was required to replace the power supply board in the module with one containing a double insulated transformer. The insured sought coverage from its liability insurer for the cost of taking the remedial action. The insurer conceded that property damage had occurred to the copiers, but asserted that there had not been an accident. The Ontario Court of Appeal agreed. Citing the decision in *Privest Properties Ltd. v. Foundation Co. of Canada*[145] with respect to the work/product *exclusion*, the Ontario Court of Appeal considered that it would be repugnant to the purpose of the policy to find that "defective design or manufacture can constitute an accident".[146] This statement must be placed in its proper context, for had the defective transformer electrocuted a person using one of the photocopiers no one could reasonably dispute the fact that there was bodily injury caused by accident, the accident consisting of the negligent manufacture of the module by the insured.[147] What is not explicitly stated by the Ontario Court of Appeal, but which clearly informs the reasons for judgment is that this was essentially a warranty claim against the insured to replace a defective product before it

---

[141] See the further discussion of this case in Chapter 8, section 4(c): Performance.

[142] [2005] B.C.J. No. 1964, [2005] I.L.R. 1-4445 (S.C.).

[143] *Supra*, note 90.

[144] [2003] O.J. No. 2820, 50 C.C.L.I. (3d) 190 (C.A.), leave to appeal to S.C.C. dismissed [2003] S.C.C.A. No. 433.

[145] [1991] B.C.J. No. 2213, 6 C.C.L.I. (2d) 23 (S.C.).

[146] *Supra*, note 44 at para. 31 (C.A.).

[147] For the purpose of this analysis I am assuming that the failure to provide the double insulated transformer was due to negligence. Whether this was so is not clear from the reasons in the case.

caused physical injury to person or property. The incorporation of the module into the photocopier did not result in any physical injury; rather, there was a notional injury to the photocopier in that its usefulness was impaired.[148] Unlike many modern policies, the policy in *Celestica* contained a definition of "property damage" which did not require physical injury. In these circumstances the insurer conceded that property damage had occurred to the photocopiers. This concession having been made, the insurer's argument that no accident had taken place had to be based upon the premise that the notional damage which occurred was the direct and expectable result of a breach of contract and was a business risk that must be assumed by the insured.

Celestica is a hard case. If one parses the insuring agreement and the exclusions in accordance with the established case law the result will be that the claim, in part, may be covered. This is plainly at odds with the general intent of a liability policy, but the language of the specific policy under consideration was created by the insurer and the insurer chose not to limit the definition of "property damage" so as preclude coverage for the notional injury that occurred in the case.

The business risk analysis of "accident" is also evident in the decision in *Kisle v. St. Paul Fire & Marine Insurance Co.*[149] The insured agreed to order the necessary pipe and repair a rancher's irrigation system. Due to illness, the insured's employee did not order the pipe, with the result that the rancher's crop was damaged before the irrigation system could be repaired. It was held that the insured's failure to perform its contract in reasonable time could not be characterized as an accident.

One view might be that the business risk analysis of "caused by accident" is flawed and that any so-called business risks for which the insurer does not wish to provide coverage ought to be addressed in the policy exclusions. There is a certain attractiveness to this view, for it would require the insurer to rely upon clear language to exclude any of the so-called business risks from coverage. Yet, no matter what language is chosen, it is impossible to set out in advance all of the categories of loss and damage which may occur. In the end, one is left with words whose meaning must be interpreted both in their popular and ordinary sense and in the context of the particular contract of insurance. In such cases, the courts should, as Estey J. put it in *Consolidated Bathurst Export Ltd. v. Mutual Boiler & Machinery Insurance Co.*, "be loath to support a construction which would ... enable ... the insured to achieve a recovery which could neither be sensibly sought nor anticipated at the time of the contract".[150] The business risk analysis of "caused by accident" may be seen as proceeding on this basis.

---

[148] See, in this chapter, section 4(b): Property Damage.

[149] 495 P.2d 1198 (Or. 1972).

[150] (1979), 112 D.L.R. (3d) 49 at 59 (S.C.C.).

(h) Reconciling the Various Tests for "Accident"

Unfortunately, in the trilogy of Supreme Court of Canada decisions in *Canada Indemnity Co. v. Walkem,*[151] *Co-operative Fire & Casualty Co. v. Saindon,*[152] and *Mutual of Omaha Insurance Co. v. Stats*[153] no attempt is made to reconcile the various tests for "accident" put forward in the three cases. In *Walkem,* the majority stated that a loss is accidental unless it was intended by the insured. In *Saindon,* the majority held that a loss is not accidental, even when it is not intended by the insured, where it is the eminently foreseeable consequence of the insured's deliberate act. In *Stats,* the majority stated that a loss is accidental unless the insured realized the danger and deliberately assumed the risk.

As a result, it has not been clear to the lower courts which test to apply in determining whether or not damage is "caused by accident". A good example of the difficulty this has created is provided by the decision in *University of Western Ontario v. Yanush.*[154] The insured, a university student, had coverage with respect to physical injury or property damage which was "caused by an accident" and which "was not expected or intended". As a prank, the insured emptied a pillow case full of toilet paper on top of a sleeping student and set it ablaze. The insured unsuccessfully attempted to extinguish the resulting fire, which was very quickly out of control, and the university building sustained over $100,000 in property damage. On the basis of *Co-operative Fire & Casualty Co. v. Saindon* one would have expected that the Court, applying the rule that a person intends the natural and probable consequence of his or her act, would have held that the damage was not "caused by accident". The *Saindon* decision, however, was not even referred to by the Court in *Yanush*. Rather, relying on *Mutual of Omaha Insurance Co. v. Stats,* the Court held that the insured did not realize the dangers of his actions, nor did he deliberately assume the risk of harm, and that the damage was therefore accidental.

Is *Yanush* correctly decided? Applying *Canadian Indemnity Co. v. Walkem,* the decision can certainly be supported on the basis that the result was not intended. Yet, common sense suggests that the loss in *Yanush* was not "caused by accident" and, if *Saindon* is good law, then the decision ought to have gone in favour of the insurer.

6. POLICY TERRITORY

Liability policies generally restrict coverage geographically. The Insurance Bureau of Canada's standard liability forms contain a provision that: "This insurance applies only to bodily injury and property damage which occurs within the policy territory." "Policy territory" is defined as follows:

---

[151] (1975), 53 D.L.R. (3d) 1 (S.C.C.).

[152] (1975), 56 D.L.R. (3d) 556 (S.C.C.).

[153] (1978), 87 D.L.R. (3d) 169 (S.C.C.).

[154] [1989] O.J. No. 19, 67 O.R. (2d) 525 (H.C.J.).

"policy territory" means:

(i)   Canada or the United States of America, its territories or possessions, or

(ii) anywhere in the world with respect to compensatory damages because of bodily injury or property damage arising out of a product which was sold for use or consumption within the territory described in paragraph (i) above, provided suit for such compensatory damages is brought within such territory.[155]

By stipulating that the injury or damage must occur in the policy territory, this wording avoids the confusion that arose in *Pickford & Black Ltd. v. Canadian General Insurance Co.*[156] In that case, the policy excluded coverage in respect of claims arising or existing by reason of an "accident occurring outside the Dominion of Canada and the United States of America". A claim was brought against the insured for its negligent storage of cargo aboard a ship within Canada which caused damage when the cargo shifted at sea while beyond the territory of Canada and the United States. The trial judge, applying a chain of causation test, held that the accident originated in Canada.[157] Both the Nova Scotia Court of Appeal[158] and the Supreme Court of Canada[159] disagreed, holding that the accident occurred at the place where the property damage was sustained.

A similar issue arose in *Cansulex Ltd. v. Reed Stenhouse Ltd.*[160] The insured, who had coverage in respect of property damage caused by an occurrence in Canada, was responsible for placing wet sulphur in the hold of a ship in Vancouver, thereby starting a process of corrosion which, it was found, did not cause actual damage until after the vessel had left Canadian waters. It was held that the policy applied to the claim, for the occurrence started the moment that the sulphur came into contact with the ship's steel. The Court referred with approval to the decision in *Sandoz Inc. v. Employers' Liability Assurance Corp.*,[161] which adopted the continuous exposure theory in an asbestosis[162] claim, but expressly declined to follow the decision in *Sandoz* on the basis that in the latter case bodily injury was presumed from the moment of ingestion or inhalation, whereas there was no actual damage in *Cansulex* until after the ship had left Canadian waters.

---

[155] See Appendix A of this book.

[156] (1973), 42 D.L.R. (3d) 360 (N.S.T.D.), revd (1974), 53 D.L.R. (3d) 277 (N.S.C.A.), affd (1976), 64 D.L.R. (3d) 179 (S.C.C.).

[157] (1973), 42 D.L.R. (3d) 360 at 392 (N.S.T.D.).

[158] (1974), 53 D.L.R. (3d) 277 at 282, 288 (N.S.C.A.).

[159] (1976), 64 D.L.R. (3d) 179 at 184 (S.C.C.).

[160] [1986] B.C.J. No. 3125, 70 B.C.L.R. 273 (S.C.).

[161] 554 F. Supp. 257 (U.S. Dist. Ct. 1983).

[162] See section 7(a): Occurrence Policies.

7. PERIOD OF COVERAGE

In general terms, liability coverage is written either on an occurrence or a claims-made basis. Under the former, coverage is provided by the policy in force at the time that the bodily injury or property damage occurs; under the latter, coverage is provided by the policy in force when the claim is made, regardless of when the injury or damage occurs.

It is important to recognize, however, that not all liability policies can be conveniently labelled in this fashion. As the Supreme Court of Canada noted in *Simcoe & Erie General Insurance Co. v. Reid Crowther & Partners Ltd.*, in every case the wording of the particular policy under consideration governs:

> At the same time, it is important to note that "claims-made" and "occurrence" are not legal labels which dictate a certain legal result once a policy is characterized as one or the other. The issue is always what the particular policy dictates, regardless of what it is called. This is particularly so due to there being disagreement between academics as to just what are "pure" "claims-made" policies, and "pure" "occurrence" policies. For instance, there is disagreement as to whether "claims-made" means claims made against the insured by third parties, or claims made by the insured against the insurer for coverage under the insurer's policy. Regarding the characterization of "pure" "occurrence" policies, one point of disagreement is whether the "occurrence" consists of a negligent act, or the resultant damage, or both.
>
> These disagreements can perhaps be resolved by recognizing that there may be different types of "claims-made" and "occurrence" policies, as well as hybrid policies that have some features of "claims-made" policies and some features of "occurrence" policies. The essential is not the label one places on the policy, but what the policy says. The courts must in each case look to the particular wording of the particular policy, rather than simply attempt to pigeonhole the policy at issue into one category or the other. Construction of policies at issue in these kinds of cases depends much more on the specific wording of the policy at issue than on a general categorizing of the policy.[163]

(a) Occurrence Policies

For many years, business liability policies were written on the basis that coverage was provided with respect to bodily injury or property damage which occurs during the policy period. In the standard form of CGL rider this is accomplished by the definitions of "bodily injury" and "property damage":

> "bodily injury" means bodily injury, sickness or disease sustained by any person which occurs during the policy period, including death at any time resulting therefrom.

---

[163] [1993] S.C.J. No. 10, [1993] I.L.R. 1-2914 at 2209. See also *Nanaimo Shipyard (1985) Ltd. v. Underwriters, Lloyd's London*, [1992] B.C.J. No. 597, 12 B.C.A.C. 179 (C.A.), leave to appeal to S.C.C. refd (1992), 17 B.C.A.C. 320*n*.

"property damage" means (1) physical injury to or destruction of tangible property which occurs during the policy period, including the loss of use thereof at any time resulting therefrom, or (2) loss of use of tangible property which has not been physically injured or destroyed provided such loss of use is caused by an accident occurring during the policy period.[164]

This type of policy is often characterized as an "occurrence" policy (as distinct from a claims-made policy rather than as distinct from an "accident" policy) because coverage depends upon the date that the injury or damage *occurs*. Under this type of policy, coverage is not triggered by the date of the wrongful act which *gives rise* to the claim,[165] nor is it triggered by the date that the claim itself is advanced.

A good example of when coverage attaches under an occurrence-based policy is provided by the decision in *Deodato v. Hartford Insurance Co.*[166] The plaintiff, a roofing contractor, had constructed a roof in 1969 while insured with the Hartford Insurance Company under a CGL policy. Some four years later, and approximately six months after cancellation of the Hartford policy, the roof came off the building and an action was commenced against Deodato. It was held that Hartford was not required to indemnify Deodato in respect of the claim because the property damage did not occur until the destruction of the roof, which was outside the policy period. The fact that the wrongful act took place while the Hartford policy was still in force was not material.

In most cases, the date upon which bodily injury or property damage occurs can be readily ascertained. In recent years, however, and particularly with respect to environmental issues, there has been an increasing number of claims which cannot be easily categorized. These claims involve injury or damage that is either continuing, or difficult to pinpoint in time, or both. The best examples of these sorts of claims are provided by the asbestosis[167] and D.E.S.[168] claims for bodily injury and the toxic waste[169] and leaky condo cases with regard to property damage.

Asbestosis is a disease which is contracted as the result of long-term exposure to asbestos. Over the period of exposure, any given tortfeasor has likely been insured by more than one insurer and, at any rate, has had a succession of

---

[164] See Appendix A of this book.

[165] Under some earlier policies coverage was triggered by the date the accident originated: See *Cdn. Indemnity Co. v. Walkem* (1975), 53 D.L.R. (3d) 1 (S.C.C.).

[166] 363 A.2d 361 (1976). Followed in *Landry v. Fenton*, [1994] B.C.J. No. 1472, 27 C.C.L.I. (2d) 304 (S.C.).

[167] See, for example, *Ins. Co. of North America v. Forty-Eight Insulations Inc.*, 633 F.2d 1212 (6th Cir. 1980), modified, 657 F.2d 814, cert. denied, 454 U.S. 1109 (1981), rehearing denied, 455 U.S. 1009 (1982).

[168] See, for example, *American Motorist Ins. Co. v. E.R. Squib & Sons Inc.*, 406 N.Y.S. 2d 658 (N.Y. Sup. Ct. 1978).

[169] See, for example, *Continental Ins. Co. v. Northeastern Pharmaceutical & Chemical Co.*, 811 F.2d 1180 (8th Cir. 1987).

policies of insurance, usually with different limits and perhaps with different insuring provisions. Which policy or policies must respond to the claim?

The same problem arises with toxic waste claims. Containers of toxic waste may be placed in landfill sites. Many years later it is often discovered that over time the containers have developed leaks and contaminated the groundwater. Over this period of time the insured may have had a variety of liability policies. Which of these policies responds to the claim?

No single answer to these questions has emerged but at least four distinct theories have been propounded:[170]

(i) Exposure[171]

The date of the occurrence is the date of first exposure to the conditions which later cause the harm.

(ii) Continuous Exposure[172] (or "Triple Trigger")[173]

The date of the occurrence is the continuous period from the date of first exposure to the date of manifestation of the harm;

(iii) Manifestation[174]

The date of occurrence is the date when the insured or third party first knows or ought to know that injury or damage has occurred;

(iv) Injury-In-Fact[175]

The date of the occurrence is the date that the bodily injury or property damage actually occurs.

The only one of these theories which is entirely consistent with the CGL policy wording is, of course, the injury-in-fact theory.[176] If it is possible, in

---

[170] *Slough Estates Canada Ltd. v. Federal Pioneer Ltd.*, [1994] O.J. No. 2147, 20 O.R. (3d) 429, [1995] I.L.R. 1-3129 (Gen. Div.); *St. Paul Fire & Marine Ins. Co. v. Durabla Can. Ltd.*, [1994] O.J. No. 1727, 19 O.R. (3d) 631, [1994] I.L.R. 1-3101 (Gen. Div.), vard, [1996] O.J. No. 2505, 137 D.L.R. (4th) 126, 29 O.R. (3d) 737, 36 C.C.L.I. (2d) 25 (C.A.); *Privest Properties Ltd. v. Foundation Co. of Can.*, [1991] B.C.J. No. 2213, 6 C.C.L.I. (2d) 23 (S.C.); *Alie v. Bertrand & Frère Construction Co.*, [2000] O.J. No. 1360, 30 C.C.L.I. (3d) 166 (S.C.J.), vard on appeal, [2003] O.J. No. 2977, [2003] I.L.R. I-4146 (C.A.), leave to appeal to S.C.C. dismissed, [2003] S.C.C.A. No. 60.

[171] See, for example, *Hancock Laboratories Inc. v. Admiral Ins. Co.*, 777 F.2d 520 (9th Cir. 1986).

[172] See, for example, *Keene Corp. v. Ins. Co. of North America*, 667 F.2d 1034 (D.C. Cir. 1981) and *Hay Bay Genetics Inc. v. MacGregor Concrete Products (Beachburg) Ltd.*, [2003] O.J. No. 2049, 6 C.C.L.I. (4th) 218 (S.C.J.)

[173] This theory is sometimes called the "triple trigger" because it triggers coverage on three events: (i) exposure; (ii) injury-in-fact (presumably this occurs after a certain period of exposure); and (iii) manifestation.

[174] *Eagle-Picher Industries Inc. v. Liberty Mutual Ins. Co.*, 682 F.2d 12 (1st Cir. 1982); *Allstate du Canada Cie D'Assurance c. Assurance Royale du Canada*, [1994] R.J.Q. 2045 (C.S.), affd [1999] R.J.Q. 2827 (C.A.).

[175] See, for example, *American Home Products Corp. v. Liberty Mutual Ins. Co.*, 748 F.2d 760 (2nd Cir. 1984); *Aetna Casualty Surety Co. v. Abbott Laboratories Inc.*, 636 F. Supp. 546 (D. Conn. 1986).

[176] *Allstate Insurance Co. of Canada v. AXA Pacific Insurance Co.*, [1998] B.C.J. No. 1762 [1998] I.L.R. 1-3608 (S.C.); *Sam Ermen Plumbing & Heating Ltd. v. Canadian General Insurance Co.*

retrospect, to pinpoint the date or dates when the injury or damage actually took place, then the other theories become irrelevant, for the wording of the CGL policy is clear — it refers to bodily injury or property damage during the policy period. An exposure to a hazard within the policy period which causes damage outside the policy period does not fit this wording. Nor should the manifestation of damage in one policy period relieve the previous insurer when the damage actually took place while that previous policy was in force.[177]

Where it is impossible to determine the actual date of bodily injury or property damage, however, then a deemed date must be selected. One will then have to choose among the exposure, continuous exposure, and manifestation theories or one of their variants for the purpose of ascertaining which policy or policies must respond to the claim.

Each of the various theories has its proponents. The exposure and manifestation theories are both easy to apply, for the date of exposure and the date of manifestation are usually clear enough. The continuous exposure theory may be favoured for reasons of public policy, in that by involving a number of insurance policies the greatest amount of coverage will be brought to bear in a particular case.

In the United States, there are a multitude of decisions in favour of each of these approaches. In reviewing these decisions one cannot help but think that the theory a court adopts in a particular case may be dictated by whatever is necessary to provide coverage rather than by a rational application of legal principle.[178]

In Canada, these issues have received considerably less attention. The manifestation theory was rejected in *St. Paul Fire & Marine Insurance Co. v. Durabla Canada Ltd.*,[179] a decision dealing with the duty to defend in asbestos-related litigation, and also in *University of Saskatchewan v. Firemen's Fund Insurance Co. of Canada*,[180] a decision under an all-risks property policy. In *Alie v. Bertrand & Frère Construction Co.*[181] and *International Comfort Products Corp. (Canada) v. Royal Insurance Co. of Canada*[182] the Court adopted the

---

[1999] N.B.J. No. 58, 535 A.P.R. 94, 209 N.B.R. (2d) 94 (Q.B); *Alie v. Bertrand & Frère Construction Co.*, *supra*, note 170.

[177] *Alie v. Bertrand & Frère Construction Co.*, [2003] I.L.R. I-4146 at para. 140 (Ont. C.A.).

[178] As the Ontario Superior Court of Justice noted in *Alie v. Bertrand & Frère Construction Co.*, *supra*, note 170 at para. 329, "The Courts in both Canada and the U.S. have done what Courts generally do and, that is, make findings that achieve the most equitable results. Therefore, in different circumstances, they have invoked different trigger theories".

[179] [1994] O.J. No. 1727, 19 O.R. (3d) 631, [1994] I.L.R. 1-3101 (Gen. Div.), vard, [1996] O.J. No. 2505, 137 D.L.R. (4th) 126, 29 O.R. (3d) 737, 92 O.A.C. 157, 36 C.C.L.I. (2d) 25 (C.A.).

[180] [1995] S.J. No. 239, 31 C.C.L.I. (2d) 217 (Q.B.), revd, [1998] S.J. No. 615, [1998] 5 W.W.R. 276, 158 Sask. R. 223, [1998] I.L.R. 1-3548, 50 C.C.L.I. (2d) 272 (C.A.), leave to appeal to S.C.C. refd (1998), 227 N.R. 287*n*, 173 W.A.C. 320*n*, 168 Sask. R. 320*n*.

[181] *Supra*, note 170.

[182] [2000] O.J. No. 893, I.L.R. 1-3828 (S.C.J.).

continuous exposure theory, which was also given tacit approval in *Cansulex Ltd. v. Reed Stenhouse Ltd.*[183]

(b) Claims-Made Policies

One of the most significant features of the Commercial General Liability Program released by the Insurance Bureau of Canada in 1986 was the introduction of a claims-made form. Traditionally, commercial risks were written on an occurrence basis. Occurrence policies, however, have what is known as a "long tail" in that the insurer may be required to respond decades later to a loss that occurred during the policy period but which did not manifest itself as a claim until much later. An illustration of the long tail of an occurrence policy is provided by the asbestosis, D.E.S. and toxic waste litigation in the United States.[184] In order to avoid this sort of unpredictable, long-term liability, some underwriters have chosen to insure commercial risks on a claims-made basis.[185]

Under a claims-made policy, the trigger of coverage is the date the claim is made[186] rather than the date when the occurrence took place. In the Insurance Bureau of Canada's Commercial General Liability policy (claims-made form) coverage is written on the following basis:

(i) Retroactive Date
A retroactive date (which will usually be the inception date of the first claims-made policy) is specified in the declarations. Coverage will not be extended to any claims, whenever made, which result from an occurrence before the retroactive date. Coverage in respect of those claims will presumably be provided by the occurrence policy in force at the relevant time.

(ii) Period of Coverage
Subject to the extended reporting periods discussed below, the policy responds only to those claims brought during the policy period.

(iii) Extended Reporting Periods
(a) 60 Day ("Mini") Tail: Coverage is automatically extended to a claim which is brought within 60 days after the expiration of the policy, provided that the claim results from an occurrence which

---

[183] [1986] B.C.J. No. 3125, 70 B.C.L.R. 273 (S.C.). Although the Court approved of the continuous exposure theory, the decision may be explained as an example of the exposure theory. See the discussion in M.B. Snowden & M.G. Lichty, *Annotated Commercial General Liability Policy* (Aurora: Canada Law Book, 1997-) at para. 11:40.2(1).

[184] See the cases cited, *supra*, in notes 167, 168 and 169. See, generally, Fagan, "Liability Insurance, Uncertainty and Long-Tail Risks" (1989) 1 C.I.L.R. 219.

[185] A helpful discussion of the rationale for claims-made policies is found in *Simcoe & Erie General Insurance Co. v. Reid, Crowther & Partners Ltd.*, [1993] S.C.J. No. 10, [1993] I.L.R. 1-2914.

[186] There is a variation on claims-made coverage known as a "claims made and reported" policy. Under the latter form the claim must be both made and reported to the insurer during the policy period for there to be coverage: *Stuart v. Hutchins* [1999] O.J. No. 3672, 164 D.L.R. (4th) 67, 40 O.R. (3d) 321, [1999] I.L.R. 1-3619 (C.A.).

took place before the end of the policy period (but not before the retroactive date).

(b)　Five Year ("Midi") Tail: Coverage is automatically extended to a claim which is brought within five years after the expiration of the policy, provided that notice of the claim was given to the insurer within 60 days after the end of the policy period and provided further that the claim results from an occurrence which took place before the end of the policy period (but not before the retroactive date).

(c)　Unlimited Tail: For an additional premium, coverage may be purchased with respect to any claims which may result in the future from occurrences which took place during the policy period. In short, this endorsement converts the claims-made policy into an occurrence policy. The extended reporting period endorsement may be purchased generally or for specific accidents, products, or locations.[187]

　　　　The word "claim" is not defined in the Commercial General Liability policy.[188] The policy provides only that: "A claim by a person or organization seeking compensatory damages will be deemed to have been made when notice of such claim is received and recorded by any insured or by us, whichever comes first". In the absence of a definition, the courts will interpret "claim" in accordance with its ordinary, plain meaning. On this basis, as a general rule, for a "claim" to be made there must be some form of written or verbal communication of a demand for compensation or other form of reparation by a third party upon the insured, or at least communication by the third party to the insured of a clear intention to hold the insured responsible for the damages in question.[189] Thus, a coroner's inquest does not constitute a claim, for the governing legislation specifically precludes a finding of legal responsibility.[190] An allegation of negligence or misconduct, in the absence of a demand for compensation, does not constitute making a claim.[191] Similarly, knowledge by the insured of

---

[187] See Appendix J of this book.

[188] In *Wright Engineers Ltd. v. U.S. Fire Ins. Co.*, [1986] B.C.J. No. 129, 19 C.C.L.I. 74 at 87 (C.A.), the British Columbia Court of Appeal noted that it is with good reason that the word "claim" is not defined in the policy, for "the number of permutations and combinations of events which may give rise to claims against a professional engineer are almost literally infinite. It may well be advantageous both to insurer and insured that a degree of flexibility be retained. So the approach should be to decide on which side of the line a given set of facts should fall without trying to specify a line applicable to all cases".

[189] *Simcoe & Erie General Insurance Co. v. Reid Crowther & Partners Ltd.*, *supra*, note 185, at page 2213; *Builders Contract Management Ltd. v. Simcoe & Erie General Ins. Co.*, [1993] S.J. No. 176, 16 C.C.L.I. (2d) 84 (Q.B.); *Gaunce v. Continental Ins. Co. of Can.* [1995] N.B.J. No. 387, 166 N.B.R. (2d) 180, [1995] I.L.R. 1-3240 (Q.B.).

[190] *Akey v. Encon Insurance Managers Inc.*, [2002] O.J. No. 2605, 43 C.C.L.I. (3d) 37 (C.A.).

[191] *Stevenson v. Simcoe & Erie General Ins. Co.*, [1981] A.J. No. 921, [1981] I.L.R. 1-1434 (Alta. Q.B.); *Defranceso v. Stivala*, [1992] O.J. No. 2116 (C.A.), revg [1989] I.L.R. 1-2524 (H.C.); *Gaunce v. Continental Ins. Co. of Can.*, *supra*, note 189; *cf. Continental Casualty Co. v. Robert McLellan & Co.*, [1973] 5 W.W.R. 475 (B.C.S.C.).

circumstances which could rise to a demand for compensation does not constitute a claim.[192] Nor is a claim made when a writ, asserting legal responsibility, is issued but not served or otherwise brought to the insured's attention.[193]

It must be emphasized that the preceding paragraph does not apply to all claims-made policies. As noted earlier,[194] regardless of the label used, all claims-made policies are not the same. Some policies define the term "claim"; others do not. Some policies contain a provision that a claim is deemed to be made when the insured provides notice of an act or omission which may give rise to liability;[195] other policies are silent on this point. In each case careful attention must be paid to the wording of the particular policy what hand. Moreover, many policies are hybrids, incorporating features of both claims-made and occurrence policies.[196] One must be careful, particularly with respect to hybrid policies, to avoid an interpretation which would create a gap in coverage in the situation where the loss and the claim are in separate policy periods.[197]

8. CONTRACTUAL LIABILITY COVERAGE

Liability insurance is a means of transferring fortuitous contingent risks. Accordingly, contractual liability insurance coverage is generally quite limited in scope. In some cases the policy is entirely silent on the matter of contractual liability. In other cases coverage in respect of certain forms of contractual liability is expressly included in the insuring agreement. In still further cases the insuring agreement makes no mention of contractual liability, but the policy contains an exclusion with respect to some, but not all, forms of contractual liability.

---

[192] *Jesuit Fathers of Upper Canada v. Guardian Insurance Co. of Canada*, [2003] O.J. No. 4534, 6 C.C.L.I. (4th) 276 (S.C.J.), [2004] O.J. No. 4641, 16 C.C.L.I. (4th) 24 (C.A.), leave to appeal to S.C.C. granted, [2005] S.C.C.A. No. 5.

[193] *St. Paul Fire & Marine Ins. Co. v. Guardian Ins. Co. of Can.*, [1983] I.L.R. 1-1711 (Ont. C.A.). Cf. *Peacock v. Roberts and Guardian Ins. of Can.*, [1985] B.C.J. No. 2836, 15 C.C.L.I. 36 (S.C.), appeal dismissed [1990] B.C.J. No. 574, I.L.R. 1-2590 (C.A.) where it was held that the phrase "claim or suit brought" contemplated coverage where the writ was issued, though not served, during the policy period.

[194] See section 7: Period of Coverage.

[195] *Kirk v. St. Paul Fire & Marine Insurance Co.*, [2002] M.J. No. 251, [2001] I.L.R. I-4016 (Man. Q.B.).

[196] *Simcoe & Erie General Insurance Co. v. Reid, Crowther & Partners Ltd.*, [1993] S.C.J. No. 10, [1993] I.L.R. 1-2914.

[197] *Canada Trustco Mortgage Co. v. Kansa General Ins. Co.*, [1994] M.J. No. 276, 25 C.C.L.I. (2d) 97 (Q.B.); *Simcoe & Erie General Ins. Co. v. Reid, Crowther & Partners Ltd., ibid.*; cf. *Nanaimo Shipyard (1985) Ltd. v. Underwriters, Lloyd's London*, [1992] B.C.J. No. 597, 12 B.C.A.C. 179 (C.A.), leave to appeal to S.C.C. refd (1992), 17 B.C.A.C. 320*n*, where the apparent result is a gap in coverage.

For both the CGL and Commercial General Liability policies, coverage with respect to contractual liability is excluded, with certain specified exceptions. The scope of the exclusion is addressed in Chapter 8.[198]

Apart from the CGL and Commercial General Liability policies, coverage with respect to contractual liability may be purchased in the form of a Contractual Liability Coverage Rider. The insuring agreement provides as follows:

> Coverage Y — Contractual Bodily Injury Liability
> To pay on behalf of the Insured all sums which the Insured, by reason of contractual liability assumed by the Insured under a contract designated in the schedule for this insurance, shall become legally obligated to pay as compensatory damages because of bodily injury.

> Coverage Z — Contractual Property Damage Liability
> To pay on behalf of the Insured all sums which the Insured, by reason of contractual liability assumed by the Insured under a contract designated in the schedule of this insurance, shall become legally obligated to pay as compensatory damages because of property damage caused by accident.

> "contractual liability" means liability expressly assumed under a written contract or agreement; provided, however, that contractual liability shall not be construed as including liability under a warranty of the fitness or quality of the Named Insured's products or a warranty that work performed by or on behalf of the Named Insured will be done in workmanlike manner.[199]

The purpose of this form of coverage is to indemnify the insured with respect to the insured's contractual assumption of the tortious liability of a third party. As is apparent from the insuring agreement and the definition of "contractual liability", coverage applies only with respect to written contracts or agreements that have been designated by schedule in the policy. Moreover, the insured's assumption of liability in the contract must be express. In *J.L. Simmons Co. v. Fidelity & Casualty Co.*[200] the Court held that even in the absence of policy wording requiring that the assumption of liability be "express", that was still the most natural interpretation of coverage Y:

> ... giving consideration to all the foregoing factors, we choose the construction of the policy language which seems to us the most natural, that is that there must be a portion of a written contract identifiable as an indemnity provision in order for liability to be deemed assumed under a written contract and covered.[201]

---

[198] See Chapter 8, section 1: Contractual Liability.

[199] I.B.C. Form 2007, June 1978. See Appendix F of this book.

[200] 511 F.2d 87 (7th Cir. 1975).

[201] *Ibid.*

The contractual liability coverage rider is subject to the same exclusions as the CGL policy.[202] With respect to contractual liability, coverage is excluded for liability arising out of professional services:

> This insurance does not apply:
>
> (a)   if the Insured or his indemnitee is an architect, engineer or surveyor, to bodily injury or property damage arising out of the rendering of or the failure to render professional services by such Insured or indemnity, including (1) the preparation or approval of maps, plans, opinion, reports, surveys, designs or specifications and (2) supervisory, inspection or engineering services.

---

[202] See, generally, Chapter 8: Exclusions.

Chapter 8

EXCLUSIONS

All commercial liability policies contain a number of exclusions designed to limit the scope of the coverage provided under the insuring agreement. Although policy exclusions do not grant coverage,[1] in some cases, particularly where there are exceptions to the exclusion, the wording of the exclusion may be used to expand the coverage otherwise available under the policy.[2]

All commercial liability policies, in general, share a number of similar exclusions. These exclusions will be discussed under the following headings:

- (i)   Contractual Liability;
- (ii)   Automobile, Watercraft and Aircraft;
- (iii) Care, Custody or Control;
- (iv)   Product and Performance;
- (v)   Recall or "Sistership";
- (vi)   Employee and Workers' Compensation;
- (vii) Intentional Injury;
- (viii) Environmental Liability;
- (ix)   Professional Services.

In addition to these exclusions, a commercial liability policy designed for a particular industry, purpose or insured may have certain other exclusions.[3]

The discussion that follows is based upon the policy language found in IBC Form 2001.[4] Where appropriate, references are made to subsequent forms.

1. CONTRACTUAL LIABILITY

In broad terms (apart from bodily injury or property damage resulting from a breach of a warranty to supply goods of suitable fitness or quality, or breach of a warranty that work be done in a workmanlike manner), commercial liability

---

[1]   *Fresard v. Michigan Millers Mutual Ins. Co.*, 327 N.W.2d 286 at 290 (1982).

[2]   See Chapter 7, section 2: Liability Imposed by Law.

[3]   See, for example, *Virgil Greenhouses Ltd. v. Westland Construction (1997) Inc.*, [2003] O.J. No. 2868, 29 C.L.R. (3d) 306 (S.C.J.), dealing with a contractor's "Hard Hat" policy containing exclusions relating to the removal or weakening of support, the moving of buildings and the performance of demolition operations.

[4]   Appendix A.

policies are not intended to protect the insured from liability arising from the insured's own breach of contract. Insurance protection may be purchased, however, with respect to the insured's assumption, by contract, of the legal liability of other persons.

The standard CGL policy contains an exclusion which removes from coverage all forms of contractual liability except those that have been specifically excepted:

> This insurance does not apply to:
>
> (a) liability assumed by the Insured under any contract or agreement except an incidental contract, but this exclusion does not apply to a warranty of fitness or quality of the Named Insured's products or a warranty that work performed by or on behalf of the Named Insured will be done in a workmanlike manner.

"Incidental Contract" is defined as:

> Any written agreement which is a lease of premises, easement agreement, agreement required by municipal ordinance, side-track agreement or elevator maintenance agreement.

The exception with respect to warranties of fitness or quality of goods is likely a consequence of the decision of the Supreme Court of Canada in *Canadian Indemnity Co. v. Andrews & George Co.*[5] Liability for property damage or bodily injury resulting from a breach of warranty to supply goods of suitable fitness or quality, or breach of warranty that work be performed in a workmanlike manner is often one of the principal areas of exposure for which insureds seek protection.[6] It must be noted, however, that coverage with respect to the breach of such warranties is still subject to the other exclusions in the policy, particularly the product and performance exclusions.[7]

The type of liability assumed by the insured under an "incidental contract", as defined in the policy, is a contractual assumption of the tortious liability of a third party.[8] Unfortunately, not all policies draw a clear distinction between the liability of others assumed by the insured under contract and the direct contractual liability of the insured.[9] Indeed, the standard form of contractual liability exclusion quoted above fails to draw this distinction, which leaves open an argument that "liability assumed ... under ... contract ..." encompasses both the contractual assumption of the tortious liability of others and the insured's own direct contractual liability.

---

[5] [1953] 1 S.C.R. 19.

[6] *Cansulex Ltd. v. Reed Stenhouse Ltd.* (1986), 70 B.C.L.R. 273 (S.C.).

[7] *Ibid.* See also *Weedo v. Stone-E-Brick Inc.*, 405 A.2d 788 (N.J. 1979).

[8] See *Acklands Ltd. v. Can. Indemnity Co.*, [1984] 4 W.W.R. 764 (Man. Q.B.), affd [1985] 4 W.W.R. 71 (Man. C.A.). It is noted that in the various types of agreements referred to in the definition of "incidental contract" it would be customary for the insured to assume the tortious liability of others.

[9] See Chapter 7, section 2: Liability Imposed by Law.

In some cases, liability may arise concurrently in tort and contract. If the contract is one for which liability has been excluded in the insurance policy, then, under the CGL policy, the exclusion applies and coverage is thereby avoided.[10] In the Commercial General Liability policy, however, coverage is expressly extended to cover tortious liability which the insured would have in the absence of contract.

In the Commercial General Liability policy, coverage in respect of contractual liability has been expanded from that available under the basic CGL policy. The contractual liability exclusion in the 1986 Commercial General Liability policy is in the following terms:

This insurance does not apply to: ...

b. "Bodily injury" or "property damage" for which the insured is obligated to pay compensatory damages by reason of the assumption of liability in a contract or agreement. This exclusion does not apply to liability for compensatory damages:

1) Assumed in a contract or agreement that is an "insured contract"; or

2) That the insured would have in the absence of the contract or agreement.

The term "insured contract" is defined as follows:

"Insured contract" means:

a. A lease of premises;

b. A sidetrack agreement;

c. An easement or license agreement in connection with vehicle or pedestrian private railroad crossings at grade;

d. Any other easement agreement;

e. An indemnification of a municipality as required by ordinance, except in connection with work for a municipality;

f. An elevator maintenance agreement; or

g. That part of any other contract or agreement pertaining to your business under which you assume the tort liability of another to pay compensatory damages because of "bodily injury" or "property damage" to a third person or organization, if the contract or agreement is made prior to the "bodily injury" or "property damage". Tort liability means a liability that would be imposed by law in the absence of any contract or agreement.

An "insured contract" does not include that part of any contract or agreement that indemnifies an architect, engineer or surveyor for injury or damage arising out of:

1) Preparing, approving or failing to prepare or approve maps, drawings, opinions, reports, surveys, change orders, designs or specifications; or

2) Giving directions or instructions, or failing to give them, if that is the primary cause of the injury or damage;

---

[10] *Dominion Bridge Co. v. Toronto General Ins. Co.* (1962), 37 W.W.R. 673 (B.C.C.A.), affd (1963), 45 W.W.R. 125 (S.C.C.).

In the 2005 revision to the Commercial General Liability form the exception in respect of "insured contracts" was expanded so as to provide for payment of defense expenses incurred by the insured on behalf of another.

Unlike the CGL policy, the Commercial General Liability form does not limit contractual coverage to written agreements alone. Nor, as noted earlier, does it operate to exclude coverage where liability is concurrent in contract and tort. Moreover, the basic coverage under the Commercial General Liability form extends generally to tortious liability of others assumed under any contract or agreement pertaining to the insured's business. Pursuant to the Contractual Liability Limitation endorsement (I.B.C. Form 2308, August 1987), however, coverage under the Commercial General Liability policy in respect of contractual liability may be narrowed to approximately that provided under the basic CGL form.

2. AUTOMOBILE, WATERCRAFT AND AIRCRAFT

A commercial liability policy is not an automobile, watercraft or aircraft liability policy. Such policies may be purchased separately. Accordingly, the standard CGL policy contains the following exclusions:

This insurance does not apply to:...
(b) bodily injury or property damage arising out of the ownership, mainte-nance, use or operation by or on behalf of the Insured of any automobile;
(c) bodily injury or property damage arising out of the ownership, maintenance, use, operation, loading or unloading by or on behalf of the Insured of any watercraft, but this exclusion does not apply to water-craft while ashore on premises owned by, rented to or controlled by the Named Insured;
(d) (1) bodily injury or property damage arising out of the ownership, main-tenance, use, operation, loading or unloading by or on behalf of the In-sured of
(i) any aircraft, or
(ii) any air cushion vehicle
(2) bodily injury or property damage arising out of the ownership, exis-tence, use or operation by or on behalf of the Insured of any premises for the purpose of an airport or aircraft landing strip and all operations neces-sary or incidental thereto.

"Automobile" is defined as follows:
"Automobile" means any self-propelled land motor vehicle, trailers or semi-trailers while attached thereto or unattached (including its equipment mounted on or attached thereto) other than any of the following or their trailers, accessories and equipment:
(i) vehicles of the crawler type (other than motorized snow vehicles);
(ii) tractors (other than road transport tractors designed to haul trailers or semi-trailers), road rollers, graders, scrapers, bulldozers, paving machines and con-crete mixers (other than concrete mixers of the mix-in-transit type);
(iii) other construction machinery or equipment mounted on wheels but not self-propelled while not attached to any self-propelled land motor vehicle;
(iv) self-propelled land motor vehicles used solely on the premises of the Insured.

The language used in the automobile exclusion is very similar to that used in the insuring agreement of an automobile liability policy. It would appear, therefore, that the policies are designed to be complementary, such that a claim excluded under the CGL policy should be covered under the automobile liability policy. In *Law, Union & Rock Insurance Co. v. Moore's Taxi Ltd.*,[11] Ritchie J. of the Supreme Court of Canada adopted the following comment of Tritschler J.A. in the Manitoba Court of Appeal:

> The comprehensive policy issued by defendant is complementary to the standard motor vehicle liability policy and the coverage of the former commences where the coverage of the latter ceases. In my opinion plaintiff could not succeed against the insurer under the standard motor vehicle liability policy for the same reason that it can in this case succeed against the defendant.[12]

The same logic was employed by the Ontario Court of Appeal in *Axa Insurance v. Dominion of Canada General Insurance Co.*[13] Dominion asserted that although the accident arose out of the ownership, use or operation of a motor vehicle so as to fall within an insuring agreement of a motor vehicle liability policy, the accident did not arise from the ownership, use or operation of a motor vehicle for the purposes of an exclusion in a homeowner's policy. The court rejected this as sophistry, noting that:

> Although the case law supports the general proposition that coverage clauses should be interpreted generously and exclusion clauses strictly, the distinction cannot be stretched to provide two completely opposite interpretations to the same words in two insurance policies applying to the same accident.[14]

The meaning of the phrase "arising out of the ownership, maintenance, use or operation ... of any automobile" has received extensive consideration in Canadian courts, both in the context of an insuring clause and in the context of an exclusion. The leading decisions are those of the Supreme Court of Canada in *Stevenson v. Reliance Petroleum Ltd.*,[15] *Law, Union & Rock Insurance Co. v. Moore's Taxi Ltd.*,[16] and *Amos v. Insurance Corp. of British Columbia.*[17]

In *Stevenson*, the issue was whether the motor vehicle policy or the general liability policy or both applied. Reliance Petroleum delivered gasoline in a tank truck to a service station. Through the negligence of an employee, the fuel hose was left unattended with the result that gasoline overflowed the station's tanks, ignited, and destroyed the premises. The Supreme Court of Canada held that the

---

[11] (1959), 22 D.L.R. (2d) 264 (S.C.C.).

[12] (1959), 20 D.L.R. (2d) 149 at 155-6 (Man. C.A.).

[13] [2004] O.J. No. 4492, 16 C.C.L.I. (4th) 28 (C.A.)

[14] *Ibid.*, at para. 32.

[15] (1956), 5 D.L.R. (2d) 673 (S.C.C.).

[16] *Supra*, note 11.

[17] [1995] S.C.J. No. 74, [1995] 9 W.W.R. 305.

motor vehicle policy responded. Applying a "purpose" test, the Court noted that the tank truck was designed so as to permit gasoline to be discharged through a hose. The negligence of the employee in the discharge of gasoline, therefore, arose from the use of a motor vehicle and fell within the coverage provided by the motor vehicle policy. Mr. Justice Rand expressed the purpose test in these terms:

> The expression "use or operation" would or should, in my opinion, convey to one reading it all accidents resulting from the ordinary and well-known activities to which automobiles are put, all accidents which the common judgment in ordinary language would attribute to the utilization of an automobile as a means of different forms of accommodation or service. [18]

The general liability policy in *Stevenson* contained an exclusion with respect to "any claim arising ... by reason of ... any motor vehicle which is owned, hired or leased by the Insured". This exclusion, although rather vaguely worded, was given a broad interpretation by the majority of the Court and was held to exclude any damage arising out of the use or operation of a motor vehicle. Accordingly, the action against the general liability insurer was dismissed.

Applying the purpose test, it has been held that unloading a tank truck delivering fuel oil,[19] improperly parking a car such that it becomes a runaway vehicle,[20] drilling a hole in a car to hook up trailer wires,[21] negligence in the course of loading a truck with household goods,[22] leaving a dog unsecured in a car with a window partly open,[23] an owner's improper installation of snow tires on a motor vehicle,[24] a deer hunter's use of a vehicle's headlights to illuminate a target[25] and draining gasoline from a motorcycle prior to repairs[26] all relate to the use or operation of a motor vehicle. On the other hand, it was held that the use of a portable barbecue inside a van,[27] the use of a cutting torch to cut a

---

[18] *Supra*, note 15, at 676-77.

[19] *Irving Oil Co. v. Can. General Ins.*, [1958] S.C.R. 590. See also *Harvey Oil Ltd. v. Lombard General Insurance Co. of Canada*, [2003] N.J. No. 273, 8 C.C.L.I. (4th) 51 (S.C.T.D.), affd [2004] N.J. No. 47 (C.A.).

[20] *Cochrane v. ING Halifax Insurance Co.*, [2004] N.B.J. No. 45, 8 C.C.L.I. (4th) 79 (Q.B.).

[21] *Gramak Ltd. v. State Farm Mutual Auto Ins. Co.* (1975), 63 D.L.R. (3d) 630 (Ont. H.C.J.), affd (1976), 69 D.L.R. (3d) 505*n* (Ont. C.A.).

[22] *Huba v. Schulze (No. 2)* (1963), 37 D.L.R. (2d) 570 (Man. Q.B.).

[23] *Boell v. Schinkel*, [1991] O.J. No. 1019, 3 O.R. (3d) 741 (Gen. Div.). See also *Taylor v. Maris*, [2004] B.C.J. No. 1431, 14 C.C.L.I. (4th) 178 (C.A.).

[24] *Strickland v. Miller*, [1998] O.J. No. 2762, [1998] I.L.R. 1-3602 (Gen. Div.).

[25] *Herbison v. Lumbermens Mutual Casualty Co.*, [2005] O.J. No. 2262, 255 D.L.R. (4th) 74 (C.A.)

[26] *Shelton v. Ins. Corp. of British Columbia*, [1993] B.C.J. No. 1169, 15 C.C.L.I. (2d) 161 (C.A.). See also *Kracson v. Pafco Ins. Co.* (1981), 121 D.L.R. (3d) 498 (Ont. Co. Ct.). *Cf. Thacker v. Lavell*, [1992] A.J. No. 1018, 13 C.C.L.I. (2d) 128, 40 M.V.R. (2d) 306 (C.A.). The latter decision, which concerns coverage under an automobile policy, is inconsistent with the authorities referred to in this section, is not well reasoned and is of dubious value as a precedent.

[27] *Chateauvert v. Economical Mutual Ins. Co.*, [1980] I.L.R. 1-1223 (Ont. H.C.J.).

vehicle in half,[28] draining gasoline from a motorcycle preparatory to dismantling it for parts,[29] and negligence in the maintenance of a truck[30] did not constitute the use or operation of a motor vehicle.

In *Law, Union & Rock Insurance Co. v. Moore's Taxi Ltd.*,[31] the Supreme Court of Canada considered the meaning of "claims arising out of the ... use or operation ... of any motor vehicle" in an exclusion clause of a commercial liability policy. The insured taxi company had contracted to transport mentally retarded children from school to their homes and to escort them right to the door. One of the taxi drivers, contrary to the escort requirement, let a child out of the car and in crossing the street to his home the child was hit by a truck. The Supreme Court of Canada held that the taxi driver's liability did not arise out of the use or operation of a motor vehicle. Rather, the liability arose from the breach of the separate duty to escort the child to his home. Ritchie J., for the Court, formulated a "chain of causation" test:

> ... the words "claims arising out of ... the ownership, use or operation ... of any motor vehicle" as used in this exclusion can only be construed as referring to claims based upon circumstances in which it is possible to trace a continuous chain of causation unbroken by the interposition of a new act of negligence and stretching between the negligent use and operation of a motor vehicle on the one hand and the injuries sustained by the claimant on the other. In the present case the motor vehicle was stationary at the time of the accident and the chain of causation originating with its use was severed by the intervening negligence of the taxi driver whose failure to escort the boy across the street was the factor giving rise to the respondent's liability. [32]

In subsequent decisions applying the chain of causation test, the automobile exclusion has been held to apply to a fire occurring while siphoning gas from a truck to a gasoline container[33] and to property damage resulting when a

---

[28] *Dobish v. Garies*, [1985] A.J. No. 757, 15 C.C.L.I. 69 (Alta. Q.B.).

[29] *Yip v. Davies*, [1999] B.C.J. No. 1836, [2000] I.L.R. 1-3757 (S.C.).

[30] *Czarnuch v. Devon Transport Ltd.*, [1989] B.C.J. No. 230, [1989] I.L.R. 1-2452 (B.C.C.A.). The exclusion in this case was limited to "use or operation" of a motor vehicle. Liability with respect to "maintenance" was not excluded. Having regard to other policy provisions (in which maintenance was specifically mentioned as a risk separate and apart from use) the Court held that the policy drew a distinction between maintenance and use, and thus found in favour of coverage. As a general rule, however, use does include maintenance: *Shelton v. Ins. Corp. of British Columbia, supra*, note 26. Moreover, in *Elias v. Ins. Corp. of British Columbia*, [1992] B.C.J. No. 1857, 12 C.C.L.I. (2d) 135 (S.C.) the Court appeared to accept that maintenance or repair also fell within a motor vehicle policy as being an incident of "ownership".

[31] (1959), 22 D.L.R. (2d) 264 (S.C.C.). *Cf. Carwardine (Litigation guardian of) v. Northumberland Clarington Board of Education*, [2001] O.J. No. 63, 25 C.C.L.I. (3d) 193 (C.A.), in which it was held that the alleged negligence of a school bus operator in failing to ensure that a child boarded the bus, with the result that the child was exposed to severe weather conditions and had his legs amputated, triggered the defence clause under an automobile policy as possibly constituting use or operation of the school bus.

[32] *Ibid.*, at 268.

[33] *Pioneer Grain Co. v. Wellington Ins. Co.*, [1988] A.J. No. 1038, [1989] I.L.R. 1-2409 (Q.B.).

carelessly stowed paving machine fell from a trailer[34] but not to a claim arising out of a passenger opening the door into the path of an oncoming vehicle,[35] nor to a claim arising out of the negligent handling of a firearm mounted on the gun rack of a pick-up truck,[36] nor to a claim against the driver of a taxi for discharging an intoxicated patron before reaching his destination.[37]

In *Amos v. Insurance Corp. of British Columbia* the Supreme Court of Canada applied a two-part test incorporating both the purpose test from *Stevenson* and a modification of the chain of causation test from *Law, Union & Rock Insurance Co.*:

1.   Did the accident result from the ordinary and well-known activities to which automobiles are put?

2.   Is there some nexus or causal relationship (not necessarily a direct or proximate causal relationship) between the appellant's injuries and the ownership, use or operation of his vehicle, or is the connection between the injuries and the ownership, use or operation of the vehicle merely incidental or fortuitous?[38]

Amos was decided in the context of a regulation providing no-fault benefits, the language of which was similar, but not identical, to the standard CGL automobile exclusion. While driving his van the insured was surrounded by a gang of thugs who began to pound on the vehicle. As he attempted to escape, the insured was shot and seriously injured. His automobile policy entitled him to accident benefits providing his injuries were "caused by an accident that arises out of the ownership, use or operation of a vehicle". At trial and in the British Columbia Court of Appeal it was held that the van was merely the situs of a random shooting. Accordingly, the injuries were not causally related to the ownership, use or operation of a motor vehicle and the benefits were not payable.

On further appeal the Supreme Court of Canada disagreed with the concurrent findings of fact in the courts below. The Supreme Court of Canada's view of the evidence was that the shooting occurred as a direct result of the assailants' failed attempt to gain entry to the van. It followed that the injuries were caused

---

[34] *Imperial Equipment Lease v. Royal Ins. Co. of Can.*, [1980] I.L.R. 1-1266 (N.B. Arbitration Award, Fredericton); revd on jurisdictional grounds [1982] I.L.R. 1-1467 (N.B.C.A.). The arbitrator's decision is an interesting application of the automobile exclusion. The paving machine in question was covered while it was being used as a paver. The arbitrator found, however, that the claim, which resulted from inadequately securing the paving machine to a trailer, arose out of the use or operation of the truck and trailer and therefore fell within the exclusion.

[35] *Watts v. Centennial Ins. Co.* (1967), 65 D.L.R. (2d) 529 (B.C.S.C.); see *Fraser v. Co-op. Ins. Assoc.* (1984), 6 C.C.L.I. 232 (Ont. H.C.J.), revd (1986), 54 O.R. (2d) 579 (C.A.), in which the Ontario Court of Appeal disagreed with the decision in *Watts*.

[36] *Yurkowski v. Federated Mutual Implement & Hardware Ins. Co.* (1975), 54 D.L.R. (3d) 728 (B.C.S.C.).

[37] *Fraser Valley Taxi Cabs Ltd. v. Ins. Corp. of British Columbia*, [1993] B.C.J. No. 84, 13 C.C.L.I. (2d) 50 (B.C.C.A.).

[38] [1995] S.C.J. No. 74, [1995] 9 W.W.R. 305 at para. 17.

by an accident arising out of the insured's ownership, use or operation of his vehicle and the benefits were therefore payable.

It bears emphasis that the causation requirement in *Amos* was not that of a direct or proximate relationship between the loss and the ownership, use or operation of an automobile. This is based upon the language used in the policy. In a case in which the policy contains a more stringent causation requirement (*e.g.*, direct causation) then the second part of the *Amos* test will not apply.[39]

A number of cases have considered whether claims for bodily injury or property damage involving negligent entrustment of a motor vehicle to another or negligent supervision of another's use of a motor vehicle fall within the automobile exclusion. There are two apparently conflicting lines of authority. One line, exemplified by the decisions in *Perkull (Guardian ad litem of) v. Gilbert*,[40] *Unger (Litigation guardian of) v. Unger*,[41] *Silverthorne v. Gore Mutual Insurance Co.*[42] and *Warren (Guardian ad litem of) v. Martin*,[43] holds that the exclusion applies on the basis that an essential element of a claim of negligent entrustment or supervision is that the loss arises from the negligent use (albeit by another) of a motor vehicle. The other line of authority, exemplified by the decisions in *Williams v. Pictou County Farmers Mutual Fire Ins. Co.*[44] and *Fitzgerald v. Co-Operators Insurance Co.*,[45] notes that in a negligent supervision case the insured may be liable even in the absence of negligence on the part of the driver. The latter cases, in order to avoid a gap in coverage and proceeding on the basis that a claim of negligent supervision does not fall within the coverage afforded by an automobile liability policy, hold that the exclusion does not apply.

The apparent conflict between these two lines of authority disappears when one takes into account the particular facts in a given case. In each of *Perkull, Unger, Silverthorne* and *Warren* the insured was the owner of the vehicle in question. Plainly, entrusting one's motor vehicle to another is an incident of ownership. Moreover, in these circumstances coverage is available to the insured under a motor vehicle liability policy. In *Williams* and *Fitzgerald*, on the other hand, the claims which were held to be potentially covered arose in circumstances under which the insured was not the owner of a motor vehicle, but, rather, exercised supervision over the child whose use of the motor vehicle resulted in bodily injury. The latter claims would not be covered under a motor vehicle liability policy.

---

[39]   *Chisholm v. Liberty Mutual Group*, [2002] O.J. No. 3135, 60 O.R. (3d) 776 (C.A.); *Greenhalgh v. ING Halifax Insurance Co.*, [2004] O.J. No. 3485, 13 C.C.L.I. (4th) 292 (C.A.).

[40]   [1993] B.C.J. No. 1078, 18 C.C.L.I. (2d) 133 (S.C.).

[41]   [2003] O.J. No. 4587, 69 O.R. (3d) 257 (C.A.).

[42]   [2001] O.J. No. 871, 28 C.C.L.I. (3d) 24 (C.A.).

[43]   [1998] N.S.J. No. 373, [1999] I.L.R. 1-3693 (S.C.).

[44]   [2001] N.S.J. No. 59, 25 C.C.L.I. (3d) 32 (C.A.).

[45]   [2003] N.S.J. No. 206, 50 C.C.L.I. (3d) 307 (S.C.).

The decision in *Cella v. McLean*[46] provides a useful example of the importance of paying attention to the facts in the individual case. The plaintiff was injured in a motor vehicle accident when her car was struck by a vehicle in which the defendant was a passenger. The defendant did not own the car, but was alleged to have been negligent in failing to prevent the driver from operating the vehicle while his faculties were impaired by alcohol or drugs. The defendant sought coverage under his homeowner's policy. The insurer declined on the basis that the claim arose out of the use or operation of a motor vehicle. The Ontario Court of Appeal did not agree, noting that the defendant did not have any aspect of control over the vehicle itself; rather, his alleged liability arose in relation to his alleged responsibility over the actions of another person. The distinction is a fine one, but it is consistent with a purposive approach to the interpretation of both general liability and automobile liability policies. The defendant was not using the motor vehicle in question so as to be covered under the owner's policy. Given the intention that the coverage clause in a motor vehicle liability policy and the automobile exclusion in a general liability policy are designed to complement one another,[47] it follows that neither should the insured be denied coverage under his or her homeowner's policy.

In its 2005 revision to the Commercial General Liability policy, the Insurance Bureau of Canada incorporated a new paragraph to specifically exclude from coverage claims relating to negligent hiring, training or supervision in relation to automobiles:

> This exclusion applies even if the claims against any insured allege negligence or other wrongdoing in the supervision, hiring, employment, training or monitoring of others by that insured, if the "occurrence" which caused the "bodily injury" or "property damage" involved the ownership, maintenance, use or entrustment to others of any "automobile" that is owned or operated by or rented or loaned to any insured.

Similar wording has been incorporated into the watercraft and aircraft exclusion in the Commercial General Liability policy.

Although the intention is that the automobile and general liability policies be complementary rather than overlapping, depending upon the particular policy language under consideration, or the characterization of the negligence involved, both insurers may be required to respond to a claim. In *Royal Insurance Co. of Canada v. Guardian Insurance Co. of Canada*[48] the insured's negligent omission to secure a towed forklift (so as to prevent it from running downhill) before unhitching it from the tow vehicle was held to be covered both under a liability policy in respect of the vehicle and a commercial liability policy in respect of the insured's operations. Although the commercial liability policy contained an automobile exclusion, there was an exception with respect to

---

[46] [1997] O.J. No. 2439, 44 C.C.L.I. (2d) 214 (C.A.).

[47] See text at note 12.

[48] [1995] O.J. No. 3207, 26 O.R. (3d) 290, 31 C.C.L.I. (2d) 42 (Gen. Div.).

attached machinery while in actual use. Thus, the decision is explained by the use of non-congruent policy wordings.

In *Whitehead v. Whitehead*[49] a claim was brought against a person insured under both an automobile policy and a homeowners' policy by a passenger who, while alighting from a vehicle, tripped over a chock block which had been left on the driveway. The insuring agreement in the automobile policy used identical language to that contained in the exclusion clause in the liability section of the homeowners' policy. Nevertheless, it was held that both policies applied. The decision may be explained on the basis that there were two acts of negligence, both of which contributed to the loss. As an occupier, the insured was negligent in leaving the chock block on the driveway where someone might trip over it. It can be argued that this negligence did not relate to the use or operation of a motor vehicle and was therefore covered under the homeowner's policy. As a driver, the insured was negligent in permitting his passenger to alight where it was dangerous to do so. This negligence arose out of the use or operation of a motor vehicle and was therefore covered under the automobile policy.

Determining whether a claim can properly be characterized in two distinct fashions so as to fall within both within a motor vehicle and a comprehensive general liability policy may involve a very subtle analysis of the nature of the insured's liability. In *Derksen v. 539938 Ontario Ltd.*,[50] the insured contractor's foreman had carelessly stowed a heavy steel plate on a compressor unit towed by a truck in the course of picking up road signs after the completion of a nearby construction project. While he was driving the truck along an icy highway the plate flew off of the compressor unit and crashed through the window of a nearby school bus, killing one child and injuring others. A claim was brought against the contractor for negligence in the operation of a motor vehicle (driving with an improperly secured load) and for negligence in the instruction and supervision of employees with respect to the cleaning up the work site. The contractor sought coverage under both a motor vehicle and a comprehensive liability policy. The parties agreed to submit the coverage issues for determination by the Court on a point of law. The Court held that both policies applied, noting that there were two sources of liability, one automobile-related and one not automobile-related. In terms of the question asked of the Court and in terms of the duty to defend this is surely correct, for there was a possibility that the non-automobile related claim could succeed. In terms of indemnity, the result would depend upon the evidence led and the findings made at trial. If, for example, there were no negligence on the part of the contractor regarding instructions and supervision (presumably the foreman needed no supervision

---

49 [1984] I.L.R. 1-1820 (B.C.S.C.). See also *Canadian Indemnity Co. v. Security National Ins. Co.*, [1994] S.J. No. 428, 9 W.W.R. 589, 122 Sask. R. 264, 26 C.C.L.I. (2d) 295 (Q.B.).

50 [1998] O.J. No. 3723, 37 M.V.R. (3d) 59 (Gen. Div.), affd, [1999] O.J. No. 2473, 123 O.A.C. 232, 45 M.V.R. (3d) 6 (C.A.), appeal dismissed, [2001] S.C.J. No. 27, [2002] I.L.R. 1-4029. See also *Twylight Pressure Controls Ltd. v. Dominion of Canada General Insurance Co.*, [2000] B.C.J. No. 120, [2000] I.L.R. I-3806 (C.A.) and *Neary v. Wawanesa Mutual Insurance Co.*, [2003] N.S.J. No. 198, 50 C.C.L.I. (3d) 176 (C.A.).

and may very well have been properly instructed as to his duties but was simply careless) then the essence of the so-called non-automobile-related negligence would consist solely of carelessly stowing the steel plate on a piece of equipment intended to be towed by a motor vehicle, in which case it is questionable whether the comprehensive general liability policy would have responded to the claim.

The scope of the automobile exclusion in personal liability policies, including homeowners' policies, is further discussed in Chapter 14.[51]

3. CARE, CUSTODY OR CONTROL

Commercial liability policies generally contain an exclusion with respect to damage to property "in the care, custody or control of the insured". There has been considerable litigation over the scope of this exclusion. On occasion, the courts have expressed the concern that a literal application of the exclusion would render coverage illusory.[52] It is noted, however, that limited coverage in respect of this risk is available under the Broad Form Property Damage Coverage endorsement[53] and, depending upon the particular circumstances, may be available under other forms as well.

The care, custody or control exclusion has undergone a number of revisions over the years. In its current form in the CGL policy, the exclusion is in the following terms:

This insurance does not apply:
(h) to property damage to
    (1) property owned or occupied by or rented to the Insured, or
    (2) property used by the Insured, or
    (3) property in the care, custody or control of the Insured or property as to which the Insured is for any purpose exercising physical control, or
    (4) any personal property or any fixtures as the result of any work performed thereon by the Insured or anyone on his behalf;

but parts (2) and (3) of this exclusion do not apply with respect to liability under a written sidetrack agreement and part (3) of this exclusion does not apply with respect to property damage (other than to elevators) arising out of the use of an elevator at premises owned by, rented to or controlled by the Named Insured.

---

[51] See Chapter 14, section 5(a): Automobile, Watercraft and Aircraft.

[52] *T.W. Thompson Ltd. v. Simcoe & Erie General Ins. Co.* (1975), 58 D.L.R. (3d) 327 (Ont. H.C.J.); affd (1976), 68 D.L.R. (3d) 240 (Ont. C.A.); *Indemnity Ins. Co. v. Excel Cleaning Service*, [1954] 2 D.L.R. 721 (S.C.C.).

[53] See Chapter 9: Endorsements.

(a) Damage to Property Owned or Occupied by or Rented to the Insured

Liability insurance is intended to cover the insured's liability to a third party; it is not meant to indemnify the insured in respect of loss or damage to the insured's own property.[54] Coverage with respect to property falling within the first part of the care, custody or control exclusion is generally available under a policy of property insurance.

The phrase "property owned or occupied by or rented to the Insured" indicates that the insured has some measure of control over the property in question. The exclusion has thus been held not to apply to cranes which were supplied to a contractor under a so-called rental agreement where the owner of the cranes provided the operators and the insured had no measure of possession or control.[55] Nor did an insured "occupy" a tank where it carried out work inside the tank but did not have the right to admit or deny access to others.[56] Although the point was not addressed in the latter case, it has been held in the United States that property "occupied", given its ordinary meaning, refers to realty not personalty.[57]

In *Romay Automotive Ltd. v. Dominion of Canada General Insurance Co.*,[58] it was held, where two persons were named as insured and one negligently damaged the property of the other, that the exclusion applied and the insurer was not liable under the policy. The result would have been otherwise had the policy contained a cross-liability clause.[59]

(b) Damage to Property Used by the Insured

In order for the second part of the exclusion to apply, the property must be used by, not for,[60] the insured. Thus, the exclusion does not apply to damage to property used by the insured's contractor, even though under the supervision of the insured.[61] The sense in which the property must be "used" in order to fall

---

[54] *Archway Holdings Ltd. v. Royal Ins. Co. of Can.*, [1992] N.B.J. No. 594, [1993] I.L.R. 1-2907 (Q.B.).

[55] *Fraser River Pile Driving Co. v. Fidelity Ins. Co. of Can.*, [1973] I.L.R. 1-519 (B.C.S.C.); *Acadia Road Contractors Ltd. v. Can. Surety Co.* (1977), 81 D.L.R. (3d) 169 (N.S.T.D.), affd (1978), 88 D.L.R. (3d) 287 (N.S.C.A.). Where the insured is in control of the rented equipment, however, the exclusion applies: See *B.C. Bridge & Dredging Co. v. Royal Exchange Assur.*, [1960] I.L.R. 1-353 (B.C.S.C.).

[56] *Interprovincial Pipe Line Co. v. Seller's Oil Field Service Ltd.* (1975), 58 D.L.R. (3d) 719 at 731 (Man. Q.B.), affd (1976), 66 D.L.R. (3d) 360 (Man. C.A.).

[57] *Indiana Lumbermen's Mutual Ins. Co. v. Gallos Plastic Corp.*, 264 S.E.2d 73 (N.C. 1980).

[58] (1974), 43 D.L.R. (3d) 346 (Ont. H.C.).

[59] See *ING Insurance Co. of Canada v. Sportsco International L.P.*, [2004] O.J. No. 2254, 12 C.C.L.I. (4th) 86 (S.C.J.) and Chapter 6, section 3(i): Severability of Insureds or "Cross-Liability".

[60] *Fraser River Pile Driving Co. v. Fidelity Ins. Co. of Can.*, *supra*, note 55.

[61] *Ibid.* See also *Kenting Drilling Ltd. v. General Accident Assur. Co. of Can.*, [1979] 5 W.W.R. 68 (Alta. S.C.), affd [1985] 3 W.W.R 286 (Alta. C.A.).

within the exclusion has not been clearly defined. It would appear that the exclusion contemplates "use" in the sense of employing the property with some aim or purpose, whether or not that purpose is one to which the property is ordinarily put.[62]

In *ING Insurance Co. of Canada v. Sportsco International L.P.*[63] the court correctly stated that application of the exclusion is limited to circumstances in which the insured is using the property which is damaged, but then further limited the exclusion to situations in which the insured was using its own property. As it is generally written, the exclusion is not confined to the insured's use of its own property; rather, the exclusion would apply to circumstances in which the insured was using another's property in its operations. An example would be a carpenter damaging a borrowed table-saw while using it to rip lumber for the construction of a building. The damage to the table-saw would be excluded from coverage.

(c) Damage to Property in the Care, Custody or Control of the Insured

The third part of the exclusion excepts from coverage damage to property in the care, custody or control of the insured or property over which the insured is for any purpose exercising physical control. The majority of American cases support the view that care, custody or control is to be interpreted in the physical or possessory sense rather than in the proprietary sense.[64] The preponderance of Canadian authority[65] also supports this view, although in an early Supreme Court of Canada decision dealing with a previous version of the exclusion (which did not include the words "or property as to which the insured is for any purpose exercising physical control") one of the majority opinions suggested that the test is proprietary rather than possessory control.[66] The additional words contained in the modern version of the exclusion leave no doubt, however, that physical possession is required before the exclusion can come into operation. Thus, it was held that the exclusion did not apply to damage to goods for which the insured was responsible but which were in the possession of a warehouse-man.[67] Nor did the exclusion apply to one of two joint bailees, where it was the

---

[62] See comments of Sheppard J.A. in *Dominion Bridge Co. v. Toronto General Ins. Co.* (1962), 37 W.W.R. 673 at 695 *et seq.* (B.C.C.A.), affd (1963), 45 W.W.R. 125 (S.C.C.).

[63] [2004] O.J. No. 2254, 12 C.C.L.I. (4th) 86 (S.C.J.).

[64] See, for example, *Stealy v. Continental Western Ins. Co.*, 417 N.W.2d 140 (Minn. 1987); and *U.S. Fidelity & Guaranty Co. v. Johnson Shoes Inc.*, 461 A.2d 85 (N.H. 1983); *Phoenix of Hartford v. Holloway Corp.*, 260 So.2d 195 (Fla. 1972).

[65] *Neil's Trailer & Equipment Ltd. v. Butler, Maveety & Meldrum Ltd.* (1977), 75 D.L.R. (3d) 151 (Alta. S.C.); *Sumitomo Can. Ltd. v. Can. Indemnity Co.*, [1983] I.L.R. 1-1594 (B.C.C.A.). *Acadia Road Contractors Ltd. v. Can. Surety Co.*, [1978] I.L.R. 1-998 (N.S.T.D.); T.W. *Thompson Ltd. v. Simcoe & Erie General Ins. Co.*, [1976] I.L.R. 1-734 (Ont. C.A.).

[66] *Indemnity Ins. Co. v. Excel Cleaning Service, supra*, note 52, at 725, *per* Rand J.

[67] *Sumitomo Can. Ltd. v. Can. Indemnity Co., supra*, note 65.

other bailee who had physical possession of the goods at the time the damage was sustained.[68]

In practice, the application of the care, custody or control exclusion often leads to a judicial splitting of hairs. The intention of the exclusion is that the insured not be covered with respect to the business risk that it may damage property over which it is exercising responsibility or control, whether as a bailee for hire or for the purpose of performing some work or service.[69] Yet, in giving effect to this purpose, the courts are concerned that coverage not be rendered nugatory.[70] Thus, consideration will be given to the operations of the insured, as disclosed in the policy declarations, so as to ensure that the application of the exclusion will not negate the purpose for which the policy was issued.[71]

As a general rule, a line is drawn between damage to property which is under the insured's control as a necessary element of the performance of the insured's work and property damage which is merely incidental thereto.[72] On this basis, where an insured was working on an inner component part of an industrial furnace, it was held that the exclusion did not apply to damage to the furnace's outer wall.[73]

(d) Damage to Personal Property or Fixtures as a Result of Work Performed Thereon

The fourth part of the exclusion is restricted to work performed on personal property or fixtures. The purpose would appear to be to avoid the result in *Indemnity Insurance Co. of North America v. Excel Cleaning Service*,[74] in which

---

[68] *W. Krause Logging Ltd. v. Tomenson Saunders Whitehead Ltd.* (1984), 9 C.C.L.I. 248 (B.C.S.C.).

[69] As the Court observed in *Stewart Warner Corp. v. Burns International Security Service Inc.*, 527 F.2d 1025 (7th Cir. 1975), one purpose of the exclusion "is to prevent the general liability insurer from becoming a guarantor of the insured's workmanship in his ordinary operations. Failures of workmanship are a normal business risk which the insured is in the best position to prevent. If such risk be transferred to the insurer via general liability provisions, the cost of general liability coverage will be greater. The 'care, custody or control' exclusion is designed to avoid such result". An example of the proper application of this exclusion is provided by the decision in *Tsubaki of Canada Ltd. v. Standard Tube Canada*, [1993] O.J. No. 1855 (Gen. Div.). The decision, however, is erroneous in other respects. See *infra* at note 186.

[70] *T.W. Thompson Ltd. v. Simcoe & Erie Gen. Ins. Co.* (1975), 58 D.L.R. (3d) 327 (Ont. H.C.J.), affd (1976), 68 D.L.R. (3d) 240 (Ont. C.A.); *Indemnity Ins. Co. v. Excel Cleaning Service*, [1954] 2 D.L.R. 721 (S.C.C.).

[71] *Newfoundland Power Inc. v. Insurance Corp. of Newfoundland Ltd.*, [2001] N.J. No. 152, 28 C.C.L.I. (3d) 107 (S.C.T.D.).

[72] *International Derrick & Equipment Co. v. Buxbaum*, 240 F.2d 536 (3d Cir. 1957); *Country Mutual Ins. Co. v. Waldman Mercantile Co.*, 430 N.E.2d 606 (Ill. App. 1981).

[73] *Ronalco Inc. v. Home Ins. Co.*, 606 S.W.2d 160 (Ky. 1980). See also *Privest Properties Ltd. v. Foundation Co. of Can.*, [1991] B.C.J. No. 2213, 6 C.C.L.I. (2d) 23 (S.C.), in which, in the context of the duty to defend, the Court, absent further evidence, was not prepared to accept the proposition that a contractor performing renovations had care, custody or control of the entire building.

[74] *Supra*, note 52.

it was held that the care, custody or control exclusion did not apply where the insured damaged a carpet it was cleaning at a customer's home. Yet it appears that this purpose has not necessarily been achieved. In *Hoegy v. General Accident Assurance Co.*[75] it was held that the insured crop sprayer was covered for damage to plants resulting from his improper application of a weed-control agent. The Court's reasoning was that growing crops were treated for some purposes as personalty and for other purposes as realty and the exclusion, therefore, did not unambiguously apply. The Court also noted that the declarations described the insured's operations as "crop spraying" and stated that it would therefore take very clear language to exclude the risk of that which occurred. Given these circumstances the decision may be sound. It nevertheless remains that the CGL policy was not intended to cover this sort of risk.

In *Day & Ross (Nfld.) Ltd. v. Insurance Corp. of Newfoundland*[76] the insured contractor was responsible for the maintenance and repair of heating equipment in a temperature-controlled trailer. In the course of performing this work, he negligently attempted to ignite a propane heater installed in the trailer, which resulted in an explosion in which the trailer was damaged. The insurer denied coverage, relying on the fourth part of the care, custody or control exclusion. The trial judge agreed with the insurer's position, noting that the insured's liability was for damage to personal property as the result of work being performed thereon. The Appeal Division of the Newfoundland Supreme Court, however, reversed the decision of the Court below on the basis that the reference in the exclusion to "personal property" must be taken to mean property owned by the insured, for coverage would otherwise be "illusory". Yet, if the fourth part of the exclusion is read in this fashion it is rendered meaningless, for coverage with respect to property owned by the insured is already excluded under the first part. Thus, the reasoning in *Day & Ross* ignores the plain meaning of the policy wording and the decision is clearly erroneous.

4. PRODUCT AND PERFORMANCE

In broad terms, commercial liability policies are designed to insure the risk that the insured's work or product might cause bodily injury or property damage to another. Such policies are not intended to cover the risk that the insured might have to make good its work or product where the work or product is defective or is not what was bargained for.[77] There are a number of exclusions designed to

---

[75] [1977] I.L.R. 1-851 (Ont. Co. Ct.).

[76] (1987), 29 C.C.L.I. 112 (Nfld. C.A.), revg (1985), 15 C.C.L.I. 85 (Nfld. T.D.).

[77] Passage applied in Royal *Insurance Co. of Canada v. Normerica Building Systems Inc.*, [1998] O.J. No. 3845, [1999] I.L.R. I-3626 (Gen. Div.), affd, [1999] O.J. No. 2323 (C.A.). See also *Carwald Concrete & Gravel Co. v. General Security Ins. Co. of Can.* (1985), 17 C.C.L.I. 241 at 261 (Alta. C.A.), supp. reasons (1986), 17 C.C.L.I. 265, application for leave to appeal to S.C.C. dismissed (1986), 17 C.C.L.I. 241n; *Quintette Coal Ltd. v. Bow Valley Resource Services Ltd.*, [1987] B.C.J. No. 2412, 21 B.C.L.R. (2d) 203 at 207 (S.C.); *Stewart Warner Corp. v. Burns*

secure this end: namely, the contractual liability, product, work performed, performance, and recall (or "sistership") exclusions. It should be noted that a Comprehensive General Liability policy may also include Broad Form Property Damage coverage, which amends certain of these exclusions.[78]

The discussion which follows is based upon the 1978 revision of the standard Comprehensive General Liability form. The Commercial General Liability form contains exclusions which are similar in concept, although the wording has been altered in accordance with the plain language philosophy of the policy.

(a) Damage to Product

The standard CGL form provides that:

> This insurance does not apply...
> (e) to property damage to the Named Insured's products arising out of such products or any part of such products.

"Named Insured's products" is defined in the policy as:

> Goods or products manufactured, sold, handled or distributed by the named Insured or by others trading under his name, including any container thereof (other than a vehicle), but shall not include a vending machine or any property other than such container, rented to or located for use of others but not sold.

The purpose of this provision is to exclude from coverage the risk that the insured will be required to replace or repair its products as the result of some defect in the products themselves.[79] There has been considerable litigation in the United States, although not in Canada, with regard to the scope of this exclusion. The exclusion is generally considered to be unambiguous[80] and to apply to all goods or products in which the insured trades or deals, whether as manufacturer or otherwise, and even if only on an occasional basis.[81]

The question often arises of what constitutes the insured's product. There are two fact patterns in particular which appear frequently throughout the cases. One is where the insured is a building contractor and the insurer asserts that the building is the insured's "product"; the other where the product consists of more than one component.

International Security Service Inc., *supra*, note 69; *Weedo v. Stone-E-Brick Inc.*, 405 A.2d 788 (N.J. 1979).

[78] See Chapter 9: Endorsements.

[79] *Weedo v. Stone-E-Brick*, *supra*, note 77; *Zandri Const. Co. Inc. v. Firemen's Ins. Co. of Newark*, 440 N.Y.S.2d 353 (1981), affd 430 N.E.2d 922 (N.Y. Supp. Ct. 1981).

[80] *Century Ins. Co. v. S. & L. Home Heating Co.*, 414 N.E.2d 1218 (Ill. App. 1980); *Fremont Indemnity Co. v. Special Earth Equipment Corp.*, 474 N.E.2d 926 (Ill. App. 1985).

[81] Henderson, "Insurance Protection for Products Liability and Completed Operations: What Every Lawyer Should Know" 15 Neb. L. Rev. 415; *Smith v. Maryland Casualty Co.*, 229 A.2d 120 (Md. 1967).

With respect to the first instance one must pay careful attention to the wording of the particular policy. Some policies specifically include or exempt real property from the definition of "product"; other policies are silent on the issue. The definition of "Named Insured's products" in the I.B.C. form set out above falls into the latter category. On its face, the I.B.C. definition appears to be directed at personalty rather than realty. Moreover, it is arguable that a general contractor enters into a services contract and is not engaged in the manufacture, sale or distribution of a product. On the other hand, as noted earlier,[82] a comprehensive general liability policy is not intended as a performance bond. In these circumstances it is not surprising that the courts both in the United States[83] and in Canada[84] are divided on the issue of whether a building is a general contractor's[85] product.

On the basis of the policy language under consideration, where the insured supplies a product consisting of several components, the exclusion applies to the entire product and not just to the component part that fails.[86] Thus, where an insured modified the chassis of a tractor truck so as to convert it to a dump truck and then sold it to a customer, there was no coverage for the damage to the truck when the chassis subsequently failed.[87] Similarly, when a general contractor was responsible for building a house, which was damaged by a faulty foundation, the exclusion applied to the entire house, and not just the foundation as the component part out of which the loss arose.[88]

The result is different where an insured's product is incorporated by someone else into a larger product. In such a case, the exclusion is generally considered to apply only in respect of damage to the component supplied by the insured. Thus, where the insured supplied a lightweight concrete product to a floating aquarium, which caused the aquarium to sink, the damage to the aquarium was not excluded.[89]

---

[82] See *supra*, note 77 and Chapter 7 at pp. 181-82.

[83] See, for example, *Indiana Ins. Co. v. DeZutti*, 408 NE.2d 1275 (Ind. 1980) (product); and *Maryland Casualty Co. v. Reeder*, 221 Cal.App.3d 961, 270 Cal. Rptr. 719 (1990) (not a product).

[84] *Privest Properties Ltd. v. Foundation Co. of Can.*, [1991] B.C.J. No. 2213, 6 C.C.L.I. (2d) 23 (S.C.) (product); *Pier Mac Petroleum Installation Ltd. v. Axa Pacific Insurance Co.*, [1997] B.C.J. No. 1611, 41 B.C.L.R. (3d) 326 (S.C.) (product); *AXA Pacific Insurance Company Ltd. v. Guildford Marquis Towers Ltd.*, [2000] B.C.J. No. 208, 74 B.C.L.R. (3d) 194, [2000] I.L.R. 1-3801 (not product).

[85] Arguably, different considerations apply to a developer engaged in the construction and sale of housing units.

[86] *Pittsburgh Bridge & Iron Works v. Liberty Mutual Ins. Co.*, 444 F.2d 1286 (3rd Cir. C.A. 1971).

[87] *Adams Tree Service Inc. v. Hawaiian Ins. & Guarantee Co.*, 573 P.2d 76 (Ariz. App. 1977).

[88] *Indiana Ins. Co. v. DeZutti*, 408 N.E.2d 1275 (Ind. 1980).

[89] *Ocean Const. Supplies Ltd. v. Continental Ins. Co.*, [1978] 5 W.W.R 681 (B.C.S.C.), affd (1980), 21 B.C.L.R. 194 (C.A.). See also *Alie v. Bertrand & Frère Construction Co.*, [2003] I.L.R. I-4146 (Ont. C.A.); leave to appeal dismissed [2003] S.C.C.A. No. 48.

(b) Work Performed

The work-performed exclusion is the counterpart to the product exclusion. The policy is not intended to cover the risk that the insured may be required to correct a deficiency in the work performed under the contract:

> This insurance does not apply ...
> (f) to property damage to work performed by or on behalf of the Named Insured arising out of the work or any portion thereof, or out of materials, parts or equipment furnished in connection therewith. [90]

The purpose underlying this exclusion was stated by Spencer J. in *Quintette Coal Ltd. v. Bow Valley Resource Services Ltd.* as follows:

> I am hesitant to think that a comprehensive general liability policy covers a contractor for the cost of having to repair or replace his own negligently done work as opposed to the cost of redressing damages caused to others through the contractor's carelessness. Were that the case a contractor could bid a job for $1 million, do it carelessly at minimal cost to itself, and then claim from the insurer the cost of redoing the work as it should have been done in the first place for $1 million. [91]

The work-performed exclusion is limited in two respects. First of all, the property damage must be to work performed by or on behalf of the insured and, secondly, the property damage must arise out of that work. Thus, the exclusion does not apply in a case in which the insured's work is not damaged but must be replaced in order to effect repairs to other damaged property.[92]

The application of the work-performed exclusion is limited to situations where the insured's "work" is represented by tangible property and has no application where the insured has provided a service only and has not created or modified any tangible property.[93] The exclusion applies to work performed by the insured or by a sub-contractor on the insured's behalf. The "work" consists of all of the work performed by or on behalf of the insured, but only that work. A general contractor's "work" was thus held to be an entire residence,[94] and the exclusion applied to settlement damage to the house resulting from defective

---

[90] *Greenan v. Maber Construction Co.*, [1992] N.B.J. No. 7, 123 N.B.R. (2d) 271, 14 C.C.L.I. (2d) 139, [1993] I.L.R. 1-2899 (C.A.).

[91] *Supra*, note 77.

[92] *Bothwell Accurate Co. v. Royal Insurance Co. of Canada*, [2001] O.J. No. 453, [2002] I.L.R. 1-4030 (S.C.J.).

[93] *International Radiography and Inspection Services (1976) Ltd. v. General Accident Assurance Co. of Canada*, [1996] A.J. No. 1053 [1997] 4 W.W.R. 115, 47 Alta. L.R. (3d) 137, 40 C.C.L.I. (2d) 282 (C.A.). The insured's services consisted of non-destructive testing of metal for hardness.

[94] *J.N.A. Distributors v. Permacool Mechanical Systems Inc.*, [1993] O.J. No. 1807, [1994] I.L.R. 1-3018 (Gen. Div.); *Indiana Ins. Co. v. DeZutti*, *supra*, note 88; *Privest Properties Ltd. v. Foundation Co. of Can.*, *supra*, note 67.

footings installed by a sub-contractor. The sub-contractor, however, had coverage with respect to the damage to the house, for its "work" was confined to the footings. The exclusion does not purport to exclude damage resulting from improper workmanship generally. Rather, the exclusion is limited to the work itself.[95]

When Broad Form Property Damage[96] coverage is obtained, the words "or on behalf of" are deleted from the exclusion. This confines the exclusion to property damage to the insured's own work that arises out of that insured's work. Thus, subject to the other exclusions (particularly the product exclusion) coverage would be provided to the general contractor where property damage arose out of a sub-contractor's work.

The application of the work-performed exclusion often involves consideration of other policy provisions, particularly the meaning of the phrase in the insuring agreement, "property damage caused by accident" and the related exclusions with respect to contractual liability, damage to the product itself, and performance. The decision of the British Columbia Court of Appeal in *Harbour Machine Ltd. v. Guardian Insurance Co. of Canada*[97] provides an illustration of the relationship between the work-performed exclusion and the insuring agreement in respect of "property damage caused by accident". The insured installed two engines in a customer's boat. The space for the propeller was inadequate, causing the propeller shaft to break. In order to remedy the insured's work the customer had the boat lengthened by four feet at considerable expense. The insured settled with its customer and then made a claim under its Comprehensive General Liability policy. The claim was not upheld. The Court noted that the only property damage caused by accident was the failure of the propeller shaft. Yet the failure of the shaft was a result of work performed by the insured and was therefore excluded. There was thus no coverage for any portion of the repairs.

(c) Performance

Coverage under a CGL policy for property damage caused by accident or occurrence includes, under the definition of "property damage", "loss of use of tangible property which has not been physically injured or destroyed provided such loss of use is caused by an accident occurring during the policy period". This grant of coverage for loss of use of tangible property not physically injured is subject to an exclusion with respect to the insured's failure to perform:

This insurance does not apply: ...

(g) to loss of use of tangible property which has not been physically injured or destroyed resulting from

---

[95] *Ultramar Can. Inc. v. Demik Const. Ltd.* (1987), 27 C.C.L.I. 161 (Ont. H.C.J.).

[96] See Chapter 9, section 4: Broad Form Property Damage Endorsement.

[97] (1985), 10 C.C.L.I. 72 (B.C.C.A.).

(1) a delay in or lack of performance by or on behalf of the Named Insured of any contract or agreement, or

(2) the failure of the Named Insured's products or work performed by or on behalf of the Named Insured to meet the level of performance, quality, fitness or durability warranted or represented by the Named Insured;

but this exclusion does not apply to loss of use of other tangible property resulting from the sudden and accidental physical injury to or destruction of the Named Insured's products or work performed by or on behalf of the Named Insured after such products or work have been put to use by any person or organization other than an Insured.

On its face, this exclusion applies solely to the loss of use of tangible property which has not been physically injured. In *Modern Agro Systems Ltd. v. Wellington Insurance Co.*[98] the insured supplied and installed a milk tank with an improperly calibrated volume gauge. This resulted in the farmer delivering more milk to his customers than he was charging them for. The farmer sued the insured, characterizing his claim as one for loss of use of the milk. The Court held that on this basis the claim fell within the performance exclusion, for the milk had not been physically injured. Had the claim been for property damage to the tank, however, the Court noted that the exclusion would not have applied.[99]

In *Carwald Concrete & Gravel Co. v. General Security Insurance Co. of Canada*[100] it was held that the performance exclusion did not apply where the insured's defective cement resulted in a concrete pad having insufficient compressive strength. The components of the pad (rebars, reinforcing steel, ducting, wiring, plumbing and anchor bolts) became useless for the purposes for which they were installed. It was held that this constituted physical injury to tangible property.

There is an exception to the exclusion with respect to sudden and accidental physical injury to the insured's work or product resulting in the loss of use of other tangible property. An example of this exception is provided by the decision in *Baldt Inc. v. American Universal Insurance Co.*[101] The insured's product, anchor chains, suddenly and accidentally failed, resulting in the loss of use of an off-shore oil rig. It was held that the policy provided coverage for the claim against the insured arising from this loss of use.

By its wording, the performance exclusion is limited to claims arising out of certain types of breach of contract and misrepresentation. In *Ellett Industries Ltd. v. Laurentian P & C Insurance Co.*,[102] the British Columbia Court of Appeal considered the scope of the performance exclusion in the context of an issue concerning the duty to defend. The action arose from the installation by the insured in the plaintiff's plant of a cooler condenser designed and manufactured

---

[98] (1986), 21 C.C.L.I. 143 (Ont. H.C.J.).

[99] *Ibid.*, at 144.

[100] (1985), 17 C.C.L.I. 241 (Alta. C.A.), supp. reasons (1986), 17 C.C.L.I. 265, leave to appeal to S.C.C. refd (1986), 17 C.C.L.I. 241*n*.

[101] 559 F. Supp. (E.D. Pa. 1985).

[102] [1996] B.C.J. No. 500, 17 B.C.L.R. (3d) 201, 34 C.C.L.I. (2d) 294 (C.A.).

by the insured. It was alleged that the condenser was defective and that these defects were the result of the insured's inadequate or improper design or fabrication of the condenser, in breach of the terms of a written agreement; alternatively, that the insured negligently designed, analyzed, fabricated and supplied the cooler. The Court of Appeal held that the alternative claim in negligence was not excluded under the policy. Accordingly, the insurer was ordered to defend.

5. RECALL (OR "SISTERSHIP")

The purpose of the CGL policy is to provide coverage with respect to bodily injury and property damage caused by accident. Once an accident has occurred, it is not intended that the policy cover the remedial expense involved in preventing similar accidents from occurring in the future. Accordingly, the policy contains the following exclusion:

> This insurance does not apply to: ...
> (1) expenses incurred for the withdrawal, inspection, repair, replacement, or amounts claimed for loss of use of the Named Insured's products or work completed by or for the Named Insured or of any property of which such products or work form a part, if such products, work or property are withdrawn from the market or from use because of any known or suspected defect or deficiency therein.

This exclusion is referred to as the "sistership" exclusion because of the practice in the aircraft industry of recalling planes for repairs when a plane of the same model (a "sister ship") exhibits a design defect.[103] In order for the sistership exclusion to apply, there must be an actual withdrawal of the insured's product. It has been held that the temporary removal of a product for purposes of repair does not constitute a withdrawal from the market within the meaning of the exclusion.[104] There are divergent opinions on whether the withdrawal must be instituted by the insured.[105] In the Commercial General Liability policy this issue is resolved in favour of the insurer, for the policy language makes it clear that the exclusion applies if the product is withdrawn from the market "by any person or organization".

---

[103] See *Arcos Corp. v. American Mutual Liability*, 350 F. Supp. 380 (E.D. Pa. 1972), affd 485 F.2d 678 (3rd Cir. 1973); *American Motorist Ins. Co. v. Trane Co.*, 544 F.Supp. 669 (D. Wis. 1982).

[104] *American Motorist Ins. Co. v. Trane Co.*, 544 F. Supp. 699 (D. Wis. 1982), affd 718 F.2d 842 (7th Cir. 1983); *Yakima Cement Products Co. v. Great American Ins. Co.*, 590 P.2d 371, revd 608 P.2d 254 (Wash. 1980).

[105] See *Arcos Corp. v. American Mutual Liability Ins. Co.*, *supra*, note 103 and *Thomas J. Lipton Inc. v. Liberty Mutual Ins. Co.*, 357 N.Y.S.2d 705 (1974) in which it was held that the exclusion applies only if the withdrawal is instituted by the insured, and *Elco Industries Inc. v. Liberty Mutual Ins. Co.*, 361 N.E.2d 589 (Ill. 1977) and *Hamilton Diecast Inc. v. U.S. Fidelity & Guarantee Co.*, 508 F.2d 417 (7th Cir. 1975) in which it was held that the exclusion applies regardless of who instituted the withdrawal.

Despite the broad language of the exclusion, which on its face speaks of the withdrawal of the insured's product from use because of a known defect, the courts have repeatedly held that the exclusion does not apply to the product that failed, but only to the "sister" products.[106] In *Carwald Concrete & Gravel Co. v. General Security Insurance Co. of Canada*[107] the Alberta Court of Appeal accepted as correct the following passage from *Honeycomb Systems Inc. v. Admiral Insurance Co.*:

> ... [the exclusion] is designed to limit the insurer's exposure in cases where, because of the actual failure of the insured's product, similar products are withdrawn from use to prevent the failure of these other products, which have not yet failed but are suspected of containing the same defect. ... The exclusion does not apply to the product that failed, only to the "sister" products. [108]

It has also been held that the sistership exclusion does not apply in respect of claims for physical injury to property. Rather, the exclusion is confined to the expenses and claims related to the cost of taking preventive action. Thus, in *Foodpro National Inc. v. General Accident Assurance Co. of Canada*[109] it was held that the loss, including loss of profits, associated with replacing and re-conditioning peanut butter due to a defect in an insured's pre-mix agent was covered under a commercial liability policy. Since it was agreed by the insurer that the peanut butter was damaged by the defective pre-mix agent, it followed that the cost of replacing and re-conditioning the damaged product did not fall within the sistership exclusion.

A similar result was reached in *Gulf Plastics Ltd. v. Cornhill Insurance Co.*[110] The insured manufactured a product known as "Masterbatch" which was used by Flexpack to make plastic film, which, in turn, was used by others to make freezer bags. Due to a defect in one of the components of the Masterbatch, the freezer bags were not sealing properly. Flexpack then recalled all of its plastic film and claimed damages from the insured, Gulf Plastics. The insurer denied coverage, citing, among other reasons, the sistership exclusion. It was held, however, that the sistership exclusion did not apply. The basis for this decision was that the plastic film sustained property damage at the time it was manufactured using the defective Masterbatch. As noted earlier,[111] the mere supply of a defective product does not constitute property damage. Where, however, the defective product is incorporated into another product and causes injury to that product, property damage will have occurred.

---

[106] *Régie des installations olympiques c. Royal & Sun Alliance du Canada Société d'Assurances*, [2001] J.Q. No. 1092.

[107] (1985), 17 C.C.L.I. 241 (Alta. C.A.).

[108] 567 F. Supp. 1400 at 1406-07 (D. Maine 1983).

[109] [1986] O.J. No. 1299, 24 C.C.L.I. 227 (H.C.J.), affd (1988), 63 O.R. (2d) 288 (C.A.).

[110] [1990] B.C.J. No. 1541, 46 C.C.L.I. 144 (S.C.), affd [1991] B.C.J. No. 3310, 3 C.C.L.I. (2d) 203 (C.A.).

[111] See Chapter 7, section 4: Bodily Injury and Property Damage.

In the Commercial General Liability policy, the sistership exclusion has been redrafted in plain language, incorporating new definitions of "product", "work" and "impaired property". The concept of "impaired property" has been devised to address situations where the insured's work or product is incorporated into someone else's work or product. In such a case, coverage is not available when the impaired property can be restored by remedying the insured's work or product.

6. EMPLOYEE AND WORKERS' COMPENSATION

The standard CGL policy contains the following exclusions:

> This insurance does not apply to: ...
>
> (e) bodily injury to any employee of the Insured arising out of and in the course of his employment by the Insured, but this exclusion does not apply to liability assumed by the Insured under an incidental contract;
>
> (f) any obligation for which the Insured or his Insurer may be held liable under any workers' compensation law.

An exclusion similar to (e) was considered by the Supreme Court of Canada in *Stolberg v. Pearl Assurance Co.*[112] There were two insureds, a corporation and its principal, Stolberg. An employee of the corporation was killed in the course of his employment. His widow obtained a judgment against Stolberg for negligence. Stolberg's insurer denied coverage on the basis that the liability fell within the employee exclusion. The Supreme Court of Canada disagreed. The Court read the exclusion on the basis that it applied only in respect of bodily injury to an employee of the particular insured against whom liability was found.

The exclusion was also considered in *Hanis v. University of Western Ontario.*[113] The plaintiff brought an action against his former employer for a number of claims, including wrongful dismissal, intentional interference with contractual relations, defamation, malicious prosecution, conversion and infringement of copyright. Some of the claims were expressly related to post-termination conduct of the defendant. The defendant's insurer refused to defend the claims on the basis of exclusion (e), set out above, as well as on the basis of the intentional injury exclusion, which is discussed in the next section. The policy contained an extended definition of "bodily injury" so as to include defamation and malicious prosecution. The insured brought an application to compel the insurer to defend the action. The court held in favour of the insured. Although the court concluded that all of the claims arose, directly or indirectly, from the plaintiff's employment with the insured, the court was not satisfied, given the wide ranging pleadings, that exclusion (e) would necessarily apply.

---

[112] [1971] I.L.R. 1-415 (S.C.C.).

[113] [2003] O.J. No. 4167, 5 C.C.L.I. (4th) 277 (S.C.J.).

Similar exclusions have been considered in the United States. It has been held that in order for exclusion (f) to apply, the liability must arise pursuant to workers' compensation legislation. Thus, where an employer failed to obtain workers' compensation insurance and a worker, pursuant to the Oregon workers' compensation statute, was given the right to sue the employer for damages, it was held that the statutory obligation brought the claim within the policy exclusion and relieved the insurer from its liability and duty to defend under the policy.[114]

In considering whether or not a person is an "employee" for the purposes of the exclusion, a court is not bound by the characterization which the parties themselves place upon their relationship. Rather, the court will determine in all of the circumstances whether the contract is one "of service" or "for services". Thus, it was held that a television actor was not an employee of the insured production company, notwithstanding the fact that the written agreement between the parties described the actor as an "employee-for-hire".[115]

7. INTENTIONAL INJURY

Liability insurance policies are not intended to provide coverage for intentionally caused harm. In the CGL policy, with respect to property damage claims, this intent is accomplished by the limitation in the insuring agreement that the property damage must be caused by accident. As noted previously, the definition of "accident" precludes coverage with respect to intentionally caused loss or damage.[116] With respect to bodily injury claims there is no similar limitation in the CGL policy that the injury be caused by accident. Instead, there is an exclusion with respect to "bodily injury caused intentionally by or at the direction of the Insured".[117]

The insuring agreement in the Commercial General Liability policy is not limited to bodily injury or property damage caused by accident. Instead, the policy contains the following exclusion:

This insurance does not apply to:

a. "Bodily injury" or "property damage" expected or intended from the standpoint of the insured. This exclusion does not apply to "bodily injury" resulting from the use of reasonable force to protect persons or property.

---

[114] *Tri-State Const. Inc. v. Columbia Casualty Co.*, 692 P.2d 899 (1984).

[115] *Walden v. Danger Bay Productions Ltd.*, [1994] B.C.J. No. 841, 114 D.L.R. (4th) 85, [1994] 6 W.W.R. 138, 90 B.C.L.R. (2d) 180, 23 C.C.L.I. (2d) 133 (C.A.).

[116] See Chapter 7, section 5(e) "Accident" and Deliberate Acts. Note that there may be a middle ground between "accident" and 'intent' such that, although a particular injury is not caused by accident, neither can it be said to have been intentionally caused.

[117] Even where the policy stipulates that the bodily injury must be caused by an accident, some insurers have unnecessarily included in their policies an exclusion with respect to intentional injuries. See, for example, *Bluebird Cabs Ltd. v. Guardian Insurance Co. of Canada*, [1999] B.C.J. No. 694, 173 D.L.R. (4th) 318, 66 B.C.L.R. (3d) 86, [1999] I.L.R. 1-3688.

This form of exclusion is often referred to as an "intentional act" exclusion. Such a characterization, however, may lead to confusion, even where the language of the policy itself refers to "... bodily injury or property damage caused by any intentional or criminal act or failure to act" by the insured.[118] Much of the law of negligence consists of the unforeseen consequences of intentional conduct. For example, a driver makes a right turn and strikes an unseen pedestrian in a crosswalk. The act of turning is deliberate but there is no intent to injure the pedestrian. No one would say that the driver's coverage is excluded by reason of an "intentional act". The language of the exclusion requires more than an intentional act which, in fact, results in injury; it requires an intent to injure.[119] The exclusion is therefore more aptly characterized as an "intentional injury" exclusion. Negligence is covered, intentional torts, generally, are not.[120]

The form of the exclusion set out above contains an exception in cases in which the insured has acted with reasonable force to protect person or property. Even in the absence of this exception some American courts have held that acts in self-defence are not encompassed by the intentional injury exclusion.[121] Since the use of reasonable force to protect person or property is generally a defence to a claim of battery, however, the exception to the exclusion will generally apply only for the purpose of requiring the insurer to defend the action on behalf of the insured.[122] In the event that the insured fails to establish self-defence in the underlying action then the exclusion will apply and the insurer will be under no obligation to indemnify the insured with respect to the intentional tort.

For the purpose of applying the intentional injury exclusion the American authorities draw a distinction between intending an act and intending a result.[123] As a general rule, the exclusion does not apply unless the insured acted with specific intent to cause harm.[124] A number of courts have held that once harm is

---

[118] As Iacobucci J. states in *Non-Marine Underwriters, Lloyd's of London v. Scalera*, [2000] S.C.J. No. 26, [2000], 1 S.C.R. 551, 185 D.L.R. (4th) 1, [2000] I.L.R. 1-3810: "... the exclusion clause must be read to require that the injuries be intentionally caused, in that they are the product of an intentional tort and not of negligence".

[119] *Hodgkinson v. Economical Mutual Insurance Co.*, [2003] O.J. No. 5125 6 C.C.L.I. (4th), (C.A.).

[120] *Misirlis (Trustee of) v. Continental Insurance Co.*, [2001] O.J. No. 2642, 30 C.C.L.I. (3d) 99 (S.C.J.), affd, [2002] O.J. No. 4830 (C.A.).

[121] James Rigelhaupt, Jr., Annotation, "Acts in Self-defense as within Provision of Liability Insurance Policy Expressly Excluding Coverage for Damage or Injury Intended or Expected by Insured" (1984) 34 A.L.R. (4th) 761.

[122] *Thorne v. Royal & Sun Alliance Insurance Co. of Canada*, [2003] N.B.J. 322, 230 D.L.R. (4th) 587 (C.A.).

[123] See generally Rigelhaupt, "Construction and Application of Provision of Liability Insurance Policy Expressly Excluding Injuries Intended or Expected by Insured" (1984) 31 A.L.R. (4th) 957.

[124] *Ibid.*

intended the exclusion applies, even though the harm which occurs may be different in character or magnitude from the intentional injury.[125]

On its face the particular form of exclusion under consideration applies only where the injury is intended or expected by "the insured". Where the policy insures more than one person (which is usually the case) and where the policy contains a "separation of insureds" or "cross-liability" provision[126] (which is also usually the case) then the exclusion does not apply to an innocent insured. Thus, the employer of a taxi driver, although vicariously liable for their driver's assault, was entitled to coverage.[127] The Court held that the basis of vicarious liability is that the liability rather than the act of the employee is it attributed to the employer.

Most commercial liability policies are drafted in this fashion, thus affording protection to the innocent co-insured. Many homeowners' policies, however, are drafted so that an intentional injury by one person insured under the policy results in a lack of coverage for all persons so insured. This result is often accomplished by a subtle change in the wording of the exclusion. As noted in *Wilkieson-Valiente v. Wilkieson*,[128] the exclusion may be expressed in terms either of "*an* insured" or "*the* insured". In the former case, if one insured is guilty of an intentional injury then coverage is also excluded with respect to an innocent co-insured. In the latter case the exclusion applies only to the particular insured guilty of the intentional wrongdoing.

With specific regard to the wording of the exclusion adopted in the Commercial General Liability policy set out above, the courts in the United States disagree on the test to be applied in determining whether the insured "expected" injury to occur. A number of courts have held that for the purposes of an intentional injury exclusion the term "expected" should be read as indicating a "substantial probability"[129] or "high degree of certainty".[130] Other courts have expressed the view that injury is expected if it is more likely to occur than not.[131]

The application of the intentional injury exclusion was addressed by the Supreme Court of Canada in the decision in *Co-operative Fire & Casualty Co. v. Saindon*,[132] discussed earlier.[133] The insured had purchased a policy which provided coverage in respect of liability imposed by law to pay damages

---

[125] *Lyons v. Hartford Ins. Group*, 310 A.2d 485 (N.J. 1973), cert. denied 315 A.2d 411 (1974).

[126] See Chapter 6, section 3(i): Severability of Insureds or "Cross-Liability".

[127] See also *Godonoaga (Litigation Guardian of) v. Khatambakhsh*, [1999] O.J. No. 2598, I.L.R. 1-3733 (S.C.J.), supp. reasons [1999] O.J. No. 3368 (S.C.J.), revd [2000] O.J. No. 2172, 49 O.R. (3d) 22 (C.A.), supp. reasons, [2000] O.J. No. 3807, 25 C.C.L.I. (3d) 37 (C.A.).

[128] [1996] I.L.R. 1-3351 (Ont. Gen. Div.).

[129] *Carter Lake (City) v. Aetna Casualty & Surety Co.*, 604 F.2d 1052 (8th Cir. C.A. 1979).

[130] *Continental Western Ins. Co. v. Toal*, 244 N.W. 2d 121 (Minn. 1976).

[131] *C. Raymond Davis & Sons Inc. v. Liberty Mutual Ins. Co.*, 467 F. Supp. 17 (1979).

[132] (1975), 56 D.L.R. (3d) 556 (S.C.C.). See also *Buchanan v. GAN Canada Insurance Co.*, [1999] O.J. No. 436 (Gen. Div.), affd, 50 O.R. (3d) 89, [2000] I.L.R. 1-3876 (C.A.).

[133] See Chapter 2, section 1(h): Public Policy; and Chapter 7, section 5(e): "Accident" and Deliberate Acts; and section 5(f): "Accident" and Courting the Risk.

because of bodily injury or property damage. The insuring agreement did not stipulate that the bodily injury or property damage must be caused by accident. There was, however, an exclusion with respect to "bodily injury or property damage caused intentionally by or at the direction of an insured". In the course of a dispute with his neighbour, the insured thrust a power lawnmower in the neighbour's face so as to give him a scare. The neighbour put up his hands in self-defence, with the result that they were seriously injured by the revolving blades. The majority of the Supreme Court of Canada held that the claim fell within the exclusion. The reasoning in the majority judgment is, however, somewhat unclear. Justice Ritchie, who gave the judgment on behalf of the majority, purported to apply the test of "accident" proposed by Phillimore L.J. in *Gray v. Barr*.[134] On this test the foreseeable consequences of an intentional act are not considered to be "caused by accident". It appears from this that Ritchie J. was proceeding on the basis that "accident" and "intent" are opposite terms. By this reasoning, since the injury was not caused by accident, it must therefore fall within the intentional injury exclusion. If this, indeed, is the basis of the decision in *Saindon* then it is erroneous for reasons discussed elsewhere.[135] There is, however, another explanation for the majority decision, namely, that it is an example of the principle, referred to earlier, that where the insured acts with the intention of causing injury or damage, however slight, then the intentional injury exclusion will apply, even though the injury which occurs is different in character or magnitude to that which was intended.[136]

A number of lower courts in Canada have had occasion to distinguish the decision of the Supreme Court of Canada in *Co-operative Fire & Casualty Co. v. Saindon*. In *Devlin v. Co-operative Fire & Casualty Co.*[137] a person insured under a motor vehicle liability policy, in order to scare his passengers, drove his car in an extremely reckless manner, ignoring stop signs and red lights as well as ignoring the pleas of his passengers to let them out. Not surprisingly, a collision occurred and one of the passengers was injured. The motor vehicle liability insurer denied coverage on the basis that indemnity would be contrary to public policy because the insured had acted with intent to bring about loss or damage. The Alberta Court of Appeal did not agree. The Court distinguished the decision in *Saindon* on the basis that in the latter case it was the very act of assault that caused the damage, whereas in *Devlin* the insured, although driving recklessly, actually sought to avoid the vehicle that he struck. Whether this distinction is a valid one is questionable. In both cases, the insured engaged in deliberate and criminal conduct for the purpose of giving a scare to another. In both cases, the conduct resulted in injury which, although not subjectively intended by the insured, was the natural and probable consequence of the insured's criminal act.

---

[134] [1971] 2 All E.R. 949 at 969 (C.A.). See the discussion in Chapter 7, section 5(e): "Accident" and Deliberate Acts.

[135] See Chapter 7, section 5(f): "Accident" and Courting the Risk.

[136] *Supra*, note 125.

[137] (1978), 90 D.L.R. (3d) 444 (Alta. C.A.), revg (1977), 78 D.L.R. (3d) 102 (Alta. S.C.).

The decision in *Saindon* was also distinguished, on rather dubious factual grounds, in *Long Lake School Div. No. 30 v. Schatz.*[138] The insured, a teenage boy, broke into a school and committed various acts of vandalism. After strewing paper over the floor he lit a number of wooden matches one by one and tossed them into the litter. A fire resulted, causing substantial damage to the school building. The trial judge accepted the boy's evidence that he was simply discarding the matches so that his parents would not find them and that he believed the matches were extinguished when he threw them on the floor. On this basis, it was held that the intentional injury exclusion did not apply and that the policy therefore covered. The decision was upheld by a majority of the Saskatchewan Court of Appeal. Although the reasoning in the dissent is compelling, the Supreme Court of Canada refused to grant leave to appeal.

In *Newcastle (Town) v. Mattatall*[139] the insured broke into a hockey arena for the purpose of committing a theft. During the course of this activity he lit two fires which, together, caused the arena to burn to the ground. The first fire started when the insured discarded a tub of glue which had caught fire when he used his lighter to peer at the contents. The insured testified that he thought that fire would extinguish itself. The second fire started when the insured lit an empty cigarette package for light and then, believing it to be out, threw it among some trash. In respect of this conduct the insured pleaded guilty to a charge of arson. Nevertheless, when he was sued by the owner of the arena for damages, it was held that the insured was covered in respect of the claim. The intentional injury exclusion did not apply, for, on a subjective test, the insured did not intend to burn down the arena. The Court distinguished *Saindon* on the grounds that in that case the act which caused the damage was the insured's act of assault in raising a lawnmower, whereas in *Mattatall* damage resulted from the negligent rather than the intentional act of the insured.

Saindon was also distinguished in *Ellis v. Pilot Insurance Co.*[140] The insured had given a bottle of methanol to a friend, knowing that it would be drunk. A number of people partook of the poison, one of whom died. The insured was convicted of criminal negligence causing death. In coverage proceedings the insurer alleged that the bodily injury had been caused intentionally by the insured and raised pleas of issue estoppel and *res judicata*. On the insured's application these pleas were struck on the basis that they had no possibility of success at trial. The Court held that the exclusionary phrase "caused intentionally" could not be equated with the "impugned intent" implicit in a finding of criminal negligence.

---

[138] [1984] S.J. No. 78, 6 C.C.L.I. 1 (Q.B.), affd, [1986] S.J. No. 138, 18 C.C.L.I. 232 (C.A.), leave to appeal to S.C.C. refd 21 C.C.L.I. *xxxiv*. See also *R.D.F. (Litigation Guardian of) v. Co-operators General Insurance Co.*, [2004] M.J. No. 382, 16 C.C.L.I. (4th) 5 (C.A.).

[139] (1987), 37 D.L.R. (4th) 528 (N.B.Q.B.), affd (1988), 52 D.L.R. (4th) 356 (N.B.C.A.). See also *Lambton Cartage & Warehousing Ltd. v. Barraclough (Litigation Guardian of)*, [1998] O.J. No. 5537, 10 C.C.L.I. (3d) 107 (Gen. Div.).

[140] [1991] O.J. No. 748, [1992] I.L.R. 1-2781 (Gen. Div.), vard [1995] O.J. No. 1040 (C.A.).

For cases concerning the application of the intentional injury and criminal act exclusions in the context of personal liability policies see Chapter 14. For cases concerning the application of the intentional injury exclusion in cases of sexual assault see Chapter 15.

8.　ENVIRONMENTAL LIABILITY

A specific exclusion with respect to environmental liability was first introduced in the United States by the Insurance Rating Board, a predecessor of the Insurance Service Office, Inc. by way of an endorsement which was generally attached to CGL policies issued on and after September, 1970.[141] When the CGL policy underwent a major revision in the United States in 1973, the so-called pollution exclusion became part of the standard policy form. The wording of the exclusion was as follows:

> It is agreed that this policy does not apply to bodily injury or property damage arising out of the discharge, dispersal, release or escape of smoke, vapours, soot, fumes, acids, alkalis, toxic chemicals, liquids or gases, waste materials or other irritants, contaminants or pollutants into or upon land, the atmosphere or any water of any description no matter where located or how contained, or into any watercourse, drainage or sewage system, but this exclusion does not apply if such discharge, dispersal, release or escape is sudden or accidental.

In Canada, the pollution exclusion came into general use in 1970, although at that time the Insurance Bureau of Canada did not include the pollution exclusion in its standard policy wording, noting that it was not clear whether exposure to pollution claims was merely a rating factor or whether the intent was that there should be no coverage at all in respect of such claims. Subsequently, in a bulletin issued April 8, 1974, the Insurance Bureau of Canada recommended that environmental exclusion clauses not be attached to liability policies for farmers, agriculturalists, or insect, pest or weed control operators or fumigation operators:

> Much concern has recently been expressed by representatives of agriculturalists and pest control operators as respects various environmental exclusions which are attached to third party public liability insurance policies. It has been contended that the wording of the endorsements limits coverage in such a way that these agriculturalists and others have no protection whatsoever if damage occurs as a result of a normal use of insecticides, pesticides, fumigation or weed control products. Although the majority of the environmental exclusions make an exception of damages caused by accident, it is contended that coverage could be denied due to the intentional nature of the use of these substances for definite purposes.

---

[141] J. Moran Jr., "Pollution Exclusion of the 1973 C.G.L. Policy: Background, Current, Interpretation, and Future Evolution" in *C.G.L. Reporter: Trial and Insurance Counsel's Handbook for the Comprehensive General Liability Insurance Policy* (Chicago: Karpowitz, 1983).

It may be recalled that environmental exclusion endorsements came into general use in 1970 when the industry decided not to provide liability protection for insureds who in the course of their operations were knowingly or intentionally polluting the environment.

However, it was never intended to take away coverages from agriculturalists and others whose unusual operations require the use of such products as those referred to above.

Until recently there has been no major objection or controversy as a result of these wordings, but the Ministry of the Environment has been in touch with the Bureau in recent months because of the aforesaid concern of farmers and others.

Having considered a report of the Liability Committee on the matter, the Board of Directors now recommends to Members that environmental exclusion endorsements should not be attached to liability policies for farmers, agriculturalists, or insect, pest or weed control or fumigation operators. In addition, the Directors recommend that any risks of this type be extended to the defined "occurrence basis" in accordance with IBC General Liability Form No. 2009.

The reason for this is that even if the environmental exclusion is omitted from a liability policy, coverage is still on an "accident" basis and it might be contended that no coverage would apply. Use of the endorsement in question extends the word "accident" to include a continuous or repeated exposure to conditions causing property damage not intended or expected from the standpoint of the insured.[142]

In 1985, along with the introduction of the new Commercial General Liability policy, the Insurance Bureau of Canada changed the environmental liability exclusion to what is colloquially known as the "absolute pollution exclusion", which was designed to further restrict coverage for pollution claims. In 1993 the Insurance Bureau of Canada issued an endorsement[143] designed to replace the absolute pollution exclusion and provide limited coverage for certain pollution risks. The latter endorsement, which contains both an exclusion and an extension of coverage, is discussed in Chapter 12. The most recent version of the pollution exclusion, published in 2005 by the Insurance Bureau of Canada, is discussed later in this section. The separate exclusions which are now commonly found with respect to asbestos and fungi or spores are set out at the end of this section.

For a full understanding of the modern exclusion it is necessary to review the case law decided under the earlier forms. Moreover, given the long tail of environmental pollution claims, there are still actions being brought today which may trigger coverage under occurrence policies issued over 20 years ago. Thus, the early case law may well be of more than mere historical interest.

---

[142] I.B.C. Bulletin No. 74-7.

[143] I.B.C. Form 2313.

The initial version of the pollution exclusion received considerable attention in the United States,[144] but, along with somewhat modified versions, has been the subject of only a relatively modest number of reported cases in Canada.[145]

On its face, the exclusion appears to be quite broad. Although there is an exception to the exclusion, it is limited to instances where the discharge of the pollutant is sudden and accidental. The exception thus focuses on the act of pollution rather than the resulting property damage.[146] Coverage is not provided for the unintended consequences of an intentional release of pollutants.[147]

Although appearing broad, the exclusion has often been given a rather narrow interpretation by the courts, particularly in the United States. This has been accomplished both by limiting the scope of the exclusion to actual or active polluters[148] and by giving considerable scope to the "sudden and accidental" exception.[149]

---

[144] See Rosenkranz, "The Pollution Exclusion Clause through the Looking Glass" (1986) 74 Geo. L.J. 1237; Goulka, "The Pollution Exclusion" (September, 1983) For the Defence 22; J. Moran Jr., "Pollution Exclusion of the 1973 C.G.L. Policy: Background, Current, Interpretation, and Future Evolution", *supra*, note 141; "Construction and Application of Pollution Exclusion Clause in Liability Insurance Policies" (1985) 39 A.L.R. (4th) 1047. There is presently an enormous, and still growing, body of American case law with respect to this exclusion.

[145] *Murphy Oil Co. v. Continental Ins. Co.* (1981), 33 O.R. (2d) 853 (Co. Ct.); *Zatko v. Paterson Springs Service Ltd.*, [1995] O.J. NO. 1327, [1986] I.L.R. 1-1997 (H.C.J.); *Grace Farms Ltd. v. Big A Tank Services* (1984), 6 C.C.L.I. 136 (B.C.S.C.); *British Petroleum Canada Inc. v. Comco Service Station Const. & Maintenance Ltd.*, [1990] O.J. No. 919, 73 O.R. (2d) 317 (H.C.J.); *Ontario v. Kansa General Ins. Co.*, [1991] O.J. No. 126, 2 O.R. (3d) 269 (Gen. Div.), revd [1994] O.J. No. 177, 111 D.L.R. (4th) 757, 17 O.R. (3d) 38 (C.A.), leave to appeal to S.C.C. refd September 8, 1994; *Uniroyal Chemical Ltd. v. Kansa General Ins. Co.*, [1996] O.J. No. 644, [1996] I.L.R. 1-3285 (C.A.); *Pier Mac Petroleum Installation Ltd. v. Axa Pacific Insurance Co.*, [1997] B.C.J. No. 1611, 47 C.C.L.I. (2d) 229 (S.C.).

[146] *Murphy Oil Co. v. Continental Ins. Co., ibid.* at 857. This point has been lost on some of the American courts interpreting the exclusion. In *Jackson Township Municipal Utilities Authority v. Hartford Accident & Indemnity Co.*, 451 A.2d 990 (N.J. 1982) the Court said that the exclusion "can be interpreted as simply a restatement of a definition of occurrence — that is, that the policy will cover claims where the injury was neither expected nor intended. It is a reaffirmation of the principle that coverage will not be provided for intended results of intentional acts, but will be provided for the unintended results of an intentional act". The language quoted disregards the plain meaning of the words used in the exclusion. It is the discharge, dispersal, release or escape which must be "sudden and accidental". The requirement that the resulting damage be accidental is already stated in the insuring agreement. Thus, not only does the Court in *Jackson Township* ignore the plain meaning of the exclusion, but the interpretation which the Court gives to the exclusion renders it entirely superfluous.

[147] *Milwaukee (City) v. Allied Smelting Corp.*, 344 N.W.2d 523 (Wis. App. 1983); *Technicon Electronics Corp. v. American Corp. Assur. Co.*, 544 N.Y.S.2d 531 (N.Y. 1989).

[148] See, for example, *Niagara County v. Utica Mutual Ins. Co.*, 439 N.Y.S.2d 538.

[149] See, for example, *Allstate Ins. Co. v. Klock Oil Co.*, 426 N.Y.S.2d 603 (1980). Other authorities, however, concentrating on the temporal element implicit in the term "sudden" have held that the discharge of pollutants over a long period does not fall within the "sudden and accidental" exception. See, for example, *International Minerals & Chemical Corp. v. Liberty Mutual Ins. Co.*, 522 N.E.2d 758 (Ill. App. Ct. 1988).

The distinction between active and passive polluters was considered by the Ontario Court of Appeal in *Ontario v. Kansa General Insurance Co.*[150] The insured province sought a declaration that its insurer defend a third party action in which it was alleged that provincial officials were negligent in failing to adequately respond to the escape of contaminants from the defendants' land, which in turn, it was alleged, had caused loss and damage to the plaintiff. The insurer argued that because the claim arose out of the escape of a pollutant, coverage was excluded by the terms of the pollution exclusion, which was in the standard CGL form. The insured, relying upon a line of American authority, responded that the exclusion was intended to apply only to active polluters. Since it was not alleged that the insured was the actual polluter, even in the sense of permitting the discharge of a pollutant, the insured submitted that the insurer was required to defend the action. The Court of Appeal, however, rejected this argument. The Court did not consider the American authorities that distinguish between active and passive polluters to be persuasive. The Court further reasoned that under the applicable Ontario legislation the insured would, in any event, be considered an "active polluter" within the meaning of the American cases. Applying the chain of causation test,[151] the Court held that the claim arose out of the discharge of pollutants and was accordingly excluded under the policy.

The distinction between active and passive polluters was also considered, although in the context of the absolute pollution exclusion, in *Palliser Regional School Division No. 26 v. Aviva Scottish & York Insurance Co.*[152] The insured owned and operated an elementary school that was situated on the same parcel of land as an exposed coal bed that was no longer used for coal mining. An action was brought against the insured by local residents alleging that wind-borne particles of coal dust emanating from the insured's premises caused damage to their homes. The insurer declined to defend this claim on the basis that the pollution exclusion applied. The court did not agree. Although it was found that coal dust was a pollutant within the meaning of the policy and that the exclusion applied to both active and passive polluters, the court held that there was no connection between the insured's business activities and the alleged release of coal dust. Applying the connotative contextual approach enunciated by the Ontario Court of Appeal in *Zurich Insurance Co. v. 686234*

---

[150] *Supra*, note 145. See also *Uniroyal Chemical Ltd. v. Kansa General Ins. Co.*, [1996] O.J. No. 644, [1996] I.L.R. 1-3285 (C.A.), in which the majority of the Ontario Court of Appeal, in very brief reasons, appears to have distinguished *Ontario v. Kansa General Ins. Co.* on the dubious basis that it did not deal with the scope of coverage for an insured actively engaged in pollution-causing activities. This might cause some to erroneously read the *Uniroyal* decision as counte-nancing the proposition that the exclusion applies only to insureds who are not alleged to have been active polluters. The true basis of the *Uniroyal* decision is that the insurer acknowledged in an affidavit that the loss might be covered under the policy and never sought to withdraw that admission.

[151] See section 2: Automobile, Watercraft and Aircraft.

[152] [2004] A.J. No. 1356, 18 C.C.L.I. (4th) 98 (Q.B.).

Ontario Ltd.[153] the court held that it was not within the reasonable commercial expectations of the policyholder and the insurer that the pollution exclusion would apply in the circumstances.

The scope of the "sudden and accidental" exception was considered in *Murphy Oil Co. v. Continental Insurance Co.*,[154] a decision of the Ottawa-Carleton County Court. A complaint was brought against an insured gasoline station for the contamination of well water on neighbouring premises. The escape of gasoline occurred over a three-month period. The gasoline station's liability insurer denied coverage pursuant to the environmental liability exclusion on the basis that the continuous leak of gasoline from a pipe was not sudden and accidental. The Court did not agree. The Court found that a leak in a pipe must always occur suddenly. At one time the pipe is functional and at another time it springs a leak. Although the Court did not address the point, it is implicit in the reasons that a leak does not lose the element of suddenness by continuing over an extended period of time, a proposition which was questioned in a subsequent decision out of Ontario.[155]

The decision in *Zatko v. Paterson Springs Service Ltd.*[156] also involves the escape of petroleum products from an underground storage tank. The plaintiff discovered oil seeping into his premises and complained to his neighbour, the defendant, who maintained an underground storage tank. The defendant acted promptly and arranged to have the tank drained and excavated. This did not resolve the problem, for the oil continued to seep into the plaintiff's premises. The defendant, who was aware of this, chose not to take any further remedial steps. The Court found that the cause of the seepage was that oil had drained out of the tank for a considerable period of time, collected on the defendant's property, and had gradually, through the action of water and the slope of the land, moved onto the plaintiff's property. In these circumstances the Court held that the original escape of oil onto the plaintiff's premises was sudden and accidental and was covered under the policy, whereas the damage that occurred after the insured became aware of the problem was not.

Whether the discharge of pollutants is accidental or not is determined from the standpoint of the insured. Thus, when vandals opened valves in a storage tank, causing an oil spill, the discharge was held to be "sudden and accidental".[157]

As a response to the narrow interpretation the courts gave to the pollution exclusion, the insurance industry drafted what became known as the "absolute pollution" exclusion, which is in the following terms:

This insurance does not apply to:

---

[153] [2002] O.J. No. 4496, 43 C.C.L.I. (3d) 174 (C.A.), application for leave to appeal to S.C.C. dismissed [2003] S.C.C.A. No. 33. See the discussion of the latter case further in this section.

[154] *Supra*, note 145.

[155] *B.P. Canada Inc. v. Comco Service Station Const. & Maintenance Ltd.*, *supra*, note 145.

[156] *Supra*, note 145.

[157] *Lansco Inc. v. Dept. of Environmental Protection*, 350 A.2d 520, affd 368 A.2d 363 (1976).

1. Pollution Liability
   a. "Bodily injury" or "property damage" arising out of the actual, alleged or threatened discharge, dispersal, release or escape of pollutants:
      1) At or from premises you own, rent or occupy;
      2) At or from any site or location used by or for you or others for the handling, storage, disposal, processing or treatment of waste;
      3) Which are at any time transported, handled, stored, treated, disposed of, or processed as waste by or for you or any person or organization for whom you may be legally responsible; or
      4) At or from any site or location on which you or any contractors or subcontractors working directly or indirectly on your behalf are performing operations:
         a) if the pollutants are brought on or to the site or location in connection with such operations; or
         b) if the operations are to test for, monitor, clean up, remove, contain, treat, detoxify or neutralize the pollutants.
   b. Any loss, cost, or expense arising out of any governmental direction or request that you test for, monitor, clean up, remove, contain, treat, detoxify or neutralize pollutants.

   "Pollutants" means any solid, liquid, gaseous or thermal irritant or contaminant, including smoke, vapour, soot, fumes, acids, alkalis, chemicals and waste. Waste includes materials to be recycled, reconditioned or reclaimed.

On its face, the "absolute pollution" exclusion is enormously broad, so much so that in certain instances its application may be contrary to the reasonable expectations of the insured and may exclude the very sort of liability for which the policy of insurance was purchased.[158] In these circumstances, for the most part, the courts have avoided a literal interpretation of the exclusion and instead have focused on the nature of the liability which the exclusion reasonably seeks to exclude from coverage. This has been referred to as the "connotative contextual approach".[159]

A number of decisions have considered the scope of the absolute pollution exclusion in the context of the duty to defend. The exclusion was held not to apply in *Medicine Hat (City) v. Continental Casualty Co.*[160] The city converted its bus fleet to operate on methanol. Lubrizol was used as a fuel additive. It was alleged that employees of the city sustained neurological problems from exposure to these substances, which, it was acknowledged, were pollutants within the meaning of the exclusion. Nevertheless, the court held that the exclusion did not apply:

> "Discharge, dispersal, release or escape of pollutants" is the language of improper or unintended events or conduct. It is not the language of intended use

---

[158] *Hay Bay Genetics Inc. v. MacGregor Concrete Products (Beachburg) Ltd.*, [2003] O.J. No. 2049, 6 C.C.L.I. (4th) 218 (S.C.J.).

[159] *Zurich Insurance Co. v. 686234 Ontario Ltd.*, *supra*, note 153.

[160] [2002] A.J. No. 350, 37 C.C.L.I. (3d) 48 (Q.B.), appeal dismissed, [2004] A.J. No. 682, 13 C.C.L.I. (4th) 52 (C.A.).

or consequences or of the normal operation of facilities or vehicles. In this case, the polluting substance or gas is part of and confined to the intended and normal operation of a transit garage and buses. This conduct and these events do not fall within the exclusion clause. In my view, the pollution exclusion clause is intended to protect the insurer from liability for the enforcement of environmental laws. The exclusion clause uses environmental terms of art because it is intended to exclude coverage only as it relates to environmental pollution and the improper disposal or contamination of hazardous waste. [161]

The most comprehensive analysis to date of the absolute pollution exclusion is that of the Ontario Court of Appeal in *Zurich Insurance Co. v. 686234 Ontario Ltd.*[162] The insured, the owner of an apartment building, was the defendant in two proposed class actions in which it was alleged that the plaintiffs suffered injuries from carbon monoxide that leaked from the apartment's furnace. The plaintiffs claimed that the insured had negligently failed to keep the furnace in good repair. The property owner carried commercial general liability coverage with Zurich. The insurer declined to defend the actions on the basis that carbon monoxide is a pollutant and that a claim for personal injury arising from the escape of carbon monoxide was excluded under the absolute pollution exclusion. The court rejected this assertion. Although, on a literal reading of the exclusion, the insurer's position might well have been correct, the court rejected the notion that the exclusion should be interpreted solely by reference to dictionary literalism:

> In my view, in construing contracts of insurance, dictionary literalism is often a poor substitute for connotative contextual construction. When the full panoply of insurance contract construction tools is brought to bear on the pollution exclusion, defective maintenance of a furnace giving rise to carbon monoxide poisoning, like related business torts such as temporarily strong odours produced by floor resurfacing or painting, fail the common sense test for determining what is "pollution". These represent claims long covered by CGL insurance policies. To apply an exclusion intended to bar coverage for claims arising from environmental pollution to carbon monoxide poisoning from a faulty furnace, is to deny the history of the exclusion, the purpose of CGL insurance, and the reasonable expectations of policyholders in acquiring the insurance.[163]

In the result, the court held that the exclusion was ambiguous and that the ambiguity should be resolved in favour of the insured:

> Accepting for the purpose of my conclusion that carbon monoxide is a "pollutant" within the meaning of the exclusion, although it is arguably clear in its plain and ordinary meaning, the exclusion is overly broad and subject to more than one compelling interpretation, as is evident from its construction by

---

[161] *Ibid.*, at para. 27

[162] *Supra*, note 153. See also *Palliser Regional School Division No. 26 v. Aviva Scottish & York Insurance Co.*, [2004] A.J. No. 1356, 18 C.C.L.I. (4th) 98 (Q.B.).

[163] *Ibid.*, at para. 37.

American courts. Given that the exclusion is capable of more than one reasonable interpretation, it is ambiguous and should be interpreted in favour of the respondent. The historical context of the exclusion suggests that its purpose is to bar coverage for damages arising from environmental pollution, and not the circumstances of this case in which a faulty furnace resulted in a leak of carbon monoxide. Based on the coverage provided by a CGL policy, a reasonable policyholder would expect that the policy insured the very risk that occurred in this case. A reasonable policyholder would, therefore, have understood the clause to exclude coverage for damage caused by certain forms of industrial pollution, but not damages caused by the leakage of carbon monoxide from a faulty furnace. In my view, the policy provisions should be construed to give effect to the purpose for which the policy was acquired. [164]

In response to the *Zurich* decision the Insurance Bureau of Canada modified its pollution exclusion so as to provide coverage for bodily injury caused by smoke, fumes, vapour or soot from equipment used to heat, cool or dehumidify the building or equipment that is used to heat water for use by a building's occupants or guests. [165]

The decision of the Ontario Court of Appeal in *Zurich Insurance Co. v. 686234 Ontario Ltd.*[166] followed the court's earlier decision in *Trafalgar Insurance Co. of Canada v. Imperial Oil Ltd.*[167] Although the court in *Zurich* barely comments upon the decision in *Trafalgar*, the reasoning in *Zurich* may well provide a better explanation for the result in *Trafalgar* than that which appears in the reasons for judgment in the latter decision.

In *Trafalgar* a majority of the Ontario Court of Appeal held that the absolute pollution exclusion did not apply in circumstances in which it was alleged that the insured, a property remediation contractor, was negligent in failing to promptly and adequately clean up a fuel oil spill for which another was responsible. The majority held that subparagraph 4 of the exclusion would not be triggered unless the insured had been responsible for a new escape of fuel oil during the clean-up operation, which it was not. The majority read into subparagraph 4 of the exclusion the temporal requirement that a new escape occur while the clean-up operation is active. The majority distinguished the court's earlier decision in *Ontario v. Kansa General Insurance Co.*[168] in which it was held that an earlier version of the pollution exclusion applied in the case of a claim against the province of Ontario for negligently failing to enforce the law so as to prevent another party from discharging pollutants. The majority reasoned that Ontario's alleged negligence in the *Kansa* case was not a new and independent cause of the loss, and as a result, the damages claimed against Ontario were excluded by the clause because they were damages arising from the discharge itself. In *Trafalgar,* on the other hand, the damage arising out of the contractor's

---

[164] *Ibid.*, at para. 38.

[165] See Appendix K.

[166] *Supra*, note 153.

[167] [2001] O.J. No. 4936, 34 C.C.L.I. (3d) 192 (C.A.).

[168] *Supra*, note 145. See discussion, *supra*, at p. 243.

alleged negligence did not arise out of the original escape of the fuel oil, but, rather, from the failure to adequately remove the oil. The dissenting judge, rejecting this analysis, would have applied the exclusion on the basis that the loss was caused by the escape of fuel oil and that the contractor's negligence was not an intervening act which broke the chain of causation. The circumstances of the claim, in his opinion, fell squarely within the plain meaning of the exclusion.

Although couched in terms of causation, the real issue in *Trafalgar* concerns the proper interpretation to be given to the exclusion clause. Whether applying the purposive approach enunciated in *Consolidated Bathurst Export Ltd. v. Mutual Boiler & Machinery Insurance Co.*,[169] the connotative contextual construction approach referred to in *Zurich Insurance Co. v. 686234 Ontario Ltd.*,[170] the rule that the words used are to be interpreted in accordance with their ordinary meaning or the rule of *contra proferentem*, it is submitted that one would reasonably conclude that the claim does not fall within the exclusion. Paraphrasing subparagraph 4(b) of the exclusion, coverage is not afforded for property damage arising out the escape of pollutants at a site at which the insured is carrying out clean-up operations. Even if one rejects the view that the most reasonable interpretation of the clause is that it is implicit that the escape occurs during the course of the insured's operations, one must concede that there is at least an ambiguity, which is resolved in favour of the insured.

The application of the absolute pollution exclusion was also rejected in *Great West Development Marine Corp. v. Canadian Surety Co.*[171] The insured, Great West, was the owner and developer of a condominium project. A subcontractor on the project made arrangements to supply excavated materials to a farmer, Ms. Swamy, who was seeking fill. Ms. Swamy later sued Great West, alleging that she had been expecting good topsoil but that the fill she received consisted of poor quality soil and contained construction debris. She further claimed that the fill would leach toxic chemicals, contaminating both her crops and the groundwater. The Court held that Great West was entitled to a defence from its insurer. The claim did not entirely rest upon the threatened escape of pollutants; indeed, the thrust of the claim appeared to be that the fill was of poor quality and contained construction debris, which, if true, did not by itself bring the claim within the confines of the exclusion.

The absolute pollution exclusion was applied, on the other hand, in *Pretty v. Ontario*.[172] The insureds were the developers of a real estate subdivision. The plaintiffs, owners of property in the subdivision, alleged that their groundwater had become contaminated from pollutants originating in a nearby landfill neither owned nor operated by the insureds. Liability was alleged against the insureds on the basis that they had failed to meet the standard of care imposed upon them

---

[169] [1980] 1 S.C.R. 888.

[170] *Supra*, note 153.

[171] [2000] B.C.J. No. 939, 19 C.C.L.I. (3d) 52 (S.C.).

[172] [2001] O.J. No. 4867 (S.C.J.).

as real estate developers. The insured tendered the defence of the claim to their liability insurer. The insurer declined to defend, asserting the claim fell within the absolute pollution exclusion. The court agreed with the assertion. Although subparagraphs 1, 3 and 4 did not apply, the court reasoned that the claim fell within subparagraph 2 in that the alleged property damage arose out of the escape of pollutants from a location used by "others" for the storage of waste. It did not matter, for the purposes of subparagraph 2, that the insured had no relation to either the property from which the pollution emanated or the "others" who were responsible for its emanation.

The most recent version of the pollution exclusion, published in 2005 by the Insurance Bureau of Canada, is in the following terms:

4. Pollution

    (1) "Bodily injury", "property damage" or "personal and advertising injury" arising out of the actual, alleged or threatened spill, discharge, emission, dispersal, seepage, leakage, migration, release or escape of "pollutants":

    (a) At or from any premises, site or location which is or was at any time owned or occupied by, or rented or loaned to, any insured. However, this subparagraph does not apply to:

       (i) "Bodily injury" if sustained within a building and caused by smoke, fumes, vapour or soot from equipment used to heat, cool or dehumidify the building, or equipment that is used to heat water for personal use, by the building's occupants or their guests;

       (ii) "Bodily injury" or "property damage" for which you may be held liable, if you are a contractor and the owner or lessee of such premises, site or location has been added to your policy as an additional insured with respect to your ongoing operations performed for that additional insured at that premises, site or location and such premises, site or location is not and never was owned or occupied by, or rented or loaned to, any insured, other than that additional insured; or

       (iii) "Bodily injury" or "property damage" arising out of heat, smoke or fumes from a "hostile fire";

    (b) At or from any premises, site or location which is or was at any time used by or for any insured or others for the handling, storage, disposal, processing or treatment of waste;

    (c) Which are or were at any time transported, handled, stored, treated, disposed of, or processed as waste by or for:

       (i) Any insured; or

       (ii) Any person or organization for whom you may be legally responsible; or

    (d) At or from any premises, site or location on which any insured or any contractors or subcontractors working directly or indirectly on any insured's behalf are performing operations if the "pollutants" are brought on or to the premises, site or location in connection with such operations by such insured, contractor or subcontractor. However, this subparagraph does not apply to:

       (i) "Bodily injury" or "property damage" arising out of the escape of fuels, lubricants or other operating fluids which are needed to perform the normal electrical, hydraulic or mechanical functions necessary for the operation of mobile equipment or its parts, if such fuels, lubricants or other operating fluids escape from a vehicle part designed to hold, store or receive them. This exception does not apply if the "bodily injury" or "property damage" arises out of the intentional discharge, dispersal or release of the fuels, lubricants or other operating fluids, or if such fuels, lubricants or other operating fluids are brought on or to the premises, site or location with the intent that they be discharged, dispersed or released as part of the operations being performed by such insured, contractor or subcontractor;

(ii) "Bodily injury" or "property damage" sustained within a building and caused by the release of gases, fumes or vapours from materials brought into that building in connection with operations being performed by you or on your behalf by a contractor or subcontractor; or

(iii) "Bodily injury" or "property damage" arising out of heat, smoke or fumes from a "hostile fire".

(e) At or from any premises, site or location on which any insured or any contractors or subcontractors working directly or indirectly on any insured's behalf are performing operations if the operations are to test for, monitor, clean up, remove, contain, treat, detoxify or neutralize, or in any way respond to, or assess the effects of, "pollutants".

(2) Any loss, cost or expense arising out of any:

(a) Request, demand, order or statutory or regulatory requirement that any insured or others test for, monitor, clean up, remove, contain, treat, detoxify or neutralize, or in any way respond to, or assess the effects of, "pollutants"; or

(b) Claim or "action" by or on behalf of a governmental authority for "compensatory damages" because of testing for, monitoring, cleaning up, removing, containing, treating, detoxifying or neutralizing, or in any way responding to, or assessing the effects of, "pollutants".

However, this Section (2) does not apply to liability for "compensatory damages" because of "property damage" that the insured would have in the absence of such request, demand, order or statutory or regulatory requirement, or such claim or "action" by or on behalf of a governmental authority.

The terms "pollutants" is defined as :

"Pollutants" mean any solid, liquid, gaseous or thermal irritant or contaminant, including smoke, odour, vapour, soot, fumes, acids, alkalis, chemicals and waste. Waste includes materials to be recycled, reconditioned or re-claimed.

It is apparent that the wording of the pollution exclusion has come a long way from its original formulation in 1970. In its present form, the exclusion applies to "personal and advertising injury", which is now incorporated in the 2005 Commercial General Liability standard coverage instead of being offered separately by way of endorsement.[173] The initial broad wording of the exclusion is modified in a number of respects in what appears to be a response to a number

---

[173] See Chapter 10: Personal Injury and Advertising Injury Liability Coverage.

of decisions which have been critical of earlier versions of the exclusion on the basis that the wording is so overly broad as to defeat the reasonable expectations of the insured.

In addition to the pollution exclusion, modern policies also generally contain exclusions with respect to asbestos and fungi or spores. The latter exclusions, as they appear in the Insurance Bureau of Canada's 2005 Commercial General Liability policy, are as follows:

> This insurance does not apply to:
> 1.   Asbestos
>   "Bodily injury", "property damage" or "personal and advertising injury" related to or arising from any actual or alleged liability for any legal remedy of any kind whatsoever (including but not limited to damages, interest, mandatory or other injunctive relief, statutory orders or penalties, legal or other costs, or expenses of any kind) in respect of actual or threatened loss, damage, cost or expense directly or indirectly caused by, resulting from, in consequence of or in any way involving, asbestos or any materials containing asbestos in whatever form or quantity.
>   This exclusion applies regardless of any other contributing or aggravating cause or event that contributes concurrently or in any sequence to the "bodily injury", "property damage" or "personal and advertising injury".
>
> 2.   Fungi or Spores
>   a.   "Bodily injury", "property damage" or "personal and advertising injury" or any other cost, loss or expense incurred by others, arising directly or indirectly from the actual, alleged or threatened inhalation of, ingestion of, contact with, exposure to, existence of, presence of, spread of, reproduction, discharge or other growth of any "fungi" or "spores" however caused, including any costs or expenses incurred to prevent, respond to, test for, monitor, abate, mitigate, remove, cleanup, contain, remediate, treat, detoxify, neutralize, assess or otherwise deal with or dispose of "fungi" or "spores".

9.   PROFESSIONAL SERVICES

Commercial liability policies are not intended to provide coverage for professional liability. Insurance in respect of professional liability is available separately from underwriters who specialize in that market, often at a substantially higher premium than that associated with the ordinary commercial risk.[174] The standard Insurance Bureau of Canada forms for the Comprehensive General Liability and Commercial General Liability policies do not contain any specific exclusion with respect to the provision of professional services. The structure of both policies is such that to some extent liability in respect of professional services is not covered in any event. Many claims against professionals are for

---

[174] *Foundation of Can. Engineering Corp. Ltd. v. Can. Indemnity Co.*, [1977] 2 W.W.R. 75 (S.C.C.).

pure economic loss, and are therefore not covered under business liability policies that limit coverage to claims concerning bodily injury or property damage. The contractual liability and performance exclusions in a business liability policy may also remove from coverage certain types of claims concerning the provision of professional services. Nevertheless, this still leaves some room within a commercial liability policy for coverage in respect of professional risks. Accordingly, most commercial liability policies contain an exclusion with respect to professional services. The Insurance Bureau of Canada has published an endorsement[175] which contains a rather sparsely worded example of such an exclusion:

> This insurance does not apply to bodily injury or property damage due to the rendering of or failure to render any professional service.

Several insurers have adopted a more elaborate wording for the professional services exclusion, a typical example of which is as follows:

> It is agreed that the insurance does not apply to bodily injury or property damage arising out of the rendering of or the failure to render any professional services by or for the named insured, including:
> 1. The preparation or approval of maps, plans, opinions, reports, surveys, designs or specifications and
> 2. Supervisory, inspection or engineering services.

The term "professional services" is usually left undefined. The meaning of the term has been considered in a number of cases, albeit in a variety of contexts. Traditionally, the term "professional" was given a restrictive meaning. In *Davenport v. McNiven* it was stated that:

> The generally accepted meaning of professional work is labour in which knowledge of some branch of science and learning is employed in the practice of an art involving a *liberal education.* [176]

The term is not given so restrictive a meaning today. The cases suggest that the question is one of fact, the test of a professional service being one which embraces "both a mental or intellectual exercise within a recognized discipline and the application of special skill, knowledge and training to the particular function in question".[177]

In determining whether or not an activity consists of "professional services" one must look at the nature of the activity rather than at the training and

---

[175] I.B.C. 2011 (7-11).

[176] [1930] 2 W.W.R 263 at 267 (B.C.C.A.).

[177] *Chemetics International Ltd. v. Commercial Union Assur. Co. of Can.* (1981), 31 B.C.L.R. 273 at 286 (S.C.), affd (1984), 55 B.C.L.R. 60 (C.A.).

education of the person performing the task.[178] In *Chemetics International Ltd. v. Commercial Union Assurance Co. of Canada*[179] the insured engineered and supplied the equipment and materials for an industrial plant. After completion, the plant was damaged and the insured was held liable for failing to give adequate operating instructions either in its operation manual or through its on-site supervisor. Notwithstanding the fact that the person who prepared the manual and provided supervision was a qualified engineer, the Court held that the professional services exclusion did not apply because the task which was being performed was not of a professional nature. As noted in *Kerr v. Law Profession Indemnity Co.*, where the same issue arose in the context of a professional liability policy:

> ... In my view the act and not the title is to be looked at to determine whether the insured is covered. ...[180]

Application of the professional services exclusion often becomes an issue with construction claims. Professionals, such as architects and engineers, engaged in the construction industry may perform a variety of professional and non-professional services. They may be insured under both a professional liability policy and a commercial liability policy. In either case, it will be a question of fact whether or not the claim arises out of the rendering of or the failure to render professional services. Services such as supervision and design, performed in the context of the provision of non-professional services, do not become professional services simply by being included in the wording of the exclusion.[181]

Examples of claims which have been denied under the professional services exclusion are: a claim by a non-client spouse against a psychologist for negligence and defamation in performing a psychological evaluation of a child and issuing a report to be used in divorce proceedings[182]; the failure to establish appropriate standards or tests for products used in the gas industry,[183] poor design of a municipal water system and failure to do a proper pre-blast sur-

---

[178] *Ibid.* See also *Tested Truss Systems Inc. v. Can. Indemnity Co.*, [1973] 4 W.W.R. 542 (Alta. S.C.), affd [1974] 2 W.W.R. 288 (Alta. C.A.); *Mercer v. Paradise (Town)*, [1991] N.J. No. 126, [1991] I.L.R. 1-2740 (Nfld. T.D.); *Station Square Developments Inc. v. Amako Construction Ltd.*, [1989] B.C.J. No. 1533, 39 B.C.L.R. (2d) 61, [1989] I.L.R. 1-2499, 40 C.C.L.I. 292 (S.C.); *Monenco Ltd. v. Commonwealth Insurance Co.*, [1997] B.C.J. No. 1971, 42 B.C.L.R. (3d) 280, 47 C.C.L.I. (2d) 12 (S.C.), affd on other grounds (1999), 198 W.A.C. 154, 8 C.C.L.I. (3d) 11 (B.C.C.A.), leave to appeal to S.C.C. granted [2001] S.C.J. No. 50.

[179] *Supra*, note 177.

[180] [1994] O.J. No. 2 22 C.C.L.I. (2d) 28 at 30 (Gen. Div.), revd, [1995] O.J. No. 2823, 128 D.L.R. (4th) 269, 25 O.R. (3d) 804, [1995] I.L.R. 1-3250 (C.A.).

[181] *Rotating Equipment Services Inc. v. Continental Insurance Co.*, [2004] A.J. No. 1340, 20 C.C.L.I. (4th) 75 (Q.B.).

[182] *Mantini-Atkinson v. Co-Operators General Insurance Co.*, [2003] O.J. No. 3858, 5 C.C.L.I. (4th) 150 (S.C.J.), appeal dismissed, [2005] O.J. No. 1858, 23 C.C.L.I. (4th) 18 (C.A.).

[183] *Canadian Gas Assn. v. Guardian Insurance Co. of Canada* [1988] O.J. No. 5260, [1999] I.L.R. 1-3633 (Gen. Div.).

vey,[184] failure of a design engineer to warn the client of the dangers inherent in the design[185] and improper application of a heat treatment to steel.[186] Examples of claims which have not been excluded are: improper supervision, direction and inspection[187] and failure to provide operating instructions.[188]

---

[184] *Mercer v. Paradise (Town), supra,* note 178.

[185] *Monenco Ltd. v. Commonwealth Insurance Co., supra,* note 178.

[186] *Tsubaki of Canada Ltd. v. Standard Tube Canada,* [1993] O.J. No. 1855 (Gen. Div.). The details of the process are not set out in the judgment, yet, with respect, it is difficult to accept that what is surely an industrial process should be captured by the professional services exclusion. This formed an alternate basis for the decision, which is better explained on other grounds. See *supra,* note 69.

[187] *Mercer v. Paradise (Town), supra,* note 178.

[188] *Chemetics International Ltd. v. Commercial Union Assur. Co. of Can., supra,* note 177.

Chapter 9

ENDORSEMENTS

There are a number of standard endorsements which, for an additional premium, may be purchased with a commercial liability policy. The parties to the insurance contract may also, from time to time, negotiate non-standard endorsements. The purpose of the endorsements is, generally, to extend coverage in some respect. There are certain endorsements, however, that have the effect of restricting coverage and which result in a lowering of the premium.[1]

In this chapter, four of the more common endorsements will be considered: the Property Damage Endorsement, the Additional Property Damage Exclusion, the Contractual Liability Endorsement, and the Broad Form Property Damage Endorsement.

1. PROPERTY DAMAGE ENDORSEMENT

Although most modern policies are written on an occurrence basis, that has not always been the case. In the past policies were written on an accident basis. The purpose of the Property Damage Endorsement was to convert an "accident" policy to an "occurrence" policy. The endorsement was worded as follows:

Property Damage Endorsement
(Defined Occurrence Basis)
It is understood and agreed this policy is amended as follows:

Additional Definition
When used in this policy (including endorsements forming a part thereof):
"accident" includes continuous or repeated exposure to conditions which results in property damage neither expected nor intended from the standpoint of the Insured.

Limits of Liability
For the purpose of determining the limit of the Insurer's liability all property damage arising out of a continuous or repeated exposure to substantially the same general conditions shall be considered as arising out of one accident.[2]

---

[1] Pursuant to the Contractual Liability Limitation endorsement, for example, coverage under the Commercial General Liability policy in respect of contractual liability may be narrowed to approach that provided under the basic CGL form.

[2] I.B.C. Form 2009, May 1978.

The effect of this endorsement is discussed in Chapter 7.[3]

2. ADDITIONAL PROPERTY DAMAGE EXCLUSION

An endorsement commonly used with the CGL policy is the Additional Property Damage Exclusion:

> This insurance does not apply to property damage arising out of
> (1) the use of explosives for blasting, or
> (2) vibration from pile driving or caisson work, or
> (3) the removal or weakening of support of any property, building or land whether such support be natural or otherwise;
> but this exclusion does not apply with respect to property damage
> (i) arising out of operations performed for the Named Insured by independent contractors;
> (ii) included within the completed operations hazard;
> (iii) for which liability is assumed by the Insured under an incidental contract. [4]

The scope of this exclusion was considered in *Johnson Construction Ltd. v. Canadian General Insurance Co.*[5] A storm sewer collapsed at the time of blasting performed by the insured's subcontractor. The insurer denied coverage for various reasons, including that the subcontractor was not a person insured under the policy. The insured then settled a number of flooding claims which resulted from the collapsed storm sewer and sought indemnity from the insurer. The Court held that the insurer was liable. Since the use of explosives for blasting is inherently dangerous, the insured was answerable for the negligence of its subcontractor. Because the policy exclusion specifically excepts property damage arising out of operations performed by independent contractors it was plain that the exclusion did not apply to the loss.

3. CONTRACTUAL LIABILITY ENDORSEMENT

The Contractual Liability Endorsement is designed to extend the scope of coverage under a CGL policy in respect of the contractual assumption of another's tortious liability.[6] The endorsement is in the following terms:

> It is agreed that: Amended Definition
> 1. The definition of "incidental contract" is amended to read as follows:

---

[3]   See Chapter 7, section 5(a): Accident versus Occurrence.

[4]   I.B.C. Form 2010, June 1978.

[5]   [1985] N.B.J. No. 118, 10 C.C.L.I. 183, 12 C.L.R. 22 (Q.B.).

[6]   *Amertec-Granada Inc. v. Older Public Ins. Co.*, 421 So. 2d 722 (Fla. 1982).

(a) which is a lease of premises, easement agreement, agreement required by municipal ordinance, sidetrack agreement, elevator maintenance agreement, or

(b) which assumes the liability of others except agreements where the Insured has assumed liability for the sole negligence of his indemnitee.

Additional Exclusion

2. The insurance afforded by this endorsement does not apply, if the Insured or his indemnitee is an architect, engineer or surveyor, to bodily injury or property damage arising out of the rendering of or failure to render professional services by such Insured or indemnitee, including (a) the preparation or approval of maps, plans, opinions, reports, surveys, designs or specifications and (b) supervisory, inspection or engineering services, but this exclusion does not apply to any of the following agreements: a lease of premises, easement agreement, agreement required by municipal ordinance, sidetrack agreement, or elevator maintenance agreement. [7]

Clause 1(a) of the endorsement merely reiterates the definition of "incidental contract" contained in the standard CGL form. By clause 1(b) the definition is extended to include any written agreement by which the insured assumes the liability of others, except where the insured has assumed liability for the sole negligence of the indemnitee. The additional exclusion set out in the endorsement is designed to prevent coverage from applying where the insured or the indemnitee is an architect, engineer or surveyor and the loss arises out of the rendering or the failure to render professional services. This exclusion does not apply where the negligence of the indemnitee is outside the scope of the professional services exclusion.[8] The exception to the exclusion provides that it does not apply to any agreements that fall within the definition of "incidental contract" found in the standard CGL form.

4. BROAD FORM PROPERTY DAMAGE ENDORSEMENT

In order to properly understand the Broad Form Property Damage endorsement it is necessary to give consideration to the history of the clause. Indeed, in one case the court went so far as to permit expert evidence from an underwriter as to the purpose for which the provision was introduced.[9]

The Broad Form Property Damage endorsement originated in the United States in the late 1960s. Three years after the 1966 revisions to its Comprehensive General Liability form, the Insurance Services Office, Inc. ("ISO")[10] drafted its Broad Form Property Damage endorsement 3006 to the standard policy form.

---

[7] I.B.C. Form 2020, June 1978.

[8] *Estrin Const. Co. v. Aetna Casualty Surety Co.*, 612 S.W.2d 413 (Mo. 1981). Note that in this case, the form of professional services exclusion found in the policy did not exclude inspection services.

[9] *Amondsen v. General Accident Assurance Co.*, [2004] O.J. No. 5633, 74 O.R. (3d) 65 (S.C.J.).

[10] ISO is an American insurance industry organization involved in the promulgation of suggested policy forms. See, further, Chapter 6, section 1: Types of Commercial Policies.

The endorsement expanded coverage by modifying the work-performed and care, custody and control exclusions.[11] The result of the modified exclusions is to limit the application of the work-performed exclusion to that particular part of the work out of which property damage arises as well as to provide an insured coverage for property damage arising out of the defective work of its subcontractors. In its 1986 revisions ISO incorporated the Broad Form Property Damage endorsement into the standard policy wording of what then became the Commercial General Liability policy. In December of 2001, ISO came full circle by introducing two new endorsements retracting the subcontractor exception, one on a blanket basis, the other on a project specific basis.

The Insurance Bureau of Canada, in its 1971 uniform general liability policy forms, followed the same format as ISO. The Broad Form Property Damage endorsement was initially suggested as an extension of coverage to a CGL policy. In 1986, with the development of the Commercial General Liability policy, the Broad Form Property Damage endorsement was incorporated into the standard policy wording. The same format has been followed in the 2005 revision.

In its original form the Broad Form Property Damage endorsement read as follows:

A.   Exclusions (h) and (j) are replaced by the following exclusions (y) and (z):
  (y)   property damage
  (1)   to property owned or occupied by or rented to the Insured, or, except with respect to the use of elevators, to property held by the Insured for sale or entrusted to the Insured for storage or safekeeping.
  (2)   except with respect to liability under a written sidetrack agreement or the use of elevators, to
      (a)   property while on premises owned by or rented to the Insured for the purpose of having operations performed on such property by or on behalf of the Insured;
      (b)   tools or equipment while being used by the Insured in performing his operations;
      (c)   property in the custody of the Insured which is to be installed, erected or used in construction by the Insured;
      (d)   that particular part of any property, not on premises owned by or rented to the Insured;
          (i)   upon which operations are being performed by or on behalf of the Insured at the time of the property damage arising out of such operations, or
          (ii)   out of which any property damage arises, or
          (iii)   the restoration, repair or replacement of which has been made necessary by reason of faulty workmanship thereon by or on behalf of the Insured;
  (z)   with respect to the completed operations hazard, to property damage to work performed by the Named Insured arising out of the work or any

---

[11]   See Chapter 8 for a discussion of these exclusions.

portion thereof, or out of materials, parts or equipment furnished in connection therewith.[12]

Any discussion of the coverage afforded with and without the Broad Form Property Damage endorsement requires a clause-by-clause comparison of the policy provisions in each case. Although the Broad Form Property Damage endorsement eliminates the previous care, custody or control and work-performed exclusions, it reintroduces some of the same exclusions, but with different policy wording.

The standard care, custody or control exclusion has four parts:

This insurance does not apply to: ...
(h) property damage to
  (1) property owned or occupied by or rented to the Insured, or
  (2) property used by the Insured, or
  (3) property in the care, custody or control of the Insured or property as to which the Insured is for any purpose exercising physical control, or
  (4) any personal property or any fixtures as the result of any work performed thereon by the Insured or anyone on his behalf;
  but parts (2) and (3) of this exclusion do not apply with respect to liability under a written sidetrack agreement and part (3) of this exclusion does not apply with respect to property damage (other than to elevators) arising out of the use of an elevator at premises owned by, rented to or controlled by the Named Insured.

The standard work performed exclusion is as follows:

This insurance does not apply to: ...
(j) property damage to work performed by or on behalf of the Named Insured arising out of the work or any portion thereof, or out of materials, parts or equipment furnished in connection therewith.

The Broad Form Property Damage endorsement, by clause (y)(1), restores the first part of the care, custody or control exclusion. The second and third parts of the standard exclusion restrict coverage generally with respect to property either used by or in the care, custody or control of the insured, whereas clauses (y)(2)(a), (b), and (c) of the Broad Form Property Damage endorsement restrict coverage only in the specific instances enumerated.

The fourth part of the care, custody or control exclusion and also the work-performed exclusion are replaced, with respect to operations generally, by clause (y)(2)(d)(i), and, with respect to completed operations, by clause (z). Under clause (y)(2)(d)(i), liability is excluded for damage to that particular part of any property (not on premises owned by or rented to the insured) on which operations are being performed by or on behalf of the insured at the time that the property damage arises out of those operations. This is sometimes referred to as the "operations exclusion". Since the exclusion refers to work done "on behalf

---

[12] Appendix H: IBC 2021.

of the insured" coverage is not available to an insured for property damage that falls within the exclusion and which results from work done by the insured's subcontractor. The exclusion does not apply to all damage to property upon which operations are being performed — rather, it is restricted to that particular part of the property upon which the insured or the insured's subcontractor is performing operations.

Under clause (y)(2)(d)(ii), coverage is excluded with respect to the particular part of the property out of which the property damage arises. This exclusion addresses the business risk that the insured may be required to repair or replace property provided under the contract as a result of some defect in the property itself.

Under clause (y)(2)(d)(iii), coverage is excluded with respect to the insured's liability to remedy defects that arise by reason of faulty workmanship by or on behalf of the insured. This addresses the concept that the policy is not intended to cover the business risk that the insured may be required to correct a deficiency in the work performed under the contract. Again, this exclusion is limited to that particular part of the property which requires restoration, repair or replacement by reason of the faulty workmanship.

Each of these exclusions requires a determination of what constitutes a "particular part", an issue which has only rarely been addressed by Canadian courts but upon which there is an abundance of American authority. When the work is with respect to an integrated structure, determining the particular part upon which the insured is performing operations, for the purpose of the application of the exclusion, is often a difficult task.

In *Amondsen v. General Accident Assurance Co.*[13] the insured contractor was hired to dismantle a riding arena at one location and reconstruct it at another location. The arena collapsed in the course of reconstruction. The cause of the collapse was determined to be inadequate temporary bracing of the roof trusses, as a result of which wind forces brought down the roof. The insurer argued that the phrase "that particular part of any property" in connection with clause (y)(2)(d)(iii) must be read as referring to the property that must be replaced because of faulty workmanship. Because the entire building had to be restored, rebuilt or replaced as a result of the faulty bracing workmanship, the insurer argued, the entire claim was excluded from coverage. The court did not agree, restricting the application of the exclusion to the bracing. A similar result was reached in *Columbia Mutual Insurance Co. v. Schauf.*[14] The insured had contracted to paint, stain or lacquer all the interior and exterior surfaces of a house. While cleaning up after lacquering the kitchen cabinets the insured inadvertently started a fire, which caused damage throughout the home. The insurer denied coverage under an exclusion similar to (y)(2)(d)(i) (but restricted to real property) on the basis that the insured was performing operations on the home; thus no part of the loss was covered. The insured argued that the entire

---

[13] [2004] O.J. No. 5633, 74 O.R. (3d) 65 (S.C.J.).

[14] 967 S.W.2d 74 (Mo. 1998).

claim was covered for, at the time of the fire, the insured was cleaning equipment instead of performing operations. The court rejected both arguments, ruling that at the time of the loss the kitchen cabinets were the particular part of the real property upon which the insured was performing operations. In the result, the loss with respect the cabinets was excluded; the balance of the loss was covered.

On the other hand, the exclusion was applied to the entire loss in *Vinsant Electrical Contractors v. Aetna Casualty & Surety Co.*[15] The insured, an electrical contractor, was engaged to install two circuit breakers in a switchboard. One of the insured's employees negligently dropped a wrench in such a fashion that it came into contact with two buss bars, resulting in an electrical short which destroyed the entire switchboard. On the basis that the insured's operations were being performed on the switchboard in its entirety the insurer denied coverage under the equivalent to clause (y)(2)(d)(i). The insured responded that the switchboard consisted of many component parts and that the exclusion should be confined to the buss bars. The court agreed with the denial, noting that to construe the exclusion more narrowly, such that it applied only to the precise spot on the switchboard on which the socket wrench fell, would completely nullify the intent of the provision.

With respect to the completed operations hazard, the Broad Form Property Damage endorsement removes coverage only in respect of property damage to work performed by the named insured. It follows that coverage is afforded for completed operations when the property damage arises out of work performed by the insured's sub-contractor. Thus, in *Mid-United Contractors Inc. v. Providence Lloyds Ins. Co.,*[16] coverage was afforded to a general contractor for moisture damage to a building as a result of defects in prefabricated panels installed by a subcontractor.[17]

---

[15] 530 S.W.2d 76 (Tenn. 1975).

[16] 754 S.W.2d 824 (Tex. 1988).

[17] See also *Lee Builders, Inc. v. Farm Bureau Mutual Insurance Co.,* 104 P.3d 997 (Kan. App. 2005).

Chapter 10

PERSONAL INJURY AND ADVERTISING INJURY LIABILITY COVERAGE

In commercial liability policies the term "personal injury" is not used in its popular sense. Rather, insurers providing commercial liability insurance make a distinction between "bodily injury" and "personal injury", the latter term being used to refer to a variety of offences against the person, including defamation of character, false arrest and imprisonment, and discrimination.

Personal injury liability coverage was first introduced by the Insurance Services Office[1] in the United States as an endorsement to the 1973 revision of the Comprehensive General Liability policy. In 1986 it was incorporated into the standard Commercial General Liability policy wording. In subsequent years the policy wording has undergone a number of changes, particularly with respect to the incorporation of what is referred to as "advertising injury" coverage. In Canada, the Insurance Bureau of Canada introduced a Personal Injury Liability Coverage rider in 1980[2] and, in 1986, incorporated this form of coverage in the standard wording of the Commercial General Liability policy.[3]

1. THE INSURING AGREEMENT

The insuring agreement published by the Insurance Bureau of Canada with respect to personal injury liability coverage, before the introduction of the 1986 Commercial General Liability Program, was in the following terms:

I.   Coverage — Personal Injury Liability
      To pay on behalf of the Insured all sums which the Insured shall become legally obligated to pay as compensatory damages because of injury (herein called "personal injury") sustained by any person or organization and arising out of one or more of the following offenses committed in the conduct of the Named Insured's business designated in the declarations:
      Group A — false arrest, detention or imprisonment, or malicious prosecution;
      Group B — the publication or utterance of a libel or slander or of other defamatory or disparaging material, or a publication or ut-

---

[1]   For a discussion of the Insurance Services Office see Chapter 6, section 1: Types of Commercial Policies.
[2]   See Appendix G.
[3]   See Appendices I and J.

terance in violation of an individual's right of privacy; except publication or utterances in the course of or related to advertising, broadcasting or telecasting activities conducted by or on behalf of the Named Insured;

Group C — wrongful entry or eviction, or other invasion of the right of private occupancy.

In the Commercial General Liability policy, personal injury coverage is included in the standard policy under Coverage B:

1. Insuring Agreement
   a. We will pay those sums that the insured becomes legally obligated to pay as compensatory damages because of "personal injury" to which this insurance applies. ...
   b. This insurance applies to "personal injury" only if caused by an offence:
      1) Committed in the "coverage territory" during the policy period; and
      2) Arising out of the conduct of your business, excluding advertising, publishing, broadcasting or telecasting done by or for you.

The term "personal injury" is defined in the Commercial General Liability policy as follows:

"Personal Injury" means injury, other than "bodily injury", arising out of one or more of the following offences:
a. False arrest, detention or imprisonment;
b. Malicious prosecution;
c. Wrongful entry into, or eviction of a person from a room, dwelling or premises that the person occupies;
d. Oral or written publication of material that slanders or libels a person or organization or disparages a person's or organization's goods, products or services; or
e. Oral or written publication of material that violates a person's right of privacy.

In 2005, the Insurance Bureau of Canada incorporated advertising injury liability with the personal injury liability coverage provisions in the standard Commercial General Liability policy.[4]

One of the striking features of personal injury liability coverage is that, on its face, the policy wording appears to extend coverage in respect of certain intentional torts. This raises two issues, one being the application of the fortuity principle[5] and the other being the public policy prohibition with respect to insurance coverage for intentional wrongdoing.[6] The first issue is one of policy interpretation; should the language so permit, coverage will be construed as extending to the unintended consequences of the intentional tort but not to any

---

[4] See the discussion in this chapter at section 3: Advertising Injury.

[5] For a discussion of the fortuity principle see Chapter 7, section 2(b): Meaning of "Accident".

[6] See Chapter 2, section 1(h): Public Policy.

losses the insured intended to bring about.[7] Pursuant to the public policy rule the courts will not enforce a contract of indemnity in circumstances in which the insured intended to bring about loss or damage. In the United States there is a division of authority on this issue. Some American courts have expressed the view that that the public policy rule is no longer valid in that there are other deterrents against intentional wrongdoing and it is in the public interest that businesses be insured with respect to these sorts of claims, particularly those involving discrimination, sexual harassment, and the like.[8] In Canada, the public policy rule does not apply unless the insured acts with the intent to bring about loss or damage. In such cases, it is not entirely clear whether the rule precludes all recovery or whether coverage would still be extended with respect to the unintended consequences of the intentional wrongdoing.[9] It is submitted that the latter view should be preferred.

Unlike the former Personal Injury Liability Coverage rider,[10] the definition of "personal injury" in the new Commercial General Liability form specifically excludes bodily injury. Thus coverage in respect of bodily injury which occurred during the course of a false arrest, for example, would fall within the insuring agreement under a Personal Injury Liability Coverage rider but would not fall within Coverage B of a Commercial General Liability policy. Under the latter form of policy, coverage in respect of such bodily injury may apply under Coverage A (covering bodily injury and property damage liability), depending on the particular facts of the case.

In the United States, there has been considerable litigation over the scope of coverage afforded with respect to malicious prosecution. In *Koehring Co. v. American Mutual Liability Insurance Co.*[11] it was held that "malicious prosecution" within the meaning of the policy provided coverage with respect to a claim for abuse of process. In *Parker Supply Co. v. Traveler's Indemnity Co.*[12] it was found, however, that abuse of process is a separate tort and is not covered under policy language referring to "malicious prosecution". The majority of American jurisdictions have concluded that for the purposes of determining the date of the occurrence, a malicious prosecution is deemed to occur at the time that the tortfeasor took the action that resulted in the application of the criminal process to the claimant.[13] Similarly, the injury in a false arrest case occurs at the time of the unlawful detention. Thus, even though the claimant is acquitted during the

---

[7]   *Liberty Mutual Insurance Co. v. Hollinger Inc.*, [2004] O.J. No. 481, 10 C.C.L.I. (4th) 200 (C.A.).

[8]   See the discussion in *Gencorp v. American National Underwriters*, 125 F.3d 983 (U.S.C.A. 6th Cir. 1999).

[9]   See Chapter 2, section 1(h): Public Policy.

[10]   I.B.C. Form 2008, August, 1980. See Appendix G of this book.

[11]   564 F. Supp. 303 (E.D. Wash. 1983).

[12]   588 F.2d 180 (5th Cir. 1979).

[13]   *Zurich Ins. Co. v. Peterson*, 232 Cal. Rptr. 807 (1986); *Southern Maryland Agricultural Assn. Inc. v. Bituminous Casualty Corp.*, 539 F. Supp. 1295 (D. Md. 1982).

policy period, coverage is not provided where the arrest took place before the policy was in force.[14]

The provision in the insuring agreement that coverage with respect to libel or slander does not extend to "publication or utterances in the course of or related to advertising" was considered in *Playboy Enterprises v. St. Paul Fire & Marine Insurance Co.*[15] *Playboy* magazine's competitor *Penthouse* alleged libel and various business torts against Playboy Enterprises based on a letter which Playboy had sent to advertisers in which it was erroneously stated that Penthouse had failed to meet its circulation guarantees. Playboy's insurer denied coverage with respect to the claim on the basis that the alleged libel arose from a publication or utterance in the course of or related to advertising activities. The Court did not agree, noting that the term "advertising" was meant to apply to the public or widespread distribution of promotional material. The Court recognized that on one interpretation Playboy's letter could be construed as being "related to advertising activities"; the Court held, however, that there were other equally plausible interpretations that could be placed on the policy exclusion and that the ambiguity must be construed in favour of the insured.

Similar reasoning was adopted by the Alberta Court of Queen's Bench in *P.C.S. Investments Ltd. v. Dominion of Canada General Insurance Co.*[16] An action for defamation was commenced against the insured by one of its competitors, in which it was alleged that the insured had obtained a copy of a promotional letter which the plaintiff had prepared, altered it so as to defame the plaintiff, and mailed it to the plaintiff's customers. The insurer denied a defence, one of its reasons being that the publication of the libel constituted "publishing" and therefore fell within the exclusionary phrase appearing in the insuring agreement, which extended coverage to the publication of a libel arising out of the conduct of the insured's business, "excluding advertising, publishing, broadcasting or telecasting done by or for you". The Court noted that on this interpretation coverage would be denied for libel and slander in all circumstances, a result which was clearly not contemplated by the drafters the policy. Rather, the Court held, the term "publishing" should be given a narrower definition than that of "publication", and should be read as requiring a widespread and public distribution.

The same exclusion was considered in *Reform Party of Canada v. Western Union Insurance Co.*[17] The insured, a political party, sought coverage in respect of an action commenced by a senator alleging that he had been defamed in an article posted on the party's web site. The insurer maintained that posting information on a web page to which the public has access constitutes both "publishing" and "broadcasting" within the meaning of the exclusion. The Court

---

[14] *S. Freedman & Sons v. Hartford Fire Ins. Co.*, 396 A.2d 195 (D.C. 1978).

[15] 769 F.2d 425 (7th Cir. 1985).

[16] [1994] A.J. No. 204, 18 Alta. L.R. (3d) 270, 25 C.C.L.I. (2d) 119 (Q.B.), vard, [1996] A.J. No. 33, 110 W.A.C. 274, 37 Alta. L.R. (3d) 38, [1996] I.L.R. 1-3308, 34 C.C.L.I. (2d) 113 (C.A.).

[17] [1999] B.C.J. No. 2794, 3 C.P.R. (4th) 289 (S.C.), revd [2001] B.C.J. No. 697, 26 C.C.L.I. (3d) 1 (C.A.).

agreed, noting that the fact that the site had received only a small number of visits was immaterial.

The violation of privacy aspect of personal injury coverage was considered in *Dyne Holdings Ltd. v. Royal Insurance Co. of Canada*[18] in the context of the duty to defend. An action had been commenced against the insured alleging, among other things, the improper use by the defendants of documents covered by solicitor-client privilege. Giving the pleadings their widest latitude, the Court held that the claim potentially fell within coverage as a violation of the plaintiff's right of privacy and directed the insurer to defend.

Personal injury coverage is often written, either on a manuscript basis or otherwise, so as to include coverage with respect to "wrongful dismissal". The scope of the coverage thus afforded has been held not to encompass the employer's liability to pay damages in lieu of reasonable notice.[19] Personal injury liability coverage is also sometimes written so as to provide coverage for claims of discrimination. In *Liberty Mutual Insurance Co. v. Hollinger Inc.*[20] it was held, applying the fortuity principle, that claims of intentional discrimination were not covered.

The Group C offences set out in the Personal Injury Liability endorsement provide coverage for damages resulting from wrongful entry or other invasion of the right of private occupancy. Some courts in the United States have held that this is broad enough to include claims in nuisance and trespass arising out of the escape of pollutants.[21] Although the newer form of personal injury coverage excludes bodily injury, there is arguably still coverage both for emotional distress and the interference with the use and enjoyment of one's premises occasioned by environmental pollution.

2. EXCLUSIONS

Personal injury liability coverage is subject to a relatively small number of exclusions. The Personal Injury Liability Coverage rider contains five exclusions as follows:

> This insurance does not apply to:
> (a) liability assumed by the Insured under any contract or agreement;

---

[18] [1995] P.E.I.J. No. 4, 127 Nfld. & P.E.I.R. 211 (P.E.I.T.D.), vard, [1996] P.E.I.J. No. 28, 135 D.L.R. (4th) 142, 138 Nfld. & P.E.I.R. 318, [1996] I.L.R. 1-3366, 34 C.C.L.I. (2d) 180 (C.A.), leave to appeal to S.C.C. refd [1997] S.C.C.A. No. 344.

[19] *Capital Regional District v. General Accident Assur. Co. of Can.*, [1985] B.C.J. No. 345, 15 C.C.L.I. 193 (S.C.), affd, [1987] B.C.J. No. 1301, 27 C.C.L.I. 81 (C.A.); *Acklands Ltd. v. Can. Indemnity Co.*, [1984] 4 W.W.R. 764 (Man. Q.B.), affd [1985] 4 W.W.R. 71 (Man. C.A.); *Ben's Ltd. v. Royal Ins. Co.*, [1985] I.L.R. 1-1969 (N.S.T.D.); *Neiman v. CGU Insurance Co.*, [2002] O.J. No. 2215 (S.C.J.).

[20] [2004] O.J. No. 481, 10 C.C.L.I. (4th) 200 (C.A.).

[21] See Chapter 12, section 1(e): Personal Injury Coverage for Pollution Claims.

(b)   personal injury arising out of the wilful violation of a penal statute or ordinance committed by or with the knowledge or consent of any Insured;

(c)   personal injury sustained by any person as a result of an offense directly or
indirectly related to the employment of such person by the Named Insured;

(d)   personal injury arising out of any publication or utterance described in
Group B, if the first injurious publication or utterance of the same or similar material by or on behalf of the Named Insured was made prior to the
effective date of this insurance;

(e)   personal injury arising out of a publication or utterance described in Group
B concerning any organization or business enterprise, or its products or
services, made by or at the direction of any Insured with knowledge of the
falsity thereof.

Coverage B under the Commercial General Liability form contains four
exclusions:

This insurance does not apply to: "Personal Injury":
1)   Arising out of oral or written publication of material, if done by or at the
direction of the insured with knowledge of its falsity;
2)   Arising out of oral or written publication of material whose first publication took place before the beginning of the policy period;
3)   Arising out of the wilful violation of a penal statute or ordinance committed by or with the consent of the insured; or
4)   For which the insured has assumed liability in a contract or agreement.
This exclusion does not apply to liability for compensatory damages that
the insured would have in the absence of the contract or agreement.

As can be seen, the exclusions under Coverage B are essentially re-worded
versions of exclusions (a), (b), (d) and (e) of the Personal Injury Liability
Coverage policy.

The exclusion of personal injury arising out of oral or written publication of
material which the insured knows to be false is of considerable significance in
defamation actions where the plaintiff often alleges that the defamatory
statement made by the insured was known to be untrue. In such cases, the claim
falls within the exclusion and the insurer is therefore not obliged to provide a
defence.[22]

The exclusion with respect to publication of material whose first publication
took place prior to the commencement of the policy period was applied in *Dyne
Holdings Ltd. v. Royal Insurance Co. of Canada.*[23]

In the 2005 version of the Insurance Bureau of Canada's Commercial General Liability policy, with the incorporation of advertising injury liability
coverage with personal injury liability coverage, the exclusions have been
modified accordingly.

---

[22]   *E.E.O.C. v. Southern Publishing Co.*, 705 F. Supp. 1213 (S.D. Miss. 1988).

[23]   *Supra*, note 18.

3. ADVERTISING INJURY

Any discussion of advertising injury liability policies must take into account the history of this form of coverage. It was introduced in the early 1970s as a separate rider to a comprehensive general liability policy. Over the years there has been a considerable evolution in the coverage provisions. In addition, advertising injury liability coverage has now been incorporated into the standard form Commercial General Liability policy published by the Insurance Bureau of Canada.

"Advertising Injury" was defined in the 1973 I.S.O.[24] Advertising Injury Endorsement as follows:

> "Advertising Injury" means injury arising out of an offence committed during the policy period occurring in the course of the named insured's advertising activities, if such injury arises out of libel, slander, defamation, invasion of right of privacy, piracy, unfair competition, or infringement of copyright, title or slogan.

The phrase "advertising activities" was undefined. This led to considerable litigation over the meaning of the phrase. Some courts interpreted the phrase to mean the widespread promotion of goods or services to the public at large.[25] Other courts, however, have interpreted the phrase more broadly, so as to include solicitation of a small group of potential customers.[26]

In the 1986 American version of the Commercial General Liability policy the definition of "advertising injury" was redrafted and "piracy" and "unfair competition" were dropped from the list of covered offences:

> "Advertising injury" means injury arising out of one or more of the following offenses:
> a. Oral or written publication or material that slanders or libels a person or organization or disparages a person's or organization's goods, products or services;
> b. Oral or written publication of material that violates a person's right of privacy;
> c. Misappropriation of advertising ideas or style of doing business; or
> d. Infringement of copyright, title or slogan.

In a separate provision, the 1986 policy wording states that coverage with respect to advertising injury applies only if caused by an offence committed in the policy territory during the policy period and in the course of the advertising of goods, products or services.

---

[24] "Insurance Services Office, Inc." See Chapter 6, section 1: Types of Commercial Policies.

[25] See, *e.g.*, *Hameid v. Nat'l Fire Ins. of Hartford*, 71 P.3d 761 (Cal. 2003) and *Zurich Am. Ins. Co. v. Amcor Sunclipse of N. Am.*, 241 F.3d 605 (7th Cir. 2000).

[26] *Charter Oak Fire Ins. Co. v. Hedeen & Cos.*, 280 F.3d 730, (7th Cir. 2002); *Solers, Inc. v. Hartford Cas. Ins. Co.*, No. 01-1862, 2002 WL 1289740 (4th Cir. June 12, 2002).

In 1998, I.S.O. introduced substantial changes to the advertising liability coverage. The requirement that the offence be committed in the course of the insured's advertising activities was changed to a requirement that the offence be committed in the named insured's "advertisement", a defined term:

> "Advertisement" means a notice that is broadcast or published in the general public or specific market segments about your goods, products or services for the purpose of attracting customers or supporters.

In addition, the description of certain of the offences was changed. Offence (c) "misappropriation of advertising ideas or style of doing business" was amended to read "use of another's advertising idea." Offence (d) "infringement of copyright, title or slogan" became "infringing upon another's copyright, trade dress or slogan". In *Central Mutual Insurance Co., v. StunFence, Inc.*,[27] the court held that the change from "title" to "trade dress" was a significant one. The reference to "title" in the earlier policy wording included most trademark infringement claims, whereas the term "trade dress" encompassed only a defined subset of such claims.

In 2001 there were further revisions to the I.S.O. advertising injury form, mostly for the purpose of responding to the phenomenon of communication via the internet. Thus, the definition of "advertisement" was extended as follows:

> For purposes of this definition: (a) notices that are published include material on the Internet, or on similar electronic means of communication; and (b) regarding web-sites, only that part of a web-site that is about your goods, products or services for the purpose of attracting customers or supporters is considered an advertisement.

The 2001 Form also added new exclusions so as to limit coverage for certain types of electronic liabilities, including liabilities arising out of electronic chatrooms or bulletin boards and the unauthorized use of another's name or product in e-mail addresses, domain names, or metatags.

In 2005 the Insurance Bureau of Canada incorporated advertising injury coverage into the personal injury liability coverage provisions of the Commercial General Liability policy. The phrase "personal and advertising injury" is defined as follows:

> "Personal and advertising injury" means injury, including consequential "bodily injury", arising out of one or more of the following offenses:
> a. False arrest, detention or imprisonment;
> b. Malicious prosecution;
> c. The wrongful eviction from, wrongful entry into, or invasion of the right of private occupancy of a room,
> dwelling or premises that a person occupies, committed by or on behalf of its owner, landlord or lessor;

---

[27]   2003 WL 22723022 (N.D. Ill. Nov. 18, 2003).

d. Oral or written publication, in any manner, of material that slanders or libels a person or organization or

disparages a person's or organization's goods, products or services;

e. Oral or written publication, in any manner, of material that violates a person's right of privacy;

f. The use of another's advertising idea in your "advertisement"; or

g. Infringing upon another's copyright, trade dress or slogan in your "advertisement".

Generally speaking, in order to fit within the insuring agreement in an advertising injury policy there must be:

(i) a legal obligation upon the insured;

(ii) to pay damages;

(iii) arising out of one or more of the specific offences enumerated in the policy;

(iv) occurring in the course of the insured's advertising activities or in the insured's advertisements;

(v) in the policy territory;

(vi) during the policy period.

Issues concerning "legally obligated to pay", "damages", "policy territory" and "policy period" are discussed in Chapter 7. To date there has been only limited jurisprudence in Canadian courts dealing with the balance of the requirements that must be met in order for a claim to fall within advertising injury coverage. In *Grayson v. Wellington Insurance Co.*[28] the British Columbia Court of Appeal considered the nature of the conduct that must be established in order to fit within the insuring agreement of what appears to have been the 1973 version of the policy. The Court noted an ambiguity in the definition of "advertising injury" in that it is not clear whether the subject described by the phrase "occurring in the course of the Named Insured's advertising activities" is intended to be the "injury" or the "offence". The Court held that it was the former; thus, the policy provided coverage for damages resulting from advertising for sale a product whose manufacture involved patent, copyright and trademark infringement and piracy. This is a result which is avoided by the 1986 and subsequent policy versions, which require that the offence itself must be committed in the course of the advertising of goods, services or products.[29] The Court in *Grayson* also commented upon the nature of the causal connection which must exist between the insured's advertising activities and the advertising injury in order for coverage to obtain. Referring to the decision of the Supreme

---

[28] [1997] B.C.J. No. 1734, [1997] 9 W.W.R. 718, 37 B.C.L.R. (3d) 49, [1998] I.L.R. 1-3516 (C.A.), leave to appeal to S.C.C. refd [1997] S.C.C.A. No. 487.

[29] *PrairieFyre Software Inc. v. St. Paul Fire and Marine Insurance Co.*, [2004] O.J. No. 2555, 10 C.C.L.I. (4th) 175 (C.A.).

Court of Canada in *Amos v. Insurance Corp. of British Columbia*,[30] the Court in *Grayson* held that the phrase "in the course of" does not require a direct causal link; rather, it is sufficient if the advertising activity contributed or added to the injuries alleged in the underlying action.

In *Reform Party of Canada v. Western Union Insurance Co.*[31] the British Columbia Court of Appeal, in the context of the duty to defend under a commercial general liability policy, gave consideration to what constitutes "advertising activities", a term not defined in the policy. The insured, a political party, allegedly defamed a senator in an article posted on a web site created by the party under the heading "Senate Scandals". The insured was not clearly identified as the sponsor of the site, nor did the article refer to the party's policy in favour of an elected senate. Rather, the article consisted entirely of negative comments about several senators. There was a link to the article, however, from the party's senate reform web page. On this basis the Court concluded that the article was arguably a part of the insured's promotion of its senate reform policy, and, as such, could be considered as constituting "advertising activities". The Court drew a distinction between those activities of political parties which are promotional and those which are merely informational or serve as an instigation to public debate of an issue. The former constitute "advertising activities", the latter do not.

The exclusions in an advertising injury policy typically relate to losses which are intentionally caused, criminal acts, infringement of copyright, and contractual liability. The latter exclusion was considered in *Corel Corp. v. Guardian Insurance Co. of Canada*.[32] It was alleged, among other things, that Corel, in breach of a non-disclosure agreement and in violation of copyright, had publicly offered for sale a software product displaying certain graphic images owned by the claimant. Corel's insurer denied coverage on the basis that the claim was for breach of contract, which was excluded under the policy. The court did not agree, noting that the claim for copyright infringement was independent of the claim for breach of the non-disclosure agreement.

---

[30]   [1995] S.C.J. No. 74, 3 S.C.R. 405, 127 D.L.R. (4th) 618, [1995] 9 W.W.R. 305, 10 B.C.L.R. (3d) 1.

[31]   *Supra*, note 17.

[32]   [2001] O.J. No. 368, 26 C.C.L.I. (3d) 39 (S.C.J.).

PART III

OTHER TOPICS

Chapter 11

DIRECTORS' AND OFFICERS' LIABILITY INSURANCE

1. IN GENERAL

Directors' and officers' ("D & O") liability insurance issues have received very little attention from Canadian courts. Yet such policies are regularly sold in Canada and, especially in recent years, a number of significant claims have been brought against directors and officers. No doubt in years to come further jurisprudence in this area will be developed.

Both at common law and under federal and provincial legislation, directors and officers owe various duties to the company, its shareholders, creditors, employees, and the public.[1] Some jurisdictions permit the company to indemnify the directors and officers, in limited circumstances, with respect to certain of these forms of liability and to purchase insurance to that end. The *Canada Business Corporations Act*,[2] for example, provides in section 124(4) as follows:

> (4) A corporation may purchase and maintain insurance for the benefit of any person referred to in subsection (1) against any liability incurred by him
> (*a*) in his capacity as a director or officer of the corporation, except where the liability relates to his failure to act honestly and in good faith with a view to the best interests of the corporation; or
> (*b*) in his capacity as a director or officer of another body corporate where he acts or acted in that capacity at the corporation's request, except where the liability relates to his failure to act honestly and in good faith with a view to the best interests of the body corporate.

In the result, directors and officers may be entitled to look to the company for indemnification with respect to some, but not all, claims. This has led to the creation of two types of insurance: the first is a type of coverage designed to protect the corporation in the event that it is required to indemnify directors and officers; the second is coverage designed to protect directors and officers with respect to those claims where they are not entitled to indemnification from the company. These two types of insurance are often combined in one policy.

---

[1] See generally, Lazar Sarna & Hillel Neuer, *Directors and Officers — A Canadian Legal Manual—Revised Edition* (Markham: LexisNexis)

[2] R.S.C. 1985, c. C-44.

Directors' and officers' liability insurance is generally regarded as a specialized market. There is not the same uniformity of policy wording as in commercial liability policies. Moreover, some forms of D & O policies may be characterized as indemnity rather than liability insurance in that there is no duty to defend claims or make settlements on behalf of the insured; rather, the policy provides only that the insurer must indemnify the insured for both an insured loss and the costs of defence.[3]

2. INSURING AGREEMENT

There are, typically, two parts to the insuring agreement of a D & O policy:

   (i) To pay on behalf of the directors and officers losses arising from claims which are covered under the policy and for which the directors and officers are not entitled to indemnification from the corporation;

   (ii) To pay on behalf of the corporation losses arising from claims which are covered under the policy and for which the corporation is liable to indemnify the directors and officers.

An example of a typical insuring agreement is as follows:

   A) To pay on behalf of the Directors and Officers of the Corporation as described in Item 1 of the Declarations any Loss (as defined herein) arising from any claim(s) for which liability may be imposed by law against the Directors and Officers jointly or severally by reason of any Wrongful Act (as defined herein) committed or alleged to have been committed during the policy period in their respective capacities of Directors and Officers.

   B) To pay on behalf of the Corporation any Loss arising from a claim or claims which may be made during the policy period against the Directors and Officers jointly or severally by reason of any Wrongful Act committed to or alleged to have been committed in their respective capacities of Directors and Officers of the Corporation, but only when the Directors and Officers have been entitled to indemnification by the Corporation for Loss, pursuant to law, or the articles or incorporation by the by-laws of the Corporation determining and defining such rights of indemnity.

The essential elements in determining coverage under this type of policy are that there be:

   (i)   a loss;
   (ii) arising from a claim;
   (iii) for which liability may be imposed by law;
   (iv) because of a wrongful act by a director or officer;
   (v)   in the capacity of director or officer.

---

[3]   See Chapter 1, section 3: Indemnity, Liability and Contingency Contracts Distinguished.

(a) Loss

The term "loss" is generally defined in the policy, and in the following way:

> (c) The term "Loss" shall mean any amount which the Directors and Officers are obligated by law to pay or for which the Corporation is required to indemnify the Directors and Officers, or for which the Corporation has, to the extent permitted by law, indemnified the Directors and Officers, for a claim or claims made against the Directors and Officers for Wrongful Acts. However, such Loss shall not include fines or penalties imposed by any provision of law, statute, rule or regulation to which the Corporation and its Directors and Officers may be subject, or matters which may be deemed uninsurable under the law pursuant to which the policy shall be construed or by which the Corporation is governed.

The term "loss" is broader than the insuring phrase "compensatory damages" which appears in many commercial liability policies. "Loss", standing alone, would encompass amounts payable in equity, at law, or pursuant to statute, without the requirement that such sums be compensatory in nature, subject to limitations placed with respect to fines or penalties or matters that may be deemed uninsurable by law. On this basis, unless otherwise excluded, punitive damages would arguably be covered under the policy. It is noted, however, that there is an issue as to whether insurance in respect of punitive damages is void for being contrary to public policy.[4] Insofar as the corporation is concerned, "loss" is limited to sums payable by way of indemnity to directors and officers. There is no coverage for claims against the corporation itself.[5]

(b) Claim

In order for there to be coverage, the loss must arise from a "claim", a term that is often not defined in the policy.[6] The term is, nevertheless, one of considerable importance, for it is also used in the notice provisions of the policy as well as in the provisions limiting the period of coverage.

Considered in its context, it appears that "claim" refers to any written or verbal demand for payment as a result of a wrongful act by a director or an officer. Since D & O policies are invariably written on a claims-made basis, the risk being insured against is not that a wrongful act will occur during the policy period; rather, it is that a claim will be brought.[7] On this basis, mere notice of a wrongful act or a request for information does not constitute a claim.[8] Nor was a

---

[4]   See Chapter 2, section 1(h): Public Policy.

[5]   *Farmer & Merchants Bank v. Home Ins. Co.*, 514 So. 2d 825 (1987 Alabama); *PLM Inc. v. National Union Fire Ins. Co.*, 848 F.2d 1243 (1988 U.S.A. 9th Cir.).

[6]   See the discussion of "claim" in Chapter 7, section 7(b): Claims-Made Policies.

[7]   *Bensalem Township v. Western World Ins. Co.*, 609 F.Supp. 1343 (ED Pa. 1985).

[8]   *Hoyt v. St. Paul Fire & Marine Ins. Co.*, 607 F.2d 864 (9th Cir. 1979).

claim held to exist where the insured, in the absence of a demand, repaid moneys obtained by fraud.[9]

(c) Liability Imposed by Law

The meaning of the phrase "liability imposed by law" depends upon the context in which it is used.[10] Where commercial liability policies are concerned, the phrase may encompass tortious, contractual or statutory liability, depending upon the other provisions of the policy. With D & O liability insurance policies, the phrase "liability imposed by law" includes at least tortious and statutory liability, for the duties of directors and officers are imposed both at law and by statute. Whether contractual liability is covered, and if so, to what extent, is an interesting, though unresolved, issue.[11]

(d) Wrongful Act

In order for there to be coverage under a D & O liability policy there must be a "wrongful act" by a director or officer. The term "wrongful act" is always defined in the policy. One example of such a definition is as follows:

> The term "Wrongful Act" shall mean any actual or alleged error, misstatement, criminal or malicious misrepresentation or fraud, civil libel, slander or defamation of character, actor omission, or neglect or breach of duty by the Directors and Officers in the discharge of their duties solely in their capacity as Directors and Officers, or any other matter claimed against them solely by reason of their being Directors and Officers.

As can be seen, the term "wrongful act" is quite broadly defined and encompasses both tortious and statutory liabilities. Coverage is not restricted merely to claims sounding in negligence.[12] "Wrongful act" may encompass contractual liability as well. In *Allyn v. Nipissing District (Roman Catholic Separate School Board)*,[13] which dealt with a different type of policy but with somewhat similar wording, it was held that "wrongful act" included breaches of duty in contract as well as in tort.

---

[9]   *MGIC Indemnity Corp. v. Home State Savings Assoc.*, 797 F.2d 285 (6th Cir. 1986).

[10] See discussion in Chapter 7, section 2: Liability Imposed by Law.

[11] In *Allyn v. Nipissing District (Roman Catholic Separate School Board)* (1986), 30 D.L.R. (4th) 458 (Ont. H.C.J.) it was held that a school board's errors-and-omissions policy, which contained wording somewhat similar to a D & O policy, provided coverage for legal fees associated with defending a claim for breach of contract. The reasons do not contain any analysis of the insuring phrase "legally obligated to pay". Since the policy contained an exclusion with respect to contractual liability, however, the insuring agreement must have been intended to include breach of contract: See the discussion in Chapter 7, section 2: Liability Imposed by Law.

[12] *Doering v. Economical Insurance Group*, [2000] O.J. No. 2820, I.L.R. 1-3878 (S.C.J.).

[13] *Supra*, note 11.

(e) In the Capacity of Director or Officer

Coverage for directors and officers is limited to wrongful acts committed by them while acting solely in the capacity of director or officer. This limitation may lead to disputes as to whether a particular act or omission by a director or officer occurred while in his or her capacity as such. This is most common when the director has a dual role as, for example, in the case of a director who is also the corporation's solicitor. In *Ross v. American Home Assurance Co.*[14] the plaintiff sought defence coverage with respect to a claim which had been brought against him by an investor for misrepresentation, breach of fiduciary duty, loss of opportunity and intentional interference with economic relations. Mr. Ross was an investment advisor with the firm of Midland Walwyn, which was also named in the suit. The investor, allegedly on the advice of Mr. Ross, had purchased shares in Diadem, a company of which Mr. Ross was a director. The court held that the claim was brought against Mr. Ross in his capacity as an investment advisor and not in his capacity as a director. Accordingly, the denial of coverage was upheld.

A somewhat unusual fact pattern is presented by the decision in *Riverwest v. Royal Insurance Co. of Canada.*[15] The plaintiff, a strata corporation, sought a defence under a directors' and officers' liability policy with respect to a claim by a strata owner that a member of the strata council had prevented a sale of the claimant's unit by making certain representations to a prospective purchaser. Although the member of the strata council was insured under the directors' and officers' liability coverage, the suit named only the strata corporation as defendant. The strata corporation itself was not covered except to the extent to which it was required to reimburse directors and officers, which, apparently, was not the case with respect to the subject claim. Nevertheless, the court found that there was a duty to defend the corporation on the basis that the claim against the strata corporation, by the operation of law, would result in a judgment against the individual strata owners, which would include the members of the strata council.

3. PERSONS INSURED

There is no uniform approach to the definition of "insured" in D & O liability policies issued by the various insurers. Some insurers require that the directors and officers to be insured under the policy be specified in the declarations. Other policies simply cover those persons who are directors and officers during the policy period. Policies may or may not include past directors and officers, and directors and officers of affiliated or subsidiary companies.

---

[14] [1999] O.J. No. 1558 (S.C.J.), affd [1999] O.J. No. 4262 (C.A.).

[15] [1996] B.C.J. No. 618, 37 C.C.L.I. (2d) 21 (S.C.).

4. PERIOD OF COVERAGE

D & O liability policies are generally written on a claims-made basis.[16] Coverage is extended not on the basis of when the wrongful act occurred but, rather, on the basis of when the claim is made. For this reason, coverage may be extended to persons who were directors at the time of the wrongful act but are no longer directors at the time when the claim is advanced.[17]

The term "claim" may not be defined in the policy. This can lead to an issue of what is meant by the term and whether it applies, for example, to mere notice of an alleged wrongful act without an accompanying demand for payment.[18]

Although in theory a claims-made policy covers all and only those claims presented during the policy period, in practice most such policies are modified. Many policies will stipulate a retroactive date before which coverage for an occurrence is not available, even though the claim is first presented during the policy period. Most policies will also provide for extended coverage beyond the termination of the policy for wrongful acts that are committed before the policy expired but which do not lead to a claim until after the expiration of the policy.

5. EXCLUSIONS

In the past there were relatively few exclusions in a D & O liability policy. Such policies generally contained exclusions with respect to claims made against directors or officers:

    (i) arising out of the dishonesty of the directors and officers;
    (ii) based upon a personal profit or advantage to the directors and officers;
    (iii) for return by the directors and officers of remuneration paid to them without proper approval;
    (iv) with respect to pollution.

Given the modern business climate, however, insurers are experimenting with a number of new exclusions, particularly in response to litigation arising out of corporate takeovers and litigation brought by corporations themselves (as opposed to shareholders or third parties) to recover losses to the corporation caused by the acts or omissions of the directors or officers. Thus, in addition to the exclusions noted above one will often find exclusions relating to claims brought by one insured against another, claims relating to insider trading and

---

[16] For a discussion of claims-made policies in the commercial liability context see Chapter 7, section 7(b): Claims-Made Policies.

[17] *Nipissing Condominium Corp. No. 18 v. Mayco Homes Ltd.*, [1999] O.J. No. 3936, [2000] I.L.R. 1-3755 (S.C.J.).

[18] See, *supra*, note 8 and accompanying text.

claims arising out of resisting takeover bids. One may also find an exclusion with respect to claims arising out of bodily injury.[19]

6. DUTY TO DEFEND

Unlike commercial liability policies, D & O policies generally give control of the defence to the insured,[20] with the insurer's requirement being limited to reimbursement of legal expenses.[21] In such cases, the policy limits are usually inclusive of defence costs.

Where the policy leaves control of the defence to the insured, there may nevertheless be some provision to protect the insurer's interest. Some policies, for example, provide that the insured must obtain the insurer's consent before selecting counsel, but that such consent must not be unreasonably withheld. Some policies may also stipulate that the insured must co-operate with the insurer in the defence of the claim. Regardless of such provisions, however, it is submitted that where the insured has conduct of the defence, it must act in good faith — which would generally include seeking the insurer's approval of any settlement.

A recurring issue with respect to D & O policies is that of allocation of defence costs between covered and uncovered claims.[22] Unlike CGL policies, D & O policies typically contain an allocation clause, an example of which is as follows:

> In any claim against both Directors and Officers and any other party or parties, Costs, Charges and Expenses for investigation or defense shall be limited to those incurred in the right of and for the principal benefit of the Directors and Officers, as distinguished from any such other party or parties, and the Insurer and the Directors and Officers will endeavour to establish, at the earliest opportunity, a proper basis for the allocation of the Costs, Charges or Expenses of counsel or others rendering services to or for the benefit of both the Directors and Officers and any such other party or parties.

---

[19] *Wellington Guarantee v. Evangelical Lutheran Church in Canada*, [1996] B.C.J. No. 872, [1996] 9 W.W.R. 373, 35 C.C.L.I. (2d) 164, [1996] I.L.R. 1-3334 (C.A.), leave to appeal to S.C.C. refd, [1996] S.C.C.A. No. 322, 207 N.R. 79*n*, 138 W.A.C. 160*n*, 39 C.C.L.I. (2d) 12*n*, [1996] I.L.R. 1-3334 at 4053*n*.

[20] *Continental Ins. Co. v. Dia Met Minerals Ltd.*, [1994] B.C.J. No. 1724, 5 B.C.L.R. (3d) 222 (S.C.).

[21] In the United States the issue often arises of whether the insured must wait until the conclusion of the litigation to seek reimbursement, or is entitled to reimbursement of interim accounts as they fall due: See, generally, Arter & Hadden, "D & O Insurance Case Law: Recent Developments", Practising Law Institute, Securities Litigation 1995.

[22] *Coronation Insurance Co. v. Clearly Canadian Beverage Corp.* [1999] B.C.J. No. 43, 168 D.L.R. (4th) 366, [1999] 6 W.W.R. 189, 57 B.C.L.R. (3d) 303 (C.A.); *New Zealand Forest Products v. New Zealand Insurance Co. Ltd.*, [1997] 3 N.Z.L.R. 1, [1997] 1 W.L.R. 1237 (P.C.).

In the absence of an allocation clause, defense costs will be apportioned in accordance with the rule that the insured is responsible only for those costs which are solely and unequivocally referable to an uncovered claim.[23] Nor, in the absence of appropriate policy wording, will a clause respecting allocation of defence costs be extended so as to permit the allocation of settlement moneys between the insurer and the insured where the corporation has received a benefit from the settlement.[24]

---

[23] See Chapter 5, section 2: Apportionment and Reimbursement of Defence Costs; and *New Zealand Forest Products v. New Zealand Insurance Co. Ltd.*, *ibid.*

[24] *Coronation Insurance Co. v. Clearly Canadian Beverage Corp.*, *supra*, note 22.

Chapter 12

ENVIRONMENTAL LIABILITY INSURANCE

Environmental claims now constitute one of the most significant hazards that businesses and insurers face. This has not always been so. In years past such claims were rarely, if ever, brought. Specialized policies for environmental risks were not available and coverage was provided instead under the standard commercial liability policies. All that has now changed. In response to the growing number and size of environmental claims the insurance industry has, over the years, restricted the coverage available under commercial forms and has introduced specialized environmental liability policies.

Even so, environmental claims have what is referred to as a "long tail".[1] A claim presented today often has its genesis in property damage that occurred many years ago but which has only recently come to light. Since most commercial policies were and are written on an occurrence basis (*i.e.,* the policy that covers is the one which was in force at the time the damage occurred rather than the one in force when the claim is made)[2] it is not unusual to see commercial liability insurers brought in to defend an environmental claim. Nor should other forms of policies be overlooked. Depending upon the circumstances, environmental liability risks may be covered under a homeowners', boiler and machinery, automobile, or directors' and officers' policy. In some cases, even a property policy may respond to the cost of cleaning up contaminants.

1. COMMERCIAL LIABILITY POLICIES

(a) Before the Pollution Exclusion

For many years, commercial liability policies did not contain any exclusions designed to limit coverage for environmental risks. Coverage under these policies for pollution-related claims depended solely upon whether the claim fell within the insuring agreement. These policies generally provided coverage with respect to: (i) liability imposed by law to pay damages (ii) because of bodily injury or property damage (iii) caused by an accident or occurrence.

---

[1] See Fagan, "Liability Insurance, Uncertainty and Long-Tail Risks" (1989) 1 Can. Ins. L. Rev. 219.

[2] See Chapter 7, section 7: Period of Coverage.

(i) Liability Imposed by Law to Pay Damages

The phrase "liability imposed by law" is generally considered to refer to tortious liability.[3] As noted in Chapter 9, however, certain forms of statutory liability, including obligations under environmental protection legislation, have been held to fall within the insuring phrase "liability imposed by law".[4] The term "damages" in a commercial liability policy is usually considered to refer to sums payable by way of compensation, whether at law or under statute.[5] Thus, compensatory damages for nuisance, for example, would fall within the insuring agreement, provided, of course, that the nuisance consisted of property damage caused by an accident or occurrence.

The extent to which clean-up and remedial costs payable under environmental protection legislation may constitute "damages" for the purposes of the insuring agreement is a serious issue. In the United States, there are conflicting decisions on this point.[6] In Canada, the issue has been raised, but not considered at any length, in only two reported cases, both of which were decided in favour of coverage.[7] It is likely that in the future this issue will have to be decided on a case-by-case basis. As far as environmental legislation allows for compensation to injured parties for the harm done, the sums thus payable would appear to fall within the insuring phrase "liability imposed by law to pay damages". Where the environmental legislation, however, goes beyond compensation and provides either for preventive measures or for fines and penalties it is unlikely that any sums thus payable will be held to constitute "damages" for the purposes of the insuring agreement.

(ii) Because of Bodily Injury or Property Damage

Coverage under a commercial liability policy generally depends upon there being "bodily injury" or "property damage", both terms usually being defined in the policy. The standard form of the CGL policy defines bodily injury as:

> Bodily injury, sickness or disease sustained by any person which occurs during the policy period, including death at any time resulting therefrom.

"Property damage" is defined as:

> (1) physical injury to or destruction of tangible property which occurs during •
> the policy period, including the loss of use thereof at any time resulting
> therefrom, or

---

3   See Chapter 7, section 2: Liability Imposed by Law.

4   See *Hildon Hotel (1963) Ltd. v. Dominion Ins. Corp.* (1968), 1 D.L.R. (3d) 214 (B.C.S.C.).

5   See Chapter 7, section 3: Damages.

6   See *Maryland Casualty Co. v. Armco*, 822 F.2d 1348 (4th Cir. 1987); cert. den. 108 S. Ct. 703; *Newcastle County v. Hartford Accident & Indemnity Co.*, 673 F. Supp. 1359 (1987).

7   *Hildon Hotel (1963) Ltd. v. Dominion Ins. Corp.* (1968), 1 D.L.R. (3d) 214 (B.C.S.C.); *Greenwood Forest Products Ltd. v. U.S. Fire Ins. Co.*, [1982] 3 W.W.R. 739 (B.C.S.C.).

(2) loss of use of tangible property which has not been physically injured or destroyed provided such loss of use is caused by an accident occurring during the policy period.

In Canada the definition of "bodily injury" set out above has been held to include psychological trauma.[8] There is some American support for this view[9] but for the most part the courts in the United States have ruled that claims for "pure" emotional distress are not covered on the basis that "bodily injury" denotes an injury to the body of a physical nature.[10] These latter courts do, however, generally permit coverage where the emotional distress results from a physical injury, physical contact or bodily pain[11] or manifests itself through physical symptomatology.[12] In cases where exposure to environmentally hazardous substances does not result in physical symptoms but does cause severe emotional distress or mental anguish, coverage may be available under a personal injury endorsement.[13]

In the United States, the majority of courts considering the issue have accepted that the term "property damage" includes environmental harm resulting from the discharge of pollutants on land, in the air or in water.[14] The point has not been directly addressed in Canada. In *Hildon Hotel (1963) Ltd. v. Dominion Insurance Corp.*[15] the insuring agreement did not define the term "property damage" but simply provided coverage with respect to "damages because of injury to or destruction of property, including loss of use thereof ...". It was held that this form of insuring agreement, with its unqualified use of the word "injury", provided coverage for the infringement of a right as well as for physical injury to property. Accordingly, the Court held that there was coverage with respect to a claim resulting from the insured's pollution of the ocean, for the act of pollution amounted to an infringement of the Crown's right to enjoy unpolluted wharves and water. Similarly, in *Greenwood Forest Products Ltd. v. U.S. Fire Insurance Co.*[16] it was held that chemical pollution of groundwater, a river and a lake constituted an infringement of the Crown's right to a clean water system and was therefore "injury to property".

---

[8]   See Chapter 7, section 4(a): Bodily Injury.

[9]   See, for example, *Lavanant v. General Accident Ins. Co. of America*, 79 N.Y.2d 623 (1992); and *Lanigan v. Snowden*, 938 S.W.2d 330 (Mo. App. W.D. 1997).

[10] *Farm Bureau Mutual Ins. Co. v. Hoag*, 356 N.W. 2d 630 (Mich. App. 1984).

[11] *National Casualty Co. v. Great Southwest Fire Ins. Co.*, 833 P.2d 741 (Colo. 1992).

[12] *Voorhees v. Preferred Mutual Ins. Co.*, 607 A.2d 1255 (N.J. 1992).

[13] See the discussion below in section 1(e): Personal Injury Coverage for Pollution Claims.

[14] See, for example, *Continental Ins. Co. v. Northeastern Pharmaceutical & Chemical Co.*, 811 F.2d 1180 (8th Cir. 1987).

[15] *Supra*, note 7, at 216.

[16] *Supra*, note 7.

(iii) *Caused by an Accident or Occurrence*

Depending upon the wording used, coverage under a commercial liability policy is triggered by either an accident or an occurrence. "Occurrence" is generally defined as "an accident, including continuous or repeated exposure to conditions, which results, during the policy period, in bodily injury or property damage neither expected nor intended from the standpoint of the insured".

The courts in the United States have generally interpreted the "occurrence" wording as contemplating coverage for claims resulting from the repeated release of pollutants, whether intentional or otherwise, provided that the resulting bodily injury or property damage was neither expected nor intended by the insured.[17] There is disagreement, however, on which test to apply in determining whether environmental harm is "expected or intended". Some courts have held that if the insured knew or ought to have known that there was a substantial probability that environmental harm would result then there has not been an "occurrence" within the meaning of the policy.[18] Other courts have held that mere foreseeability of damage may be sufficient to render the damage "expected or intended" and consequently outside of coverage.[19] The unsatisfactory state of the Canadian jurisprudence is discussed in Chapter 7.[20]

Once the insured has knowledge of the environmental harm for which the insured is responsible and fails to take preventive action, then any subsequent harm is not within coverage. Thus, in *Zatko v. Paterson Springs Service Ltd.*,[21] the Ontario Supreme Court held that while there was coverage for the initial escape of oil from an underground tank, coverage ceased once the insured knew of the leak and failed to act promptly to correct the situation.

It is often difficult, with respect to claims involving environmental damage, to determine when the damage occurred. Since most comprehensive general liability policies are written on an occurrence rather than a claims-made basis, the date of the occurrence is vital to a determination of which policy responds to the loss. This matter is discussed in Chapter 7.[22]

(b) Exclusion of Environmental Liability

As noted in Chapter 8,[23] an exclusion with respect to environmental liability was generally included in commercial liability policies issued after 1970. The wording of that exclusion is as follows:

---

[17] See, for example, *Grand River Lime Co. v. Ohio Casualty Ins. Co.*, 289 N.E.2d 360 (Ohio 1972).

[18] *Carter Lake (City) v. Aetna Casualty & Surety Co.*, 604 F.2d 1052 (8th Cir. C.A. 1979); *Millard Warehouse Inc. v. Hartford Fire Ins. Co.*, 283 N.W.2d 56 (Neb. 1979); *American Mutual Liability Ins. Co. v. Neville Chemical Co.*, 650 F. Supp. 929 (W.D.P.A. 1987).

[19] See *Gassaway v. Travelers Ins. Co.*, 439 S.W.2d 605 (Tenn. 1969); *Tieton (Town) v. General Ins. Co.*, 380 P.2d 127 (Wash. 1963).

[20] Sections 5(e)-(h).

[21] [1985] O.J. No. 1327, [1986] I.L.R. 1-1997 (H.C.J.).

[22] See section 7(a): Occurrence Policies.

[23] Chapter 8, section 8: Environmental Liability.

It is agreed that this policy does not apply to bodily injury or property damage arising out of the discharge, dispersal, release or escape of smoke, vapours, soot, fumes, acids, alkalis, toxic chemicals, liquids or gases, waste materials or other irritants, contaminants or pollutants into or upon land, the atmosphere or any water of any description no matter where located or how contained, or into any watercourse, drainage or sewage system, but this exclusion does not apply if such discharge, dispersal, release or escape is sudden and accidental.

As also noted in Chapter 8,[24] the courts have given a narrow scope to the exclusion both in Canada and in the United States. The response of the insurance industry was to redraft the exclusion as follows:

This insurance does not apply to:
1. Pollution Liability
    a. "Bodily injury" or "property damage" arising out of the actual, alleged or threatened discharge, dispersal, release or escape of pollutants:
        1) At or from premises you own, rent or occupy;
        2) At or from any site or location used by or for you or others for the handling, storage, disposal, processing or treatment of waste;
        3) Which are at any time transported, handled, stored, treated, disposed of, or processed as waste by or for you or any person or organization for whom you may be legally responsible; or
        4) At or from any site or location on which you or any contractors or subcontractors working directly or indirectly on your behalf are performing operations:
            a) if the pollutants are brought on or to the site or location in connection with such operations; or
            b) if the operations are to test for, monitor, clean up, remove, contain, treat, detoxify or neutralize the pollutants.
    b. Any loss, cost, or expense arising out of any governmental direction or request that you test for, monitor, clean up, remove, contain, treat, detoxify or neutralize pollutants.

Pollutants means any solid, liquid, gaseous or thermal irritant or contaminant, including smoke, vapour, soot, fumes, acids, alkalis, chemicals and waste. Waste includes materials to be recycled, reconditioned or reclaimed.[25]

This form of environmental liability exclusion is often referred to as the "absolute pollution exclusion" because it eliminates the exception relating to the sudden and accidental discharge of pollutants. In addition, unlike the earlier form, it applies to threatened as well as actual discharge of pollutants and specifically applies to any loss, cost or expense arising out of a governmental direction to take clean-up or remedial steps. The scope of the absolute pollution exclusion is discussed in Chapter 8.[26]

---

[24] *Ibid.*

[25] I.B.C. Bulletin 85-11, December 30, 1985. See Appendix K for the latest version of this exclusion.

[26] See Chapter 8, section 8: Environmental Liability.

(c) Environmental Damage Endorsement

In 1981, in response to environmental protection legislation under consideration in Ontario and Saskatchewan, the Insurance Bureau of Canada drafted a form of Environmental Damage Endorsement for use with commercial liability policies:

> It is agreed that the insurance applies to liability to pay compensation for loss, damage or expense arising out of damage or a perceived threat of damage, to the environment, imposed by or under a law of a province or of the federal government in Canada or of the Northwest Territories or Yukon Territory, any such liability being deemed to be because of bodily injury or property damage, subject to all the provisions of the Policy, except as modified by this endorsement, and subject to the following additional provisions: —
>
> 1. Notwithstanding Condition 3(c) of the Policy, any expense required to be incurred by the Insured under any law referred to in the opening paragraph of this endorsement shall be deemed to be a legal liability of the Insured to pay compensation.
> 2. The Environmental Liability Exclusion is deleted and the following substituted therefor: —
>   > "It is agreed that the insurance does not apply to bodily injury or property damage arising out of the discharge, dispersal, release or escape of smoke, vapours, soot, fumes, acids, alkalis, toxic chemicals, liquids or gases, waste materials or other irritants, contaminants or pollutants into or upon land, the atmosphere or any water of any description no matter where located or how contained, or into any watercourse, drainage or sewage system, but this exclusion does not apply if such discharge, dispersal, release or escape is accidental."
> 3. The insurance does not apply to
>   (a) expenses incurred in connection with the prevention, control, repair, clean-up or restoration of environmental damage on property owned or occupied by or rented to the Insured;
>   (b) fines or penalties;
>   (c) liability assumed by the Insured under any contract or agreement; or
>   (d) liability arising out of any discharge, dispersal, release or escape from a waste disposal site.[27]

This endorsement amends the environmental liability exclusion by removing the word "sudden". The intention is that the slow, undetected leak be covered.[28] Of course, as has already been noted, some courts have held that slow leaks are covered notwithstanding that the exception to the exclusion is limited to those which are "sudden".[29]

The opening paragraph of the endorsement negates the requirement of bodily injury or property damage. Thus, coverage is extended to clean-up costs that may be payable under environmental protection legislation.

---

[27] I.B.C. Form 2033, April 1981.

[28] I.B.C. Bulletin 81-8.

[29] See Chapter 8, section 8: Environmental Liability.

There are four exclusions to the endorsement. The first exclusion relates to liability for property damage to property owned, occupied by or rented to the insured. That liability, if it is covered at all, would have to be covered under a property policy. The second exclusion relates to fines or penalties, which traditionally have not been covered by liability policies, and in any event are subject to the rule of public policy.[30] Presumably, this exclusion could be deleted where underwriting considerations so warrant. The last exclusion is with respect to liability arising out of any discharge, dispersal, release or escape from a waste disposal site. This would exclude coverage for the insured's liability as a waste generator. Again, it may be that in the appropriate circumstances an insured could bargain for the deletion of this exclusion.[31]

(d) Limited Pollution Liability Coverage

In 1993 the Insurance Bureau of Canada issued an endorsement[32] designed to replace the absolute pollution exclusion and provide limited coverage for certain pollution risks. In general terms the endorsement is designed to cover the accidental discharge of pollutants of a quality and quantity not routine to the insured's business, provided the discharge is detected and reported to the insurer within 120 hours of its occurrence. In *Groupe Pétrolier Nirom Inc. v. Cie d'Assurance du Québec*,[33] which involved a leak from an underground storage tank, it was held that the 120-hour time limit commences when the insured either knows or ought to know of the leak. In *Irving Oil Ltd. v. London & Hull Maritime Insurance Co.*,[34] however, which concerned different policy wording containing a requirement that the incident be detected by the insured within 180 days of its occurrence and be reported to the insurer within a further period of 180 days, the Court ruled that the inability of the insured to establish when a leak from an underground tank commenced was fatal to coverage. The latter decision is consistent with the plain meaning of the words used in the policy; the former, although not entirely consistent with the policy language, introduces an element of commercial reality to the policy. It is often impossible to establish, especially in terms of the day and hour, when a leak in an underground storage tank commenced. Holding the insured to such a requirement effectively renders coverage nugatory.[35]

Pilot Insurance Co. v. Tyre King Recycling Ltd.[36] is another case decided under a form of "limited pollution" insurance. The insured operated a tire recycling business, where it stored literally walls of tires. These were set on fire by vandals, resulting in an enormous conflagration and substantial clean-up

---

[30] See Chapter 2, section 1(h): Public Policy.

[31] *Supra*, note 28.

[32] I.B.C. Form 2313.

[33] [1999] Q.J. No. 1222 (C.A.).

[34] [1998] N.B.J. No. 521, 207 N.B.R. (2d) 301, [1999] I.L.R. 1-3670 (Q.B.).

[35] See Chapter 2, section 3(b): Construction According to Purpose.

[36] [1992] O.J. No. 807, 8 O.R. (3d) 236, [1992] I.L.R. 1-2851, 10 C.C.L.I. (2d) 264 (Gen. Div.).

costs both on and off the premises. The policy provided coverage for the insured's legal obligation to pay damages because of property damage caused by a "pollution incident", which was defined as:

> an unexpected or unintentional discharge of any "pollutants" from or out of a structure or container provided ...
> (c) Such discharge does not occur in a quantity or with a quality that is routine to the insured's operation.

The coverage was subject to various exclusions, two of which were at issue in the proceeding:

> This insurance does not apply to:
> (b) "bodily injury", "property damage" or "clean-up costs" arising out of a "pollution incident" which "pollution incident" is expected or intended from the standpoint of the insured; ...
> (q) "bodily injury", "property damage" or "clean-up costs" caused by a "pollution incident" resulting from war, invasion, act of foreign enemy, hostilities (whether war be declared or not), civil war, rebellion, revolution, insurrection or military power, riot or civil commotion, sabotage or any other act of deliberate destruction of property or terrorism.

The insurer argued that the policy did not respond because the fire was deliberately set, the pollutants were not discharged from or out of a structure or container, the damage was expected or intended by the insured, and the loss arose out of a deliberate destruction of property. All of these arguments were rejected by the Court. Although the fire was deliberately set, it was unexpected or unintentional from the standpoint of the insured and therefore fell within the parameters of the insuring agreement. The tires formed a "structure" within the meaning of the policy, for the policy described the risk as "used tires — storage in open" and the tires were arranged into clearly defined "walls". The "expected or intended damage" exclusion did not apply, for that exclusion, by its very wording, applies only "from the standpoint of the insured", and therefore does not apply to the actions of third parties. Finally, the "war risk" exclusion did not apply because, applying the interpretive rule of *ejusdem generis,* vandalism was held not to be similar in character to the other acts enumerated in the exclusion.

(e) Personal Injury Coverage for Pollution Claims

The Personal Injury Liability endorsement to the CGL policy provides coverage for a variety of "personal injury" offences, including, under Group C, "wrongful entry or eviction, or other invasion of the right of private occupancy".[37] In the Commercial General Liability form personal injury coverage is provided as a matter of course, but unlike the earlier form, specifically excludes bodily injury claims. Moreover, in the latter form the former Group C offences are restated as

---

[37] See Chapter 10: Personal Injury and Advertising Injury Liability Coverage.

"wrongful entry into, or eviction of a person from a room, dwelling or premises that the person occupies".

In the United States there are differing opinions as to the circumstances, if any, under which environmental liability claims may fall within personal injury liability coverage. Some courts have held that claims involving the contamination of property by a pollutant are covered on the basis that the third party's right of private occupancy has been interfered with.[38] In accepting this argument, some courts have held that the environmental liability exclusion does not apply with respect to personal injury coverage.[39] Other courts have expressly rejected this view.[40] The most recent Canadian version of the Commercial General Liability policy specifically provides that the pollution exclusion applies to the personal injury and advertising injury provisions in the policy.

2. ENVIRONMENTAL IMPAIRMENT LIABILITY POLICIES

During the 1970s, the insurance industry began to develop policies specifically designed to provide liability coverage for environmental risks. These policies, which are sometimes referred to as "environmental impairment liability policies", have not been standardized, unlike commercial liability policies.

There are significant differences between the types of coverage offered in this regard. The policies vary not only among insurers, but also depending on the particular industry for which they are written. One feature that environmental impairment liability policies appear to have in common, however, is that they are issued on a claims-made basis.[41] This poses a significant difficulty for the insured who, for whatever reason, wishes to change carriers. Notwithstanding that a claim is made during the policy period, a claims-made policy does not provide coverage if the claim results from an occurrence that took place before the "retroactive date" specified in the policy. If the new insurer does not agree to a retroactive date earlier than the inception date of the new policy, then the insured may be left with a significant gap in coverage.

3. OTHER POLICIES

Environmental liability claims may be covered under a variety of other types of insurance policies. Homeowners' policies typically provide a broad range of coverage without any specific exclusion of environmental risks. Directors and

---

[38] See, generally, N.L. Quackenbush, "The Personal Injury Endorsement: Breathing New Life into CGL Coverage For Pollution-Related Offenses" (1994) 29 Gonz. L. Rev. 385.

[39] See, for example, *Pipefitter Welfare Educ. Fund v. Westchester Fire Ins. Co.*, 976 F.2d 1037 (7th Cir. 1992).

[40] See, for example, *Columbia (County) v. Continental Ins. Co.*, 595 N.Y.S.2d 988 (1993); and *Union Oil Co. of California v. International Ins. Co.*, 44 Cal. Rptr.2d 4 (1995).

[41] See Chapter 7, section 7(b): Claims-Made Policies.

officers of corporations who are subject to civil liability for environmental claims may be able to find coverage under a directors' and officers' liability policy.[42] Transporters of hazardous waste may find coverage under a motor vehicle liability policy. Environmental consultants may be insured under a professional liability policy.[43]

In recent years, property policies have been a frequent source of coverage for environmental hazards. Even though a property policy is designed to indemnify the insured only with respect to damage to the insured's own property, remedying the loss to the insured's property may also satisfy the insured's liability in respect of an environmental hazard. The debris removal clause, for example, may cover the cost of cleaning up the damage to the insured's property caused by pollution.[44]

---

[42] Directors' and officers' liability policies, however, now typically contain an exclusion for environmental claims.

[43] *Temple Insurance Co. v. Sirman Associates Ltd.*, [2003] O.J. No. 4257, [2004] I.L.R. 1-4255 (C.A.).

[44] See, for example, *Compass Ins. Co. v. Cravens, Dargan & Co.*, 748 P.2d 724 (Wyo. 1988).

Chapter 13

PROFESSIONAL LIABILITY INSURANCE

Premises, operations and products liability is covered under a commercial liability policy. Such policies, however, invariably contain an exclusion with respect to the provision of professional services.[1] The liability that a professional faces for failing to exercise the requisite degree of care and skill is recognized as presenting a hazard significantly different to that of the ordinary commercial risk.[2] Typically, professional liability risks are underwritten only by a few insurers specializing in that particular market. In addition, and especially in recent years, self-insurance is common among professional organizations.

Because of the great variety of professional liability policies and the surprising lack of Canadian jurisprudence with respect to such policies, the topic is addressed here in general terms only.

1. "PROFESSIONAL" DEFINED

The term "professional" is not limited to those engaged in the traditional professions of law, medicine and the Church. For the purposes of insurance contracts the test of a "professional" service is one which embraces "both a mental or intellectual exercise within a recognized discipline and the application of special skill, knowledge and training to the particular function in question".[3] Lawyers, barbers, beauticians, doctors, dentists, nurses, massage therapists, optometrists, physiotherapists, chiropractors, veterinarians, architects, engineers, surveyors, environmental consultants, real estate agents, insurance agents and accountants are all eligible for insurance under professional liability policies. This list is not exhaustive but merely illustrative of the diversity of services that fall under the rubric "professional".

---

[1]   See Chapter 8, section 9: Professional Services.

[2]   *Foundation of Can. Engineering Corp. v. Can. Indemnity Co.*, [1977] 2 W.W.R. 75 (S.C.C.).

[3]   *Chemetics International Ltd. v. Commercial Union Assur. Co. of Can.* (1982), 31 B.C.L.R. 273 (S.C.) at 286, affd (1984), 55 B.C.L.R. 60 (C.A.).

2. INSURING AGREEMENT

Unlike commercial liability policies, which are typically triggered by an accident or occurrence and limited to bodily injury or property damage,[4] professional liability policies generally define coverage in terms of sums of money which the insured becomes legally obligated to pay as damages because of injury or loss arising out of an act or omission by the insured in the provision of professional services. Typically, the term "professional services" is defined in the policy.

An example of an insuring agreement in a professional liability policy is provided by the lawyers' compulsory professional liability policy used in British Columbia:

> We shall pay on your behalf all sums which you become legally obligated to pay as damages because of any claim first made against you and reported during the policy period arising out of an error by you in performing or failing to perform professional services for others.

The term "professional services" is defined in the policy in the following way:

(a) the practice of law as defined in the *Legal Profession Act* of British Columbia;

(b) acting as an Official Administrator, a custodian under Part 8 of the *Legal Profession Act* in British Columbia, an arbitrator, mediator or conciliator, by a member;

(c) acting as:
    (i) a receiver or receiver manager;
    (ii) an administrator, conservator, executor, guardian, trustee or committee or in any similar fiduciary capacity;
    (iii) a patent or trademark agent;
    (iv) agent for any record keeping or filing duty imposed by any provincial or federal statute;
    provided that such services are connected with and incidental to the Individual Insured's profession as a lawyer;

(d) performing any other activity deemed to be the practice of law by the Law Society.

As can be seen from this example, coverage under the lawyers' professional liability policy is limited to the provision of professional services. The policy does not extend coverage for all liability that a lawyer may incur as a business person. Thus, in *Hazelwood v. Travelers Indemnity Co.*[5] it was held that a

---

[4] See Chapter 7, section 1: Structure of the Insuring Agreement.

[5] [1979] 2 W.W.R. 271 (B.C.C.A.). See also *General Accident Ins. Co. v. Namesulk*, 790 F.2d 197 (9th Cir. 1986) in which it was held that a lawyer's professional liability policy did not provide coverage with respect to her liability to a client who made an investment in certain corporations owned by the lawyer. In *Continental Casualty Co. v. Burton*, 795 F.2d 187 (4th Cir. 1986),

solicitor who guaranteed an investment in his capacity as a commission agent was not entitled to indemnity under a professional liability policy covering his omissions in his capacity as a lawyer.

The giving of a solicitor's undertaking, however, as opposed to a guarantee, does fall within the insuring agreement as "... arising out of the performance ... of professional services for others ... in the Insured's capacity as a lawyer...". Thus, in *Pollon v. American Home Assurance Co.*[6] a solicitor recovered from the insurer her loss arising from an undertaking she gave to the Ministry of Revenue on behalf of her client to pay land transfer tax in a real estate transaction.

Whether the insured acted in a professional capacity and rendered professional services is a question of fact in each case. The court will focus on the proximate cause of the loss and determine whether that cause may be characterized as a "professional service". An example of this sort of analysis is provided by the decision in *Marx v. Hartford Accident & Indemnity Co.*[7] An insured physician's employee mistakenly filled a hot water sterilizer with benzine instead of water. A fire resulted, which damaged the building. The Court held that the loss did not arise out of rendering or failing to render professional services, for the act of boiling water does not require any professional knowledge or training. Hence, the loss was not covered under the physician's professional liability policy. Presumably, it was covered under his commercial liability policy, if he had one. Liability of health care professionals in respect of sexual torts is addressed in Chapter 15.[8]

Other examples of the meaning of "professional services" include *Albert J. Schiff Associates Inc. v. Flack*,[9] in which it was held that an insurance agent's unauthorized use of another agent's marketing plan is not covered under an agent's professional liability policy; *Transamerica Insurance Co. v. Sayble*,[10] in which it was held that a lawyer's professional liability policy did not apply to a dispute between two former partners over their entitlement to compensation; *Karpel v. Rumack*,[11] in which it was held that acting as a mortgage broker could conceivably be considered a professional service rendered by a lawyer; *Brumer v. Gunn*,[12] in which it was held that held that a lawyer was acting in his capacity as a solicitor while providing investment advice; and *Kerr v. Law Profession*

---

however, a lawyer was covered by a professional liability policy when he accepted funds from a client for the purpose of investing them. The policy in question provided coverage to the lawyer in his capacity as a fiduciary.

[6] [1991] O.J. No. 531, 79 D.L.R. (4th) 178 (C.A.), leave to appeal to S.C.C. refd (1991), 85 D.L.R. (4th) viii*n*; see also *Wolinsky v. General Security Ins. Co.*, [1983] 2 W.W.R. 761 (Man. Q.B.).

[7] 157 N.W.2d 870 (Neb. 1968).

[8] Chapter 15, section 3: Coverage under Professional Liability Policies.

[9] 435 N.Y.S.2d 972 (1980).

[10] 193 Cal. App. 3d 1562 (1987).

[11] (1994), 19 O.R. (3d) 555 (Gen. Div.).

[12] [1983] 1 W.W.R. 424 (Man. Q.B.).

Indemnity Co.,[13] in which it was held that the duties of a corporate secretary are of an administrative nature and do not constitute professional services for the purposes of a lawyer's professional liability policy.

Typically, the insuring agreement in a professional liability policy applies only in respect of claims for damages. Thus, a lawyers' professional liability policy was held not to respond to a claim by a former client seeking a declaration that the lawyer was not entitled to fees.[14]

3. NOTICE REQUIREMENTS

As is the case with business liability policies, professional liability policies invariably require the insured to provide notice of circumstances which may give rise to a claim. Typically, professional liability policies are written on a claims-made basis.[15] Under such policies coverage is usually triggered by the earlier of the date when the claim is made and the date when the insured becomes aware of circumstances which might reasonably be expected to be the basis of a claim.[16] Invariably, there will be a provision that the insured, as soon as is reasonably practicable, give notice to the insurer of any such circumstances.[17] Failure to provide such notice may result in a forfeiture of coverage.

The test applied by the courts in determining whether there has been a breach of the notice requirement combines subjective and objective elements. The subjective element is that the insured must be actually aware of the circumstances which gave rise to the claim. The objective element is whether a reasonably prudent practitioner, with knowledge of those circumstances, would consider that they would likely give rise to a claim. These requirements were discussed in *Moore v. Canadian Lawyers Insurance Assn.*[18] as follows:

> First that the insured lawyer had actually become aware that he had likely breached a duty to his client in the performance of legal services. Otherwise, it could not be said that he had "learned" of such a circumstance. A court could infer such knowledge from the evidence. Secondly, after learning of his probable breach of duty, a lawyer must measure up to the standard of a reasonably prudent lawyer in assessing whether his deficient conduct will likely give rise to a claim; at this stage an objective test applies. The insurer must adduce evi-

---

[13] [1994] O.J. No. 2, 22 C.C.L.I. (2d) 28 (Gen. Div.), revd, [1995] O.J. No. 2823, [1995] I.L.R. 1-3250 (C.A.).

[14] *Warren v. Alberta Lawyers' Public Protection Assn.* [1997] A.J. No. 1041, 56 Alta. L.R. (3d) 52, 48 C.C.L.I. (2d) 107 (Q.B).

[15] For a discussion of claims-made policies see Chapter 7, section 7(b): Claims-Made Policies.

[16] This is a general statement and is not necessarily applicable to all policies. In each case careful attention must be paid to the wording of the particular policy under consideration.

[17] See Chapter 3, section 3: Notice of Accident, Occurrence, Claim or Suit.

[18] [1993] N.S.J. No. 290, 18 C.C.L.I. (2d) 1 (C.A.). See also *Fellowes, McNeil v. Kansa General International Insurance Co.*, 2000 CarswellOnt 3093 (Ont. C.A.), leave to appeal allowed 272 N.R. 194.

dence from which a court could conclude that the lawyer did not meet this test. The lawyer cannot be absolved from the contractual responsibility of reporting as soon as practicable simply because, although he had learned of his probable breach of duty to his client, he did not believe a claim was likely; such a belief must be a belief that would be reasonably held by a prudent solicitor under the circumstances . Thirdly, the insurer must prove the insured failed to report as soon as practicable. If the delay in reporting, after learning of an apparent breach of duty is lengthy, as in this case, the lawyer, as a rule, must adduce some evidence that would support a finding that he acted as a reasonably prudent solicitor would have under the circumstances.[19]

A breach by the insured of the notice requirement does not necessarily result in a forfeiture of coverage. Under statute law the court, where it is equitable to do so, may grant relief against forfeiture.[20]

The decision in *McNish & McNish v. American Home Assurance Co.*[21] provides a good illustration of the notice and relief against forfeiture issues which can arise in the case of a professional liability policy written on a claims-made basis. The insured, a law firm, was covered in successive years under policies obtained by the Law Society of Upper Canada. The law firm received notice of a potential claim in 1981, arising out of an act or omission occurring in 1979. Believing the claim to have been resolved, the law firm did not give notice to its insurers until 1983. The policy in force at the time the notice was given to the insurer provided that there was no coverage with respect to acts or omissions committed prior to the policy period if the insured, on the effective date of this policy, had knowledge that such acts or omissions might be expected to be the basis of a claim or suit. Since the insured had such knowledge, the latter policy did not apply to the claim. Relief against forfeiture was not available because the coverage under the latter policy was never triggered. Coverage was triggered under the policy in force at the time that notice of the claim was received by the insured, even though the insured did not give the insurer notice of the claim during the policy period, but that policy contained, as a condition precedent to any action against the insurer, compliance with a condition requiring the insured to give the insurer prompt notice of any claims. Although the insured was in breach of this condition, the court granted relief against forfeiture on the basis that it was not inequitable to do so.

4. EXCLUSIONS

Professional liability policies contain a number of exclusions designed to:

(i) exclude liability for activities which are separately insured;

---

[19] *Ibid.*, at 5.

[20] See Chapter 3, section 13, Relief Against Forfeiture.

[21] 1989 CarswellOnt 654 (S.C.J.), appeal dismissed 1991 CarswellOnt 647 (C.A.).

(ii) exclude liability for extraordinary risks; and

(iii) exclude liability for "moral" risks, that is, fraud, dishonesty and criminal or malicious acts.

An example of the first sort of exclusion is provided by the kind typically found in a lawyers' professional liability policy with respect to any claims arising out of the insured's activities as an officer or director of a corporation, company or business, other than the practice of law. If the insured requires coverage for that sort of claim then it will be necessary to purchase a directors' and officers' liability policy.[22] A further example, in the context of an errors an omissions policy for environmental consultants, is provided by the decision in *Temple Insurance Co. v. Sirman Associates Ltd.*[23] In addition to providing environmental consulting services, the insured was involved in remediation work with respect to the project. The policy contained a "Design/Build" exclusion, the effect of which was to preclude coverage for any claim arising from services involving physical performance of work on the property. Separate coverage is available with respect to construction risks.

An example of the second sort of exclusion is provided by the "business enterprise" exclusion in a lawyers' professional liability policy, by which coverage is excluded with respect to claims made by a business that is owned or operated by the insured or in which the insured has what the policy deems to be a substantial or controlling interest. The scope of this sort of exclusion was considered in the context of the duty to defend in *Douglas Symes & Brissenden v. LSBC Captive Insurance Co.*[24] The chambers judge gave a broad reading to the exclusion, holding that it applied to most of the claims set out in the pleadings. The British Columbia Court of Appeal appears not to have agreed with this interpretation but did not offer any definitive opinion in that regard. Instead, focusing on the deficiencies in the pleadings, the Court of Appeal held that it could not determine the issue of the duty to defend on the basis of the pleadings as they then stood.[25] In the result, the decision of the chambers judge as to the scope of the exclusion cannot be regarded as having been affirmed.

A similar exclusion in a professional liability policy providing coverage to a real estate agent was considered in *Potts v. Kansa General Insurance Co.*[26] The insured was held liable for negligence in her capacity as a realtor in connection with the sale of a house that she and her husband owned. Although the claim fell within the insuring agreement it was held that coverage was excluded by a provision disallowing claims arising out of "professional services performed by or on behalf of a joint venture of which the insured is a member".

---

[22] See Chapter 11: Directors' and Officers' Liability Insurance.

[23] [2003] O.J. No. 4257, [2004] I.L.R. 1-4255 (C.A.).

[24] [1999] B.C.J. No. 1424, 13 C.C.L.I. (3d) 228 (S.C. in chambers), vard, [2000] B.C.J. No. 1874, 24 C.C.L.I. (3d) 178 (C.A.).

[25] The pleadings were subsequently amended and the issue of the duty to defend was resolved by agreement between the insurer and the insured.

[26] [1987] O.J. No. 1133, 29 C.C.L.I. 94 (H.C.J.).

The third category of exclusion proceeds on the same basis as the intentional injury exclusion in a general liability policy.[27] Professional liability insurance policies are not designed to indemnify the insured in respect of dishonesty, fraud or criminal wrongdoing.[28] In *Fisher v. Guardian Insurance Co. of Canada*,[29] a lawyer was held to be in breach of fiduciary duty when he facilitated the investment of a client's money into a mortgage loan to a corporation in which the lawyer had a large financial interest. The lawyer did not disclose this interest to the client, nor did he advise the client to obtain independent legal advice. The Court noted that an allegation of dishonest intent, as with fraud, must be proven to a high degree of probability. On this basis, the Court was unable to reach the conclusion that the non-disclosure was carried out with a dishonest intent; accordingly, it was held that the exclusion did not apply.

In *Jon Picken v. Guardian Insurance Co. of Canada*,[30] which dealt with a real estate broker's errors and omissions policy, it was held that a breach of fiduciary duty by a real estate agent amounting to constructive fraud fell within the insuring agreement as a "negligent act, error, or omission (including constructive fraud)" and was not caught by an exclusion with respect to "actual fraudulent, criminal or malicious acts". The alleged breach of fiduciary duty in *Jon Picken* was that the real estate agent had presented a purchase offer without disclosing the existence of another purchaser to whom the property was resold a few days later at a substantial profit.

In *Misirlis (Trustee of) v. Continental Insurance Co.*[31] the insured, an insurance agent, placed a policy of credit insurance on behalf of his client with an unlicensed offshore insurer. This was contrary to Ontario law. The client suffered a loss which was not honoured due to the offshore insurer becoming bankrupt. The insurance agent, having been held liable for the loss, sought coverage under his errors and omissions policy. The insurer denied on the basis of an exclusion which provided: "this Policy does not apply to the consequences of any intentional wrongful act, error or omission committed by the Insured." The court found against the insurer, however, on the basis that the insured was merely negligent, that he did not intend to harm his client and his conduct was not reckless.

---

[27] See Chapter 8, section 7: Intentional Injury.

[28] As in *Nichols v. American Home Assur. Co.*, [1988] O.J. No. 90, 30 C.C.L.I. 79 (H.C.J.), affd [1989] O.J. No. 238, 36 C.C.L.I. 204 (C.A.), revd [1990] S.C.J. No. 33, 68 D.L.R. (4th) 321 and *Sternthal c. Boreal Insurance Inc.*, [2004] Q.J. No. 4340 (C.A.).

[29] [1993] B.C.J. No. 1830, [1994] 3 W.W.R. 336, 87 B.C.L.R. (2d) 34, [1994] I.L.R. 1-3006, 18 C.C.L.I. (2d) 305 (S.C.), vard, [1995] B.C.J. No. 651, 123 D.L.R. (4th) 336, [1995] 5 W.W.R. 576, 3 B.C.L.R. (3d) 161, 28 C.C.L.I. (2d) 74 (C.A.).

[30] [1993] O.J. No. 1952, 17 C.C.L.I. (2d) 167 (C.A.).

[31] [2001] O.J. No. 2642, 30 C.C.L.I. (3d) 99 (S.C.J.), appeal dismissed [2002] O.J. No. 4830, [2003] I.L.R. 1-4237 (C.A.).

Chapter 14

PERSONAL LIABILITY INSURANCE

1. FORM OF THE POLICY

Personal liability insurance is available under a variety of forms. It is invariably included as part of the omnibus policy sold to homeowners and tenants. It may also be purchased separately under a comprehensive personal liability form. Some business policies, for example the Farmer's Personal Liability Coverage rider, provide coverage for personal as well as business (farm) risks.

Although the policy wording may differ both among insurers and among the various policy forms, the general purpose of personal liability policies is the same: namely, to provide coverage with respect to certain of the personal activities of the insured, including the risks associated with the occupation of premises, but excluding the risks associated with the operation of a business. This is achieved by a combination of the various insuring agreements with the exclusions from coverage.

2. INSURING AGREEMENT: PERSONAL AND PREMISES LIABILITY

The precise wording of the insuring agreement will depend both upon the particular type of policy purchased and the particular insurer involved. The Insurance Bureau of Canada has adopted a so-called "clear language" program, which has been followed by most underwriters. Under this program, the format of homeowners' and tenants' insurance policies has been substantially altered. Although the intention is that the policies cover the same risks as before, it must be recognized that the different policy wordings may produce different judicial results.

Under the clear language format, instead of just one insuring agreement (as is typical of commercial liability policies) the policy contains a series of insuring agreements, each addressing a different aspect of liability. Coverage is typically provided for compensatory damages that the insured is liable to pay because of bodily injury or property damage arising out of one of the hazards included in the policy. The primary hazards covered in a homeowners' or tenants' policy are bodily injury or property damage resulting from the insured's personal activities anywhere in the world, as well as bodily injury or property damage resulting from the insured's ownership, use or occupancy of premises. Coverage is also generally extended to bodily injury or property damage for which the insured is obligated to pay compensation by reason of the assumption of liability in a written contract or agreement. In addition, most policies extend coverage to include bodily injury to residence employees arising out of and in the course of their employment by the insured and to bodily injury or property damage arising out of the insured's employment by someone else as a sales representative, collector, messenger, clerk or teacher. The term "bodily injury" is typically given an extended definition so as to include coverage for the "personal injury"[1] offences of false arrest and imprisonment, defamation,[2] invasion of right of private occupancy and the like.

An example of the typical personal liability coverage available under a homeowners' or tenants' policy is provided by the Insurance Bureau of Canada's residential policy:

Coverage E — Legal Liability
We will pay all sums which you become legally liable to pay as compensatory damages because of bodily injury or property damage.

The amount of insurance is the maximum amount we will pay, under one or more selections of Coverage E, for all compensatory damages in respect of one accident or occurrence other than as provided under defence, settlement, supplementary payments.

You are insured for claims made against you arising from:
1.   Personal Liability — legal liability arising out of your personal actions anywhere in the world.

You are not insured for claims made against you arising from:
a.   the ownership, use or operation of any motorized vehicle, trailer or watercraft, except those for which coverage is shown in this form;
b.   damage to property you own, use, occupy or lease;
c.   damage to property in your care, custody or control;
d.   damage to personal property or fixtures as a result of work done on them by you or anyone on your behalf;
e.   bodily injury to you or to any person residing in your household other than a residence employee.

2.   Premises liability — legal liability arising out of your ownership, use or occupancy of the premises defined in Section II. This insurance also applies if you assume, by a written contract, the legal liability of other persons in relation to your premises.

You are not insured for claims made against you arising from:
a.   damage to property you own, use, occupy or lease;
b.   damage to property in your care, custody or control;
c.   damage to personal property or fixtures as a result of work done on them by you or anyone on your behalf;
d.   bodily injury to you or to any person residing in your household other than a residence employee.

---

[1]   See Chapter 10: Personal Injury and Advertising Injury Liability Coverage.

[2]   See *Wilkinson v. Security National Insurance Co.*, [1999] A.J. No. 1022 [2000] 9 W.W.R. 127, 81 Alta. L.R. (3d) 149, [2000] I.L.R. 1-3758 (Q.B.) for an example of coverage issues under a homeowners' policy with respect to a defamation claim.

3. Tenants' Legal Liability — legal liability for property damage to premises or their contents which you are using, renting or have in your custody or control caused by fire, explosion, water escape or smoke. This means smoke due to a sudden unusual and faulty operation of any heating or cooking unit in or on the premises, but not smoke from fireplaces. Water escape has the same meaning as in Section I.

You are not insured for liability you have assumed by contract unless your legal liability would have applied even if no contract had been in force.

4. Employers' Liability — legal liability for bodily injury to residence employees arising out of and in the course of their employment by you.

You are not insured for claims made against you resulting from the ownership, use or operation of aircraft, while being operated or maintained by your employee.

You are not insured for liability imposed upon or assumed by you under any Workers Compensation Statute.[3]

For the purposes of liability coverage, the term "premises" is defined as follows:

"Premises" in this Section means all premises where the person(s) named as Insured on the Coverage Summary page, or his or her spouse, maintains a residence. It also includes:
1. other residential premises specified on the Coverage Summary page, except business property and farms;
2. individual or family cemetery plots or burial vaults;
3. vacant land you own or rent, excluding farm land;
4. land where an independent contractor is building a one or two-family residence to be occupied by you;
5. premises you are using or where you are temporarily residing if you do not own such premises.

This extended definition of "premises" was considered in *Woodside v. Gibraltar General Insurance Co.*[4] The insured owned two houses. He was trying to sell the one in which he lived, after which he planned to move into the other. He had purchased liability insurance for the second house but had allowed his coverage for the first house to lapse. An accident occurred at the first house. Noting a term of the policy to the effect that "there are no additional residences except as stated in [the] declaration page" the Court held that the first house did not fall within the extended definition of "premises" and the insured was therefore not able to look to his liability insurer for coverage.

The requirement that the claim be one for bodily injury or property damage was considered in *Ritchie (Litigation Guardian of) v. Barill.*[5] The insureds, as

---

[3] I.B.C. Form 1105.

[4] [1988] O.J. No. 1806, 66 O.R. (2d) 630 (H.C.J.), revd [1991] O.J. No. 114, [1991] I.L.R. 1-2693 (C.A.).

[5] [2002] O.J. No. 1778, [2002] I.L.R. I-4115 (S.C.J.).

trustees, delivered trust funds to an investment advisor for the purchase of bonds. The investment advisor converted the funds to his own use. The beneficiary of the trust brought an action against the trustees for negligence. One of the trustees sought coverage under his homeowner's policy, his argument being that the money had been lost as surely as if it had been destroyed by fire. The court did not agree, noting that as there was no physical damage to or destruction of tangible property, the claim fell outside the insuring agreement.

3. ADDITIONAL COVERAGE FOR VOLUNTARY PAYMENTS

As well as providing coverage for certain forms of contractual and tortious liability, homeowners' and tenants' packages generally provide coverage for voluntary medical payments assumed by the insured where the insured unintentionally injures another person or that person is accidentally injured on the insured's premises, even though the insured is not legally liable for the injuries. The Insurance Bureau of Canada's residential policy provides coverage for voluntary medical payments as follows:

> Coverage F — Voluntary Medical Payments
> We will pay reasonable medical expenses incurred within 1 year of the date of the accident, if you unintentionally injure another person or if they are accidentally injured on your premises. This coverage is available even though you are not legally liable. Medical expenses include surgical, dental, hospital, nursing, ambulance service and funeral expenses. Medical expenses for residence employees are insured.
>
>   The amount of insurance shown on the Coverage Summary page is the maximum amount we will pay for each person in respect of one accident or Occurrence.
>
>   We will not pay expenses covered by any medical, dental, surgical or hospitalization plan or law, or under any other insurance contract.
>
>   We will not pay your medical expenses or those of persons residing with you, other than residence employees.
>
>   We will not pay medical expenses of any person covered by any Workers Compensation Statute.
>
>   You are not insured for claims arising out of the ownership, use or operation of any motorized vehicle, trailer or watercraft, except those for which coverage is shown in this policy.
>
> You shall arrange for the injured person, if requested, to:
> 1.   give us, as soon as possible, written proof of claim, under oath if required;
> 2.   submit to physical examination at our expense by doctors we select as often as we may reasonably require;
> 3.   authorize us to obtain medical and other records.
>
> Proofs and authorizations may be given by someone acting on behalf of the injured person.

It is noted that this coverage is not available to the insured or persons residing with the insured, other than residence employees. The policy does not require, however, that the injury to the residence employee arise in the course and scope of employment.

The policy limits applicable to voluntary medical payments are modest. This type of coverage is valuable, nevertheless, where someone is unintentionally injured by the insured or at the insured's premises.

A similar type of coverage, also with modest limits, is available with respect to voluntary payment for property damage. The Insurance Bureau of Canada's residential policy provides:

> We will pay for unintentional direct damage you cause to property even though you are not legally liable. You may also use this coverage to reimburse others for direct property damage caused intentionally by anyone included in the definition of "you" and "your" in Section II of this form, 12 years of age or under.
>
> You are not insured for claims:
> 1. resulting from the ownership, use or operation of any motorized vehicle, trailer or watercraft, except those for which coverage is provided by this form;
> 2. for property you or your tenants own or rent;
> 3. which are insured under Section I;
> 4. caused by the loss of use, disappearance or theft of property.

4. DEFENCE AND SUPPLEMENTARY PAYMENTS

In addition to paying compensatory damages and voluntary medical payments, homeowners' policies provide coverage for the expenses incurred in defending actions, for all costs charged against the insured in an action defended by the insurer, and for post-judgment interest. The wording of the Insurance Bureau of Canada's residential policy with respect to these matters is as follows:

> We will defend you against any suit which makes claims against you for which you are insured under Coverage E and which alleges bodily injury or property damage and seeks compensatory damages even if it is groundless, false or fraudulent. We reserve the right to investigate, negotiate and settle any claim or suit if we decide this is appropriate.
>
> In addition to the limit of insurance under Coverage E, we will pay:
> 1. all expenses which we incur;
> 2. all costs charged against you in any suit insured under Coverage E;
> 3. any interest accruing after judgment on that part of the judgment which is within the amount of insurance of Coverage E;
> 4. premiums for appeal bonds required in any insured lawsuit involving you and bonds to release any property that is being held as security up to the amount of insurance, but we are not obligated to apply for or provide these bonds;
> 5. expenses which you have incurred for emergency medical or surgical treatment to others following an accident or occurrence insured by this form;

6.　reasonable expenses, except loss of earnings, which you incur at our request.

There is not a uniform practice among insurers with respect to coverage for pre-judgment interest. Some insurers provide coverage for pre-judgment interest in addition to the policy limits;[6] others do not.[7] In some cases the policy language with regard to interest is somewhat obscure. In *Hopkins v. Dockendorff* [8] it was held that a policy that provided coverage for interest that "accrues from the date of action" provided coverage for pre-judgment interest that commenced not with the date of action but on the date that the cause of action arose. Where the policy was silent on the matter of pre-judgment interest, it was held that the policy did, nevertheless, provide coverage with respect to pre-judgment interest, but only within the limits of the policy.[9]

5.　EXCLUSIONS

Personal liability policies of insurance contain a number of exclusions, generally designed to exclude coverage for perils that may be insured separately (for example, business and professional activities) or which are not the sort of perils that insurers wish to cover (for example, intentional injury or transmission of communicable diseases).

(a)　Automobile, Watercraft and Aircraft

As a general rule, homeowners' and tenants' policies of insurance exclude liability arising in any way out of the ownership, maintenance, use, operation, or entrustment to others of motor vehicles or aircraft. Coverage is also excepted for watercraft beyond a specified length or equipped with motors beyond a specified horsepower rating.[10] The reason for these exceptions is that coverage is separately available with respect to the risks imposed by automobiles, aircraft and watercraft. There are certain classes of vehicles, however, such as trailers and all-terrain vehicles, which may be covered under a homeowner's policy, notwithstanding that such vehicles may also be eligible for coverage under an automobile policy.

Thus, in the Insurance Bureau of Canada's residential policy there is an exclusion with respect to claims arising from "the ownership, use or operation of any motorized vehicle, trailer or watercraft except those for which coverage is provided in this form". Coverage is typically extended with respect to liability

---

6　*Schmidt v. Home Ins.* Co., [1984] O.J. No. 586, [1985] I.L.R. 1-1869 (H.C.J.), affd [1986] I.L.R. 1-2033 (C.A.); *Mayo v. Ins. Corp. of B.C.* (1982), 38 B.C.L.R. 376 (S.C.).

7　*United Realty Ltd. v. Guardian Ins. Co. of Can.*, [1986] B.C.J. No. 847, [1987] I.L.R. 1-2193 (C.A.).

8　[1989] B.C.J. No. 800, 40 C.C.L.I. 110 (S.C.).

9　*United Realty Ltd. v. Guardian Ins. Co. of Can.*, *supra*, note 7.

10　In *Pennock v. General Accident Assur. Co. of Can.*, [1994] I.L.R. 1-3054 (Ont. Gen. Div.) the insured tried, unsuccessfully, to have the "or" read as conjunctive rather than disjunctive.

arising out of the use or operation of a trailer, provided it is not being towed by, attached to or carried on a motorized vehicle.[11]

The term "motorized vehicle" is not defined in the policy. In *Gore Mutual Insurance Co. v. Deane*[12] it was held that it should be given its "plain, ordinary, everyday meaning and not a restrictive definition dependent on external conditions or intrinsic problems or defects that determine whether it is at any particular point in time capable of being operated or driven through its own power". On this basis it was held that a homeowner's liability policy did not provide coverage for a claim brought resulting from an automobile chassis being pushed down a hill and striking a pedestrian. In another case, however, coverage was afforded under a tenants' policy in respect of the insured's liability for starting a fire in the course of draining gas from a motorcycle while dismantling it for parts.[13] Because the motorcycle was being dismantled for parts it was no longer being "used" as a motor vehicle.[14]

The scope of the automobile exclusion has been addressed in Chapter 8 with respect to commercial liability policies.[15] The same considerations apply to personal liability policies. Generally speaking, a homeowner's policy, being a comprehensive liability policy, is complementary to a standard automobile policy.[16] Where more than one category of negligence is involved, however, the policies may overlap.[17]

The decision in *Healy v. Blake*[18] provides an interesting example of the coverage considerations which may arise in this context. The insured built a trailer at home which then came apart and caused an accident while being towed by his motor vehicle. The statement of claim alleged that the trailer came apart as a result of improper construction. Nevertheless, it was held that the homeowners' policy did not respond to the claim. An essential element of the insured's negligence was his use of the trailer, without which the loss would not have occurred. Thus the claim arose out of the use of the trailer and coverage was excluded.

An example of the limited coverage that is provided for watercraft and motorized vehicles in a typical homeowner's policy is as follows:

---

[11] In *Masih v. Allstate Insurance Co. of Canada*, [2001] O.J. No. 4357, [2002] I.L.R. 1-4019 (S.C.J.) it was held that a homeowner's policy applied in a case in which the insured left his trailer at the side of the road with a flat tire and a person was fatally injured when struck buy another vehicle while he was changing the tire on the trailer.

[12] [1993] O.J. No. 1457, [1993] I.L.R. 1-2967 at 2447 (Gen. Div.).

[13] *Yip v. Davies*, [1999] B.C.J. No. 1836, [2000] I.L.R. I-3757 (B.C.S.C.).

[14] See also *Meadowview Heights Limited v. Revivo*, [2004] O.J. No. 4742, [2005] I.L.R. I-4354 (S.C.J.).

[15] Section 2: Automobile, Watercraft and Aircraft.

[16] *Cella (Litigation Guardian of) v. McLean*, [1994] O.J. No. 1822, 20 O.R. (3d) 357, [1995] I.L.R. 1-3124 (Gen. Div.), affd, [1997] O.J. No. 2439, 148 D.L.R. (4th) 514, 34 O.R. (3d) 327, [1997] I.L.R. 1-3465, 29 M.V.R. (3d) 292 (C.A.).

[17] *Whitehead v. Whitehead*, [1980] B.C.J. No. 1760, [1984] I.L.R. 1-1820 (S.C.); *Canadian Indemnity Co. v. Security National Ins. Co.*, [1994] 9 W.W.R. 589, 26 C.C.L.I. (2d) 295 (Q.B.).

[18] [2000] O.J. No. 1475, 48 O.R. (3d) 307, 4 M.V.R. (4th) 260 (S.C.J.).

Watercraft

Watercraft You Own. You are insured against claims arising out of your ownership, use or operation of watercraft equipped with an outboard motor or motors of not more than 12 kW (16 HP) in total when used with or on a single watercraft. You are also insured if your watercraft has an inboard or an inboard-outboard motor of not more than 38 kW (50 HP) or for any other type of watercraft not more than 8 metres (26 feet) in length.

If you own any motors or watercraft larger than those stated above, you are insured only if they are shown on the policy. If they are acquired after the effective date of this policy, you will be insured automatically for a period of 320 days only from the date of their acquisition.

Watercraft You Do Not Own. You are insured against claims arising out of your use or operation of watercraft which you do not own, provided:
1.　the watercraft is being used or operated with the owner's consent;
2.　the watercraft is not owned by anyone included in the definition of "you" or "your" in Section II of this form.
You are not insured for damage to the watercraft itself.

Motorized Vehicles

Vehicles You Own. You are insured against claims arising out of your ownership, use or operation of the following including their trailers or attachments:
1.　self-propelled lawn mowers, snow blowers, garden-type tractors of not more than 25 HP, used or operated mainly on your property, provided they are not used for compensation or hire;
2.　motorized golf carts while in use on a golf course;
3.　motorized wheelchairs.

Vehicles You Do Not Own. You are insured against claims arising out of your use or operation of any self-propelled land vehicle, amphibious vehicle or air cushion vehicle including their trailers, which you do not own, provided that:
1.　the vehicle is not licensed and is designed primarily for use off public roads;
2.　you are not using it for business or organized racing;
3.　the vehicle is being used or operated with the owner's consent;
4.　the vehicle is not owned by anyone included in the definition of "you" or "your" in Section II of this form.
You are not insured for damage to the vehicle itself.

Trailers

You are insured against claims arising out of your ownership, use or operation of any trailer or its equipment, provided that such trailer is not being towed by, attached to or carried on a motorized vehicle.

As with most homeowners' policies, this policy language extends coverage with respect to the use of non-owned motor vehicles designed principally for use off public roads, *i.e.*, vehicles such as snowmobiles and all-terrain vehicles. The rationale behind this grant of coverage is that such motor vehicles may not have been registered and insured by the owner. In *Cleworth v. Zackariuk*[19] an issue arose as to whether the motor vehicle exclusion applied in circumstances where

---

[19]　[1987] B.C.J. No. 126, 11 B.C.L.R. (2d) 125 (C.A.).

the insured's 16-year-old son was operating a snowmobile owned by his father. The exclusion provided that there was no coverage with respect to "the use by an insured of any automobile, except in respect of an automobile not owned by the Insured, designed for use principally off public roads". The term "Insured" was defined to include the Named Insured, that is, the father, and residents of his household, which included his son. The insurer argued that the use of the capital "I" in the term "Insured" indicated that the term was to be read in conjunction with the definition accorded that term in the policy. On that basis, there would be no coverage with respect to the use by one insured of a snowmobile owned by another person insured under the same policy. The British Columbia Court of Appeal, however, did not agree. It was held that the exclusion applied only with respect to the use by an insured of a snowmobile owned by that particular insured. While this decision is perhaps a proper application of the rule of *contra proferentem*, it does lead to the somewhat unusual result that all members of a household would enjoy insurance protection with respect to off-road vehicles except the owner, who, presumably, is the person most in need of it.

In *Smith v. Dewitt*[20] it was asserted on behalf of the insured that the watercraft coverage provisions were ambiguous and that the phrase "any other type of watercraft not more than 8 metres (26 feet) in length" should include coverage for a 19-foot boat with a 120-horsepower engine. The Court did not agree, holding that the intent of the policy was to provided coverage with respect only to three types of watercraft, namely those with an outboard motor of not more than 16 horsepower, those with an inboard or inboard-outboard motor of not more than 50 horsepower, and unmotorized watercraft of not more than 26 feet in length.

(b) Business Pursuits and Professional Activities

As a general rule, personal liability policies are not designed to provide coverage for liability arising out of the insured's business or professional activities. Coverage for those activities may be purchased separately. Accordingly, personal liability policies typically contain exclusions with respect to liability arising out of business pursuits or professional services. In past years, the business pursuits exclusion usually contained an exception with respect to activities of the insured which, although they occur in the course of a business, are ordinarily incidental to non-business pursuits.

The Insurance Bureau of Canada's residential policy provides limited coverage for business activities as follows:

> You are insured against claims arising out of:
> 1.   your work for someone else as a sales representative, collector, messenger or clerk, provided that the claim does not involve injury to a fellow employee;
> 2.   your work as a teacher, provided the claim does not involve physical disciplinary action to a student or injury to a fellow employee;

---

[20]   [1997] I.L.R. 1-3472, [1997] O.J. No. 1588 (Gen. Div.).

3. the occasional rental of your residence to others; rental to others of a one or two-family dwelling usually occupied in part by you as a residence, provided no family unit includes more than 2 roomers or boarders;
4. the rental of space in your residence to others for incidental office, school or studio occupancy;
5. the rental to others, or holding for rent, of not more than 3 car spaces or stalls in garages or stables;
6. activities during the course of your trade, profession or occupation which are ordinarily considered to be non-business pursuits;
7. the temporary or part time business pursuits of an insured person under the age of 21 years;

Claims arising from the following business pursuits are insured only if the properties or operations are declared on the Coverage Summary page:
1. the rental of residential buildings containing not more than 6 dwelling units;
2. the use or part of your residence by you for incidental office, school or studio occupancy.

Apart from this coverage, liability is excluded with respect to claims arising from business or professional activities:

You are not insured for claims arising from: ...
3. Your business or any business use at your premises except as specified in this policy;
4. The rendering or failure to render any professional service. ...

The term "business" is defined as "any continuous or regular pursuit undertaken for financial gain including a trade, profession or occupation". The business exclusion has received extensive consideration in the United States.[21] In determining what constitutes a business, the courts have generally been guided by two factors: (1) that the activity is one in which the insured is regularly engaged and (2) that the activity is carried out for the purpose of earning income.[22] On this basis, a variety of activities conducted at home have been held to be business pursuits, including babysitting,[23] craft-making[24] and real estate sales.[25]

---

[21]   "Construction and Application of 'Business Pursuits' Exclusion Provision in General Liability Policy" (1973) 48 A.L.R. (3d) 1096; Frazier, "The Business-Pursuits Exclusion Revisited" (February 1977) 579 Ins. L.J. 88; David J. Marchitelli, Annotation, "Construction and Application of 'Business Pursuits' Exclusion Provision in General Liability Policy" (1996) 35 A.L.R. (5th) 375.

[22]   *State Farm Fire & Casualty Co. v. Moore*, 430 N.E.2d 641 (1981); *Fadden v. Cambridge Mutual Ins.*, 51 Misc.2d 858, 274 N.Y.S.2d 235 (1966), affd 27 App. Div. 2d 487, 280 N.Y.S.2d 209 (1967).

[23]   *Tam (Litigation guardian of) v. Lee*, [1998] O.J. No. 4567, 167 D.L.R. (4th) 353, [1999] I.L.R. 1-3684 (Gen. Div.); *State Farm Fire & Casualty Co. v. Moore, ibid.*

[24]   *Riverside Ins. Co. v. Kolonich*, 329 N.W.2d 528 (1982).

[25]   *Callahan v. American Motorist Ins. Co.*, 289 N.Y.S.2d 1005 (1968).

The scope of the exception to the exclusion of activities ordinarily incidental to business pursuits has also received considerable attention in the American courts, with conflicting results. Some courts have found the exception obscure,[26] others have found it to be clear and unambiguous.[27] Considered in context, it would seem that the exception should be applied whenever the act or omission giving rise to the claim is not one that falls within the insured's business duties. As one court noted, "the appropriate inquiry is not whether the insured was engaged in a business pursuit at the time of the accident, but whether the particular activity was nevertheless one ordinarily incidental to non-business pursuits".[28]

The activity that most often generates discussion on the business pursuits exclusion is in-home babysitting for remuneration. Most courts agree that such activity, if conducted on a regular basis, clearly constitutes a business pursuit.[29] There is disagreement, however, on the circumstances in which the exception as to incidental activities should apply. Many injuries which occur during the course of babysitting at home could be characterized as either negligent supervision of the child (in which case there would be no coverage) or as incidental to a non-business pursuit (in which case coverage would be available). For example, in *Allstate Insurance Co. v. Kelsey*[30] the majority of the Oregon Court of Appeals was of the view that the business pursuits exclusion precluded coverage for an insured babysitter where the child she was babysitting was crushed to death by a ladder which fell on him in his playpen. The majority rejected the argument that the ladder, being the instrument causing the death, was not connected to the babysitting. Rather, the majority characterized the cause as being the insured's failure to maintain the premises in a safe condition. The dissenting opinion expressed the view that coverage should be provided, for the harm-producing activity, that is, the placement of the ladder, was not incidental to a business pursuit.

In Canada, the business pursuits exclusion has been considered on a number of occasions. It has been held to apply in *Tam v. Lee*,[31] *Kaler v. Red River Valley Mutual Insurance Co.*,[32] *Seeton v. Commercial Union Assurance Co. of Canada*,[33] *Canadian Universities' Reciprocal Insurance v. Halwell Mutual Insurance Co.*[34] and *Stoyka v. General Accident Assurance Co. of Canada*.[35] The

---

[26] *State Farm Fire & Casualty Co. v. MacDonald*, 230 N.E.2d 513 (1967).

[27] *Aetna Ins. Co. v. Janson*, 377 N.E.2d 296 (1978).

[28] *State Farm Fire & Casualty Co. v. Moore, supra*, note 22

[29] *State Farm Fire & Casualty Co. v. Moore, supra*, note 22. *Tam (Litigation guardian of) v. Lee, supra*, note 23.

[30] 67 Or. App. 349 (1984).

[31] *Supra*, note 23. Child care was provided on an almost daily basis for six months.

[32] [1995] M.J. No. 284, 102 Man. R. (2d) 136 (C.A.).

[33] [1999] N.W.T.J. No. 57, 41 C.P.C. (4th) 361 (S.C.).

[34] [1998] O.J. No. 5322 [1999] I.L.R. 1-3663 (Gen. Div.), appeal dismissed [2002] O.J. No. 3306, [2003] I.L.R. 1-4133 (C.A.).

[35] [2002] O.J. No. 539, 36 C.C.L.I. (3d) 296 (S.C.J.). The insured performed electrical services in exchange for legal fees.

exclusion was held not to apply in *Wilkinson v. Security National Insurance Co.*[36] and *Rocovitis v. Dominion of Canada General Insurance Co.*[37]

In *Kaler* the insured, a taxi driver, fatally injured a passenger during an altercation over the passenger's failure to pay the fare. Although the altercation took place in a convenience store some 20 minutes after the passenger left the vehicle, the Court held that this did not break the chain of causation; the injury arose directly as a result of the insured's business activities.

The decision in *Seeton* arose out of a wrongful death action commenced following a deliberate explosion which occurred during a labour dispute at the Giant Mine in Yellowknife. The insureds, all union members and including a union officer, sought a defence under their homeowners' policies with respect to a claim alleging that their negligence created an atmosphere which led to the explosion. The Court held that the claim, being in connection with the insureds' employment, arose out of business pursuits and coverage was thereby excluded.

In *Canadian Universities' Reciprocal Insurance v. Halwell Mutual Insurance Co.* the insured, a university student, was president of a residence, a paid position. An action seeking damages was commenced against him by a student seriously injured in an initiation game. The university's insurer sought contribution from the insured's homeowners' policy. It was held, however, that the claim arose out of the insured's paid position as president of the residence and was therefore excluded.

In *Rocovitis* the insured provided occasional handyman services to a single customer. Over the course of three years he issued approximately 30 invoices for a total of approximately $2,200, a substantial portion of which consisted of reimbursement for parts. Labour charges were nominal. The court considered that the insured's activities in this regard were casual and irregular and in the nature of a hobby. The business pursuits exclusion was held not to apply.

(c) Intentional Injury or Criminal Act

Whether by a specific exclusion or by the terms used in the insuring agreement, liability for intentionally caused harm is not covered under a personal liability policy. Coverage is also generally excluded for bodily injury or property damage resulting from a criminal act or failure to act. The Insurance Bureau of Canada's residential policy contains the following exclusion:

> You are not insured for claims arising from: ...
>
> 5.   bodily injury or property damage caused by any intentional or criminal act or failure to act by:
>
>   a.   any person insured by this policy; or

---

[36]   [1999] A.J. No. 1022, [2000] 9 W.W.R. 127, 81 Alta. L.R. (3d) 149, [2000] I.L.R. 1-3758 (Q.B.). The insured uttered statements, alleged to be defamatory, after he had left his employment.

[37]   [2003] O.J. No. 297, 46 C.C.L.I. (3d) 310 (S.C.J.); affd, [2004] O.J. No. 4326, 16 C.C.L.I. (4th) 207 (C.A.).

b.   any other person at the direction of any person insured by this policy.

Cases considering this and similar exclusions are noted in Chapter 8[38] and Chapter 15.[39] As noted in *Wilkieson-Valiente v. Wilkieson*[40] the exclusion may be expressed in terms either of "*an* insured" or "*the* insured". This slight difference in wording has a profound impact on coverage for a co-insured, innocent of the intentional injury, but alleged to be liable in negligence for the actions of the other insured person. In the case in which the exclusion is with respect to "*an* insured", then if one insured is guilty of an intentional injury coverage is also excluded with respect to the innocent co-insured.[41] In the case in which the exclusion is with respect to "*the* insured", however, it will apply only to the particular insured guilty of the intentional wrongdoing.[42] The reference to "criminal act" in the exclusion above appears to be intended to further restrict coverage where the injury or damage, although not subjectively intended by the insured, is the result of the insured's criminal act.

The application of this exclusion often involves issues of causation. As noted in Chapter 8,[43] provided the insured acts with the intention of causing injury or damage, however slight, then the intentional injury exclusion will apply, even though the injury which is caused by the act is different in character or magnitude to that which was intended. The same principle applies with respect to the "criminal act" component to the exclusion set out above. In *British Columbia Insurance Corporation v. Kraiger*[44] the insured set a fire in the forest with the intention that it burn until firefighters arrived to extinguish it. The fire burned out of control and soon engulfed a number of homes. The insured, who plead guilty to arson, argued that he did not intend for the fire to escape the forest and spread to the residential area; indeed, when he realized how quickly the fire was spreading he unsuccessfully tried to put it out. In these circumstances, the insured argued that the criminal act exclusion should apply only in respect of the fire damage in the forest and not to the damage to the homes. The British Columbia Court of Appeal did not agree. The cause of the loss was the arson fire started by the insured. His attempt to put out the fire could not be said to be an intervening or supervening act serving to legally isolate him from the consequences of starting the fire. Rather, he simply failed at trying to undo what he had started.

Whether proof of a criminal conviction is conclusive evidence for the application of the exclusion was considered in *The Halifax Insurance Co. v. O'Don-*

---

[38] See Chapter 8, section 7: Intentional Injury.

[39] See Chapter 15, section 2(d): Intentional Injuries.

[40] [1996] O.J. No. 2102 I.L.R. 1-3351 (Gen. Div.).

[41] *Thompson v. Warriner*, [2002] O.J. No. 1769 (C.A.); *D.C. v. Royal & Sun Alliance Insurance Co. of Canada*, [2004] O.J. No. 4587 (S.C.J.).

[42] *Godonoaga (Litigation Guardian of) v. Khatambakhsh*, [2000] O.J. No. 2172, 20 C.C.L.I. (3d) 262 (C.A.).

[43] See Chapter 8, section 7: Intentional Injury.

[44] [2002] B.C.J. No. 2132, 41 C.C.L.I. (3d) 10 (C.A.).

nell. [45] The insured, while hunting, fired his rifle at what he took to be a deer. In fact he shot at a vehicle, a passenger of which was seriously injured. In a civil action the insured was held liable for negligence. In criminal proceedings, in which he did not testify, he was found guilty under the *Criminal Code* of Canada of the offence of careless use of a firearm. The insurer argued that by proving the conviction it brought the claim within the criminal act exclusion. The New Brunswick Court of Appeal did not agree. Although the conviction was *prima facie* evidence that the offence had been committed, it was open to the insured to lead evidence to the contrary. The Court of Appeal held that the trial judge's findings of fact were consistent with civil liability for negligence but did not demonstrate such a marked departure from the standard of a reasonable person so as to invoke criminal liability.

(d) Claims by One Insured against Another Insured

Depending upon the application of any cross-liability clause[46] a homeowner's policy will usually not provide coverage for a property damage claim brought by one insured against another person insured under the same policy.[47] In addition, most homeowners' policies contain an exclusion with respect to claims arising from bodily injury to the insured or to any person residing in the insured's household, other than a residence employee. These exclusions may appear either separately in the policy or combined in one clause.

The scope of these exclusions was considered by the Ontario Court of Appeal in the twin appeals in *Sheppard v. The Co-Operators General Insurance Co.; Quick v. MacKenzie.*[48] In *Sheppard* the insured's four-year-old son was struck by a car while he was playing in the street. Proceedings were commenced on his behalf against the driver of the vehicle. The driver, in turn, brought a counterclaim against the child's mother alleging that she was negligent in the supervision of her child. She sought coverage under her homeowners' policy, which contained the following exclusion:

> You are not insured for claims arising from:
>
> ... or between any person(s) insured by this policy named or not;

The insurer maintained that the exclusion applied to the claim brought by the defendant driver against the insured on the basis that the claim "arose" from the infant plaintiff, who was a person insured under the policy. The Court did not agree; in the Court's view the claim arose from the insured mother's alleged

---

[45] [2001] N.B.J. No. 432, [2002] I.L.R. I-4057 (C.A.).

[46] See Chapter 6, section 3(i): Severability of Insureds or "Cross-Liability".

[47] This was the result in *Romay Automotive Ltd. v. Dominion of Can. General Ins. Co.* (1974), 2 O.R. (2d) 506 (H.C.J.).

[48] [1995] O.J. No. 1024, 23 O.R. (3d) 117, [1995] I.L.R. 1-3231 (Gen. Div.), revd, [1997] O.J. No. 1600, 33 O.R. (3d) 362, [1997] I.L.R. 1-3437 (C.A.).

negligent supervision. The fact that the child's presence was necessary for the claim to arise did not mean that it arose *from* him.

In *Quick* the insured plaintiffs' infant daughter was bitten by the defendant's dog. The defendant filed a counterclaim against the insureds, alleging vicarious liability for the actions of their nanny and direct responsibility for their lack of supervision of their daughter. The homeowners' policy contained the following exclusion:

> You are not insured for claims made against you arising from:
> e.   bodily injury to you or to any person residing in your household other than a residence employee.

The insurer maintained that it was not required to defend the counterclaim, for it arose out of bodily injury to the insureds' daughter, who was a resident of the household. The lower Court disagreed, noting that although the injury was a precondition to the counterclaim, the counterclaim "arose", to use the language of the policy, for vicarious liability and lack of supervision, which is quite apart from the injury itself. The Court of Appeal, however, took a different view of the matter. The latter Court was of the opinion that the claim had its origin in the bodily injury to the insureds' daughter and therefore fell within the exclusion. The Court justified the different results reached in the *Sheppard* and *Quick* appeals on the basis that in the former case the exclusion was broad to the point of being almost meaningless, whereas in the latter case the wording of the exclusion was precisely focused.

There has been considerable litigation over the meaning of the terms "household" and "resident", for, in addition to being used in an exclusion clause, these terms are often used to extend coverage by defining the class of insured persons covered by the liability portion of the policy. Of course, the meaning of a word is affected by the context in which it is found; therefore, a decision interpreting "household" in a provision extending coverage may not be authority for the interpretation of the same term in an exclusionary provision, and vice versa.

The leading Canadian case on the meaning of "household" in a policy exclusion is *Wawanesa Mutual Insurance Co. v. Bell*,[49] a decision concerning a provision in a motor vehicle liability policy extending coverage to automobiles temporarily used by the owner provided that the automobile was "not owned by the insured nor by any person or persons of the household of which the insured was a member". The Court was unanimous in finding that a man who paid room and board to his brother while living in his brother's house was not "of the household". Justice Rand stated that:

> The "household", in the broad sense of a family, is a collective group living in a home, acknowledging the authority of a head, the members of which, with few exceptions, are bound by marriage, blood, affinity or other bond, between

---

[49]   [1957] S.C.R. 581.

whom there is an intimacy and by whom there is felt a concern with and an interest in the life of all that gives it a unity. It may, for example, include such persons as domestic servants, and distant relatives permanently residing within it. To some degree they are all admitted and submit to the collective body, its unity and its conditions, particularly that of the general discipline of the family head.[50]

Justice Rand went on to draw a distinction between persons who are "of the household" and persons who are "in a household", the latter category being the larger as it may include relatives or outsiders who are temporarily guests in the household.

Justice Rand's characterization of a household being determined largely by submission to the general discipline of the "family head" should now be considered as archaic. It appears, nevertheless, that there must be some sort of intimacy, community or domestic nexus between persons in order to constitute a household.[51] Thus, in *McWhirter v. State Farm Mutual Automobile Insurance Co.*,[52] it was held that two unmarried men who roomed together, having their separate interests and leading separate lives, did not constitute a household. Nor was a separated spouse a part of a household when he was a frequent visitor at his estranged wife's premises strictly for the purpose of seeing his son.[53] Where an estranged spouse did intend to return, however, and where the marriage was marked by a series of cohabitations, separations and reconciliations, a household was held to exist.[54]

The meaning of the term "resident" has also been considered in a number of cases. The issue usually arises with respect to persons who are temporarily either at or away from the insured premises. In order to be considered a "resident" there must be a notion of permanence or an intention to stay for an indefinite period of time.[55] Persons who are merely visitors to the insured premises are not residents, even though they may stay in the premises for a period of weeks or months,[56] and even though they do not reside anywhere else. In *Appel (Guardian ad litem of) v. Dominion of Canada General*

---

[50] *Ibid.*, at 584.

[51] *Wade v. Canadian Northern Shield Ins. Co.*, [1986] B.C.J. No. 3004, (1986), 5 B.C.L.R. (2d) 62, 18 C.C.L.I. 173 (S.C.); *Murphy v. Beaton*, [1992] N.S.J. No. 251, 114 N.S.R. (2d) 187 (T.D.); *Snair v. Halifax Ins. Nationale-Nederlanden North America Corp.*, [1995] N.S.J. No. 424, 145 N.S.R. (2d) 132, [1996] I.L.R. 1-3286 (S.C.); *Wait v. Travelers Ins. Co.*, 331 N.W.2d 643 (1983); *Quinlen v. Cooms*, 314 N.W.2d 125 (1981).

[52] (1959), 21 D.L.R. (2d) 743 (Ont. H.C.J.).

[53] *Sullivan v. Sask. Mutual Ins. Co.*, [1975] I.L.R. 1-651 (B.C.S.C.).

[54] *Boasley v. British America Ins. Co.* (1976), 15 O.R. (2d) 120 (Co. Ct.), leave to appeal dismissed (1976), 15 O.R. (2d) 120n (C.A.).

[55] *Appel (Guardian ad litem of) v. Dominion of Can. General Ins. Co.*, [1995] B.C.J. no. 1760, 32 C.C.L.I. (2d) 92 (S.C.), affd, [1997] B.C.J. No. 1794, [1998] 1 W.W.R. 592, 39 B.C.L.R. (3d) 113 (C.A.); *Sequeira v. Sequeira*, [1995] B.C.J. No. 58, 30 C.C.L.I. (2d) 298 (S.C.); *Wright v. Canadian Group Underwriters Insurance Co.*, [2000] I.L.R. 1-3858, [2000] B.C.J. No. 1441 (S.C.).

[56] *Puente v. Arroyo*, 366 So.2d 857 (1979).

Insurance Co.[57] a mother and her child lived with the child's grandparents temporarily while they were looking for a new home. For the purposes of an exclusion clause in the grandparents' homeowners' policy it was held that the child was not "residing" in the household. On the other hand, persons who are absent from the premises, even for an extended period of time, such as students, may still be residents of the household.[58] In determining whether a child has left home, the factors considered by the courts include whether a child keeps belongings at the premises, has a key to the premises, is free to return without making special arrangements, and intends to return to the premises.[59]

6. PERSONS INSURED

The persons insured under the liability portion of a homeowners' policy are usually defined by class rather than by name. This leads to disputes over whether a particular person does or does not fall within the insured class.

The class of persons in addition to the named insured covered under a homeowners' policy generally includes members of the household who are either relatives of the insured or are under the age of 21 and in the care of an insured. In addition, persons engaged in various activities may be covered under the liability portion of the policy; for example, residence employees while performing their duties as such, and persons legally responsible for watercraft owned by an insured.

In the Insurance Bureau of Canada's residential policy those persons insured by the policy are referred to as "you", which is defined as follows:

> "You" or "your" means the person(s) named as Insured on the Coverage Summary page and while living in the same household, his or her husband or wife, the relatives of either or any person under 21 in their care. Husband and wife include a man and a woman who are living together as husband and wife and have so lived together continuously for a period of 3 years or if a child was born of their union for a period of 1 year. Only the person(s) named on the Coverage Summary page may take legal action against us.

> "You" or "your" in this Section have the same meanings as in Section I. In addition, the following persons are insured:
>
> 1. any person or organization legally liable for damages caused by a water-craft or animal owned by you, and to which this insurance applies. This does not include anyone using or having custody of the watercraft or animal in the course of any business or without the owner's permission;
>
> 2. a residence employee while performing duties in connection with the ownership, use or operation of motorized vehicles and trailers for which coverage is provided in this form;

---

[57] *Supra*, note 55.
[58] *Sullivan v. Sask. Mutual Ins. Co.*, *supra*, note 53; *Schoemann v. Skate Country Inc.*, 459 So.2d 743 (1984).
[59] *Flannigan v. Valiant*, 371 So.2d 349 (1979).

3. your legal representative having temporary custody of the insured premises, if you die while insured by this form, for legal liability arising out of the insured premises;

4. any person who is insured by this form at the time of your death and who continues residing on the insured premises.

The meanings of the terms "household" and "resident" are discussed above.[60]

---

[60] Section 5(d): Claims by One Insured against Another Insured.

Chapter 15

INSURANCE COVERAGE FOR SEXUAL TORTS

The 1990s witnessed an unprecedented number of actions brought before the courts in Canada concerning civil liability for sexual torts. For the most part these claims involve the alleged sexual molestation of children. The category of sexual torts, however, also includes claims concerning sexual interference with adults by, for example, a doctor, therapist or pastoral counsellor, as well as claims concerning sexual harassment, often in a workplace setting.

Determining what insurance coverage, if any, is available to a defendant in such an action is often a daunting task. Where the claim involves matters which took place many years in the past it is often difficult for the parties to obtain details of the insurance policy in force at the relevant time. Even when the policy is located it may be in a form which is no longer in use today and which is not at all familiar to modern day practitioners. Issues may well arise over what persons and activities are covered by the policy. Moreover, because molesters often have a number of victims and commit their offences over a number of years, issues frequently arise as to when the loss or damage occurs and what constitutes an occurrence for the purposes of the application of the policy. There is some similarity in this regard to the issues that arise with respect to environmental claims.[1]

The defendants named in actions concerning sexual torts frequently extend beyond the individual alleged to have committed the offence. Employers, institutions, government bodies and even spouses are often alleged to be responsible, whether vicariously or for some independent act of negligence or breach of fiduciary duty. When determining insurance coverage in a particular case, close attention must be paid to the particular nature of the claim. As a general rule, no coverage will be available for a defendant guilty of committing an intentional tort,[2] but it may be available to someone responsible whether (i) vicariously, or (ii) for negligence in hiring, supervision or failing to warn, or (iii) for breach of fiduciary duty.

1. PROVING THE POLICY

In cases involving sexual abuse alleged to have occurred many years in the past, the parties may encounter difficulty in proving either the existence of a policy or

---

[1] See Chapter 7, section 7: Period Coverage.

[2] See section 2(d): Intentional Injuries.

the nature of its terms. Although claims-made coverage is now available for sexual abuse claims, in most historical abuse cases, if coverage is available at all it will be found in the policy which existed when the injury occurred.

The burden of proving the terms of the policy rests with the insured.[3] Where the policy document is still in the possession of the insured this burden is easily met. But where the insured no longer has the policy, it will be necessary to either obtain it through other means or prove its terms with secondary evidence, which is admissible provided the insured can establish that the original documents did exist, that they have been lost or destroyed, and that a diligent and appropriate search for them has been made.[4] In cases where secondary evidence is relied upon, a number of American authorities favour the view that the standard of proof is that of the balance of probabilities rather than the more onerous standard, applied in the case of lost deeds, of clear and convincing evidence.[5] The balance of probabilities approach has also been followed in Canada.[6]

Generally speaking, insurers do not keep copies of each individual policy of insurance which they sell. Instead, because the policies are for the most part pre-printed forms, insurers simply keep track of the designation of the particular form which was sold to the insured along with the information set out in the declarations.[7] Provided that this information has been kept on file, and provided that a copy of the particular coverage form is still available, then the policy can be accurately reconstructed. Given the inevitable purging of files that has taken place over the years, especially with the development of computerization, this is often easier said than done.

Another source for details of insurance coverage is the insured's agent or broker. Typically the agent will have the information set out in the declarations and, possibly, copies of the various policy forms in use. If the policy is in manuscript form then the agent may very well have a copy of the very policy itself.

The more difficult cases are those in which the existence of the policy is known (whether through invoices, cancelled cheques or otherwise) but neither the insured, the insurer nor the agent is able to locate copies of the policy

---

[3] *W. (T.) v. W. (K.R.J.)*, [1996] O.J. No. 2102, 29 O.R. (3d) 277, [1996] I.L.R. 1-3351, 39 C.C.L.I. (2d) 272 (Gen. Div.); *Synod of the Diocese of Edmonton v. Lombard General Insurance Co. of Canada*, [2004] A.J. No. 1287, 20 C.C.L.I. (4th) 221 (Q.B.).

[4] *Catholic Children's Aid Society of Hamilton-Wentworth v. Dominion of Canada General Insurance Co.*, [1998] O.J. No. 3720, 7 C.C.L.I. (3d) 11 (Gen. Div.).

[5] *Rubenstein v. Royal Insurance Co.*, 44 Mass. App. Ct. 842 (1998), [1998] M.A.-QL 173 (Mass. C.A.); *Gold Fields American Corp. v. Aetna Casualty & Surety Company*, [1997] NY-QL 11437 (New York); *National American Insurance Company of California v. Underwriters at Lloyd's London*, 60 F.3d 536 (9th Cir. C.A. 1995); *cf. W.M. Barr & Co. v. Commercial Union*, [1997] TN-QL 2278 (Tenn. C.A.).

[6] *Catholic Children's Aid Society of Hamilton-Wentworth v. Dominion of Canada General Insurance Co.*, *supra*, note 4; *Synod of the Diocese of Edmonton v. Lombard General Insurance Co. of Canada*, *supra*, note 3.

[7] See Chapter 2, section 2(a)(i): Declarations.

wording.[8] In such cases the insured will have to expand the search so as to include other sources where the policy form may be found. These sources include old claim files and litigation files involving the same insured or even another insured who may have purchased the same policy.

In *M. (E.) v. Reed* [9] the policy in question was in manuscript form and was issued in 1963. An issue arose as to whether the insurer was required to defend the insured in the underlying litigation. The insured had kept the manuscript wording but had thrown away the policy jacket, which, on the evidence, typically contained the provision relating to the duty to defend. The court, noting that the policy had been negotiated by a broker on the insured's behalf, that the broker would have been alert to something as basic as a missing defence provision and that it would have been remarkable for such a policy not to contain a defence provision, ruled in favour of the insured.

2. COVERAGE UNDER COMMERCIAL LIABILITY POLICIES

Only in recent years have commercial liability insurers directly addressed coverage considerations pertaining to sexual torts. Depending upon the type of coverage purchased, there may be either a partial or complete exclusion with respect to liability arising from sexual abuse[10] or sexual harassment or there may be policy wording designed to specifically cover such claims.

Many of the claims currently before our courts, however, had their genesis at a time when business liability policies were written on an occurrence basis and were silent on the issue of sexual torts. In these cases coverage should be analyzed in the fashion set out in Chapter 6.[11] When dealing with policies other than the Comprehensive General Liability form,[12] especially policy forms which pre-date the development of the CGL form, very close attention must be paid to the wording of the insuring agreement. Unlike that in the CGL form, coverage may be restricted to liability arising out of certain designated operations or out of the occupation of certain designated premises, and coverage in respect of bodily injury may not be on the same broad basis as found in CGL policies.[13]

---

[8]   As in *Navy League of Canada v. Citadel General Assurance Co.*, [2003] O.J. No. 3192 (S.C.J.).

[9]   [2000] O.J. No. 4791, 24 C.C.L.I. (3d) 229 (S.C.J.), affd [2003] O.J. No. 1791 (C.A.), leave to appeal to S.C.C. dismissed, [2003] S.C.C.A. No. 334.

[10]   See *Children's Aid Society of Halifax v. Boreal Insurance Company* [1996] N.S.J. No. 508, 155 N.S.R. (2d) 221, [1997] I.L.R. 1-3431 (S.C.) for an example of a clause excluding liability for claims "resulting from ... or alleging sexual behaviour or physical, mental or emotional abuse".

[11]   Section 2: Structure of a Commercial Liability Policy.

[12]   See Chapter 6, section 1: Types of Commercial Policies.

[13]   See, for example, *American Empire Surplus Lines Ins. v. Bay Area Cab Lease*, 756 F.Supp. 1287 (ND Cal. 1991) in which it was held that coverage under an Owners', Landlords' and Tenants' policy was restricted to accidents occurring on the defendant taxicab company's premises and therefore did not provide coverage to the company when its employee molested a child in a taxicab.

With respect to CGL policies in general, coverage is provided for damages resulting from accidents or occurrences that take place during the policy period.[14] In the context of sexual abuse claims, coverage issues often arise concerning what constitutes a "bodily injury", what constitutes an "occurrence" for the purpose of triggering coverage and determining policy limits, and whether the claim falls within any exclusions pertaining to criminal acts or intentional injuries. Issues may also arise as to coverage under other forms of commercial liability insurance such as employment practices liability and personal injury liability insurance.

(a) Bodily Injury

The standard form of the CGL policy provides coverage in respect of "bodily injury", which is typically defined as:

> Bodily injury, sickness or disease sustained by any person which occurs during the policy period, including death at any time resulting therefrom.

In Canada it has been held that this definition extends "bodily injury" beyond mere physical trauma, such that any sickness or disease, physical or mental, is included. The Manitoba Queen's Bench, in *Victoria General Hospital v. General Accident Assurance Co. of Canada*,[15] held that the insuring agreement in a comprehensive general liability policy in respect of "bodily injury, sickness or disease" provided coverage for a claim for severe emotional trauma consequent upon incidents of sexual abuse. The British Columbia Court of Appeal, in *Wellington Guarantee v. Evangelical Lutheran Church in Canada*,[16] held that nervous shock, depression and psychological trauma resulting from sexual abuse amounted to "bodily injury, sickness or disease" for the purposes of an *exclusion* in a directors' and officers' liability policy. Both Courts noted that "sickness" includes the impairment of mental health. Although both decisions stand for the proposition that "bodily" modifies solely "injury", they could arguably be explained on the alternative basis that severe psychological trauma is often accompanied by physical symptoms so as to result in "bodily injury".[17]

(b) Whether Sexual Abuse Is an Occurrence

Commercial liability insurance policies typically provide coverage for property damage caused by an occurrence. With respect to bodily injury claims, however, the insuring agreement may be written either in terms of bodily injury caused by

---

[14] For a detailed analysis of the CGL insuring agreement see Chapter 7.

[15] [1995] M.J. No. 276, [1995] 8 W.W.R. 106, 103 Man. R. (2d) 168 (Q.B.). See also *Children's Aid Society of Halifax v. Boreal Insurance Co.*, *supra*, note 10.

[16] (1995), 29 C.C.L.I. (2d) 93 (B.C.S.C.), revd [1996] B.C.J. No. 872 [1996] 9 W.W.R. 373 (C.A.); leave to appeal to S.C.C. refd (1996), 39 C.C.L.I. (2d) 12*n*.

[17] *Voorhees v. Preferred Mutual Insurance Co.*, 607 A.2d 1255 (N.J. 1992). See also the discussion in Chapter 7, section 4(a): Bodily Injury.

an occurrence or simply as bodily injury with no qualification as to how it arises. In the latter case there is invariably an exclusion with respect to intentional injuries; in the former case there may also be such an exclusion, even though it would be superfluous, given that the concept of an occurrence already precludes intentionally caused harm.[18]

In those cases where coverage for bodily injury is expressed in terms of having been caused by an "occurrence", this is generally defined along the lines of "an accident, including continuous or repeated exposure to substantially the same general harmful conditions". In the context of the present discussion, the issue that arises is whether an injury arising from sexual abuse can ever be characterized as having been caused by an accident.

In the United States there are, not surprisingly, two schools of thought with respect to this issue. The majority view is that whether an accident took place is determined from the standpoint of the insured. Thus, in the case of an employer liable for negligent supervision of an employee guilty of a sexual assault, the incident would be treated as an accident from the point of view of the employer, and, subject to any applicable exclusions, the employer would be covered with respect to the claim.[19] The minority position, although not always expressed in terms of proximate cause, appears to be based on the premise that there can be only one proximate cause of the injury, that cause being the sexual abuse.[20] According to this logic, the negligent employer is not covered, for the negligent supervision was not the proximate cause of the loss.

Insurers in Canada may take some comfort from the fact that the minority position in the United States is sometimes expressed in terms of the negligence claim as "deriving from" the intentional sexual abuse, a concept which was adopted by the Supreme Court of Canada in *Non-Marine Underwriters, Lloyd's of London v. Scalera*,[21] albeit in a somewhat different context. Nevertheless, in principle the majority position in the United States is the correct one. The idea that an employer's negligence could be the cause of a victim's loss for the purposes of tort law but not insurance law defies logic. Commercial liability policies are intended, in broad general terms, to provide coverage in respect of negligence. Such policies typically provide that the insurance afforded applies separately to each person insured.[22] It stands to reason, therefore, that the innocent but negligent employer is covered but the employee who is an intentional tortfeasor is not.

---

[18] See Chapter 7, section 5: Accident and Occurrence; and Chapter 8, section 7: Intentional Injury.

[19] *Silverball Amusement, Inc. v. Utah Home Fire Insurance Co.*, 842 F. Supp. 1151 (W.D. Ark. 1994), affd *per curiam*, 33 F.3d 1476 (8th Cir. 1994); *U.S. Fidelity & Guaranty Co. v. Open Sesame Child Care Center*, 819 F. Supp. 756 (N.D. Ill. 1993); *Allstate Ins. Co. v. Patterson*, 904 F. Supp. 1270 (D. Utah 1995).

[20] *Mutual of Enumclaw v. Wilcox*, 843 P.2d 154 (Idaho 1992).

[21] [1997] B.C.J. No. 2481, 47 B.C.L.R. (3d) 187, [1998] I.L.R. 1-3519 (S.C.), affd, [2000] 1 S.C.R. 551, 185 D.L.R. (4th) 1, [2000] I.L.R. 1-3810, 253 N.R. 1.

[22] See Chapter 6, section 3(i): Severability of Insured or "Cross-Liability".

(c) Trigger of Coverage

Coverage under a commercial liability policy is typically written with respect to bodily injury occurring during the policy period. In addition, the insurer's liability in respect of bodily injury is invariably subject to a monetary limit, which is often expressed on a per occurrence basis, with the term "occurrence" given an extended definition such that all bodily injury arising out of continuous or repeated exposure to substantially the same general conditions is considered as arising out of one occurrence.[23]

There is considerable American jurisprudence on the issue of what constitutes an occurrence in this context. At least three theories have emerged, and within each theory there are variations on the theme:

(i) First Encounter
There is only one occurrence and it takes place when abuse first begins;
(ii) *Pro Rata*
There is a separate occurrence for each policy period during which the abuse continues;
(iii) Manifestation
The occurrence takes place when the symptoms of abuse become manifest.

When giving consideration to these theories it must always be borne in mind that the trigger of coverage is ordinarily the *injury* not the *act.*[24] Although one might expect that the two would almost always go together, there may be cases in which the injury does not occur until many years after the abuse. That will be a matter to be determined by the evidence presented in any given case. It must also be borne in mind that the extent to which each successive act of abuse causes further loss or damage to the victim will be a matter of evidence in any particular case.

The first encounter theory typically holds that the repeated abuse of a single victim constitutes a single occurrence for the purposes of the application of a liability insurance policy. Thus, under the first encounter theory, one occurrence exists for each victim of abuse and the occurrence takes place at the time of the initial act of molestation.[25] In an extreme form the first encounter theory has been interpreted so as to find only one occurrence in circumstances where over a three year period a pedophile molested over 40 children in a daycare facility.[26] The decision is an anomaly and is perhaps best explained by the fact that the insured had a self-retention of $50,000 per occurrence and each of the claims was settled for less than $50,000. Thus the only basis upon which the insurer could be held liable was that there was but one occurrence.

---

[23] See Chapter 4, section 2(d): Limit per Accident or Occurrence.

[24] See Chapter 7, section 7(a): Occurrence Policies.

[25] *Cigna Property & Casualty Ins. Co. v. Diocese of Crookston*, Civil Action No. 3-94-382 (D. Minn. May 3, 1994); *Lee v. Interstate Fire & Casualty Co.*, 826 F. Supp. 1156 (N.D. Ill. 1993).

[26] *Washoe County v. Transcontinental Ins. Co.*, 110 Nev. 798, 878 P. 2d 306 (Nev. 1994).

The proponents of the first encounter theory rely upon the clause typically found in CGL policies stating that "... all bodily injury arising out of continuous or repeated exposure to substantially the same general conditions shall be considered as arising out of one occurrence". Those courts which have rejected the first encounter theory, however, and favour the *pro rata* approach, have held that the language of this clause must be restricted to multiple exposures during the period of coverage.[27] Thus, a period of abuse which spans policy periods gives rise to a separate occurrence in each of those periods.

Of the two theories the *pro rata* approach has achieved the greater acceptance. It is also more consistent with the wording and intent of the policy. Each policy is a separate contract applying to occurrences of bodily injury taking place during the policy period. When a new policy is issued it does not, by its terms, provide that repeated injuries which began under a previous policy are excluded under the new one. Instead it provides that the injuries which take place during the currency of the policy as a result of exposure to the same general conditions are treated as a single occurrence. If this were not the case then it would follow that the insurer whose policy was in place at the time the abuse began would be solely responsible for all subsequent incidents of abuse notwithstanding that they occurred at a time when another insurer's policy was in place and resulted in additional injury.

In addition to these theories some insureds have contended in favour of a manifestation theory, that is, that the policy in force when the symptoms of the abuse first become manifest is the one that should respond to the claim. The manifestation theory was rejected by an American court on the ground that the mental realization that one was sexually abused in the past does not constitute bodily injury.[28] Given the broad meaning ascribed to "bodily injury" by Canadian courts,[29] this reasoning would not necessarily apply in this country. In principle, provided that the mental injury was suffered when the victim first learned of the abuse, then the policy in force when the injury became manifest would provide coverage. This is to be distinguished from the situation in which the injury occurred at the time of the abuse but the effects of the injury continue through multiple policy periods. In the latter case the continuing effects are not treated as a new injury in each policy period, no more than an ongoing physical disability resulting from a motor vehicle accident triggers coverage in more than one policy period.[30]

---

[27] *Interstate Fire & Cas. Co. v. Portland Archdiocese*, 35 F.3d 1325 (9th Cir. 1994), on remand, 899 F. Supp. 498 (1995); *Society of Roman Catholic Church (Diocese of Lafayette & Lake Charles) v. Interstate Fire & Cas. Co.*, 26 F.3d 1359 (5th Cir. 1994).

[28] *Servants of Paraclete, Inc. v. Great American Ins. Co.*, 857 F. Supp. 822 (D.N.M. 1994), on reconsideration, 866 F. Supp. 1560 (D.N.M. 1994).

[29] See *Victoria Gen. Hospital v. Gen. Accident Assur. Co. of Can.*, *supra*, note 15 and *Children's Aid Soc. of Halifax v. Boreal Ins. Co.*, [1996] N.S.J. No. 508, 155 N.S.R. (2d) 221, [1997] I.L.R. 1-3431 (S.C.); and *Wellington Guarantee v. Evangelical Lutheran Church in Can.*, (1995), 29 C.C.L.I. (2d) 93 (B.C.S.C.), revd [1996] B.C.J. No. 872 (C.A.).

[30] *Synod of the Diocese of Edmonton v. Lombard General Insurance Co. of Canada*, [2004] A.J. No. 1287, 20 C.C.L.I. (4th) 221 (Q.B.).

The issue of what triggers coverage in a sexual abuse claim was considered by the Ontario Superior Court in *Chippewas of Nawash First Nation v. Scottish & York Insurance Co.*[31] The decision concerns the duty to defend in actions alleging multiple incidents of sexual abuse by a priest against a number of victims between 1960 and 1985. The insurer sought to restrict coverage to injuries occurring on or after the effective date of its policy, which was issued in 1984. In the absence of any reference to authority by counsel for either party the Court ruled that the insurer must defend all the incidents on the basis that the pleadings alleged continuing injuries. Unfortunately, the reasons for judgment contain little reference to the facts in the underlying claims. As noted above, the continuing effects of a previous injury (as distinct from a new injury) do not constitute an occurrence for the purposes of coverage under a liability insurance policy.

(d) Intentional Injuries

As a general rule, liability insurance policies are not intended to provide coverage for intentionally caused harm. There may be an exception to this general rule in cases in which the policy is specially written to cover assault and battery.[32]

As noted previously, where the insuring agreement provides coverage for loss or damages caused by an accident or an occurrence the definition of "accident" and "occurrence" will preclude coverage with respect to intentionally caused loss or damage.[33] Where the insuring agreement is not restricted to damage "caused by accident", however, liability policies invariably contain an exclusion with respect to intentionally caused harm.[34] Thus, the standard CGL policy contains an exclusion with respect to "bodily injury caused intentionally by or at the direction of the Insured". In the Commercial General Liability policy the exclusion reads as follows:

> This insurance does not apply to:
>
> a. Bodily injury" or "property damage" expected or intended from the stand-point of the insured. This exclusion does not apply to "bodily injury" re-sulting from the use of reasonable force to protect persons or property.

This form of exclusion is often referred to as an "intentional act" exclusion. As noted earlier, however, such a characterization may lead to confusion.[35] The exclusion is meant to remove from coverage intentionally caused harm; it is not

---

[31] [1999] O.J. No. 1596, I.L.R. 1-3738 (S.C.J.).

[32] See the discussion later in this section.

[33] See Chapter 7, section 5(e) "Accident" and Deliberate Acts.

[34] Even where the policy stipulates that the bodily injury must be caused by an accident some insurers, unnecessarily, have included in their policies an exclusion with respect to intentional injuries. See, for example, *Bluebird Cabs Ltd. v. Guardian Insurance Co. of Canada*, [1999] B.C.J. No. 694, 173 D.L.R. (4th) 318, 66 B.C.L.R. (3d) 86, [1999] I.L.R. 1-3688 (C.A.).

[35] See Chapter 8, section 7: Intentional Injury.

meant to apply to negligence.[36] Since much of the law of negligence consists of the unforeseen consequences of intentional conduct the exclusion is more aptly characterized as an "intentional injury" exclusion.

(i) Whether Intent Is Determined Subjectively or Objectively

Some courts in the United States have held that the application of the exclusion depends upon the insured's subjective intent: if the abuser did not subjectively intend to harm the victim then the exclusion does not apply.[37] This is consistent with the policy wording, which typically provides that whether an injury is "expected or intended" is to be determined "from the standpoint of the insured". The majority view in the United States, however, is that an intent to injure must be inferred in every case of child molestation.[38] This is also the approach followed by the Supreme Court of Canada in the companion cases of *Non-Marine Underwriters, Lloyd's of London v. Scalera*[39] and *Sansalone v. Wawanesa Mutual Insurance Co.*[40] Both cases involved bus drivers who had been sued by the same young woman for allegedly having non-consensual intercourse with her. The bus drivers sought coverage under their homeowners' policies on the basis that the pleadings in the action presented a claim in negligence as well as in battery. The Supreme Court of Canada, however, noted that the claim in negligence was not legally viable. The fact of intercourse was not disputed; the only issue was whether it was consensual. In these circumstances the Court held that the intentional injury exclusion applied so as to preclude the duty to defend. Iacobucci J., in a concurring judgment which was adopted by the majority on this point, stated:

> One who engages in non-consensual sexual activity will be presumed to have intended harm; whether or not he subjectively intended harm will not change the injurious nature of his actions, and will not deny an insurer its bargained-for exclusion of intentionally injurious activities.[41]

In *Scalera* and *Sansalone* the Supreme Court of Canada was dealing with adult males of full mental capacity. The Supreme Court did not comment upon whether the same result would apply in cases involving minors or persons of diminished mental capacity. In those jurisdictions in the United States which

---

[36] As Iacobucci J. states in *Non-Marine Underwriters, Lloyd's of London v. Scalera*, [2000] S.C.J. No. 26, [2000] 1 S.C.R. 551, 185 D.L.R. (4th) 1, [2000] I.L.R. 1-3810, at para. 92: "... the exclusion clause must be read to require that the injuries be intentionally caused, in that they are the product of an intentional tort and not of negligence".

[37] See, for example, *State Auto Mut. Insurance Co. v. McIntyre*, 652 F. Supp. 1177 (N.D. Ala. 1987).

[38] *State Farm Fire & Casualty Co. v. Abraio*, 874 F.2d 619 (9th Cir. 1989); *J.C. Penny Casualty Insurance Co. v. M.K.*, 52 Cal. 3rd 1009, 278 Cal. Rptr. 64, 804 P.2d 689 (Cal. 1991).

[39] *Supra*, note 36.

[40] [2000] S.C.J. No. 27, 18 C.C.L.I. (3d) 107.

[41] *Supra*, note 36, at para. 133.

have adopted the inferred intent rule with respect to sexual abuse claims, the age or mental capacity of the abuser is generally considered to be irrelevant.[42] Some American courts, however, have refused to apply the inferred intent doctrine in these circumstances.[43] In the United States the courts also generally reject the argument that pedophilia is a mental illness which renders the perpetrator of child sexual abuse incapable of forming the intent to injure.[44] Nor is voluntary intoxication generally considered as negativing intent.[45]

In principle, if the inferred intent rule is to be followed at all, its application should be limited to cases involving the sexual abuse of children by otherwise mentally competent adults. The basis of the rule is that because the child lacks the capacity to give consent to engage in sexual activity, the sexual abuse of the child by an adult raises the irrebuttable presumption that the adult intended harm.[46] Indeed, any mentally competent adult must appreciate that sexual activity with children is likely to be harmful even though the child may consent. To apply the same rule in a case where a child is the perpetator of the abuse, however, as one court has noted,[47] results in cognitive dissonance: a child, in a consensual sexual relationship with an adult, is deemed to lack sufficient understanding of the consequences of sexual activity to give a valid consent, yet the same child, in a consensual sexual relationship with another child, will be deemed to have intended harm. Moreover, as one court noted in a case involving a perpetrator at ages six, seven and nine years:

> Understanding that parents and television often have a major effect on children's lives, this child found himself in a position in which he was exposed to media images of sexual conduct, in which he was himself exploring sexual conduct, and yet in which he was uninformed of the potential consequences of such conduct. Because of a child's developmental status, it is likely that many minors may be exposed to aspects of sexual activity, attempt to experiment with such activity, and yet not have the capacity to understand the consequences of their sexual acts.[48]

---

[42] See, for example, *State Farm Fire & Casualty v. Robin R.*, 264 Cal. Rptr. 326 (Cal.App. 1989), in which the Court found an irrebuttable inference of intent, which could not be overcome by evidence of the lack of a subjective intent to harm, in circumstances where a 14-year-old male babysitter performed acts of oral copulation on three girls ranging in age from one to five years, and *State Farm & Casualty Co. v. Watters*, 268 Ill. App. 3d 501, 644 N.E.2d 492 (Ill. App. 1994), appeal denied, 161 Ill. 2d 540, 649 N.E.2d 425 (Ill. 1995), in which the Court stated that when the insured's intent to injure is inferred as a matter of law, evidence of the insured's mental retardation is irrelevant.

[43] In *Allstate Insurance Co. v. Jack S.*, 709 F. Supp. 963 (D. Nev. 1989), for example, the Court refused to infer an intent to injure on the part of a 14-year-old female babysitter who fellated a three-year-old child.

[44] *State Farm Fire & Casualty Co. v. Brown*, 905 P.2d 527 (Ariz. App. 1995).

[45] *Wiley v. State Farm Fire & Cas. Co.*, 995 F.2d 457 (3rd Cir. 1993).

[46] *Aetna Life and Cas. Co. v. Barthelemy*, 33 F.3d 189 (3rd Cir. 1994).

[47] *Allstate Insurance Co. v. Jack S.*, *supra*, note 43.

[48] *Fire Insurance Exchange v. Diehl*, 450 Mich. 678, 545 N.W.2d 602 (Mich. 1996).

The inferred intent rule is limited to cases involving non-consenual sexual activity. It does not apply to cases involving the alleged negligent transmission of a sexually communicable disease.[49]

(ii) Mixed Allegations: Intentional Wrongdoing and Negligence

In actions concerning sexual torts it is common to see allegations of both negligence and intentional wrongdoing in the same complaint. Frequently the claim in negligence is a charade, presented solely as an attempt to trigger the defence obligation under a liability insurance policy. Even where there is no practical possibility of being required to indemnify the insured with respect to the claim, the insurer may consider it more economical to settle the claim rather than incur substantial defence costs. Faced with this problem in the *Scalera* and *Sansalone* cases, Iacobucci J. in the Supreme Court of Canada formulated a test for determining when the claim in negligence should be considered independent of the claim in sexual battery so as to trigger coverage under a liability insurance policy:

> Having construed the pleadings, there may be properly pleaded allegations of both intentional and non-intentional tort. When faced with this situation, a court construing an insurer's duty to defend must decide whether the harm allegedly inflicted by the negligent conduct is derivative of that caused by the intentional conduct. In this context, a claim for negligence will not be derivative if the underlying elements of the negligence and of the intentional tort are sufficiently disparate to render the two claims unrelated. If both the negligence and intentional tort claims arise from the same actions and cause the same harm, the negligence claim is derivative, and it will be subsumed into the intentional tort for the purposes of the exclusion clause analysis. If, on the other hand, neither claim is derivative, the claim of negligence will survive and the duty to defend will apply. Parenthetically, I note that the foregoing should not preclude a duty to defend simply because the plaintiff has pleaded in the alternative. As Pryor, "The Stories We Tell: Intentional Harm and the Quest for Insurance Funding", *supra*, points out at p. 1752, "[p]laintiffs must have the freedom to plead in the alternative, to develop alternative theories, and even to submit alternative theories to the jury". A claim should only be treated as "derivative", for the purposes of this analysis, if it is an ostensibly separate claim which nonetheless is clearly inseparable from a claim of intentional tort.[50]

In *Godonoaga v. Khatambakhsh*,[51] the Ontario Court of Appeal described the concept of derivative claims as "problematic" and stated that it was probably confined to the facts in *Scalera*. As noted earlier,[52] the concept of "derivative" claims does not transfer well to non-sexual torts. Even with respect to sexual torts, however, the test may be difficult to apply. Some acts or omissions in the

---

[49] *Loveridge v. Chartier*, 468 NW.2d 146, 161 Wis.2d 150 (Wisc. 1991).

[50] *Scalera, supra*, note 36 at para. 85.

[51] *Godonoaga (Litigation Guardian of) v. Khatambakhsh* [2000] O.J. No. 2172, 188 D.L.R. (4th) 706, 49 O.R. (3d) 22, [2000] I.L.R. 1-3864 (C.A.).

[52] See Chapter 5, section 1(a): The Pleadings Rule.

course of ongoing sexual misconduct can be conceived of as merely negligent, while others are clearly within the realm of intentional sexual torts. In such cases it will be necessary to determine whether the negligence is so intertwined with the tortfeasor's sexual exploitation of the victim as to be inseparable from and derivative of the intentional tort or whether it can truly be characterized as being independent of the intentional wrongdoing. Perhaps a useful guide to resolving such cases is to consider whether the negligence claim can stand if the claim in respect of an intentional sexual tort is dismissed.

The decision in *Scalera* was applied by the Alberta Court of Appeal in *S. (J.A.) v. Gross*,[53] The defendant Gross, a former United Church minister, tendered to his insurer the defence of an action in which the plaintiff alleged that in the guise of providing therapy the minister had subjected her to humiliation, cruelty and degradation, including acts in the nature of sexual assault. The statement of claim contained pleas of negligence and breach of fiduciary duty in addition to the plea of an intentional tort, but no particulars of negligence were given. The Alberta Court of Appeal held that, properly construed, the claim was for an intentional tort and fell outside of the coverage provided.

On the other hand, *Scalera* was distinguished in *Sommerfield v. Lombard Insurance Group*.[54] In the latter case it was alleged that each of four insured teachers, independent of one another, sexually molested a student. It was further alleged that each of the teachers knew or ought to have known that the student was being sexually molested by the others and negligently failed to take protective measures. The claims of sexual molestation, plainly, were not covered under the policy. The negligence claims, however, were held not to be derivative, for the alleged negligence of a particular teacher in failing to report the abuse by one or more of the other teachers was independent of the allegation that the particular teacher was also guilty of sexually abusing the student. Accordingly, the insurer was held liable to pay the portion of the defence costs relating to the negligence claims.

(iii) The Innocent Co-insured

The intentional injury exclusion applies to at least those insureds guilty of causing intentional injury. Depending upon how it is worded the exclusion can also apply to a co-insured who is innocent of the intentional wrongdoing but who may be independently liable in negligence. Commercial liability policies are typically drafted with a "separation of insureds" or "cross-liability" clause, the intent of which is that the policy be read as if applying separately to each insured.[55] In these policies the intentional injury exclusion is often drafted so as to apply only to the guilty insured. In many modern homeowners' policies, however, even those incorporating a "separation of insureds" clause, the

---

[53] [2002] I.L.R. 1-4061 (Alta. C.A.), revg [1998] A.J. No. 1466, [1999] 6 W.W.R. 613 (Q.B.).

[54] [2005] O.J. No. 1131, 20 C.C.L.I. (4th) 301 (S.C.J.).

[55] See Chapter 6, section 3(i): Severability of Insureds or "Cross-Liability".

exclusion often purports to deny coverage to *all* insureds when *any* insured is guilty of intentionally bringing about harm.

Both of these wordings are illustrated in the case of *W. (T.) v. W. (K.R.J.)*[56] The decision deals with the duty to defend against allegations by the plaintiff that she was subjected to a series of sexual assaults by her stepfather and that her mother negligently failed to prevent them. These defendants were both insured under four separate insurance policies which were in place during the period of the alleged assaults. One of the policies (a Comprehensive Farm Liability policy) could not be located; another was silent on the obligation of the insurer to defend.[57] Of the remaining two policies, one excluded coverage with respect to liability for intentional conduct "by or at the direction of *an* insured", the other for intentional conduct "by or at the direction of *the* insured" (emphasis added). The Court held that the former wording excluded coverage for both insureds whereas the latter wording excluded coverage only for the stepfather. No reference is made in the reasons for judgment to the prior Ontario decision in *Jupp v. Firth*,[58] which was affirmed by the Ontario Court of Appeal subsequent to the decision in *W. (T) v. W. (K.R.J.)*, but the same analysis was followed in the two decisions.

In *Jupp v. Firth* the insured homeowner, Mrs. Firth, babysat on a casual basis for others in her home. An action alleging negligent supervision was commenced against her on behalf of two young children who had been sexually abused by Mrs. Firth's 13-year-old son while in Mrs. Firth's care. Mrs. Firth sought a defence under her homeowners' policy. The insurer denied coverage on the basis of two exclusions, one with respect to business use of the premises,[59] the other with respect to "bodily injury or property damage caused intentionally by or at the direction of an insured". Because the son was an insured person under the policy and the sexual assault was committed intentionally by him, the Court held that the conditions of the latter exclusion clause had been met and coverage for Mrs. Firth had been properly denied.

In both cases the Courts applied the decision of the Supreme Court of Canada in *Scott v. Wawanesa Mutual Insurance Co.*,[60] a case dealing with similar language in a homeowners' policy but in the context of a property loss rather than a liability claim.

The same issue arose in the decision of the Ontario Court of Appeal in *Godonoaga (Litigation guardian of) v. Khatambakhsh*, a case dealing with non-sexual intentional harm. The insureds were covered under a tenants' policy which provided that:

> You are not insured for claims arising from:

---

[56] [1996] O.J. No. 2102, 29 O.R. (3d) 277, [1996] I.L.R. 1-3351, 39 C.C.L.I. (2d) 272 (Gen. Div.).

[57] See Chapter 5, note 1.

[58] *Sub nom. Firth v. Westminster Mut. Fire Ins. Co.*, [1993] O.J. No. 4473 (Gen. Div.), affd, [1996] O.J. No. 3078 (C.A.).

[59] See Chapter 14, section 5(b): Business Pursuits and Professional Activities.

[60] [1989] S.C.J. No. 55, [1989] 1 S.C.R. 1445, 59 D.L.R. (4th) 660.

. . . . .

(5) Bodily Injury or Property Damage caused intentionally by or at your direction or resulting from your criminal acts or omissions;

The terms "you" and "your" were defined as follows:

> "You" and "your" mean the person(s) named as Insured on the Declaration page and, while living in the same household, his or her wife or husband, the relatives of either or any person under 21 in their care. ...[61]

An action was commenced against the insured parents for negligence in the upbringing, discipline and supervision of their children, who allegedly assaulted the plaintiff. Since the children were also insured under the policy, the insurer argued that their act of assault triggered the intentional injury exclusion not just with respect to themselves but also with respect to their parents. The basis for this argument was that the references to "you" and "your" embrace all four of the insured defendants and if any one of the four is excluded from coverage, all four are excluded. The Court did not agree. Noting that the policy contained a provision that "Each person is a separate Insured but this does not increase the limit of insurance", the Court held that the exclusion clause must be read as pertaining separately to each insured.

(iv) Coverage for Assault and Battery

Some policies expressly provide coverage for bodily injury resulting from assault and battery. An example of such a clause is found in *Medhurst v. Children's Aid Society of London and Middlesex:*

> To pay on behalf of the Insured all sums which the Insured shall become obligated to pay by reason of the liability imposed upon the Insured by law or assumed under an Insured Contract as defined below, for damages because of bodily injury, sickness, disease, shock, mental anguish, mental injury, *assault and battery* and death at any time resulting therefrom, and sustained during the policy period by any person.[62]

A somewhat similar insuring agreement is found in *M. (E.) v. Reed:*

> To pay on behalf of the Insured, all sums which the Insured shall become obligated to pay by reason of any liability imposed by law upon the Insured for damages, including damages for care and loss of services because of bodily injury, sickness, disease, mental anguish and/or mental suffering, including death at any time resulting therefrom, sustained by any person or persons, and occurring during the policy period, caused by an occurrence including *assault and battery* by a person, arising out of or in the course of his duties as an employee of the Insured, *unless committed by or at the direction of the Insured.* Without restricting the generality thereof "occurrence" shall include bodily

---

[61] [2000] O.J. No. 2172, 49 O.R. (3d) 22 at 25-26 (C.A.).

[62] [2001] O.J. No. 1382, 53 O.R. (3d) 631 (S.C.J.) (emphasis added).

injury, sickness or disease, and death at any time resulting therefrom sustained within the policy period and caused by any act or acts of omission or commission whether due to negligence, lack of skill, training or qualification, *or any other cause*, in connection with the rendering of or omitting to render any skilful, trained or professional service which is ordinarily rendered on or to the person of an individual, or in connection with the dispensing of any prescription, remedy, drug or medical supplies.[63]

These sorts of policies present issues both of interpretation and of public policy. In the *Medhurst* case the policy contained an exclusion with respect to intentional injuries. The insured, a warden of a group home, was convicted of the sexual assault of a child in his care. A civil action was brought against him claiming damages for both physical and sexual assault. It was held that the insurer was required to defend the insured because the insuring agreement in the policy extended coverage to claims for damages because of "assault and battery". The court did not apply the intentional injury exclusion on the basis that to do so would render nugatory the express grant of coverage for assault and battery. There was no discussion of the public policy prohibition with respect to insurance against intentionally caused harm.[64]

In *Reed* it was alleged that the insured, a priest, entered into a sexual relationship with a teenage parishioner suffering from mental problems. The action settled part way through a lengthy and complex trial. Reed sought indemnification under a policy issued to his diocese, under which he was added as an additional insured. The insurer resisted on the grounds that Reed's action were criminal in nature, so as to invoke both an exclusion and the rule of public policy, and, further, that Reed's actions constituted sexual battery "... committed by or at the direction of the Insured ...", thus falling within the exception in the insuring agreement. Both grounds were rejected by the court. As to the first ground, the court held that no criminal act had occurred. As to the second ground, the court interpreted the phrase "the Insured" as referring to the diocese, which was named as "Insured" in the policy. Reed was an "Additional Insured". As such, the court reasoned, the exception did not apply to Reed unless his battery had been performed at the direction of the diocese. With respect, the latter reasoning is erroneous. The insuring agreement provides coverage to "the Insured". There is no reference in the insuring agreement to an "Additional Insured", which is the class in which Reed was included in an endorsement to the policy. The only way of interpreting the insuring agreement so as to extend coverage to Reed, then, is to read the phrase "the Insured" as including "Additional Insureds". As such, for Reed to take advantage of the grant of coverage to "the Insured", he would also be subject to the exception with respect to battery "...committed by or at the direction of the Insured...".

---

[63] [2000] O.J. No. 4791, 24 C.C.L.I. (3d) 229 (Ont. S.C.J.), affd [2003] O.J. No. 1791 (C.A.), leave to appeal to S.C.C. dismissed, [2003] S.C.C.A. No. 334 (emphasis added).

[64] See Chapter 2, Section 1(h): Public Policy.

(e) Criminal Act Exclusion

Liability insurance policies often contain an exclusion, either incorporated with the intentional injury exclusion or standing on its own, that pertains to bodily injury resulting from a criminal act[65] on the part of the insured or, under some wordings, on the part of any person insured under the policy.[66] The wording of the exclusion may or may not require that the criminal violation occur with the knowledge and the consent of the insured. Depending upon its wording, the criminal act exclusion may in some circumstances remove from coverage a claim that would not be caught by the intentional injury exclusion, for instance, a claim in which the injury, although not intended by the insured, resulted from a criminal act.

(f) Sexual Molestation Exclusions

In response to the avalanche of sexual abuse claims in recent years general liability insurers have begun to attach sexual molestation exclusions to their policies. A properly worded exclusion will remove from coverage the employer's liability in negligence for a claim arising out of the sexual molestation of a third party by an employee.[67] Nevertheless, issues may still arise as to whether the proximate cause of the loss was sexual molestation or some other cause.[68]

An example of such an exclusion clause is provided by the decision in *Clausen v. Royal & SunAlliance Insurance Co. of Canada.*[69] The insured mother provided babysitting services in her home. On two occasions she briefly left children in the care of her teenage son, who was also insured under the policy. On both of these occasions her son sexually touched a child. He subsequently plead guilty to sexual assault. A claim in negligence was made against the insured parents on the basis that the mother failed in her supervision duties and both parents knew of their son's aberrant activities and had failed to warn the parents of the two young children. The policy contained, among others, the following exclusion:

> You are not insured for claims arising from actual or alleged sexual molestation, sexual harassment, corporal punishment or physical or mental abuse or harassment by any person insured by this policy.

It was held that the exclusion applied. The characterization of the claims against the parents as being based on negligence did not alter the fact that they arose

---

[65] See also the discussion in Chapter 14, section (c): Intentional Injury or Criminal Act.

[66] See discussion above in section 2(d)(iii): The Innocent Co-Insured.

[67] *Thompson v. Warriner*, [2002] O.J. No. 1769 (C.A.); *McAuliffe v. Northern Ins. Co.*, 69 F.3d 277 (Missouri 8th Cir. 1995).

[68] See, for example, *IPCI Ltd. v. Old Republic Ins. Co.*, 758 F. Supp. 478, dismissed, 777 F. Supp. 1451 (E.D. Wis. 1991); and *Lopez v. N.M. Public Schools Ins. Auth.*, 870 P.2d 745 (N.M. 1994).

[69] 2004 CarswellOnt 4597 (S.C.J.).

from an event for which coverage is expressly excluded, namely, "sexual molestation...by any person insured by this policy".

(g) Late Notice

In cases involving historical sexual abuse, especially those involving allegations of a conspiracy or a cover-up, an issue may arise as to whether the insured is in breach of the condition requiring prompt notice be given of an accident or occurrence.[70] As a general rule, in the case of a breach of condition, the courts will relieve against forfeiture of coverage provided that no prejudice has resulted to the insurer.[71] Yet in historical sexual abuse claims the potential for such prejudice is high. With the passage of time witnesses may have either passed away or become impossible to locate and physical or documentary evidence may have become lost or destroyed. Since the triggering event of the notice requirement, however, is knowledge on the part of the insured, no breach will have occurred unless the insured was aware of circumstances which ought to have been reported to the insurer.

(h) Coverage under Other Commercial Policies

Sexual torts are not confined to bodily injury claims. Nor are they confined to claims in negligence and battery. Occasionally claims are presented for false imprisonment, sexual harassment or intentional infliction of emotional distress. There are various forms of commercial liability policies which may respond to such claims.

As noted in Chapter 10, despite their appellation, personal injury liability policies do not ordinarily provide coverage for bodily injury claims. Instead they cover a variety of offences against the person, including false imprisonment, defamation and certain violations of a person's right of privacy. Under appropriate circumstances coverage could be extended for a claim alleging sexual harassment. Although sexual harassment is not typically named as one of the personal injury offences, one or more of the acts comprising the sexual harassment could conceivably fall within one or more of offenses which are defined in the policy.

A form of policy which usually provides explicit coverage for sexual harassment claims is Employment Practices Liability insurance. As its title indicates, this form of coverage is restricted to claims arising in the workplace setting. The intent of the policy is to provide coverage to an employer with respect to a variety of claims which can arise out of the relationship between employer and employee, including discrimination, invasion of privacy, and sexual and other forms of harassment. Bodily injury claims may or may not be covered.

---

[70] See Chapter 3, section 3: Notice of Accident, Occurrence, Claim or Suit.

[71] *Ibid.*

A typical insuring clause in an Employment Practices Liability policy is as follows:

> We will pay for any loss that you are legally obligated to pay to a claimant as a result of any claim brought against you arising out of the claimant's capacity as your past or present employee or as an applicant to be your employee.
>
> We will pay for loss only if a claim is first made during the Annual Policy Period. Such claim must result from any of the following wrongful employment practices:
>
> a) Discrimination; or
> b) Actual or constructive termination of an employment relationship; refusal to hire; failure to promote; demotion; discipline; misrepresentation; evaluation; deprivation of a career opportunity; or
> c) Sexual or work place harassing of any kind; intimidating, creating or condoning an offensive or hostile work environment; coercion; or
> d) Defamation, infliction of emotional distress; bad faith; unfair or wrongful dealing: invasion of privacy; or retaliatory treatment,
>
> which violates Canadian federal, provincial, local or common law.

The losses covered by an Employment Practices Liability policy generally include defence costs and non-pecuniary damages but may exclude pecuniary damages in addition to fines, penalties and punitive damages. This form of coverage may be incorporated with a Directors' and Officers' policy.

3. COVERAGE UNDER PROFESSIONAL LIABILITY POLICIES

Sexual activity between a doctor, counsellor or psychotherapist and his or her patient may form the basis of a claim in tort and for breach of fiduciary duty. The claim in tort may be advanced either in negligence or for sexual battery. Coverage in respect of such claims may be provided under a professional liability policy. Recent policies sometimes address coverage specifically in respect of sexual torts, either in the insuring agreement or in an exclusion.[72]

Professional liability policies are intended to provide coverage for liability arising out of the provision of professional services. Ordinarily, sexual activity with patients does not fit within this description.[73] Some courts in the United States, however, have found that claims involving sexual torts brought against health care practitioners may fall within the ambit of coverage depending upon the degree of connection between the sexual activity and the professional

---

[72] See, for example, *B. (J.) v. Co-operators General Insurance Co.* [1999] N.B.J. No. 507, 222 N.B.R. (2d) 203, [2000] I.L.R. 1-3807 (Q.B.).

[73] *Snyder v. Major*, 789 F. Supp. 646 (S.D.N.Y. 1992), modified, 818 F. Supp. 68 (S.D.N.Y. 1993); David S. Florig, "Insurance Coverage for Sexual Abuse or Molestation" (1994) 30 Tort & Ins. L.J. 699; Debra E. Wax, Annotation, "Coverage and Exclusions of Liability or Indemnity Policy on Physicians, Surgeons, and Other Healers" (1984) 33 A.L.R. (4th) 14.

services provided. In a number of these cases liability arose out of the mishandling by the doctor or therapist of the transference phenomenon, which is the term used by mental health professionals to describe the patient's emotional reaction to the therapist, in some cases leading to feelings of erotic attraction.[74]

The test frequently applied in determining coverage in these cases is stated by the Minnesota Supreme Court in *St. Paul Fire & Marine Insurance Co. v. Love*.

> In determining whether the patient's claim results from professional services provided or which should have been provided, we believe the focus must be on the therapist's entire conduct. The question then becomes whether the sexual aspect of that conduct is inextricably related to the professional services provided or withheld. If the linkage is absent or slight, the patient's claim cannot be said to result from professional services provided or withheld. On the other hand, if there is a substantial connection, the claim results from the professional services, and the sexual conduct is seen as a consequence of those services provided or withheld. In applying this test, the factors to be considered include the patient's health problem, the nature of the professional services involved, and how the sexual conduct arises within the context of the patient's problem and the prescribed treatment.[75]

Examples of cases in which coverage has been found include a physician's engaging in improper clitoral manipulation during a gynecological examination[76] and a therapist's engaging in sexual activity with a patient.[77] Examples of cases in which coverage has been denied include sexual assault by a dentist upon a patient while performing a filling,[78] by an EEG technician upon a patient[79] and by a physician upon young male patients in the course of treating assorted medical problems.[80]

In Canada the majority of medical doctors do not carry medical malpractice insurance. Instead, they purchase protection against malpractice claims from the Canadian Medical Protective Association, which is incorporated by federal statute,[81] does not issue insurance policies[82] and is not treated as an insurer by regulatory agencies. The Association provide doctors with a defence and indemnity with respect to malpractice claims on a discretionary basis. As a

---

[74] *Simmons v. United States*, 805 F.2d 1363 (9th Cir. 1986); *Zipkin v. Freeman*, 436 S.W.2d 753 (Mo. 1968).

[75] 459 NW.2d 698 (Minn. 1990).

[76] *St. Paul Fire & Marine Ins. Co. v. Asbury*, 149 Ariz. 565, 720 P.2d 540 (Ct. App. 1986).

[77] *L.L. v. Medical Protective Co.*, 362 NW.2d 174 (Wis. Ct. App. 1984).

[78] *Niedzielski v. St. Paul Fire & Marine Insurance Co.*, 134 NH 141, 589 A.2d 130 (N.H. 1991).

[79] *St. Paul Fire & Marine Insurance Co. v. Quintana*, 419 NW.2d 60, 165 Mich. App. 719 (1988), appeal denied, 430 Mich. 885 (1988).

[80] *Smith v. St. Paul Fire & Marine Insurance Co.*, 353 NW.2d 130 (Minn. 1984).

[81] *An Act to Incorporate the Canadian Medical Protective Association*, S.C. 1913, c. 91.

[82] *Qureshi v. Nickerson*, [1991] B.C.J. No. 264, 77 D.L.R. (4th) 1, 53 B.C.L.R. (2d) 379, 47 C.P.C. (2d) 69 (C.A.).

general rule the Association will provide a defence to a doctor with respect to a claim alleging sexual battery but, if the claim is proven, the Association may refuse to provide indemnity.

Coverage under professional liability policies is generally written on a claims-made basis. The trigger of coverage is not when the damage occurs, but, rather, when a claim is made. The term "claim" may or may not be defined in the policy. In *Jesuit Fathers of Upper Canada v. Guardian Insurance Co. of Canada*[83] the plaintiff had been involved in the operation and administration of a residential school for aboriginal children. The school, which was known as the Spanish school, closed in 1958. In the early 1990s the plaintiff became aware of broad-based allegations of physical and sexual abuse committed by Jesuit brothers against aboriginal children generally. The plaintiff commenced an investigation, as a result of which, in 1994, the plaintiff identified ten persons who may have been sexually molested by a Jesuit brother at the Spanish school. One of the 10, Mr. Cooper, had given notice through a lawyer of an intention to seek compensation; the remaining nine had not given such notice but were aware that the plaintiff accepted responsibility and was seeking to provide redress. Other potential claimants had not been identified, but could reasonably be expected. The plaintiff provided full details to its insurer. The policy required the insurer:

> To pay on behalf of the Insured all sums which the Insured shall become legally obligated to pay as damages, because of injury arising out of the rendering of, or failure to render professional services in the practice of the Insured's profession, provided however, that coverage as provided herein shall apply only to claims which are first made against the Insured during the policy period as stated in the Declarations.

After receiving notice of the potential claims the insurer chose not to renew the policy. After the policy had thus expired the plaintiff received approximately 100 claims. The plaintiff sought a declaration requiring the insurer to defend all of them, but was successful only in part. The court analyzed the claims in three categories, namely, (i) Mr. Cooper's claim, of which express notice had been given to the insured, (ii) the other nine potential claimants, who had been identified by name, and (iii) the unnamed potential claimants. The court held that the first two categories constituted claims made against the insured during the policy period but that the third category did not. The court reasoned that a general belief that other unidentified persons might have complaints against the insured lacked the necessary specificity to be considered a "claim" under the policy.

---

[83] [2003] O.J. No. 4534, 6 C.C.L.I. (4th) 276 (S.C.J.), affd [2004] O.J. No. 4641, 16 C.C.L.I. (4th) 24 (C.A.), leave to appeal to S.C.C. granted [2005] S.C.C.A. No. 5.

4. COVERAGE UNDER HOMEOWNERS' AND TENANTS' POLICIES

In limited circumstances coverage in respect of certain sexual torts may be available under a homeowners' or tenants' policy. As noted in Chapter 14, these policies typically include coverage for legal liability to pay compensatory damages for bodily injury arising outside of business or professional activities.[84] Depending upon the wording of the policy, if the claim arises out of an intentional injury inflicted by an insured person, the coverage is excluded at least with respect to that person and possibly to other insureds as well.[85] The policy may also have an exclusion which removes coverage with respect to claims brought by one insured against another.[86] The coverage considerations reviewed above with respect to commercial liability policies, may, depending upon the particular policy wording, apply in the case of homeowners' policies.

---

[84] See Chapter 14, section 5(b): Business Pursuits and Professional Activities.

[85] See discussion above in section 2(d): Intentional Injuries.

[86] See Chapter 14, section 5(d): Claims by One Insured against Another Insured.

APPENDICES

APPENDIX A

LIABILITY POLICY

INSURANCE CO.

HEAD OFFICE — CANADA
(hereinafter called the Insurer)

POLICY NO.

Agent

The Insurer, in consideration of the payment of the premium, in reliance upon the statements in the declarations made a part hereof and subject to all the terms of this policy, agrees with the Named Insured as follows:

DECLARATIONS

1. Named Insured

   Address

2. Business of Named Insured is

   The Named Insured is   INDIVIDUAL ☐;   PARTNERSHIP ☐;   CORPORATION ☐;   JOINT VENTURE ☐;

   OTHER ....

	Day	Month	Year	Day	Month	Year	12:01 A.M., Standard Time, at the address of the Named Insured as stated herein.
3. Policy Period From				To			

4. Coverage and Premium — The insurance afforded under this policy is only with respect to the coverage rider(s) indicated below and for which a premium charge is specified.

RIDER(S)	PREMIUM
	$
TOTAL OR ADVANCE PREMIUM	$

Countersigned by _____ Authorized Representative

IBC 2000
1-83

DEFINITIONS

When used in this policy (including endorsements forming a part hereof):

"automobile" means any self-propelled land motor vehicle, trailers or semi-trailers while attached thereto or unattached (including its equipment mounted on or attached thereto) other than any of the following or their trailers, accessories and equipment:

(i) vehicles of the crawler type (other than motorized snow vehicles);

(ii) tractors (other than road transport tractors designed to haul trailers or semi-trailers), road rollers, graders, scrapers, bulldozers, paving machines and concrete mixers (other than concrete mixers of the mix-in-transit type);

(iii) other construction machinery or equipment mounted on wheels but not self-propelled while not attached to any self-propelled land motor vehicle.

(iv) self-propelled land motor vehicles used solely on the premises of the Insured.

"bodily injury" means bodily injury, sickness or disease sustained by any person which occurs during the policy period, including death at any time resulting therefrom.

"completed operations hazard" includes bodily injury or property damage arising out of operations, but only if the bodily injury or property damage occurs after such operations have been completed or abandoned and occurs away from premises owned by or rented to the Named Insured. Operations include materials, parts or equipment furnished in connection therewith. Operations shall be deemed completed at the earliest of the following times:

(i) when all operations to be performed by or on behalf of the Named Insured under the contract have been completed;

(ii) when all operations to be performed by or on behalf of the Named Insured at the site of the operations have been completed;

(iii) when the portion of the work out of which the bodily injury or property damage arises has been put to its intended use by any persons or organization other than another contractor or subcontractor engaged in performing operations for a principal as a part of the same project.

Operations which may require further service or maintenance work, or correction, repair or replacement because of any defect or deficiency, but which are otherwise complete shall be deemed completed.
The completed operations hazard shall not include:

(i) operations in connection with the pick up and delivery of property;

(ii) the existence of tools, uninstalled equipment or abandoned or unused materials.

"elevator" means any hoisting or lowering device to connect floors or landings whether or not in service, and all appliances thereof, including

any car, platform, shaft, hoistway, stairway, runway, power equipment and machinery, but shall not include:

(i) dumbwaiters, the floor area of which does not exceed 1 square metre (10.76 square feet), and used exclusively for carrying property;

(ii) hod or material hoists used in connection with alterations, construction or demolition operations;

(iii) inclined conveyors used exclusively for carrying property;

(iv) automobile servicing hoists.

"incidental contract" means any written agreement which is a lease of premises, easement agreement, agreement required by municipal ordinance, sidetrack agreement or elevator maintenance agreement.

"insured" means any person or organization qualifying as an Insured in the "Persons Insured" provision of the applicable coverage rider. The insurance afforded applies separately to each Insured against whom claim is made or suit is brought.

"Named Insured" means the person or organization named in the Declarations of this policy.

"Named Insured's products" means goods or products manufactured, sold, handled or distributed by the Named Insured or by others trading under his name, including any container thereof (other than a vehicle), but shall not include a vending machine or any property other than such container, rented to or located for use of others but not sold.

"policy territory" means:

(i) Canada or the United States of America, its territories or possessions, or

(ii) anywhere in the world with respect to compensatory damages because of bodily injury or property damage arising out of a product which was sold for use or consumption within the territory described in paragraph (i) above, provided suit for such compensatory damages is brought within such territory.

"products hazard" includes bodily injury and property damage arising out of the Named Insured's products but only if such bodily injury or property damage occurs away from premises owned by or rented to the Named Insured and after physical possession of such products has been relinquished to others.

"property damage" means (1) physical injury to or destruction of tangible property which occurs during the policy period, including the loss of use thereof at any time resulting therefrom, or (2) loss of use of tangible property which has not been physically injured or destroyed provided such loss of use is caused by an accident occurring during the policy period.

ENVIRONMENTAL LIABILITY EXCLUSION

It is agreed that this policy does not apply to bodily injury or property damage arising out of the discharge, dispersal, release or escape of smoke, vapours, soot, fumes, acids, alkalis, toxic chemicals, liquids or gases, waste materials or other irritants, contaminants or pollutants into or upon land, the atmosphere or any water of any description no matter where located or how contained, or into any watercourse, drainage or sewage system, but this exclusion does not apply if such discharge, dispersal, release or escape is sudden and accidental.

NUCLEAR ENERGY LIABILITY EXCLUSION

(Applicable to all coverage riders other than Comprehensive Personal Liability, Farmer's Comprehensive Liability and Storekeepers' Liability.)
It is agreed that this policy does not apply:

(a) to liability imposed by or arising under the Nuclear Liability Act; nor

(b) to bodily injury or property damage with respect to which an Insured under this policy is also insured under a contract of nuclear energy liability insurance (whether the Insured is unnamed in such contract and whether or not it is legally enforcible by the Insured) issued by the Nuclear Insurance Association of Canada or any other insurer or group or pool of insurers or would be an Insured under any such policy but for its termination upon exhaustion of its limit of liability; nor

(c) to bodily injury or property damage resulting directly or indirectly from the nuclear energy hazard arising from:

(i) the ownership, maintenance, operation or use of a nuclear facility by or on behalf of an Insured;

(ii) the furnishing by an Insured of services, materials, parts or equipment in connection with the planning, construction, maintenance, operation or use of any nuclear facility; and

(iii) the possession, consumption, use, handling, disposal or transportation of fissionable substances, or of other radioactive material (except radioactive isotopes, away from a nuclear facility, which have reached the final stage of fabrication so as to be useable for any scientific, medical, agricultural, commercial or industrial purpose) used, distributed, handled or sold by an Insured.

As used in this policy:

1. The term "nuclear energy hazard" means the radioactive, toxic, explosive, or other hazardous properties of radioactive material;

2. The term "radioactive material" means uranium, thorium, plutonium, neptunium, their respective derivatives and compounds, radioactive isotopes of other elements and any other substances that the Atomic Energy Control Board may, by regulation, designate as being prescribed substances capable of releasing atomic energy, or as being requisite for the production, use or application of atomic energy;

3. The term "nuclear facility" means:

(a) any apparatus designed or used to sustain nuclear fission in a self-supporting chain reaction or to contain a critical mass of plutonium, thorium and uranium or any one or more of them;

(b) any equipment or device designed or used for (i) separating the isotopes of plutonium, thorium and uranium or any one or more of them, (ii) processing or utilizing spent fuel, or (iii) handling, processing or packaging waste;

(c) any equipment or device used for the processing, fabricating or alloying of plutonium, thorium or uranium enriched in the isotope uranium 233 or in the isotope uranium 235, or any one or more of them if at any time the total amount of such material in the custody of the Insured at the premises where such equipment or device is located consists of or contains more than 25 grams of plutonium or uranium 233 or any combination thereof, or more than 250 grams of uranium 235;

(d) any structure, basin, excavation, premises or place prepared or used for the storage or disposal of waste radioactive material; and includes the site on which any of the foregoing is located, together with all operations conducted thereon and all premises used for such operations.

4. The term "fissionable substance" means any prescribed substance that is, or from which can be obtained, a substance capable of releasing atomic energy by nuclear fission.

Page 2 of 4

IBC 2000
1-83

CONDITIONS

1. **Premium and Adjustment of Premiums:**

   (a) Unless otherwise stated, the premium stated in the declarations is an estimated deposit premium only. Adjustment of premium shall be made at least annually and for this purpose the premium bases and rates shown in the declarations or in any endorsement attached hereto, shall be used in ascertaining the earned premium with respect to the specific hazards mentioned herein.

   (b) In the case of any hazards existing and covered under coverage rider(s) attached but not specified in the declarations, or in any endorsement the earned premium with respect thereto shall be computed in accordance with the Insurer's rules, rates, rating plans and minimum premiums applicable to such hazards.

   (c) Subject to the retention by the Insurer of the minimum premium provided for in the declarations, if the earned premium for this policy thus computed exceeds the estimated deposit premium paid, the Named Insured shall pay such excess to the Insurer; on the other hand, if the estimated deposit premium exceeds the earned premium, the Insurer shall return to the Named Insured such excess.

   (d) The Named Insured shall maintain for each hazard hereby insured against, a record of the information necessary for premium computation on the basis stated, and shall submit such record to the Insurer at the end of the policy period and at such other times during the policy period as the Insurer may direct.

2. **Inspection -- Audit:**

   The Named Insured shall permit the Insurer to inspect the insured premises, operations and elevators and to examine and audit the Named Insured's books and records at any time during the policy period (and any extension thereof and within one year after the termination of this policy), as far as they relate to the premium basis or the subject matter of this insurance. The Insurer assumes no responsibility and waives no rights by reason of such inspection, examination, audit or the omission thereof.

3. **Insured's Duties in the event of Accident, Occurrence, Claim or Suit:**

   (a) In the event of an accident or occurrence, written notice containing particulars sufficient to identify the Insured and also reasonably obtainable information with respect to the time, place and circumstances thereof, and the names and addresses of the injured and of available witnesses, shall be given promptly by or for the Insured to the Insurer or any of its authorized agents.

   (b) If claim is made or suit is brought against the Insured, the Insured shall immediately forward to the Insurer every writ, letter, document or advice received by him or his representative.

   (c) The Insured shall co-operate with the Insurer and, upon the Insurer's request, assist in making settlements, in the conduct of suits and in enforcing any right of contribution or indemnity against any person or organization who may be liable to the Insured because of injury or damage with respect to which insurance is afforded under this policy; and the Insured shall attend hearings and trials and assist in securing and giving evidence and obtaining the attendance of witnesses. The Insured shall not, except at his own cost, voluntarily make any payment, assume any obligation or incur any expenses other than for the first aid to others at the time of accident.

4. **Action against Insurer:**

   No action shall lie against the Insurer under any Insuring Agreement of this policy including the Insuring Agreement relating to "Defense — Settlement — Supplementary Payments" unless, as a condition precedent thereto, there shall have been full compliance with all of the terms of this policy, nor until the amount of the Insured's obligation to pay shall have been finally determined either by judgment against the Insured after actual trial or by written agreement of the Insured, the claimant and the Insurer. Every action or proceeding against the Insurer shall be commenced within one year next after the date of such judgment or written agreement and not afterwards. If this policy is governed by the law of Quebec, every action or proceeding against the Insurer shall be commenced within three years from the time the right of action arises. Nothing contained in this policy shall give any person or organization any right to join the Insurer as a co-defendant in any action against the Insured to determine the Insured's liability.

   Bankruptcy or insolvency of the Insured or of the Insured's estate shall not relieve the Insurer of any of its obligations hereunder.

5. **Subrogation:**

   In the event of any payment under this policy, the Insurer shall be subrogated to all the Insured's rights of recovery therefor against any person or organization and the Insured shall execute and deliver instruments and papers and do whatever else is necessary to secure such rights. The Insured shall do nothing after loss to prejudice such rights.

6. **Other Insurance:**

   The insurance afforded by this policy is primary insurance, except when stated to apply in excess of or contingent upon the absence of other insurance. When this insurance is primary and the Insured has other insurance which is stated to be applicable to the loss on an excess or contingent basis the amounts of the Insurer's liability under this policy shall not be reduced by the existence of such other insurance. When both this insurance and other insurance apply to the loss on the same basis, whether primary, excess or contingent, the Insurer shall not be liable under this policy for a greater proportion of the loss than that stated in the applicable contribution provision below:

   (a) Contribution by Equal Shares:

   If all of such other valid and collectible insurance provides for contribution by equal shares, this Insurer shall not be liable for a greater proportion of such loss than would be payable if each insurer contributes an equal share until the share of each insurer equals the lowest applicable limit of liability under any one policy or the full amount of the loss is paid, and with respect to any amount of loss not so paid the remaining insurers then continue to contribute equal shares of the remaining amount of the loss until each such insurer has paid its limit in full or the full amount of the loss is paid.

   (b) Contribution by Limits:

   If any of such other insurance does not provide for contribution by equal shares, this Insurer shall not be liable for a greater proportion of such loss than the applicable limit of liability under this policy for such loss bears to the total applicable limit of liability of all valid and collectible insurance against such loss.

7. **Changes:**

   Notice to any agent or knowledge possessed by any agent or by any other person shall not effect a waiver or a change in any part of this policy or estop the Insurer from asserting any right under the terms of this policy; nor shall the terms of this policy be waived or changed, except by endorsement issued to form a part of this policy.

8. **Assignment:**

   Assignment of interest under this policy shall not bind the Insurer until its consent is endorsed hereon; if, however, the Named Insured shall die or be adjudged bankrupt or insolvent within the policy period, this policy, unless cancelled, shall, if written notice be given to the Insurer within sixty days, after the date of such death or adjudication, cover the Named Insured's legal representative as the Named Insured except in the Province of Quebec where no notice is required.

9. **Notice:**

   Any written notice to the Insurer may be delivered at or sent by registered mail to the agent through whom this policy was issued or to any branch of the Insurer in Canada. Written notice may be given to the Named Insured by letter personally delivered to him or by registered letter addressed to him at his last post office address notified to the Insurer; or, except in Quebec, where no address is notified and the address is not known, addressed to him at the post office of the agency, if any, from which the application was received. In this condition the expression "registered" shall mean registered within or without Canada. Notice to the first Named Insured shall constitute notice to all Insureds.

10. **Cancellation — Termination:**

    (a) This policy may be terminated,

    (i) by the Insurer giving to the Named Insured 15 days written notice of termination by registered mail or personal delivery;

    (ii) by the Named Insured at any time on written request.

    (b) Where the policy is terminated by the Insurer,

    (i) and where the premium is developed on other than an estimated basis, the Insurer will refund the excess of the paid premium for the time the policy has been in force, calculated pro rata; or

    (ii) where the premium is developed on an estimated basis, the Insurer will refund the excess of the premium above the premium earned, when determined.

    (c) Where the policy is terminated by the Named Insured,

    (i) and where the premium is developed on other than an estimated basis, the Insurer will refund the excess of the paid premium above the short rate premium for the time the policy has been in force calculated in accordance with the short rate premium table in use by the Insurer, and except in Quebec, subject to the retention of the minimum premium, if any, provided by the policy; or

Page 3 of 4

IBC 2000
1-83

(ii) where the premium is developed by an estimated basis, the Insurer will refund the excess of the paid premium above the premium earned, when determined, and except in Quebec, subject to the retention of the minimum premium, if any, provided by the policy.

(d) Refund of premium may be made by money, postal or express company money order or by cheque payable at par.

(e) Except in Quebec, the 15 days mentioned above in this condition commences to run on the day following the receipt of the registered letter at the post office to which it is addressed.

(f) In Quebec, the Notice of Cancellation from the Insurer takes effect 15 days after receipt by the Insured at the last known address.

(g) premium adjustment may be made at the time cancellation is effected and if not then made shall be made as soon as practicable after cancellation becomes effective but payment or tender of unearned premium is not a condition of cancellation.

11. **Declarations:**

By acceptance of this policy, the Named Insured agrees that the statements in the declarations are his agreements and representations, that this policy is issued in reliance upon the truth of such representations and that this policy embodies all agreements existing between himself and the Insurer or any of its agents relating to this insurance.

IN WITNESS WHEREOF, the Insurer has caused this policy to be signed by its [describe officer(s)], but the same shall not be binding upon the Insurer unless countersigned by an authorized representative of the Insurer.

APPENDIX B

COMPREHENSIVE GENERAL LIABILITY COVERAGE RIDER
Attached to and forming part of this Policy

ADDITIONAL DECLARATIONS

The following discloses all hazards insured hereunder known to exist at the effective date of this policy, unless otherwise stated herein.

SCHEDULE

The insurance afforded is only with respect to such of the following Coverages as are indicated by specific premium charge or charges. The limit of the Insurer's liability against each such Coverage shall be as stated herein, subject to all the terms of this policy having reference thereto.

Coverages		Limits of Liability	Advance Premium

Separate Limits	A. Bodily Injury Liability	$ each person
		$ each occurrence
		$ aggregate
			$

	B. Property Damage Liability	$ each accident $ aggregate	$

Inclusive Limit	A. Bodily Injury Liability
	and
	B. Property Damage Liability
		$ bodily injury
		each occurrence
		property damage
		each accident
		$ aggregate
			$

Minimum Premium $		Total Advance Premium	$

Description of Hazards	Premium Bases	Rates		Advance Premium	
		B.I.	P.D.	B.I.	P.D.
Premises—Operations (List all locations owned, rented or controlled by Named Insured stating interest as owner, lessee or tenant.)	(a) Area (sq. ft.) (b) Remuneration (c) Receipts (d)	(a) Per 100 sq. ft. of Area (b) Per $1000. Remuneration (c) Per $1000. of Receipts (d)			
Elevators (Describe)	Number	Per Elevator			
Independent Contractors (Let or Sub-let work)	Cost of Work	Per $1,000 of Cost of Work			
Products	Sales	Per $1,000 of Sales			
Completed Operations	Receipts	Per $1,000 of Receipts			
Other hazards or endorsements					

IBC 2001 (Continued)
6—78

INSURING AGREEMENTS

I. Coverage A — Bodily Injury Liability

To pay on behalf of the Insured all sums which the Insured shall become legally obligated to pay as compensatory damages because of bodily injury.

Coverage B — Property Damage Liability

To pay on behalf of the Insured all sums which the Insured shall become legally obligated to pay as compensatory damages because of property damage caused by accident.

II. Defence — Settlement — Supplementary Payments

As respects insurance afforded by this policy, the Insurer shall:

(1) defend in the name and on behalf of the Insured and at the cost of the Insurer any civil action which may at any time be brought against the Insured on account of such bodily injury or property damage but the Insurer shall have the right to make such investigation, negotiation and settlement of any claim as may be deemed expedient by the Insurer;

(2) pay all premiums on bonds to release attachments for an amount not in excess of the applicable limit of liability of this policy, all premiums on appeal bonds required in any such defended suit, but without any obligation to apply for or furnish such bonds;

(3) pay all costs taxed against the Insured in any civil action defended by the Insurer and any interest accruing after entry of judgment (or, in those jurisdictions where statute prescribes interest from some other date, from such prescribed date) upon that part of the judgment which is within the limits of the Insurer's liability;

(4) pay expenses incurred by the Insured for such immediate medical and surgical relief to others as shall be imperative at the time of accident;

(5) pay reasonable expenses incurred by the Insured at the Insurer's request in assisting the Insurer in the investigation or defense of any claim or suit, including actual loss of earnings not to exceed $25. per day.

The amounts so incurred except settlement of claims or suits are payable in addition to the applicable limits of liability.

III. Persons Insured

Each of the following is an Insured under this insurance to the extent set forth below:

(1) if the Named Insured is designated in the declarations as an individual, the person so designated but only with respect to the conduct of a business of which he is the sole proprietor;

(2) if the Named Insured is designated in the declarations as a partnership or joint venture, the partnership or joint venture so designated and any partner or member thereof but only with respect to his liability as such;

(3) if the Named Insured is designated in the declarations as other than an individual, partnership or joint venture, the organization so designated and any executive officer, director or stockholder thereof while acting within the scope of his duties as such;

(4) any person (other than an employee of the Named Insured) or organization while acting as real estate manager for the Named Insured.

This insurance does not apply to bodily injury or property damage arising out of the conduct of any partnership or joint venture of which the Insured is a partner or member and which is not designated in this policy as a Named Insured.

IV. Policy Territory

This insurance applies only to bodily injury and property damage which occurs within the policy territory.

EXCLUSIONS

This insurance does not apply to:

(a) liability assumed by the Insured under any contract or agreement except an incidental contract, but this exclusion does not apply to a warranty of fitness or quality of the Named Insured's products or a warranty that work performed by or on behalf of the Named Insured will be done in a workmanlike manner;

(b) bodily injury or property damage arising out of the ownership, maintenance, use or operation by or on behalf of the Insured of any automobile;

(c) bodily injury or property damage arising out of the ownership, maintenance, use, operation, loading or unloading by or on behalf of the Insured of any watercraft, but this exclusion does not apply to watercraft while ashore on premises owned by, rented to or controlled by the Named Insured;

(d) (1) bodily injury or property damage arising out of the ownership, maintenance, use, operation, loading or unloading by or on behalf of the Insured of
    (i) any aircraft, or
    (ii) any air cushion vehicle;
(2) bodily injury or property damage arising out of the ownership, existence, use or operation by or on behalf of the Insured of any premises for the purpose of an airport or aircraft landing strip and all operations necessary or incidental thereto;

(e) bodily injury to any employee of the Insured arising out of and in the course of his employment by the Insured, but this exclusion does not apply to liability assumed by the Insured under an incidental contract;

(f) any obligation for which the Insured or his Insurer may be held liable under any workmen's compensation law;

(g) bodily injury caused intentionally by or at the direction of the Insured;

(h) property damage to
    (1) property owned or occupied by or rented to the Insured, or
    (2) property used by the Insured, or
    (3) property in the care, custody or control of the Insured or property as to which the Insured is for any purpose exercising physical control, or
    (4) any personal property or any fixtures as the result of any work performed thereon by the Insured or anyone on his behalf;
    but parts (2) and (3) of this exclusion do not apply with respect to liability under a written sidetrack agreement and part (3) of this exclusion does not apply with respect to property damage (other than to elevators) arising out of the use of an elevator at premises owned by, rented to or controlled by the Named Insured;

(i) property damage to the Named Insured's products arising out of such products or any part of such products;

EXCLUSIONS (Continued)

(j) property damage to work performed by or on behalf of the Named Insured arising out of the work or any portion thereof, or out of materials, parts or equipment furnished in connection therewith;

(k) to loss of use of tangible property which has not been physically injured or destroyed resulting from

(1) a delay in or lack of performance by or on behalf of the Named Insured of any contract or agreement, or

(2) the failure of the Named Insured's products or work performed by or on behalf of the Named Insured to meet the level of performance, quality, fitness or durability warranted or represented by the Named Insured;

but this exclusion does not apply to loss of use of other tangible property resulting from the sudden and accidental physical injury to or destruction of the Named Insured's products or work performed by or on behalf of the Named Insured after such products or work have been put to use by any person or organization other than an Insured;

(l) expenses incurred for the withdrawal, inspection, repair, replacement, or amounts claimed for loss of use of the Named Insured's products or work completed by or for the Named Insured or of any property of which such products or work form a part, if such products, work or property are withdrawn from the market or from use because of any known or suspected defect or deficiency therein;

(m) bodily injury or property damage due to war, invasion, act of foreign enemy, hostilities (whether war be declared or not), civil war, rebellion, revolution, insurrection or military power;

(n) Nuclear Energy Liability — see exclusion herein.

(o) Environmental Liability — see exclusion herein.

LIMITS OF LIABILITY

Regardless of the number of (1) Insureds under this policy (2) persons or organizations who sustain bodily injury or property damage or (3) claims made or suits brought on account of bodily injury or property damage, the Insurer's liability is limited as follows:

1. **Limits of Liability Coverage A** The limit of bodily injury liability stated in the schedule as applicable to "each person" is the limit of the Insurer's liability for all compensatory damages, including compensatory damages for care and loss of services, arising out of bodily injury sustained by one person in any one occurrence; the limit of such liability stated in the schedule as applicable to "each occurrence" is, subject to the above provision respecting each person, the total limit of the Insurer's liability for all compensatory damages, including compensatory damages for care and loss of services, arising out of bodily injury sustained by two or more persons in any one occurrence.

2. **Limits of Liability Coverage B** The limit of property damage liability stated in the schedule as applicable to "each accident" is the total limit of the Insurer's liability for all compensatory damages arising out of property damage, as the result of any one accident, or series of accidents arising out of one event.

3. Subject to the above provision respecting "each person" and "each occurrence" under Coverage A, and "each accident" under Coverage B, the limits of bodily injury liability and property damage liability stated in the schedule as "aggregate" are respectively the total limits of the Insurer's liability for all compensatory damages arising out of the products hazard and completed operations hazard in any one period of twelve months terminating on an anniversary of the inception date of the policy.

4. **Limits of Liability Coverages A and B** The inclusive limit of liability stated in the schedule as applicable to "bodily injury each occurrence property damage each accident" is the total limit of the Insurer's liability under Coverages A or B or Coverages A and B combined for all compensatory damages, including compensatory damages for care and loss of services, arising out of bodily injury in any one occurrence or property damage as a result of any one accident or series of accidents arising out of one event.

5. Subject to the above provision respecting "bodily injury each occurrence property damage each accident" under Coverage A and B combined, the limit of bodily injury and property damage liability combined stated in the schedule as "aggregate" is the total limit of the Insurer's liability for all compensatory damages arising out of the products hazard and completed operations hazard in any one period of twelve months terminating on an anniversary of the inception date of the policy.

6. All compensatory damages arising out of one lot of goods or products prepared or acquired by the Named Insured or by another trading under his name, shall be considered as arising out of one occurrence as regards bodily injury liability and one accident as regards property damage liability.

7. For the purpose of determining the limit of the Insurer's liability, all bodily injury arising out of continuous or repeated exposure to substantially the same general conditions shall be considered as arising out of one occurrence.

DESCRIPTION OF TERMS USED FOR PREMIUM BASES

1. "Area" means the square footage of the buildings to be insured excluding that portion of the basement used exclusively for storage or that portion of the premises used for heating or air conditioning plant purposes.

2. "Cost of work" means the total cost of all operations performed for the Named Insured during the policy period by independent contractors, including materials used or delivered for use by whomsoever supplied, except maintenance or ordinary alterations and repairs on premises owned or rented by the Named Insured.

3. "Receipts" means the gross amount of money charged by the Named Insured for such operations as are rated on a receipts basis during the policy period.

4. "Remuneration" means the total earnings during the policy period for each owner, partner, executive officer or employee.

5. "Sales" means the gross amount of money charged for all goods and products sold and distributed by the Named Insured or by others trading under his name during the policy period.

APPENDIX C

IBC 2002
6—78

MANUFACTURERS' AND CONTRACTORS' LIABILITY COVERAGE RIDER
(RIDER A)

Coverage for Premises and for Operations in Progress Including Operations of Independent Contractors

Attached to and forming part of this Policy

ADDITIONAL DECLARATIONS

The following discloses all hazards insured hereunder known to exist at the effective date of this policy, unless otherwise stated herein.

SCHEDULE

The insurance afforded is only with respect to such of the following Coverages as are indicated by specific premium charge or charges. The limit of the Insurer's liability against each such Coverage shall be as stated herein, subject to all the terms of this policy having reference thereto.

Coverages		Limits of Liability	Advance Premium
Separate Limits	A. Bodily Injury Liability	$ each person	
		$ each occurrence	$
	B. Property Damage Liability	$ each accident	
			$
Inclusive Limit	A. Bodily Injury Liability and B. Property Damage Liability	$ { bodily injury each occurrence property damage each accident	$
Minimum Premium $		Total Advance Premium	$

Description of Hazards	Premium Bases	Rates		Advance Premium	
		B.I.	P.D.	B.I.	P.D.
Premises—Operations (List all locations owned, rented or controlled by Named Insured stating interest as owner, lessee or tenant.)	(a) Remuneration (b) Receipts (c)	(a) Per $1,000. Remuneration (b) Per $1,000. of Receipts (c)			
Elevators (Describe)	Number	Per Elevator			
Independent Contractors (Let or Sub-let work)	Cost of Work	Per $1,000. of Cost of Work			
Other hazards or endorsements					

IBC 2003 (Continued)
6-78

INSURING AGREEMENTS

I. Coverage A — Bodily Injury Liability

To pay on behalf of the Insured all sums which the Insured shall become legally obligated to pay as compensatory damages because of bodily injury.

Coverage B — Property Damage Liability

To pay on behalf of the Insured all sums which the Insured shall become legally obligated to pay as compensatory damages because of property damage caused by accident.

II. Defence — Settlement — Supplementary Payments

As respects insurance afforded by this policy, the Insurer shall:

(1) defend in the name and on behalf of the Insured and at the cost of the Insurer any civil action which may at any time be brought against the Insured on account of such bodily injury or property damage but the Insurer shall have the right to make such investigation, negotiation and settlement of any claim as may be deemed expedient by the Insurer;

(2) pay all premiums on bonds to release attachments for an amount not in excess of the applicable limit of liability of this policy, all premiums on appeal bonds required in any such defended suit, but without any obligation to apply for or furnish such bonds;

(3) pay all costs taxed against the Insured in any civil action defended by the Insurer and any interest accruing after entry of judgment (or, in those jurisdictions where statute prescribes interest from some other date, from such prescribed date) upon that part of the judgment which is within the limits of the Insurer's liability;

(4) pay expenses incurred by the Insured for such immediate medical and surgical relief to others as shall be imperative at the time of accident;

(5) pay reasonable expenses incurred by the Insured at the Insurer's request in assisting the Insurer in the investigation or defense of any claim or suit, including actual loss of earnings not to exceed $25. per day.

The amounts so incurred except settlement of claims or suits are payable in addition to the applicable limits of liability.

III. Persons Insured

Each of the following is an Insured under this insurance to the extent set forth below:

(1) if the Named Insured is designated in the declarations as an individual, the person so designated but only with respect to the conduct of a business of which he is the sole proprietor;

(2) if the Named Insured is designated in the declarations as a partnership or joint venture, the partnership or joint venture so designated and any partner or member thereof but only with respect to his liability as such;

(3) if the Named Insured is designated in the declarations as other than an individual, partnership or joint venture, the organization so designated and any executive officer, director or stockholder thereof while acting within the scope of his duties as such;

(4) any person (other than an employee of the Named Insured) or organization while acting as real estate manager for the Named Insured.

This insurance does not apply to bodily injury or property damage arising out of the conduct of any partnership or joint venture of which the Insured is a partner or member and which is not designated in this policy as a Named Insured.

IV. Policy Territory

This insurance applies only to bodily injury and property damage which occurs within the policy territory.

EXCLUSIONS

This insurance does not apply to:

(a) liability assumed by the Insured under any contract or agreement except an incidental contract, but with respect to bodily injury or property damage occurring while work performed by the Named Insured is in progress, this exclusion does not apply to a warranty that such work will be done in a workmanlike manner;

(b) bodily injury or property damage arising out of the ownership, maintenance, use or operation by or on behalf of the Insured of any automobile;

(c) bodily injury or property damage arising out of the ownership, maintenance, use, operation, loading or unloading by or on behalf of the Insured of any watercraft, but this exclusion does not apply to watercraft while ashore on premises owned by, rented to or controlled by the Named Insured;

(d) (1) bodily injury or property damage arising out of the ownership, maintenance, use, operation, loading or unloading by or on behalf of the Insured of
(i) any aircraft, or
(ii) any air cushion vehicle;

(2) bodily injury or property damage arising out of the ownership, existence, use or operation by or on behalf of the Insured of any premises for the purpose of an airport or aircraft landing strip and all operations necessary or incidental thereto;

(e) bodily injury to any employee of the Insured arising out of and in the course of his employment by the Insured, but this exclusion does not apply to liability assumed by the Insured under an incidental contract;

(f) any obligation for which the Insured or his Insurer may be held liable under any workmen's compensation law;

(g) bodily injury caused intentionally by or at the direction of the Insured;

(h) property damage to
(1) property owned or occupied by or rented to the Insured, or
(2) property used by the Insured, or
(3) property in the care, custody or control of the Insured or property as to which the Insured is for any purpose exercising physical control, or
(4) any personal property or any fixtures as the result of any work performed thereon by the Insured or anyone on his behalf;

but parts (2) and (3) of this exclusion do not apply with respect to liability under a written sidetrack agreement and part (3) of this exclusion does not apply with respect to property damage (other than to elevators) arising out of the use of an elevator at premises owned by, rented to or controlled by the Named Insured;

(i) property damage to the Named Insured's products arising out of such products or any part of such products;

(j) property damage to work performed by or on behalf of the Named Insured arising out of the work or any portion thereof, or out of materials, parts or equipment furnished in connection therewith;

LIMITS OF LIABILITY

Regardless of the number of (1) Insureds under this policy (2) persons or organizations who sustain bodily injury or property damage or (3) claims made or suits brought on account of bodily injury or property damage, the Insurer's liability is limited as follows:

1. **Limits of Liability Coverage A**   The limit of bodily injury liability stated in the schedule as applicable to "each person" is the limit of the Insurer's liability for all compensatory damages, including compensatory damages for care and loss of services, arising out of bodily injury sustained by one person in any one occurrence; the limit of such liability stated in the schedule as applicable to "each occurrence" is, subject to the above provision respecting each person, the total limit of the Insurer's liability for all compensatory damages, including compensatory damages for care and loss of services, arising out of bodily injury sustained by two or more persons in any one occurrence.

2. **Limits of Liability Coverage B**   The limit of property damage liability stated in the schedule as applicable to "each accident" is the total limit of the Insurer's liability for all compensatory damages arising out of property damage, as the result of any one accident, or series of accidents arising out of one event.

3. **Limits of Liability Coverages A and B**   The inclusive limit of liability stated in the schedule as applicable to "bodily injury each occurrence property damage each accident" is the total limit of the Insurer's liability under Coverages A or B or Coverages A and B combined for all compensatory damages, including compensatory damages for care and loss of services, arising out of bodily injury in any one occurrence or property damage as a result of any one accident or series of accidents arising out of one event.

4. For the purpose of determining the limit of the Insurer's liability, all bodily injury arising out of continuous or repeated exposure to substantially the same general conditions shall be considered as arising out of one occurrence.

ADDITIONAL DEFINITION

When used in reference to this insurance (including endorsements forming a part of the policy):

"insured premises" means (1) the premises designated in the schedule, and (2) premises as to which the Named Insured acquires ownership or control provided the Named Insured notifies the Insurer within 30 days following the effective date of such acquisition, but the insurance with respect to the newly acquired premises does not apply to any loss against which the Named Insured has other valid and collectible insurance; and includes the ways immediately adjoining such premises.

DESCRIPTION OF TERMS USED FOR PREMIUM BASES

1. "Area" means the square footage of the buildings to be insured excluding that portion of the basement used exclusively for storage or that portion of the premises used for heating or air conditioning plant purposes.

2. "Receipts" means the gross amount of money charged by the Named Insured for such operations as are rated on a receipts basis during the policy period.

3. "Remuneration" means the total earnings during the policy period for each owner, partner, executive officer or employee.

IBC 2003
6–78

MANUFACTURERS' AND CONTRACTORS' LIABILITY COVERAGE RIDER
(RIDER B)

Coverage for Premises and for Named Insured's Operations in Progress.

Attached to and forming part of this Policy

ADDITIONAL DECLARATIONS

The following discloses all hazards insured hereunder known to exist at the effective date of this policy, unless otherwise stated herein.

SCHEDULE

The insurance afforded is only with respect to such of the following Coverages as are indicated by specific premium charge or charges. The limit of the Insurer's liability against each such Coverage shall be as stated herein, subject to all the terms of this policy having reference thereto.

Coverages		Limits of Liability		Advance Premium
Separate Limits	A. Bodily Injury Liability	$	each person	
		$	each occurrence	$
	B. Property Damage Liability			
		$	each accident	$
Inclusive Limit	A. Bodily Injury Liability and B. Property Damage Liability	$	bodily injury each occurrence property damage each accident	$
Minimum Premium $			Total Advance Premium	$

Description of Hazards	Premium Bases	Rates		Advance Premium	
		B.I.	P.D.	B.I.	P.D.
Premises—Operations (List all locations owned, rented or controlled by Named Insured stating interest as owner, lessee or tenant.)	(a) Receipts (b) Remuneration (c)	(a) Per $1,000. of Receipts (b) Per $1,000. Remuneration (c)			
Elevators (Describe)	Number Insured	Per Elevator			
Other hazards or endorsements					

IBC 2003 (Continued)
6−78

INSURING AGREEMENTS

I. Coverage A — Bodily Injury Liability

To pay on behalf of the Insured all sums which the Insured shall become legally obligated to pay as compensatory damages because of bodily injury.

Coverage B — Property Damage Liability

To pay on behalf of the Insured all sums which the Insured shall become legally obligated to pay as compensatory damages because of property damage caused by accident.

II. Defence — Settlement — Supplementary Payments

As respects insurance afforded by this policy, the Insurer shall:

(1) defend in the name and on behalf of the Insured and at the cost of the Insurer any civil action which may at any time be brought against the Insured on account of such bodily injury or property damage but the Insurer shall have the right to make such investigation, negotiation and settlement of any claim as may be deemed expedient by the Insurer;

(2) pay all premiums on bonds to release attachments for an amount not in excess of the applicable limit of liability of this policy, all premiums on appeal bonds required in any such defended suit, but without any obligation to apply for or furnish such bonds;

(3) pay all costs taxed against the Insured in any civil action defended by the Insurer and any interest accruing after entry of judgment (or, in those jurisdictions where statute prescribes interest from some other date, from such prescribed date) upon that part of the judgment which is within the limits of the Insurer's liability;

(4) pay expenses incurred by the Insured for such immediate medical and surgical relief to others as shall be imperative at the time of accident;

(5) pay reasonable expenses incurred by the Insured at the Insurer's request in assisting the Insurer in the investigation or defense of any claim or suit, including actual loss of earnings not to exceed $25. per day.

The amounts so incurred except settlement of claims or suits are payable in addition to the applicable limits of liability.

III. Persons Insured

Each of the following is an Insured under this insurance to the extent set forth below:

(1) if the Named Insured is designated in the declarations as an individual, the person so designated but only with respect to the conduct of a business of which he is the sole proprietor;

(2) if the Named Insured is designated in the declarations as a partnership or joint venture, the partnership or joint venture so designated and any partner or member thereof but only with respect to his liability as such;

(3) if the Named Insured is designated in the declarations as other than an individual, partnership or joint venture, the organization so designated and any executive officer, director or stockholder thereof while acting within the scope of his duties as such;

(4) any person (other than an employee of the Named Insured) or organization while acting as real estate manager for the Named Insured.

This insurance does not apply to bodily injury or property damage arising out of the conduct of any partnership or joint venture of which the Insured is a partner or member and which is not designated in this policy as a Named Insured.

IV. Policy Territory

This insurance applies only to bodily injury and property damage which occurs within the policy territory.

This insurance does not apply to: **EXCLUSIONS**

(a) liability assumed by the Insured under any contract or agreement except an incidental contract, but with respect to bodily injury or property damage occurring while work performed by the Named Insured is in progress, this exclusion does not apply to a warranty that such work will be done in a workmanlike manner;

(b) bodily injury or property damage arising out of the ownership, maintenance, use or operation by or on behalf of the Insured of any automobile;

(c) bodily injury or property damage arising out of the ownership, maintenance, use, operation, loading or unloading by or on behalf of the Insured of any watercraft, but this exclusion does not apply to watercraft while ashore on premises owned by, rented to or controlled by the Named Insured;

(d) (1) bodily injury or property damage arising out of the ownership, maintenance, use, operation, loading or unloading by or on behalf of the Insured of
   (i) any aircraft, or
   (ii) any air cushion vehicle;

(2) bodily injury or property damage arising out of the ownership, existence, use or operation by or on behalf of the Insured of any premises for the purpose of an airport or aircraft landing strip and all operations necessary or incidental thereto;

(e) bodily injury to any employee of the Insured arising out of and in the course of his employment by the Insured, but this exclusion does not apply to liability assumed by the Insured under an incidental contract;

(f) any obligation for which the Insured or his Insurer may be held liable under any workmen's compensation law;

(g) bodily injury caused intentionally by or at the direction of the Insured;

(h) property damage to
(1) property owned or occupied by or rented to the Insured, or
(2) property used by the Insured, or
(3) property in the care, custody or control of the Insured or property as to which the Insured is for any purpose exercising physical control, or
(4) any personal property or any fixtures as the result of any work performed thereon by the Insured or anyone on his behalf,
but parts (2) and (3) of this exclusion do not apply with respect to liability under a written sidetrack agreement and part (3) of this exclusion does not apply with respect to property damage (other than to elevators) arising out of the use of an elevator at premises owned by, rented to or controlled by the Named Insured;

(i) property damage to the Named Insured's products arising out of such products or any part of such products;

(j) property damage to work performed by or on behalf of the Named Insured arising out of the work or any portion thereof, or out of materials, parts or equipment furnished in connection therewith;

EXCLUSIONS (Continued)

(k) bodily injury or property damage included within the completed operations hazard or the products hazard;

(l) to loss of use of tangible property which has not been physically injured or destroyed resulting from

    (1) a delay in or lack of performance by or on behalf of the Named Insured of any contract or agreement, or

    (2) the failure of the Named Insured's products or work performed by or on behalf of the Named Insured to meet the level of performance, quality, fitness or durability warranted or represented by the Named Insured;

    but this exclusion does not apply to loss of use of other tangible property resulting from the sudden and accidental physical injury to or destruction of the Named Insured's products or work performed by or on behalf of the Named Insured after such products or work have been put to use by any person or organization other than an Insured;

(m) property damage arising out of

    (1) the use of explosives for blasting, or

    (2) vibration from pile driving or caisson work, or

    (3) the removal or weakening of support of any property, building or land whether such support be natural or otherwise;

    but this exclusion does not apply to property damage for which liability is assumed by the Insured under an incidental contract;

(n) bodily injury or property damage arising out of operations performed for the Named Insured by independent contractors or acts or omissions of the Named Insured in connection with his general supervision of such operations, other than bodily injury or property damage which occurs in the course of

    (i) maintenance and repairs at premises owned by or rented to the Named Insured, or

    (ii) structural alterations at such premises which do not involve changing the size of or moving buildings or other structures;

(o) bodily injury or property damage due to war, invasion, act of foreign enemy, hostilities (whether war be declared or not), civil war, rebellion, revolution, insurrection or military power;

(p) Nuclear Energy Liability — see exclusion herein;

(q) Environmental Liability – see exclusion herein.

LIMITS OF LIABILITY

Regardless of the number of (1) Insureds under this policy (2) persons or organizations who sustain bodily injury or property damage or (3) claims made or suits brought on account of bodily injury or property damage, the Insurer's liability is limited as follows:

1. **Limits of Liability** The limit of bodily injury liability stated in the schedule as applicable to "each person" is the limit of the Insurer's
    Coverage A liability for all compensatory damages, including compensatory damages for care and loss of services, arising out of bodily injury sustained by one person in any one occurrence; the limit of such liability stated in the schedule as applicable to "each occurrence" is, subject to the above provision respecting each person, the total limit of the Insurer's liability for all compensatory damages, including compensatory damages for care and loss of services, arising out of bodily injury sustained by two or more persons in any one occurrence.

2. **Limits of Liability** The limit of property damage liability stated in the schedule as applicable to "each accident" is the total limit of the
    Coverage B Insurer's liability for all compensatory damages arising out of property damage, as the result of any one accident, or series of accidents arising out of one event.

3. **Limits of Liability** The inclusive limit of liability stated in the schedule as applicable to "bodily injury each occurrence property
    Coverages A and B damage each accident" is the total limit of the Insurer's liability under Coverages A or B or Coverages A and B combined for all compensatory damages, including compensatory damages for care and loss of services, arising out of bodily injury in any one occurrence or property damage as a result of any one accident or series of accidents arising out of one event.

4. For the purpose of determining the limit of the Insurer's liability, all bodily injury arising out of continuous or repeated exposure to substantially the same general conditions shall be considered as arising out of one occurrence.

DESCRIPTION OF TERMS USED FOR PREMIUM BASES

1. "Receipts" means the gross amount of money charged by the Named Insured for such operations as are rated on a receipts basis during the policy period.

2. "Remuneration" means the total earnings during the policy period for each owner, partner, executive officer or employee.

APPENDIX D

IBC 2004
6-78

OWNERS', LANDLORDS' & TENANTS' LIABILITY COVERAGE RIDER

Coverage for Designated Premises and Related Operations in Progress

Attached to and forming part of this Policy

SCHEDULE

The insurance afforded is only with respect to such of the following Coverages as are indicated by specific premium charge or charges. The limit of the Insurer's liability against each such Coverage shall be as stated herein, subject to all the terms of this policy having reference thereto.

Coverages		Limits of Liability		Advance Premium
Separate Limits	A. Bodily Injury Liability	$	each person	$
		$	each occurrence	
	B. Property Damage Liability	$	each accident	
				$
Inclusive Limit	A. Bodily Injury Liability and B. Property Damage Liability	$	bodily injury each occurrence property damage each accident	$
Minimum Premium $			Total Advance Premium	$

Description of Hazards	Premium Bases	Rates		Advance Premium	
		B.I.	P.D.	B.I.	P.D.
Premises—Operations (List all locations owned, rented or controlled by Named Insured stating interest as owner, lessee or tenant.)	(a) Area (sq. ft.) (b) Remuneration (c) Receipts (d)	(a) Per 100 sq. ft. of Area (b) Per $1000. Remuneration (c) Per $1000. of Receipts (d)			
Elevators (Describe)	Number	Per Elevator			
Endorsement(s)					

INSURING AGREEMENTS

I. **Coverage A — Bodily Injury Liability**

To pay on behalf of the Insured all sums which the Insured shall become legally obligated to pay as compensatory damages because of bodily injury arising out of the ownership, maintenance or use of the insured premises and all operations necessary or incidental thereto.

Coverage B — Property Damage Liability

To pay on behalf of the Insured all sums which the Insured shall become legally obligated to pay as compensatory damages because of property damage caused by accident and arising out of the ownership, maintenance or use of the insured premises and all operations necessary or incidental thereto.

IBC 2004 (Continued)
6-78

II. Defence — Settlement — Supplementary Payments

As respects insurance afforded by this policy, the Insurer shall:

(1) defend in the name and on behalf of the Insured and at the cost of the Insurer any civil action which may at any time be brought against the Insured on account of such bodily injury or property damage but the Insurer shall have the right to make such investigation, negotiation and settlement of any claim as may be deemed expedient by the Insurer;

(2) pay all premiums on bonds to release attachments for an amount not in excess of the applicable limit of liability of this policy, all premiums on appeal bonds required in any such defended suit, but without any obligation to apply for or furnish such bonds;

(3) pay all costs taxed against the Insured in any civil action defended by the Insurer and any interest accruing after entry of judgment (or, in those jurisdictions where statute prescribes interest from some other date, from such prescribed date) upon that part of the judgment which is within the limits of the Insurer's liability;

(4) pay expenses incurred by the Insured for such immediate medical and surgical relief to others as shall be imperative at the time of accident;

(5) pay reasonable expenses incurred by the Insured at the Insurer's request in assisting the Insurer in the investigation or defense of any claim or suit, including actual loss of earnings not to exceed $25. per day.

The amounts so incurred except settlement of claims or suits are payable in addition to the applicable limits of liability.

III. Persons Insured

Each of the following is an Insured under this insurance to the extent set forth below:

(1) if the Named Insured is designated in the declarations as an individual, the person so designated but only with respect to the conduct of a business of which he is the sole proprietor;

(2) if the Named Insured is designated in the declarations as a partnership or joint venture, the partnership or joint venture so designated and any partner or member thereof but only with respect to his liability as such;

(3) if the Named Insured is designated in the declarations as other than an individual, partnership or joint venture, the organization so designated and any executive officer, director or stockholder thereof while acting within the scope of his duties as such;

(4) any person (other than an employee of the Named Insured) or organization while acting as real estate manager for the Named Insured.

This insurance does not apply to bodily injury or property damage arising out of the conduct of any partnership or joint venture of which the Insured is a partner or member and which is not designated in this policy as a Named Insured.

IV. Policy Territory

This insurance applies only to bodily injury or property damage which occurs within the policy territory.

EXCLUSIONS

This insurance does not apply to:

(a) liability assumed by the Insured under any contract or agreement except an incidental contract, but this exclusion does not apply to a warranty of fitness or quality of the Named Insureds products with respect to consumption, handling or use thereof on the insured premises;

(b) bodily injury or property damage arising out of the ownership, maintenance, use or operation by or on behalf of the Insured of any automobile;

(c) bodily injury or property damage arising out of the ownership, maintenance, use, operation, loading or unloading by or on behalf of the Insured of any watercraft, but this exclusion does not apply to watercraft while ashore on premises owned by, rented to or controlled by the Named Insured;

(d) (1) bodily injury or property damage arising out of the ownership, maintenance, use, operation, loading or unloading by or on behalf of the Insured of

    (i) any aircraft, or

    (ii) any air cushion vehicle;

   (2) bodily injury or property damage arising out of the ownership, existence, use or operation by or on behalf of the Insured of any premises for the purpose of an airport or aircraft landing strip and all operations necessary or incidental thereto;

(e) bodily injury to any employee of the Insured arising out of and in the course of his employment by the Insured, but this exclusion does not apply to liability assumed by the Insured under an incidental contract;

(f) any obligation for which the Insured or his Insurer may be held liable under any workmen's compensation law;

(g) bodily injury caused intentionally by or at the direction of the Insured;

(h) property damage to

(1) property owned or occupied by or rented to the Insured, or

(2) property used by the Insured, or

(3) property in the care, custody or control of the Insured or property as to which the Insured is for any purpose exercising physical control, or

(4) any personal property or any fixtures as the result of any work performed thereon by the Insured or anyone on his behalf;

but parts (2) and (3) of this exclusion do not apply with respect to liability under a written sidetrack agreement and part (3) of this exclusion does not apply with respect to property damage (other than to elevators) arising out of the use of an elevator at premises owned by, rented to or controlled by the Named Insured;

(i) property damage to the Named Insured's products arising out of such products or any part of such products;

(j) property damage to work performed by or on behalf of the Named Insured arising out of the work or any portion thereof, or out of materials, parts or equipment furnished in connection therewith;

(k) bodily injury or property damage included within the completed operations hazard or the products hazard;

(l) bodily injury or property damage arising out of operations on or from premises (other than the insured premises) owned by, rented to or controlled by the Named Insured, or to liability assumed by the Insured under any contract or agreement relating to such premises;

(m) bodily injury or property damage arising out of structural alterations which involve changing the size of or moving buildings or other structures, new construction or demolition operations performed by or on behalf of the Named Insured;

(n) to loss of use of tangible property which has not been physically injured or destroyed resulting from

(1) a delay in or lack of performance by or on behalf of the Named Insured of any contract or agreement, or

(2) the failure of the Named Insured's products or work performed by or on behalf of the Named Insured to meet the level of performance, quality, fitness or durability warranted or represented by the Named Insured;

but this exclusion does not apply to loss of use of other tangible property resulting from the sudden and accidental physical injury to or destruction of the Named Insured's products or work performed by or on behalf of the Named Insured after such products or work have been put to use by any person or organization other than an Insured;

(o) bodily injury or property damage due to war, invasion, act of foreign enemy, hostilities (whether war be declared or not), civil war, rebellion, revolution, insurrection or military power;

(p) Nuclear Energy Liability — see exclusion herein.

(q) Environmental Liability — see exclusion herein.

LIMITS OF LIABILITY

Regardless of the number of (1) Insureds under this policy (2) persons or organizations who sustain bodily injury or property damage or (3) claims made or suits brought on account of bodily injury or property damage, the Insurer's liability is limited as follows:

1. **Limits of Liability Coverage A** The limit of bodily injury liability stated in the schedule as applicable to "each person" is the limit of the Insurer's liability for all compensatory damages, including compensatory damages for care and loss of services, arising out of bodily injury sustained by one person in any one occurrence; the limit of such liability stated in the schedule as applicable to "each occurrence" is, subject to the above provision respecting each person, the total limit of the Insurer's liability for all compensatory damages, including compensatory damages for care and loss of services, arising out of bodily injury sustained by two or more persons in any one occurrence.

2. **Limits of Liability Coverage B** The limit of property damage liability stated in the schedule as applicable to "each accident" is the total limit of the Insurer's liability for all compensatory damages arising out of property damage, as the result of any one accident, or series of accidents arising out of one event.

3. **Limits of Liability Coverages A and B** The inclusive limit of liability stated in the schedule as applicable to "bodily injury each occurrence property damage each accident" is the total limit of the Insurer's liability under Coverages A or B or Coverages A and B combined for all compensatory damages, including compensatory damages for care and loss of services, arising out of bodily injury in any one occurrence or property damage as a result of any one accident or series of accidents arising out of one event.

4. For the purpose of determining the limit of the Insurer's liability, all bodily injury arising out of continuous or repeated exposure to substantially the same general conditions shall be considered as arising out of one occurrence.

ADDITIONAL DEFINITION

When used in reference to this insurance (including endorsements forming a part of the policy):

"insured premises" means (1) the premises designated in the schedule, and (2) premises as to which the Named Insured acquires ownership or control provided the Named Insured notifies the Insurer within 30 days following the effective date of such acquisition, but the insurance with respect to the newly acquired premises does not apply to any loss against which the Named Insured has other valid and collectible insurance; and includes the ways immediately adjoining such premises.

DESCRIPTION OF TERMS USED FOR PREMIUM BASES

1. "Area" means the square footage of the buildings to be insured excluding that portion of the basement used exclusively for storage or that portion of the premises used for heating or air conditioning plant purposes.

2. "Receipts" means the gross amount of money charged by the Named Insured for such operations as are rated on a receipts basis during the policy period.

3. "Remuneration" means the total earnings during the policy period for each owner, partner, executive officer or employee.

APPENDIX E

IBC 2005
6-78

PRODUCTS AND COMPLETED OPERATIONS
LIABILITY COVERAGE RIDER

Attached to and forming part of this Policy

SCHEDULE

The insurance afforded is only with respect to such of the following Coverages as are indicated by specific premium charge or charges. The limit of the Insurer's liability against each such Coverage shall be as stated herein, subject to all the terms of this policy having reference thereto.

Coverages		Limits of Liability		Advance Premium
Separate Limits	A. Bodily Injury Liability	$	each person	$
		$	each occurrence	
		$	aggregate	
	B. Property Damage Liability	$	each accident	
		$	aggregate	$
Inclusive Limit	A. Bodily Injury Liability and B. Property Damage Liability	$	bodily injury each occurrence property damage each accident	$
		$	aggregate	
Minimum Premium $			Total Advance Premium	$

Description of Hazards	Premium Bases	Rates		Advance Premium	
		B.I.	P.D.	B.I.	P.D.
Products	Sales	Per $1,000 of Sales			
Completed Operations	Receipts	Per $1,000 of Receipts			
Endorsements					

INSURING AGREEMENTS

I. Coverage A — Bodily Injury Liability

To pay on behalf of the Insured all sums which the Insured shall become legally obligated to pay as compensatory damages because of bodily injury and arising out of (a) the products hazard, or (b) the completed operations hazard.

Coverage B — Property Damage Liability

To pay on behalf of the Insured all sums which the Insured shall become legally obligated to pay as compensatory damages because of property damage caused by accident and arising out of (a) the products hazard, or (b) the completed operations hazard.

II. Defence — Settlement — Supplementary Payments

As respects insurance afforded by this policy, the Insurer shall:

(1) defend in the name and on behalf of the Insured and at the cost of the Insurer any civil action which may at any time be brought against the Insured on account of such bodily injury or property damage but the Insurer shall have the right to make such investigation, negotiation and settlement of any claim as may be deemed expedient by the Insurer;

(2) pay all premiums on bonds to release attachments for an amount not in excess of the applicable limit of liability of this policy, all premiums on appeal bonds required in any such defended suit, but without any obligation to apply for or furnish such bonds;

(3) pay all costs taxed against the Insured in any civil action defended by the Insurer and any interest accruing after entry of judgment (or, in those jurisdictions where statute prescribes interest from some other date, from such prescribed date) upon that part of the judgment which is within the limits of the Insurer's liability;

(4) pay expenses incurred by the Insured for such immediate medical and surgical relief to others as shall be imperative at the time of accident;

(5) pay reasonable expenses incurred by the Insured at the Insurer's request in assisting the Insurer in the investigation or defense of any claim or suit, including actual loss of earnings not to exceed $25. per day.

The amounts so incurred except settlement of claims or suits are payable in addition to the applicable limits of liability.

IBC 2005 (Continued)
6 – 78

III. Persons Insured

Each of the following is an Insured under this insurance to the extent set forth below:

(1) if the Named Insured is designated in the declarations as an individual, the person so designated but only with respect to the conduct of a business of which he is the sole proprietor;

(2) if the Named Insured is designated in the declarations as a partnership or joint venture, the partnership or joint venture so designated and any partner or member thereof but only with respect to his liability as such;

(3) if the Named Insured is designated in the declarations as other than an individual, partnership or joint venture, the organization so designated and any executive officer, director or stockholder thereof while acting within the scope of his duties as such.

This insurance does not apply to bodily injury or property damage arising out of the conduct of any partnership or joint venture of which the Insured is a partner or member and which is not designated in this policy as a Named Insured.

IV. Policy Territory

This insurance applies only to bodily injury and property damage which occurs within the policy territory.

EXCLUSIONS

This insurance does not apply to:

(a) liability assumed by the Insured under any contract or agreement, but this exclusion does not apply to a warranty of fitness or quality of the Named Insured's products or a warranty that work performed by or on behalf of the Named Insured will be done in a workmanlike manner;

(b) bodily injury to any employee of the Insured arising out of and in the course of his employment by the Insured;

(c) any obligation for which the Insured or his Insurer may be held liable under any workmen's compensation law;

(d) property damage to the Named Insured's products arising out of such products or any part of such products;

(e) property damage to work performed by or on behalf of the Named Insured arising out of the work or any portion thereof, or out of materials, parts or equipment furnished in connection therewith;

(f) to loss of use of tangible property which has not been physically injured or destroyed resulting from

(1) a delay in or lack of performance by or on behalf of the Named Insured of any contract or agreement, or

(2) the failure of the Named Insured's products or work performed by or on behalf of the Named Insured to meet the level of performance, quality, fitness or durability warranted or represented by the Named Insured;

but this exclusion does not apply to loss of use of other tangible property resulting from the sudden and accidental physical injury to or destruction of the Named Insured's products or work performed by or on behalf of the Named Insured after such products or work have been put to use by any person or organization other than an Insured;

(g) expenses incurred for the withdrawal, inspection, repair, replacement, or amounts claimed for loss of use of the Named Insured's products or work completed by or for the Named Insured or of any property of which such products work form a part, if such products, work or property are withdrawn from the market or from use because of any known or suspected defect or deficiency therein;

(h) bodily injury or property damage due to war, invasion, act of foreign enemy, hostilities (whether war be declared or not), civil war, rebellion, revolution, insurrection or military power;

(i) Nuclear Energy Liability — see exclusion herein.

(j) Environmental Liability — see exclusion herein.

LIMITS OF LIABILITY

Regardless of the number of (1) Insureds under this policy (2) persons or organizations who sustain bodily injury or property damage or (3) claims made or suits brought on account of bodily injury or property damage, the Insurer's liability is limited as follows:

1. **Limits of Liability Coverage A** The limit of bodily injury liability stated in the schedule as applicable to "each person" is the limit of the Insurer's liability for all compensatory damages, including compensatory damages for care and loss of services, arising out of bodily injury sustained by one person in any one occurrence; the limit of such liability stated in the schedule as applicable to "each occurrence" is, subject to the above provision respecting each person, the total limit of the Insurer's liability for all compensatory damages, including compensatory damages for care and loss of services, arising out of bodily injury sustained by two or more persons in any one occurrence.

2. **Limits of Liability Coverage B** The limit of property damage liability stated in the schedule as applicable to "each accident" is the total limit of the Insurer's liability for all compensatory damages arising out of property damage, as the result of any one accident, or series of accidents arising out of one event.

3. Subject to the above provision respecting "each person" and "each occurrence" under Coverage A, and "each accident" under Coverage B, the limits of bodily injury liability and property damage liability stated in the schedule as "aggregate" are respectively the total limits of the Insurer's liability for all compensatory damages arising out of the products hazard and completed operations hazard in any one period of twelve months terminating on an anniversary of the inception date of the policy.

4. **Limits of Liability Coverages A and B** The inclusive limit of liability stated in the schedule as applicable to "bodily injury each occurrence property damage each accident" is the total limit of the Insurer's liability under Coverages A or B or Coverages A and B combined for all compensatory damages, including compensatory damages for care and loss of services, arising out of bodily injury in any one occurrence or property damage as a result of any one accident or series of accidents arising out of one event.

5. Subject to the above provision respecting "bodily injury each occurrence property damage each accident" under Coverage A and B combined, the limit of bodily injury and property damage liability combined stated in the schedule as "aggregate" is the total limit of the Insurer's liability for all compensatory damages arising out of the products hazard and completed operations hazard in any one period of twelve months terminating on an anniversary of the inception date of the policy.

6. All compensatory damages arising out of one lot of goods or products prepared or acquired by the Named Insured or by another trading under his name, shall be considered as arising out of one occurrence as regards bodily injury liability and one accident as regards property damage liability.

7. For the purpose of determining the limit of the Insurer's liability, all bodily injury arising out of continuous or repeated exposure to substantially the same general conditions shall be considered as arising out of one occurrence.

DESCRIPTION OF TERMS USED FOR PREMIUM BASES

1. "Receipts" means the gross amount of money charged by the Named Insured for such operations as are rated on a receipts basis during the policy period.

2. "Sales" means the gross amount of money charged for all goods and products sold and distributed by the Named Insured or by others trading under his name during the policy period.

APPENDIX F

CONTRACTUAL LIABILITY COVERAGE RIDER

Designated Contracts Only

Attached to and forming part of this Policy

SCHEDULE

The insurance afforded is only with respect to such of the following Coverages as are indicated by specific premium charge or charges. The limit of the Insurer's liability against each such Coverage shall be as stated herein, subject to all the terms of this policy having reference thereto.

Coverages		Limits of Liability	Advance Premium
Separate Limits	Y. Bodily Injury Liability	$ each person $ each occurrence	$
	Z. Property Damage Liability	$ each accident	
Inclusive Limit	Y. Bodily Injury Liability and Z. Property Damage Liability	$ { bodily injury each occurrence property damage each accident	$
Minimum Premium $		Total Advance Premium	$

Designation of Contracts	Premium Bases	Rates		Advance Premiums	
		B.I.	P.D.	B.I.	P.D.
	(a) Number (b) Cost	(a) Per Contract (b) Per $1000. of Cost			
Endorsements					

INSURING AGREEMENTS

I. Coverage Y — Contractual Bodily Injury Liability

To pay on behalf of the Insured all sums which the Insured, by reason of contractual liability assumed by the Insured under a contract designated in the schedule for this insurance, shall become legally obligated to pay as compensatory damages because of bodily injury.

Coverage Z — Contractual Property Damage Liability

To pay on behalf of the Insured all sums which the Insured, by reason of contractual liability assumed by the Insured under a contract designated in the schedule for this insurance, shall become legally obligated to pay as compensatory damages because of property damage caused by accident.

II. Defence — Settlement — Supplementary Payments

As respects insurance afforded by this policy, the Insurer shall:

(1) defend in the name and on behalf of the Insured and at the cost of the Insurer any civil action which may at any time be brought against the Insured on account of such bodily injury or property damage but the Insurer shall have the right to make such investigation, negotiation and settlement of any claim as may be deemed expedient by the Insurer;

(2) pay all premiums on bonds to release attachments for an amount not in excess of the applicable limit of liability of this policy, all premiums on appeal bonds required in any such defended suit, but without any obligation to apply for or furnish such bonds;

(3) pay all costs taxed against the Insured in any civil action defended by the Insurer and any interest accruing after entry of judgment (or, in those jurisdictions where statute prescribes interest from some other date, from such prescribed date) upon that part of the judgment which is within the limits of the Insurer's liability;

(4) pay expenses incurred by the Insured for such immediate medical and surgical relief to others as shall be imperative at the time of accident;

(5) pay reasonable expenses incurred by the Insured at the Insurer's request in assisting the Insurer in the investigation or defense of any claim or suit, including actual loss of earnings not to exceed $25. per day.

The amounts so incurred except settlement of claims or suits are payable in addition to the applicable limits of liability.

III. Persons Insured

Each of the following is an Insured under this insurance to the extent set forth below:

(1) if the Named Insured is designated in the declarations as an individual, the person so designated but only with respect to the conduct of a business of which he is the sole proprietor;

(2) if the Named Insured is designated in the declarations as a partnership or joint venture, the partnership or joint venture so designated and any partner or member thereof but only with respect to his liability as such;

(3) if the Named Insured is designated in the declarations as other than an individual, partnership or joint venture, the organization so designated and any executive officer, director or stockholder thereof while acting within the scope of his duties as such.

IV. Policy Territory

This insurance applies only to bodily injury and property damage which occurs within the policy territory.

IBC 2007 (Continued)
8-78

EXCLUSIONS

This insurance does not apply:

(a) if the Insured or his indemnitee is an architect, engineer or surveyor, to bodily injury or property damage arising out of the rendering of or the failure to render professional services by such Insured or indemnitee, including (1) the preparation or approval of maps, plans, opinion, reports, surveys, designs or specifications and (2) supervisory, inspection or engineering services;

(b) to any obligation for which the Insured or his Insurer may be held liable under any workmen's compensation law;

(c) to bodily injury caused intentionally by or at the direction of the Insured;

(d) to property damage to
   (1) property owned or occupied by or rented to the Insured, or
   (2) property used by the Insured, or
   (3) property in the care, custody or control of the Insured or property as to which the Insured is for any purpose exercising physical control, or
   (4) any personal property or any fixtures as the result of any work performed thereon by the Insured or anyone on his behalf;

   but parts (2) and (3) of this exclusion do not apply with respect to liability under a written sidetrack agreement and part (3) of this exclusion does not apply with respect to property damage (other than to elevators) arising out of the use of an elevator at premises owned by, rented to or controlled by the Named Insured;

(e) to property damage to the Named Insured's products arising out of such products or any part of such products;

(f) to property damage to work performed by or on behalf of the Named Insured arising out of the work or any portion thereof, or out of materials, parts or equipment furnished in connection therewith;

(g) to loss of use of tangible property which has not been physically injured or destroyed resulting from
   (1) a delay in or lack of performance by or on behalf of the Named Insured of any contract or agreement, or
   (2) the failure of the Named Insured's products or work performed by or on behalf of the Named Insured to meet the level of performance, quality, fitness or durability warranted or represented by the Named Insured;

   but this exclusion does not apply to loss of use of other tangible property resulting from the sudden and accidental physical injury to or destruction of the Named Insured's products or work performed by or on behalf of the Named Insured after such products or work have been put to use by any person or organization other than an Insured;

(h) to expenses incurred for the withdrawal, inspection, repair, replacement, or amounts claimed for loss of use of the Named Insured's products or work completed by or for the Named Insured or of any property of which such products or work form a part, if such products, work or property are withdrawn from the market or from use because of any known or suspected defect or deficiency therein;

(i) to bodily injury or property damage due to war, invasion, act of foreign enemy, hostilities (whether war be declared or not), civil war, rebellion, revolution, insurrection or military power;

(j) to Nuclear Energy Liability – see exclusion herein;

(k) Environmental Liability – see exclusion herein.

LIMITS OF LIABILITY

Regardless of the number of (1) Insureds under this policy (2) persons or organizations who sustain bodily injury or property damage or (3) claims made or suits brought on account of bodily injury or property damage, the Insurer's liability is limited as follows:

1. **Limits of Liability Coverage Y** The limit of bodily injury liability stated in the schedule as applicable to "each person" is the limit of the Insurer's liability for all compensatory damages, including compensatory damages for care and loss of services, arising out of bodily injury sustained by one person in any one occurrence; the limit of such liability stated in the schedule as applicable to "each occurrence" is, subject to the above provision respecting each person, the total limit of the Insurer's liability for all compensatory damages, including compensatory damages for care and loss of services, arising out of bodily injury sustained by two or more persons in any one occurrence.

2. **Limits of Liability Coverage Z** The limit of property damage liability stated in the schedule as applicable to "each accident" is the total limit of the Insurer's liability for all compensatory damages arising out of property damage, as the result of any one accident, or series of accidents arising out of one event.

3. **Limits of Liability Coverages Y and Z** The inclusive limit of liability stated in the schedule as applicable to "bodily injury each occurrence property damage each accident" is the total limit of the Insurer's liability under Coverages Y or Z or Coverages Y and Z combined for all compensatory damages, including compensatory damages for care and loss of services, arising out of bodily injury in any one occurrence or property damage as a result of any one accident or series of accidents arising out of one event.

4. For the purpose of determining the limit of the Insurer's liability, all bodily injury arising out of continuous or repeated exposure to substantially the same general conditions shall be considered as arising out of one occurrence.

ADDITIONAL DEFINITION

When used in reference to this insurance (including endorsements forming a part of the policy):

"contractual liability" means liability expressly assumed under a written contract or agreement; provided, however, that contractual liability shall not be construed as including liability under a warranty of the fitness or quality of the Named Insured's products or a warranty that work performed by or on behalf of the Named Insured will be done in a workmanlike manner.

DESCRIPTION OF TERM USED FOR PREMIUM BASIS

"cost" means the total cost to any indemnitee with respect to any contract which is insured of all work let or sub-let in connection with each specific project, including the cost of all labour, materials and equipment furnished, used or delivered for use in the execution of such work, whether furnished by the owner, contractor or the sub-contractor, including all fees, allowances, bonuses or commissions made, paid or due.

APPENDIX G

Attached to and forming part of this Policy

Schedule

Coverage	Limits of Liability	Advance Premiums
P. Personal Injury Liability The insurance afforded is only with respect to personal injury arising out of an offense included within such of the following groups of offenses as are indicated by specific premium charge or charges.	$ aggregate	
Groups of Offenses		
A. False Arrest, Detention or Imprisonment or Malicious Prosecution		$
B. Libel, Slander, Defamation or Violation of Right of Privacy		$
C. Wrongful Entry or Eviction or Other Invasion of Right of Private Occupancy		$
Insured's Participation % Minimum Premium $	Total Advance Premium	$
Endorsements		

INSURING AGREEMENTS

I. Coverage P — Personal Injury Liability

To pay on behalf of the Insured all sums which the Insured shall become legally obligated to pay as compensatory damages because of injury (herein called "personal injury") sustained by any person or organization and arising out of one or more of the following offenses committed in the conduct of the Named Insured's business designated in the declarations:

Group A—false arrest, detention or imprisonment, or malicious prosecution;

Group B—the publication or utterance of a libel or slander or of other defamatory or disparaging material, or a publication or utterance in violation of an individual's right of privacy; except publications or utterances in the course of or related to advertising, broadcasting or telecasting activities conducted by or on behalf of the Named Insured;

Group C—wrongful entry or eviction, or other invasion of the right of private occupancy.

II. Defence — Settlement — Supplementary Payments

As respects insurance afforded by this policy, the Insurer shall:

(1) defend in the name and on behalf of the Insured and at the cost of the Insurer any civil action which may at any time be brought against the Insured on account of such personal injury but the Insurer shall have the right to make such investigation, negotiation and settlement of any claim as may be deemed expedient by the Insurer;

(2) pay all premiums on bonds to release attachments for an amount not in excess of the applicable limit of liability of this policy, all premiums on appeal bonds required in any such defended suit, but without any obligation to apply for or furnish such bonds;

(3) pay all costs taxed against the Insured in any civil action defended by the Insurer and any interest accruing after entry of judgment (or, in those jurisdictions where statute prescribes interest from some other date, from such prescribed date) upon that part of the judgment which is within the limits of the Insurer's liability;

(4) reimburse the Insured for all reasonable expenses, other than loss of earnings, incurred at the Insurer's request.

The amounts so incurred except settlement of claims or suits are payable in addition to the applicable limits of liability.

III. Persons Insured

Each of the following is an Insured under this insurance to the extent set forth below:

(1) if the Named Insured is designated in the declarations as an individual, the person so designated;

(2) if the Named Insured is designated in the declarations as a partnership or joint venture, the partnership or joint venture so designated and any partner or member thereof but only with respect to his liability as such;

(3) if the Named Insured is designated in the declarations as other than an individual, partnership or joint venture, the organization so designated and any executive officer, director or stockholder thereof while acting within the scope of his duties as such.

This insurance does not apply to personal injury arising out of the conduct of any partnership or joint venture of which the Insured is a partner or member and which is not designated in this policy as a Named Insured.

IV. Policy Period: Territory

This insurance applies only to personal injury arising out of an offense committed during the policy period within the policy territory.

EXCLUSIONS

This insurance does not apply to:

(a) liability assumed by the Insured under any contract or agreement;

(b) personal injury arising out of the wilful violation of a penal statute or ordinance committed by or with the knowledge or consent of any Insured;

(c) personal injury sustained by any person as a result of an offense directly or indirectly related to the employment of such person by the Named Insured;

(d) personal injury arising out of any publication or utterance described in Group B, if the first injurious publication or utterance of the same or similar material by or on behalf of the Named Insured was made prior to the effective date of this insurance;

(e) personal injury arising out of a publication or utterance described in Group B concerning any organization or business enterprise, or its products or services, made by or at the direction of any Insured with knowledge of the falsity thereof.

LIMITS OF LIABILITY

Regardless of the number of (1) Insureds under this policy, (2) persons or organizations who sustain personal injury, or (3) claims made or suits brought on account of personal injury, the limit of "personal injury" liability stated in the schedule as "aggregate" is the total limit of the Insurer's liability for all compensatory damages arising out of personal injury in any one period of twelve months terminating on the anniversary of the inception date of the policy.

INSURED'S PARTICIPATION

If a participation percentage is stated in the schedule for the Insured, the Insurer shall not be liable for a greater proportion of any loss than the difference between such percentage and one hundred percent and the balance of the loss shall be borne by the Insured; provided, the Insurer may pay the Insured's portion of a loss to effect settlement of the loss, and, upon notification of the action taken, the Named Insured shall promptly reimburse the Insurer therefor.

APPENDIX H

IBC 2021
6-78

BROAD FORM PROPERTY DAMAGE ENDORSEMENT

(including Completed Operations)

It is agreed that:

A. Exclusions (h) and (j) are replaced by the following exclusions (y) and (z):

    (y) property damage

        (1) to property owned or occupied by or rented to the Insured, or, except with respect to the use of elevators, to property held by the Insured for sale or entrusted to the Insured for storage or safekeeping.

        (2) except with respect to liability under a written sidetrack agreement or the use of elevators, to

            (a) property while on premises owned by or rented to the Insured for the purpose of having operations performed on such property by or on behalf of the Insured;

            (b) tools or equipment while being used by the Insured in performing his operations;

            (c) property in the custody of the Insured which is to be installed, erected or used in construction by the Insured;

            (d) that particular part of any property, not on premises owned by or rented to the Insured;

                (i) upon which operations are being performed by or on behalf of the Insured at the time of the property damage arising out of such operations, or

                (ii) out of which any property damage arises, or

                (iii) the restoration, repair or replacement of which has been made necessary by reason of faulty workmanship thereon by or on behalf of the Insured;

    (z) with respect to the completed operations hazard, to property damage to work performed by the Named Insured arising out of the work or any portion thereof, or out of materials, parts or equipment furnished in connection therewith.

B. The insurance afforded by this endorsement shall be excess insurance over any valid and collectible Property insurance (including any deductible portion thereof) available to the Insured, such as but not limited to Fire and Extended Coverage, Builder's Risk Coverage or Installation Risk coverage, and the Other Insurance condition is amended accordingly.

For use with Comprehensive General Liability Coverage Rider

APPENDIX I

IBC 2100
8-87

Commercial General Liability Policy

INSURANCE CO.

Head Office - Canada

POLICY NO.
Agent/Broker

In return for the payment of the premium, and subject to all the terms of this policy, we agree with you to provide the insurance as stated in this policy.

DECLARATIONS

1. Named Insured

   Address

	Day	Month	Year		Day	Month	Year	
2. Policy Period From				To				12:01 A.M., Standard Time, at your address shown above.

3. LIMITS OF INSURANCE

AGGREGATE LIMIT	Each Occurrence Limit	Personal Injury Limit	Tenants' Legal Liability Limit	Medical Expense Limit
$	$	$	$ Any One Premises	$ Any One Person

4. Form of Business:

   INDIVIDUAL ☐;   JOINT VENTURE ☐;   PARTNERSHIP ☐;   ORGANIZATION ☐;   (Other than Partnership or Joint Venture)

5. Business Description: _____

6. Location of All Premises You Own, Rent or Occupy:

   _____

   _____

7. Classification	Code No.	Premium Basis	Rate	Advance Premium

8. Minimum Premium $_____   TOTAL PREMIUM $_____

9. Endorsements Attached To This Policy:

COUNTERSIGNED BY _____   by _____
                 (Date)   (Authorized Representative)

_____
(Insurer's Signature)

IBC 2100
9-87

COMMERCIAL GENERAL LIABILITY POLICY
Read Your Policy Carefully

DECLARATIONS PAGE
  Named Insured and Address
  Policy Period
  Coverages and Limits of Insurance
  Form, Description and Location of Business

IBC 2100
8-87

Commercial General Liability Policy

Various provisions in this policy restrict coverage. Read the entire policy carefully to determine rights, duties and what is and is not covered.

Throughout this policy the words "you" and "your" refer to the Named Insured shown in the Declarations. The words "we", "us" and "our" refer to the Company providing this insurance.

The word "insured" means any person or organization qualifying as such under SECTION II - WHO IS AN INSURED.

Other words and phrases that appear in quotation marks have special meaning.

SECTION I - COVERAGES
COVERAGE A. BODILY INJURY AND PROPERTY DAMAGE LIABILITY

1. **Insuring Agreement.**

   a. We will pay those sums that the insured becomes legally obligated to pay as compensatory damages because of "bodily injury" or "property damage" to which this insurance applies. No other obligation or liability to pay sums or perform acts or services is covered unless explicitly provided for under SUPPLEMENTARY PAYMENTS - COVERAGES A, B AND D. This insurance applies only to "bodily injury" and "property damage" which occurs during the policy period. The "bodily injury" or "property damage" must be caused by an "occurrence". The "occurrence" must take place in the "coverage territory". We will have the right and duty to defend any "action" seeking those compensatory damages but:

      1) The amount we will pay for compensatory damages is limited as described in SECTION III - LIMITS OF INSURANCE.

      2) We may investigate and settle any claim or "action" at our discretion; and

      3) Our right and duty to defend end when we have used up the applicable limit of insurance in the payment of judgments or settlements under Coverages A, B or D or medical expenses under Coverage C.

   b. Compensatory damages because of "bodily injury" include compensatory damages claimed by any person or organization for care, loss of services or death resulting at any time from the "bodily injury".

   c. "Property damage" that is loss of use of tangible property that is not physically injured shall be deemed to occur at the time of the "occurrence" that caused it.

2. **Exclusions.**

   This insurance does not apply to:

   a. "Bodily injury" or "property damage" expected or intended from the standpoint of the insured. This exclusion does not apply to "bodily injury" resulting from the use of reasonable force to protect persons or property.

   b. "Bodily injury" or "property damage" for which the insured is obligated to pay compensatory damages by reason of the assumption of liability in a contract or agreement. This exclusion does not apply to liability for compensatory damages:

      1) Assumed in a contract or agreement that is an "insured contract"; or

      2) That the insured would have in the absence of the contract or agreement.

   c. Any obligation of the insured under a workers-compensation, disability benefits or unemployment compensation law or any similar law.

   d. "Bodily injury" to an employee of the insured arising out of and in the course of employment by the insured.

      This exclusion applies:

      1) Whether the insured may be liable as an employer or in any other capacity; and

      2) To any obligation to share compensatory damages with or repay someone else who must pay compensatory damages because of the injury.

      This exclusion does not apply:

      i) To liability assumed by the insured under an "insured contract"; or

      ii) To employees on whose behalf contributions are made by or required to be made by the insured under the provisions of any workers compensation law.

   e. 1) "Bodily injury" or "property damage" arising out of the ownership, use or operation by or on behalf of any insured of:

      a) Any "automobile";

      b) Any motorized snow vehicle or its trailers;

      c) Any vehicle while being used in any speed or demolition contest or in any stunting activity or in practice or preparation for any such contest or activity; or

      d) Any vehicle which if it were to be insured would be required by law to be insured under a contract evidenced by a motor vehicle liability policy, or any vehicle insured under such a contract, but this exclusion does not apply to the ownership, use or operation of machinery, apparatus or equipment mounted on or attached to any vehicle while at the site of the use or operation of such equipment.

      2) "Bodily injury" or "property damage" with respect to which any motor vehicle liability policy is in effect or would be in effect but for its termination upon exhaustion of its limit of liability or is required by law to be in effect.

      This Exclusion e. does not apply to "bodily injury" to an employee of the insured on whose behalf contributions are made by or required to be made by the insured under the provisions of any workers compensation law.

   f. "Bodily injury" or "property damage" arising out of the ownership, maintenance, use, operation, loading or unloading, or entrustment to others, by or on behalf of any insured of any watercraft.

      This exclusion does not apply to:

      1) A watercraft while ashore on premises you own or rent;

      2) A watercraft you do not own that is:

         a) Less than 8 metres long; and

         b) Not being used to carry persons or property for a charge.

      3) "Bodily injury" to an employee of the insured on whose behalf contributions are made by or required to be made by the insured under the provisions of any workers compensation law.

   g. 1) "Bodily injury" or "property damage" arising out of the ownership, maintenance, use, operation, loading or unloading, or the entrustment to others, by or on behalf of any insured of:

      a) Any aircraft; or

      b) Any air cushion vehicle.

      2) "Bodily injury" or "property damage" arising out of the ownership, existence, use or operation by or on behalf of any insured of any premises for the purpose of an airport or aircraft landing area and all operations necessary or incidental thereto.

IBC 2100
8-87

h. "Property damage" to:

   1) Property you own, rent, or occupy;

   2) Premises you sell, give away or abandon, if the "property damage" arises out of any part of those premises;

   3) Property loaned to you;

   4) Personal property in your care, custody or control;

   5) That particular part of real property on which you or any contractor or subcontractor working directly or indirectly on your behalf is performing operations, if the "property damage" arises out of those operations; or

   6) That particular part of any property that must be restored, repaired or replaced because "your work" was incorrectly performed on it.

   Paragraph 2) of this exclusion does not apply if the premises are "your work" and were never occupied, rented or held for rental by you.

   Paragraphs 3), 4), 5) and 6) of this exclusion do not apply to liability assumed under a sidetrack agreement.

   Paragraph 6) of this exclusion does not apply to "property damage" included in the "products-completed operations hazard"

i. "Property damage" to "your product" arising out of it or any part of it.

j. "Property damage" to "your work" arising out of it or any part of it and included in the "products-completed operations hazard".

   This exclusion does not apply if the damaged work or the work out of which the damage arises was performed on your behalf by a subcontractor.

k. "Property damage" to "impaired property" or property that has not been physically injured, arising out of:

   1) A defect, deficiency, inadequacy or dangerous condition in "your product" or "your work"; or

   2) A delay or failure by you or anyone acting on your behalf to perform a contract or agreement in accordance with its terms.

   This exclusion does not apply to the loss of use of other property arising out of sudden and accidental physical injury to "your product" or "your work" after it has been put to its intended use.

l. Any loss, cost or expense incurred by you or others for the loss of use, withdrawal, recall, inspection, repair, replacement, adjustment, removal or disposal of:

   1) "Your product";

   2) "Your work"; or

   3) "Impaired property";

   if such product, work, or property is withdrawn or recalled from the market or from use by any person or organization because of a known or suspected defect, deficiency, inadequacy or dangerous condition in it.

m. Pollution Liability - See Common Exclusions.

n. Nuclear Liability - See Common Exclusions.

o. War Risks - See Common Exclusions.

COVERAGE B. PERSONAL INJURY LIABILITY

1. **Insuring Agreement.**

   a. We will pay those sums that the insured becomes legally obligated to pay as compensatory damages because of "personal injury" to which this insurance applies. No other obligation or liability to pay sums or perform acts or services is covered unless explicitly provided for under SUPPLEMENTARY PAYMENTS - COVERAGES A, B AND D. We will have the right and duty to defend any "action" seeking those compensatory damages but:

     1) The amount we will pay for compensatory damages is limited as described in SECTION III - LIMITS OF INSURANCE;

     2) We may investigate and settle any claim or "action" at our discretion; and

     3) Our right and duty to defend end when we have used up the applicable limit of insurance in the payment of judgments or settlements under Coverages A, B or D or medical expenses under Coverage C.

   b. This insurance applies to "personal injury" only if caused by an offence:

     1) Committed in the "coverage territory" during the policy period; and

     2) Arising out of the conduct of your business, excluding advertising, publishing, broadcasting or telecasting done by or for you.

2. **Exclusions.**

   This insurance does not apply to:

   "Personal injury":

   1) Arising out of oral or written publication of material, if done by or at the direction of the insured with knowledge of its falsity:

   2) Arising out of oral or written publication of material whose first publication took place before the beginning of the policy period;

   3) Arising out of the wilful violation of a penal statute or ordinance committed by or with the consent of the insured; or

   4) For which the insured has assumed liability in a contract or agreement. This exclusion does not apply to liability for compensatory damages that the insured would have in the absence of the contract or agreement.

COVERAGE C. MEDICAL PAYMENTS

1. **Insuring Agreement.**

   a. We will pay medical expenses as described below for "bodily injury" caused by an accident:

     1) On premises you own or rent;

     2) On ways next to premises you own or rent; or

     3) Because of your operations;

   provided that:

     a) The accident takes place in the "coverage territory" and during the policy period;

     b) The expenses are incurred and reported to us within one year of the date of the accident; and

     c) The injured person submits to examination, at our expense, by physicians of our choice as often as we reasonably require.

   b. We will make these payments regardless of fault. These payments will not exceed the applicable limit of insurance. We will pay reasonable expenses for:

     1) First aid at the time of an accident;

     2) Necessary medical, surgical, x-ray and dental services, including prosthetic devices; and

     3) Necessary ambulance, hospital, professional nursing and funeral services.

IBC 2100
8-87

2. **Exclusions.**

We will not pay expenses for "bodily injury":

a. To any insured.

b. To a person hired to do work for or on behalf of any insured or a tenant of any insured.

c. To a person injured on that part of premises you own or rent that the person normally occupies.

d. To a person, whether or not an employee of any insured, who at the time of injury is entitled to benefits under any workers compensation or disability benefits law or a similar law.

e. To a person injured while taking part in athletics.

f. The payment of which is prohibited by law.

g. Included within the "products-completed operations hazard".

h. Excluded under Coverage A.

COVERAGE D. TENANTS' LEGAL LIABILITY

1. **Insuring Agreement.**

We will pay those sums that the insured becomes legally obligated to pay as compensatory damages because of "property damage" to which this insurance applies. No other obligation or liability to pay sums or perform acts or services is covered unless explicitly provided for under SUPPLEMENTARY PAYMENTS - COVERAGES A,B AND D. This insurance applies only to "property damage" caused by fire, explosion, smoke or leakage from fire protective equipment to premises rented to you or occupied by you. This insurance applies only to "property damage" which occurs during the policy period. The "property damage" must be caused by an "occurrence". The "occurrence" must take place in the "coverage territory". We will have the right and duty to defend any "action" seeking those compensatory damages but:

a. The amount we will pay for compensatory damages is limited as described in SECTION III - LIMITS OF INSURANCE;

b. We may investigate and settle any claim or "action" at our discretion; and

c. Our right and duty to defend end when we have used up the applicable limit of insurance in the payment of judgments or settlements under Coverages A. B or D or medical expenses under Coverage C.

2. **Exclusions.**

This insurance does not apply to:

a. "Property damage" expected or intended from the standpoint of the insured.

b. "Property damage" for which the insured is obligated to pay by reason of the assumption of liability in a contract or agreement. This exclusion does not apply to liability for compensatory damages that the insured would have in the absence of the contract or agreement.

c. Pollution Liability - See Common Exclusions.

d. Nuclear Energy Liability - See Common Exclusions.

e. War Risks - See Common Exclusions.

COMMON EXCLUSIONS - COVERAGES A, C AND D

This insurance does not apply to:

1. **Pollution Liability**

a. "Bodily injury" or "property damage" arising out of the actual, alleged or threatened discharge, dispersal, release or escape of pollutants:

   1) At or from premises owned, rented or occupied by an insured;

   2) At or from any site or location used by or for an insured or others for the handling, storage, disposal, processing or treatment of waste;

   3) Which are at any time transported, handled, stored, treated, disposed of, or processed as waste by or for an insured or any person or organization for whom the insured may be legally responsible; or

   4) At or from any site or location on which an insured or any contractors or subcontractors working directly or indirectly on behalf of an insured are performing operations:

      a) if the pollutants are brought on or to the site or location in connection with such operations; or

      b) if the operations are to test for, monitor, clean up, remove, contain, treat, detoxify or neutralize the pollutants.

b. Any loss, cost, or expense arising out of any governmental direction or request that an insured test for, monitor, clean up, remove, contain, treat, detoxify or neutralize pollutants.

   "Pollutants" means any solid, liquid, gaseous or thermal irritant or contaminant, including smoke, vapour, soot, fumes, acids, alkalis, chemicals and waste. Waste includes materials to be recycled, reconditioned or reclaimed.

   Sub-paragraphs 1) and 4)a) of paragraph a. of this exclusion do not apply to "bodily injury" or "property damage" caused by heat, smoke or fumes from a hostile fire. As used in this exclusion, a "hostile fire" means one which becomes uncontrollable or breaks out from where it was intended to be.

2. **Nuclear Energy Liability**

a. Liability imposed by or arising under the Nuclear Liability Act;

b. "Bodily injury" or "property damage" with respect to which an insured under this policy is also insured under a contract of nuclear energy liability insurance (whether the insured is unnamed in such contract and whether or not it is legally enforceable by the insured) issued by the Nuclear Insurance Association of Canada or any other insurer or group or pool of insurers or would be an insured under any such policy but for its termination upon exhaustion of its limit of liability;

c. "Bodily injury" or "property damage" resulting directly or indirectly from the nuclear energy hazard arising from:

   1) the ownership, maintenance, operation or use of a nuclear facility by or on behalf of an insured;

   2) the furnishing by an insured of services, materials, parts or equipment in connection with the planning, construction, maintenance, operation or use of any nuclear facility;

   3) The possession, consumption, use, handling, disposal or transportation of fissionable substances, or of other radioactive material (except radioactive isotopes, away from a nuclear facility, which have reached the final stage of fabrication so as to be useable for any scientific, medical, agricultural, commercial or industrial purpose) used, distributed, handled or sold by an insured.

As used in this policy:

   1) The term "nuclear energy hazard" means the radioactive, toxic, explosive, or other hazardous properties of radioactive material;

   2) The term "radioactive material" means uranium, thorium, plutonium, neptunium, their respective derivatives and compounds, radioactive isotopes of other elements and any other substances that the Atomic Energy Control Board may, by regulation, designate as being prescribed substances capable of releasing atomic energy, or as being requisite for the production, use or application of atomic energy;

IBC 2100
8-87

3) The term "nuclear facility" means:

   a) any apparatus designed or used to sustain nuclear fission in a self-supporting chain reaction or to contain a critical mass of plutonium, thorium and uranium or any one or more of them;

   b) any equipment or device designed or used for (i) separating the isotopes of plutonium, thorium and uranium or any one or more of them, (ii) processing or utilizing spent fuel, or (iii) handling, processing or packaging waste;

   c) any equipment or device used for the processing, fabricating or alloying of plutonium, thorium or uranium enriched in the isotope uranium 233 or in the isotope uranium 235, or any one or more of them if at any time the total amount of such material in the custody of the insured at the premises where such equipment or device is located consists of or contains more than 25 grams of plutonium or uranium 233 or any combination thereof, or more than 250 grams of uranium 235;

   d) any structure, basin, excavation, premises or place prepared or used for the storage or disposal of waste radioactive material;

   and includes the site on which any of the foregoing is located, together with all operations conducted thereon and all premises used for such operations.

4) The term "fissionable substance" means any prescribed substance that is, or from which can be obtained, a substance capable of releasing atomic energy by nuclear fission.

3. War Risks

"Bodily injury" or "property damage" due to war, invasion, act of foreign enemy, hostilities (whether war be declared or not), civil war, rebellion, revolution, insurrection or military power.

SUPPLEMENTARY PAYMENTS - COVERAGES A, B AND D

We will pay, with respect to any claim or "action" we defend:

   a. All expenses we incur.

   b. The cost of bonds to release attachments, but only for bond amounts within the applicable limit of insurance. We do not have to furnish these bonds.

   c. All reasonable expenses incurred by the insured at our request to assist us in the investigation or defence of the claim or "action", including actual loss of earnings up to $100 a day because of time off from work.

   d. All costs taxed against the insured in the "action" and any interest accruing after entry of judgment upon that part of the judgment which is within the applicable limit of insurance.

These payments will not reduce the limits of insurance.

SECTION II - WHO IS AN INSURED

1. If you are designated in the Declarations as:

   a. An individual, you and your spouse are insureds, but only with respect to the conduct of a business of which you are the sole owner.

   b. A partnership or joint venture, you are an insured. Your members, your partners, and their spouses are also insureds, but only with respect to the conduct of your business.

   c. An organization other than a partnership or joint venture, you are an insured. Your executive officers and directors are insureds, but only with respect to their duties as your officers or directors. Your stockholders are also insureds, but only with respect to their liability as stockholders.

2. Each of the following is also an insured:

   a. Your employees, other than your executive officers, but only for acts within the scope of their employment by you. However, none of these employees is an insured for:

     1) "Bodily injury" or "personal injury" to you or to a co-employee while in the course of his or her employment; or

     2) "Bodily injury" or "personal injury" to any person who at the time of injury is entitled to benefits under any workers compensation or disability benefits law or a similar law; or

     3) "Bodily injury" or "personal injury" arising out of his or her providing or failing to provide professional health care services; or

     4) "Property damage" to property owned or occupied by or rented or loaned to that employee, any of your other employees, or any of your partners or members (if you are a partnership or joint venture).

   b. Any person (other than your employee), or any organization while acting as your real estate manager.

   c. Any person or organization having proper temporary custody of your property if you die, but only:

     1) With respect to liability arising out of the maintenance or use of that property; and

     2) Until your legal representative has been appointed.

   d. Your legal representative if you die, but only with respect to duties as such. That representative will have all your rights and duties under this policy.

3. Any organization you newly acquire or form, other than a partnership or joint venture, and over which you maintain ownership or majority interest, will be deemed to be a Named Insured if there is no other similar insurance available to that organization. However:

   a. Coverage under this provision is afforded only until the 90th day after you acquire or form the organization or the end of the policy period, whichever is earlier;

   b. Coverages A and D do not apply to "bodily injury" or "property damage" that occurred before you acquired or formed the organization; and

   c. Coverage B does not apply to "personal injury" arising out of an offense committed before you acquired or formed the organization.

No person or organization is an insured with respect to the conduct of any current or past partnership or joint venture that is not shown as a Named Insured in the Declarations.

SECTION III - LIMITS OF INSURANCE

1. The Limits of Insurance stated in the Declarations and the rules below fix the most we will pay regardless of the number of:

   a. Insureds;

   b. Claims made or "actions" brought; or

   c. Persons or organizations making claims or bringing "actions".

2. The Aggregate Limit is the most we will pay for the sum of:

   a. Medical expenses under Coverage C; and

   b. Compensatory damages under Coverage A, Coverage B and Coverage D.

3. Subject to 2. above, the Each Occurrence Limit is the most we will pay for the sum of:

   a. Compensatory damages under Coverage A and Coverage D; and

IBC 2100
8-87

b. Medical expenses under Coverage C;

because of all "bodily injury" and "property damage" arising out of any one "occurrence".

4. Subject to 2. above, the Personal Injury Limit is the most we will pay under Coverage B for the sum of all compensatory damages because of all "personal injury" sustained by any one person or organization.

5. Subject to 3. above, the Tenants' Legal Liability Limit is the most we will pay under Coverage D for compensatory damages because of "property damage" to any one premises.

6. Subject to 3. above, the Medical Expense Limit is the most we will pay under Coverage C for all medical expenses because of "bodily injury" sustained by any one person.

The limits of this policy apply separately to each consecutive annual period and to any remaining period of less than 12 months, starting with the beginning of the policy period shown in the Declarations, unless the policy period is extended after issuance for an additional period of less than 12 months. In that case, the additional period will be deemed part of the last preceding period for purposes of determining the Limits of Insurance.

SECTION IV - COMMERCIAL GENERAL LIABILITY CONDITIONS

1. **Bankruptcy.**

Bankruptcy or insolvency of the insured or of the insured's estate will not relieve us of our obligations under this policy.

2. **Canadian Currency Clause.**

All limits of insurance, premiums and other amounts as expressed in this policy are in Canadian currency.

3. **Cancellation.**

a. The first Named Insured shown in the Declarations may cancel this policy by mailing or delivering to us advance written notice of cancellation.

b. We may cancel this policy by mailing or delivering to the first Named Insured written notice of cancellation at least:

1) 15 days before the effective date of cancellation if we cancel for nonpayment of premium; or

2) 30 days before the effective date of cancellation if we cancel for any other reason.

Except in Quebec, if notice is mailed, cancellation takes effect 15 or 30 days after receipt of the letter by the post office to which it is addressed, depending upon the reason for cancellation. Proof of mailing will be sufficient proof of notice.

In Quebec, cancellation takes effect either 15 or 30 days after receipt of the notice at the last known address of the first Named Insured, depending upon the reason for cancellation.

c. We will mail or deliver our notice to the first Named Insured's last mailing address known to us.

d. The policy period will end on the date cancellation takes effect.

e. If this policy is cancelled, we will send the first Named Insured any premium refund due. If we cancel, the refund will be pro rata. If the first Named insured cancels, the refund may be less than pro rata. The cancellation will be effective even if we have not made or offered a refund.

4. **Changes.**

This policy contains all the agreements between you and us concerning the insurance afforded. The first Named Insured shown in the Declarations is authorized to make changes in the terms of this policy with our consent. This policy's terms can be amended or waived only by endorsement issued by us and made a part of this policy.

5. **Duties in the Event of Occurrence, Claim or Action.**

a. You must see to it that we are notified promptly of an "occurrence" which may result in a claim. Notice should include:

1) How, when and where the "occurrence" took place; and

2) The names and addresses of any injured persons and of witnesses.

b. If a claim is made or "action" is brought against any insured, you must see to it that we receive prompt written notice of the claim or "action".

c. You and any other involved insured must:

1) Immediately send us copies of any demands, notices, summonses or legal papers received in connection with the claim or "action";

2) Authorize us to obtain records and other information;

3) Cooperate with us in the investigation, settlement or defence of the claim or "action"; and

4) Assist us, upon our request, in the enforcement of any right against any person or organization which may be liable to the insured because of injury or damage to which this insurance may also apply.

d. No insureds will, except at their own cost, voluntarily make a payment, assume any obligation, or incur any expense, other than for first aid, without our consent.

6. **Examination of Your Books and Records.**

We may examine and audit your books and records as they relate to this policy at any time during the policy period and up to three years afterward.

7. **Inspections and Surveys.**

We have the right but are not obligated to:

a. Make inspections and surveys at any time;

b. Give you reports on the conditions we find; and

c. Recommend any changes.

Any inspections, surveys, reports or recommendations relate only to insurability and the premiums to be charged. We do not make safety inspections. We do not undertake to perform the duty of any person or organization to provide for the health or safety of workers or the public. And we do not warrant that conditions:

a. Are safe or healthful; or

b. Comply with laws, regulations, codes or standards.

This condition applies not only to us, but also to any rating, advisory, rate service or similar organization which makes insurance inspections surveys, reports or recommendations.

8. **Legal Action Against Us.**

No person or organization has a right under this policy:

a. To join us as a party or otherwise bring us into an "action" asking for compensatory damages from an insured; or

b. To sue us on this policy unless all of its terms have been fully complied with.

IBC 2100
8-87

A person or organization may sue us to recover on an agreed settlement or on a final judgment against an insured obtained after an actual trial; but we will not be liable for compensatory damages that are not payable under the terms of this policy or that are in excess of the applicable limit of insurance. An agreed settlement means a settlement and release of liability signed by us, the insured and the claimant or the claimant's legal representative. Every "action" or proceeding against us shall be commenced within one year next after the date of such judgment or agreed settlement and not afterwards. If this policy is governed by the law of Quebec every action or proceeding against us shall be commenced within three years from the time the right of action arises.

9. **Other Insurance.**

   If other valid and collectible insurance is available to the insured for a loss we cover under Coverages A, B or D of this policy our obligations are limited as follows:

   a. **Primary Insurance**

   This insurance is primary except when b. below applies. If this insurance is primary, our obligations are not affected unless any of the other insurance is also primary. Then, we will share with all that other insurance by the method described in c. below.

   b. **Excess Insurance**

   This insurance is excess over any of the other insurance, whether primary, excess, contingent or on any other basis:

   1) That is Property Insurance such as, but not limited to, Fire, Extended Coverage, Builder's Risk, Installation Risk or similar coverage for "your work" or for premises rented to you; or

   2) If the loss arises out of the maintenance or use of watercraft to the extent not subject to Exclusion f. of Coverage A (Section 1).

   When this insurance is excess, we will have no duty under Coverage A, B or D to defend any claim or "action" that any other insurer has a duty to defend. If no other insurer defends, we will undertake to do so, but we will be entitled to all the insured's rights against all those other insurers.

   When this insurance is excess over other insurance, we will pay only our share of the amount of the loss, if any, that exceeds the sum of:

   1) The total amount that all such other insurance would pay for the loss in the absence of this insurance; and

   2) The total of all deductible and self-insured amounts under all that other insurance.

   We will share the remaining loss, it any, with any other insurance that is not described in this Excess Insurance provision and was not bought specifically to apply in excess of the Limits of Insurance shown in the Declarations of this policy.

   c. **Method of Sharing**

   If all of the other insurance permits contribution by equal shares, we will follow this method also. Under this approach each insurer contributes equal amounts until it has paid its applicable limit of insurance or none of the loss remains, whichever comes first.

   If any of the other insurance does not permit contribution by equal shares, we will contribute by limits. Under this method, each insurer's share is based on the ratio of its applicable limit of insurance to the total applicable limits of insurance of all insurers.

10. **Premium Audit.**

    a. We will compute all premiums for this policy in accordance with our rules and rates.

    b. Premium shown in this policy as advance premium is a deposit premium only. At the close of each audit period we will compute the earned premium for that period. Audit premiums are due and payable on notice to the first Named Insured. If the sum of the advance and audit premiums paid for the policy term is greater than the earned premium, we will return the excess to the first Named Insured subject to the retention of the minimum premium shown in the Declarations of this policy.

    c. The first Named Insured must keep records of the information we need for premium computation, and send us copies at such times as we may request.

11. **Premiums.**

    The first Named Insured shown in the Declarations:

    a. Is responsible for the payment of all premiums; and

    b. Will be the payee for any return premiums we pay.

12. **Representations.**

    By accepting this policy, you agree:

    a. The statements in the Declarations are accurate and complete;

    b. Those statements are based upon representations you made to us; and

    c. We have issued this policy in reliance upon your representations.

13. **Separation of Insureds, Cross Liability.**

    Except with respect to the Limits of Insurance, and any rights or duties specifically assigned to the first Named Insured, this insurance applies:

    a. As of each Named Insured were the only Named Insured; and

    b. Separately to each insured against whom claim is made or "action" is brought.

14. **Transfer of Rights of Recovery Against Others to Us.**

    If the insured has rights to recover all or part of any payment we have made under this policy, those rights are transferred to us. The insured must do nothing after loss to impair them. At our request, the insured will bring "action" or transfer those rights to us and help us enforce them.

15. **Transfer of your Rights and Duties Under this Policy.**

    Your rights and duties under this policy may not be transferred without our written consent except in the case of death of an individual Named Insured.

    If you die, your rights and duties will be transferred to your legal representative but only while acting within the scope of duties as your legal representative. Until your legal representative is appointed, anyone having proper temporary custody of your property will have your rights and duties but only with respect to that property.

SECTION V - DEFINITIONS

1. **"Action"** means a civil proceeding in which compensatory damages because of "bodily injury", "property damage" or "personal injury" to which this insurance applies are alleged. "Action" includes an arbitration proceeding alleging such damages to which you must submit or submit with our consent.

2. **"Automobile"** means any self-propelled land motor vehicle, trailer or semi-trailer (including machinery, apparatus, or equipment attached thereto) which is principally designed and is being used for transportation of persons or property on public roads.

3. **"Bodily injury"** means bodily injury, sickness or disease sustained by a person, including death resulting from any of these at any time.

4. **"Coverage territory"** means:

   a. Canada and the United States of America (including its territories and possessions);

   b. International waters or airspace, provided the injury or damage does not occur in the course of travel or transportation to or from any place not included in a. above; or

   c. All parts of the world if:

Page 6 of 7

IBC 2100
8-87

1) The injury or damage arises out of:

   a) Goods or products made or sold by you in the territory described in a. above; or

   b) The activities of a person whose home is in the territory described in a. above, but is away for a short time on your business; and

2) The insured's responsibility to pay compensatory damages is determined in an "action" on the merits, in the territory described in a. above or in a settlement we agree to in writing.

5. "Impaired property" means tangible property, other than "your product" or "your work", that cannot be used or is less useful because:

  a. It incorporates "your product" or "your work" that is known or thought to be defective, deficient, inadequate or dangerous; or

  b. You have failed to fulfill the terms of a contract or agreement;

if such property can be restored to use by:

  a. The repair, replacement, adjustment or removal of "your product" or "your work"; or

  b. Your fulfilling the terms of the contract or agreement.

6. "Insured contract" means:

  a. A lease of premises;

  b. A sidetrack agreement;

  c. An easement or license agreement in connection with vehicle or pedestrian private railroad crossings at grade;

  d. Any other easement agreement;

  e. An indemnification of a municipality as required by ordinance, except in connection with work for a municipality;

  f. An elevator maintenance agreement; or

  g. That part of any other contract or agreement pertaining to your business under which you assume the tort liability of another to pay compensatory damages because of "bodily injury" or "property damage" to a third person or organization, if the contract or agreement is made prior to the "bodily injury" or "property damage". Tort liability means a liability that would be imposed by law in the absence of any contract or agreement.

An "insured contract" does not include that part of any contract or agreement that indemnifies an architect, engineer or surveyor for injury or damage arising out of:

   1) Preparing, approving or failing to prepare or approve maps, drawings, opinions, reports, surveys, change orders, designs or specifications; or

   2) Giving directions or instructions, or failing to give them, if that is the primary cause of the injury or damage;

7. "Occurrence" means an accident, including continuous or repeated exposure to substantially the same general harmful conditions.

8. "Personal Injury" means injury, other than "bodily injury", arising out of one or more of the following offences:

  a. False arrest, detention or imprisonment;

  b. Malicious prosecution;

  c. Wrongful entry into, or eviction of a person from, a room, dwelling or premises that the person occupies;

  d. Oral or written publication of material that slanders or libels a person or organization or disparages a person's or organization's goods, products or services; or

  e. Oral or written publication of material that violates a person's right of privacy.

9. a. "Products-completed operations hazard" includes all "bodily injury" and "property damage" occurring away from premises you own or rent and arising out of "your product" or "your work" except:

   1) Products that are still in your physical possession; or

   2) Work that has not yet been completed or abandoned.

  b. "Your work" will be deemed completed at the earliest of the following times:

   1) When all of the work called for in your contract has been completed.

   2) When all of the work to be done at the site has been completed if your contract calls for work at more than one site.

   3) When that part of work done at a job site has been put to its intended use by any person or organization other than another contractor or subcontractor working on the same project.

Work that may need service, maintenance, correction, repair or replacement, but which is otherwise complete, will be treated as completed.

  c. This hazard does not include "bodily injury" or "property damage" arising out of the existence of tools, uninstalled equipment or abandoned or unused materials.

10. "Property damage" means:

  a. Physical injury to tangible property, including all resulting loss of use of that property; or

  b. Loss of use of tangible property that is not physically injured.

11. "Your product" means:

  a. Any goods or products, other than real property, manufactured, sold, handled, distributed or disposed of by:

   1) You;

   2) Others trading under your name; or

   3) A person or organization whose business or assets you have acquired; and

  b. Containers (other than vehicles), materials, parts or equipment furnished in connection with such goods or products.

"Your product" includes warranties or representations made at any time with respect to the fitness, quality, durability or performance of any of the items included in a. and b. above.

"Your product" does not include vending machines or other property rented to or located for the use of others but not sold.

12. "Your work" means:

  a. Work or operations performed by you or on your behalf; and

  b. Materials, parts or equipment furnished in connection with such work or operations.

"Your work" includes warranties or representations made at any time with respect to the fitness, quality, durability or performance of any of the items included in a. or b. above.

APPENDIX J

IBC 2200
4-89

Commercial General Liability Policy

INSURANCE CO.

Head Office - Canada

POLICY NO.
Agent/Broker

In return for the payment of the premium, and subject to all the terms of this policy, we agree with you to provide the insurance as stated in this policy.

DECLARATIONS

1. Named Insured

   Address

2. Policy Period From	Day	Month	Year	To	Day	Month	Year	12:01 A.M., Standard Time, at your address shown above.

3. LIMITS OF INSURANCE

AGGREGATE LIMIT	Each Occurrence Limit	Personal Injury Limit	Tenants' Legal Liability Limit	Medical Expense Limit
$	$	$	$ Any One Premises	$ Any One Person

4. Retroactive Date:

   Coverages A and D of this insurance do not apply to "bodily injury" or "property damage" which occurred before the Retroactive Date, if any, shown below:

   Retroactive Date: _____ (Enter Date or "None" if no Retroactive Date applies.)

5. Form of Business:

   INDIVIDUAL ☐;   JOINT VENTURE ☐;   PARTNERSHIP ☐;   ORGANIZATION ☐;   (Other than Partnership or Joint Venture)

6. Business Description: _____

7. Location of All Premises You Own, Rent or Occupy:
   _____
   _____

8. Classification	Code No.	Premium Basis	Rate	Advance Premium

9. Minimum Premium $_____   TOTAL PREMIUM $ _____

10. Endorsements Attached To This Policy:

COUNTERSIGNED BY _____   by   _____
                          (Date)   (Authorized Representative)

                                                        _____
                                                          (Insurer's Signature)

IBC 2200
4-89

COMMERCIAL GENERAL LIABILITY POLICY
Read Your Policy Carefully

DECLARATIONS PAGE
  Named Insured and Address
  Policy Period
  Coverages and Limits of Insurance
  Form, Description and Location of Business

IBC 2200
8-87

COMMERCIAL GENERAL LIABILITY POLICY

COVERAGES A and D Provide Claims Made Coverage. Please Read The Entire Policy Carefully.

Various provisions in this policy restrict coverage. Read the entire policy carefully to determine rights, duties and what is and is not covered.

Throughout this policy the words "you" and "your" refer to the Named Insured shown in the Declarations. The words "we", "us" and "our" refer to the Company providing this insurance.

The word "insured" means any person or organization qualifying as such under SECTION II - WHO IS AN INSURED.

Other words and phrases that appear in quotation marks have special meaning.

SECTION I - COVERAGES
COVERAGE A. BODILY INJURY AND PROPERTY DAMAGE LIABILITY

1. **Insuring Agreement.**

    We will pay those sums that the insured becomes legally obligated to pay as compensatory damages because of "bodily injury" or "property damage" to which this insurance applies but only if a claim for these compensatory damages is first made against any insured during the policy period. No other obligation or liability to pay sums or perform acts or services is covered unless explicitly provided for under SUPPLEMENTARY PAYMENTS - COVERAGES A, B AND D. This insurance does not apply to "bodily injury" or "property damage" which occurred before the Retroactive Date, if any, shown in the Declarations or which occurs after the policy period. The "bodily injury" or "property damage" must be caused by an "occurrence". The "occurrence" must take place in the "coverage territory". We will have the right and duty to defend any "action" seeking those compensatory damages but:

    a. The amount we will pay for compensatory damages is limited as described in SECTION III - LIMITS OF INSURANCE;

    b. We may investigate and settle any claim or "action" at our discretion; and

    c. Our right and duty to defend end when we have used up the applicable limit of insurance in the payment of judgments or settlements under Coverages A, B or D or medical expenses under Coverage C.

    A claim by a person or organization seeking compensatory damages will be deemed to have been made when notice of such claim is received and recorded by any insured or by us, whichever comes first.

    All claims for compensatory damages because of "bodily injury" to the same person, including damages claimed by any person or organization for care, loss of services, or death resulting at any time from the "bodily injury", will be deemed to have been made at the time the first of those claims is made against any insured.

    All claims for compensatory damages because of "property damage" causing loss to the same person or organization as a result of an "occurrence" will be deemed to have been made at the time the first of those claims is made against any insured.

2. **Exclusions.**

    This insurance does not apply to:

    a. "Bodily injury" or "property damage" expected or intended from the standpoint of the insured. This exclusion does not apply to "bodily injury" resulting from the use of reasonable force to protect persons or property.

    b. "Bodily injury" or "property damage" for which the insured is obligated to pay compensatory damages by reason of the assumption of liability in a contract or agreement. This exclusion does not apply to liability for compensatory damages:

        1) Assumed in a contract or agreement that is an "insured contract"; or

        2) That the insured would have in the absence of the contract or agreement.

    c. Any obligation of the insured under a workers compensation, disability benefits or unemployment compensation law or any similar law.

    d. "Bodily injury" to an employee of the insured arising out of and in the course of employment by the insured.

        This exclusion applies:

        a) Whether the insured may be liable as an employer or in any other capacity; and

        b) To any obligation to share compensatory damages with or repay someone else who must pay compensatory damages because of the injury.

        This exclusion does not apply:

        i) To liability assumed by the insured under an "insured contract"; or

        ii) To employees on whose behalf contributions are made by or required to be made by the insured under the provisions of any workers compensation law.

    e. 1) "Bodily injury" or "property damage" arising out of the ownership, use or operation by or on behalf of any insured of:

        a) Any "automobile";

        b) Any motorized snow vehicle or its trailers;

        c) Any vehicle while being used in any speed or demolition contest or in any stunting activity or in practice or preparation for any such contest or activity; or

        d) Any vehicle which if it were to be insured would be required by law to be insured under a contract evidenced by a motor vehicle liability policy, or any vehicle insured under such a contract, but this exclusion does not apply to the ownership, use or operation of machinery, apparatus or equipment mounted on or attached to any vehicle while at the site of the use or operation of such equipment.

        2) "Bodily injury" or "property damage" with respect to which any motor vehicle liability policy is in effect or would be in effect but for its termination upon exhaustion of its limit of liability or is required by law to be in effect.

    This Exclusion e. does not apply to "bodily injury" to an employee of the insured on whose behalf contributions are made by or required to be made by the insured under the provisions of any workers compensation law.

    f. "Bodily injury" or "property damage" arising out of the ownership, maintenance, use, operation, loading or unloading, or entrustment to others, by or on behalf of any insured of any watercraft.

        This exclusion does not apply to:

        1) A watercraft while ashore on premises you own or rent;

        2) A watercraft you do not own that is:

            a) Less than 8 metres long; and

            b) Not being used to carry persons or property for a charge.

        3) "Bodily injury" to an employee of the insured on whose behalf contributions are made by or required to be made by the insured under the provisions of any workers compensation law.

IBC 2200
8-87

g. 1) "Bodily injury" or "property damage" arising out of the ownership, maintenance, use, operation, loading or unloading, or the entrustment to others, by or on behalf of any insured of:

    a) Any aircraft; or

    b) Any air cushion vehicle.

  2) "Bodily injury" or "property damage" arising out of the ownership, existence, use or operation by or on behalf of any insured of any premises for the purpose of an airport or aircraft landing area and all operations necessary or incidental thereto.

h. "Property damage" to:

  1) Property you own, rent, or occupy;

  2) Premises you sell, give away or abandon, if the "property damage" arises out of any part of those premises;

  3) Property loaned to you;

  4) Personal property in your care, custody or control;

  5) That particular part of real property on which you or any contractor or subcontractor working directly or indirectly on your behalf is performing operations, if the "property damage" arises out of those operations; or

  6) That particular part of any property that must be restored, repaired or replaced because "your work" was incorrectly performed on it.

Paragraph 2) of this exclusion does not apply if the premises are "your work" and were never occupied, rented or held for rental by you.

Paragraphs 3), 4), 5) and 6) of this exclusion do not apply to liability assumed under a sidetrack agreement.

Paragraph 6) of this exclusion does not apply to "property damage" included in the "products-completed operations hazard".

i. "Property damage" to "your product" arising out of it or any part of it.

j. "Property damage" to "your work" arising out of it or any part of it and included in the "products-completed operations hazard".

This exclusion does not apply if the damaged work or the work out of which the damage arises was performed on your behalf by a subcontractor.

k. "Property damage" to "impaired property" or property that has not been physically injured, arising out of:

  1) A defect, deficiency, inadequacy or dangerous condition in "your product" or "your work"; or

  2) A delay or failure by you or anyone acting on your behalf to perform a contract or agreement in accordance with its terms.

This exclusion does not apply to the loss of use of other property arising out of sudden and accidental physical injury to "your product" or "your work" after it has been put to its intended use.

l. Any loss, cost or expense incurred by you or others for the loss of use, withdrawal, recall, inspection, repair, replacement, adjustment, removal or disposal of:

  1) "Your product";

  2) "Your work"; or

  3) "Impaired property";

if such product, work, or property is withdrawn or recalled from the market or from use by any person or organization because of a known or suspected defect, deficiency, inadequacy or dangerous condition in it.

m. Pollution Liability - See Common Exclusions.

n. Nuclear Liability - See Common Exclusions.

o. War Risks - See Common Exclusions.

COVERAGE B. PERSONAL INJURY LIABILITY

1. **Insuring Agreement.**

a. We will pay those sums that the insured becomes legally obligated to pay as compensatory damages because of "personal injury" to which this insurance applies. No other obligation or liability to pay sums or perform acts or services is covered unless explicitly provided for under SUPPLEMENTARY PAYMENTS - COVERAGES A, B AND D. We will have the right and duty to defend any "action" seeking those compensatory damages but:

  1) The amount we will pay for compensatory damages is limited as described in SECTION III - LIMITS OF INSURANCE;

  2) We may investigate and settle any claim or "action" at our discretion; and

  3) Our right and duty to defend end when we have used up the applicable limit of insurance in the payment of judgments or settlements under Coverages A, B or D or medical expenses under Coverage C.

b. This insurance applies to "personal injury" only if caused by an offence:

  1) Committed in the "coverage territory" during the policy period; and

  2) Arising out of the conduct of your business, excluding advertising, publishing, broadcasting or telecasting done by or for you.

2. **Exclusions.**

This insurance does not apply to:

"Personal injury":

  1) Arising out of oral or written publication of material, if done by or at the direction of the insured with knowledge of its falsity;

  2) Arising out of oral or written publication of material whose first publication took place before the beginning of the policy period;

  3) Arising out of the wilful violation of a penal statute or ordinance committed by or with the consent of the insured; or

  4) For which the insured has assumed liability in a contract or agreement. This exclusion does not apply to liability for compensatory damages that the insured would have in the absence of the contract or agreement.

COVERAGE C. MEDICAL PAYMENTS

1. **Insuring Agreement.**

a. We will pay medical expenses as described below for "bodily injury" caused by an accident:

  1) On premises you own or rent;

  2) On ways next to premises you own or rent; or

  3) Because of your operations;

provided that:

  a) The accident takes place in the "coverage territory" and during the policy period;

  b) The expenses are incurred and reported to us within one year of the date of the accident; and

IBC 2200
8-87

   c) The injured person submits to examination, at our expense, by physicians of our choice as often as we reasonably require.

  b. We will make these payments regardless of fault. These payments will not exceed the applicable limit of insurance. We will pay reasonable expenses for:

    1) First aid at the time of an accident;

    2) Necessary medical, surgical, x-ray and dental services, including prosthetic devices; and

    3) Necessary ambulance, hospital, professional nursing and funeral services.

2. **Exclusions.**

  We will not pay expenses for "bodily injury":

  a. To any insured.

  b. To a person hired to do work for or on behalf of any insured or a tenant of any insured.

  c. To a person injured on that part of premises you own or rent that the person normally occupies.

  d. To a person, whether or not an employee of any insured, who at the time of injury is entitled to benefits under any workers compensation or disability benefits law or a similar law.

  e. To a person injured while taking part in athletics.

  f. The payment of which is prohibited by law.

  g. Included within the "products-completed operations hazard".

  h. Excluded under Coverage A.

COVERAGE D. TENANTS' LEGAL LIABILITY

1. **Insuring Agreement.**

We will pay those sums that the insured becomes legally obligated to pay as compensatory damages because of "property damage" to which this insurance applies but only if a claim for these compensatory damages is first made against any insured during the policy period. No other obligation or liability to pay sums or perform acts or services is covered unless explicitly provided for under SUPPLEMENTARY PAYMENTS - COVERAGES A, B AND D. This insurance applies only to "property damage" caused by fire, explosion, smoke or leakage from fire protective equipment to premises rented to you or occupied by you. This insurance does not apply to "property damage" which occurred before the Retroactive Date, if any, shown in the Declarations or which occurs after the policy period. The "property damage" must be caused by an "occurrence". The "occurrence" must take place in the "coverage territory". We will have the right and duty to defend any "action" seeking those compensatory damages but:

  a. The amount we will pay for compensatory damages is limited as described in SECTION III - LIMITS OF INSURANCE.

  b. We may investigate and settle any claim or "action" at our discretion; and

  c. Our right and duty to defend end when we have used up the applicable limit of insurance in the payment of judgments or settlements under Coverages A, B or D or medical expenses under Coverage C.

A claim by a person or organization seeking compensatory damages will be deemed to have been made when notice of such claim is received and recorded by any insured or by us, whichever comes first.

All claims for compensatory damages because of "property damage" causing loss to the same person or organization as a result of an "occurrence" will be deemed to have been made at the time the first of those claims is made against any insured.

2. **Exclusions.**

  This insurance does not apply to:

  a. "Property damage" expected or intended from the standpoint of the insured.

  b. "Property damage" for which the insured is obligated to pay by reason of the assumption of liability in a contract or agreement. This exclusion does not apply to liability for compensatory damages that the insured would have in the absence of the contract or agreement.

  c. Pollution Liability - See Common Exclusions.

  d. Nuclear Energy Liability - See Common Exclusions.

  e. War Risks - See Common Exclusions.

COMMON EXCLUSIONS - COVERAGES A, C AND D

This insurance does not apply to:

1. **Pollution Liability**

  a. "Bodily injury" or "property damage" arising out of the actual, alleged or threatened discharge, dispersal, release or escape of pollutants:

    1) At or from premises owned, rented or occupied by an Insured;

    2) At or from any site or location used by or for an Insured or others for the handling, storage, disposal, processing or treatment of waste;

    3) Which are at any time transported, handled, stored, treated, disposed of, or processed as waste by or for an Insured or any person or organization for whom the Insured may be legally responsible; or

    4) At or from any site or location on which an Insured or any contractors or subcontractors working directly or indirectly on behalf of an Insured are performing operations:

      a) if the pollutants are brought on or to the site or location in connection with such operations; or

      b) if the operations are to test for, monitor, clean up, remove, contain, treat, detoxify or neutralize the pollutants.

  b. Any loss, cost, or expense arising out of any governmental direction or request that an Insured test for, monitor, clean up, remove, contain, treat, detoxify or neutralize pollutants.

  "Pollutants" means any solid, liquid, gaseous or thermal irritant or contaminant, including smoke, vapour, soot, fumes, acids, alkalis, chemicals and waste. Waste includes materials to be recycled, reconditioned or reclaimed.

  Sub-paragraphs 1) and 4)a) of paragraph a. of this exclusion do not apply to "bodily injury" or "property damage" caused by heat, smoke or fumes from a hostile fire. As used in this exclusion, a "hostile fire" means one which becomes uncontrollable or breaks out from where it was intended to be.

2. **Nuclear Energy Liability**

  a. Liability imposed by or arising under the Nuclear Liability Act;

  b. "Bodily injury" or "property damage" with respect to which an insured under this policy is also insured under a contract of nuclear energy liability insurance (whether the insured is unnamed in such contract and whether or not it is legally enforceable by the insured) issued by the Nuclear Insurance Association of Canada or any other insurer or group or pool of insurers or would be an insured under any such policy but for its termination upon exhaustion of its limit of liability;

  c. "Bodily injury" or "property damage" resulting directly or indirectly from the nuclear energy hazard arising from:

IBC 2200
8-87

1) the ownership, maintenance, operation or use of a nuclear facility by or on behalf of an insured;

2) the furnishing by an insured of services, materials, parts or equipment in connection with the planning, construction, maintenance, operation or use of any nuclear facility;

3) the possession, consumption, use, handling, disposal or transportation of fissionable substances, or of other radioactive material (except radioactive isotopes, away from a nuclear facility, which have reached the final stage of fabrication so as to be useable for any scientific, medical, agricultural, commercial or industrial purpose) used, distributed, handled or sold by an insured.

As used in this policy:

1) The term "nuclear energy hazard" means the radioactive, toxic, explosive, or other hazardous properties of radioactive material;

2) The term "radioactive material" means uranium, thorium, plutonium, neptunium, their respective derivatives and compounds, radioactive isotopes of other elements and any other substances that the Atomic Energy Control Board may, by regulation, designate as being prescribed substances capable of releasing atomic energy, or as being requisite for the production, use or application of atomic energy;

3) The term "nuclear facility" means:

   a) any apparatus designed or used to sustain nuclear fission in a self-supporting chain reaction or to contain a critical mass of plutonium, thorium and uranium or any one or more of them;

   b) any equipment or device designed or used for (i) separating the isotopes of plutonium, thorium and uranium or any one or more of them, (ii) processing or utilizing spent fuel, or (iii) handling, processing or packaging waste;

   c) any equipment or device used for the processing, fabricating or alloying of plutonium, thorium or uranium enriched in the isotope uranium 233 or in the isotope uranium 235, or any one or more of them if at any time the total amount of such material in the custody of the insured at the premises where such equipment or device is located consists of or contains more than 25 grams of plutonium or uranium 233 or any combination thereof, or more than 250 grams of uranium 235;

   d) any structure, basin, excavation, premises or place prepared or used for the storage or disposal of waste radioactive material;

   and includes the site on which any of the foregoing is located, together with all operations conducted thereon and all premises used for such operations.

4) The term "fissionable substance" means any prescribed substance that is, or from which can be obtained, a substance capable of releasing atomic energy by nuclear fission.

3. **War Risks**

"Bodily injury" or "property damage" due to war, invasion, act of foreign enemy, hostilities (whether war be declared or not), civil war, rebellion, revolution, insurrection or military power.

SUPPLEMENTARY PAYMENTS - COVERAGES A, B AND D

We will pay, with respect to any claim or "action" we defend:

a. All expenses we incur.

b. The cost of bonds to release attachments, but only for bond amounts within the applicable limit of insurance. We do not have to furnish these bonds.

c. All reasonable expenses incurred by the insured at our request to assist us in the investigation or defence of the claim or "action", including actual loss of earnings up to $100. a day because of time off from work.

d. All costs taxed against the insured in the "action" and any interest accruing after entry of judgment upon that part of the judgment which is within the applicable limit of insurance.

These payments will not reduce the limits of insurance.

SECTION II - WHO IS AN INSURED

1. If you are designated in the Declarations as:

   a. An individual, you and your spouse are insureds, but only with respect to the conduct of a business of which you are the sole owner.

   b. A partnership or joint venture, you are an insured. Your members, your partners, and their spouses are also insureds, but only with respect to the conduct of your business.

   c. An organization other than a partnership or joint venture, you are an insured. Your executive officers and directors are insureds, but only with respect to their duties as your officers or directors. Your stockholders are also insureds, but only with respect to their liability as stockholders.

2. Each of the following is also an insured:

   a. Your employees, other than your executive officers, but only for acts within the scope of their employment by you. However, none of these employees is an insured for:

      1) "Bodily injury" or "personal injury" to you or to a co-employee while in the course of his or her employment; or

      2) "Bodily injury" or "personal injury" to any person who at the time of injury is entitled to benefits under any workers compensation or disability benefits law or a similar law; or

      3) "Bodily injury" or "personal injury" arising out of his or her providing or failing to provide professional health care services; or

      4) "Property damage" to property owned or occupied by or rented or loaned to that employee, any of your other employees, or any of your partners or members (if you are a partnership or joint venture).

   b. Any person (other than your employee), or any organization while acting as your real estate manager.

   c. Any person or organization having proper temporary custody of your property if you die, but only:

      1) With respect to liability arising out of the maintenance or use of that property; and

      2) Until your legal representative has been appointed.

   d. Your legal representative if you die, but only with respect to duties as such. That representative will have all your rights and duties under this policy.

3. Any organization you newly acquire or form, other than a partnership or joint venture, and over which you maintain ownership or majority interest, will be deemed to be a Named Insured if there is no other similar insurance available to that organization. However:

   a. Coverage under this provision is afforded only until the 90th day after you acquire or form the organization or the end of the policy period, whichever is earlier;

   b. Coverages A and D do not apply to "bodily injury" or "property damage" that occurred before you acquired or formed the organization; and

   c. Coverage B does not apply to "personal injury" arising out of an offense committed before you acquired or formed the organization.

No person or organization is an insured with respect to the conduct of any current or past partnership or joint venture that is not shown as a Named Insured in the Declarations.

IBC 2200
8-87

SECTION III - LIMITS OF INSURANCE

1. The Limits of Insurance stated in the Declarations and the rules below fix the most we will pay regardless of the number of:
   a. Insureds;
   b. Claims made or "actions" brought; or
   c. Persons or organizations making claims or bringing "actions".
2. The Aggregate Limit is the most we will pay for the sum of:
   a. Medical expenses under Coverage C; and
   b. Compensatory damages under Coverage A, Coverage B and Coverage D.
3. Subject to 2. above, the Each Occurrence Limit is the most we will pay for the sum of:
   a. Compensatory damages under Coverage A and Coverage D; and
   b. Medical expenses under Coverage C;
   because of all " bodily injury" and "property damage" arising out of any one "occurrence".
4. Subject to 2. above, the Personal Injury Limit is the most we will pay under Coverage B for the sum of all compensatory damages because of all "personal injury" sustained by any one person or organization.
5. Subject to 3. above, the Tenants' Legal Liability Limit is the most we will pay under Coverage D for compensatory damages because of "property damage" to any one premises.
6. Subject to 3. above, the Medical Expense Limit is the most we will pay under Coverage C for all medical expenses because of "bodily injury" sustained by any one person.

The limits of this policy apply separately to each consecutive annual period and to any remaining period of less than 12 months, starting with the beginning of the policy period shown in the Declarations, unless the policy period is extended after issuance for an additional period of less than 12 months. In that case, the additional period will be deemed part of the last preceding period for purposes of determining the Limits of Insurance.

SECTION IV - COMMERCIAL GENERAL LIABILITY CONDITIONS

1. **Bankruptcy.**
   Bankruptcy or insolvency of the insured or of the insured's estate will not relieve us of our obligations under this policy.
2. **Canadian Currency Clause.**
   All limits of insurance, premiums and other amounts as expressed in this policy are in Canadian Currency.
3. **Cancellation.**
   a. The first Named Insured shown in the Declarations may cancel this policy by mailing or delivering to us in advance written notice of cancellation.
   b. We may cancel this policy by mailing or delivering to the first Named Insured written notice of cancellation at least:
      1) 15 days before the effective date of cancellation if we cancel for nonpayment of premium; or
      2) 30 days before the effective date of cancellation if we cancel for any other reason.

      Except in Quebec, if notice is mailed, cancellation takes effect 15 or 30 days after receipt of the letter by the post office to which it is addressed, depending upon the reason for cancellation. Proof of mailing will be sufficient proof of notice.

      In Quebec, cancellation takes effect either 15 or 30 days after receipt of the notice at the last known address of the first Named Insured, depending upon the reason for cancellation.
   c. We will mail or deliver our notice to the first Named Insured's last mailing address known to us.
   d. The policy period will end on the date cancellation takes effect.
   e. It this policy is cancelled, we will send the first Named Insured any premium refund due. If we cancel, the refund will be pro rata. If the first Named Insured cancels, the refund may be less than pro rata. The cancellation will be effective even if we have not made or offered a refund.
4. **Changes.**
   This policy contains all the agreements between you and us concerning the insurance afforded. The first Named Insured shown in the Declarations is authorized to make changes in the terms of this policy with our consent. This policy's terms can be amended or waived only by endorsement issued by us and made a part of this policy.
5. **Duties in the Event of Occurrence, Claim or Action.**
   a. You must see to it that we are notified as soon as practicable of an "occurrence" which may result in a claim. Notice should include:
      1) How, when and where the "occurrence" took place; and
      2) The names and addresses of any injured persons and witnesses; and
      3) The nature and location of any injury or damage arising out of the "occurrence".
         Notice of an "occurrence" is not notice of a claim.
   b. If a claim is received by any insured you must:
      1) Immediately record the specifics of the claim and the date received; and
      2) Notify us as soon as practicable.
      You must see to it that we receive written notice of the claim as soon as practicable.
   c. You and any other involved insured must:
      1) Immediately send us copies of any demands, notices, summonses or legal papers received in connection with the claim or an "action";
      2) Authorize us to obtain records and other information;
      3) Cooperate with us in the investigation, settlement or defence of the claim or "action"; and
      4) Assist us, upon our request, in the enforcement of any right against any person or organization which may be liable to the insured because of injury or damage to which this insurance may also apply.
   d. No insureds will, except at their own cost, voluntarily make a payment, assume any obligation, or incur any expense, other than for first aid, without our consent.
6. **Examination of Your Books and Records.**
   We may examine and audit your books and records as they relate to this policy at any time during the policy period and up to three years afterward.

IBC 2200
8-87

7. Inspections and Surveys.

We have the right but are not obligated to:

a. Make inspections and surveys at any time;

b. Give you reports on the conditions we find; and

c. Recommend any changes.

Any inspections, surveys, reports or recommendations relate only to insurability and the premiums to be charged. We do not make safety inspections. We do not undertake to perform the duty of any person or organization to provide for the health or safety of workers or the public. And we do not warrant that conditions:

a. Are safe or healthful; or

b. Comply with laws, regulations, codes or standards.

This condition applies not only to us, but also to any rating, advisory, rate service or similar organization which makes insurance inspections, surveys, reports or recommendations.

8. Legal Action Against Us.

No person or organization has a right under this policy:

a. To join us as a party or otherwise bring us into an "action" asking for compensatory damages from an insured; or

b. To sue us on this policy unless all of its terms have been fully complied with.

A person or organization may sue us to recover on an agreed settlement or on a final judgment against an insured obtained after an actual trial; but we will not be liable for compensatory damages that are not payable under the terms of this policy or that are in excess of the applicable limit of insurance. An agreed settlement means a settlement and release of liability signed by us, the insured and the claimant or the claimant's legal representative. Every "action" or proceeding against us shall be commenced within one year next after the date of such judgment or agreed settlement and not afterwards. If this policy is governed by the law of Quebec every "action" or proceeding against us shall be commenced within three years from the time the right of action arises.

9. Other Insurance.

If other valid and collectible insurance is available to the insured for a loss we cover under Coverages A, B or D of this policy, our obligations are limited as follows:

a. Primary Insurance

This insurance is primary except when b. below applies. If this insurance is primary, our obligations are not affected unless any of the other insurance is also primary. Then, we will share with all that other insurance by the method described in c. below.

b. Excess Insurance

This insurance is excess over any of the other insurance, whether primary, excess, contingent or on any other basis:

1) That is effective prior to the beginning of the policy period shown in the Declarations of this insurance and applies to "bodily injury" or "property damage" on other than a claims made basis, if:

    a) No Retroactive Date is shown in the Declarations of this insurance; or

    b) The other insurance has a policy period which continues after the Retroactive Date shown in the Declarations of this insurance;

2) That is Property Insurance such as, but not limited to, Fire, Extended Coverage, Builder's Risk, Installation Risk or similar coverage for "your work" or for premises rented to you; or

3) If the loss arises out of the maintenance or use of watercraft to the extent not subject to Exclusion f. of Coverage A (Section I).

When this insurance is excess, we will have no duty under Coverage A, B or D to defend any claim or "action" that any other insurer has a duty to defend. If no other insurer defends, we will undertake to do so, but we will be entitled to all the insured's rights against all those other insurers.

When this insurance is excess over other insurance, we will pay only our share of the amount of the loss, if any, that exceeds the sum of:

1) The total amount that all such other insurance would pay for the loss in the absence of this insurance; and

2) The total of all deductible and self-insured amounts under all that other insurance.

We will share the remaining loss, if any, with any other insurance that is not described in this Excess Insurance provision and was not bought specifically to apply in excess of the Limits of Insurance shown in the Declarations of this policy.

c. Method of Sharing

If all of the other insurance permits contribution by equal shares, we will follow this method also. Under this approach each insurer contributes equal amounts until it has paid its applicable limit of insurance or none of the loss remains, whichever comes first.

If any of the other insurance does not permit contribution by equal shares, we will contribute by limits. Under this method, each insurer's share is based on the ratio of its applicable limit of insurance to the total applicable limits of insurance of all insurers.

10. Premium Audit.

a. We will compute all premiums for this policy in accordance with our rules and rates.

b. Premium shown in this policy as advance premium is a deposit premium only. At the close of each audit period we will compute the earned premium for that period. Audit premiums are due and payable on notice to the first Named Insured. If the sum of the advance and audit premiums paid for the policy term is greater than the earned premium, we will return the excess to the first Named Insured subject to the retention of the minimum premium shown in the Declarations of this policy.

c. The first Named Insured must keep records of the information we need for premium computation, and send us copies at such times as we may request.

11. Premiums.

The first Named Insured shown in the Declarations:

a. Is responsible for the payment of all premiums; and

b. Will be the payee for any return premiums we pay.

12. Representations.

By accepting this policy, you agree:

a. The statements in the Declarations are accurate and complete;

b. Those statements are based upon representations you made to us; and

c. We have issued this policy in reliance upon your representations.

13. Separation of Insureds, Cross Liability.

Except with respect to the Limits of Insurance, and any rights or duties specifically assigned to the first Named Insured, this insurance applies:

a. As if each Named Insured were the only Named Insured; and

IBC 2200
8-87

b. Separately to each insured against whom claim is made or "action" is brought.

14. Transfer of Rights of Recovery Against Others to Us.

If the insured has rights to recover all or part of any payment we have made under this policy, those rights are transferred to us. The insured must do nothing after loss to impair them. At our request, the insured will bring "action" or transfer those rights to us and help us enforce them.

15. Transfer of Your Rights and Duties Under this Policy.

Your rights and duties under this policy may not be transferred without our written consent except in the case of death of an individual Named Insured.

If you die, your rights and duties will be transferred to your legal representative but only while acting within the scope of duties as your legal representative. Until your legal representative is appointed, anyone having proper temporary custody of your property will have your rights and duties but only with respect to that property.

SECTION V - EXTENDED REPORTING PERIODS

1. We will provide an automatic Extended Reporting Period as described in paragraph 3 or, if you purchase it, an Extended Reporting Period Endorsement as described in paragraph 4, only if:

   a. This policy is cancelled or not renewed for any reason except non payment of the premium;

   b. We renew or replace this policy with other insurance that:

   1) Provides claims made coverage for Bodily Injury and Property Damage Liability; and

   2) Has a Retroactive Date later than the one shown in this policy's Declarations; or

   c. We replace this policy with other insurance that applies to "bodily injury" or "property damage" on other than a claims made basis.

2. If we provide an Extended Reporting Period, the following is added to paragraph 1 of SECTION I - COVERAGES A AND D:

   A claim first made during the Extended Reporting Period will be deemed to have been made on the last day of the policy period provided that the claim is for compensatory damages because of "bodily injury" or "property damage" that occurred before the end of the policy period of this policy(but not before any applicable Retroactive Date).

   The Extended Reporting Period will not reinstate or increase the Limits of Insurance or extend the policy period.

3. The automatic Extended Reporting Period will be as set forth in either a. or b. below:

   a. 60 days, starting with the end of the policy period of this policy.

   b. Five years, starting with the end of the policy period of this policy. This automatic Extended Reporting Period applies only to claims as a result of an "occurrence" of which we are notified after the Retroactive Date, if any, shown in the Declarations but not later than 60 days after the end of the policy period of this policy. Notification of the "occurrence" must be in accordance with paragraph 5.a. of SECTION IV - COMMERCIAL GENERAL LIABILITY CONDITIONS (Duties In The Event of Occurrence, Claim or Action).

   These automatic Extended Reporting Periods apply only if no subsequent insurance you purchase applies to the claim, or would apply but for the exhaustion of its applicable limit of insurance.

   These automatic Extended Reporting Periods may not be cancelled.

4. If you purchase the optional Extended Reporting Period Endorsement, the extended reporting period will be an unlimited time, starting with the end of the policy period of this policy. We will issue that Endorsement if the first Named Insured shown in the Declarations:

   a) Makes a written request for it which we receive within 60 days after the end of the policy period; and

   b) Promptly pays the additional premium when due.

   The Extended Reporting Period Endorsement will not take effect unless the additional premium is paid when due. If that premium is paid when due,the endorsement may not be cancelled.

   The Extended Reporting Period Endorsement will also amend paragraph 9.b. of SECTION IV -COMMERCIAL GENERAL LIABILITY CONDITION (Other Insurance) so that the insurance provided will be excess over any other valid and collectible insurance available to the insured, whether primary, excess, contingent or on any other basis, whose policy period begins or continues after the Endorsement takes effect.

We will determine the actual premium for the Extended Reporting Period Endorsement in accordance with our rules and rates.

The premium for the Extended Reporting Period Endorsement will not exceed 200% of the annual premium for this policy to which the endorsement would be attached and will be fully earned when the Endorsement takes effect.

SECTION VI - DEFINITIONS

1. "Action" means a civil proceeding in which compensatory damages because of "bodily injury", "property damage" or "personal injury" to which this insurance applies are alleged. "Action" includes an arbitration proceeding alleging such damages to which you must submit or submit with our consent.

2. "Automobile" means any self-propelled land motor vehicle, trailer or semi-trailer (including machinery, apparatus, or equipment attached thereto) which is principally designed and is being used for transportation of persons or property on public roads.

3. "Bodily Injury" means bodily injury, sickness or disease sustained by a person, including death resulting from any of these at any time.

4. "Coverage territory" means:

   a. Canada and the United States of America (including its territories and possessions);

   b. International waters or airspace, provided the injury or damage does not occur in the course of travel or transportation to or from any place not included in a. above; or

   c. All parts of the world if:

   1) The injury or damage arises out of:

   a) Goods or products made or sold by you in the territory described in a. above; or

   b) The activities of a person whose home is in the territory described in a. above, but is away for a short time on your business; and

   2) The insured's responsibility to pay compensatory damages is determined in an "action" on the merits, in the territory described in a. above or in a settlement when we agree to in writing.

5. "Impaired property" means tangible property, other than "your product" or "your work", that cannot be used or is less useful because:

   a. It incorporates "your product" or "your work" that is known or thought to be defective, deficient, inadequate or dangerous; or

   b. You have failed to fulfill the terms of a contract or agreement;

   if such property can be restored to use by:

   a. The repair, replacement, adjustment or removal of "your product" or "your work"; or

   b. Your fulfilling the terms of the contract or agreement.

IBC 2200
8-87

6. "Insured contract" means:

a. A lease of premises;

b. A sidetrack agreement;

c. An easement or license agreement in connection with vehicle or pedestrian private railroad crossings at grade;

d. Any other easement agreement;

e. An indemnification of a municipality as required by ordinance, except in connection with work for a municipality;

f. An elevator maintenance agreement; or

g. That part of any other contract or agreement pertaining to your business under which you assume the tort liability of another to pay compensatory damages because of "bodily injury" or "property damage" to a third person or organization, if the contract or agreement is made prior to the "bodily injury" or "property damage." Tort liability means a liability that would be imposed by law in the absence of any contract or agreement.

An "insured contract" does not include that part of any contract or agreement that indemnifies an architect, engineer or surveyor for injury or damage arising out of:

1) Preparing, approving or failing to prepare or approve maps, drawings, opinions, reports, surveys, change orders, designs or specifications; or

2) Giving directions or instructions, or failing to give them, if that is the primary cause of the injury or damage;

7. "Occurrence" means an accident, including continuous or repeated exposure to substantially the same general harmful conditions.

8. "Personal Injury" means injury, other than "bodily injury", arising out of one or more of the following offences:

a. False arrest, detention or imprisonment;

b. Malicious prosecution;

c. Wrongful entry into, or eviction of a person from, a room, dwelling or premises that the person occupies;

d. Oral or written publication of material that slanders or libels a person or organization or disparages a person's or organization's goods, products or services; or

e. Oral or written publication of material that violates a person's right of privacy.

9. a. "Products-completed operations hazard" includes all "bodily injury" and "property damage" occurring away from premises you own or rent and arising out of "your product" or "your work" except:

1) Products that are still in your physical possession; or

2) Work that has not yet been completed or abandoned.

b. "Your work" will be deemed completed at the earliest of the following times:

1) When all of the work called for in your contract has been completed.

2) When all of the work to be done at the site has been completed if your contract calls for work at more than one site.

3) When that part of work done at a job site has been put to its intended use by any person or organization other than another contractor or subcontractor working on the same project.

Work that may need service, maintenance, correction, repair or replacement, but which is otherwise complete, will be treated as completed.

c. This hazard does not include "bodily injury" or "property damage" arising out of the existence of tools, uninstalled equipment or abandoned or unused materials.

10. "Property damage" means:

a. Physical injury to tangible property, including all resulting loss of use of that property; or

b. Loss of use of tangible property that is not physically injured.

11. "Your product" means:

a. Any goods or products, other than real property, manufactured, sold, handled, distributed or disposed of by:

1) You.

2) Others trading under your name; or

3) A person or organization whose business or assets you have acquired; and

b. Containers (other than vehicles), materials, parts or equipment furnished in connection with such goods or products.

"Your product" includes warranties or representations made at any time with respect to the fitness, quality, durability or performance of any of the items included in a. and b. above.

"Your product" does not include vending machines or other property rented to or located for the use of others but not sold.

12. "Your work" means:

a. Work or operations performed by you or on your behalf; and

b. Materials, parts or equipment furnished in connection with such work or operations.

"Your work" includes warranties or representations made at any time with respect to the fitness, quality, durability or performance of any of the items included in a. or b. above.

APPENDIX K

IBC 2100
03-2005

COMMERCIAL GENERAL LIABILITY POLICY

Throughout this policy the words "you" and "your" refer to the Named Insured shown in the Declarations, and any other person or organization qualifying as a Named Insured under Paragraph **3.** of Section **II** – Who is an Insured. The words "we", "us" and "our" refer to the company providing this insurance.

The word "insured" means any person or organization qualifying as such under Section **II** – Who Is An Insured.

Other words and phrases that appear in quotation marks have special meaning. Refer to Section **V** –Definitions.

Various provisions in this policy restrict coverage. Read the entire policy carefully to determine rights, duties and what is and is not covered.

SECTION I – COVERAGES

COVERAGE A. BODILY INJURY and PROPERTY DAMAGE LIABILITY

1. **Insuring Agreement**
   a. We will pay those sums that the insured becomes legally obligated to pay as "compensatory damages" because of "bodily injury" or "property damage" to which this insurance applies. We will have the right and duty to defend the insured against any "action" seeking those "compensatory damages". However, we will have no duty to defend the insured against any "action" seeking "compensatory damages" for "bodily injury" or "property damage" to which this insurance does not apply. We may, at our discretion, investigate any "occurrence" and settle any claim or "action" that may result. But:
      (1) The amount we will pay for "compensatory damages" is limited as described in Section **III** – Limits Of Insurance; and
      (2) Our right and duty to defend ends when we have used up the applicable limit of insurance in the payment of judgments or settlements under Coverages **A**, **B** or **D** or medical expenses under Coverage **C**.

      No other obligation or liability to pay sums or perform acts or services is covered unless explicitly provided for under Supplementary Payments – Coverages **A**, **B** and **D**.
   b. This insurance applies to "bodily injury" and "property damage" only if:
      (1) The "bodily injury" or "property damage" is caused by an "occurrence" that takes place in the "coverage territory"; and
      (2) The "bodily injury" or "property damage" occurs during the policy period; and
      (3) Prior to the policy period, no insured listed under Paragraph **1.** of Section **II** – Who Is An Insured and no "employee" authorized by you to give or receive notice of an "occurrence" or claim, knew that the "bodily injury" or "property damage" had occurred, in whole or in part. If such a listed insured or authorized "employee" knew, prior to the policy period, that the "bodily injury" or "property damage" occurred, then any continuation, change or resumption of such "bodily injury" or "property damage" during or after the policy period will be deemed to have been known prior to the policy period.
   c. "Bodily injury" or "property damage" which occurs during the policy period and was not, prior to the policy period, known to have occurred by any insured listed under Paragraph **1.** of Section **II** – Who Is An Insured or any "employee" authorized by you to give or receive notice of an "occurrence" or claim, includes any continuation, change or resumption of that "bodily injury" or "property damage" after the end of the policy period.
   d. "Bodily injury" or "property damage" will be deemed to have been known to have occurred at the earliest time when any insured listed under Paragraph **1.** of Section **II** – Who Is An Insured or any "employee" authorized by you to give or receive notice of an "occurrence" or claim:
      (1) Reports all, or any part, of the "bodily injury" or "property damage" to us or any other insurer;
      (2) Receives a written or verbal demand or claim for "compensatory damages" because of the "bodily injury" or "property damage"; or

(3) Becomes aware by any other means that "bodily injury" or "property damage" has occurred or has begun to occur.

e. "Compensatory damages" because of "bodily injury" include "compensatory damages" claimed by any person or organization for care, loss of services or death resulting at any time from the "bodily injury".

2. Exclusions

This insurance does not apply to:

a. Expected or Intended Injury

"Bodily injury" or "property damage" expected or intended from the standpoint of the insured. This exclusion does not apply to "bodily injury" resulting from the use of reasonable force to protect persons or property.

b. Contractual Liability

"Bodily injury" or "property damage" for which the insured is obligated to pay "compensatory damages" by reason of the assumption of liability in a contract or agreement. This exclusion does not apply to liability for "compensatory damages":

(1) That the insured would have in the absence of the contract or agreement; or

(2) Assumed in a contract or agreement that is an "insured contract", provided the "bodily injury" or "property damage" occurs subsequent to the execution of the contract or agreement. Solely for the purposes of liability assumed in an "insured contract", reasonable legal fees and necessary litigation expenses incurred by or for a party other than an insured are deemed to be "compensatory damages" because of "bodily injury" or "property damage", provided:

    (a) Liability to such party for, or for the cost of, that party's defense has also been assumed in the same "insured contract"; and

    (b) Such legal fees and litigation expenses are for defense of that party against a civil or alternative dispute resolution proceeding in which "compensatory damages" to which this insurance applies are alleged.

c. Workers' Compensation and Similar Laws

Any obligation of the insured under a workers' compensation, disability benefits or unemployment or employment compensation law or any similar law.

d. Employer's Liability

"Bodily injury" to:

(1) An "employee" of the insured arising out of and in the course of:

    (a) Employment by the insured; or

    (b) Performing duties related to the conduct of the insured's business; or

(2) The spouse, child, parent, brother or sister of that "employee" as a consequence of Paragraph 2. d. (1) above.

This exclusion applies:

(i) Whether the insured may be liable as an employer or in any other capacity; and

(ii) To any obligation to share "compensatory damages" with or repay someone else who must pay "compensatory damages" because of the injury.

This exclusion does not apply to:

(a) Liability assumed by the insured under an "insured contract"; or

(b) A claim made or an "action" brought by a Canadian resident "employee" on whose behalf contributions are made by or required to be made by you under the provisions of any Canadian provincial or territorial workers' compensation law, if cover or benefits have been denied by any Canadian Workers' Compensation Authority.

e. Aircraft or Watercraft

"Bodily injury" or "property damage" arising out of the ownership, maintenance, use or entrustment to others by or on behalf of any insured of:

(i) Any aircraft, air cushion vehicle or watercraft owned or operated by or rented or loaned to any insured; or

(ii) Any premises for the purpose of an airport or aircraft landing area and all operations necessary or incidental thereto.

Use includes operation and "loading or unloading".

This exclusion applies even if the claims against any insured allege negligence or other wrongdoing in the supervision, hiring, employment, training or monitoring of others by that insured, if the "occurrence" which caused the "bodily injury" or "property damage" involved the ownership, maintenance, use or entrustment to others of any aircraft or watercraft that is owned or operated by or rented or loaned to any insured.

This exclusion does not apply to:

(1) A watercraft while ashore on premises you own or rent;

(2) A watercraft you do not own that is:

    (a) Less than 8 metres long; and

    (b) Not being used to carry persons or property for a charge;

(3) "Bodily injury" to an "employee" of the insured on whose behalf contributions are made by or required to be made by the insured under the provisions of any Canadian provincial or territorial workers' compensation law, if the "bodily injury" results from an "occurrence" involving watercraft.

f. Automobile

"Bodily injury" or "property damage" arising directly or indirectly, in whole or in part, out of the ownership, maintenance, use or entrustment to others of any "automobile" owned or operated by or rented or loaned to any insured. Use includes operation and "loading or unloading". This exclusion applies regardless of any other contributing or aggravating cause or event that contributes concurrently or in any sequence to the "bodily injury" or "property damage".

This exclusion applies to any motorized snow vehicle or its trailers and any vehicle while being used in any speed or demolition contest or in any stunting activity or in practice or preparation for any such contest or activity.

This exclusion applies even if the claims against any insured allege negligence or other wrongdoing in the supervision, hiring, employment, training or monitoring of others by that insured, if the "occurrence" which caused the "bodily injury" or "property damage" involved the ownership, maintenance, use or entrustment to others of any "automobile" that is owned or operated by or rented or loaned to any insured.

This exclusion does not apply to:

(1) "Bodily injury" to an "employee" of the insured on whose behalf contributions are made by or required to be made by the insured under the provisions of any Canadian provincial or territorial workers' compensation law.

(2) "Bodily injury" or "property damage" arising out of a defective condition in, or improper maintenance of, any "automobile" owned by the Insured while leased to others for a period of 30 days or more provided the lessee is obligated under contract to ensure that the "automobile" is insured.

(3) the ownership, use or operation of machinery, apparatus or equipment mounted on or attached to any vehicle while at the site of the use or operation of such equipment, but this exception does not apply when such equipment is used for the purpose of "loading or unloading".

g. Damage To Property

"Property damage" to:

(1) Property you own, rent, or occupy, including any costs or expenses incurred by you, or any other person, organization or entity, for repair, replacement, enhancement, restoration or maintenance of such property for any reason, including prevention of injury to a person or damage to another's property;

(2) Premises you sell, give away or abandon, if the "property damage" arises out of any part of those premises;

(3) Property loaned to you;

(4) Personal property in your care, custody or control;

(5) That particular part of real property on which you or any contractors or subcontractors working directly or indirectly on your behalf are performing operations, if the "property damage" arises out of those operations; or

Page 3 of 21

(6) That particular part of any property that must be restored, repaired or replaced because "your work" was incorrectly performed on it.

Paragraph **(2)** of this exclusion does not apply if the premises are "your work" and were never occupied, rented or held for rental by you.

Paragraphs **(3)**, **(4)**, **(5)** and **(6)** of this exclusion do not apply to liability assumed under a sidetrack agreement.

Paragraph **(6)** of this exclusion does not apply to "property damage" included in the "products-completed operations hazard".

h. Damage To Your Product

"Property damage" to "your product" arising out of it or any part of it.

i. Damage To Your Work

"Property damage" to "your work" arising out of it or any part of it and included in the "products-completed operations hazard".

This exclusion does not apply if the damaged work or the work out of which the damage arises was performed on your behalf by a subcontractor.

j. Damage To Impaired Property or Property Not Physically Injured

"Property damage" to "impaired property" or property that has not been physically injured, arising out of:

(1) A defect, deficiency, inadequacy or dangerous condition in "your product" or "your work"; or

(2) A delay or failure by you or anyone acting on your behalf to perform a contract or agreement in accordance with its terms.

This exclusion does not apply to the loss of use of other property arising out of sudden and accidental physical injury to "your product" or "your work" after it has been put to its intended use.

k. Recall of Products, Work or Impaired Property

"Compensatory damages" claimed for any loss, cost or expense incurred by you or others for the loss of use, withdrawal, recall, inspection, repair, replacement, adjustment, removal or disposal of:

(1) "Your product";

(2) "Your work"; or

(3) "Impaired property";

if such product, work, or property is withdrawn or recalled from the market or from use by any person or organization because of a known or suspected defect, deficiency, inadequacy or dangerous condition in it.

l. Electronic Data

"Compensatory damages" arising out of the loss of, loss of use of, damage to, corruption of, inability to access, or inability to manipulate electronic data.

m. Personal and Advertising Injury

"Bodily injury" arising out of "personal and advertising injury".

n. Professional Services

"Bodily injury" (other than "incidental medical malpractice injury"), or "property damage" due to the rendering of or failure to render by you or on your behalf of any "professional services" for others, or any error or omission, malpractice or mistake in providing those services.

o. Abuse

a. Claims or "actions" arising directly or indirectly from "abuse" committed or alleged to have been committed by an insured, including the transmission of disease arising out of any act of "abuse".

b. Claims or "actions" based on your practices of "employee" hiring, acceptance of "volunteer workers" or supervision or retention of any person alleged to have committed "abuse".

c. Claims or "actions" alleging knowledge by an insured of, or failure to report, the alleged "abuse" to the appropriate authority(ies).

p. Asbestos – see Common Exclusions

q. Fungi or Spores – see Common Exclusions

r. **Nuclear** – see Common Exclusions

s. **Pollution** – see Common Exclusions

t. **Terrorism** – see Common Exclusions

u. **War Risks** – see Common Exclusions

COVERAGE B. PERSONAL and ADVERTISING INJURY LIABILITY

1. Insuring Agreement

a. We will pay those sums that the insured becomes legally obligated to pay as "compensatory damages" because of "personal and advertising injury" to which this insurance applies. We will have the right and duty to defend the insured against any "action" seeking those "compensatory damages". However, we will have no duty to defend the insured against any "action" seeking "compensatory damages" for "personal and advertising injury" to which this insurance does not apply. We may, at our discretion, investigate any offense and settle any claim or "action" that may result. But:

(1) The amount we will pay for "compensatory damages" is limited as described in Section III – Limits Of Insurance; and

(2) Our right and duty to defend end when we have used up the applicable limit of insurance in the payment of judgments or settlements under Coverages **A, B** or **D** or medical expenses under Coverage **C.**

No other obligation or liability to pay sums or perform acts or services is covered unless explicitly provided for under Supplementary Payments – Coverages **A, B** and **D.**

b. This insurance applies to "personal and advertising injury" caused by an offense arising out of your business but only if the offense was committed in the "coverage territory" during the policy period.

2. Exclusions

This insurance does not apply to:

a. **Knowing Violation Of Rights Of Another**

"Personal and advertising injury" caused by or at the direction of the insured with the knowledge that the act would violate the rights of another and would inflict "personal and advertising injury".

b. **Material Published With Knowledge Of Falsity**

"Personal and advertising injury" arising out of oral or written publication of material, if done by or at the direction of the insured with knowledge of its falsity.

c. **Material Published Prior To Policy Period**

"Personal and advertising injury" arising out of oral or written publication of material whose first publication took place before the beginning of the policy period.

d. **Criminal Acts**

"Personal and advertising injury" arising out of a criminal act committed by or at the direction of the insured.

e. **Contractual Liability**

"Personal and advertising injury" for which the insured has assumed liability in a contract or agreement. This exclusion does not apply to liability for "compensatory damages" that the insured would have in the absence of the contract or agreement.

f. **Breach Of Contract**

"Personal and advertising injury" arising out of a breach of contract, except an implied contract to use another's advertising idea in your "advertisement".

g. **Quality Or Performance Of Goods – Failure To Conform To Statements**

"Personal and advertising injury" arising out of the failure of goods, products or services to conform with any statement of quality or performance made in your "advertisement".

h. **Wrong Description Of Prices**

"Personal and advertising injury" arising out of the wrong description of the price of goods, products or services stated in your "advertisement".

i. Infringement Of Copyright, Patent, Trademark or Trade Secret

"Personal and advertising injury" arising out of the infringement of copyright, patent, trademark, trade secret or other intellectual property rights.

However, this exclusion does not apply to infringement, in your "advertisement", of copyright, trade dress or slogan.

j. Insureds In Media and Internet Type Businesses

"Personal and advertising injury" committed by an insured whose business is:

(1) Advertising, broadcasting, publishing or telecasting;

(2) Designing or determining content of web-sites for others; or

(3) An Internet search, access, content or service provider.

However, this exclusion does not apply to Paragraphs **21. a., b.** and **c.** of "personal and advertising injury" under the Definitions Section.

For the purposes of this exclusion, the placing of frames, borders or links, or advertising, for you or others anywhere on the Internet, is not by itself, considered the business of advertising, broadcasting, publishing or telecasting.

k. Electronic Chatrooms or Bulletin Boards

"Personal and advertising injury" arising out of an electronic chatroom or bulletin board the insured hosts, owns, or over which the insured exercises control.

l. Unauthorized Use Of Another's Name or Product

"Personal and advertising injury" arising out of the unauthorized use of another's name or product in your e-mail address, domain name or metatag, or any other similar tactics to mislead another's potential customers.

m. Asbestos – see Common Exclusions

n. Fungi or Spores – see Common Exclusions

o. Nuclear– see Common Exclusions

p. Pollution – see Common Exclusions

q. Terrorism – see Common Exclusions

r. War Risks – see Common Exclusions

COVERAGE C. MEDICAL PAYMENTS

1. Insuring Agreement

a. We will pay medical expenses as described below for "bodily injury" caused by an accident:

(1) On premises you own or rent;

(2) On ways next to premises you own or rent; or

(3) Because of your operations;

provided that:

(1) The accident takes place in the "coverage territory" and during the policy period;

(2) The expenses are incurred and reported to us within one year of the date of the accident; and

(3) The injured person submits to examination, at our expense, by physicians of our choice as often as we reasonably require.

b. We will make these payments regardless of fault. These payments will not exceed the applicable limit of insurance as described in Section III – Limits of Insurance. We will pay reasonable expenses for:

(1) First aid administered at the time of an accident;

(2) Necessary medical, surgical, x-ray and dental services, including prosthetic devices; and

(3) Necessary ambulance, hospital, professional nursing and funeral services.

2. Exclusions

We will not pay expenses for "bodily injury":

a. **Any Insured**

To any insured, except "volunteer workers".

b. **Hired Person**

To a person hired to do work for or on behalf of any insured or a tenant of any insured.

c. **Injury On Normally Occupied Premises**

To a person injured on that part of premises you own or rent that the person normally occupies.

d. **Workers Compensation and Similar Laws**

To a person, whether or not an "employee" of any insured, if benefits for the "bodily injury" are payable or must be provided under a workers' compensation or disability benefits law or a similar law.

e. **Athletics Activities**

To a person injured while practicing, instructing or participating in any physical exercises or games, sports or athletic contests.

f. **Products-Completed Operations Hazard**

Included within the "products-completed operations hazard".

g. **Coverage A Exclusions**

Excluded under Coverage **A.**

COVERAGE D. TENANTS' LEGAL LIABILITY

1. **Insuring Agreement**

a. We will pay those sums that the insured becomes legally obligated to pay as "compensatory damages" because of "property damage" to which this insurance applies. This insurance applies only to "property damage" to premises of others rented to you or occupied by you. We will have the right and duty to defend the insured against any "action" seeking those "compensatory damages". However, we will have no duty to defend the insured against any "action" seeking "compensatory damages" for "property damage" to which this insurance does not apply. We may, at our discretion, investigate any "occurrence" and settle any claim or "action" that may result. But:

(1) The amount we will pay for "compensatory damages" is limited as described in Section III – Limits Of Insurance; and

(2) Our right and duty to defend ends when we have used up the applicable limit of insurance in the payment of judgments or settlements under Coverages **A, B** or **D** or medical expenses under Coverage **C.**

No other obligation or liability to pay sums or perform acts or services is covered unless explicitly provided for under Supplementary Payments – Coverages **A, B** and **D.**

b. This insurance applies to "property damage" only if:

(1) The "property damage" is caused by an "occurrence" that takes place in the "coverage territory";

(2) The "property damage" occurs during the policy period; and

(3) Prior to the policy period, no insured listed under Paragraph **1.** of Section II – Who Is An Insured and no "employee" authorized by you to give or receive notice of an "occurrence" or claim, knew that the "property damage" had occurred, in whole or in part. If such a listed insured or authorized "employee" knew, prior to the policy period, that the "property damage" occurred, then any continuation, change or resumption of such "property damage" during or after the policy period will be deemed to have been known prior to the policy period.

c. "Property damage" which occurs during the policy period and was not, prior to the policy period, known to have occurred by any insured listed under Paragraph **1.** of Section II – Who Is An Insured or any "employee" authorized by you to give or receive notice of an "occurrence" or claim, includes any continuation, change or resumption of that "property damage" after the end of the policy period.

d. "Property damage" will be deemed to have been known to have occurred at the earliest time when any insured listed under Paragraph **1.** of Section II – Who Is An Insured or any "employee" authorized by you to give or receive notice of an "occurrence" or claim:

(1) Reports all, or any part, of the "property damage" to us or any other insurer;

(2) Receives a written or verbal demand or claim for "compensatory damages" because of the "property damage"; or

(3) Becomes aware by any other means that "property damage" has occurred or has begun to occur.

2. Exclusions

This insurance does not apply to:

a. Expected or Intended Injury

"Property damage" expected or intended from the standpoint of the insured.

b. Contractual Liability

"Property damage" for which the insured is obligated to pay "compensatory damages" by reason of the assumption of liability in a contract or agreement. This exclusion does not apply to liability for "compensatory damages":

(1) That the insured would have in the absence of the contract or agreement; or

(2) Assumed in a contract or agreement that is an "insured contract", provided the "property damage" occurs subsequent to the execution of the contract or agreement. Solely for the purposes of liability assumed in an "insured contract", reasonable legal fees and necessary litigation expenses incurred by or for a party other than an insured are deemed to be "compensatory damages" because of "property damage", provided:

(a) Liability to such party for, or for the cost of, that party's defense has also been assumed in the same "insured contract"; and

(b) Such legal fees and litigation expenses are for defense of that party against a civil or alternative dispute resolution proceeding in which "compensatory damages" to which this insurance applies are alleged.

c. Asbestos – see Common Exclusions

d. Fungi or Spores – see Common Exclusions

e. Nuclear– see Common Exclusions

f. Pollution – see Common Exclusions

g. Terrorism – see Common Exclusions

h. War Risks – see Common Exclusions

COMMON EXCLUSIONS – COVERAGES A, B, C and D

This insurance does not apply to:

1. Asbestos

"Bodily injury", "property damage" or "personal and advertising injury" related to or arising from any actual or alleged liability for any legal remedy of any kind whatsoever (including but not limited to damages, interest, mandatory or other injunctive relief, statutory orders or penalties, legal or other costs, or expenses of any kind) in respect of actual or threatened loss, damage, cost or expense directly or indirectly caused by, resulting from, in consequence of or in any way involving, asbestos or any materials containing asbestos in whatever form or quantity.

This exclusion applies regardless of any other contributing or aggravating cause or event that contributes concurrently or in any sequence to the "bodily injury", "property damage" or "personal and advertising injury".

2. Fungi or Spores

a. "Bodily injury", "property damage" or "personal and advertising injury" or any other cost, loss or expense incurred by others, arising directly or indirectly from the actual, alleged or threatened inhalation of, ingestion of, contact with, exposure to, existence of, presence of, spread of, reproduction, discharge or other growth of any "fungi" or "spores" however caused, including any costs or expenses incurred to prevent, respond to, test for, monitor, abate, mitigate, remove, cleanup, contain, remediate, treat, detoxify, neutralize, assess or otherwise deal with or dispose of "fungi" or "spores";

b. Any supervision, instructions, recommendations, warnings, or advice given or which should have been given in connection with **a.** above; or

c. Any obligation to pay damages, share damages with or repay someone else who must pay damages because of such injury or damage referred to in **a.** or **b.** above.

This exclusion applies regardless of any other contributing or aggravating cause or event that contributes concurrently or in any sequence to the "bodily injury", "property damage" or "personal and advertising injury".

3. Nuclear Energy Liability

a. Liability imposed by or arising from any nuclear liability act, law or statute, or any law amendatory thereof;

b. "Bodily injury", "property damage" or "personal and advertising injury" with respect to which an insured under this policy is also insured under a contract of nuclear energy liability insurance (whether the insured is unnamed in such contract and whether or not it is legally enforceable by the insured) issued by the Nuclear Insurance Association of Canada or any other insurer or group or pool of insurers or would be an insured under any such policy but for its termination upon exhaustion of its limit of liability;

c. "Bodily injury", "property damage" or "personal and advertising injury" resulting directly or indirectly from the "nuclear energy hazard" arising from:

1) The ownership, maintenance, operation or use of a "nuclear facility" by or on behalf of an insured;
2) the furnishing by an insured of services, materials, parts or equipment in connection with the planning, construction, maintenance, operation or use of any "nuclear facility";
3) the possession, consumption, use, handling, disposal or transportation of "fissionable substances", or of other "radioactive material" (except radioactive isotopes, away from a nuclear facility, which have reached the final stage of fabrication so as to be useable for any scientific, medical, agricultural, commercial or industrial purpose) used, distributed, handled or sold by an insured.

This exclusion applies regardless of any other contributing or aggravating cause or event that contribute concurrently or in any sequence to the "bodily injury", "property damage" or "personal and advertising injury".

4. Pollution

(1) "Bodily injury", "property damage" or "personal and advertising injury" arising out of the actual, alleged or threatened spill, discharge, emission, dispersal, seepage, leakage, migration, release or escape of "pollutants":

(a) At or from any premises, site or location which is or was at any time owned or occupied by, or rented or loaned to, any insured. However, this subparagraph does not apply to:

(i) "Bodily injury" if sustained within a building and caused by smoke, fumes, vapour or soot from equipment used to heat, cool or dehumidify the building, or equipment that is used to heat water for personal use, by the building's occupants or their guests;

(ii) "Bodily injury" or "property damage" for which you may be held liable, if you are a contractor and the owner or lessee of such premises, site or location has been added to your policy as an additional insured with respect to your ongoing operations performed for that additional insured at that premises, site or location and such premises, site or location is not and never was owned or occupied by, or rented or loaned to, any insured, other than that additional insured; or

(iii) "Bodily injury" or "property damage" arising out of heat, smoke or fumes from a "hostile fire";

(b) At or from any premises, site or location which is or was at any time used by or for any insured or others for the handling, storage, disposal, processing or treatment of waste;

(c) Which are or were at any time transported, handled, stored, treated, disposed of, or processed as waste by or for:

(i) Any insured; or

(ii) Any person or organization for whom you may be legally responsible; or

(d) At or from any premises, site or location on which any insured or any contractors or subcontractors working directly or indirectly on any insured's behalf are performing operations if the "pollutants" are brought on or to the premises, site or location in connection with such operations by such insured, contractor or subcontractor. However, this subparagraph does not apply to:

(i) "Bodily injury" or "property damage" arising out of the escape of fuels, lubricants or other operating fluids which are needed to perform the normal electrical, hydraulic or mechanical functions necessary for the operation of mobile equipment or its parts, if such fuels, lubricants or other operating fluids escape from a vehicle part designed to hold, store or receive them. This exception does not apply if the "bodily injury" or "property damage" arises out of the intentional discharge, dispersal or release of the fuels, lubricants or other operating fluids, or if such fuels, lubricants or other operating fluids are brought on or to the premises, site or location with the intent that they be discharged, dispersed or released as part of the operations being performed by such insured, contractor or subcontractor;

(ii) "Bodily injury" or "property damage" sustained within a building and caused by the release of gases, fumes or vapours from materials brought into that building in connection with operations being performed by you or on your behalf by a contractor or subcontractor; or

(iii) "Bodily injury" or "property damage" arising out of heat, smoke or fumes from a "hostile fire".

(e) At or from any premises, site or location on which any insured or any contractors or subcontractors working directly or indirectly on any insured's behalf are performing operations if the operations are to test for, monitor, clean up, remove, contain, treat, detoxify or neutralize, or in any way respond to, or assess the effects of, "pollutants".

(2) Any loss, cost or expense arising out of any:

(a) Request, demand, order or statutory or regulatory requirement that any insured or others test for, monitor, clean up, remove, contain, treat, detoxify or neutralize, or in any way respond to, or assess the effects of, "pollutants"; or

(b) Claim or "action" by or on behalf of a governmental authority for "compensatory damages" because of testing for, monitoring, cleaning up, removing, containing, treating, detoxifying or neutralizing, or in any way responding to, or assessing the effects of, "pollutants".

However, this Section (2) does not apply to liability for "compensatory damages" because of "property damage" that the insured would have in the absence of such request, demand, order or statutory or regulatory requirement, or such claim or "action" by or on behalf of a governmental authority.

5. Terrorism

"Bodily injury", "property damage" or "personal and advertising injury" arising directly or indirectly, in whole or in part, out of "terrorism" or out of any activity or decision of a government agency or other entity to prevent, respond to or terminate "terrorism". This exclusion applies regardless of any other contributing or aggravating cause or event that contributes concurrently or in any sequence to the "bodily injury", "property damage" or "personal and advertising injury".

6. War Risks

"Bodily injury", "property damage" or "personal and advertising injury" arising directly or indirectly, in whole or in part, out of war, invasion, act of foreign enemy, hostilities (whether war be declared or not), civil war, rebellion, revolution, insurrection or military power. This exclusion applies regardless of any other contributing or aggravating cause or event that contributes concurrently or in any sequence to the "bodily injury", "property damage" or "personal and advertising injury".

SUPPLEMENTARY PAYMENTS – COVERAGES A, B and D

1. We will pay, with respect to any claim we investigate or settle, or any "action" against an insured we defend:

a. All expenses we incur.

b. The cost of bonds to release attachments, but only for bond amounts within the applicable limit of insurance. We do not have to furnish these bonds.

c. All reasonable expenses you incur at our request to assist us in the investigation or defense of the claim or "action", including actual loss of earnings up to $250 a day because of time off from work.

d. All costs assessed or awarded against you in the "action".

e. Any interest accruing after entry of judgment upon that part of the judgment which is within the applicable limit of insurance and before we have paid, offered to pay, or deposited in court the part of the judgment that is within the applicable limit of insurance.

These payments will not reduce the limits of insurance.

2. If we defend an insured against an "action" and an indemnitee of the insured is also named as a party to the "action", we will defend that indemnitee if all of the following conditions are met:

   a. The "action" against the indemnitee seeks "compensatory damages" for which the insured has assumed the liability of the indemnitee in a contract or agreement that is an "insured contract";

   b. This insurance applies to such liability assumed by the insured;

   c. The obligation to defend, or the cost of the defense of, that indemnitee, has also been assumed by the insured in the same "insured contract";

   d. The allegations in the "action" and the information we know about the "occurrence" are such that no conflict appears to exist between the interests of the insured and the interests of the indemnitee;

   e. The indemnitee and the insured ask us to conduct and control the defense of that indemnitee against such "action" and agree that we can assign the same counsel to defend the insured and the indemnitee; and

   f. The indemnitee:

      (1) Agrees in writing to:

         (a) Cooperate with us in the investigation, settlement or defense of the "action";

         (b) Immediately send us copies of any demands, notices, summonses or legal papers received in connection with the "action";

         (c) Notify any other insurer whose coverage is available to the indemnitee; and

         (d) Cooperate with us with respect to coordinating other applicable insurance available to the indemnitee; and

      (2) Provides us with written authorization to:

         (a) Obtain records and other information related to the "action"; and

         (b) Conduct and control the defense of the indemnitee in such "action".

   So long as the above conditions are met, legal fees incurred by us in the defense of that indemnitee, necessary litigation expenses incurred by us and necessary litigation expenses incurred by the indemnitee at our request will be paid as Supplementary Payments. Notwithstanding the provisions of Paragraph **2.b. (2)** of Section I – Coverage **A** – Bodily Injury and Property Damage Liability, such payments will not be deemed to be "compensatory damages" for "bodily injury" and "property damage" and will not reduce the limits of insurance.

   Our obligation to defend an insured's indemnitee and to pay for legal fees and necessary litigation expenses as Supplementary Payments ends when:

   a. We have used up the applicable limit of insurance in the payment of judgments or settlements; or

   b. The conditions set forth above, or the terms of the agreement described in Paragraph **f.** above, are no longer met.

SECTION II – WHO IS AN INSURED

1. If you are designated in the Declarations as:

   a. An individual, you and your spouse are insureds, but only with respect to the conduct of a business of which you are the sole owner.

   b. A partnership, limited liability partnership or joint venture, you are an insured. Your members, your partners, and their spouses are also insureds, but only with respect to the conduct of your business.

   c. A limited liability company, you are an insured. Your members are also insureds, but only with respect to the conduct of your business. Your managers are insureds, but only with respect to their duties as your managers.

   d. An organization other than a partnership, limited liability partnership, joint venture or limited liability company, you are an insured. Your "executive officers" and directors are insureds, but only with respect to their duties as your officers or directors. Your shareholders are also insureds, but only with respect to their liability as shareholders.

   e. A trust, you are an insured. Your trustees are also insureds, but only with respect to their duties as trustees.

2. Each of the following is also an insured:

a. Your "volunteer workers" only while performing duties related to the conduct of your business, or your "employees", other than either your "executive officers" (if you are an organization other than a partnership, limited liability partnership, joint venture or limited liability company) or your managers (if you are a limited liability company), but only for acts within the scope of their employment by you or while performing duties related to the conduct of your business. However, none of these "employees" or "volunteer workers" are insureds for:

    (1) "Bodily injury" or "personal and advertising injury":

        (a) To you, to your partners or members (if you are a partnership, limited liability partnership or joint venture), to your members (if you are a limited liability company), to a co-"employee" while in the course of his or her employment or performing duties related to the conduct of your business, or to your other "volunteer workers" while performing duties related to the conduct of your business;

        (b) To the spouse, child, parent, brother or sister of that co-"employee" or "volunteer worker" as a consequence of Paragraph **(1) (a)** above;

        (c) For which there is any obligation to share "compensatory damages" with or repay someone else who must pay "compensatory damages" because of the injury described in Paragraphs **(1)(a)** or **(b)** above;

        (d) Arising out of his or her providing or failing to provide professional health care services; or

        (e) To any person who at the time of injury is entitled to benefits under any workers' compensation or disability benefits law or a similar law.

    (2) "Property damage" to property:

        (a) Owned, occupied or used by,

        (b) Rented to, in the care, custody or control of, or over which physical control is being exercised for any purpose by

        you, any of your "employees", "volunteer workers", any partner or member (if you are a partnership, limited liability partnership or joint venture), or any member (if you are a limited liability company).

b. Any person (other than your "employee" or "volunteer worker"), or any organization while acting as your real estate manager.

c. Any person or organization having proper temporary custody of your property if you die, but only:

    (1) With respect to liability arising out of the maintenance or use of that property; and

    (2) Until your legal representative has been appointed.

d. Your legal representative if you die, but only with respect to duties as such. That representative will have all your rights and duties under this policy.

3. Any organization you newly acquire or form, other than a partnership, limited liability partnership or joint venture or limited liability company, and over which you maintain ownership or majority interest, will qualify as a Named Insured if there is no other similar insurance available to that organization. However:

    a. Coverage under this provision is afforded only until the 90th day after you acquire or form the organization or the end of the policy period, whichever is earlier;

    b. Coverage **A** and **D** does not apply to "bodily injury" or "property damage" that occurred before you acquired or formed the organization; and

    c. Coverage **B** does not apply to "personal and advertising injury" arising out of an offense committed before you acquired or formed the organization.

No person or organization is an insured with respect to the conduct of any current or past partnership, limited liability partnership, joint venture or limited liability company that is not shown as a Named Insured in the Declarations.

SECTION III – LIMITS OF INSURANCE

1. The Limits of Insurance shown in the Declarations and the rules below fix the most we will pay regardless of the number of:

    a. Insureds;

    b. Claims made or "actions" brought; or

    c. Persons or organizations making claims or bringing "actions".

2. The General Aggregate Limit is the most we will pay for the sum of:

    a. "Compensatory damages" under Coverage **A**, except "compensatory damages" because of "bodily injury" or "property damage" included in the "products-completed operations hazard";

    b. "Compensatory damages" under Coverage **B**; and

    c. Medical expenses under Coverage **C**.

3. The Products-Completed Operations Aggregate Limit is the most we will pay under Coverage **A** for "compensatory damages" because of "bodily injury" and "property damage" included in the "products-completed operations hazard".

4. Subject to **2.** or **3.** above, whichever applies, the Each Occurrence Limit is the most we will pay for the sum of:

    a. "Compensatory damages" under Coverage **A**; and

    b. Medical expenses under Coverage **C**

    because of all "bodily injury" and "property damage" arising out of any one "occurrence".

5. Subject to **2.** above, the Personal and Advertising Injury Limit is the most we will pay under Coverage **B** for the sum of all "compensatory damages" because of all "personal and advertising injury" sustained by any one person or organization.

6. The Tenants' Legal Liability Limit is the most we will pay under Coverage **D** for "compensatory damages" because of "property damage" to any one premises.

7. Subject to **4.** above, the Medical Expense Limit is the most we will pay under Coverage **C** for all medical expenses because of "bodily injury" sustained by any one person

The Limits of Insurance of this policy apply separately to each consecutive annual period and to any remaining period of less than 12 months, starting with the beginning of the policy period shown in the Declarations, unless the policy period is extended after issuance for an additional period of less than 12 months. In that case, the additional period will be deemed part of the last preceding period for purposes of determining the Limits of Insurance.

8. **Deductible**

    a. Our obligation under Property Damage Liability and Tenants' Legal Liability to pay "compensatory damages" on your behalf applies only to the amount of "compensatory damages" in excess of any deductible amounts stated in the Declarations as applicable to such coverages, and the limits of insurance applicable to each "occurrence" for Property Damage Liability and any one premises for Tenants' Legal Liability will be reduced by the amount of such deductible.

    b. The deductible amount applies as follows:

        1) Under Coverage **A**: To all "compensatory damages" because of "property damage" as the result of any one "occurrence", regardless of the number of persons or organizations who sustain "compensatory damages" because of that "occurrence".

        2) Under Coverage **D**, Tenants' Legal Liability, to all "compensatory damages" because of "property damage" as the result of any one "occurrence", regardless of the number of persons or organizations who sustain "compensatory damages" because of that "occurrence".

    c. The terms of this insurance, including those in respect to:

        1) our right and duty to defend any "action" seeking those "compensatory damages"; and

        2) your duties in the event of an "occurrence", claim or "action"

        apply irrespective of the application of the deductible amount.

    d. We may pay any part or all of the deductible amount to effect settlement of any claim or "action" and, upon notification of the action taken, you shall promptly reimburse us for such part of the deductible amount as has been paid by us.

SECTION IV – COMMERCIAL GENERAL LIABILITY CONDITIONS

1. Bankruptcy

Bankruptcy or insolvency of the insured or of the insured's estate will not relieve us of our obligations under this policy.

2. Canadian Currency Clause

All limits of insurance, premiums and other amounts as expressed in this policy are in Canadian currency.

3. Changes.

This policy contains all the agreements between you and us concerning the insurance afforded. The first Named Insured shown in the Declarations is authorized to make changes in the terms of this policy with our consent. This policy's terms can be amended or waived only by endorsement issued by us and made a part of this policy.

4. Duties In The Event Of Occurrence, Offense, Claim or Action

a. You must see to it that we are notified as soon as practicable of an "occurrence" or an offense which may result in a claim. To the extent possible, notice should include:

(1) How, when and where the "occurrence" or offense took place;

(2) The names and addresses of any injured persons and witnesses; and

(3) The nature and location of any injury or damage arising out of the "occurrence" or offense.

b. If a claim is made or "action" is brought against any insured, you must:

(1) Immediately record the specifics of the claim or "action" and the date received; and

(2) Notify us as soon as practicable.

You must see to it that we receive written notice of the claim or "action" as soon as practicable.

c. You and any other involved insured must:

(1) Immediately send us copies of any demands, notices, summonses or legal papers received in connection with the claim or "action";

(2) Authorize us to obtain records and other information;

(3) Cooperate with us in the investigation or settlement of the claim or defense against the "action"; and

(4) Assist us, upon our request, in the enforcement of any right against any person or organization which may be liable to the insured because of injury or damage to which this insurance may also apply.

d. No insured will, except at that insured's own cost, voluntarily make a payment, assume any obligation, or incur any expense, other than for first aid, without our consent.

5. Examination Of Your Books and Records.

We may examine and audit your books and records as they relate to this policy at any time during the policy period and up to three years afterward.

6. Inspections and Surveys

1. We have the right to:

a. Make inspections and surveys at any time;

b. Give you reports on the conditions we find; and

c. Recommend changes.

2. We are not obligated to make any inspections, surveys, reports or recommendations and any such actions we do undertake relate only to insurability and the premiums to be charged. We do not make safety inspections. We do not undertake to perform the duty of any person or organization to provide for the health or safety of workers or the public. And we do not warrant that conditions:

a. Are safe or healthful; or

b. Comply with laws, regulations, codes or standards.

3. Paragraphs 1. and 2. of this condition apply not only to us, but also to any rating, advisory, rate service or similar organization which makes insurance inspections, surveys, reports or recommendations.

4. Paragraph 2. of this condition does not apply to any inspections, surveys, reports or recommendations we may make relative to certification, under provincial or municipal statutes, ordinances, bylaws or regulations, of boilers, pressure vessels or elevators.

7. Legal Action Against Us

No person or organization has a right under this policy:

a. To join us as a party or otherwise bring us into an "action" asking for "compensatory damages" from an insured; or

b. To sue us on this policy unless all of its terms have been fully complied with.

A person or organization may sue us to recover on an agreed settlement or on a final judgment against an insured; but we will not be liable for "compensatory damages" that are not payable under the terms of this policy or that are in excess of the applicable limit of insurance. An agreed settlement means a settlement and release of liability signed by us, the insured and the claimant or the claimant's legal representative.

8. Other Insurance

If other valid and collectible insurance is available to the insured for a loss we cover under Coverages **A**, **B** or **D** of this policy, our obligations are limited as follows:

a. Primary Insurance

This insurance is primary except when **b.** below applies. If this insurance is primary, our obligations are not affected unless any of the other insurance is also primary. Then, we will share with all that other insurance by the method described in **c.** below.

b. Excess Insurance

This insurance is excess over:

(1) Any of the other insurance, whether primary, excess, contingent or on any other basis:

    (a) That is Fire, Extended Coverage, Builder's Risk, Installation Risk or similar coverage for "your work";

    (b) That is Fire insurance for premises rented to you or temporarily occupied by you with permission of the owner;

    (c) If the loss arises out of the maintenance or use of watercraft to the extent not subject to Exclusion **e.** of Section I – Coverage **A** – Bodily Injury and Property Damage Liability.

(2) Any other primary insurance available to you covering liability for "compensatory damages" arising out of the premises or operations or products-completed operations for which you have been added as an additional insured by attachment of an endorsement.

When this insurance is excess, we will have no duty under Coverages **A**, **B** or **D** to defend the insured against any "action" if any other insurer has a duty to defend the insured against that "action". If no other insurer defends, we will undertake to do so, but we will be entitled to the insured's rights against all those other insurers.

When this insurance is excess over other insurance, we will pay only our share of the amount of the loss, if any, that exceeds the sum of:

(1) The total amount that all such other insurance would pay for the loss in the absence of this insurance; and

(2) The total of all deductible and self-insured amounts under all that other insurance.

We will share the remaining loss, if any, with any other insurance that is not described in this Excess Insurance provision and was not bought specifically to apply in excess of the Limits of Insurance shown in the Declarations of this policy.

c. Method Of Sharing

If all of the other insurance permits contribution by equal shares, we will follow this method also. Under this approach each insurer contributes equal amounts until it has paid its applicable limit of insurance or none of the loss remains, whichever comes first.

If any of the other insurance does not permit contribution by equal shares, we will contribute by limits. Under this method, each insurer's share is based on the ratio of its applicable limit of insurance to the total applicable limits of insurance of all insurers.

9. Premium Audit

a. We will compute all premiums for this policy in accordance with our rules and rates.

    b. Premium shown in this policy as advance premium is a deposit premium only. At the close of each audit period we will compute the earned premium for that period. Audit premiums are due and payable on notice to the first Named Insured. If the sum of the advance and audit premiums paid for the policy period is greater than the earned premium, we will return the excess to the first Named Insured subject to the retention of the minimum retained premium shown in the Declarations of this policy.

    c. The first Named Insured must keep records of the information we need for premium computation, and send us copies at such times as we may request.

10. Premiums

The first Named Insured shown in the Declarations:

    a. Is responsible for the payment of all premiums; and

    b. Will be the payee for any return premiums we pay.

11. Representations

By accepting this policy, you agree:

    a. The statements in the Declarations are accurate and complete;

    b. Those statements are based upon representations you made to us; and

    c. We have issued this policy in reliance upon your representations.

12. Separation Of Insureds, Cross Liability

Except with respect to the Limits of Insurance, and any rights or duties specifically assigned in this policy to the first Named Insured, this insurance applies:

    a. As if each Named Insured were the only Named Insured; and

    b. Separately to each insured against whom claim is made or "action" is brought.

13. Termination

    a. The first Named Insured shown in the Declarations may terminate this policy by mailing or delivering to us advance written notice of termination.

    b. We may terminate this policy by mailing or delivering to the first Named Insured written notice of termination at least:
        1) 15 days before the effective date of termination if we terminate for nonpayment of premium; or
        2) 30 days before the effective date of termination if we terminate for any other reason.
        Except in Quebec, if notice is mailed, termination takes effect 15 or 30 days after receipt of the letter by the post office to which it is addressed, depending upon the reason for termination. Proof of mailing will be sufficient proof of notice.

        In Quebec, termination takes effect either 15 or 30 days after receipt of the notice at the last known address of the first Named Insured, depending upon the reason for termination.

    c. We will mail or deliver our notice to the first Named Insured's last mailing address known to us.

    d. The policy period will end on the date termination takes effect.

    e. If this policy is terminated, we will send the first Named Insured any premium refund due. If we terminate, the refund will be pro rata. If the first Named Insured terminates, the refund may be less than pro rata. The termination will be effective even if we have not made or offered a refund.

14. Transfer Of Rights Of Recovery Against Others To Us

If the insured has rights to recover all or part of any payment we have made under this policy, those rights are transferred to us. The insured must do nothing after loss to impair them. At our request, the insured will bring "action" or transfer those rights to us and help us enforce them.

15. Transfer Of Your Rights and Duties Under This Policy

Your rights and duties under this policy may not be transferred without our written consent except in the case of death of an individual Named Insured.

If you die, your rights and duties will be transferred to your legal representative but only while acting within the scope of duties as your legal representative. Until your legal representative is appointed, anyone having proper temporary custody of your property will have your rights and duties but only with respect to that property.

SECTION V – DEFINITIONS

1. "Abuse" means any act or threat involving molestation, harassment, corporal punishment or any other form of physical, sexual or mental abuse.

2. "Action" means a civil proceeding in which "compensatory damages" because of "bodily injury", "property damage" or "personal and advertising injury" to which this insurance applies are alleged. "Action" includes:

   a. An arbitration proceeding in which such "compensatory damages" are claimed and to which the insured must submit or does submit with our consent; or

   b. Any other alternative dispute resolution proceeding in which such "compensatory damages" are claimed and to which the insured submits with our consent.

3. "Advertisement" means a notice that is broadcast or published to the general public or specific market segments about your goods, products or services for the purpose of attracting customers or supporters. For the purposes of this definition:

   a. Notices that are published include material placed on the Internet or on similar electronic means of communication; and

   b. Regarding web-sites, only that part of a web-site that is about your goods, products or services for the purposes of attracting customers or supporters is considered an advertisement.

4. "Automobile" means a land motor vehicle, trailer or semitrailer that is required by law to be insured under a contract evidenced by a motor vehicle liability policy, or any vehicle insured under such a contract, including any attached machinery or equipment.

5. "Bodily injury" means bodily injury, sickness or disease sustained by a person, including death resulting from any of these at any time.

6. "Compensatory damages" means damages due or awarded   in payment for actual injury or economic loss. "Compensatory damages" does not include punitive or exemplary damages or the multiple portion of any multiplied damage award.

7. "Coverage territory" means:

   a. Canada and the United States of America (including its territories and possessions).

   b. International waters or airspace, but only if the injury or damage occurs in the course of travel or transportation between any places included in **a.** above; or

   c. All other parts of the world if the injury or damage arises out of:

      (1) Goods or products made or sold by you in the territory described in **a.** above;

      (2) The activities of an insured person whose home is in the territory described in **a.** above, but is away for a short time on your business; or

      (3) "Personal and advertising injury" offenses that take place through the Internet or similar electronic means of communication

   provided the insured's responsibility to pay "compensatory damages" is determined in an "action" on the merits, in the territory described in **a.** above or in a settlement we agree to.

8. "Employee" includes a "leased worker" and a "temporary worker".

9. "Executive officer" means a person holding any of the officer positions created by your charter, constitution, by-laws or any other similar governing document.

10. "Fissionable substance" means any prescribed substance that is, or from which can be obtained, a substance capable of releasing atomic energy by nuclear fission.

11. "Fungi" includes, but is not limited to, any form or type of mould, yeast, mushroom or mildew whether or not allergenic, pathogenic or toxigenic, and any substance, vapour or gas produced by, emitted from or arising out of any "fungi" or "spores" or resultant mycotoxins, allergens or pathogens.

12. "Hostile fire" means one which becomes uncontrollable or breaks out from where it was intended to be.

13. "Impaired property" means tangible property, other than "your product" or "your work", that cannot be used or is less useful because:

   a. It incorporates "your product" or "your work" that is known or thought to be defective, deficient, inadequate or dangerous; or

   b. You have failed to fulfill the terms of a contract or agreement;

if such property can be restored to use by:

a. The repair, replacement, adjustment or removal of "your product" or "your work"; or

b. Your fulfilling the terms of the contract or agreement.

14. "Incidental medical malpractice injury" means "bodily injury" arising out of the rendering of or failure to render, during the Policy Period, the following services:

i) medical, surgical, dental, x-ray or nursing services or treatment or the furnishing of food or beverages in connection therewith; or

ii) the furnishing or dispensing of drugs or medical, dental or surgical supplies or appliances;

by any insured or any indemnitee causing the "incidental medical malpractice injury" who is not engaged in the business or occupation of providing any of the services described in i) and ii) above.

15. "Insured contract" means:

a. A contract for a lease of premises. However, that portion of the contract for a lease of premises that indemnifies any person or organization for damage to premises while rented to you or temporarily occupied by you with permission of the owner is not an "insured contract";

b. A sidetrack agreement;

c. An easement or license agreement in connection with vehicle or pedestrian private railroad crossings at grade;

d. Any other easement agreement;

e. An obligation, as required by ordinance or bylaw, to indemnify a municipality, except in connection with work for a municipality;

f. An elevator maintenance agreement;

g. That part of any other contract or agreement pertaining to your business (including an indemnification of a municipality in connection with work performed for a municipality) under which you assume the tort liability of another party to pay for "compensatory damages" because of "bodily injury" or "property damage" to a third person or organization, provided the "bodily injury" or "property damage" is caused, in whole or in part, by you or by those acting on your behalf. Tort liability means a liability that would be imposed by law in the absence of any contract or agreement.

Paragraph g. does not include that part of any contract or agreement:

(1) That indemnifies an architect, engineer or surveyor for injury or damage arising out of:

(a) Preparing, approving, or failing to prepare or approve, maps, shop drawings, opinions, reports, surveys, field orders, change orders or drawings and specifications; or

(b) Giving directions or instructions, or failing to give them, if that is the primary cause of the injury or damage; or

(2) Under which the insured, if an architect, engineer or surveyor, assumes liability for an injury or damage arising out of the insured's rendering or failure to render "professional services", including those listed in (1) above and supervisory, inspection, architectural or engineering activities.

16. "Leased worker" means a person leased to you by a labour leasing firm under an agreement between you and the labour leasing firm, to perform duties related to the conduct of your business. "Leased worker" does not include a "temporary worker".

17. "Loading or unloading" means the handling of property:

a. After it is moved from the place where it is accepted for movement into or onto an aircraft, watercraft or "automobile";

b. While it is in or on an aircraft, watercraft or "automobile"; or

c. While it is being moved from an aircraft, watercraft or "automobile" to the place where it is finally delivered;

but "loading or unloading" does not include the movement of property by means of a mechanical device, other than a hand truck, that is not attached to the aircraft, watercraft or "automobile".

18. "Nuclear energy hazard" means the radioactive, toxic, explosive, or other hazardous properties of radioactive material;

19. "Nuclear facility" means:

a) any apparatus designed or used to sustain nuclear fission in a self-supporting chain reaction or to contain a critical mass of plutonium, thorium and uranium or any one or more of them;

b) any equipment or device designed or used for (i) separating the isotopes of plutonium, thorium and uranium or any one or more of them, (ii) processing or packaging waste;

c) any equipment or device used for the processing, fabricating or alloying of plutonium, thorium or uranium enriched in the isotope uranium 233 or in the isotope uranium 235, or any one or more of them if at any time the total amount of such material in the custody of the insured at the premises where such equipment or device is located consists of or contains more than 25 grams of plutonium or uranium 233 or any combination thereof, or more than 250 grams of uranium 235;

d) any structure, basin, excavation, premises or place prepared or used for the storage or disposal of waste radioactive material;

and includes the site on which any of the foregoing is located, together with all operations conducted thereon and all premises used for such operations.

20. "Occurrence" means an accident, including continuous or repeated exposure to substantially the same general harmful conditions.

21. "Personal and advertising injury" means injury, including consequential "bodily injury", arising out of one or more of the following offenses:

   a. False arrest, detention or imprisonment;

   b. Malicious prosecution;

   c. The wrongful eviction from, wrongful entry into, or invasion of the right of private occupancy of a room, dwelling or premises that a person occupies, committed by or on behalf of its owner, landlord or lessor;

   d. Oral or written publication, in any manner, of material that slanders or libels a person or organization or disparages a person's or organization's goods, products or services;

   e. Oral or written publication, in any manner, of material that violates a person's right of privacy;

   f. The use of another's advertising idea in your "advertisement"; or

   g. Infringing upon another's copyright, trade dress or slogan in your "advertisement".

22. "Pollutants" mean any solid, liquid, gaseous or thermal irritant or contaminant, including smoke, odour, vapour, soot, fumes, acids, alkalis, chemicals and waste. Waste includes materials to be recycled, reconditioned or reclaimed.

23. "Products-completed operations hazard":

   a. Includes all "bodily injury" and "property damage" occurring away from premises you own or rent and arising out of "your product" or "your work" except:

   (1) Products that are still in your physical possession; or

   (2) Work that has not yet been completed or abandoned. However, "your work" will be deemed completed at the earliest of the following times:

   (a) When all of the work called for in your contract has been completed.

   (b) When all of the work to be done at the job site has been completed if your contract calls for work at more than one job site.

   (c) When that part of the work done at a job site has been put to its intended use by any person or organization other than another contractor or subcontractor working on the same project.

   Work that may need service, maintenance, correction, repair or replacement, but which is otherwise complete, will be treated as completed.

   b. Does not include "bodily injury" or "property damage" arising out of:

   (1) The transportation of property, unless the injury or damage arises out of a condition in or on a vehicle not owned or operated by you, and that condition was created by the "loading or unloading" of that vehicle by any insured; or

   (2) The existence of tools, uninstalled equipment or abandoned or unused materials.

24. "Professional services" shall include but not be limited to:

   a. Medical, surgical, dental, x-ray or nursing service or treatment, or the furnishing of food or beverages in connection therewith;

b. Any professional service or treatment conducive to health;

c. Professional services of a pharmacist;

d. The furnishing or dispensing of drugs or medical, dental or surgical supplies or appliances;

e. The handling or treatment of deceased human bodies including autopsies, organ donations or other procedures;

f. Any cosmetic, body piercing, tonsorial, massage, physiotherapy, chiropody, hearing aid, optical or optometrical services or treatments;

g. The preparation or approval of maps, shop drawings, opinions, reports, surveys, field orders, change orders or drawings and specifications;

h. Supervisory, inspection, architectural, design or engineering services;

i. Accountant's, advertiser's, notary's (Quebec), public notary's, paralegal's, lawyer's, real estate broker's or agent's, insurance broker's or agent's, travel agent's, financial institution's, or consultant's professional advices or activities;

j. Any computer programming or re-programming, consulting, advisory or related services; or

k. Claim, investigation, adjustment, appraisal, survey or audit services.

25. "Property damage" means:

   a. Physical injury to tangible property, including all resulting loss of use of that property. All such loss of use shall be deemed to occur at the time of the physical injury that caused it; or

   b. Loss of use of tangible property that is not physically injured. All such loss of use shall be deemed to occur at the time of the "occurrence" that caused it.

   For the purposes of this insurance, electronic data is not tangible property.

   As used in this definition, electronic data means information, facts or programs stored as or on, created or used on, or transmitted to or from computer software, including systems and applications software, hard or floppy disks, CD-ROMS, tapes, drives, cells, data processing devices or any other media which are used with electronically controlled equipment.

26. "Radioactive material" means uranium, thorium, plutonium, neptunium, their respective derivatives and compounds, radioactive isotopes of other elements and any other substances which may be designated by any nuclear liability act, law or statute, or any law amendatory thereof, as being prescribed substances capable of releasing atomic energy, or as being requisite for the production, use or application of atomic energy;

27. "Spores" includes, but is not limited to, any reproductive particle or microscopic fragment produced by, emitted from or arising out of any "fungi".

28. "Temporary worker" means a person who is furnished to you to substitute for a permanent "employee" on leave or to meet seasonal or short-term workload conditions.

29. "Terrorism" means an ideologically motivated unlawful act or acts, including but not limited to the use of violence or force or threat of violence or force, committed by or on behalf of any group(s), organization(s) or government(s) for the purpose of influencing any government and/or instilling fear in the public or a section of the public.

30. "Volunteer worker" means a person who is not your "employee", and who donates his or her work and acts at the direction of and within the scope of duties determined by you, and is not paid a fee, salary or other compensation by you or anyone else for their work performed for you.

31. "Your product":

   a. Means:

      (1) Any goods or products, other than real property, manufactured, sold, handled, distributed or disposed of by:

         (a) You;

         (b) Others trading under your name; or

         (c) A person or organization whose business or assets you have acquired; and

      (2) Containers (other than vehicles), materials, parts or equipment furnished in connection with such goods or products.

   b. Includes

      (1) Warranties or representations made at any time with respect to the fitness, quality, durability, performance or use of "your product"; and

      (2) The providing of or failure to provide warnings or instructions.

   c. Does not include vending machines or other property rented to or located for the use of others but not sold.

32. "Your work":

   a. Means:

      (1) Work or operations performed by you or on your behalf; and

      (2) Materials, parts or equipment furnished in connection with such work or operations.

   b. Includes

      (1) Warranties or representations made at any time with respect to the fitness, quality, durability, performance or use of "your work", and

      (2) The providing of or failure to provide warnings or instructions.

INDEX